MUSIC AND MIND

ALSO BY RENÉE FLEMING

The Inner Voice

MUSIC
AND
MIND

Harnessing the Arts
for Health and Wellness

Edited by

RENÉE FLEMING

VIKING

VIKING

An imprint of Penguin Random House LLC

penguinrandomhouse.com

Selection and introduction copyright © 2024 by Renée Fleming

LIBRARY OF CONGRESS CATALOGING-IN-PUBLICATION DATA

Names: Fleming, Renée, editor.
Title: Music and mind: harnessing the arts for
health and wellness / edited by Renée Fleming.
Description: New York: Viking, 2024. |
Includes bibliographical references and index.
Identifiers: LCCN 2023042349 (print) | LCCN 2023042350 (ebook) |
ISBN 9780593653197 (hardcover) | ISBN 9780593653203 (ebook)
Subjects: LCSH: Music therapy. | Art therapy. |
Music—Psychological aspects. | Music—Physiological aspects.
Classification: LCC ML3920 .M874 2024 (print) |
LCC ML3920 (ebook) | DDC 615.8/5154—dc23/eng/20230908
LC record available at https://lccn.loc.gov/2023042349
LC ebook record available at https://lccn.loc.gov/2023042350

Printed in the United States of America
1st Printing

Book design by Daniel Lagin

*To the countless researchers, practitioners, and organizations
dating back to the nineteenth century, who have led the way,
often conquering skepticism, to demonstrate the value of
creative arts therapies in health-care settings;
and to those who continue this vital work today.*

Contents

HOW AND WHY
Experts Explain the Basic Science Connecting Arts and Health,
Including Origins in Evolution

THE MEDICAL MUSE
Health Professionals and Artists Share Impacts of the Arts in Hospitals
and Clinical Settings

HEALTH IN THE SPOTLIGHT
Artists and Leading Presenters Discuss Key Health and Community Initiatives

CREATIVE LEARNING
Educators and Researchers Illuminate the Effects of Arts Engagement on the Developing Brain

MUSIC AS THERAPY
Experiences and Applications

SCIENCE: A DEEPER DIVE

Researchers Reveal Their Methodology and Compelling Results

THE ROAD AHEAD

Integrated Approaches to Arts, Technology, Community, and Health for the Future

For source notes to all essays in *Music and Mind*, please see

prh.com/musicandmindsourcenotes

Foreword

Nurturing New Horizons
for Science and the Arts

FRANCIS S. COLLINS, MD, PhD

Senior Investigator, National Human Genome Research Institute

Former Director, National Institutes of Health

It was Saturday, June 27, 2015. My wife and I were invited to a dinner of Washingtonian professionals, held at an elegant country inn. Attending the event were three Supreme Court justices—Ruth Bader Ginsburg, Anthony Kennedy, and Antonin Scalia. But the evening was fraught with significance—the day before, the Supreme Court decision in favor of same-sex marriage had been announced. Justice Ginsburg ("RBG," as she will always be known) described the scene in a subsequent interview: "Justice Kennedy wrote the opinion for the court. I joined him. Justice Scalia dissented—vigorously—that's an understatement. And yet we were all together that evening at this wonderful dinner."

As a physician-scientist, I had been invited to join this diverse group as the director of the National Institutes of Health, the largest supporter of biomedical research in the world. Prior to taking on that role, I had had the privilege of leading the International Human Genome Project, which read out all the letters of the human DNA instruction book, providing a historic resource with the potential over the coming decades to revolutionize our understanding of how life works and how disease occurs.

The air at the dinner table was a bit tense. But it was a beautiful evening, and afterward we moved outside to continue the conversation over brandy and cordials. A three-person band was off to the side running through some bluegrass standards—"John Henry," "Red Wing," "Soldier's Joy." While you might be surprised to learn that those tunes were familiar to me, my father was a fiddler and folk song collector, and I grew up surrounded by traditional American music. As a child I learned to sing and play guitar and keyboards, and throughout my life I have found taking part in music to be a joyful experience, especially when other people joined in. The dinner hosts knew of my history, and so had invited me to bring along my acoustic six-string guitar. After a while I joined the band, and we ran through a couple of tunes.

Then the most remarkable thing happened. A stunning and elegant woman approached us and suggested that some group singing might help to bring everyone together, and that she would join us. I soon realized that this was none other than Renée Fleming, the leading operatic soprano of our era. Oh my. Not being very well versed in opera, I feared we might not have much of a shared repertory, but I needn't have worried—Renée had deep familiarity with many genres of music, including Americana. We quickly settled on an opening duet of one of the oldest English folk songs, "The Water Is Wide." The assembled dignitaries, hearing the most exquisite voice imaginable (not mine) lifted into the night air, were transfixed. I don't remember what we sang next—maybe it was "Country Roads," maybe "Shenandoah." Everyone began to join in, including the three justices. The tone of the evening changed dramatically. Justice Scalia, with cigar in one hand and brandy in the other, sang lustily, and then announced with great bravado that Renée had wasted her time in opera, and folk music was a much better choice. He also suggested that I should keep my day job. In return, perhaps with a bit of mischief intended, I suggested the next song. Everyone joined on the final line of each verse as we sang ("rather raucously," according to RBG) the Dylan anthem "The Times They Are A-Changin'." Scalia got the joke, grinned, and lifted his glass.

I have taken part in other events where a shared musical experience changed the atmosphere in wonderful ways, but this one was truly memorable. When Renée told me later that evening that she had just accepted an invitation to serve as an advisor to the Kennedy Center and would like to explore ways that music could be even more effective in the healing arts, I was thrilled. And so our partnership began. We started by assessing achievements in the music therapy field, reviewing exciting new findings in neuroscience that were beginning to identify the mechanisms by which music exerts powerful effects on the brain, and developing a shared sense that the time was right to put more energy and resources into this field.

I put out a call to my NIH scientist colleagues to see who might be interested in exploring new research initiatives in this area. I was surprised and delighted by the outpouring of responses. Compared to the general population, scientists traditionally are more likely to play a musical instrument and consider music an important part of their life experience, and so many of my colleagues were delighted that we might be able to bring these two passions together.

With lots of input from Renée and NIH staff, and a burgeoning interest from the Kennedy Center, especially president Deborah Rutter, we prepared an agenda for a two-day workshop at NIH. Sunil Iyengar of the National Endowment for the Arts became an important partner. The Sound Health workshop in January 2017 was truly electrifying, covering a wide swath of current knowledge on the basic science and clinical applications of music therapy across the life span. New revelations were shared, like the fact that music may have had evolutionary advantages, and that the brain seems to have a "music room" where musical sounds receive special attention. The workshop outcome was summarized subsequently in the highly respected journal *Neuron*, which laid out a detailed set of recommendations for research that could enhance future progress.

Since then, the NIH has funded twenty-one new research grants across a variety of applications, and as I write this a new program on music-based interventions for pain or Alzheimer's disease is soliciting applications. Renée herself spent hours in an NIH MRI machine so that the activity of her brain could be recorded during listening, singing, and imagining singing. (Flash: It was imagining singing that activated the greatest part of the brain!) A series of three NIH workshops produced a tool kit for researchers seeking to carry out clinical studies of music-based interventions for particular health applications, emphasizing the key aspects of research design that can lead to results that can be broadly applied.

The Kennedy Center has creatively designed and produced three major events, including concerts and workshops, that have brought together performers like Ben Folds, Mickey Hart, and esperanza spalding with neuroscientists and music therapists. Our colleagues at the National Endowment for the Arts have funded the Sound Health Network at the University of California San Francisco, convening a broad range of multidisciplinary stakeholders to promote research and public awareness about the impact of music on health and wellness.

And now we have the publication of this landmark book. With themes including the science of arts and health; creative arts therapies; artists, healing, and humanity; singing for health; and arts across the life span, *Music and Mind* has assembled the voices of leading figures in neuroscience and the musical and visual arts, providing an inspiring view of the emerging synthetic possibilities. You will find much here to love.

A challenge for this still young field is to contemplate where our joint efforts should be directed in the next five to ten years. Reviewing the contents of this book, and discussing the future with other Sound Health colleagues, I have a few suggestions about potential areas of research:

1. Progress in understanding the eighty-six billion neurons in the human brain is proceeding at a remarkable rate, stimulated by the NIH-funded human BRAIN Initiative, which involves about five hundred leading neuroscientists and bioengineers. But a focus on how to incorporate the effects of musical input to the brain has not yet been prioritized. The time is right to do that.

2. The most dramatic advances in science and medicine often arise when two previously unconnected disciplines intersect, learn each other's language, and achieve insights that neither could have managed alone. This seems like the right moment for that to happen with experts in neuroscience and music therapy. There have been some encouraging early examples, but the full flowering of these potential collaborations still lies ahead.

3. A clear demonstration of the success of Sound Health would be the appearance of a set of peer-reviewed publications that demonstrate the benefits of music and art therapy for particular health conditions, based upon well-designed and well-powered studies that can move past the now mostly anecdotal history of the field. The tool kit can help with this. Such published studies will also be the best foundation for the evidence needed to make music and art therapy interventions

reimbursable by third-party payers, which would be a major benefit to patients and the profession.

I want to express my sincere thanks to colleagues who have come alongside this bold effort. Many of them are authors of chapters in this book. But a special thanks goes to Renée Fleming, Deborah Rutter, Sunil Iyengar, and the three leaders of the NIH Working Group on Music and Health: Tom Cheever, Emmeline Edwards, and Bob Finkelstein. We may have started as colleagues, but along the way we have become friends and joint owners of a shared vision. Truly, for an expanded appreciation of how the arts and sciences can now intersect and learn from each other, all for the benefit of humanity, that same song sung to Justice Scalia reverberates: The Times They Are A-Changin'!

Overture

Music and Mind

RENÉE FLEMING

The rectangular table filled the conference room at the National Institutes of Health (NIH), the largest public funder of biomedical research in the world. I was seated at the head of the table between Dr. Francis Collins, then director of the NIH, and Deborah Rutter, president of the John F. Kennedy Center for the Performing Arts. It was January 2017, and the three of us were hosting a convening examining the current state of research on the intersection of music and health. It was the first time that scientists, music therapists, and these two great institutions had gathered, joined by representatives from the National Endowment for the Arts (NEA). Though many at the table had also studied the arts or pursued them as an avocation, I was the only professional performer in the room, and I felt incredibly privileged to be there.

The researchers and therapists who presented their work during this two-day conference made for an extraordinary overview, especially for someone like me, who knew nothing at all about the subject. In fact, I walked in expecting that I wouldn't be able to understand a word of the science. Apologies were even made in advance by presenters for the alphabet soup of acronyms, but I followed the general content and was fascinated by the presentations.

Decades of research on the health and wellness benefits of the arts had already been conducted, but too often yielded only unheralded, unpublicized, or siloed results. "Soft science" was the term used by those in medicine to ascribe a perceived lack of seriousness to the notion that arts can contribute to health care. But in recent years, the exploding field of neuroscience, with a new understanding of brain plasticity, has begun to bring the research into focus. Now there are multiple noninvasive ways of looking at the brain, and the scanning technology continues to develop at a rapid pace. When I met Francis Collins for the first time at the dinner party he describes in the foreword, my burning question to him was, "Why are scientists studying music? Don't they have more important things to do?" His answer: "The NIH has a new brain initiative, and music can teach us more about the brain, the most complex known object in the universe." As Dan Levitin writes in his chapter in this book, music's impact can be found in every region of the brain as it has been mapped to date.

The many of us who appreciate, create, or perform the arts intuitively understand their therapeutic effects on our lives. For me, experiencing art—whether musical, theatrical, or visual—can invoke bliss, a heart-filling satiation, and the gift of being fully present. Additionally, as a performer, I know well how it can produce a flow state, a sense of being in the zone, with my voice transported on long breaths as I attempt to paint a landscape of sound. As a singer, my body is my instrument, so I came to the conference table hoping to understand what science could teach me about the biological need to express and create. The ideas I encountered that day gave form and language to questions I had long harbored, sparking a passion that is continuing to enrich my life.

Music currently has the largest footprint within arts research because of its extensive history. Millennia ago, Pythagoras discovered the system of harmonics that forms the basis of modern music and studied the healing properties of vibration. Music therapy itself began in the late nineteenth century, developing further in response to both world wars to aid veterans experiencing physical and emotional trauma. So why, then, aren't these practices and therapies more widely accepted, utilized, and reimbursable by insurance?

The major pillars of current study are childhood development, disorders of aging, mental health, and basic science, comprising the building blocks of research. Who hasn't delighted in the sight of a toddler joyously bobbing

and dancing to a strong beat? Rhythm is the basis of language and movement as we develop. I can still recall the cover art on my favorite album
from childhood. As I played the record repeatedly, I stared at the image
hoping to find more meaning there, but my brain was already creating its
own meaning through listening and imagination—and shaping my taste
for classical music, because the album was Prokofiev's *Peter and the Wolf.*

I discovered at the meeting why hearing was the last of our senses to be
researched: we generally think of it as being passive, unlike other major
senses. Additional takeaways included the value of music training for developing children's brains; the use of music therapy for teens with cancer
and their families; the impacts of music on treating chronic pain, anxiety, and
depression; and the applications of melodic intonation therapy (using singing to regain speech lost as the result of brain trauma or stroke). A brief film
demonstrated a further use of this technique, helping a nonverbal child with
autism spectrum disorder to speak using tone, rhythm, and movement.

I was stunned to discover that the performing arts I was raised on and
that became my career were being leveraged far beyond artistic experience,
to impact hearts, minds, and bodies for the health and wellness of all! I
remembered then how many letters I've received throughout my years of
performing from listeners who said my recordings helped them through
periods of tragic loss or illness, often cancer. They are the best reviews I could
ever have gotten.

Though I was fortunate to grow up in an enriched musical environment,
I was innately shy and developed stage fright as a teen. I suffered again from
periods of intense discomfort onstage in graduate school and during a challenging time in the late 1990s. Acutely aware of the effect fear had on my
body, I began to read about various explorations of the mind-body connection, which was only beginning to be accepted by the medical establishment. While I was attending Juilliard, my back went into spasm the day
before an important audition. I happened to read a brief article on John
Sarno's work on physical manifestations of anxiety, and the pain lifted
within minutes. This wasn't the only bout I was to have with somatic pain.
It continued to threaten my performances more than stage fright, persisting
for many years—typically in the form of tension in the neck and trapezius
muscles, which affected my ability to sing. Science now understands that
the mind has control over the body in many ways; not all of them are helpful.

One of the most striking aspects of the material that was presented at the NIH conference was the granularity of the research. I had imagined that if it worked, *voila!* It was proven. But halfway through the first day, I came to understand that research is effectively a mosaic of discrete pieces that painstakingly, over time, form a compelling picture, to either support or disprove what we hypothesize. Or, in architectural terms, tiny bricks of solid, factual discoveries gradually lay a strong foundation for building a reliable structure of knowledge. I learned that the standards that form the basis of medical research—randomized double-blind studies, large study groups, and a fine-tuning of customized protocols and dosages—help to strengthen this developing field. I heard so much new terminology, including the consistent use of the word "intervention" as an activity targeted to produce an effect and create change.

In the wake of that event, twenty-two of the twenty-seven NIH institutes would join in an unprecedented collaboration to contribute to music and neuroscience research. I left that day incredibly inspired and determined to advocate for the field, promoting the work of these dedicated practitioners and scientists. Since then, I have worked with the NIH, the Kennedy Center, and the NEA to share the growing scientific understanding of arts and health with the public. A follow-up convening was organized in December 2023, to examine the next steps in the development of this research.

Because my primary work is now touring for orchestral concerts and recitals, I thought to bring the news on the road and see if arts and community organizations, local health-care providers, and researchers could collaborate as well. The resulting series of Music and Mind presentations offers audiences a chance to learn how the art forms they love can contribute to health care, and what researchers are discovering. These events have also helped me meaningfully engage with the communities in which I perform. I've given more than fifty presentations to date throughout North America, Europe, and China, and this extracurricular learning experience is met with enthusiasm by audiences everywhere. Performing arts and health-care institutions are all service providers in their communities—so when collaborations continue, such as with Los Angeles Opera and Los Angeles County initiating an annual Arts and Health Week, it's a win for the public they serve.

I believe that the arts should be embedded in our health-care system and broadly accessible, given that integrative and preventive medicine are now increasingly being adopted as part of standard treatment. With quality research, doctors and health-care providers who recognize the benefits of these personalized, low-cost, noninvasive procedures can refer more patients to creative arts therapists. My hope is that this anthology will introduce readers to the scope of current research and practices that result in powerful health benefits of music and the arts, so that they might share the awakening that I experienced when I discovered the extraordinary breadth of this emerging field and its implications. Science and the arts have so much in common. The spark of inspiration is the same: teasing out the quality and "bones" of a project's validity, followed by disciplined application and execution of the plan. I never cease to marvel at what medical research has achieved: the hundreds of diseases that are now curable, ever more effective treatments for cancer and other illnesses and disorders, and our increasing longevity and quality of life. Every new finding begets another, and evolving technology feeds these advances. Creativity and innovation are inextricably linked.

We are now in the midst of a vast mental health crisis around the world, including an epidemic of addiction. Chronic pain, anxiety, and depression are increasing at an alarming rate and have fueled the opioid crisis sweeping the United States. Joke Bradt is a leading researcher on chronic pain and music, an area that shows some of the greatest promise. Her research has found that music is more than just a distraction from pain; it also has long-lasting effects on the brain. The loneliness and isolation made more acute by the COVID-19 pandemic have exacerbated what were already growing trends. One important benefit of arts therapies, beyond targeted interventions, is the opportunity for forming crucial social connection. I would encourage arts presenters and institutions to expand opportunities that prioritize social interaction and create community that is sorely needed in an increasingly divided world.

Visual art therapy is also effective at enabling veterans, children, and teens to express pain and trauma, sometimes more easily than with talk therapy. Anjan Chatterjee and Juliet King use the visual arts, psychology, and neuroscience to aid veterans coping with PTSD and/or traumatic brain injury. In some interventions, patients create their own personalized masks. These works of art express what is too difficult to verbalize. When I toured

Walter Reed National Military Medical Center and saw them, both the skilled craft and hidden emotion were profound.

This introduction provides an overview of the book, beginning with basic science and evolution, which gave me a needed entryway for understanding these discoveries. Leaders in research, health care, and the performing arts recount in the following chapters the real-world application of arts interventions for the health and well-being of patients and communities. A number of artists, whose intellectual curiosity has taken them far beyond performing, have also contributed their insights. I'm grateful for their willingness to share the journey this inquiry has inspired.

To bring all these endeavors together for the future, the NeuroArts Blueprint, a collaboration of Johns Hopkins University and the Aspen Institute, led by Susan Magsamen and Ruth Katz, is a detailed road map for creating a new field of arts and health. This is not unprecedented; climate change research is itself a recently created field. Neuroarts stems from the biology of neuroaesthetics, and it broadly maps a plan to bring together the many siloed factions that currently exist into an organized and functional ecosystem, including educational and career pathways and new policy frameworks. I'm a co-chair of the project, and I'm proud to support them in this endeavor.

EVOLUTION AND BASIC SCIENCE

The fundamental question of "Why music?" is addressed in large part by Ani Patel's explanation of evolution as a way of understanding the continued power of art to affect our minds and bodies. On an evolutionary timeline, we humans likely sang before we spoke. Ani shares both the why and the how of our history as creative and musical beings, from cave paintings dating back more than sixty thousand years to the first known musical instrument, dating from forty thousand years ago. He is currently studying animals as a model to unlock the secrets of human development, and he makes his case eloquently.

Many of us are familiar with Dan Levitin's bestseller *This Is Your Brain on Music*. His chapter sets the stage for us by mapping the brain, instructing us on the elements of musicality, and combining his skill as a producer and musician with neuroscience. Michael Thaut describes his pivotal work in establishing neurologic music therapy; he has continued to be an innovator on the highest level. Robert Zatorre, who has contributed greatly to advances in research, explores the intricacies of brain processes and the connection between reward circuits and our love of music. Neuroscientist and author Antonio Damasio and neurologist Hanna Damasio, with researchers Assal Habibi and Beatriz Ilari, share the breadth of their work at the University of Southern California on childhood, language development, and aging. Nina Kraus introduces us to the brain's ability to decipher sound, with a nod to human survival throughout history. Who hasn't walked down a dark street at night without a heightened awareness of the importance of this sense? Chapters by Emmeline Edwards and Coryse St. Hillaire-Clarke, from NIH institutes, focused on integrated health and aging, respectively, offer a wealth of information on research and knowledge in these areas. NIH institutes are responsible for funding the research that ultimately advances our health care. I often consult the NIH website now for the latest on health research. And in partnership with my foundation, the NIH has also developed a tool kit for improving the rigor of future music and health research, starting with brain disorders of aging.

Mickey Hart of the Grateful Dead has long been involved with the Institute for Music and Neurologic Function in Westchester County, New York. In 1991, he was part of a presentation to the U.S. Congress with famed neurologist and author Oliver Sacks, making the case for music therapy for disorders of aging. Mickey introduced me to Concetta Tomaino, who founded the institute with Sacks. Their focus has been on how attention, emotion, and memory are linked, a correlation I naturally understood from years of memorizing poetry and libretti in foreign languages. I had also witnessed how, in a patient with dementia, songs remain from youth, a period when music is powerfully linked to identity. In her final convalescence, my husband's Aunt Hat sang "I'm Looking Over a Four-Leaf Clover" and "You Made Me Love You" with her eyes closed and word-perfect lyrics, while otherwise unable to speak or recognize her family. During acute cognitive decline, patients can be brought back to themselves when hearing music that is meaningful to them. Concetta's work seeks to extend memory in patients with dementia by strengthening these musical memory pathways. Great strides have been made in research on this plasticity of the brain, which we now know continues throughout our lives.

ARTISTS

Just as my own experiences have informed this journey for me, I have invited other artists to share their ideas and discoveries. Yo-Yo Ma is a visionary artist who has inspired me to think more deeply about what it means to be a musician. He writes about the wisdom of Indigenous cultures and shares a global vision for climate change and planetary health. Drawing on the power of neuroaesthetics, famed architect Liz Diller describes the importance of green space and the future of architecture from the perspective of art, health, and well-being. It doesn't surprise me that architecture can induce awe, an emotion with the power to make us feel connected to something greater than ourselves.

Writers share the emotional impact of the arts, beginning with my brilliant friend and co-writer of my memoir *The Inner Voice*, Ann Patchett. She relates the genesis of her novel *Bel Canto*, in which music is the unifying force for hostages and their captors. I consider that book an essential work to understand the power of music to create and sustain community. Polymath Richard Powers, who won the Pulitzer Prize for *The Overstory*, celebrates the beauty of folk song and nature's chorus as proxies for pain and loss, with the music teaching us how to grieve. In many of his novels, he artfully weaves together themes of music, science, and nature. And President's Committee on the Arts and Humanities appointee Anna Deavere Smith has created her own unique place in our cultural landscape; she recently composed her first libretto, for *Proximity*, at Lyric Opera of Chicago. She amplifies voices of those marginalized by racism, violence, and inequality, perspectives that deserve the widest platforms.

Other singers and artists share their own powerful journeys. Rosanne Cash candidly recounts her harrowing experience of undetected illness, brain surgery, rehabilitation, and her struggle to perform again. esperanza spalding and music therapy researcher Marisol Norris bring creative perspective to trauma, the roots of identity, and the challenges of a capitalist society. Pulitzer Prize winner Rhiannon Giddens describes music as a great social equalizer and a crucial repository of our cultural history. Tabla virtuoso Zakir Hussain discusses the mysticism and spirituality of music and musicians in his native India, as well as some of the secrets of his mastery.

Because of the very interdisciplinary nature of this field, you will find other artists' perspectives highlighted throughout this section.

HEALTH-CARE INSTITUTIONS

The institutions represented in this anthology are also embracing the inclusion of arts in health care. Christopher Bailey, who is building an international arts and health network through the World Health Organization, utilizes monologues and his own story of late-onset blindness in his moving testimony of resilience. In my new role as the first WHO Goodwill Ambassador for Arts and Health, I collaborate with Christopher frequently.

When Todd Frazier from Houston Methodist Hospital first recommended that a music therapist be added to the staff, the benefits quickly became apparent with a stroke patient who had aphasia. The stroke had damaged Broca's area, the brain's speech center. In one session with a music therapist, the patient was able to begin to communicate, because singing was unaffected by the stroke. How many people would benefit if this noninvasive, nonpharmaceutical, low-cost intervention were immediately available to stroke patients? Joanne Loewy, at the Louis Armstrong Center for Music and Medicine at Mount Sinai Beth Israel, has developed multiple music therapy programs to serve both patients and exhausted health-care providers. I witnessed a drumming circle that clearly brought stress relief to the employees who participated. I was also incredibly moved by her work with premature, incubated infants born with addiction. Touch is an unbearable stimulus for them because they are in withdrawal. The therapist's soothing voice, entrained with a baby's cries, can calm the infant and slow their breathing.

Programs like these raise patient satisfaction and Press Ganey scores (a widely used measure of the perceived effectiveness of health-care services), which also contribute favorably to the bottom line.

EDUCATION AND PERFORMING ARTS

The advantages of arts and health benefit us throughout our life span. In addition to aging, another major pillar of this research is childhood development. Education is central to understanding why the impact of artistic training takes us beyond entertainment. Ken Elpus provides key statistics that illuminate the current state of music education in our schools; Indre Viskontas—scientist and opera stage director, and communications lead for the Sound Health Network at UCSF—writes on the power of music education for childhood development and for success with other school subjects. Miriam Lense and Sara Beck's research focuses on early development and childhood disorders. Their chapter also shares practical tools using play for parents with young children to enhance bonding and development. And Stanford Thompson, who established an El Sistema–inspired music education program in Philadelphia, speaks about the change possible when young people develop skills and are supported in this community model.

Performing arts organizations are contributing in meaningful ways to the field. Deborah Rutter and her team at the Kennedy Center, where I am an artistic advisor, share accounts of programming that seeks to mend the fabric of society and create an inclusive environment. The Kennedy Center's Office of Accessibility and VSA is the national standard-bearer for best practices around disability and access. Musician Ben Folds, also a Kennedy Center advisor, lobbies for the importance of the orchestra as a source of community connection, prioritizing the well-being of orchestral musicians.

Sarah Johnson at Carnegie Hall gives an impassioned account of her journey to create two uniquely effective programs: one working with expectant teen mothers to write their own lullabies, and the other with incarcerated men at Sing Sing Correctional Facility. World-renowned choreographer Mark Morris writes evocatively about music and movement; with the Mark Morris Dance Group, he and David Leventhal founded Dance for PD (Parkinson's Disease). David describes the development of that program and how it expanded significantly during the COVID-19 pandemic. In addition to its use within the Parkinson's population, this program could be an asset for every elder-care facility. Another successful professional dancer, Courtney Platt, underlines the importance of creative arts therapies for improving motor function with her advocacy for patients with MS.

SINGING AND MUSIC THERAPY

In addition to instrumental music, singing has an especially significant role in several chapters. It's something most everyone can do in a group or alone, and it's expressive. Francisco Núñez created the Young People's Chorus of New York City as a way of bringing children from different socioeconomic groups together through choral singing. It's an ambitious program that builds equity and community, as well as offering international touring opportunities for these fortunate young people.

Prolific music therapist and researcher Sheri Robb focuses in her chapter on the patient experience, using singing and songwriting to improve anxiety, mood, pain, and fatigue during cancer treatment. Researcher Julene Johnson from UCSF shares the international path she took to her groundbreaking career, and she remains at the forefront of research on aging populations and the benefits of group singing. Cardiologist Jacquelyn Kulinski has discovered something about voice that surprised even me. Singing is athletic to a degree, certainly for classical singers' unamplified voices, but Jacquelyn has shown the benefits of singing in a study with patients with cardiovascular disease. Just thirty minutes improves endothelial function, or blood vessel health, in otherwise sedentary patients.

Everyone knows that breathing is essential to singing, but lung disorders—including COPD, pulmonary fibrosis, and now long COVID—are far more prevalent than is publicly acknowledged. During the heart of the pandemic, I worked with Google Arts and Culture to create a star-studded video series of renowned vocalists and actors sharing their favorite breathing exercises with a song. The aim was to inspire people to use the techniques performers have relied on for centuries to maximize breath capacity and control. I then worked with Johns Hopkins School of Medicine and the Three Lakes Foundation to examine the current state of breathing rehabilitation and the potential for much-needed early-detection tools for pulmonologists.

Music therapist Tom Sweitzer found resilience and a profession as a highly creative and visionary music therapist. His work is the best example of community building I know, using his talent as a music theater composer and performer to serve young patients with disabilities, host groups with long COVID on telehealth, and even write a musical aimed at stemming teen suicide. The documentary *Music Got Me Here* tells the story of Tom's work with Forrest, a teen who suffered extensive brain trauma in a snowboarding accident. Stacie Yeldell tells of her creative injury as a budding pop star, and her inspired work as a music therapist with vocal psychotherapy.

She serves both patients and their families, helping them with grief and the complexities of treatment.

TECHNOLOGY AND THE FUTURE

What's ahead? The intersection of arts and health is now growing exponentially; it is already well established in other countries, with the potential for extraordinary scale and sustainability. "Arts on prescription," where doctors and other health-care professionals can directly prescribe activities such as artistic and nature-based experiences for improved health outcomes, is one such encouraging development; this is currently being implemented in areas of the United States, the United Kingdom, and Canada. Additionally, initiatives such as the NeuroArts Blueprint and the Sound Health Network are building cohesive systems for the field through databases and summaries of research.

One result of the initial gathering in 2017 was a request from researchers at the NIH for me to participate in the fMRI experiment referenced by Dr. Collins in his foreword. The finding that imagining singing activated more regions in my brain than singing or speaking was surprising to the scientists. They hypothesized that this is because singing is second nature to me, whereas imagining singing, especially with the distraction of the fMRI noise, required more focus. Imagination is also how I memorize complete opera roles. If I can hear the score with every detail correct in my "mind's ear" while, say, driving, I've got it! (As an aside, the earworms that plague me when I'm rehearsing a new role come from my colleagues' lines, and not my own. And they are persistent!)

Technology will continue to benefit the field. Tod Machover, Rébecca Kleinberger, and Alexandra Rieger from MIT show in their chapter how technology, music, and creative design can address intractable problems, from stuttering to Alzheimer's and autism. I have performed Tod's composition *VocaGammified*, which uses the 40-hertz vibration that has been found to reduce plaques and tangles in the brain by researchers at MIT. Imagine attending a concert and practicing brain hygiene at the same time!

In addition to increasingly powerful scanning tools that will teach us more about what is happening in the brain and nervous system when we engage with art, there are also applications for artificial intelligence and virtual reality. Adam Gazzaley of Neuroscape at UCSF has developed virtual reality video games for doctors to prescribe for ADHD in youth and for cognitive decline in our aging population. It does seem counterintuitive that gaming would stem attention deficit disorder, but these games use our reward system to keep us on track. For aging, it's rhythm that tunes up the brain. I'm hoping that learning new, rhythmically challenging music does the trick for me. We all know that continued learning, activity, and strong social support are keys to healthy aging. Interestingly, rhythm makes its presence known through the spinal cord before it reaches the brain, and before we're even aware of its presence. I experienced this recently while walking, when I saw that I was in sync, or entrained, with a woman across the street, and only then realized we were both hearing the same subtle background pop music coming from a restaurant!

CAREERS

Embedding the arts in health care can also offer artists a professional alternative to the competitive and often grueling path of the performer. Creative arts therapies, for example, represent a robust and expanding career opportunity. There are more than nine thousand licensed music therapists in the United States with the Music Therapy Board Certification (MT-BC) credential. Scores of colleges and universities now offer music therapy, visual art therapy, and other creative arts therapy degree programs at the bachelor's, master's, and doctoral levels. A growing number of states officially recognize creative arts therapy certifications through licensure, registry, or title protection. Nearly half of U.S. states also allow for limited Medicare and Medicaid arts therapy coverage for certain conditions and populations, but reimbursement is often on a case-by-case basis; this is also true for private insurance. For many patients, the costs of these therapies must still be paid out of pocket or supported by philanthropy. However, many state legislatures, regulatory agencies, and insurance groups have expressed interest in expanding recognition and coverage of creative arts therapies, not only for benefits to patients but also for cost savings.

An important distinction exists between licensed disciplines such as creative arts therapies, which apply arts-based interventions for specific clinical outcomes, and the nonclinical use of arts in health. In music medicine, for example, performers and other artists share their talents in health-care settings, offering comfort, calm, and an alternative to the beeps and alarms typically heard in a hospital. There are also many visual art displays in health-care settings; the Laurie M. Tisch Illumination Fund's Healing Walls (a series of murals in NYC Health + Hospitals) and the Cleveland Clinic's extensive Arts and Medicine initiative are just two examples. More artists will begin to create work that is designed to benefit patients and caregivers, such as drumming circles, group dance activities, and general performances for social cohesion and an environment more conducive to healing.

The Eastman School of Music at the University of Rochester and the Peabody Institute of Johns Hopkins University, among others, are now encouraging students to engage with arts and health, finding another way of serving their communities. Many educational institutions, as well as the National Organization for Arts in Health (NOAH), are developing degree programs or certificates to formalize training and best practices for delivering arts in health-care environments. Mentorship and the sharing of knowledge from one generation to the next are core traditions of classical singing. In classes and coachings with young performers, in addition to breathing exercises and stylistic guidance, I now share the idea that they might integrate arts and health into a fulfilling life in music.

Crossing the steps of the Lincoln Memorial on December 31, 1999, I worked to catch the breeze with my silver stole, like any self-respecting diva. On this night in particular, I was filled with hope as well as adrenaline. It seemed that the twenty-first century had the potential to bring peace and the culmination of all we had learned as a species, enabling us to solve problems in a cooperative spirit embodied by the newly popular term "globalization." I was singing that night in a truly star-studded event, joining my own voice with those of Kathleen Battle and Jessye Norman. There was little thought of violence or political division; climate change was still called global warming and in the limelight for barely a decade. In fact, the biggest fear was a looming Y2K computer bug.

We would all soon receive a series of devastating reality checks. However, we are a creative and collaborative species, and science still gives me hope. The great minds who created vaccines at unprecedented speed to reduce the suffering from COVID demonstrate our potential, as do the scientists pursuing ways to preserve our planet. These are all areas that need the best minds and hearts of our brilliant researchers. I am in awe of them, and they deserve our support and respect.

Performers know how intrinsically healing the arts can be. Many of history's prodigies didn't survive much past age thirty and dealt with crippling illnesses themselves, and yet they left the world with works of art that fill us with wonder, are stunning in their craft and genius, and still resonate with us today. How fortunate, then, that science is now exploring the mechanisms behind human engagement with the arts. This is what I wanted to share with you: the vast potential of creative arts therapies in the context of health and well-being.

I recently visited my idol, Leontyne Price, at her home. I hadn't seen her since before the COVID pandemic began, and I honestly didn't know what to expect. She had helped me enormously at a critical period in my career, when I felt overwhelmed by the constant, competing demands on my time, voice, and energy, which she dismissed as merely noise. "Your job is to focus on this," she said, pointing to her golden throat. "You need to protect yourself, because if you don't, the noise stops overnight, and you are no longer in demand." She had realigned my priorities and kept my goal simple. Nearly ninety-six, she answered the door this day singing a sustained high C. She told me she begins each day by singing, exercising the gift that God gave her, and she means to take care of it until her last breath. She said how truly blessed she is to be surrounded by many grand- and great-grandnieces and nephews. Leontyne had given me yet another gift. She is the perfect example of how art can be a sustaining force in life, and I left feeling uplifted, hopeful, and full of joy.

HOW AND WHY

Experts Explain the Basic Science
Connecting Arts and Health,
Including Origins in Evolution

Musicality, Evolution, and Animal Responses to Music

ANIRUDDH D. PATEL, PhD

Professor, Department of Psychology, Tufts University

Fellow, CIFAR Program in Brain, Mind, and Consciousness

ARE WE AN INHERENTLY MUSICAL SPECIES?

Claude Lévi-Strauss called music "the supreme mystery in the science of humankind." Music pervades human culture, and growing evidence shows it can benefit brain function in important ways. Musical activities can help nonverbal autistic children speak, aid cognitive recovery after a stroke, and improve gait in people with Parkinson's disease. Why does music have these powers? The young field of music neuroscience is beginning to reveal the mechanisms behind such effects, and these findings will help us design even more effective music-based interventions for brain health.

A major mystery remains, however. What are the origins of our species' strong affinity for music? While scientific research on this question is in its infancy, it does seem that human musicality may be the product of an important process in human evolution that we are just beginning to understand. This process is called "gene-culture coevolution," and it is an interplay between cultural invention and biological evolution over long spans of time. A growing body of biologists, cognitive scientists, and philosophers believe this process gave rise to many of our species' key mental traits (including our gift for language), yet finding solid evidence for this has proven difficult. Research on musicality might help us unlock the mystery of how cognitive gene-culture coevolution works. For this research to progress, the first step is to determine if musical behavior is part of our biological human nature. That is, we must first answer the question, "Are we an inherently musical species?" That foundational question is the focus of this chapter.

We know that every society has music, from the largest cultures to the smallest tribes. We also know that humans have been musical for a very long time. The oldest known instruments are bone flutes made by Ice Age hunter-gatherers around forty thousand years ago. Singing is probably much more ancient but leaves no trace. Is musical behavior, like spoken language, part of human nature? Or is music a purely cultural invention, a cherished tradition passed between generations but not engraved by evolution into our genes and minds? This is an old debate, with prominent thinkers on opposite sides. Darwin believed we evolved to be musical. In *The Descent of Man* (1871), he argued that wordless songs arose in our prehuman ancestors as a display to attract mates, laying the foundations for our strong emotional responses to music and paving the way for the evolution of speech. In contrast, William James, who greatly admired Darwin and favored his idea that human minds were full of evolved instincts, had a very different view. James touched lightly on music in *The Principles of Psychology* (1890), but what he wrote made it clear that he saw human musicality as a by-product of how our minds work, a "mere incidental peculiarity of the nervous system." In short, Darwin claimed that we are an inherently musical species, while James claimed we are not.

Darwin and James never debated their positions: Darwin died before *Principles* was published, and no correspondence between the two has ever been found. Yet their opposing views persist to this day. While Darwin's theory that music originated in mating calls has waned, other "adaptationist" theories of musicality are still very much in play. Such theories propose that we are musical today because musical behaviors had survival value for human ancestors, e.g., enhancing adult social bonds or serving an important role in parent-infant communication. These theories see musicality, like language, as part of our evolved psychology. Two major papers along these lines were published in 2021 in the prominent journal *Behavioral and Brain Sciences*, synthesizing a wide range of ideas and findings in support of these views. Many scholars remain unconvinced, however, and James's "by-product" view has morphed into a number of detailed arguments proposing that musical behaviors are purely cultural inventions built using brain functions that evolved for other reasons. Steven Pinker is a prominent voice in this latter camp. Fittingly enough, he maintains this position from his Harvard office in William James Hall.

The Darwin-James debate is now over one hundred and fifty years old and is still unresolved. I believe, however, we are approaching a turning point. A growing stream of studies from several fields, including research on how animals process aspects of music, is casting new light on the debate. What started in the 1980s as a trickle of studies is on track to become a river. If it does, within the next few decades I think we will be able to decisively answer whether we evolved to be musical.

All the research in this chapter builds on a fundamental idea in evolutionary studies of music, namely the distinction between *music* and *musicality*. "Music" refers to specific cultural products, such as American jazz, Italian opera, or Tuvan throat singing. Music is always deeply shaped by social and historical forces and varies in important ways around the world, as explored by the field of ethnomusicology. "Musicality," on the other hand, refers to the cognitive and neural mechanisms that support basic musical behaviors and that develop without formal instruction. Evolutionary biology focuses on musicality in this biological sense.

An example of biological musicality comes from melody perception. Humans effortlessly recognize a familiar melody when it is played in low or high registers even if they have never heard it played that low or high before (e.g., the "Happy Birthday" tune played on a tuba or piccolo). This ability to recognize "transposed" melodies is present in infants and is widespread across cultures. While the ability may seem so simple as to be neurologically trivial, cross-species studies and neuroscientific research prove otherwise. Songbirds, for example, have complex auditory systems resembling those of mammals and can learn to recognize human melodies with ease, yet they fail to recognize a familiar melody when it is transposed. This shows that the ability to recognize transposed melodies is not an automatic consequence of having a sophisticated auditory system. Consistent with this, human neuroimaging shows that recognizing transposed melodies engages complex brain circuitry (linking auditory cortical regions to distant regions of the brain, including the parietal cortex). In other words, the brain mechanisms supporting a basic aspect of musical processing are surprisingly complex and rare in animal cognition, a finding that also applies to musical beat perception, as we shall see later in this chapter.

Why do music-relevant processing mechanisms like those supporting recognition of transposed melodies develop spontaneously in human brains? Thinkers who take a Jamesian view of musicality argue that the mechanisms have "day jobs" in other brain functions such as language, and that they are used *by* music without having been shaped by natural selection *for* music. For example, such theorists might argue that recognizing transposed melodies is based on brain circuits that evolved to process speech. When we speak, our voice rises and falls in pitch to convey important information such as word emphasis or emotion (and in tone languages such as Mandarin, pitch also shapes word meaning). Since these pitch patterns occur in higher or lower registers depending on a speaker's biological sex and age, listeners need to recognize pitch patterns independent of absolute pitch height. This task seems similar to recognizing transposed melodies in music. Thus one could plausibly argue that recognizing transposed melodies involves putting language processing mechanisms to use in music, without evolution shaping those circuits for music processing.

This borrowing of evolved brain circuits to support cultural inventions is well known in brain science, and takes advantage of the human brain's remarkable degree of neural plasticity. Your ability to read this chapter depends on a purely cultural invention: literacy. Writing is only a few thousand years old, and just two hundred years ago almost 90 percent of the world was illiterate. Neuroscientists agree that we did not evolve to read: no brain mechanisms have been specialized over evolutionary time to support learning this skill. As you learned to read, however, certain regions of your brain became specialized for this ability (a topic I will discuss more later in this chapter). That is, learning to read "neurally recycled" brain circuits that originally evolved to support skills important for our ancestors' survival, such as fine visual discrimination and object recognition, language, and selective attention. Even though literacy is of enormous value to human life today, we are not an inherently literate species.

By analogy, asking if we are an inherently musical species is not a question about the value of music in human life today. Rather, it is a question about evolution and the brain: Does human musicality draw on any brain mechanisms specialized by evolution to support music processing? If so, this leads to a second question: Why would musical behaviors have been favored by natural selection in our ancestors? These two questions are deeply related, yet a key step in determining if we are an inherently musical species is to realize that answering the first question does not require decisively answering the second. Indeed, this is one of four concepts that provide a framework for thinking about evolutionary research on music. I briefly explore these four concepts before turning to specific animal research that provides insight into the question "Are we are an inherently musical species?"

EVOLUTION AND MUSICALITY: FOUR KEY CONCEPTS

Concept 1: Evolutionary Specialization and Adaptive Function Are Distinct Issues

In debates over the evolution of musicality, the lion's share of attention has been given to questions of adaptive value. What possible survival benefit could musical behaviors have had for human ancestors, such that natural (or sexual) selection made musicality part of our evolved psychology? This question vexed Darwin, who famously wrote in *The Descent of Man* that our faculties for enjoying and producing music "must be ranked among the most mysterious with which we are endowed." While Darwin argued that music originated in wordless songs for mate attraction, today the most prominent adaptationist theories of musicality focus on other ideas, including the efficacy of music in social bonding, in signaling group strength, or in soothing infants. These ideas have stimulated interesting empirical studies of the effects of group synchrony on social behavior and of the effect of music on infants: such studies are reviewed in the two 2021 papers in *Behavioral and Brain Sciences* mentioned above. As the numerous commentaries published along with these papers make clear, however, many remain skeptical that music had survival value in human evolution. Even among those who believe humans evolved to be musical, there is little agreement on the adaptive advantages musical behaviors offered. One challenge to resolving such debates is that competing theories of adaptive function are often not mutually exclusive.

Must we await the resolution of adaptationist debates to determine if we are an inherently musical species? The simple answer is no. Biologists can reach consensus that humans are biologically specialized for a trait without agreeing on the original adaptive value of that trait. For example, there is universal consensus among evolutionary biologists that human bodies are specialized for bipedal locomotion, even though debates over *why* bipedalism was advantageous to human ancestors are far from resolved. Climate change and the survival value of being able to efficiently locomote between distant forest patches is a prominent hypothesis for the original adaptive value of bipedalism, but there are other hypotheses, and indeed, we may never know with certainty why bipedalism was advantageous at a particular point in our ancestors' history. Yet converging and convincing evidence that we are biologically specialized for bipedalism comes from multiple fields, including comparative anatomy, biomechanics, developmental biology, and genetics. By analogy, I believe we can answer the question "Have we evolved any neural specializations for music processing?" without awaiting the resolution of adaptationist debates. Just as with bipedalism, answering this question will require synthesizing evidence across a range of fields, as discussed below.

In conducting such synthetic research, the word "any" in "Have we evolved any neural specializations for music processing?" is an important one. As illustrated by our discussion of the recognition of transposed melodies, some neurological components of musicality may be borrowed from other brain functions (such as language) and used *by* music without being evolutionarily specialized *for* music. Music cognition draws on a wide array of brain mechanisms having to do with melody, rhythm, movement, emotion, memory, and so on. It is very unlikely that all these mechanisms are specialized for music. It is also highly unlikely all of them emerged at the same time in evolution. Rather, different components likely arose at different times for different reasons, including reasons unrelated to music (e.g., brain circuits for recognizing transposed melodies may have first arisen to support speech processing). In addition, as music-relevant circuits emerged in evolution, they likely supported simpler forms of music making than exist today. The key question is not if *all* of these brain mechanisms became specialized over evolutionary time to support musical behaviors, but if *any* of them did. If so, this would be evidence that we are an inherently musical species.

Concept 2: Abilities Relying on Evolved Specializations Can Involve Learning and Vary Widely Among People

An evolved ability need not be "innate" in the sense of "present at birth," and can rely heavily on learning for its emergence. Consider bipedalism: our bodies are specialized for this ability, but babies take around a year to learn to walk and show considerable variability in how they learn this fundamental human skill. Also consider language: babies are biologically predisposed to speak but must learn to do so via social interaction with caregivers. As every parent knows, different children learn speech at different rates and in different ways. Thus claiming that humans have evolved neural specializations for musicality is not the same as saying musical behaviors are innate.

Turning to issues of individual variation, a common objection to the idea that humans have evolved to be musical is the observation that musical abilities vary widely among adults, much more so than language abilities. This objection often implicitly focuses on musicality in the informal sense, i.e., special interest or talent in music. When one focuses on components of musicality in the biological sense, such as the ability to move in time with a musical beat or to find music emotionally rewarding, variance is lower. Yet even these sorts of abilities can show substantial variation. Does this show that humans have not evolved neural specializations for musicality? No, because it is common for mental abilities supported by evolved neural specializations to vary widely in a population. Indeed, evolved mental abilities are likely to vary far more than evolved physical abilities, such as bipedalism, because brains are far more complex to build than bodies, leaving more room for genetic and environmental variation (and chance) to influence development. Face recognition illustrates this point. There is compelling evidence that human face recognition relies on brain circuits specialized over evolutionary time to acquire this function. Yet face recognition abilities vary widely in neurologically healthy individuals, ranging from those with great difficulties to "super-recognizers," as vividly discussed by Oliver Sacks in his essay "Face-Blind." Even though twin studies show a substantial genetic contribution to face recognition deficits, and despite the importance of face recognition in human social interaction, individuals with poor facial recognition have not been "weeded out" by natural selection. This illustrates how there are individuals who struggle with complex mental abilities that evolved in our species. It would not be surprising if musicality followed this pattern as well.

Concept 3: Brain Science Alone Cannot Reveal If Music Processing Relies on Evolved Neural Specializations

Exciting advances in brain science have revealed neural specializations for music processing in adult human brains, yet these findings cannot by themselves prove that we have evolved to be musical. For example, researchers measuring neural activity directly from the surface of human brains (in patients being treated for epilepsy) recently found neural populations that respond more strongly to singing than to any other category of sound. Even more intriguing is that these patients were played a wide variety of familiar sounds, including environmental sounds and animal sounds, but the only sound categories that elicited selective neural responses were speech, instrumental music, and singing. Given the large body of research suggesting humans have evolved to process speech, it is tempting to think that these recent findings show that we evolved to process music too. Yet while the findings are of great interest to evolutionary studies, they cannot prove we are inherently musical. This is because during child development the brain can acquire neural specializations for activities that humans did not evolve to do, via experience-dependent neural plasticity. For example, when a person learns to read, a region in their inferior temporal cortex begins to respond more strongly to orthography in their language than to other visual stimuli, even though orthography is a purely cultural invention. This "visual word form area" is involved in interpreting visual patterns as written characters and is connected to brain regions that process these characters in terms of meaning, grammar, and sound. Thus, finding neural populations that respond selectively to music does not challenge a view of music as a purely cultural invention.

If music-selective regions were found in young infants, this would be more suggestive of a biological predisposition for music, but even this would not be conclusive. Infants begin hearing and learning about music before birth and are regularly exposed to music throughout infancy and early childhood, when the brain is rapidly developing. In sum, convincing evidence that we have evolved neural specializations for music requires more than brain science, though brain science is of course a key source of relevant evidence.

Concept 4: Determining If We Are an Inherently Musical Species Requires Synthesizing Research from at Least Five Disciplines

No single academic discipline can decisively answer if we are an inherently musical species. Answering this question requires synthesizing research from at least five different fields: developmental psychology, ethnographic and cross-cultural studies of music, cognitive neuroscience, genomics, and cross-species research. *Developmental psychology* can reveal which aspects of music processing emerge robustly and without formal training, a fundamental issue in the biological study of musicality. For example, children begin singing without any formal instruction, and recent research using wearable recording devices on infants finds that singing can start surprisingly early and can sometimes occur without being noticed by parents, meaning we have likely underestimated how early and how much babies sing. *Ethnographic and cross-cultural studies of music* are needed to determine which aspects of music processing emerge reliably around the world. For example, synchronizing rhythmic body movements to musical beats (e.g., in dance) is a widespread aspect of musical behavior across cultures and time, and emerges in children without any formal instruction. This is relevant to evolutionary studies because beat-based synchrony of movement and vocalization among people is central to several adaptationist theories of musicality, including social bonding theories and coalition signaling theories. *Cognitive neuroscience* is essential for determining if a given component of musicality can easily be accounted for as a secondary use of a brain mechanism whose "day job" lies in more obviously adaptive cognitive functions, such as speech. As discussed above, this kind of neurological borrowing is well known in brain science and might explain our ability to recognize transposed melodies. At the same time, such explanations are less plausible for some other aspects of musicality, including the human tendency to synchronize movement with auditory beats, since ordinary speech does not have periodic beats and does not lead us to tap our feet or dance.

Genomic studies can help determine if variation in basic musical abilities is influenced by genetic variation. This is important because claiming that musicality is part of human nature is tantamount to claiming that there are genetically influenced neural specializations for music processing in human brains. Note that "genetically influenced" does not mean "genetically determined." For example, a recent large-scale genome-wide association study (GWAS) found that about 15 percent of variation across individuals in beat synchronization ability could be attributed to genetic factors. This means experience plays a more important role than genetic differences in shaping this ability, but it also means the ability has genetic influences on which natural selection could have acted. Finally, *cross-species research* is essential for determining if humans are inherently musical. Such research can reveal which components of musicality are restricted to humans among primates, and thus which are candidates for being supported by evolved neural specializations for musicality. For example, if the ability to move in synchrony with periodic auditory beats were readily attainable by chimpanzees or rhesus monkeys, this would speak against the idea that humans had evolved neural specializations for this ability. Moving to a beat is not a natural behavior for chimpanzees or rhesus monkeys; they do not synchronize movements to auditory beats in the wild. If these primates could easily learn to move to a beat in a humanlike way, it would suggest the ability was a by-product of their basic perceptual and motor skills. As we shall see, however, beat synchronization does not come easily to nonhuman primates, and cross-species studies of this ability provide intriguing clues about the evolutionary origins of this (and other) aspects of human musicality.

ANIMAL RESPONSES TO MUSIC

This section gives a taste of current research on animals and music. It aims to show how such work is illuminating the evolutionary foundations of human musicality and is also giving us new insights into animal minds. While this line of work is still in its infancy, there are already many more studies than I can cover here. For those who want to learn more about research on animals and music, I have referenced some recent reviews in the endnotes.

THE BIOLOGY OF THE BEAT: RESEARCH ON BIRDS, PRIMATES, AND HORSES

One of the most widespread and familiar aspects of music is the beat, i.e., a periodic underlying pulse often perceived in complex rhythms, which can stimulate movement such as bobbing or dancing. This "beat perception and synchronization" (BPS) occurs cross-culturally and may seem simple, especially since it emerges without instruction in young children and can involve basic movements like head bobbing. Cognitive and neural research shows BPS is anything but simple, however. BPS involves highly precise prediction of beat times, which is why we spontaneously clap or tap in close alignment with beat (and often a little ahead of it) and can do this flexibly across a range of musical tempi. Neurologically, beat perception, even in the absence of movement, strongly activates motor planning regions in the human brain. These motor regions interact with auditory regions to form a circuit that is likely involved in predicting the timing of beats. Thus while BPS feels primal, moving to a beat predictively and flexibly is not simple from a brain's perspective.

In 2006, drawing on what was known about the cognitive neuroscience of beat processing, I hypothesized that only certain kinds of animals were capable of humanlike BPS, i.e., synchronizing movements predictively and flexibly to auditory beats perceived in complex rhythms. These were animals with "complex vocal learning," i.e., species (like songbirds and parrots) that learn to produce complex sound patterns based on listening to and imitating the sounds of others. Complex vocal learning is supported by evolved neural specializations in motor planning regions of the brain and in connections between these regions and auditory regions. In nonhuman species these auditory-motor networks were reminiscent of those used in beat processing in humans. I hypothesized that the brain specializations for complex vocal learning laid the neural foundations for BPS, as both were forms of sophisticated auditory-motor processing.

A provocative prediction of this hypothesis was that nonhuman primates were not capable of BPS, because humans are the only primates with complex vocal learning. This prediction is counterintuitive, because primates often make rhythmic sounds as part of their natural behavior (such as the drumming and pant-hooting of chimpanzees) and are quite capable of rhythmic movement, as seen in their walking and running. Intuitively it seemed BPS would come easily to them with training. Within a few years after my hypothesis was published, studies began emerging that were consistent with its predictions. For example, when macaque monkeys were trained to synchronize movements with a metronome, they showed a spontaneous tendency to move after each event and required special training to synchronize predictively. This is unlike humans, who synchronize predictively with no special instruction or training. Chimpanzees tested in similar work showed some evidence of predictive synchronization, but only when beats were near their natural tapping frequency. They lacked tempo flexibility, however: they did not stay synchronized when the tempo of the metronome changed.

In 2009 my colleagues and I conducted a study of an animal that did BPS to musical rhythms. A parrot named Snowball, who lived in a pet shelter, had spontaneously developed synchronized rhythmic movements to beats in human music. We tested Snowball by playing him beat-based music at many different tempi and found he synchronized predictively and flexibly across tempi. Parrots are famous for their complex vocal learning skills, so this finding supported the vocal learning hypothesis. A paper by a Harvard lab appeared alongside our paper in *Current Biology* and also supported the hypothesis: they searched the internet looking for videos of animals moving in sync with musical beats, and only found vocal learning species (mostly parrots). Notably they looked at many videos of dogs hearing rhythmic music and found no signs of synchronization to the beat. This fits the hypothesis, since dogs are not vocal learners. (Sadly, the hypothesis predicts no dog will ever fully boogie to the beat, which is a shame, because there is an entire sport devoted to teaching dogs to dance: "canine freestyling.")

To date, parrots and humans are the only animals known to spontaneously develop BPS to human music. Parrots are more closely related to dinosaurs than to humans, so why is this the case? Neuroscience has revealed parrots have an unusually complex vocal learning system (surpassing that of songbirds), with some striking parallels to the human vocal learning system. I think this is why parrots and humans are closer in beat processing abilities than chimpanzees and humans, even though we share 98 percent of our DNA with chimpanzees. Importantly, however, it is only the occasional parrot that develops BPS when raised by humans, and parrots like

Snowball often do BPS in short "bouts" of a few seconds, separated by stretches of rhythmic movements not synced to the beat. In contrast, BPS develops widely in human children, and most adults can stay synchronized for prolonged periods when moving to a beat. Thus in a recent paper I argued the capacity for spontaneous BPS originated as a by-product of the circuitry for complex vocal learning, but in human ancestors, BPS-relevant brain circuitry was gradually elaborated and specialized by natural selection to support musical beat-based processing. These enhancements made sustained (versus "bout-like") BPS develop reliably, and also made sustained BPS intrinsically rewarding. This took BPS from a "sometimes thing" occasionally emerging in a vocal learning brain to part of our biological human nature, reflecting an evolved neural specialization for musicality.

I continue to test the vocal learning hypothesis with colleagues. For example, a team at Mount Holyoke College (led by Professor Mara Breen) and I are testing if horses synchronize their trotting to music, as claimed by some horse owners. If horses spontaneously synchronize their footfalls to musical beats in a predictive and tempo-flexible way, this would refute the vocal learning hypothesis, because no equines are complex vocal learners. Turning to avian research, Professor Mimi Kao at Tufts and I have recently shown that zebra finches, a vocal learning songbird extensively studied by neuroscientists, can learn to recognize periodic rhythms flexibly across tempi. Even though these birds don't move in synchrony with such rhythms, we hypothesize they recognize periodic rhythms by predicting the timing of periodic sounds using their motor planning systems, akin to what humans do when we perceive beats. If this proves true, then these animals could provide a model system for understanding how auditory and motor regions interact during rhythm perception. This in turn could lead to a better understanding of how and why beat-based rhythms help people with certain neurological disorders, such as Parkinson's disease, to move more fluidly.

THE EVOLUTION OF SINGING:
RESEARCH ON DOG HOWLING

Singing is found in every human culture and singing in groups is widespread. In group singing it is very common for individuals to adjust the pitch of their voice in relation to other voices. This adjustment often involves pitch matching, but sometimes involves deliberate nonmatching, as when purposefully singing dissonant intervals, as happens in some Eastern European traditional music. Such pitch adjustments are not part of ordinary speech, where we take turns and try to avoid overlap. This means the ability to align (or misalign) voice pitch with other simultaneous voices is unlikely to be a by-product of neural specializations for speech. Where might this ability have come from? When we look in the animal world, do we see any other species making sustained pitched vocalizations in groups? This sort of behavior is rare in primates but is common in many howling canine species, including wolves. Like humans and unlike most mammals, wolves are intensely social and live in complex, long-lasting groups. Howling is used for social communication: it can advertise a wolf's location and other information. Group howling is also thought to have a social bonding function, reminiscent of social bonding theories of the origins of music.

Interestingly, some researchers have suggested that when wolves howl together they purposefully *misalign* their voice pitch with those of other pack members, which helps signal multiple wolves are present and therefore better conveys the size and strength of the pack. If wolves and humans share the capacity to adjust voice pitch in relation to other simultaneous voices, this would suggest the origins of this component of musicality could lie in simultaneous group vocalizations serving important social functions.

It would be difficult to study voluntary control of voice pitch in wild wolves, but this can be studied in dogs, who share a common ancestor with wolves as recently as thirty thousand years ago. Everyone knows dogs often howl when hearing certain human sounds, including sirens. Many dogs also howl to specific pieces of music, perhaps because they perceive something howl-like in the music. Performing at the Met in New York, Renée Fleming once heard a Russian wolfhound onstage howl along as she sang "Je marche sur tous les chemins" from Massenet's *Manon*, which led to the 2004 children's book *The Dog Who Sang at the Opera* about this unplanned cross-species duet.

In a 2016 paper my colleagues and I reported acoustic measurements of dogs howling to music and suggested an experiment to study if dogs adjust their howling pitch in relation to the sounds they are hearing. By playing a dog's howl-triggering music at different pitch levels—the original level, then transposed up or down—and acoustically measuring their howl pitches in these three conditions, one could determine if dogs adjust their vocal pitch accordingly. In collaboration with Professor Erin Hecht at Harvard, who researches behavioral and brain evolution in canines, we are now studying this question in a citizen science experiment. Owners test their dogs at home using our methods and send us videos, which are often a joy to watch. (If you would like to participate in this research, search for "howling study Harvard Tufts.") Data collection and analyses are under way, and we hope to have results this year. The results will inform evolutionary theories of human singing and give us new insights into canine vocal control.

Perhaps early human singing started as a social group vocalization and sounded more like wolf howling than the songs we are used to hearing today. If pitch-coordinated singing had some survival value for our ancestors, neural specializations for more precise pitch control in group singing may have emerged gradually via natural selection. Intriguingly, coordinated group singing appears to have psychological benefits for humans compared to individual singing and may be especially beneficial for older adults, though more research on this topic is needed.

THE EVOLUTION OF EMOTIONAL RESPONSES TO MUSIC: RESEARCH ON DOG RESPONSES TO STRESS

The claim that nonhuman animals respond emotionally to human music dates back to ancient Greek, Roman, and Chinese writings, but is it true? And if so, what would this teach us about the evolution of human musicality? Most people find music emotionally rewarding, and many use it for emotion regulation. There are, however, some people who are not moved by music of any sort even though they can get pleasure from other things and show no deficits in basic tests of melody and rhythm perception. Neurobiological research on these "specific musical anhedonics" is helping reveal which brain pathways are crucial for musical pleasure in humans.

How instinctive is our emotional response to music? Most people start responding emotionally to music early in life. Darwin took notes on the emotional expressions his infants made to music, which fueled his belief that we evolved to be musical. Empirical studies have confirmed that early emotional reactions to music don't depend on cultural familiarity with music. For example, physiological measurements show American infants around four to ten months of age are soothed by lullabies even when they come from unfamiliar musical traditions. (Intriguingly, physiological studies also indicate hearing a song after a stressful event is more soothing to infants than hearing infant-directed speech.) Also, growing research on newborns in neonatal intensive care units finds that calming music is physiologically soothing, with lasting beneficial effects on brain development. Such findings indicate music can have emotional effects on minds with minimal linguistic or cultural experience. Like our infants, our pets have little understanding of our language or culture. If they find human music soothing it would suggest some of music's emotional power comes from ancient biological responses to sound that predate human evolution.

In collaboration with Sidney Beecy, Seana Dowling-Guyer, and Emily McCobb at Tufts' Cummings School of Veterinary Medicine, I have recently begun to investigate this issue in pet dogs. Many dog owners believe calm music can soothe their pets, and commercial CDs of "music for dogs" capitalize on this fact, but convincing evidence is lacking. We designed a study where owners brought their dogs to the vet school for a simulated vet visit. Soon after arriving, the dogs were left alone in a room for fifteen minutes, which can be stressful for them. During this time the dogs heard either music from a commercial CD marketed to dog owners for its calming powers, human relaxation music (from the popular *Liquid Mind* collection), or silence. We used video to measure behavior and special collars to measure physiology, including heart-rate variability. As with the howling study, data analyses are under way and we hope to have results later this year.

Perhaps only a minority of dogs are soothed by calming music, in contrast to human infants, where a majority seem to show this response (though more cross-cultural work is needed to test this idea). This would raise the question of what neurobiological changes took place in evolution to give young human brains such reliable emotional sensitivity to music, and why such changes occurred.

CONCLUSION

Research on animals and music is shedding new light on old questions about the evolution of human musicality. Together with research in human cognitive neuroscience, cross-cultural studies, and other fields, a picture is emerging suggesting that musicality is an evolved part of human nature. While much work remains to be done before we can be sure if this is true, I believe scholars will reach consensus in the next few decades about whether humans are inherently musical.

If we have evolved neural specializations for music processing, this is likely due to a profound interplay of cultural invention and biological evolution in shaping the human brain. In the past few decades several prominent evolutionists have argued that such gene-culture coevolution shaped key aspects of the human mind, including language and our unusual capacity to cooperate with unrelated individuals. As of yet, however, strong evidence for cognitive gene-culture coevolution has been hard to find. Musicality may be the first domain where this theory of mental evolution is convincingly demonstrated.

As noted at the start of this chapter, Claude Lévi-Strauss called music "the supreme mystery in the science of humankind." *Why* our species became musical may always be a mystery. But if we *are* inherently musical, research on musicality could illuminate the coevolutionary dynamic that made humans who we are.

ACKNOWLEDGMENTS

I thank Renée Fleming and Michael Pollan for comments on this chapter, and Jennifer Burton for skillful editing. I am grateful to the organizations that have given me the time and resources to explore the evolutionary foundations of musicality: the Guggenheim Foundation, the Radcliffe Institute for Advanced Study, the Canadian Institute for Advanced Research, the Tufts Faculty Research Awards Committee, and the Center for the Humanities at Tufts.

What Does It Mean to Be Musical?

DANIEL J. LEVITIN, PhD, FRSC

James McGill Professor Emeritus of Psychology, McGill University

Music is a human universal: it exists in every society we know of, both now and throughout tens of thousands of years of human history. And just as languages differ across societies, so do their musics. The richness and breadth of musical expression is astonishing, and its ubiquity tells us that it is an important part of what it means to be human. Many of us find that our musical experiences are the most profound in our lives. As Friedrich Nietzsche famously said, "Without music, life would be a mistake."

To get started, we should probably define what we mean by the word "music." And yet, for all of music's intimacy with us, trying to define it is fiendishly difficult. The music of the Cameroon Pygmies has little in common with the music of the Tuvan throat singing of Mongolia, and neither would appear to have much in common with a Mozart opera or the music of Nine Inch Nails. The definition I have gravitated to is that of composer Edgard Varèse, who said that "music is organized sound." This inclusive definition allows us to accept as music anything that the creator intends to be music. That doesn't mean we will like it, but it skirts the problem of trying to find common rhythmic, timbral, or spectral features that unite so many different forms of expression. (It is the same definition that allows the work of Marcel Duchamp to be considered visual art.)

Whatever music is, we have clear tastes and preferences, much as we do for visual art or food—even those of us who consider ourselves musical omnivores don't like all music equally. We have our favorites. And we have our favorite musicians, the ones who can move us emotionally more often, more deeply, and who can move us to states of ecstasy where we lose all sense of self, time, and space. When this happens, we might say that the music creator is highly musical. And that those people who, as listeners, are moved, must also be highly musical, even if they don't play an instrument or compose themselves. They are receptive musically.

Our culture shares in a collective myth, that musical talent is something you're born with. This is a topic that has fascinated me for decades and what drove me to the field. As a child, I took music lessons alongside my friends in school. It became clear by seventh grade that some of the kids were just better than others, and it seemed to have little to do with practice. I'd see classmates practice an hour a day or more and get nowhere, while others never practiced but made great progress on their instruments, just on the fifty minutes a day that we all had in school band. In my twenties I entered the music business, working as a record producer and arranger, and eventually was hired as an A&R manager for a record label (a fancy name for "talent scout"). During that hair decade of the '80s when I was at Columbia/CBS Records, I started to wonder why some people just seemed to be better than others. Did Ella Fitzgerald and Ray Charles have something in their brains that no one else had? Or did they just have *more* of some special substance? In the parlance of cognitive science, were these differences of *kind* or differences of *degree*?

As I sat in the control room of the Automatt, the former CBS studios in San Francisco, Carlos Santana was on the other side of the glass playing a solo. And as he did so, I felt the hair stand up on the back of my neck. My body shivered as if I were cold. I looked at my bare arms and saw goose bumps. There he was, plucking on some metal wires stretched across a piece of wood, and there I was, having a powerful physiological reaction. Later that afternoon he offered to let me play his guitar—a very special instrument, wired through a very particular chain of amplifier electronics, a system he had worked for years to hone. That guitar and that amp were famous, and now I would be able to play them and create the same sounds he did! I picked it up, fully expecting to sound like Carlos Santana, but I didn't—I just sounded like me. I handed it back to him. He played a few notes and sounded like Carlos. He handed it back to me, and when I played it, I still sounded like me. "Wait a minute," I said. I went to the other room and got my guitar and amp. "Would you play this?" He did. And he still sounded unmistakably like Carlos. It wasn't the equipment; it was the fingers and the brain and the body and the *experiences* of Carlos that gave him his sound. But of course the sound, Carlos's tone and timbre, were just the medium through which he sent his message, a message that reaches millions of people around the world. From a technical standpoint, there are thousands of guitarists who can do what he does—go to any bar and listen to the band playing a Santana song, and they can play his solos note for note. It is something else. If it's musicality, where does that musicality come from?

Environmental factors such as deliberate practice certainly play a role in musical ability, yet most individuals do not become experts despite many hours of practice. Growing empirical evidence suggests variables other than practice (e.g., intelligence, personality, or physical traits) influence performance (and many of these expertise-related traits are highly genetic). Simply put, genetic factors are essential for outstanding levels of musical ability.

Music is a model system for understanding what genes can accomplish and how they relate to experience. Increasingly, neuroscientists are collaborating with geneticists to understand the links between genes, brain development, cognition, and behavior. Identifying genetic components that underlie musical ability can help us to predict who will succeed or, more interestingly, what types of musical instruction and intervention will be most effective for individuals according to their genetic profiles.

Successful genotyping (determining differences in genetic makeup by examining DNA sequences) requires an accurately described phenotype (observable characteristics or traits). Unfortunately the latter has not yet been accomplished for musicality, creating a significant hurdle to further progress. Part of the difficulty in describing the musical phenotype is its heterogeneity, the wide variety of ways in which musicality presents itself. Several questionnaires have been designed to assess specific aspects of musical behaviors—such as music receptivity, music preferences, music sophistication, music perception skills, music engagement, music involvement, absorption in music, and use of music for mood regulation. A comprehensive and psychometrically validated instrument to assess the multidimensional nature of musicality across a broad range of individuals is still needed to fully acknowledge this construct in future research and practice in the field.

In the meantime, as science works out the various ways to reliably and validly measure musical behaviors and musicality, we can go to the source. We can ask musicians what *they* think is going on. Over the last thirty years, I've asked every musician I know whether they think that their talent is a product of "talent"—meaning that they were "just born with it"—or the product of hard work, or some combination of both. Every single musician I asked, with one exception, said that music never came easy to them, it was always a lot of work. If there is a musician alive today who would just *seem* to be a naturally born musical genius, someone from whom music oozes and who can't *help* but be musical, it would probably be Stevie Wonder. When I asked him, he said, "I think that we're all put here to do the thing that we do. It gets to us just discovering what that is. And believing in what that is, and holding on to what that is and nurturing what that is." He recalled the thousands, possibly tens of thousands of hours of hard work he had to put into that nurturing and that it didn't always come easy or naturally. Surely if Stevie Wonder thinks musicality isn't the product of a particular brain region, if Stevie believes that musical ability comes as a result of a lot of practice, that should tell us something. Other musicians scoffed at the idea that they were "just born with it": Paul Simon, Rosanne Cash, Bobby McFerrin, Sonny Rollins. (The one exception was Joni Mitchell, who said it just came easy to her—but then, in the next breath, admitted that she sometimes worked on a single lyric for six months.)

Also in the meantime, we can begin to look at, and hopefully better understand, what goes on in the brains of musicians.

A BRIEF OVERVIEW OF THE FUNCTIONAL NEUROANATOMY OF MUSIC

Music appears to activate nearly every region of the brain that has so far been mapped, not just a single "music center." Like vision, music is processed component by component, with specific neural circuits handling pitch, duration, loudness, and timbre. Higher brain centers bring this information together, binding it into representations of contour, melody, rhythm, tempo, meter, and, ultimately, phrases and whole compositions. The idea that music processing can be broken down into component operations was first proposed as a conceptual tool by cognitive theorists and has been confirmed by neuroimaging studies.

The early distinction that music processing is right hemisphere lateralized and that language is left hemisphere lateralized has been replaced by a more nuanced understanding that music processing is bilateral. There is evidence that learning to name pitches, intervals, and chords invokes left hemisphere regions due to the language component. Pitch is represented by tonotopic maps, virtual piano keyboards stretched across the cortex that represent pitches in a low-to-high spatial arrangement. The sounds of different musical instruments (timbres) are processed in well-defined regions of the auditory cortex. Tempo and rhythm are believed to invoke hierarchical oscillators in the cerebellum and basal ganglia. Loudness is processed in a network of neural circuits beginning at the brain stem and midbrain, extending to the temporal lobes. The localization of sounds and the perception of distance cues are handled by a network that attends to (among other cues) differences in interaural time of arrival, changes in frequency spectrum, and changes in the temporal spectrum, such as are caused by reverberation. One can attain world-class expertise in one of these component operations without necessarily attaining world-class expertise in others.

Higher cognitive functions in music, such as musical attention, musical memory, and the tracking of temporal and harmonic structure, have been linked to specific neural processing networks. Listening to music activates reward and pleasure circuits, modulating production of dopamine. The generation of musical expectations develops in childhood. It is a largely automatic process in adults and is believed to be critical to the enjoyment of music. Tasks that require the tracking of tonal, harmonic, and rhythmic expectations activate a cortical network that also involves prefrontal regions, limbic structures, and the cerebellum.

Musical training is associated with changes in gray matter volume and cortical representation. Musicians exhibit changes in the white matter structure of the corticospinal tract. Cerebellar volumes in keyboard players increase as a function of practice. Learning to name notes and intervals is accompanied by a leftward shift in processing as musical concepts become

THIS IS YOUR BRAIN ON MUSIC

FRONTAL LOBE
Prefrontal Cortex
creation of expectations; violation
and satisfaction of expectations
Motor Cortex
movement (e.g., foot tapping, dancing,
playing an instrument)

BASAL GANGLIA &
LIMBIC SYSTEM
reward and pleasure circuit activation
modulates production of dopamine;
tracking of tonal, harmonic, and
rhythmic expectations; tempo and
rhythm processing
Amygdala emotional reactions to music
Nucleus Accumbens emotional reactions to music
Striatum motor planning and reward perception
Hippocampus* memory for music, musical experiences,
and contexts

TEMPORAL LOBE
Auditory Cortex
first stages of listening to sounds; perception and analysis of tones;
spatial acoustic feature processing; auditory motion perception
Heschl's Gyrus loudness perception; timbre perception; pitch perception
Superior Temporal Gyrus auditory processing

*Some sources include hippocampus in limbic system; there remains some controversy

PARIETAL LOBE
Sensory Cortex
tactile feedback from playing an
instrument or dancing

WHITE MATTER TRACTS
Corpus Callosum
connects right and left hemispheres
Corticospinal tracts
connects motor areas with spinal cord
Short fibers
connect motor and sensory areas

OCCIPITAL LOBE
Visual Cortex
reading music; looking at
a performer's movements (including
your own)

CEREBELLUM
movement coordination and motor
learning; emotional reactions to music;
tempo and rhythm processing

BRAINSTEM
Loudness processing starts here and
extends through midbrain to temporal
lobe; frisson ("chills")

lexicalized. Writing music involves circuits distinct from other kinds of writing, and there are clinical reports of individuals who have musical agraphia—an impairment or loss of a previous ability to write music—without loss of the ability to write other texts. Double dissociations have also been reported between musical agraphia and musical alexia (losing the ability to comprehend written materials while preserving the ability to write and vice versa). Indeed, the patient literature is rich with accounts of individuals who have lost one specific aspect of musical processing while others remain intact, bolstering claims of distinct, componential processing of music.

Each of the components mentioned above—for example, reading or remembering music, listening to various attributes of a musical performance, playing an instrument—seem intuitively to be involved in constructing a profile of musical abilities. The fact that they are distinguishable neuroanatomically lends credence to them as real, not merely theoretical, concepts, and suggests the possibility of genetic correlates influencing neural development and differentiation. Rather than there being a single "music gene," the most likely scenario is that we will discover genes that support component brain structures and thereby, by extension, component musical behaviors.

DEFINING MUSICALITY

In order to study musicality in the brain we need to define what we mean by that term. The problem is that musicality presents itself in a large number of ways that may to some degree be independent of one another. Casually, we might say that someone is musical if they play an instrument or sing, compose, orchestrate, or conduct at what we consider a "high level." That gets messy, because as John Sloboda has pointed out, defining "high level" becomes a social judgment about what we in a particular society consider expertise, and that is often confounded not with what we find skillful, but simply what we like.

Taking even just this short list of musical attributes or skills, we can further divide them into subskills. For example, some performers excel as soloists, and others as ensemble players or accompanists; some excel at sight reading, and others (in fact, most musicians in the world) play only by ear. Within the domain of music reading, some musicians are good sight readers, and others are better at reading slowly and deliberately in the service of preparing pieces; some read single lines, and others can read many lines simultaneously, as conductors must do when scanning an orchestral score. Some musicians improvise, and many others do not. Many outstanding musicians are better known for a sense of rhythm than pitch (e.g., Cindy Blackman, Charlie Watts). Composers tend to excel at a particular style or genre—popular, jazz, classical, film music, hip-hop, country—and a test of classical music ability, for example, would exclude not only many of the best-known composers of our era, but also most of the world's musicians who neither read nor write music. It is also worth noting the manifest lack of a correlation among these abilities. Instrumentalists (e.g., Arthur Rubinstein) do not typically compose or arrange, and composers do not even necessarily play instruments: the composer Irving Berlin ("White Christmas," "God Bless America") famously was unable to play his own songs.

An adequate theory of musicality must account for all the different ways musicality presents itself. So far, my list shows a production bias; it does not account for the many individuals who show an intense receptive sensitivity to music. In our studies of individuals with the neurogenetic disorder Williams syndrome, for example, we have seen people who are powerfully moved by music. Tantalizing early evidence indicates that it is the disorder itself that causes such sensitivity, among other things, by removing social inhibitions and due to connectivity changes in the amygdala. After listening to sad music, parents report that their children with Williams syndrome stay in a sad mood much longer than typically developing individuals, and, similarly, happy music "lifts them up" and allows them to maintain a positive mood state significantly longer than others. Other examples of people with receptive musicality include disc jockeys, music critics, recording engineers, film music supervisors, and record company talent scouts. Lacking formal musical training or the ability to play an instrument does not necessarily put them at a disadvantage, and yet their professions require various sorts of receptive (perceptual) musical skills. Choreographers and dancers, who set bodily movements to music, may constitute a separate category of cross-modal musical artists with distinct skill sets and neurocognitive processes to support their work.

There also exist individuals with the auditory equivalent of photographic memory, what I've previously dubbed *phonographic memory*. Some DJs can listen to the briefest excerpt of a musical piece, often one second or less, and identify the title, composer, and performers and distinguish several different performances of the same piece by the same group. DJs can introduce new connections between music we might not otherwise notice and introduce us to new music we might not otherwise discover. The connection, for example, between the Baroque composer Foscarini and the classic rock band Led Zeppelin only becomes apparent when Foscarini's "Toccata in E" is played back-to-back with Led Zeppelin's "Gallows Pole." The rhythms, articulation, and chords are hauntingly close, despite being separated by three hundred and fifty years. To discover these connections, a person requires a detailed musical memory coupled with the ability to extract certain elements of the music. While hearing one song, the listener must be consciously or unconsciously searching a vast mental repertoire of music to find a template match for chords, melodies, rhythms, timbres, or other component features, while performing mental transpositions to place them into equivalent keys and tempi. Recognizing these sorts of musical connections is not something that all musicians and not even all great musicians can do.

It has been suggested that the primary purpose of music is to convey emotion, and this must also be considered in evaluating musicality. Some musicians are extraordinarily adept at communicating emotions through music, and this becomes especially clear when those musicians lack some of the other attributes we would normally associate with high levels of musical ability. Consider, for example, Bruce Springsteen and Britney Spears, whose voices entrance millions of listeners. Both of them lack the beautiful voice and vocal clarity one traditionally associates with singers. Springsteen's raspy voice communicates great emotional depth and nuance, and even though it may not seem so, he does sing on pitch. Spears's highly processed voice, relying on a great deal of Auto-Tune, is less about conveying nuanced aspects of emotion than about making a pop record.

Another important notion concerns a cluster of attributes surrounding distinctiveness, novelty, and innovativeness. Not all great musicians possess these qualities, but those who do are highly prized in our society and by other musicians. Mozart, Louis Armstrong, and Joni Mitchell are appreciated for these qualities, quite apart from the other musical skills they possessed. That is, they were able to bring uncommon amounts of creativity to their music (despite the technical limitations that the latter two had as instrumentalists).

AMUSIA

An adequate, overarching theory of musicality should account for the entire range of abilities observed in the population, including those at the low end of the spectrum. A small percentage of the population appears to lack musical ability or sensitivity completely, and this condition of amusia has been known for over a century. In the popular press the terms "tone deafness" and "tin-ear syndrome" have also been used. However, the amusias comprise a heterogeneous set of disabilities with distinct causes, sometimes present from birth and sometimes acquired following injury, disease, or other organic trauma. Some individuals simply cannot identify songs. For example, Ulysses S. Grant quipped, "I only know two tunes: one of them is 'Yankee Doodle' and the other one isn't." Some people can identify a song but cannot sing in tune, producing abnormal variability in the tones they generate. Some individuals have an inability to detect a single aberrant note falling outside of a musical key. This is believed to be associated with abnormal gray and white matter in the auditory cortex and inferior frontal cortex.

Based on one small aggregation study, such "wrong note" detection appears to have a hereditary component. Specific deficits in rhythm, pitch, and timbre have also been observed, as a result of either brain injury or congenital defect. The characterization of amusia remains an active area of research.

QUANTIFYING MUSICALITY AND THE FUTURE OF MUSIC PHENOTYPING

The most commonly used musical assessment tests over the last century have been based on Seashore's standardized tests. These are narrowly focused on perception, although there is no firm evidence that perception and production are correlated. Moreover, the tests allow no opportunity for the test taker to demonstrate individuality, emotion, or creativity. In one module of the test, for example, individuals listen to a sequence of tones that play a simple melody. A second sequence is played, and students simply answer whether the two sequences are "same" or "different." As the test progresses, the sequences become increasingly difficult. A parallel version is administered in which musical rhythms are presented.

The chief measurement problem is that many individuals who would be considered musical (e.g., those making a living as professional orchestral musicians) only score in the middle range of the Seashore tests, while many without musical training or externally observable ability do very well on them. On three of six Seashore items, professional symphony players scored below the fiftieth percentile, making their performance indistinguishable from that of nonmusicians. Correlations between standardized musical aptitude tests and real-world musical achievement are consistently low. I believe that in an effort to control stimuli and reduce music to its atomic elements, the makers of standardized tests have removed its essence, its dynamic and emotional nature. In short, they have removed the muse from music.

We need to be more sensitive to the variety of ways that musicality can present itself, distinguishing production from perception, and technical ability from emotional ability. Assessments need to allow for spontaneity and creativity. Consider the ways that musicians evaluate one another: it is not through objective yes/no testing, but through auditions and a process of subjective evaluation. After a century of cognitive psychology and psychophysics embracing objective methods as the gold standard, I believe the time is right to reintroduce the opinions and ratings of qualified observers. To build on what Justice Potter Stewart famously said, we may not be able to define musicality, but we know it when we hear it. Subjective evaluations, properly done with blind coding and tests of interrater reliability, can yield repeatable and rigorous results that have greater real-world validity.

Musicality should also be evaluated for individuals who are not players. Disc jockeys already compile demonstration tapes to exhibit their ability to create meaningful playlists and segues. Potential music critics are given assignments, and their work output is evaluated by more experienced critics and editors. The future of music phenotyping should allow for inclusive definitions of musicality, with subjective ratings made by experienced professionals according to replicable scoring guidelines.

The Goldsmiths Musical Sophistication Index (Gold-MSI) is a self-report inventory designed to assess individual differences in musical sophistication. The authors move away from commonly used terms such as musicality, musical talent, ability, aptitude, or musical potential, adopting "musical sophistication" as a term that has been used less frequently and is presumably less biased. They define musical sophistication as a psychometric construct that can refer to musical skills, expertise, achievements, and related behaviors across a range of facets. The Gold-MSI assesses the ability of nonmusicians to engage with music in a flexible, effective, and comprehensive way. It measures general musical sophistication, as well as Active Engagement, Perceptual Abilities, Musical Training, Singing Abilities, and Emotions. This is an important move in the right direction.

Designing a suitable test to assess the broad spectrum from amusics to expert musicians would ideally recruit the involvement of experts from music perception and cognition, education, performance, statistics, and psychometrics. It would involve several steps:

1. Cataloging those behaviors that we regard as musical. A partial list might include: (a) playing a musical instrument or singing; (b) composing; (c) arranging and orchestrating music; (d) conducting; (e) programming music for aesthetic purposes or for finding connections between songs (disc jockeys, film supervisors); (f) great receptive sen-

sitivity to music and its emotional content; (g) ability to detect out-of-tune or out-of-key notes; (h) cross-modal practices, such as writing about or choreographing music.

2. Creating test items and batteries that tap into these behaviors.

3. Creating a set of guidelines by which performance can be assessed by qualified, independent judges.

4. Performing standard psychometric test construction operations, such as test-retest reliability, interrater reliability, face validity, and construct validity.

5. Cataloging objective measures of success that one might use to correlate the items of (1) above. Examples include being a member of a world-class symphony orchestra, winning awards (such as the Polar Prize, Kennedy Center Honors, a Grammy Award, or the Gershwin Prize), or having the respect of peers. The validity of the measures of (1) would be supported with such real-world achievements. The point is not that everyone who performs well on the tests will have achieved real-world recognition, but that we would expect that those who have achieved such recognition should do well on the tests (modus ponens).

6. Norming the test against a suitable number of participants drawn from a range of musical backgrounds and abilities

7. Conducting factor analysis (or similar data-reduction techniques) to uncover latent mathematical relations among variables. Factor analysis will allow the researcher to bind together variables that are intercorrelated, that is, groups of two or more test items that are tapping into some common, underlying neurocognitive process.

8. Association studies should then be conducted on the reduced set of supervariables or orthogonal factors obtained from the previous step.

CONCLUSION

In summary, musicality is a complex interaction of physical, emotional, cognitive, and psychosocial traits, including some that are overtly "musical," and others that are not but that contribute to musicality in a variety of supporting ways. Musicality presents as both productive and receptive ability, and skill can manifest itself as primarily technical, cognitive, intuitive, or emotional, or in various combinations. If research is to provide an adequate account of how music, genes, environment, and neural development inter-act, it must embrace the full variety of musical experiences and contexts. More accurately quantifying the musical phenotype is a necessary precur-sor to performing rigorous genetic studies.

Studies of the genetics of music promise both practical and theoretical benefits. They can help in music education through identifying those stu-dents with high potential in specific areas of musical endeavor and can ultimately help teachers to select the most efficient instructional methods based on a student's background and aptitudes. The important theoretical promise is in identifying and learning to measure component musical abil-ities more accurately so that musical behaviors can be correctly linked to genetics, to brain structures, and to other, nonmusical behaviors. In this latter case, there has been great interest in the question of cognitive trans-fer, that is, whether "music makes you smarter." Questions such as these would benefit by a fractionating of musical ability, so that we can know which aspects of music correlate specifically with which other cognitive abilities.

ACKNOWLEDGMENTS

The author would like to thank Lindsay Fleming for her assistance in re-searching and editing this chapter, as well as drawing the Brain on Music figure. The author is also grateful to Dr. Richard Ivry for feedback on the figure. Updated and adapted from an article that originally appeared in *Neuron* 73, no. 4, February 23, 2012.

The Parting Glass

RICHARD POWERS

Pulitzer Prize and National Book Award–Winning Novelist

It's morning, and dozens of thrushes, wrens, and warblers are singing their hearts out in the trees beneath the window of my house in the foothills of the Great Smoky Mountains. Spring in Appalachia, and you know how that piece goes. Some of the singers live here year-round. Others are passing through on long journeys. I listen as the dawn chorus reaches its wild peak. No one is conducting. The music exhilarates me, and clearly the singers are thrilling one another. If you ask a scientist why birds sing, the answer will deal in courtship and territory. But if you asked the *bird*, and if you could understand its reply, it would probably be something like, "Because I have to, and it feels so good."

I put on some music of my own, adding a descant to the morning mayhem. Here's a miracle that I hope I'll never get used to: I can stream just about any song ever recorded, any time I want, in every season, from any room in my house in the woods. I call up a fine old Scottish-Irish song that always goes right through me: "The Parting Glass." The song is at least four hundred years old, and no one is sure who wrote the music or the words. *Traditional*, as they say. And I have dozens of covers to choose from. I play one by three Canadian women singing a cappella, in crystalline harmony, as if they're already a step or two beyond the grave.

The song partakes of an old Celtic tradition. When a guest rose to leave the party and climbed up in the stirrups of his horse, he'd be given a *stirrup cup* or *parting glass,* one more drink to fortify him for the night's trip back home. The song is in the voice of a guest taking such a leave:

> *So fill to me the parting glass*
> *And drink a health whate'er befall,*
> *And gently rise and softly call*
> *Good night and joy be to you all.*

Words fill my house and spill out into the woods. It's just a folk song—plaintive, playful, a little melancholy. The tune traces out the basic moves of tonal expectation, traveling from home and back again with open grace. The harmonies are steadfast and simple, with no great surprises. The lyrics, however, are a little cheeky, a nice mix of sass, stoicism, and self-effacement, even though it's easy to hear that this singer is setting out on a journey somewhat longer than a night's ride:

> *Of all the money that e'er I spent,*
> *I spent it in good company.*
> *And all the harm that e'er I've done,*
> *Alas it was to none but me.*
> *And all I've done for want of wit*
> *To mem'ry now I can't recall.*
> *So fill to me the parting glass:*
> *Good night and joy be with you all!*

A summing up, then, with the singers taking stock before a last departure. The words could be about nothing at all—they might be in a foreign language, and I would still hear the farewell. It's there in the suspended harmonies, in the way the chords waver between major and minor. *I'm off now, out of here: drink to me, drink to my disappearance.* The Celts have always been good at emigration and goodbyes.

For reasons that science may never quite put its finger on, I get chills and my eyes start to water. It happens to me with music, far more than with any other art. Music has a startling ability to make a listener sad over nothing, simply by unfolding chords in a certain order and weaving them through with a tuneful filigree. It's not clear what the adaptive advantage of this might be, but the right pitches in the right rhythm can overwhelm us with sorrow. And we love every minute of that harmonious grief.

I'm reassured by a quick online search that reveals at least twenty health benefits of crying. The sheer abundance of weeping's benefits makes me laugh and laughing brings at least ten benefits more. I don't know why I chose this song—an evening's last farewell—to add to the birds' exuberant morning chorus. I don't understand why I would willingly choose sadness. But it feels so good. It's a bracing dive into a cold spring, a glimpse of midnight just before breakfast.

Countless clinical studies have now tied the secret of health to moving. There is also great health in *being moved*, something that produces similar physiology. Think about the old meanings buried in the etymology of "emotion." To move and to feel are complements, and the emotion that a tune triggers is a tune-up in how to move more deeply through the wider world. Music makes us *go* somewhere. It propels us into new states, new vantages, new emotional affordances. If you ask a scientist why music is healthy, the answer will come in units of cortisol and heart rate and blood-oxygen levels. But if you ask this listener, I'd say that music is an off-line cognitive therapy. By making us sad in the absence of real tragedy, it leaves us more adept in sadness when life calls for the real thing.

Being moved by a song holds the key to mental health. Music says: "Here's what happens to us. We and those around us move like chords unfolding in time, throwing off fantastic sparks and harmonies. And then the chords end. Here's how to feel sad about that. And how to hear how that sadness, too, will pass."

I suspect that none of the dozen species of birds singing outside my window know that one day their song will stop. But every human does. We carry the knowledge of our own death with us all life long. Awareness of mortality is the first and hardest challenge to our sanity. In my life, the best consolation for my approaching death has always been to sing it and to hear it being sung. I think that's why the world's great sacred ways of coping with death are so often built around music. So many times in this life I've heard friends say, "I love this piece. Play this at my funeral." Music can train us in goodbyes. In giving us a little taste of our own finitude, it lets us, for a moment, feel the infinite.

"The Parting Glass" lasts only two and a half minutes. Soon enough, it reaches its final stanza. But in those one hundred and fifty seconds, the song lights up my brain in several ways. First, there is the sheer glory of the sound: three clear voices tuned tightly to each other. Then there is the stepwise tune and its dramatic pauses, its phrases always taking their leave, always coming home. Those simple syncopations lay out the plainest two-step dance, reminding me of all the dancing I won't be doing when I no longer have a body. A good song—a great *movement*—is a way of saying, *Dance now, if only in your mind, for there is no dancing where you're going.* Finally, there is music's uniquely vertical trick, stacking up companion lines in step with the one that my ear keys to. The tune contains its own accompaniment, and all the regions of my brain fire in harmony. It reminds me of what good company I've spent my life in.

> *Of all the comrades that e'er I've had*
> *Are sorry for my going away.*
> *And all the sweethearts that e'er I've had*
> *They'd wish me one more day to stay.*
> *But since it falls unto my lot*
> *That I should rise and you should not,*
> *I'll gently rise and softly call*
> *Good night and joy be with you all!*

Of all music's health benefits, teaching us how to be okay with our own disappearance may be the deepest. A good song lets me hear how the chords go on, far beyond the double bar. As another good song puts it:

> *Music, music for a while*
> *Will all our cares beguile.*

That it can do so with sadness is a pure delight.

"The Parting Glass" does what all good songs do: it ends. It gets up in the stirrups, takes a last deep drink, and is off. My Canadian singers spring a surprise minor final cadence, and the tune is done. The morning chorus starts to disperse. I land back on Earth, turn from the window, and get on with my full day's work. For what it's worth, I get a ton done.

As I fall asleep, the night is all melancholy owls and mournful whip-poor-wills. Birdsong, too, knows the uses of sadness. At two a.m., when I briefly wake, there is nothing but dead silence. I'm fine with that. The song is ended, but the melody lingers on. Even in the long rests, I can hear how the morning chorus will begin again in the dark, just before sunrise, for whoever may or may not be there to listen.

Sound Connects Us

NINA KRAUS, PhD

Hugh Knowles Professor of Communication Sciences,
Northwestern University

CONNECTION TODAY

I find myself thinking more and more about connections. People tell me they have difficulty making and keeping connections. Even before a pandemic turned us inward, physical connections with people were waning. Why meet up with friends when you can keep up with their doings on social media? Why shoot hoops at the corner court when you can curl up with an Xbox and talk trash through your headset? Yet depression and alienation are rising.

In his book *Lost Connections*, Johann Hari tells us this increase in depression goes beyond a simple increase in diagnosis. He attributes the rise in depression in part to a decrease in connectedness with others. Medication will help in some cases. But medication does not treat loneliness. It does not treat the lack of belonging that is increasingly prevalent.

Traditional ways of belonging—such as religion and church membership—provide connection to people who see you and value you, and whom you, in turn, see and value. They position your life and your future as parts of something that makes sense. But this kind of belonging and connectedness, not just religion but bowling teams or Moose Lodge membership, is disappearing. Children tend to disperse as they age out of living at home. Long-standing intergenerational communities are rare. The concept of the place you grew up being a "hometown" has little meaning when no one you were close to as a child, including your siblings, still lives there. Increasingly prevalent are parasocial relationships—those with people you don't know, such as feeling an affinity for a celebrity or an athlete or a politician. Relationships can become less important than social media contacts, the Twitter accounts we follow, or our Facebook Likes.

So how do we—how do *I*—make connections in this less-connected moment? Whether in person or by phone, Zoom, or Skype, I find that sound is at the root of how I make and keep connections. In my book *Of Sound Mind*, I define the sound mind as the brain that evolves from our experience with sound throughout our lives. The sound mind is vast—interconnected with neural systems that underlie each of our senses: the motor system, the limbic (emotional) system, and the cognitive (memory, attention) systems. I make the case that the sound mind influences and is influenced by how we sense, feel, move, and think. Sound connects us. It is continuous, integrative, and expansive. It shapes who we are and how we connect to the world.

We feel disconnected in part because we have moved away from our sonic roots. Sound is supplanted by visioncentric social forces. Nuanced listening is impeded by a rise in noise. Yet the deep neural interconnectedness embodied in the sound mind gives me hope. Hearing is not an isolated sensory process, a cog in interpreting the sensory world, but is a lead player in every part of us. When the world is falling apart, sound can connect us. Sound holds one key to fostering the sense of community we're looking for.

THE HOLISTIC POWER OF SOUND

Sound has been of mighty importance for us for a long time. It has deep biological roots. We've been communicating with sound for hundreds of thousands of years—way before it occurred to anyone to start writing down our thoughts and messages. Throughout the ages religions have relied on sound imagery, like "the word of God" and "the word made flesh." Ancient bards did not write their tales down. They memorized the important themes and composed tales anew with each telling in the songs they sang. Sound is mnemonic—it helps us remember. When listening, one must rely on memory—you cannot go back and replay what you have heard in the same

way you can reread the last page of a book. Socrates worried that writing would come to supplant the oral traditions of teaching and learning and would produce a citizenry with poor memory. Historian and philosopher Walter Ong wrote that sound has been eclipsed by vision. Maybe he is right; maybe we have lost our way.

Indeed such a concern about not exercising our memory applies anew in the digital assistant era. Why bother racking our brains trying to remember an elusive fact or how to get to an upcoming appointment when we can simply turn to Google?

Sound fills the space surrounding you and me and connects us when we speak. Sound is alive. Sound is a presence. We have no script when we talk. A good conversation has a rhythm and is outside either person's control to direct. When we're truly listening to each other there is reciprocity, reverberation, and tunedness; psychiatrist and scholar Iain McGilchrist calls it "betweenness." It is probably the most precious form of communication there is. I feel betweenness every time I take my position in the front of a classroom. I try to create a dialogue with my students, to facilitate interactive sessions where deep discussions can take place without adhering too closely to the day's syllabus or the clock on the wall. Since the publication of *Of Sound Mind*, I have been a guest on many podcasts. I am finding the connections I build in these conversations, with sound as the medium, to be much more real than I expected.

Hearing evolved as a means to keep us fed, to keep us safe from predators, to warn us of danger, and to connect us with potential mates. Today, hearing is unnecessary for most of those activities. Can being attuned to the power of sound give us a better chance of solving alienation, isolation, depression, anxiety, and division? My argument is sound can heal and strengthen our humanity if we relearn to value it.

With the ancient Greeks' recognition of sound as a powerful force in the body and mind as inspiration, and the study of biology to guide me, I have dedicated my career to better understanding how sound impacts our lives. And I have seen evidence of sound operating for both good and bad in my own research and that of colleagues from around the world. I have assembled here examples that, for better or worse, illustrate the power of sound.

DISRUPTING THE SOUND MIND

Noise

Noise, which can be defined as unwanted sound, is so, *so* pervasive. Coming from the same linguistic root as nausea, noise can literally be sickening.

Few people realize there are two types of noise. Everyone knows about the danger of loud sounds. If you spend too much time in a noisy place, using noisy tools, or listening to loud music, your ears may be damaged. NIOSH (the occupational safety watchdog) is very clear that noise above ninety decibels causes hearing loss. There is no mistaking an ear-damaging noise when you hear it. It is LOUD.

The sound of my neighbor's leaf blower on the other hand, at least from the vantage point of my backyard, does not meet or exceed the NIOSH's accepted threshold of "unsafe." It is the sort of sound most would consider background noise. For this reason, we tend to ignore it. But are we really tuning it out, or are we simply adapting our lives to a constant state of low-level alarm? We have all had the experience of noticing a sound only when it goes away. Often it is an air conditioner or an idling truck. The air conditioner cycles off or the ignition is cut, and suddenly we "hear" the silence. And we sigh in relief. We momentarily revel in the peace until it starts up again or is replaced by the next aural annoyance. If our ears are not being damaged and we can mostly tune them out, why should these noises concern us? We should be concerned for the sake of our brains.

Chronic noise exposure—such as might be experienced by individuals who live on a bus- and taxi-filled street or near an airport—can lead to an overall decrease in perceived quality of life, elevated stress hormones, problems with memory and learning, difficulty performing challenging tasks, and stiffening of blood vessels and other cardiovascular diseases. According to the World Health Organization, noise exposure and its secondary outcomes, such as hypertension and reduced cognitive performance, account for an astounding number of work years lost due to ill health, disability, or early death.

This type of noise exposure is especially devastating for the developing brain. Children's brains are primed to extract meaning from sound and are typically good at doing so. But the ability to take meaning from sound can be compromised by chronic exposure to meaningless sound. There is an elementary school in New York City that, on one end, abuts a busy elevated subway track. Reading scores of children in classrooms on the noisy side of the school lagged those of their peers on the quiet side of the building by up to eleven months. Noise mitigation efforts that included rubber rail padding and noise abatement materials in the classrooms erased the learning gap. Young animals exposed to moderate noise (typical of commercial white noise machines) fail to develop precise neural differentiation of the constituent parts of common sounds.

Birds and other animals change their vocalizations in response to human-made noise. Birds, frogs, and whales—like humans—increase the loudness of their voices as the environment gets noisier. Animals change their call rates or pitches, or devise other changes, just to make themselves heard over us. Some animals simply give up. Ship sonar can cause whales to go silent. It also interferes with the echolocation they rely on for navigation. Human-created noise has forced hundreds of species of animals around the world to alter their behavior, with dire consequences for mating, migrating, and their continued existence on Earth.

Sound is one of the vectors by which all living organisms are linked in a unified ecology. Even plants emit and sense sounds in the interest of nourishment and pollination. Plants' roots seek out water; that is why regular augering of the main sewer line is often necessary. We now have learned that roots will grow toward the *sound* of water. Certain species of flowering plants will release nectar only when a bee buzzes at a particular pitch, which it uses to ensure that the bee species is a known good pollen spreader. All living things respond to sound and vibration. Human-made sound exerts its unseen sway well beyond the human community, deep into the community of all living things.

Sound is underrecognized largely because it is invisible. We notice more obvious environmental causes—forests, fossil fuels—while ignoring the impact of noise on animal communication, mating, and, indeed, survival. Once aware of the noise that surrounds us, we can then ask ourselves, is it necessary? Do we need music playing in the grocery store or while on hold on the phone? Do we need to let everyone nearby know we are unlocking our car door?

Finnish architect Juhani Pallasmaa wrote, "Every city has its echo which depends on the pattern and scale of its streets and the prevailing architecture styles and materials. The echo of a Renaissance city differs from that of a Baroque city. But our cities have lost their echo altogether. The wide, open spaces of contemporary streets do not return sound, and in the interiors of today's buildings echoes are absorbed and censored. The programmed recorded music of shopping malls and public spaces eliminates the possibility of grasping the acoustic volume of space. Our ears have been blinded." Noise disconnects us from the places we live in.

Have you felt it is becoming more difficult to focus your attention? Sound is our alerting sense. It evolved to keep us safe. Of course, being on perpetual sonic alert will distract us from what we're doing.

Concussion

Making sense of sound is one of the hardest jobs we ask our brain to do. The ingredients of sound—pitch, timing, timbre, loudness—occur simultaneously, and the brain has to make sense of what is said with microsecond precision. A concussive blow to the head can disrupt this delicate processing. With scalp electrodes it is possible to measure how concussion can disorganize the brain's response to sound. Assessment of sound processing in the brain can be used to inform concussion diagnosis and treatment.

Germane to music, concussion can disrupt rhythm processing. A few years ago I attended a fundraiser for the Concussion Legacy Foundation, which seeks to reduce the incidence of concussion in sports. After the speakers, the music started, and I found myself on the dance floor surrounded by football players. To a man they were phenomenal dancers, responding much more fluidly to the beat of the music than I would have thought possible of these mountains of men. This experience, along with the power of music to strengthen the brain discussed in the next section, led us to look at rhythm in concussed athletes. Namely, we looked at their ability to clap along to a metronome, a marriage of sound and motion. Sure enough, this ability was disrupted in concussed athletes, a finding that supports the consideration of rhythm training to speed concussion recovery. A merging of the arts and science, exemplified by organizations like Athletes and the Arts, is likely to go a long way to enhance athlete health through music.

STRENGTHENING THE SOUND MIND

Making Music

Making music changes us profoundly. I am talking about strengthening our senses, our bodies, our cognition, and our ability to learn.

Making music alters *how our brain processes sound*. Regular music making creates lasting changes in our vast hearing brain—our sound mind. We see stronger neural processing of the harmonics in sounds, and that the timing of processing of certain sound components is faster. Harmonics are what distinguish the sounds of a flute and a tuba playing the same note. Harmonics help us distinguish one consonant from another, such as *d* from *g*. Timing cues ranging from microseconds to seconds are everywhere in both speech and music. These brain changes span all types of musicians—instrumentalists and vocalists—and span genres too.

There is specialization as well. If you are an instrumentalist, your brain is tuned to the sound of your own instrument. If you play the flute, your brain will encode the sound of a flute more richly than will the brain of a nonflautist. If you are a music conductor, you will be able to localize sound better in space—in the orchestra!—than a nonconductor musician or a nonmusician. Your own personal way of making music changes the sound mind in ways we have yet to discover.

Playing music influences how we see. People who regularly make music can more quickly perform tests involving detection of subtle movement than those who don't. They also can combine the input from their eyes and ears more efficiently.

Playing an instrument affects our motor and somatosensory (touch) systems. We know the left hand is controlled largely by the right side of the brain and vice versa. Playing the violin requires both hands, but the movements of the left hand require more control of individual fingers compared to the bowing motion of the right hand. In violinists, the right motor cortex—controlling the left fingers—expands and takes over neighboring regions ordinarily devoted to the palm.

Music making affects our emotions. Indeed, listening to music activates the reward circuitry of the brain. Musicians can learn to process emotional cues in others' voices better than nonmusicians. Their brains are more attuned, for example, to the emotion-bearing components of a crying baby.

Making music exercises attention and memory. Musicians are able to focus attention better while avoiding distractions. They outperform nonmusicians in memory tasks, including verbal memory, working memory, and sequencing. Gaining an edge in working memory helps you listen. If your working memory is good, you will probably be better at following conversations in noisy places like a crowded bar or restaurant. And indeed, science has found this to be the case. Studies of musicians' ability to listen to speech in noise, for the most part, have found they perform this task better than nonmusicians.

Musician students tend to do better than their nonmusician peers in reading, measures of overall intelligence, and academic achievement. Changes in academics and brain function don't happen overnight. I saw this firsthand in the students enrolled in the Harmony Project in Los Angeles. The Harmony Project is a community music education program that brings music instruction to youth from low-income families and under-resourced communities. School-age children enrolled in the Harmony Project showed heightened neural processing of sound compared to their equally motivated but wait-listed peers after only two years of high-quality music instruction. We replicated these findings in a similar study conducted with Chicago high school students. The musicians were compared to students in the same

schools engaged in another enriching activity. After two years of in-school music instruction, notable changes were found in the neural processing of crucial sound ingredients—such as harmonics and timing—together with improvements in language metrics such as phonological awareness.

How does music make all this possible? The sound mind is vast. Making music engages not just our ears, but our motor and visual systems. Making music depends on focused attention, it involves memory, and it engages our emotions. Perhaps uniquely, music does an exceptional job connecting all these systems.

The illustration above depicts the connection that arises when singers join their voices in harmony. The singers' voices and their movements join in a continuous back-and-forth, a give-and-take that dynamically shapes the flow of a piece of music. Indeed, this give-and-take, with practice, can become a transcendent aural experience. And there is "blood harmony"—the sublime, close harmonies that seem to be unique among families, especially siblings. The Everly Brothers, the Louvin Brothers, and the Carter Sisters (along with mom, Maybelle) can produce harmonies rarely achievable by nonrelated singers. A genetic component is likely involved, but I believe that living under the same roof for years tunes one's experience with the voices of one's family members and influences how siblings' voices blend.

SPEAKING MORE THAN ONE LANGUAGE

If I could choose a superpower, I would like to have the ability to speak any language. A person's language is that person's sense of belonging and of home. Sharing a language means sharing a way to make sense of another person's world. People who speak more than one language naturally use sound to connect with more people. They also use sound to tune their hearing brains. First, bilinguals tend to be masters of pitch. In many cases, bilinguals will speak one language at a higher pitch than the other. Stronger neural processing of the fundamental frequency in sound (an important pitch cue) tunes them into the pitch of others' voices, which helps distinguish between similar voices, and to hear "auditory objects," like your brother's voice or the singer in the band. They also, by virtue of having a larger inventory of sounds available to them, have richly tuned sound minds. This shows up in different ways, but the most salient is in the domain of attention and, in particular, inhibitory control. Bilinguals can suppress distractions when accomplishing a task—to get down to the business at hand—while ignoring other demands on their attention. Their experience suppressing interference in one language when speaking or writing in another hones focus to a sharp point.

EXERCISING THE BODY

A group of people you might not immediately think of as sound experts are athletes. There is growing understanding that the sound mind is shaped by athletic activity. An athlete must listen and respond to teammates' cues and coaches' instructions, and to the sound of activity on the playing field itself. We have discovered that athletes have uncommonly "quiet" brains—ones with a lower level of turbulence in its resting state. When you are resting, perhaps sitting quietly lost in thought or perhaps not really thinking of anything at all, the brain does not rest—it is always *on*. Synapses continue firing randomly here, there, and everywhere in the brain. This neural activity is not in reaction to anything you are seeing or hearing or touching, but it is there nonetheless, including in the sound mind. Think of it as electrical static. When you are at rest, this neural noise ideally is minimal,

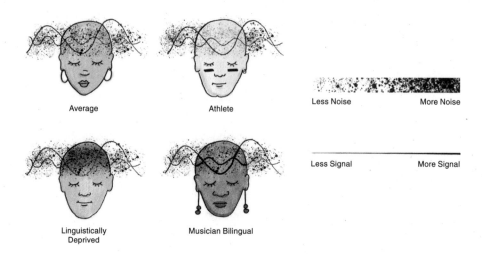

Average

Athlete

Less Noise

More Noise

Linguistically
Deprived

Musician Bilingual

Less Signal

More Signal

like a clean desk before you start to work. With this tidy cognitive desk, an athlete can get right to it when some work comes along.

In the figure above, I have depicted a "signal," a desired sound, as a pair of undulating waves. "Noise" is the swirl of foggy dots around the signal that represents the background noise in our own brains. Desired signals must always compete with some degree of noise created inside the head in addition to the noise outside the head, in the environment.

An incoming signal is processed in the brain with various levels of success, depending on the individual. A musician's brain and a bilingual's brain will strengthen the signal. In the image that depicts the musician and bilingual, an enhanced signal stands out starkly against the noise, enabling an ease of signal processing. In contrast, an individual who has been linguistically deprived, perhaps due to growing up in impoverished circumstances, has the noise in the brain turned up, making the signal more difficult to discern. Our athlete, on the other hand, has less noise in competition with the signal. Taken together with an enhanced signal, the message gets through loud and clear, landing on a quiet neural runway.

OUR SOUND MIND MAKES US *US*

The brain is an organ of prediction. Our behavior—how we react in any circumstance—is based on who we have become, based on what we have learned throughout our lives. We operate from this bedrock using a com-

The BEAMS Hypothesis

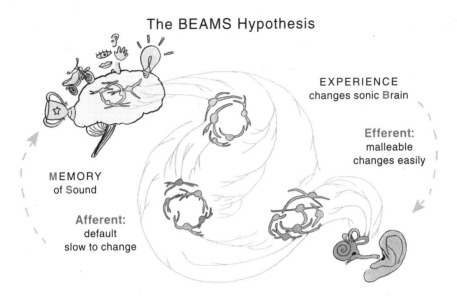

EXPERIENCE
changes sonic Brain

Efferent:
malleable
changes easily

MEMORY
of Sound

Afferent:
default
slow to change

bination of intuition and logic built up from experience. Based on probabilities and past outcomes, our brain is equipped to do what it must do at any given moment.

How do we form this bedrock of who we are? In part from our memories. When we hear a sound, our ear—the cochlea—sends a neural signal to the brain. This ear-to-brain (afferent) pathway is complemented by the pathway going in the other direction, from the brain to the ear (the efferent pathway). Why does the brain need to talk to the ear? A chief role of the efferent pathway is to prepare the ear to gather the right information under the circumstances. It quickly alters the sound mind's response based on the importance of the sound. Over time an important sound—perhaps your mother's voice—earns preference in processing due to careful sculpting of the afferent pathway by efferent signaling. The memory of the sound of your mother's voice now resides in your automatic neural circuitry. Primed to respond optimally to your mother's voice, your brain gives precedence to that sound. You are likely to hear it even if you're asleep. A prediction is made, based on memory, that it is a voice of consequence.

I have summarized auditory learning in the BEAMS hypothesis. The hearing brain interacts with the other senses, the motor, emotion, and cognitive systems of the Brain. This experience with sound effects changes through the Efferent (brain-to-ear) circuitry—which is massive. Over time, as importance is established, the Afferent (ear-to-brain) pathways change, representing Memories of the Sounds of our lives.

Our history with sound, then, is crucial to how our brain works. Our neural pathways are sculpted by our lives in sound. This process doesn't happen quickly. You do not gain the advantages described above with a week of musical instruction or a half semester of Spanish or a month at the gym. But over time it adds up. Memories for sounds are made, neural pathways are altered, and automaticity replaces labor. The signal overtakes the noise. Eventually, with music practice, with athletic competition, as we get older, the sounds of our past bring about a foundation of sound processing in the present. The sound mind continues to accrue wisdom, building on the foundation of memories that makes us *us*. The sounds of our lives shape our brains.

BIOLOGICAL CONNECTIONS

I opened this piece with the premise that sound connects us. We connect with our loved ones by speaking with them. We connect with the sounds of home. These sound connections have a biological basis. Music engages broadly similar cognitive, motor, and limbic activity in all of us. Our brains operate in sync with our fellow concertgoers in an orchestra hall or a concert venue. Not only do we nod our heads or tap our feet in synchrony, but we are connected in our brain rhythms. The friendly feelings of bonding at a concert come in part from the biological synchrony engendered by the rhythm in music.

We are *built* to connect with sound. Consider the voice. A group of researchers studied the sound components of the spoken word by analyzing speech samples of over seven thousand speakers from around the world. The sample included speakers of English, Farsi, French, German, Hindi, Japanese, Korean, Mandarin Chinese, Spanish, Tamil, and Vietnamese. They found that whether male or female, young or old, and irrespective of language, human speech shares certain consistent, universal vocal resonances. In other words, all of us have the raw materials—the esophagus, the larynx, the oral and nasal cavities, and their accompanying resonant properties—to connect with sound. We all own the same instrument.

And what's more, the sounds we make with these instruments are musical. When we speak, we produce a fundamental frequency (what we perceive as voice pitch—generally higher for women, lower for men) and harmonics of the fundamental frequency. We shape the relative sizes of these harmonics with our tongues and the shape of our mouths; this is how we form the sounds of speech. The resonances in our speech occur at ratios aligning with the most consonant musical intervals, like the octave (2:1), the perfect fifth (3:2), and the perfect fourth (4:3). This musicality in speech spans speakers of all languages. Human music naturally echoes the human voice.

Our group wondered whether vocal resonances might be affected by musicianship. We applied the same analysis that revealed musicality in speech to the speech and song of musicians and nonmusicians. While all the participants had the same prominent vocal resonances, defined by distinct peaks at consonant intervals such as octaves, fourths, and fifths, the musicians had *less acoustic noise in the troughs between the resonant peaks.* Instrumentalists had less noise than nonmusicians. Singers' voices had the least noise of all. This was true whether the participants were singing or speaking. Thus there are both individualities and commonalities contributing to the sounds we make and connect with.

Observing the alignment of brains in Egyptian fruit bats has revealed some biological underpinnings of how these connections are made. Collectives of bats, which form long-lasting social bonds with members of their group, synchronize their neural activity in the frontal areas in their brains when one of them emits a call. Interestingly, bats that are socially closer to the caller have stronger brain coupling than members of the group that are more socially distant in their relationship to the caller. We are biologically wired to connect to one another using sound.

SCIENCE IS AN ART

As an undergraduate comparative literature major, I never would have found my love of biology if I hadn't been forced to take it as a distribution requirement. Education has become specialized at the expense of a broader view. Art and science used to be more tightly coupled. Today science is estranged from the humanities, and it is becoming less human as a result. In the public eye, science is often seen as the domain of tangible facts and hard-won truths, while the humanities, including art and music, are where imagination comes first and the intangible reigns. But both science and art have tangible and intangible properties.

There is something marvelous about music that defies the type of quantification the scientific process requires. Every scientific perspective must acknowledge both what it can measure and what it cannot. Einstein wrote, "There comes a point where the mind takes a leap—call it intuition or what you will—and comes out upon a higher plane of knowledge, but can never prove how it got there. All great discoveries have involved such a leap." He also said, "At times I feel certain I am right while not knowing the reason," and "Imagination is more important than knowledge. For knowledge is limited, whereas imagination embraces the entire world, stimulating progress, giving birth to evolution. It is, strictly speaking, a real factor in scientific research." (Incidentally, Einstein claimed to think in music.) Good scientists use imagination and embrace the intangibles—what we cannot measure—that are part of the system we are investigating.

Metrics such as reading scores and brain scans go a long way toward making the argument that music training should be provided in schools. However, learning to play music provides many intangible benefits that are hard to measure. What about the focus and discipline that years of practice engender, the satisfaction of being a part of a musical group, the confidence hard won from performing on a stage? These intangibles count as benefits even though they are difficult to quantify on an MRI or on a standardized test.

Policies, laws, and regulations are often made based on the tangible—what we can measure—and are often in response to complex incentives. Sometimes this focus on the tangible comes at the expense of a more holistic appraisal of its impact on our relationships and our communities.

Consider how the logic of what we can measure makes itself heard in the beeping trucks we all listen to every day. It is much easier to measure deaths from accidents involving reversing trucks—a measurable outcome—than damage to the sound mind or to the hearing of people who drive trucks or live or work around them. So OSHA regulations require that nearly all commercial trucks must beep when reversing.

There are also marginal decreases in the responsibility of truck drivers and pedestrians, who now rely on beeps. This further erodes notions of our roles in caring for ourselves and the people around us. It moves employers closer to hiring a zero-liability employee, and an employee who can do no harm surely can be less skilled, and maybe paid a little less—a measurable outcome. In the contemporary world, those of us who care about our sound minds have no basis for arguing against the beeping. What matters is how many or how few truck accidents have been prevented.

But meanwhile, we tune the beeps out. We all become that much more likely to put on our headphones, close our windows, turn on white noise, or just stop listening altogether. Worse, some listeners no longer notice. If we are tuning that out, what else is passing us by? How much connection, peace, and agency have been lost in the process? *Just because it cannot be measured does not mean it's not important!*

In an example of misplaced metrics, some years ago, in an attempt to manage public spending, the Arts Council of England imposed objective "quality metrics" on art to determine whom to fund. The worthiness of a piece of art or an artist was determined by a series of checkboxes on a form. If Stravinsky or Warhol or Gaudí had to rely on a clipboard-wielding functionary to proceed with their art, can you imagine how much more impoverished the world would be? I have a difficult time believing an Arts Council metric that would adequately anticipate *The Rite of Spring*, soup can silkscreens, or Casa Milà. What makes art *art* is often unmeasurable and also unforeseeable in advance.

One of the biggest challenges facing music research is you can rarely get two people to agree on a definition of what music is. The temptation is to limit variables, either by restricting your definition of "musician" or by creating in-lab instruction. Neither option is particularly good. If we find out that classically trained French horn players with between thirteen and fifteen years of experience can solve crossword puzzles 30 percent faster than nonmusicians, does this really tell us anything about *musicians* generally? If we create a music training regimen that involves undergraduate nonmusicians coming to the lab to follow a thirty-minute music training course three days a week for four weeks, have we really learned anything about the brain of a musician "in the wild"? Science demands tight control when it comes to clinical trials. If you are testing a drug to treat a disease, there are rigorous protocols about dosage, controls, strictly defined primary and secondary outcomes and endpoints. Studying music systematically defies nearly all those requirements. Paradoxically, every layer of control added to music experiments can obscure the intangibles that make music what it is. Balancing competing priorities is hard, requiring nuanced thinking and decision making.

This does not mean we should not research music. On the contrary. Happily, initiatives to study music in the context of medicine and healing are beginning to cross disciplinary boundaries and embrace leaps of intuition. The Sound Health Initiative—a collaboration between the National Institutes of Health, the John F. Kennedy Center for the Performing Arts, and the National Endowment for the Arts—is working to expand our understanding of how music impacts the brain and how this knowledge can be harnessed for health and wellness. When NIH director Francis Collins called upon his twenty-seven institutes to gauge their interest, twenty-two indicated they could envision a place for music in their institute portfolios.

Renée Fleming embodies the very borderless mindset I embrace. This is evident in her musical expression—opera, musicals, lieder, jazz vocals, Christmas carols, indie rock, and improvised sing-alongs with family and heads of state. Fleming is an inspiring ambassador for the arts. But also, as a key member of this initiative, she has shown a deep understanding of what can be gained by marrying art, science, and policy—as they were during the Renaissance—and looking toward a broader, more flexible view of what can be. Because of the nature of the arts, this initiative will enable us to value what can't be measured as well as what can.

For example, one way of striking a balance between measurement and the intangible dimensions of music is to set up a science lab in the space where art is being produced. We chose to work in the context of existing, successful music programs in Los Angeles and in Chicago, not fabricated conditions. At the same time, our chief biological metrics were objective, unambiguous electric signals.

Having taken part in the Sound Health Initiative since its inception, I am hopeful the study of music in medicine and education will clarify how music and biological health coincide. Science and the arts are reinforced by embracing and guiding each other. We discover new truths by making connections with seemingly disparate ideas. It is an *asset* that music doesn't lend itself easily to the clinical trial blueprint appropriate for drug studies. This requires scientists to evaluate converging evidence and reach decisions using a combination of intuition and experience instead of searching for *the* answer or *the* proof in a single conclusive study. We can think in new ways to maintain scientific rigor while still allowing music to be *music*. By its very nature, sound, and thus music, flows; it cannot be captured. Yet considering what we can measure and what defies measurement *simultaneously*, we can honor the depth, the nuance, and the context embodied in music and in science.

THAT'S SOME BRAIN!

Remember the story of *Charlotte's Web*? A family wakes up one morning to see "Some Pig" woven in the spiderweb above their piglet, Wilbur. Word gets around, and soon everyone is convinced that Wilbur is a special pig indeed. He is treated with respect and ultimately saved from slaughter thanks to his friend Charlotte's silken message. Only one person—the mom—actually articulates that Wilbur, although remarkable in his own way, isn't the only special one here. She says, "That's some spider!"

This story came to mind while listening to a discussion of the wonders of cochlear implants. These are amazing devices that convert sounds into electrical impulses stimulating the auditory nerve directly, bypassing a nonfunctioning ear. With them, the deaf are able to hear—a triumph of biomedicine.

Indeed, the technology behind cochlear implants is remarkable; however, it's the *sound mind* that makes them possible. Cochlear implants—from the portable device that uses real-time audio processing to turn acoustic signals into twenty-some streams of electrical pulses, to the skilled surgeons who accomplish delicate precision surgery to place these pulse-delivering electrodes—are truly a testament to human ingenuity. But the cochlear implant would not work without the adaptability, complexity, and interoperability of the sound mind making sense of this unfamiliar input. What a cochlear implant sends to the brain is wildly different from what an ear sends to it. I find myself thinking, *That's some brain!*

The sound mind thrives on connections within the brain, to how we think, move, feel, and combine our senses. And it excels in helping us forge connections to others, which can be strengthened by honoring silence, and by engaging in activities such as playing music, speaking another language, and athletics. Tune the sound mind by exercising it!

How Music Shows Us
What It Means to Be Human

RHIANNON GIDDENS

Pulitzer Prize and Grammy Award–Winning Singer,
Instrumentalist, and Composer

In 2022 I embarked on my first tour with the Silkroad Ensemble, an incredible multicultural group of performers spreading a message of equity using the power of musical connection. In between tour dates we occasionally did daytime events in community spaces as a way of trying to share that message with as many people as possible. One time, during one of these little shows at this space in Bedford Hills, Connecticut, harpist Maeve Gilchrist was making the most incredible sounds on her instrument; the audience was enrapt and completely silent. You could hear a pin drop—but then I started to hear the jangling of keys. It was faint at first, but grew louder, and insistent—and I remember thinking, *Who on earth thinks it's okay to jangle keys at a concert?!?* And then I realized—the person jangling the keys was a guard, and I was brought back to the fact that the show was being performed in a correctional facility; the audience was full of incarcerated individuals, there were bars over the windows, and only some of us were walking out of there after the show. In that moment, I had completely forgotten where we actually were. In that moment, I was in the same exact space as those women—in awe of someone's talent, and receiving a spiritual experience. In that moment, I was reminded of why we were in that prison—to be in a relation with those women that had nothing to do with where they were and everything to do with who they were—fellow human beings responding to music.

When there's a perceived difference among people, a feeling of superiority tends to follow—an urge to rank one higher than the other. In the work of playing in prisons, for example, there's often this false idea that the musicians are offering a priceless gift to the poor incarcerated communities and that the energy only flows one way. This is never, ever true. The relationship of performer and audience is always a reciprocal one, no matter the background or the population. Everyone involved is actually supposed to come out of a performative experience a winner; no matter where, no matter who, no matter how. Music has this inherent power to bring humans together—at a concert, whether onstage or off, we are all equal.

This is one of the biggest reasons why I have focused on the banjo so often in different phases of my career. Far from the simplistic symbol of stereotypical mountain life as it's often portrayed, the banjo is the ultimate symbol of how people in America have found connections with one another. A brief walk through its unbelievably rich history and cultural importance (that has been largely forgotten, suppressed, and erased) will show why.

As Kristina Gaddy describes in her book *Well of Souls*, the banjo began as a ritual instrument used in ceremonies to link the spirituality and religion of different African faiths. Enslaved Africans brought their knowledge and know-how of their ancestral cultural instruments with them across the ocean and created this new version on Caribbean soil.

While these banjos were simple instruments, built using a gourd body and wooden stick neck, their music helped players and listeners make sense of a new and complex universe, and always attracted the notice of the dominant culture around them. As people from the African diaspora were moved around the various colonies of Turtle Island, they brought the banjo and its attendant music with them, spreading it from Brazil to Maine. It was noticed and written about by the European and burgeoning American elite, often in a paternalistic, barely tolerant way, but the real culture transfer happened among the poor. Poverty is the great leveler, and is the true issue at the heart of the great American problem—racism is a tool, albeit a very efficient tool—which is to enforce class distinctions and keep most of the resources in the hands of the few. Poor white Americans (often one generation or less away from massive subjugation issues of their own across the sea) and poor black Americans shared the same space and began to share the same music. Working-class, cross-cultural collaboration is at the heart of American music of all kinds—it's one of the best examples of how humans connect, regardless of perceived and enforced differences such as the amount of melanin someone has in their skin.

The banjo, the only instrument completely unique to America as a political state, became a product of that collaboration, not only musically but in engineering and form, transforming ultimately into a hybrid of European, Indigenous, and African ideas that represents beautifully so much of what America really is. When I play my banjo, particularly my handmade gourd or minstrel banjo, I feel the connection to all that history flow through my fingers; I feel the spirit of countless nameless people who tried to make life a little bit better by plucking its strings; by listening to one another, and trading licks; I feel the power of sound. And to a brain steadily fed a diet of instant, digital, and shallow connections, it is deeply calming.

Music, when being created or actively listened to, has been a time-honored way to help us find the path to inner peace; over the innumerable centuries of human existence, we have used music to help process the events of the world around us. This was very evident during the COVID pandemic, particularly in the early lockdowns. We listened to records, we watched streams of concerts, we made the music that made us feel better.

Every day I sang the old songs that brought me comfort; I played ancient tunes on my banjo; I created duets with my partner, Francesco; all these things helped me face the challenges we were going through in ways I can't even quantify. I'm fascinated by the ways music is a coping mechanism, not just in the pandemic, but throughout history.

For centuries in Southern Italy, for example, there was an ancient healing ritual centered on hypnotic, tambourine-driven music. Someone (often a woman) would be said to be bitten by a specific spider (whether real or psychological is not to be gone into here) and fall into a hysterical state—the only cure was music to make her dance the poison away. This lasted for days. Across the ocean to the southern United States and you find echoes in the ecstatic tambourine playing and dancing in certain African American churches, driving the devil out and raising the Holy Spirit. Trance dance and music from Sufi mosques to the mosh pits at Bonnaroo take people to a different plane; create ecstatic states; put us in touch with that infinite other that we cannot explain but must be able to feel.

Music is often assumed to be a universal language—it's not, but if you listen hard enough, you can always figure it out. Just like verb forms in speech, the way people think of beats and tones in India is different from the way they think about them in Germany or Alaska. The instruments that are native to each culture influence the expression of music. The interesting part is that, although not everybody processes or makes music in the same way, you will always find that point of connection.

Music has created connections between humans for thousands of years. You don't have to read it. You don't have to look at it. You don't even need to understand it. You can just sit there and absorb the sound.

During the pandemic, people were grateful for the concerts we streamed to help them through tough times. While the music helped to bring people together, the concerts were hard for us performers. There is something extra-sensory, almost spiritual, about a live physical performance that you can't replicate through a screen. There's a feeling of alchemy when actual molecules are disturbed directly by the sounds in the room, and that those changed molecules are journeying from instrument to ear. Francesco and I found it too difficult to play the songs we'd played in front of live audiences; the difference was too great. So I started singing the old and old-style songs and ballads that had been bringing me comfort, like "Calling Me Home" and "O Death." Francesco brought tunes that made him feel his home country of Italy. Folk songs like these tap into experiences that people have been dealing with for thousands of years—death, heartbreak, love, despair.

Francesco and I decided we needed to record these songs. We managed to escape into a studio with our engineer, Ben, during a brief relaxation of lockdown rules; on an isolated farm outside of Dublin, it was just the three of us, our instruments, microphones, and some homemade bread and soup. We wanted to share how we felt in that moment, so we left each live take very raw, with few alterations or studio edits. For each song we were listening to one another and reacting in a way that was born from the emotional state that we were in and the need to create together, which can be heard in the record. So we just let the music and the energy tell the story, with the hope that it would help others too.

"Calling Me Home," by veteran musician and songwriter Alice Gerrard, is the first song on this project, and it focuses on the idea of a "good" death. That when it's time to go, the best way is to be surrounded by your friends and to say goodbye with no regrets. It's a reminder that in addition to millions of people dying before their time, there was also an interruption of how the family they left behind could grieve them—people couldn't see their loved ones for one last time, they couldn't talk to them, they couldn't even see their bodies in a lot of instances, all of which was deeply traumatic.

An interviewer told me that her mother had died during the COVID pandemic, but that she hadn't been able to properly grieve for her until she listened to this song in preparation for the interview. That for the first time in the seven months since her mother's death, she was able to actually cry. That, in a nutshell, is the power of music. It creates emotional pathways for people to help them cope with the ups and downs of life. For me these songs remind me that I'm just one of billions, over thousands and thousands of years of human history, and there's an odd comfort in that. I'm still singing these songs in concerts, to give people the space to grieve and come to terms with the holes the pandemic left behind. I do think as a society we will be processing this trauma for a lot longer than we think.

The cessation of normal life the pandemic brought also became a highlighting focus for a lot of people. Personally I didn't realize how burnt out I had become in my musical life until the pandemic forced me to stop. It made me really think about the importance of that emotional connection between myself and the audience. Not only that, but even just the subject of live music, how it's performed—I suddenly had the luxury of thinking about all these things. We, as a society, musicians and everyone else, suddenly had no way to reach other people except through technology—streams, recordings, videos, TikToks. . . . The form music takes has shifted radically in the last hundred years, with ramifications that I don't even think we are aware of.

We've commodified it. We've electrified it. We've recorded and ossified it. In the past, if you wanted music, human hands and human voices had to be employed in real time, in the real space, for you to hear it. It could be played by anyone, anywhere. But now there's a massive transformation of the millennia-old idea of how we use music to relate to one another as human beings. Instead of playing banjo in the parlor or singing in the car, people now buy or stream music. With a push of a button listeners can hear whatever they want, without a human interaction, or in many instances without any knowledge of the skill and effort that went into making the music. Technology will always be a double-edged sword—the same wizardry that enabled us to share our lockdown album with the world also contributes to the "wallpapering" and devaluing of music that is upending the industry.

At the end of the day, it's essential to remember that technology is just a tool. It's the music itself and the corresponding emotional responses that are important.

Perhaps that's why humans have used music over the ages to tell their stories. Folk music is ideally suited to this role, as the songs are passed down from one generation to the next. Over the course of time, all the extraneous parts are gradually smoothed away, and you're left with a honed story—it's like a stone in a stream being tumbled over centuries until it's smooth and the essence of itself. I often find inspiration for my songs in historical sources, as I feel connected to the people in those stories. Even though I'm never going to know them, and they will never know me, I can resonate with what they were going through. It's an emotional tie that speaks to a wider human experience, making it universally accessible. My audience might never read the book I got the story from, so it's my job to bring these people to life through my music. Knowing that teachers have used my historical work in their classes thrills me and makes me feel useful! Part of the reason I am still alive in the music industry is because of this mission and these songs.

Recently I had the opportunity to explore one of these vital stories in a deeper way. In 2017, Spoleto Festival USA commissioned me to write an opera about the remarkable man Omar ibn Said. A scholar and a student of the Qur'an, he lived peacefully in his homeland of Futa Toro, in modern-day Senegal, when, at the age of thirty-seven, he was captured and sold into slavery. He lived the rest of his long life in North Carolina, dying in his eighties before the end of the Civil War. By itself, the story isn't as uncommon as people might think—between one fifth and one quarter of the souls brought to the Americas from Africa were Muslim; but what he left behind—an autobiography in Arabic—is extraordinary. With that and a lot of research, advisors, and the collaboration of my co-composer, Michael Abels, I looked to find a way to tell his story that would resonate for a modern audience, no matter what religion or cultural background: a story of maintaining a spiritual identity in the midst of incredible hardship. I composed by singing, playing my banjo, my viola, my guitar, my piano . . . trying to embody the voices of Omar and the enslaved American world he stepped into; and as I have followed the productions around the country I have been struck by how not only the audiences but the singers and creators involved have talked about the intense emotional connections they are feeling during the opera. It makes me proud to be part of a piece that not only gathers critical acclaim, like the 2023 Pulitzer for Music (pinch me, still), but that has been received with gratitude by Muslims and Christians alike.

Telling these stories can be exhausting—but ultimately musical drama and long-form storytelling can really take everyone involved into a different place. For me, there's a big difference between the songs I sing and the stage pieces I have been involved in. I recently played Bess in Gershwin's opera *Porgy and Bess*, which deals with many intense topics, like drug addiction, domestic violence, and systemic racism. It felt less emotionally draining to me to portray Bess, a devastatingly wounded character in a difficult world, than to sing one of my historically inspired songs day in, day out. I can maintain a distance from a character that is harder to navigate when I am the one who has created and is embodying a real-life story. It makes it bearable in a certain way. I've come really close to a few nervous breakdowns, which were stark reminders that I have been leaving myself last throughout the course of my career, and that, as a society, we don't always take care of our artists. We don't make it easy for our artists to take care of themselves— they have to hustle 24/7 just to keep the lights on, and when you add deeply felt cultural work that is rooted in generational trauma, it can snowball quickly. So I've started to reach out to people doing similar work, fellow performers, to try to support their mental health so we can help each other not burn out.

While science has begun to understand how music affects the brain and the body, it's still got a long way to go—its only beginning to put words and numbers to things we have known instinctively as a species for a long time. Music is steeped in history. It's been used to tell stories, pass on traditions, and bring comfort. For generations, humans have been soothed by music. It helps us relate to one another as human beings, to understand one another, and to realize that, at the end of the day, we're not that different from one another. We're all going through life in the same way. And music is the key that holds us together.

During a dark moment of self-doubt and despair one day, I met a woman who told me that when her mum was on her deathbed, she wanted to hear one of my songs over and over again. I was humbled, honored, and . . . healed by hearing that. It was an incredible reminder of the necessity of the vibrations we make as musicians—whether live or recorded—and just how powerful they can be.

With the collaboration of Joanna L. Patterson-Cross, PhD, MBiochem.

THE
MEDICAL MUSE

Health Professionals and Artists
Share Impacts of the Arts in Hospitals
and Clinical Settings

Sounding Joy

CHRISTOPHER BAILEY

Arts and Health Lead, World Health Organization

While my ophthalmologist was peering into my eye one day to view my optic nerve, I heard him gasp. My heart sank.

"Mr. Bailey," he told me, "you have lost ninety five percent of the mass of your optic nerve. If we do not intervene immediately, you will be totally blind in six months, one year tops."

With 20/20 hindsight, I now know that my terminal glaucoma had been gradually reducing my vision for years, but so slowly and so painlessly that I was able to write off the symptoms as the product of fatigue, stress, or natural aging. What I also didn't know then, but realize now, is that as I was slowly losing my vision, the sense-making ability of my brain was working overtime to fill in the gaps. My perception of my vision was becoming better than the actuality of my vision, sometimes resulting in strange mistakes in cognition that had a kind of hallucinatory intensity. I might walk by a grove of pine trees here in Switzerland, and while my brain could recognize a "tree pattern," drawing from my memory an image that would fit the faint pattern I was perceiving, instead of seeing a pine tree, I would perceive a palm tree. I would know I was experiencing a hallucination because it would be clearer than the actual image of the pine.

What does one do when you are told you are going blind? I grew up in museums, I have been over the years a film buff, I enjoy light and color and images of beautiful people and things as much as anyone. Eighty percent of the way we experience the world and enjoy it in our contemporary society is visual. The visual cortex represents one fifth of the brain's capacity. Much of our cognition and pleasure are neurologically centered around sight. But my world had slowly become corrupted, eroded, and decayed into a dull, dirty, cloudy consistency. When I eventually lost the ability to recognize faces, I felt cast out from society, a pariah, and abandoned. My sense of loss grew so deep that its vortex threatened to pull me into the darkness. When my son left home at Christmas that year, the thought that I might literally never see his face again passed over my mind like a cold fog.

But equal to the profound loss was also an all-consuming dread. How would I provide for my family? How would I read and write, or even eat and walk? Or exercise? How could I navigate the world, let alone enjoy it? Some days the dread and anxiety became so overwhelming, it took an act of will simply to go about the daily tasks that I could still do . . . but for how long?

I had recently begun a new program on Arts and Health at the World Health Organization, which now seemed completely at risk. How could I accomplish this with no sight? We had commissioned the foundational research of the field, outlining the evidence base for the health benefits of the arts, and much of it was quite promising, showing how performance in drama, music, dance, or engagement in the visual arts could help people who have experienced conflict and violence—accidental, personal, or organized—process and eventually transcend their traumatic experiences. We saw through controlled studies how appropriate visual art could lower cortisol levels in hospital environments, and how physical rehabilitation could be accelerated and assist mood enhancement when music was added. From a range of physical and mental conditions, and across a range of social interventions, we learned how music, story, movement, and visual representation could provide comfort, perhaps contextualize a difficult situation, build community, or even transform identity and give authentic personal meaning to an unavoidable catastrophe. To explore the growing body of evidence, we have been building an ever-increasing network of research centers around the world to collaborate with WHO in all forms of artistic expression and in all aspects of well-being, from effectiveness of an arts-based intervention, to exploring the biochemistry and neurology of why we react in certain ways to aesthetic engagement. Increasingly we have worked in communities around the world to find culturally relevant approaches to help people make sense of difficult situations, and have engaged the global media to promote pro-health messaging within communities, particularly in those less fortunate. The most public example was the Together at Home concert held at the beginning of the pandemic, curated by Lady Gaga, which was the largest single internet-based global event in history, raised the most money for an online benefit, but most importantly, communicated the key health messages of hand hygiene, social distancing, staying at home, and honoring health-care workers, at a key moment in the pandemic. But perhaps the most powerful element was the implied message of common solidarity, no matter who you are or where you live.

And yet no amount of exposure to the arts would ever have a hope of regenerating my frayed optic nerve.

Which brings us to an important question. When we say the arts can heal, what do we actually mean? When we talk of healing, we are not necessarily talking about curing anything, particularly when it comes to the use of the arts in a health context. In English, "heal" and "health" come from an Anglo-Saxon root word cognate with the word "whole." In its original meaning, to be "healthy" did not mean to be without disease or infirmity, but to be a complete person. This original notion of health is reflected in its WHO definition from our 1947 Constitution, which defines health as not merely the absence of disease or infirmity, but the attainment of the highest personal level of physical, mental, and social well-being. The WHO definition of mental health goes even further. When you ask yourself if you are mentally healthy, the question isn't whether or not you have any diagnosable conditions (if you look hard enough, you will find plenty), but more simply, whether you can cope with the everyday stresses of life. Can you maximize your abilities? Are you productive? Do you contribute to your community? Do these things bring you joy?

When I lost my sight, all of these aspects of day-to-day living were thrown into chaotic doubt.

Somehow I was able in the beginning to separate my personal catastrophe from the professional tasks at hand. Over the next few years, through our Healing Arts initiative, we are building a network of research centers doing rigorous work measuring the actual effects of aesthetic engagement on key health indicators for individuals and communities in every region of the world. We are engaging with practitioners in all genres of the arts, from clinical clowns to arts therapists to community curators. We engaged the global media at the height of the pandemic not only to build a sense of community but to combat misinformation by better telling the science story.

But as I began losing my ability to carry out basic human functions— walking, communicating, even cooking and eating—a sinking feeling was growing inside of me that I would not be able to keep up this work for long.

At first I declined help. When the hospital for the blind in Lausanne recommended that I adopt tinted glasses to help sharpen my vision so that the glare of light would not so easily overwhelm my fractured optic nerve, and that I start using a white cane, I rejected these notions. I couldn't imagine myself as a blind person, and I did not want to start assuming the paraphernalia of the role.

Then one day when I arrived for a checkup at the eye doctor, he asked me what the marks across my forehead were. What marks? I asked. Apparently there was a row of bruises, a red one, a yellow one, a green one, a blue one, a purple one, strung across my forehead like a row of Christmas tree lights.

"Oh, this one was when I hit the corner of a kitchen cupboard. This one was when I hit my head on the wall plugging in an electrical cord. This one was when I fell down the stairs. This one was when I ran into a light pole . . ."

The doctor firmly told me it was time to use the cane.

The road to accepting my condition and managing my situation began that day. I began training in "how to be blind." Each week I would come in with some unsolvable problem, and my coach would show me how other visually impaired people managed the situation. Even unlocking my door had become a stressful situation, as I could no longer see the keyhole. My coach would say, "Don't try to see it. Just touch it." I had despaired when I could no longer see when the bread I was baking was done, and by the time I would smell it burning, it would be too late. "So learn the smell of bread being done," she urged me, and so on.

At night my coach would take me to a busy street in Lausanne and blindfold me, guiding me to teach myself to navigate the streets by using only sound. She told me to reach out with my hearing, and listen to how the passing cars reverberate on the pavement, the buildings around me, even the trees. Hear how the sound opens out when we approach the intersection. Like a child, I slowly learned how to navigate the world again. Echolocation, the ability to imagine the world through sound, is not an intellectual enterprise. It is not something you can turn on and off with a thought. It is literally the slow rewiring of the neural pathways of the brain from the visual cortex to the auditory sensors of the brain. To some degree this happens naturally to people who lose their sight. When the visual cortex does not get the information it needs from the optic nerve to form a conception of the world, it slowly reaches out through new neural pathways to the auditory center to use sound to create an aural landscape. While not nearly as detailed as the visual world, still, it has its own strange beauty.

Although I had for weeks been consciously practicing the beginning stages of echolocation as I moved about the city, progress was slow, frustrating, and often imperceptible. The actual transformation happened in a moment.

It was an Easter performance of Mozart's *Requiem*, one of my favorite pieces, and to my mind a perfect expression of grief, coming in waves that crescendo to an unmanageable crest of sorrow, which then subsided in peace and exhaustion, only to rise up again in a tidal force of woe. As I listened to this music and was transported by this musical expression of my own grieving for the visual life I had lost, I suddenly was no longer hearing just the music, the tone, the volume, the tempo, the words, but hearing for the first time the actual sound itself, reverberating and caressing the Gothic architecture of the church, the soft textures of the fabric, and the bodies of the audience around me. I was no longer listening to music, I was experiencing the Mozart literally passing through the physical space and living beings around me, creating an aural picture in my mind, creating the world around me. The music was not about life—it literally recreated the world for me.

Sight is deceptive. It literally captures only the surface of things. It is registering the light reflecting from an object. Sound, however, is an energy that passes through matter. It is more palpable, more immediate. Once I entered fully this new world of sound, rather than feeling exiled and outcast, I found myself more intimately connected to it, sensing the sound that

I hear passing through the objects and people around me, connecting us all, not as objects, but as one continuous song.

At about this time I was also rehearsing for a show that I had been cast in prior to my diagnosis. I had offered to quit, not sure if I could manage the lead in a stage play in my condition, but after researching how blind performers manage, we worked out with the technical staff how I might accomplish it. I could not see glow tape backstage, so that was replaced with bits of cut carpet that I could feel with my hands, and on the floor with my feet, to guide me. I spent endless hours memorizing the paces between pieces of furniture and set pieces on the stage, so I would not give myself away as blind by bumping into a chair or a couch.

But my biggest worry was how I was going to accomplish the craft of acting if I couldn't react to the expressions on the other actors' faces. I could react to their voices, obviously, but subtle gestures or expressions were lost to me.

And yet, through the rehearsal process, I began to notice that my own body's reaction to my fellow actors was changing. When a character was lying, I began to feel ill inside. When there was attraction, I could feel it, even without visual or audible cues. Anger would stoke a burning fire inside me even when I couldn't see any sign of it.

I slowly realized that my body was responding to the changing smells of the other actors as they changed emotional states.

In the first preview with a live audience, when the lights went up, the brightness shocked my fragile optic nerves and wiped out what little of my vision remained. At first, rather desperately, I relied completely on my memorized steps on the stage and the sound of the actors' voices. At one point, when my character delivered a line that sparked a laugh from the audience, the sound of the rolling laughter covered the theater and rolled onto the stage and its inhabitants, creating an aural image of the scene for me. Just as I and the company were creating a scene for the audience, through echolocation so, too, were the audible reactions of the audience creating the scene for me.

I don't think it was an accident that acting helped waken the nonvisual part of my sense-making abilities. Stanislavsky, Proust, and Freud all noted within a decade or so of one another how smell, taste, or sound could summon ancient memories and powerful primal emotions. These observations were made prior to our modern understanding of neurology, and even today we are learning how visual information takes a different path in the brain, from the optic nerve to the visual cortex and back to the frontal lobes for problem-solving and use in conscious thought and immediate decision making. But smell and sound have the ability to go more directly to the midbrain, the seat of identity, long-term memory, and the primal drives. Stanislavsky reverse-engineered this process in what he called "sense memory," whereby an artist could unlock memories and emotional states by consciously introducing smells or tastes to help in the preparatory moments before entering a scene. Even the ability to make empathic connection, to elicit mirror neurons of the emotional states between people, became heightened for me, to the extent that when I would enter a room with heightened emotions, I might become overwhelmed, like staring into headlights.

Of course when I described my discoveries to my coach, her response was to congratulate me, but she suggested that maybe next time I should play the role as a blind person, and not pretend to be sighted. It would be a lot easier and make a very powerful statement.

Music and theater were having a transformative effect on my journey through blindness. As I gained confidence, my fears began to subside. Music in particular helped shape my transforming identity as I accepted, then managed, and soon transcended my condition. When the Baroque composer Rameau spoke of music, he described the pleasure experienced by the listener as hearing a melody as pleasing because of both what you hear and what you don't hear. (Modern neurology actually maps these states to production of discrete biochemical reactions.) The memory of the note just passed, combined with the present experience of a note currently heard with the anticipation of the note yet to be played, forms a harmony in our imaginations even when the sounds do not exist at the same time. All the arts to some degree unify past, present, and future, but music in particular does this with a powerful healing effect. In the temporal lobe, evolution has given our species a great gift in our sense of a past and a future. Through our sense of the past, we can learn from our experience, and from our conception of a future, we can plan. And yet these abilities are a double-edged sword, and come at a great cost. With the conception of a past also comes the conception of loss, and with the notion of a future comes a feeling of profound dread. The state of peace that we associate with contentment and happiness is related to a conception of the present moment. Sadly in our society we spend increasing amounts of time in the past and in the future and less and less focused attention on the present, resulting in a higher degree of dread and anxiety, the source of much of human suffering. The arts can help bridge these states, bringing our conception of past, present, and future into a unified whole, grasping the emotional challenges of expectation and misfortune, and easing anxiety and dread, with windows of profound luxuriating in the deep aesthetic flow of presence.

I achieved this memorably through a visit to a museum.

In the week before the first lockdown of the pandemic, I was preparing for a performance at the Wellcome Collection in London. To calm myself before the performance, I decided to go to a midday concert at St. Martin-in-the-Fields. Trafalgar Square was still packed with people, and as I tried to make my way through the crowd, I became disoriented and buffeted about by the mob. I became confused, my heart began racing, my breathing rushed, and I realized I was having a panic attack. Finally I made my way out of the crowd but found myself on the wrong side of the square, a castaway at the entrance of the National Gallery. My heart sank. I had been avoiding museums for years. As a severely visually impaired person, and having spent so many joyous moments in museums, I did not want to be reminded of how much I had lost by seeing familiar paintings, polluted, blurred, and soiled. And yet, to take refuge from the crowd, I went in.

Wandering the galleries, I came to a section that seemed familiar. I perceived large monumental paintings. As I came close to them, I was able to make out stormy seascapes and shipwrecks, and scenes of ocean fog. I then recognized where I was. It was the Turner wing. As I looked at the mist and the fog in the paintings, I began to taste salt water on my cheek, and realized it was not from the ocean spray but from the tears streaming down my cheeks.

I had adapted to my blindness by now, but in that moment, I realized that how Turner painted the world was identical to how I now see it in my advanced state of glaucoma. For the first time, through Turner's eyes, I could imagine the way I see the world as beautiful. Somehow, in that triangulation between a long-dead artist, an object he created, and my own imagination observing it, I could now navigate to an emotional safe harbor.

I now not only accepted my blindness, I embraced it. Rather than feeling exiled from the world, I luxuriated in the peace and opportunity for profound contemplation without the noise and distraction of sight. My transformation was complete.

Just as you willingly close your eyes to better listen to a beautiful piece of music. Just as you willingly close your eyes to better savor a glass of red wine. Just as you willingly close your eyes to better trace the gentle slope of a lover's forearm, so, too, do I accept the closing of my eyes to better share this moment with you.

To me, this is the healing power of art.

Can Singing Touch the Heart?

JACQUELYN KULINSKI, MD, FASPC

Associate Professor of Medicine (Cardiology)
Director, Preventive Cardiology Program
Medical College of Wisconsin

DISCLOSURE

I am not a trained or professional musician or performer, nor do I claim to be an expert in music, singing, or music therapy. I am a board-certified cardiologist and physician researcher. Team science and cross-disciplinary collaborations with music performers, music therapists, and music experts are instrumental to research at the intersection of music and health.

INTRODUCTION

The health benefits of exercise are irrefutable. Everyone has heard the phrase "Exercise is medicine." It's true. Exercise lowers the risk of developing hypertension (high blood pressure), heart disease, stroke, diabetes, Alzheimer's dementia, and certain cancers (breast and colon cancer). Exercise improves mood, sleep, and quality of life. Engaging in one hundred and fifty minutes of moderate-intensity (e.g., brisk walking, yoga, yardwork) exercise per week lowers overall mortality by 30 percent, with additional mortality reductions achieved above one hundred and fifty minutes of exercise per week. From 1950 to 2019, there were over 479,000 scientific publications on physical activity, many supporting the myriad health benefits just mentioned. But what about singing as a form of exercise? At least one definition of exercise is *activity requiring physical effort*. Just ask Renée Fleming—singing absolutely requires physical effort (lots of it, in her case)! Singing requires both passive and active breathing, muscle coordination, and various breathing techniques, including breath holds. So could singing have similar health benefits to exercise?

As a clinician researcher trained in cardiovascular medicine, one of the first places I go to access peer-reviewed, evidence-based scientific research is PubMed, a free search engine with databases of references and abstracts on life sciences and biomedical topics. The U.S. National Library of Medicine at the National Institutes of Health maintains this resource.

If I perform a simple search using the keywords in the table on the next page, I can get a rough estimate of the number of scientific abstracts and articles on a specific topic. Scientific research on the intersection of singing and health pales in comparison to that concerning exercise and health. The numbers are even more dismal when focusing solely on singing and cardiovascular health. Cardiovascular disease is the leading cause of death across the globe, in both men and women, claiming more lives each year than cancer and chronic respiratory diseases combined. What most people do not appreciate is that 80 percent of cardiovascular disease is preventable with achievement of ideal cardiovascular health. Ideal cardiovascular health comprises seven pillars, otherwise known as Life's Essential 8, as defined by the American Heart Association. These pillars include: no smoking, getting sufficient physical activity, following a healthful diet, maintenance of a healthy weight, getting healthy sleep, optimizing cholesterol and blood pressure, and preventing (or having good control of) diabetes. The disheartening (no pun intended) reality is that less than 1 percent of U.S. adults can check all eight boxes. This reality is the reason I now focus on preventive cardiology, in both clinical and research settings. Traditional cardiovascular medicine has focused primarily on treatment of manifest disease rather than on prevention of heart disease and cardiac events. The field of preventive cardiology aims to promote prevention of heart disease and preserve (ideal) cardiovascular health. It involves individual risk assessment and early initiation of interventions (behavioral and/or medical) to prevent, delay, or modify the development of atherosclerosis (the buildup of fats, cholesterol, and other substances in the artery walls). This is referred to as *primary prevention*. Preventive cardiology also includes optimizing treatment of individuals after manifestation of symptomatic heart disease (heart attack, coronary stent placement, coronary bypass surgery), termed *secondary prevention.*

RESEARCH STUDIES ON PHYSICAL ACTIVITY, EXERCISE, AND SINGING: THE NUMBERS.*

Keywords	Search Results
Physical activity AND health	267,396
Exercise AND health	215,041
Singing AND health	779
Physical activity AND cardiovascular health	35,361
Exercise AND cardiovascular health	28,195
Singing AND cardiovascular health	12

*Search performed in PubMed on March 8, 2022.

With an aging population heavily burdened by cardiovascular disease, *exercise as medicine* is frequently hindered by arthritis, chronic lung disease, diabetic neuropathy, disability, polypharmacy, frailty, and physical deconditioning. Furthermore, only 24 percent of U.S. adults meet the recommended minimum of one hundred and fifty minutes of moderate-intensity exercise (or equivalent) per week. Alternative or adjunctive therapies are therefore necessary. Music is a universal art form that is pervasive in every society. Because of its low cost, accessibility, ease of use, and minimal risk, music has immense potential for a safe, nonpharmacologic intervention to improve health. However, music intervention, and more specifically the act of singing, and its potential impact on cardiovascular health, have not been adequately explored to the same extent as traditional exercise. With singing there is almost no reliance on mobility or skeletal muscle strength, so mobility issues are not prohibitive. Because the heart and lung systems are intimately related and work together to deliver oxygen to all cells in the body, singing would be anticipated to have favorable effects on cardiovascular health. This is what I aim to investigate.

SURROGATE MARKERS OF CARDIOVASCULAR HEALTH

A surrogate marker can be defined as a laboratory or imaging measurement or physical sign that is used in research trials as a substitute for a hard clinical end point (e.g., heart attack, cardiac death, stroke). It is measurable, recordable, and often changes more rapidly than the hard end point in response to interventions. In short, it serves as an indicator of disease status. Surrogate markers are needed in medical research because they are more cost-effective than waiting for hard clinical end points, which can take several years. An important surrogate marker in cardiovascular health is measurement of endothelial function.

The endothelium constitutes the largest organ system in the body. The endothelium is a single layer of cells that line the interior surface of the entire circulatory system of blood vessels, from the heart to the smallest capillaries. This single layer of cells has numerous important functions, including prevention of blood clotting, and constriction and dilation of the blood vessels, which contribute to blood flow and blood pressure, all a result of secreting diverse bioactive substances. Exercise, low-fat diets, and some medications (statins for high cholesterol, ACE inhibitors for hypertension, aspirin) are known to improve endothelial function. Sedentary lifestyle, obesity, high cholesterol, hypertension, diabetes, smoking, and aging are associated with endothelial dysfunction. Endothelial dysfunction is regarded as the key early event in the development of atherosclerosis. One of the main mechanisms of endothelial dysfunction is impaired nitric oxide (NO) production and activity. NO is a vasodilator (increases blood flow) and an antioxidant with anti-inflammatory and antithrombotic actions. Clinical measurements of endothelium-dependent vasodilation (a NO-mediated process) by a variety of different techniques provide a marker of endothelial health and integrity.

Ultrasound measurement of brachial artery (upper arm) reactivity is currently the best-validated noninvasive technique to assess endothelium-dependent vasodilation. This technique requires training, experience, and technical expertise in specialized laboratories with strict adherence to standardized protocols. After a five-minute period of forearm occlusion with a blood pressure cuff inflated to suprasystolic pressures (often over 200 mm Hg) to restrict blood flow, rapid cuff release causes shear stress through the brachial artery, stimulating the endothelial cells to release NO, which then causes dilation of the brachial artery (FMD, flow-mediated dilation). The dilator response (measuring changes in brachial artery diameter) is representative of endothelial function, where more is better. What does this mean long term? Well, just a 1 percent increase in brachial artery FMD translates into an 8 to 13 percent lower risk of cardiovascular events, in individuals both with and without cardiovascular disease.

Finger plethysmography, which measures endothelial function at the level of the fingertips using pneumatic probes, has gained increased attention. The method uses a proprietary device, requiring much less technical expertise than the brachial artery FMD technique, and it also comes at a lower cost. It calculates a reactive hyperemia index (RHI) in response to forearm occlusion of blood flow (with a blood pressure cuff, like the FMD technique). It reflects changes in the microvessels rather than larger artery "macro" vessels. RHI only modestly correlates with FMD, likely measuring different aspects of vascular biology. Nonetheless, its lower cost and ease of use make it more attractive as a research tool.

THE "SINGING HEART" PILOT STUDY

In 2017 one of my cardiology fellows-in-training approached me with an interest in doing research on music and the heart. The idea was novel and brilliant, given the paucity of literature in this area. Music listening and health did have research "hits," but singing and health, far fewer. We needed several things to get started: pilot funding, research subjects, a hypothesis, and perhaps most importantly, a music expert to join our team. With the recruitment of a professor of voice from a neighboring institution and a small pilot funding award from the Research Affairs Committee within my institution, the Medical College of Wisconsin (MCW), along with easy access to potential research subjects (adult patients visiting our cardiology clinics), we now had a means. The surrogate end point was easy—endothelial function! We have a world-renowned vascular laboratory, the Human Vascular Translational Research Center (HVTRC) at MCW. The center has full-time technicians who are well versed in the modalities described above. Our professor of voice created a fourteen-minute coaching video, which included vocal warm-up exercises followed by "The Star-Spangled Banner," repeated at various tempos and pitches. The song was chosen because of its familiarity. Lyrics were displayed along the bottom of the video while subjects sang in a seated position. Our hypothesis was that singing would improve endothelial function acutely (just as exercise does).

Over the course of several years, sixty patients were enrolled (mean age 61 ± 13 years, 68 percent women). Subjects had a wide range of medical diagnoses, including hypertension in 60 percent, diabetes in 25 percent, known coronary artery disease in 43 percent, and chronic physical or orthopedic limitations (43 percent). At baseline, 57 percent of subjects had abnormal baseline endothelial function. Subjects with this condition demonstrated the most significant improvement in endothelial function after just fourteen minutes of singing when compared to subjects with normal baseline endothelial function. These data suggest that subjects with healthier endothelium at baseline may need a larger stimulus to effect change or cannot augment their vascular endothelial function further. While the acute vascular response to a single bout of singing may be predictive of the vascular adaptation to longer and more sustained singing interventions, this remains to be confirmed in large, randomized trials. Interestingly, there was no correlation between level of enjoyment (of the singing intervention) and changes in endothelial function. Similar to exercise, you may not need to enjoy singing to reap the benefits! This is the tip of the iceberg . . .

LESSONS LEARNED

It turns out that the national anthem is one of the most difficult songs to sing, at least in part due to its wide-ranging melody. Furthermore, subjects in our pilot study would have preferred to have a choice of musical genre to sing. Individual responses to music are likely influenced by these personal preferences, familiarity with music, environment, prior music experience, personality, and other health factors. Furthermore, the construct of singing is complex. Singing often happens in social contexts, which complicates an objective assessment of the effects of singing itself. Other factors, including vocal contagion (the potential for vocalizations—or singing—to influence the emotional state of surrounding individuals to match that of the singer), social cohesion, alterations in breathing, other physiological changes, and song structure, further add to this complexity. These intricacies are what may give music a great deal of power in its application to health and disease, but it also poses a challenge in the design of rigorous research protocols, because it may not be clear which components of music are responsible for any given effect. It also highlights the importance of team science and interdisciplinary collaborations necessary to pursuing music-based intervention research in general. I am certainly not a musician of any kind (unless you count singing to my toddlers or in the car). This is precisely why I have recruited a team of musical experts to these investigative endeavors.

NATIONAL COLLABORATION

In 2016 the National Institutes of Health (NIH), the John F. Kennedy Center for the Performing Arts, and the National Endowment for the Arts formed a collaborative partnership (Sound Health) and organized a workshop to evaluate the state of basic and applied music research. At this meeting a diverse panel of experts discussed three overlapping periods of life (childhood, adulthood, and aging) and made recommendations for enhancing research in each of these domains. The group developed a set of recommendations intended to highlight research opportunities and promote rigorous investigation in these areas. In 2017 a trans-NIH Music and Health working group was formed to capitalize on these recommendations and promote their implementation. To achieve this goal, NIH issued related funding opportunity announcements in 2019. The purpose: to promote innovative studies on music and health with an emphasis on developing music interventions aimed at understanding their mechanisms of action and clinical applications for the treatment of many diseases, disorders, and conditions.

This was the perfect chance to continue propelling my own work forward. I had pilot data to support ongoing research, and the results looked promising. I was growing my multidisciplinary team of clinician scientists and music experts, and I had lots of ideas about the next steps and potential long-term implications of this research. Given the pilot findings, in which we learned that participants with baseline endothelial dysfunction had the most improvement in vascular function after singing, I would focus on older patients with established (atherosclerotic) heart disease—a *secondary prevention* population.

Furthermore, this population is in need of alternative or adjunctive therapies. Older adults nationwide are the least likely to participate in cardiac rehabilitation programs, which are a recommended treatment after a cardiac event (heart attack, coronary stent, valve replacement, coronary artery bypass surgery, stable angina, recent heart failure, etc.). These outpatient programs, typically twelve weeks long, provide supervised exercise training in conjunction with physical activity counseling, risk-factor reduction with nutritional counseling and weight management, and psychosocial support. Education regarding the purpose of medications and reinforcement for medication adherence is also offered. The programs are safe and effective and designed to speed recovery after an acute cardiac event. Program participation lowers morbidity and mortality, improves quality of life, and prevents readmissions to the hospital for recurrent events or worse symptoms. Despite these important improvements in health outcomes, less than one in four Medicare beneficiaries participate. Heart diseases in older adults are often complicated by age-related complexities, including multimorbidities: arthritis, chronic lung disease, diabetes, polypharmacy, frailty, deconditioning, falls, disability, and other challenges that make participation (or the perception of participation) difficult. Older patients opt out of cardiac rehab as a result. What if singing, as a form of cardiac rehabilitation, were an option? Would patients be interested in this? What would the benefits to the cardiovascular system be?

Before we could trial a singing rehabilitation program, we needed to find the right dose and the right format to optimize benefits. Because the recommended daily dose of exercise for adults is at least thirty minutes, this would be reasonable to consider. Further, I wanted to look for differences in the delivery format (individualized music therapy sessions versus prerecorded singing videos). Live music could be more impactful, but singing along to an instructional video could expand the possibilities for delivering the therapy (i.e., virtually, in the patient's home). This round, we would also allow subjects to choose songs from a variety of genres to match their preferences. (We suspect —though cannot say for certain yet—that preference is important to the magnitude of benefit.)

My team and I landed a funding award from NIH (specifically, NCCIH, the National Center for Complementary and Integrative Health) for the study we titled "Evaluating the Impact of Singing Interventions on Markers of Cardiovascular Health in Older Patients with Cardiovascular Disease." We have begun enrollment of elderly patients with known cardiovascular disease, each of whom will undergo three study visits for the following interventions: (1) a thirty-minute period of guided singing from an in-person music therapist, (2) a thirty-minute period of singing along to an instructional video showing a professor of voice and "inexperienced, older singing student," and (3) a thirty-minute sham visit during which the participant would undergo a tablet-based hearing test. This sham-like arm is meant to isolate the specific effects of the treatment rather than the potential "incidental" effects related to the research setting and measurements.

The grant is a phased study. The first (a two-year phase) will assess the feasibility of the proposed study design with a focus on implementation, practicality, and acceptability of the singing interventions by the target population. This will be followed by a three-year phase, which will involve the clinical trial results, powered for vascular function outcomes using the noninvasive gold standard of brachial artery FMD. We are also collecting heartrate variability, blood pressure, oxygenation, salivary cortisol and cytokine levels (to understand the stress response to singing), and visual mood scores from all participants. These additional measures will allow us to explore the role of emotion in singing on endothelial function. If singing is anxiety provoking for some, would this change the measured outcome results? Perhaps it doesn't matter?

Alternatively, singing may directly activate the vagus nerve via innervation of the larynx and lungs, bypassing any impact of emotion or mood.

The vagus nerve, also referred to as the vagal nerve, is the longest cranial nerve in the body. It runs from the brain stem all the way to part of the colon. It is a component of the parasympathetic nervous system ("rest and digest"). This important nerve has both sensory and motor functions. Sensory functions include: (1) providing sensation for the skin behind the ear, the external part of the ear canal, and certain parts of the throat, and (2) supplying sensation information for the larynx, esophagus, lungs, trachea, heart, and digestive tract. Motor functions of the vagus nerve include: (1) stimulating muscles in the pharynx, larynx, and soft palate, which is the fleshy area near the back of the roof of the mouth, (2) stimulating the heart, where it helps lower resting heart rate, and (3) stimulating involuntary muscle contractions in the digestive tract, including the esophagus, stomach, and most of the intestines. So, it is easy to see how a nerve that stimulates and/or senses parts of the body involved in singing (lungs, larynx, pharynx, soft palate, etc.) likely has a mechanistic role in the impact of singing on our body. Further, using your diaphragm (the breathing muscle) activates the vagus nerve—think of "deep breathing" to relax and lower or counter your body's stress response. Detailed heartrate variability analysis could provide insight into physiologic connections occurring between the brain and heart, as they relate to singing.

RESULTS

All the projected feasibility milestones were met in the first phase of the study. An impressive 100 percent of study visits (seventy-five visits for twenty-five study subjects) were completed. We have had zero dropouts to date. The singing interventions are safe and have had no serious adverse events.

Finally, we achieved 21 percent participation rates (25/120 subjects) of those subjects who were deemed eligible to participate (and were made aware of the study), exceeding the projected rate of 20 percent. Because the above feasibility milestones were met, we were approved for the second (three-year) phase of our research. The trial is expected to be completed by August 2024. Until then, there will be no interim analyses of data. Stay tuned!

CRITICISM AND SKEPTICISM

I will start by saying that my research on singing and heart disease, while both promising and exciting, represents just the tip of the iceberg. More work remains to be done. Are there some skeptics out there? Of course there are. In science, however, being skeptical does not mean doubting the validity of everything, nor does it mean being cynical. Rather, to be skeptical is to judge the validity of a claim based on objective empirical evidence. Rigorously conducted research is necessary to drive medicine and evidence-based interventions, such as mine. It is required for therapies to come to fruition (and to be covered by health insurance payers).

For example, singing is not the same as physical exercise. Exercise enhances flexibility, joint mobility, balance, stability, muscle strength and tone, and neuromuscular coordination, which may lessen the propensity for falling and permit increased participation in the activities of daily living. Singing probably won't improve these abilities much, if at all. However, we cannot forget the other benefits of exercise. Namely, improvement in or prevention of age-related endothelial dysfunction through enhanced NO availability. Improvements in endothelial function translate into lower future risk of cardiovascular events, which in turn reduces hospitalizations, lowers health-care costs, and keeps patients out of the hospital, where they are at risk for further deconditioning and social isolation. Furthermore, depression that follows an acute cardiac event in 20 to 30 percent of patients can potentially be prevented. Singing may also have the potential to improve cognitive function and mental well-being, lessen anxiety and depression, and improve quality of life. All these things are important for the physical, mental, and emotional health of anyone living with heart disease—and other chronic diseases.

CONCLUSION

The impact of singing on different kinds of heart disease remains unknown. There are very few studies that have been conducted with the scientific rigor required to discover the truth (so to speak) and establish best practices in this field at this time. However, with important initiatives such as the Sound Health partnership with the NIH, support from the National Endowment for the Arts, Renée Fleming, and engaged scientists, we will continue to learn more about the role of music in heart disease and other disease processes as well. I am optimistic that singing has the potential to benefit the spectrum of cardiovascular diseases. Furthermore, we know that singing is safe. My advice—sing your heart out (no pun intended)!

Rabbit Hole

ROSANNE CASH

Grammy Award–Winning Singer-Songwriter

Around 1977 I started noticing that certain frequencies—particularly around 200 hertz—really bothered me. During sound checks for my concerts, I held my hands over my ears if that frequency went rogue and was ringing out in the overtones coming from a guitar, or bass, or the house sound. Low rumbles also disturbed me. Then, very high frequencies started to grate on me in the studio, onstage, on the street. I was getting to the point that my range of sonic tolerance had become very narrow. The problem seemed to be affecting my left ear; it was as if that ear were having a constant anxiety attack, while my right one was doing just fine.

I could also *hear* higher frequencies than many of the musicians I worked with. Once, as a guest on a recording session with a lot of people I had never collaborated with in the past, I had headphones on while the guitarist was adjusting his amplifier before we began the session. There was a very high frequency running through every twist of the dials he made, and I waited for the producer to tell him about it before we started recording. I became increasingly uncomfortable, but the producer said nothing. Finally, we were ready for a take, and I said timidly, "Sorry, but there is a very high tone coming out of the amp." The producer came into the studio and couldn't hear anything, and then put headphones on and squeezed them to his ears.

He looked up at me. "Well," he said, "I don't hear it, but I FEEL it." They jiggled the dials until I told them it was gone.

I loved yoga. I'd done it for fifteen years, and was doing strenuous power yoga three or four times a week, but I had recently begun to find myself in pain all the time. The instructor was also a physical therapist, so I booked a session with him. I lay down, and he put his hands under my neck. He immediately pulled them away and said, "I don't know what's going on with your neck, but you need to find out." To deal with the pain I became a spa junkie. In every town we played, if I had a spare moment, I found a massage therapist or a chiropractor who could see me. I felt a little guilty and thought it was decadent to spend hundreds of dollars a month on bodywork. I started having more frequent migraines, some that lasted days. They began with an intense pain down my left arm, and then my senses went haywire: I could smell a single crayon from ten feet away, sounds evoked color, and light was unbearable. I saw neurologists, one who attributed them to hormones, one who diagnosed them as "atypical migraines" and observed that my cerebellum was "hanging a little low," and another who said I had too much stress in my life. One gave me a shot of a powerful pain medicine, to which I had an allergic reaction.

I gave birth to my son, Jake, in 1999, and after the epidural I received during labor, the headaches got even worse. I had a migraine-level one that lasted for months. I tried everything to get relief—meds, meditation, massage. Nothing worked. Eventually I gave up yoga classes and tried to do it at home. Eventually, I abandoned that as well. I started having other symptoms besides chronic pain—sometimes it was hard to swallow or catch my breath. My neck hurt all the time. "New Age" massage therapists told me my problem was unresolved issues from my childhood, or that I wore too many dark colors and it was affecting my kidneys, or that it was my fault and I should change my attitude, or that I was going through menopause. I tried bizarre, even dangerous therapies. I had a kind of balloon inserted in my nose and slowly opened to "move my sphenoid bone back into place." I drove a hundred miles to see a special chiropractor who would "adjust my atlas." They both only made things worse. I thought I was losing my mind. I didn't tell my husband, John, even a fraction of what I was going through, as we had enough stress in our lives from dealing with two difficult adolescents, and I didn't want him to think that I was a hypochondriac or a whiner.

Performing was getting harder and harder. Often I would sit in my dressing room staring in the mirror at a puffy, haggard face I barely recognized. The fatigue was pervasive, and I had lost enthusiasm for nearly everything. I just managed pain and exhaustion all day, every day.

One morning I was trying to stretch and discovered I couldn't move. I started to cry and went to John and said, "I can't go on."

I went to my internist and asked him to test for every single thing he could think of. He called me in a few days and said, "It looks like you have Lyme disease." I went to an infectious disease specialist who looked at my labs, came around the desk, went down on one knee next to my chair, and said, "I'm going to explain this to you because you're a smart lady. You don't have Lyme disease." I walked out and these many years later I still feel my blood pressure rise when I think of her staggering condescension. I googled and googled and googled. In August 2007 I came across the name of a neurologist at Cornell in New York City, where I live—Dr. Norman Latov—and the name of my father in the same article. I was startled. I had no idea my father had seen a neurologist, or that it had been public knowledge. He had been seeking help for symptoms that turned out to be an autonomic immune disorder. Dr. Latov's biography noted that he was a specialist in Lyme disease. It seemed like a sign, and I made an appointment. After my labs came back, he confirmed that I did in fact have Lyme disease, but he was more alarmed at how low my T-cells were, and sent me that very moment to a lab to see if I was HIV-positive. I was not. He ordered a series of MRIs and various nerve-conduction tests and a few days later asked me to come in to discuss the results.

He was writing on my chart when I sat down, and he said, "You have a condition called Chiari malformation. It requires surgery, and you should do it soon."

"Is it a tumor?" I asked.

"No, it's not a tumor," he told me. "You need to find a surgeon who treats a lot of Chiari patients. It's not that common, and you want someone really good. I have a couple of recommendations, but you should consult with a few people."

He then explained what the condition was: my cerebellum was very low in my skull, pressing into my brain stem, and the crowding was causing not only the pain, but it was affecting the autonomic reflexes of the body, like swallowing, breathing, and balance. The pressure from the location of the cerebellum was blocking the flow of cerebrospinal fluid and causing a swelling around the length of my spine, which was called a syringomyelia. I was not in good shape.

"What about the Lyme?" I asked.

He looked at me. "You have bigger fish to fry."

He put me on six weeks of doxycycline for the Lyme, and I started consulting with neurosurgeons around the country by phone. John's brother-in-law, James Davis, a family practice doctor at the University of Wisconsin, took my images to a neurosurgeon there who said he had seen quite a few children and young people with the condition over the years, but never a woman my age. I was fifty-two.

One of the doctors I consulted pointed to my scan and said, "You see that thin trickle of white going from your spine to your head? That's cerebrospinal fluid. It's nearly blocked, and it's what keeps you alive."

My friend Liz Tirrell in Austin knew a neurologist at Johns Hopkins, Dr. Guy McKhann. When I called him, he was incredibly kind, gentle, and thoughtful. He agreed that I needed surgery soon, and said, "I hate to practice nepotism, but since you live in New York City, my son, Guy, is a neurosurgeon at Columbia-Presbyterian."

Guy McKhann II was my guy. I knew it from the moment we met at the Department of Neurosurgery at Columbia-Presbyterian. He was as kind as his father, personable, and attentive. I felt safe with him. After looking at my films, we scheduled the surgery for November 27, 2007.

My sister came from Portland, and my daughter Chelsea came from Nashville. I was angry that my parents were dead and weren't there for me. (After the surgery, I was relieved they weren't there to see what I went through.) On the day of the surgery we got up early, and the babysitter arrived to take care of my eight-year-old son. I took a selfie in my kitchen—a "before" photo. I look at that photo now and am shocked at how bad I looked—wasted, exhausted, and in terrible pain.

On the drive to the hospital, I put headphones on and listened to a hypnosis recording I'd had made: "You are on a beach. The sound of the waves calms you. The surgery is successful. There are no problems. You recover quickly." Etcetera, bullshit, etcetera.

"Wake up, Rosanne. Where are you?" Dr. McKhann was leaning over me. I looked at the blue walls behind him.

"I'm in my kitchen."

He laughed and later told me that during the surgery, as he watched the computer hooked up to my brain, a signal from my brain to my left ear changed, and the signal improved. He said, "Damn! I thought it was an artifact, but it was real."

I had a dream a couple of weeks later that I was onstage, and there were a half dozen men around me with shovels and hammers, beating my head. I told Dr. McKhann about the dream. He laughed. "I promise you, that didn't happen." Depends on your definition of "shovel" and whom you talk to, I suppose.

After six days in the hospital, I went home with morphine, steroids, a drug for nerve pain, and various other potions and chemicals. For my entire life I have had a lot of health hubris. Even given the deterioration in my mobility, the fatigue and pain, I still thought I was in incredibly good shape and could recover from any illness much faster than other people. I didn't believe I could ever be truly sick, against all current evidence. I had a show booked for March, and I left it on the books. Three and a half months should be enough time to recover.

I started gaining weight immediately. My face and body were terribly swollen and I spent a lot of time lying on my sofa and ordering loose comfort clothes online. I couldn't bear to listen to music with voices. Lyrics were complicated and annoying. I was drawn to Samuel Barber, Arvo Pärt, and Chopin's nocturnes. Looking back now, I understand that I wanted to hear melancholy compositions that tapped into my acute, aching sense of the passage of time. I felt old. I felt I had lost years of vigor, joy, and intimacy. I didn't like how I looked. I couldn't easily climb a flight of stairs or take a walk more than a few blocks. I had a credit card–size piece of skull missing in the back of my head, filled in by what was basically Gore-Tex, and a partially removed top vertebra. I cried to John that, strangely, I missed that piece of my skull.

"You didn't need it," he said. "Fuck it."

I wouldn't pick up my guitar, but I was drawn to our piano in the living room. I opened the piano bench seat and pulled out my practice book from second grade. Why had I kept this, and how had I held on to it for all these decades? I had no idea, but it was exactly what I needed at this moment in my life.

I started with the simplest pieces. I hadn't bothered to actually read music in years, so I struggled to reacquaint myself with the notes on the staff.

I looked up the unknown composers of these pieces and found nothing at all about them online. I remembered the nun who had taught me piano, and how once, when I had forgotten it was my lesson time, she had rung a bell by remote in my classroom to remind me, and everyone thought it was a fire drill. My teacher said with annoyance, "It's not a fire drill. It's only Rosanne's piano lesson reminder." Everyone stared at me. I was mortified.

I remembered being at my piano lesson one day when an older girl opened the door to the room where I was practicing with Sister seated beside me. The girl was crying, and Sister got up and ushered her out and closed the door, but not before I heard "President Kennedy was shot." I looked at the windows behind me to see if the Russians were coming in to kidnap children. The Russians were always in the news, and all the adults around me had been talking about them incessantly since the Cuban Missile Crisis.

I remembered how I had begged my mother to let me stop taking piano lessons. I hated them, and I was always a disappointment to Sister because I didn't practice and made the same mistakes over and over. All these memories came back as I worked slowly through relearning the exasperating compositions of my childhood. I felt myself putting little pieces of a puzzle together—of memory and spatial recognition, sound and rhythm, fear and frustration, time and space. I was at a fork in the road of regaining my cognition and clarity. Some of it was out of my control, some of it was purely physical, and some of it was within my power to orchestrate.

It has taken me decades to realize that my life as a performer has been an extended, painstaking project to free myself of shame. I didn't know that was what I was doing and what I am still doing, on more subtle and intricate levels than when I began. I was even ashamed of the word "shame." Shame was so ingrained in me, perhaps from early childhood, perhaps cellular, that I couldn't even identify it as something separate from myself. I still can't say exactly what it is, where it started, or why. Some broad strokes make sense—my mother's intense reserve, how easily she was humiliated, how she hated fame, her own shame at being the daughter of an alcoholic, my father's drug addiction and his shame about that, his wounds over his own father's coldness and abuse, and how I, a profoundly sensitive child, absorbed all this. My mother made acute what was already endemic by unconsciously off-loading her own shame onto the nearest receptacle: me, her oldest child. I believed, like so many children, that the adult despair and rage in my house were due to me.

It makes counterintuitive sense that people who suffer from shame, who have an impulse, conscious or not, to heal it, and who are intensely shy and private, become performers. It's true for me, and it's true for many, many performers I know. It's *how* we heal ourselves, as well as how we find a community of those who resonate with the inner unrest and suffering and the soul's desire to shake off destructive limitations and expand into our potential.

The brain surgery, it turned out, opened a parallel track of shame: physical, along with the psychic disturbance that was already deep within. My body betrayed me, so I thought. My body revealed things I had hidden and avoided for my entire life. I'm five foot five and I swelled from 135 to 175 pounds after the surgery. Weight, which was a constant obsession since my early teens, and something I kept an iron grip on by carefully limiting how much I ate—suddenly rose up like a rogue wave and engulfed me. My face disappeared into what looked like water damage, like wood that bloats and cracks after being submerged. I was an attractive woman who turned, almost overnight, into someone I didn't recognize or like. I felt like a dumpy, tired eighty-year-old, and grieved that my creative and sexual energy seemed to be at an end. I was ashamed that I had deteriorated so rapidly and I thought I saw my friends begin to avert their eyes from me. Maybe they did, maybe they didn't, but the floodgates of dormant self-loathing opened, and I was adrift.

I still couldn't expand my playlist beyond Elisabeth Leonskaja's performances of Chopin's nocturnes, and Arvo Pärt's *Spiegel im Spiegel*, along with the simple pieces in my elementary piano books, which I still played badly, but I had daydreams about musical collaborations I might create one day, as a self-soothing technique, even though the idea of writing or singing actual words was unsettling.

John and I did do the concert that I had kept booked for March 2008, a collaboration with musician and composer Mark O'Connor. After I left the stage I sat in my dressing room shaking violently, feeling that I might come out of my body with anxiety and pain, and there was a buzz in my head that was so loud I thought it must be audible to those around me. My nervous system crashed. I canceled everything else on the books until October. I called Guy McKhann and told him what had happened at the gig, and he said, "I didn't want to tell you that you couldn't do it, but I was surprised you thought you could."

Lying on the sofa a few days later, drifting in and out of sleep, an image formed in my head of me with two dear friends—Elvis Costello and Kris Kristofferson. I pictured us collaborating on something. The idea stuck, and the image kept coming back. I emailed them asking if they wanted to write something together. They both said yes, and we emailed lyrics to one another. We finished the untitled song and decided we should record it together. After some travel and schedule juggling, we realized we could all be in New York City on April 5.

We gathered at the now defunct New York Noise recording studio downtown on Gansevoort Street with John as producer, guitarist, and keyboard player, engineer Rick DePofi, bass player Zev Katz, and drummer Joe Bonadio. The song was very easy to perform, and it was a comfortable, fluid recording experience. John guided the session with a deft hand and open heart. The music he wrote and arranged and what he captured on tape (or on the computer, actually) were a gift to me, and he knew it. We tossed around ideas for a title and decided to call it "April 5th," memorializing the day we recorded it. While in the studio I showed Kris and Elvis the first verse of another song I had written about a child who was a victim of gun violence—"8 Gods of Harlem"—and asked if they wanted to each write a verse. I thought that my verse could be told from the point of view of the grieving mother, Kris's verse as the father, and Elvis as the brother. Their verses came together rapidly, and we recorded that song on the same day. I felt shaky and as if my head were in a vise, but the whole process lifted me up and gave me just a tiny peek into a possible future of recovery and inspiration.

After April 5 I was still not able to travel, perform, or do much of anything. There was one concert date on my calendar that was virtually impossible for me to remove, in October, in Bochum, Germany. It was an important festival, and I had been booked on it long before my diagnosis and surgery. My friend Joe Henry was musical director and curator of the event. Another friend, Billy Bragg, was booked to perform the same evening, solo, and then with Joe and me. In April there was no reason to think that I wouldn't be able to perform with them, as nearly a year would have passed since my surgery.

October came, and my progress was not what I had hoped. I had planned to go alone to Germany and realized at the last minute that I could not lift my suitcase, pull it, or carry anything heavier than my handbag. I sent my luggage by air freight ahead to the hotel. The trip to Europe was excruciating—the noise, the pressure, and the immobility of a long flight were deeply distressing. It was as if my nervous system were still set on 10 all the time, and any extra input hiked it beyond my capacity to assimilate or tolerate.

When I got to the hotel, where my bag was waiting, I stood in the middle of the room and turned slowly in a circle, trying to see through the haze behind my eyes, trying to establish myself in reality, trying to understand my life. I stared into the middle distance, then the mirror, for a long time. I felt despair fill me up, from my feet to my head. I had to push through; there was a rehearsal with Joe and Billy that afternoon.

I walked into the rehearsal room and Joe and Billy were there, smiling, rock and roll elegant/scruffy, happy to see me, ready to play. The first song we were going to rehearse was Bob Dylan's "Girl from the North Country." I lifted my head a little, and the first notes brought tears to my eyes. There was something in this world that could rouse me, something that lightened the darkness. I felt hope.

That was the beginning of recovery. It was a rhythm, a melody, two gentle friends. I wrote a song for them called "Rabbit Hole":

> *I just want a road that bends*
> *a love that wins*
> *an honest friend.*
> *I just want a night of peace*
> *blessed relief*
> *I want to make you see*
> *that you, in your crumpled splendor*

when you sing to the farthest rafter
with your big life full of love and laughter
you pull me up from the rabbit hole.

Much later I participated in a conversation and performance with my friend, Dr. Dan Levitin, at a conference about music and the brain. I told him about my weird left ear, and how I had been so worried that I would lose my sensitivity and understanding of music during the brain surgery, but that after those initial couple of years of fried nerves, searing pain, and hopelessness, that my sensitivity had actually *increased* in the most beautiful, breathtaking way, that my left ear calmed down and opened up like a blossom, that I stood at a crucial fork in my life, and that music and love had guided me onto the path that fit my chosen destiny.

Shame subsided. I can't say it's gone—sometimes that girl who thought it was all her fault still rises up and bends under the imagined weight of the wrong note or the wrong clothes or the wrong word at a fancy dinner—but I have compassion for her. She went through hell, she came back, and she sings to the farthest rafter, with a big life full of love and laughter.

Music for Chronic Pain Management

JOKE BRADT, PhD, MT-BC

Professor, Creative Arts Therapies Department, Drexel University

It just amazes me that the music has always been a part of my life, but I never thought that music could help with my pain.

People with chronic pain, often after becoming disillusioned with traditional medical treatments, are increasingly seeking alternative options. Participants in my research studies on music therapy for chronic pain management frequently state that they listen to music all the time, but never considered using it for their pain. At times participants express initial skepticism: How could it be that something as simple as music can offer relief for something as complex and elusive as chronic pain? If even the most advanced (and expensive, I would add) medical treatments cannot bring any relief, surely music will not be able to do so. Yet a survey of music listening habits in 318 people with chronic pain found that those who engaged more frequently in listening to music, and for whom music was important, reported better quality of life and needed less medical treatment. The findings also suggested that this group reported a greater enjoyment of life, more energy, lower levels of depression, and less interference of pain with daily activities.

Achieving adequate relief for chronic pain presents a major challenge and requires a multidisciplinary approach. The purpose of this chapter is to help bring understanding of how multifaceted engagement with music can help improve the management of chronic pain in adults. Before we delve into discussions of music interventions, it is important to define music therapy and differentiate it from the use of music outside of a therapeutic relationship. The use of music in health care can be situated along a continuum of care, namely from music listening initiated by patients, to music medicine (prerecorded music offered by medical personnel for relaxation and symptom management), to music therapy. Music therapy is the clinical use of music interventions to help people optimize their health within a relationship with a trained music therapist. Music therapy requires a therapeutic process developed between the client and the music therapist through personally tailored music experiences, including listening to live, improvised, or prerecorded music; playing musical instruments; singing; improvising music; and composing music. Some of the music-based strategies discussed below can be easily applied without the intervention of a music therapist. However, as chronic pain is often exacerbated by a multitude of psychosocial stressors and may be accompanied by significant psychological health issues such as depression and anxiety, the guidance of a music therapist may be indicated.

CHRONIC PAIN: THE FAILURE OF MODERN MEDICINE

More than one hundred million Americans live with chronic pain, presenting a staggering cost to society. In the United States alone, chronic pain carries an estimated health-care expense of over half a trillion dollars annually. Billions of dollars are spent on traditional pain treatments such as opioids, spine surgeries, and epidural injections, yet research indicates that such treatments bring relief to only a small percentage of people. Moreover, many of these interventions have undesirable side effects and may lead to complications. In addition, there has been an alarming increase in prescription-opioid deaths in the United States.

The picture was not always this bleak. In the 1960s and '70s multidisciplinary pain clinics became a successful treatment model. However, several economic factors (e.g., the introduction of a coding system for reimbursement of health-care services in the 1980s, which led to highly lucrative modality-specific pain clinics) and marketing efforts by drug companies to reduce fears of addiction to prescribed opioids led to a rapid increase in opioid prescriptions for chronic pain. Today the management of chronic pain mostly falls into two buckets—namely the use of opioids and the utilization of invasive pain management intervention, even though evidence of treatment efficacy of these interventions is mostly lacking and the risk for addiction and complications is high. A detailed discussion about the economic and historical facts that led to the current opioid epidemic in the United States and the failure of modern medicine to treat chronic pain effectively is beyond the scope of this chapter, but suffice to say that we urgently need to shift away from an overreliance on opioid-based pain management and from insurance companies reimbursing invasive interventions. Instead, I hope to shed light on how music therapy and music-based self-management interventions can play a role in returning to a multidisciplinary approach to pain management. But first, let me briefly explain why a multimodal approach driven by a biopsychosocial framework to chronic pain management is essential to successful treatment. The biopsychosocial model, which was first introduced by George Engel in 1977, suggests that it is important to acknowledge the interaction of biological, psychological, as well as social factors when treating or managing a medical condition.

OUR BRAIN: THE PAIN ORCHESTRA

Most people think that pain is located in a specific part of their body, meaning that if they have low back pain, they believe that the pain is located in their back. Neural signals may indeed travel from the back up to the brain, but our backs, in and of themselves, cannot *feel* pain. Instead, the experience of pain is always created in our brain as it orchestrates inputs from three major sources—namely, biological, psychological, and social. On the podcast *Dolorology* (the study of pain), Rachel Zoffness, a pain psychologist, uses an effective analogy. She likens the pain experience to a volume button on the radio. Any of the three major inputs (i.e., biological, psychological, and social) can turn the pain volume up or down. Zoffness is, of course, not the first to emphasize the importance of a biopsychosocial approach to pain management (see the Gate Control Theory of Pain, the Neuromatrix Theory, etc.), but the visual of a radio dial is a helpful image to keep in mind as we explore how music can help to turn down the pain volume.

Biological factors that contribute to the experience of pain include injury, tissue damage, sleep, and epigenetics. But the presence of an injury and the extent of tissue damage are not major determinants of the intensity of pain a person experiences. The fact that people with similar bodily injuries report very different levels of pain, and the fact that pain is frequently reported in the absence of tissue damage (e.g., phantom pain), suggest that pain perception is more complex than simply a neural transmission of noxious stimuli.

Psychological factors that may influence pain perception include a wide gamut of factors. How we think and how we feel at any given moment have a major impact on how much pain we experience. Research has shown that negative mood states such as depression, anxiety, and anger make pain worse. Stress makes our muscles tense up and places additional pressure on nerve endings, leading to a heightened sensation of pain. Our mood also affects how our body feels. For example, when we are depressed, our body may feel heavy. When we feel sad and are holding back tears, we may feel pain in our throat. When we are angry, we may feel our heart pounding. Unfortunately, a focus on psychological factors and how they contribute to chronic pain is often interpreted as pain being "in the head." Pain is indeed created by our brain and thus literally lives in our head, but this does not mean that pain is imagined. Chronic pain is very real and causes significant suffering. Addressing psychological factors in the management of chronic pain is of paramount importance to effective pain management.

Feeling supported by others and being able to engage in social activities also affect how we feel. Chronic pain can have devastating effects on relationships and may lead to the collapse of a person's social networks. Furthermore, chronic pain might be exacerbated by issues like job loss, low socioeconomic status, and lack of access to medical care. Biological, psychological, and social factors never act in isolation. Focusing on just one of them in pain management, as many medical treatments do, will likely be doomed to fail. Music therapy and music-based strategies can help address these biopsychosocial components of chronic pain.

MUSIC FOR STRESS REDUCTION

Many people use music to help them relax. In fact, research shows that when people experience high levels of stress, they tend to listen more to music. The survey by Laura Mitchell and colleagues about music listening habits in people with chronic pain found that, besides deriving enjoyment from listening to music, most respondents indicated that they listen to music to relax and relieve tension and stress. When we listen to relaxing music, several neurochemical pathways are activated, which helps reduce our perceived stress. It is believed that the anxiety-reducing effect of music is achieved through its suppressive action on the sympathetic nervous system (i.e., the part of our nervous system that is responsible for setting fight-or-flight responses into motion), leading to decreased adrenergic activity (e.g., lowered heart rate) and decreased neuromuscular arousal. Consequently, music listening may decrease stress hormones such as cortisol and enable our body to recover more quickly from a stressful event.

Several music-based strategies can be used for stress reduction. The most obvious one is to listen to relaxing music in a space that promotes relaxation. I am often asked what type of music people should listen to for this purpose. The most effective music for relaxation is music that an individual likes and identifies as calming. In other words, there is not a prescriptive way of determining the "right" type of music. It is true that certain musical characteristics, such as slow tempo, predictable harmonies, and particular timbre (e.g., strings instead of brass instruments), are more conducive to relaxation, yet music that relaxes one person might irritate another. Another misconception is that classical music must be superior to other genres for facilitating relaxation. It is important to note that whereas calm and soothing music is often associated with relaxation, a wide variety of music styles and ways of engaging with music can promote stress relief. For example, singing and dancing to an upbeat song can be equally effective in releasing stress as listening to a calm, soothing piece of instrumental music. Therefore, it is important to consider whether one wants to release stress or whether one wants to achieve a more deep, relaxed state.

Other music-based strategies for stress reduction include music-guided deep breathing and music-guided imagery or visualization. Music therapists will often use live music in these interventions. For music-guided deep breathing, the music therapist may match improvised music to the client's observed breathing and then gradually slow down the tempo to promote deeper breathing through a process called entrainment. For music-guided visualization, the music therapist may use improvised or precomposed music to evoke and accompany imagery experiences that lead to relaxation. An initial imagery focus is selected based on the client's preferences for a relaxing scene or a favorite place with associated memories of peacefulness and calm. Music is used to amplify, deepen, support, and provide structure for the imagery. The use of imagery can provide a powerful means to help a person relax, find refuge from the pain, and become empowered in their healing process.

Besides music listening experiences, active engagement with music can provide a powerful means for stress reduction. Most of my research studies with people with chronic pain, for example, include humming and toning. Toning is the singing of extended vowel sounds. This produces vibrations that can be felt in our bodies, with particular vowels and tones resonating with different areas of the body. Humming and toning promote deep breathing, which helps to slow down physiological responses, inducing a state of relaxation. Second, feeling vibrations promotes somatic awareness and helps people connect with their body in a positive manner. This stands in sharp contrast with a desire to disconnect or "not feel" a painful body. Embodied experiences help develop a more caring and accepting attitude toward one's body. Acceptance has been found to play an important role in adjustment to chronic pain, in that patients who report greater acceptance of living with this pain also report less distress, disability, and overall, greater well-being and everyday functioning. Finally, humming and toning help to create a sense of calm and peacefulness, as reflected in this quote by a participant in a study on vocal music therapy for chronic pain: "The humming made me feel like I was back in my mother's womb . . . very safe." This sense of emotional safety is often absent in people with chronic pain, due to the chaos it causes and the disbelief that they are often confronted with by others regarding their pain.

MUSIC FOR SUSTAINED ATTENTION

Attentional state is probably the psychological variable that has been the most frequently researched in terms of its potential to modulate pain. When people with chronic pain were asked how they think music helps to relieve pain, the most common response was "distraction." Indeed, clinical and experimental studies show that distraction can have a powerful effect on pain perception. (However, it is important to note that many of these studies use other forms of distracting stimuli, e.g., smells, movies, that also affect emotional state.) Distraction is frequently cited as an important mechanism of the analgesic effects of music. However, in a study comparing the effects of pleasant and unpleasant music on experimentally induced pain, only pleasant music reduced pain perception. This suggests that distraction alone cannot explain the pain-reducing effects of music, since unpleasant music is distracting as well. Instead, it appears that it is the combination of music's capacity to hold one's attention and its ability to evoke experiences of pleasure, thereby activating the reward circuitry in our brains, that plays a role in music-induced analgesic effects.

Several authors have argued against the use of the word "distraction." Distraction implies a quick diversion, one that can be easily interrupted. Since music is a temporal experience, it has the potential to sustain our attention moment to moment. It is this sustained focus that is important when using music for pain management. Music that is merely playing in the background will likely not impact the pain experience. Instead, purposeful listening or active engagement with music is required, as described by a participant in one of our studies with advanced cancer and chronic pain:

> Well, it helps because when I really allow myself to get into the music, I forget about everything else that's going on. I don't think about how sick I am; I don't think about the pain, I just think about, in that moment, where I am in that song.

Joanne Loewy argues that distraction implies that attention is drawn away from the pain, whereas it may be more beneficial for people to learn how their focus on specific elements of music (e.g., rhythm, melody) can help them deal with pain related to medical procedures. I would like to extend this idea to dealing with chronic pain, and specifically breakthrough pain. Teaching people, for example, how to sustain focus on music to help them breathe through the pain or to follow a melody to stimulate visualization will often be more successful in helping them manage the pain than telling them to use music to divert attention away from the pain. When pain is intense, distraction may not be a viable option. Finally, teaching people how to actively "use" music rather than letting music distract them is empowering and offers coping strategies that imply active engagement in their healing process.

MUSIC FOR MOOD ENHANCEMENT AND EMOTIONAL EXPRESSION

Chronic pain can cause significant emotional suffering and may lead to feelings of depression, frustration, and anger. In fact, depression and chronic pain coexist in up to 60 percent of people with chronic pain. Often people with chronic pain have been catapulted from a period in their life characterized by strength, well-being, and independence to one of insecurity, chaos, reduced mobility, and, sometimes, dependence. Chronic pain may also significantly impact a person's role in the world due to a reduced ability to carry out tasks expected of their role (e.g., parent, caregiver) and/or job loss. Finally, because chronic pain is invisible, people who live with it find themselves being questioned and judged about the veracity of their pain. Indeed, the experiences of people with chronic pain are often trivialized by doctors as well as family and friends. The inability to function in areas that had previously given meaning and purpose to their life as well as social stigma and disbelief may result in significant emotional turmoil, which, in turn, amplifies pain. When nociceptive signals travel from the body to the brain, they pass through the limbic system (our brain's emotion center) before they become the experience we know as pain. Brain imaging research has demonstrated that listening to pleasant music also activates structures in the limbic system involved with reward, emotion, and arousal. This overlap between neural networks involved with pain perception and those involved with music-evoked emotions may be one of the reasons why music can help reduce pain perception.

However, because of the severity of emotional exhaustion, anxiety, depression, and anger that often accompany chronic pain, addressing these issues and improving a person's mental health require more than listening to music. Music listening may bring temporary relief, but psychotherapeutic work with a music therapist may be indicated to address concerns and stressors underlying psychological health issues. Music therapists are specifically trained to engage clients in music experiences that help them explore and express their emotions. For example, a music therapist may musically accompany the participant's emotional expression, audibly reflecting their emotions and providing a safe musical container for continued exploration. Or a therapist may invite a client to identify a song that expresses how they are feeling. After singing the song, the therapist may invite discussion about the meaning of the song and subsequently engage the client in music experiences that may deepen the emotional exploration.

In a study we conducted with people with cancer, we compared their experiences of listening to a playlist of their preferred music versus engaging in active music making with a music therapist. Through improvised music making and singing with a music therapist, participants reported that they were able to access and release suppressed emotions, especially emotions related to grief. In contrast, they shared that listening to prerecorded music evoked many emotions and, at times, traumatic memories. Without a music therapist present to help process these emotions and memories, the music left them feeling vulnerable.

Many people may also find it difficult to verbalize what their pain feels like. Being able to "sound out" the pain in music therapy allows people to share pain that is otherwise invisible and so difficult for others to relate to. Externalizing the pain and subsequently being able to manipulate it by changing the sound or musical elements can be an empowering experience. One specific technique in music therapy called music entrainment for pain management does exactly that. In music entrainment, live improvised music progresses from music that expresses a person's pain into music predetermined by the person as healing. This gradual change in the music may create a shift in the cognitive perception of the presence of pain. By its focus on sounding out the sensory aspects of the pain, this technique also helps a person to directly confront the pain and work with or through it, instead of trying to escape from it. By assisting the client in creating an auditory reflection of the pain and by taking part in the music improvisation of the pain, the therapist enters directly into the person's pain and resonates with it in a unique way. This can offer important validation and support for the client.

Finally, creative engagement in music making helps people tap into their inner playfulness and creative selves. These are important resources that, when strengthened, may facilitate resilience in the face of psychosocial stressors that exacerbate chronic pain.

MUSIC TO REDUCE ISOLATION

Due to reduced physical functioning and ability to enjoy social and family activities, people with chronic pain may become isolated and feel disconnected from the world. Feelings of loneliness may be further exacerbated by depression and fatigue. This often creates a vicious cycle that leads to worsening of pain perception. Music can combat these feelings of loneliness in several ways. First, by improving one's mood, music may help dial down the pain volume sufficiently to motivate a person to engage in social activities. Second, listening to music that has personal meaning and is comforting may help create a sense of support and validation, possibly combating feelings of loneliness. Finally, the act of creating music with others, whether in group or individual music therapy sessions or community music activities (e.g., community choir), provides a sense of support and activates social engagement. Research has shown that singing with others stimulates the release of oxytocin, a hormone that promotes bonding. In the context of our discussion here, it is interesting to note that low oxytocin levels have been associated with higher pain intensity.

MUSIC THERAPY FOR CHRONIC PAIN MANAGEMENT: RESEARCH EVIDENCE

Although there are a large number of clinical and laboratory studies that demonstrate music's efficacy for the reduction of acute pain, far fewer studies exist on music therapy and music-based interventions for chronic pain management. A recent systematic review on music for chronic pain included fourteen studies, all of which used listening to prerecorded or live music as the intervention. The results suggest that listening to music reduces self-reported pain, anxiety, and depression symptoms in a diverse range of people with chronic pain. The pain-reducing effects of music were found to be the greatest for music selected by study participants compared to researcher-selected music.

Few studies have examined the impact of music therapy interventions that involve active music making on people with chronic pain. The findings of two recent studies on sickle cell disease (SCD) suggest that music therapy is an effective intervention for pain management in this population. In a randomized controlled trial, Samuel Rodgers-Melnick and colleagues compared the effects of (1) a single-session electronic music improvisation led by a music therapist with (2) listening to patient-selected recorded music and (3) standard care in sixty adults with SCD receiving treatment in an outpatient infusion center. Participants in the electronic music improvisation intervention reported significant improvements in pain and mood, whereas participants in the music listening treatment reported significant improvements in mood but not in pain. Moreover, effects on mood were greater in those people who participated in the music improvisation intervention. The authors explained that greater efficacy of the music improvisation intervention might have been due to the fact that music improvisation required higher levels of active participation and focused attention than listening and may have been more emotionally engaging. This is supported by findings from a randomized crossover study conducted by my lab in which people with cancer expressed that they preferred participation in music therapy sessions in which they engaged in instrumental or vocal improvisation and sang songs with the music therapist over music listening sessions. In another study with twenty-four adults with SCD, Samuel Rodgers-Melnick and colleagues examined the effects of a six-week music therapy treatment program compared to a wait-list control group in which patients received standard care. The music therapy treatment involved music-based breathing exercises, progressive muscle relaxation, imagery, and active music making. All music experiences were personalized to participants' preferred music genres. Participants in the music therapy intervention reported greater improvements in pain interference, self-efficacy, sleep, and social functioning than those who received standard care.

A research group in Germany has developed and tested several music therapy treatment manuals for chronic pain management in adults and children. These manuals center around the use of music improvisation. An integrative review of their research was published in 2013. Overall, their studies have demonstrated efficacy of their protocols for reducing pain intensity as well as associated psychological distress.

Research in my lab has also focused on developing and testing music therapy protocols that capitalize on active music making to address core outcomes in chronic pain management such as pain-related self-efficacy and pain interference. Self-efficacy refers to beliefs about one's ability to do things despite the pain. Pain interference is the extent to which pain interferes with completing daily activities and how significantly it has changed one's enjoyment of life and social activities. One such protocol is an eight-week group vocal music therapy program. It involves a sequential layering of humming, toning, music-guided deep breathing, group singing, and vocal improvisations, as well as verbal processing of feelings and thoughts evoked by the music experiences to address biopsychosocial factors of chronic pain management. In addition, psychoeducational information about how music can help chronic pain management is interwoven throughout the sessions. Findings from two studies that compared a vocal music therapy treatment program with a wait-list control treatment arm suggest a large treatment effect of vocal music therapy on pain-related self-efficacy. One of the studies also indicated that vocal music therapy had a moderate treatment effect on pain interference. These are important findings as greater levels of self-efficacy in people with chronic pain have been associated with better physical functioning, increased participation in social activities, enhanced health and work status, and decreased pain intensity. In one of our studies, a participant shared in a post-study interview the following about the power of music to motivate: "Learning the different songs that are uplifting. Some of them are inspirational . . . it gives you a sense of you, a sense of being, and makes you realize you have the key to your own destiny." Many participants in that study also commented on the joy that music brings and how that made a difference in their lives, as reflected in this quote: "The music therapy gave me joy so I think that was a change for me. I was shutting down and it gave me the gumption to feel better again and smile again." Participants also commented on how the music therapy sessions helped to combat isolation. For example, a participant with severe chronic pain shared: "I got out of [the sessions] that I can still be around people and interact. I don't have to close myself off like I've been doing before. I have been for about eight years that way . . . isolating myself and I pretty much didn't do anything, but now I can go to work." In a recent mechanistic trial we completed with ninety-two people with advanced cancer with chronic pain, we compared individual interactive music therapy sessions with individual verbal support sessions. We found that the positive impact of a six-week interactive music therapy program on participants' pain interference and pain intensity could be explained through enhanced pain-related self-efficacy. This means that participants assigned to the interactive music therapy sessions reported higher levels of pain-related self-efficacy after four weeks than those assigned to verbal support sessions. These higher levels of pain-related self-efficacy were then associated with less subsequent pain intensity and pain interference at the conclusion of the six-week program. Thus, it seems that the music therapy sessions first helped people feel more in control over their pain, and this, in turn, helped them experience less pain and less negative impact of pain on their daily activities. Finally, in a pilot study examining the effects of a ten-week interactive music therapy program compared to verbal support in twenty-six cancer survivors who were chronic opioid users, we found that interactive music therapy had a medium treatment effect on participants' pain interference and self-efficacy and a large effect on participants' daily opioid intake (i.e., music therapy reduced the amount of opioid pain medication they used each day). Treatment benefits were sustained at a three-month follow-up. The results of this pilot study are encouraging but need further investigation using a large-scale clinical trial before conclusions can be drawn.

In summary, research to date suggests that music-based interventions may help improve important outcomes in chronic pain management, including pain interference, pain-related self-efficacy, pain intensity, and possibly opioid use. More research on the use of music therapy treatments that include active music making is needed. In addition, more music therapy studies are needed that target opioid tapering in people with chronic pain.

Music Across the Continuum of Care: A Hospital Setting

J. TODD FRAZIER

Director, Center for Performing Arts Medicine,
Houston Methodist Hospital

It is well known that music in hospitals can have social, emotional, therapeutic, and educational benefits for patients, but it is unique to find an organization that provides entry points for music as diverse and broad as the Center for Performing Arts Medicine (CPAM). CPAM is an integrated arts-in-health department within the eight-hospital system of Houston Methodist. The overarching mission of CPAM is to effectively translate the collaborative potential of arts and medicine to the holistic health-care environment of Houston Methodist. In support of its mission, CPAM produces intentional programs that utilize the arts across the continuum of care to enhance and transform the patient and employee experience. Although CPAM uses all art forms in its applications, the following road map shows how environmental music, music medicine, and music therapy work independently and in collaboration at CPAM.

MUSIC IN THE HOSPITAL ENVIRONMENT

Take a moment and imagine you are a patient entering a hospital for an appointment or procedure. If you are like most of us, you'll feel a heightened level of anxiety just arriving at the building. As you gather your appointment papers and personal items, your mind rushes with thoughts of the day's schedule. Then, taking a glance at your watch, you speed up, not wanting to be late. Your heart rate rises, and you can feel the effect of added stress on your body. However, as you enter the lobby, you hear soothing music rolling from a grand piano. The pianist gives you a welcoming nod as you pass by. You sense that he is playing for you and others like you—it is comforting. This music has become a positive distraction from your previous stressors and transforms what you imagined would be a sterile and intimidating environment into one that is calming. Or perhaps you arrive at noon and hear a choir singing as people eat lunch, walk to their next appointment, and pause to look over the railing while you listen to the unexpected gift. Looking around, you realize the environment feels welcoming and you take a moment to exhale as you move through your day's activities. How would this instantly change your perception of a hospital experience? For many, it may humanize the place and experience and speak to the mission and overall goals of the hospital. It could even transition the perception of a hospital from a place where one goes when sick to a place that supports one's physical and mental health and well-being as a natural part of life.

At CPAM this is exactly what the environmental music programs strive to achieve. Environmental music describes music curated to enhance the public settings across the hospital. Professional staff and volunteer pianists provide live music 365 days a year across the hospital system in public lobbies and strategic community or gathering spaces. In addition, the Margaret Alkek Williams Crain Garden Performance Series, a fully endowed concert program in the hospital's public spaces, offers upwards of a hundred performances per year by professional and student ensembles. In support of the global clientele at Houston Methodist, the genres of music presented reflect the diversity of patients, guests, and employees within the organization. While a classical music group may perform in one tower, a staff pianist may be improvising jazz in another, and in a third, Hispanic Heritage Month is being celebrated with a guest guitarist from Mexico.

We know music can be a powerful agent, stimulating emotion, memory, and attention in both positive and potentially negative ways. Therefore, great care and consideration are taken to determine the role and appropriateness of music programming. Instead of a "show must go on" attitude, CPAM's environmental music is defined by being high quality and purposeful. The high-quality aspect turns the idea of what it takes to be a performing artist away from the standard concert hall definition and focuses on the intention and adaptability of the musician. Similarly described here, "excellence can instead be evaluated by the quality of musicians' and listeners' engagement, and the extent to which a musician has been a catalyst for personally meaningful experiences with music." "Purposeful" refers to the goal of the music presented—to relieve anxiety by creating a welcoming environment of solace, offering emotional rejuvenation and spiritual inspiration supporting the journey of healing and caregiving for all.

The use of music as an environmental agent has been documented throughout various health-care environments. In a compelling 2007 study, researchers examined how environmental music could change respondents' mood states within a hospital. The majority of respondents reported positive emotional states after experiencing the music, 82 percent reported music helped them to relax, 59 percent stated music made them feel happier, 47 percent felt more positive, 29 percent more energized, and 19 percent felt part of a group. Additionally, positive physical and emotional reactions were noted while listening to live music, including respondents feeling their body relax and smiling. CPAM conducts similar internal evaluations of its environmental music's efficacy with standardized patient and guest surveys as well as routine ArtObs analysis, a mixed-methods tool to evaluate performing arts activities in health-care settings. In CPAM internal surveys, questions focused on a patient's likelihood to recommend the musical programs and overall enjoyment of the experience receive consistently high scores. Combining its internal surveys and citations in the Hospital Consumer Assessment of Healthcare Providers and Systems (HCAHPS) surveys, CPAM tracks how the environmental music programming contributes to the patient experience—and financial strength—of the organization. HCAHPS surveys are used to set reimbursement rates by the federal government to a hospital; the higher a hospital's overall HCAHPS score is, the higher the percentage of reimbursement the organization will receive. While there are no specific questions regarding music programming on the HCAHPS survey, positive citations referencing music in the open comments section can be regarded as a factor in the individual's overall experience as a patient.

In 2016 CPAM published a guide for all musicians that outlines the specifics of performing in a hospital environment (what one might see, hear, or experience) and parameters for music that has proven effective in this space, including examples. For instance, atonal or dissonant selections may trigger anxiety, and sudden loud sounds, high volumes, dissonant chords, extended sections of harmonic dissonance, and intense rhythmic activity can be challenging or uncomfortable for lay audiences. In addition, the ambient noise of a coffee bar's grinder, loud conversations from other patients and visitors, or hurried footsteps on loud floors may create a chaotic soundscape. Music can be used to mitigate those common environmental sounds.

Musicians may initially feel constrained by this rethinking of their role as a performer to more of a caregiver through music, but over time the musicians who embrace this transition find themselves humbled and rewarded in new and deeply meaningful ways. For example, recently a CPAM pianist was playing in an open lobby that is overlooked by a surgical waiting room. This space offers significant challenges when programming, as the first floor is often filled with employees or visitors eating lunch while the second-floor visitors often feel heightened anxiety or stress as they await news of their loved ones post-surgery. A young woman walked from the second floor to the first-floor area visibly upset and shaking. This prompted the pianist to segue from playing a familiar popular song into a calming, spiritual piece. Seated only a few feet from the piano, the young woman slowly became less physically agitated and more composed. By the end of the piece, she was moving her head with the music and breathing normally. This brief interaction is one example of how our CPAM performers help create a welcoming and supportive space for patients, even through brief interactions.

Environmental music is not limited only to public areas. In response to the COVID-19 pandemic, one's hospitalization became limited to the confines of a patient's room, as people were discouraged or restricted from visiting or gathering in public areas. Beyond the traditional stress of hospitalization, these changes intensified anxiety and deepened isolation for patients and their loved ones. CPAM responded by reimagining how to safely reach patients and offer support through music. One avenue was the patient TVs. CPAM gained full access, twenty-four hours a day, to a hospital patient and waiting room TV channel and used this medium to further support the patient experience. The channel was repurposed to feature outdoor performances at well-known Houston locations as well as live painting set to music highlighting local ecosystems. The meal tray also became a mechanism for delivering art activities with lunch. Some examples include a musical tour of Europe through a QR code connection or writing your own song "Mad-Lib" style, where CPAM would record and send back your individualized musical piece. Additionally, each patient room at Houston Methodist was outfitted with a Patient Empowerment iPad, which offered self-guided CPAM-curated art content at the patient's fingertips by a connection to an internal CPAM website. These programming examples were specifically curated to reduce anxiety and isolation and provide patients with a constructive way to reflect upon and humanize their time in the hospital. Many of these resources were also taken home or accessed from home by patients who wished to continue their relationship with music beyond their hospital stay.

MUSIC MEDICINE

Music medicine complements environmental music programming by expanding the possibilities of how music can enhance the patient experience and patient care. Music medicine can be defined as a patient's passive music listening to prerecorded music provided by a medical team. Music medicine is usually less interactive than music therapy and focuses on monitoring the effects of music listening on patients without verbal processing of the music experience. Therefore, the music is provided similarly to how a pharmaceutical prescription is given to a patient. Playlists are developed or selected in consultation with medical professionals, arts-in-health specialists, artists, or creative arts therapists who are part of the medical team for generalized, individual, or group off-the-shelf use. These playlists become tools to promote relaxation or rejuvenation to combat common conditions that may accompany a clinical environment.

Music medicine has been used extensively in health care for everything from anxiety reduction to pain management. For example, it can support a patient who is nervous about an upcoming procedure. Imagine the patient is greeted by a friendly nurse, who assures her that the preparations are under way and offers her a curated music-for-relaxation playlist to listen to before she returns. Or perhaps in a chemotherapy waiting area, a patient care assistant encourages a patient waiting on his lab results to listen to a specific anxiety-reducing playlist created by his doctor in coordination with the hospital music therapist or artist in residence. These musical interventions personalize the patient care experience and harness the power of music to improve the treatment experience.

Looking to the future of music medicine, in a study partnership between CPAM, the Houston Methodist Imaging Core, and Rice University, researchers began using fMRI scans to better understand functional connectivity in the brain—in this case, changes in oxygenated blood flow when listening to familiar and unfamiliar music. When the blood supply to an area of one's brain is interrupted, as in a stroke, that brain tissue doesn't receive vital oxygen, causing the cells to begin to die. While medical advances continue to improve and strokes are not as deadly as in the past, they can cause a significant decrease in the quality of life. CPAM asked: What if music—in particular music medicine—could play a role in supporting rehabilitation after a stroke? While listening to music has been reported to improve stroke recovery, the research team looked for the causes behind that phenomenon. Starting with healthy subjects, participants listened to a variety of auditory samples of music and spoken word while the researchers examined what differences in brain activation appeared. Some of the auditory samples were selected in line with the music preferences of the subjects, and other pieces were consistent nonfamiliar selections for all participants. Differences in activation and functional connectivity may help explain previously observed beneficial effects in stroke recovery and be related to increased oxygenated blood flow to damaged brain areas stimulated by music listening. The research team has now moved forward to examining individual responses to a wide variety of auditory stimuli, focusing on familiar and nonfamiliar music and the corresponding increase or decrease in blood flow to emotion, memory, and focused attention areas of the brain. The hypothesis is that through increasing activation of those areas of the brain, a patient's progress through stroke or brain injury rehabilitation may be improved. This step could prove transformative to what noninvasive and inexpensive interventions patients can follow, potentially administered by an app, to support healing. This research, funded by philanthropic donations to the Center for Performing Arts Medicine, could be adapted into at-home, off-the-shelf music medicine for improving neurologic health and wellness outside of a hospital, enabling anyone, regardless of hospital affiliation, access to healing benefits.

MUSIC THERAPY

The final aspect of music integration across the continuum of care at Houston Methodist is music therapy. The overall practice of music therapy utilizes individualized music choices specific to the patient's culture and preferences to effect neurologic, physiological, and emotional changes. This field features a board-certified clinical professional (a music therapist) who works at the bedside with patients to achieve clinical goals through music interventions. Because an understanding of the patient's emotional connection with music plays a vital role in the therapy, the therapist must develop a rapport that allows for vulnerability within the session. This is achieved through the therapeutic relationship, which is the primary differentiator between music therapy and music medicine. A music therapist uses music as a tool to achieve clinical goals within a therapeutic relationship—rather than the prescribed use of music for listening outside an individualized, therapeutic relationship.

One might wonder what a music therapy intervention looks like. In most cases, music therapists use live music, whether that be in a receptive, recreative, newly composed, or improvisational intervention, and are trained to make musical changes in real time to meet a patient's needs. Certain techniques are practiced in music therapy, a common one being the technique of entrainment. Entrainment is the process of coordinating the external music that the therapist is playing with the body's internal rhythms. Through this technique, the therapist can purposefully adjust these internal rhythms by changing the tempo and characteristics of the music.

For example, one of our CPAM music therapists recently received a referral for a patient who was struggling with anxiety associated with an upcoming spontaneous breathing trial. This is a procedure where a patient is removed from a machine that provides artificial support to induce breathing. Upon arriving in the room, the therapist noted that the patient had a rosary and picture of St. Lidwina, patron saint for suffering from chronic pain, taped to the side of his bed. Using this information to start building rapport, the therapist introduced herself and pointed to the rosary, making the connection to the patient's strong Catholic faith. The patient's wife shared that his favorite hymn was "Let There Be Peace on Earth." Paying close attention to the heart monitor, the therapist began playing the song live, at first matching the quickened heart rate of the patient. Over the next few minutes, the therapist, using the concept of entrainment, slowed her tempo, and the patient's heart rate followed, helping him achieve a more relaxed state. Now that the patient was calm, the respiratory therapist was able to decrease the settings on the ventilator, transitioning the patient to a spontaneous breathing trial where he would practice breathing on his own. During this transition, the therapist continued to adjust the music to maintain an optimal respiratory rate, or breaths per minute, supporting the patient in continuing to breathe without the need for ventilator support.

On another unit of the hospital, a music therapist focuses on behavioral health on the inpatient psychiatric unit. Patients are admitted here for a variety of reasons, one being suicidal thoughts or attempts, as was the case in this next example. The music therapist, after receiving a referral for a new patient in a withdrawn state, reviewed the chart and headed to the patient's room. The man was lying in bed, staring at the ceiling. Without speaking, the therapist pulled a chair over and sat next to him. The patient, noticing the therapist's guitar, asked, "Do you play?" which opened the door to conversation and rapport building. In the next half hour, the therapist learned that this patient had always wished to learn to play guitar and that music was a powerful influence in his life. The patient also expressed sadness and fear regarding his attempted suicide. To further explore his feelings, the therapist helped him compose an original song that allowed them to journey through events in his recent past and build awareness around his hopes for the future. He was able to share this song with his family and psychologist to help them understand what he was going through and ask for accountability in specific areas of his life that would set him on a path for continued recovery.

While physiologic and psychiatric changes can often be a music therapy goal in the medical setting, so can neurologic recovery. Recently a patient in the neurologic intensive care unit was experiencing left-sided weakness after a motor vehicle accident that affected her ability to walk. The music therapist engaged in conversation with the patient to learn about her background, likes, dislikes, and culture. With this information, the therapist and patient chose songs together that were motivating and evoked positive memories for her. One was the Beatles' "Yellow Submarine." Focusing on the rhythmic components of the song allowed the music therapist to prime the brain's motor cortex in preparation for physical therapy. As the physical therapist provided physical cueing for the patient's gait or pattern of walking, the music therapist provided audio cueing to the brain. Together the physical therapist, music therapist, and patient more efficiently achieved the patient's clinical goal of walking a full lap around the unit. Over the course of two weeks, the patient utilized music therapy in conjunction with physical therapy to increase her endurance, balance, and tempo and ultimately reduce her time in the hospital.

Speech recovery is another common referral for music therapists to receive. After a stroke, patients may suffer from expressive aphasia, or the inability to produce clear and congruent speech. Much research has centered around the use of music to treat aphasia. One leading theory on why music is so successful for speech recovery involves the study of neural overlap. Parts of the neurologic pathways for speech have evolved to be used for music or vice versa. Music is also structured in a way that provides memory cues such as repetition and patterns. Because these two pathways run close to each other in the brain and have points at which they cross over each other, music training can influence speech recovery.

In a recent example at Houston Methodist, music therapy was provided to a patient with expressive aphasia after a stroke. Again the therapist began by engaging with the patient and his family to understand their relationship with music and identify songs that would be positively salient and ingrained in the patient's mind. One song that was special to him was "Amazing Grace." Prior to his stroke, he sang "Amazing Grace" as part of his daily Bible study. The therapist began treatment by introducing the technique of therapeutic singing, the "use of singing activities to facilitate initiation, development, and articulation in speech and language." The patient was able to hum and then sing along with the therapist, demonstrating that he would be a good candidate for melodic intonation therapy. This intervention allows patients to "learn a new way to speak through singing by using language-capable regions of the right cerebral hemisphere." In time the patient was able to chant phrases like "I am in pain" and "I want water," which gave him the ability to communicate during his hospital stay, and over multiple therapy sessions his speech became more confident, normalized, and articulate through his newly found method of communication.

Patient acuity defines the severity of illness or medical condition a patient is experiencing. This includes how stable the patient is both physiologically and psychologically, as well as their need for assistance to accomplish everyday tasks. Patients in the highest acuity settings throughout the Houston Methodist system engage in music therapy for recovery both medically and emotionally. Additionally, music therapists can provide support for family members coping with the difficulty of having a loved one in the hospital and the stressors of maintaining life outside of hospital visits. With one of the largest and most comprehensive music therapy teams in the country, serving the areas of mental health (in- and outpatient), rehabilitation (inpatient, neurologic, and stroke), cancer (outpatient infusion and bone marrow transplant), ICU (NICU, SLICU, MICU, CIVICU), and palliative care, CPAM is proud to provide this clinical service to a growing number of patients daily.

CONTINUUM OF CARE

At Houston Methodist we imagine a hospital setting where music is part of the continuum of care for all patients and visitors. Environmental music shapes the overall public experience, music medicine is administered to support the treatment process, and music therapy is utilized to achieve individualized clinical goals through a therapeutic relationship. These programs do not happen in silos, however. These dynamic teams work together at CPAM and across hospital departments to meet unique hospital needs.

As an example, CPAM was recently called to support a patient at end of life. A music therapist was working closely with the patient on a legacy-building project. Legacy building describes an opportunity for a patient to reflect on their unique life experiences and what legacy they want to leave for their family. The music therapist worked with the patient to create a heartbeat recording that was laid over a patient-selected song. The recording represented both a physical aspect of the patient (his heartbeat) with how he wanted to be remembered (his song). Through the therapeutic relationship, the music therapist learned that the patient was an avid music fan. He shared that he would love to be able to hear one last live performance. When the music therapist brought this wish to the arts integration team, CPAM engaged an artist for a live, virtual, one-on-one concert for the patient at the bedside via an iPad. Music therapy and environmental music worked together to create a memorable, specialized experience for this patient and his family.

Another example of collaboration across the continuum of care involves a music therapy intervention carried out in collaboration with a nursing unit. Due to an increase in patients under medical sedation and on neuromuscular blockers throughout COVID, the CPAM music therapy team created a novel protocol that uses the patient's sung name, sensory-rich stories told by family and friends, related salient songs, and a comfort message from next of kin to be played at consistent intervals during sedation and the process of weaning from sedation to decrease the potential for post-sedation delirium. This approach, called Positive Stimulation for Medically Sedated Patients, or PSMSP, has gained fast interest among our critical care staff for its ability to prime a patient's brain while they are under medical sedation and decrease post-sedation delirium and emotional confusion and agitation that is common during and after the weaning process. To implement PSMSP, the music therapist first reviews a patient's medical history and completes an assessment. The therapist then works with the patient's support system to record and create a PSMSP CD. The CD is played three times per day for sedated patients, and response data such as blood pressure, heart rate, and behavioral responses are tracked. Because the music therapy team did not have the capacity to administer these playlists thrice a day across the hospital system for each patient, they partnered with and trained the nursing staff to administer the CDs as well as look for contraindicators that would require the music therapist to reevaluate the patient and make adjustments to the playlist. This partnership between music therapy and a music medicine application through nursing allowed more patients to participate in this innovative, personalized intervention and progress toward their health goals, exemplifying the power of collaboration.

It is exciting to know that the field of arts in health is growing and bringing a much-needed human-centric side to specialized care throughout

America. Notable work to support the field as a whole is being done by national organizations such as the NOAH (National Organization for Arts in Health) and AMTA (American Music Therapy Association), other large medical centers such as the Cleveland Clinic and AdventHealth system in Florida, and on the education front with established institutions such as the University of Florida Center for Arts in Medicine, and new programs like the EPAM (Eastman Performing Arts Medicine) and at the University of Houston, where they have recently launched an Arts and Health Certificate and Music Therapy degree as part of their College of the Arts (COTA). At CPAM we see a bright future for the field of arts in health and hope more and more hospitals, environments of care, universities, medical schools, and arts organizations will broaden their programming and teaching to embrace this growth. The field not only supports the healing journey for patients and caregivers in a cost-effective, innovative, and impactful way, but it also offers meaningful career opportunities to artists and broadens the arenas in which music brings value to our lives and our communities.

::::::::::

For more information about CPAM and its programs, including access to an educational video portal, please visit: houstonmethodist.org/performing -arts.

With the collaboration of Shay Thornton Kulha, MBA, MFA, and Jennifer Townsend, MMT, MT-BC.

"I Sing the Body Electric": Music Psychotherapy in Medicine

JOANNE LOEWY, DA, LCAT, MT-BC

Director, Louis Armstrong Center for Music and Medicine

I sing the body electric,
The armies of those I love engirth me and I engirth them,
They will not let me off till I go with them, respond to them,
And discorrupt them, and charge them full with the charge of the soul.
Was it doubted that those who corrupt their own bodies conceal themselves?
And if those who defile the living are as bad as they who defile the dead?
And if the body does not do fully as much as the soul?
And if the body were not the soul, what is the soul?

—WALT WHITMAN

Music therapy has gained traction in both medical research and practice, affirming its distinction as an integrative discipline, and the field continues to expand and evolve. Through extensive clinical trials among collaborative medical teams, music therapy interventions have led to important evidence-based outcomes informing and spurring new research. As a music psychotherapist at the Louis Armstrong Center for Music and Medicine, I work with music-based mechanisms, using specific musical instruments as part of treatment. Our investigations have yielded significant advancements in how we approach care in a wide range of medical scenarios.

Music therapy is an integrative field. Historically, medical doctors were trained as generalists. In fact, there is no evidence of any significant development of specialties in the United States prior to 1855. To this day the

primary care offered by general practitioners in internal medicine is comprehensive rather than segmented into distinct specialties. As such, the
broad reach of internal medicine is vastly integrative and driven by a focus
on family-centered care.

In my role as a medical music therapist over the last twenty-nine years,
I have found the generalist-specialty relationship to be crucial in the development of a gestalt of best-treatment regimens. The continuous expansion
of knowledge in specialty areas has provided a context for our initiating,
testing, and implementing incentives, alongside doctors and nurses who have
collectively investigated the power of music's potency in treating symptoms
belonging to specific diseases. At the same time, work in settings where
medical specialties require immediate integration with one another to provide care—such as critical care ICUs, or population-based practices (e.g.,
neonatal, pediatric, adolescent, and geriatric)—has expanded collaboration
and how practitioners consider the collective wellness that music therapy
can provide in the rehabilitation of mind, body, and spirit. The importance
of integrative medicine in providing holistic care is central to the field of
music psychotherapy and affords numerous opportunities for integrating
specialty practices within a general medicine orientation.

To use a musical metaphor, the body is both a collection of individual
instruments and an ensemble as well—a variety of distinct parts ideally
functioning together to produce a unified, harmonious result. Instrumentalists and vocalists are disciplined to develop their expertise in a particular
area. The outcome is not only a talented solo performer, but also a musician
who has the advanced sensitivity to meld his individual sound within an
ensemble. The human body is likewise composed of distinct instruments
(organs) situated within an orchestra of discrete systems (e.g., spleen within
a digestive system). These systems are tasked to either create, regulate, or
respond to sound vibrations. The heart, as the central conductor of periodicity (rhythm), informs pulmonary function and vice versa. The brain, akin
to a "theme instructor," regulates emotions and organizes how systems connect. When each system is "in tune" and monitored to stay functional and
healthy, the likelihood of influencing an ailing organ and integrating it into
a harmonic forum increases.

Western medicine defines the systems of our body as skeletal, muscular,
nervous, endocrine, cardiovascular, lymphatic, respiratory, digestive, uri-

nary, and reproductive. Ancient Eastern spiritual practice roots physical body with energy perception in the chakras. There are seven chakras that start from the sacrum and work up to the crown, and correlate to a "wheel" and succinct points of energy anchored in the body. Chakras—defined literally as spinning disks of moving energy—are used in esoteric healing practices and can influence the perception of how one feels, connecting the physical and emotional aspects of "being." Our incentive to practice rituals that maintain alignment and receptivity to energy affects our capacity to stay well and open to the universe. Music, most particularly when applied in a live format, has a unique and distinguishable impact on each system of the body. Our bodies are vessels with numerous sound apertures—from the scalp; to our eyes, nose, and ear sockets; to the mouth and anus. Skin, as our largest organ, has millions of pores susceptible to vibration and air, which enhance opportunities for absorption.

The energy involved in thinking, feeling, breathing, heartbeat, smelling, hearing, tasting all have functional qualities that integrate as unique systems of our living experience. When we use consciousness to realize and attend to the inherently musical components of function, we begin to realize our bodies are truly composed of a symphony of sounds that are informed by our brain intentionally or unconsciously, and the "music" of our conditions also infers functions involuntarily and autonomically.

ENTRAINMENT

A central aspect of integrative work that is essential to music psychotherapy is the concept of entrainment. Michael Thaut and his colleagues have written about entrainment as being "defined by a temporal locking process in which one system's motion or signal frequency entrains the frequency of another system." An example of this in a nonbiological system comes from seventeenth-century Dutch scientist Christiaan Huygens, who demonstrated that pairs of moving pendulums become synchronized independent of human physical intervention.

In current times entrainment is no longer a phenomenon attributed solely to moving objects or materials; its effects are considered to be patterns of nature and evolution. For example, we synchronize and calibrate the rhythm of our internal biological clock to actual systematic, external time cues informed by ticking clocks. We calibrate our sleep and wake cycles based on rhythmic cycles of light and darkness in the morning and evening. The rhythm and predictability of sequences are notable in music mechanisms. It is precisely why participants playing live music over Zoom experience bandwidth delays that interrupt the natural interaction of parts. There is less efficacy in playing in "virtual time" than playing live in real time, because the entrainment mechanism is hampered, and the synchrony within the interactive audio experience results in a musically disorganized experience.

Participation in a live music experience incorporates entrainment in real time, through which a music therapist can calibrate the accentuating vibrations of synchrony and support for therapeutic effect. This includes the essential impacts of timing, the unique timbres of the voice in singing and speaking, and the importance of melodic and harmonic sequencing in designing music experiences. These distinct musical characteristics, involving distinct neurological perceptions, have the capacity to collectively alter the "ensembling" of the body's systems.

Thaut's studies of entrainment look at correlations between the human sensory and motor systems. His research in people with Parkinson's revealed that the inherent periodicity of auditory rhythmic patterns could entrain movement patterns in the experience of movement disorders. In simple terms, the rhythms in a piece of music could be employed to enhance control of movement, with promising ramifications for a major symptom of Parkinson's. His revelations in music synchrony and entrainment led to the development of Neurologic Music Therapy, an international training protocol for music therapists. It includes twenty standardized clinical techniques for sensorimotor, speech, and language training.

NEUROLOGIC FUNCTION AND MUSIC MEMORY

In recent years neuroscience and the study of neurologic mechanisms in medicine have moved into a leading position in health science disciplines. The recent Neuroscience and Music international conferences have included music therapy and its applications in research. This quote from the *Journal of Neuroscience* reflects neuroscience's integrative stance:

Beyond examining the complexity of the nervous system itself, we must ask ourselves how we study this system of systems. When considering the approach that other scientific fields with seemingly infinite complexity have taken . . . collaboration across disciplines and countries likely contributed to the great strides made thus far. Borrowing from this example, interdisciplinary approaches, with teams of mathematicians, engineers, computer scientists, biologists, and chemists, are key to the continued advancement of neuroscience. Presently, neuroscience is funded in many countries through numerous agencies; however, recent national and international initiatives facilitating large-scale interdisciplinary neuroscience are emerging . . . [These initiatives] have not focused on one specific area of neuroscience but instead embraced participation from researchers spanning science, engineering, math, and technology.

The vitality of [the Society for Neuroscience], whose annual meeting has grown from 1395 to >30,000 attendees per year, highlights its immense value as a central space for scientific dialog and collaboration. Expansion of these centrally coordinated efforts to accelerate brain research as well as a strong community of scientists will be instrumental in elevating the quality and capability of neuroscience research as it continues to explore the unknown.

A major theme throughout this chapter is the importance of integration—not only in addressing systems of physiology, or a symptom within a disease, but also when implementing a strategy involving music or a music therapy intervention. The "therapy" orientation is based on clinical training; it is what distinguishes simply implementing selected music (based on a request or inference) from the distinct psychological orientation that informs the treatment. Such decisions involve advanced training and define the essential elements affecting respective treatment options, including culture, personal history, trauma, past hospitalizations, and the assessment of support systems or lack thereof. For example, a music therapist could incorporate familiar songs and support parents to use their voices by framing their singing in a comfortable key to enhance attachment opportunities in the parent-child relationship—or use music with a particular meter to elongate the breathing patterns of a teen or adult with pulmonary challenges.

The increased interest in neurology research in the past decade stems not only from technological improvements, but also from the awareness that, with longer human life spans, neurological functions are more likely to become compromised. Movement and memory are a central focus of a growing number of research studies involving rehabilitation, and music and music therapy are playing an advanced role in this neurologic research.

Concetta Tomaino, a pioneer in neurologic music therapy practice, was among the first to study the impacts of live music on memory retrieval and speech engagement. Her research spans several decades and demonstrates how both words and syntax can be cued through implementation of songs with familiar melodies. This effect was conspicuous when sentences were embedded in a familiar musical phrase. The improved performance reflected in word retrieval—especially on the downbeats of tunes, or the beginnings and cadences of phrases—shows "therapeutic efficacy of coupling the semantic component of words with the musical syntax (form)."

Several years ago, the Louis Armstrong Center for Music and Medicine developed a collaboration with Lincoln Center to create a program for adults with Alzheimer's disease. Members of our team traveled to Lincoln Center, bringing adults with dementia and their caregivers to attend concerts. After the hour-long programs, we instituted group music therapy experiences with actual music themes taken from the concerts, and occasionally organized additional wellness programs in conjunction with performing artists. We saw a marked enhancement of social investment and quality-of-life involvement of participants in these groups postparticipation: they could sustain musical ideas contextualized within themes from the concert. This program, Lincoln Center Moments, continues in New York City today.

A large, multinational study from 2021 supports these observations and has provided a novel investigation of the effects of music interventions delivered by trained, informal caregivers on the behavioral and psychological symptoms of people living with dementia. Four hundred and ninety-five dyads (caregiver-patient pairs) from Australia, Germany, the UK, Poland, and Norway were randomized into either a standard care (SC) regimen, a home-based music program plus SC, or a home-based reading program plus SC for twelve weeks. This trial is unique in comparing similar neurologic efforts (singing and reading), utilizing a context emphasizing music mechanisms. It also examines the integration of caregivers, which could have an impact on activities of daily living and quality of life outside of research time.

Additional studies from Teppo Särkämö and his colleagues examined music ensemble singing in stroke and early dementia; these have shown the positive impacts of music interventions, particularly when the music utilized is familiar. Särkämö has surmised a distinct mnemonic impact that can be strategically implemented when songs are utilized as a verbal learning tool for rehabilitation.

The Louis Armstrong Center is currently studying the effects of ensemble singing and personalized playlists in similar clinical trials involving patients and caregivers, for adults with mild cognitive impairment (MCI) and adults with stroke. The MCI study includes use of journals, weekly music therapy, and home daily listening with caregivers. Our stroke study includes stroke survivors and their caregivers and a weekly choir. In both of these investigations we assess past music experience and music genre preference, in order to personalize music therapy treatment. These studies seek also to examine the impact of music therapy on caregivers' compassion fatigue, as well as patients' mood and quality of life.

PAIN AND ANXIETY

In my first years of working on a pediatric unit, my patients were often children who were fearful of medical procedures. Since fear and anxiety exacerbate a patient's perception of pain, I saw my music therapy role as twofold: treating the child and treating the fear. The International Association for the Study of Pain defines pain as "an unpleasant sensory and emotional experience arising from actual or potential tissue damage or described in terms of such damage." As such, pain is not solely a perceived uncomfortable stimulus. Rather, the duration and level of pain depend on one's subjective emotional response it.

Some psychosocial orientations are rooted in *distracting* children from particular procedures, assuming that parents in the exam room will help alleviate the children's anxiety. However, attempting to provide a distraction from pain can make a child, and virtually patients of any age, feel manipulated instead of heard. Having supported hundreds of procedures where we assessed child, teen, and adult patients' developmental and emotional levels, we learned that in many instances children and adults fare better—with stronger capacity and endurance—when participating in procedures or sessions individually. Furthermore, children's experience of pain was often seemingly exacerbated by their perceived lack of safety and their concerns about parents in the room. Instead of focusing on the worried faces of anxious parents, children can be afforded a sense of agency in individual music-based sessions.

During a hospitalization, where matters of safety and mortality become amplified, commonplace personal experiences can be felt more intensely than usual. In these situations, the relevance and importance of the use of music may become more critical. The relationship a patient has with a music therapist is unique; the expression of music and the nuances of sharing a meaningful song are highly personal, which can be important in maintaining one's sense of endurance and wellness. For example, active songwriting and drumming often serve as vehicles that prompt the authentic release of emotions, from joy to anger. Therefore, it may be effective to structure an experience where medical staff who are perceived to be frightening become part of a musical ensemble prior to a venipuncture or other possibly painful procedure. The timing of treatment regimens for patients experiencing significant pain or fear should be coordinated between music therapists and the team of doctors, nurses, social workers, etc.

Music can enhance a patient's sense of self-expression and agency, conveying physical and emotional control that is critical for all stages of disease treatment. When patients feel in control of the music, and subsequently in control of the accompanying medical procedures, they develop a sense of autonomy and resilience. When a moment of predictable pain is forthcoming—for instance, a venipuncture—the nurse or technician can encourage a patient to count off to the beat of the music, which can instill control, trust, and safety in the context of an aesthetically meaningful music experience.

Lullabies and significant themes related to one's culture can also often be comforting during times of extreme stress, or in palliative care and end-of-life transitions. A music psychotherapy assessment provides a trusting context whereby therapeutic interventions and recommendations can be made sensitively and accurately, and the results are far-reaching.

Medical staff also benefit from music interventions, such as community jams or preprocedure music sessions. We have generated close alliances and various music ensembles with medical teams who have welcomed creative opportunities to "play" during the day, and not only for their patients. This important realization has evolved post-9/11 with our "Caring for the Caregiver" approach for staff and continues to the present day in times of COVID. For doctors and nurses who have experienced trauma during the pandemic, as well as others who have faced excessive burden or post-traumatic stress from the impacts of COVID, our team has provided "Louis Zoom Rooms" for music meditations, clinical improvisation, singing, and PATH (Pause, Align, Treat, Heal), a program exclusively for staff who experienced trauma during and after COVID. The web brochure is shown in the figure below.

THE LOUIS ARMSTRONG CENTER FOR MUSIC AND MEDICINE

(LACMM) is providing staff with several short consecutive, 4-day, 30-minute sessions, to help monitor our transitions. Music will reduce stress & foster psychological first-aid via private zoom rooms. Any and all staff: first responders, incident commanders, primary and emergency health care providers, ICU staff, clinical teams and administrators may pre-register confidentially for each series.

Email info@musicandmedicine.org to register.

PATHs (Pause, Align, Treat, Heal) is a trauma-based music psychotherapy model highlighting social, cognitive and neurobiological mechanisms; emotion regulation, anxiety-reduction, pleasure inducing contexts for staff who have experienced direct or vicarious trauma exposure, or who are dealing with symptoms of PTSD. The LACMM has historically directed disaster-response efforts for staff, with support from the Grammy Foundation, including 9-11, Hurricane Sandy and Katrina. Through music and your confidential participation, we will help to foster resilience and engage our staff, including those who are struggling with stress, as we develop new patterns that incorporate strategies for daily wellness.

Weekly Sessions

Mon - Thurs | 12:00 - 12:30 PM

PATH (Pause, Align, Treat, Heal)

PULMONARY FUNCTION: BREATHING, WIND PLAY, AND SINGING

Breath is perhaps the most central mechanism of integrative activity within our bodies. This is because it informs connections between bodily systems, creating a sense of flow. While cardiac disease is still the most prevalent killer of humans worldwide, our capacity to manage heart health and regulate heart rhythms has improved significantly with diet, exercise, and the development of medical devices. The breath and respiratory function can also affect and help regulate cardiac function, an integration that is increasingly recognized in medical research. As breathing is one of the few physiological processes that can be voluntarily controlled, it is a perfect access point for singing and wind-based music therapy interventions.

When a patient with asthma or COPD plays a harmonica or recorder, the reward of play can be extended into motivating music making. The use of musical wind instruments in our research with children and adults with asthma and COPD, respectively, has validated music therapy's potency in wind play interventions, such as pursed lip breathing (PLB) techniques. The American Thoracic Society guidelines describe the technique of PLB as "involving a nasal inhalation followed by expiratory blowing against partially closed lips, avoiding forceful exhalation." Easy-to-play wind instruments—including the harmonica, melodica, recorder, and slide whistle—provide an incentive to address diaphragmatic breathing and body posture voluntarily and creatively, which can increase expiratory airways pressure. Furthermore, rather than experiencing a lack of physical control of breath agency, participation in a musical improvisation, such as a blues on harmonica, can invite a creative forum for self-expression and collaborative play with others, and an experience that can build pulmonary endurance.* Benefits of music therapy, with playing and singing in a psychotherapy forum for children with asthma and adults with COPD, have included improvements in oxygen use and lung volume enhancement, resulting in better school attendance and enhanced quality of life, respectively.

Wind play can additionally serve as a warm-up to singing. The voice is the most accessible and uniquely personal instrument, as it is the only musical instrument that is part of the body. Therefore, when one sings, all aspects of bodily function are integrating simultaneously; all the organs are vibrating, which incentivizes blood flow. Singing also invites exploration of chakra vibration. I have developed a method called tonal intervallic synthesis, which implements dissonant intervals of musical tones to points of pain in the body. Moving the dissonant intervals into consonance, in accordance with the patient's sung response, can increase blood flow and transform an experience of tension into a relaxation response.

---

*artsandculture.google.com/story/egURR_fnglOtCQ.

Another technique employed in music therapy that actively influences breathing is guided visualization, in which a person's imagination is drawn upon to achieve a certain goal, usually relaxation. Remo ocean drums (frame drums containing beads that simulate the sound of surf) are often utilized for this type of music therapy, as they can induce a relaxation response when the wavelike sound of the instrument is entrained with a patient's respiratory rate. Eventually, with repetition, the patient's breathing can be subtly elongated; their favorite place can then be visualized and explored within this meditative state.

SEDATION AND SONGS OF KIN

It is no secret that "music has charms to soothe the savage breast." In 2003 our pediatric neurologist used to refer babies and toddlers to us prior to medical tests daily. One day we had a two-year-old who was so anxious that I decided to follow her up to the EEG unit. I continuously sang lullabies to her on the elevator as the porter rolled her on a stretcher. As we arrived, she was nearly asleep, but as we neared the room where the EEG was to take place, audible recorded music was playing, fast-pulsed and with a heavy bassline. When I requested that the technician turn the music lower, she replied that attaching the leads in preparation for the EEG would take some time, and that the music would "tire the patient out." It did quite the opposite; the resident had to be paged, and more chloral hydrate (a sedative) was administered. The EEG took three hours to complete, because the young girl had the opposite reaction to the sedative. This opposite desired effect is called "emergence delirium" and unfortunately is not uncommon.

Several days later at rounds (our daily patient report meeting), it was mentioned that another patient, this time an eighteen-month-old, was due for a second EEG, but his parents were refusing because they felt sedatives might have negative repercussions on their baby's neurologic function. The father of this infant was a nutritionist and was likely well informed.

These two situations occurring in the same week inspired a research study with our neurologist and nurse, which led to a protocol ensuring that pediatric patients needing EEG could be sedated with music therapy. This not only ensured safer, more cost-effective outcomes, but encouraged the inclusion of parents to accompany their children if they so desired. The music therapist would help the parent select a "song of kin" (a term later developed from further study) and provide details on how the parents could use their singing in a sedative way. A familiar, parent-selected song with meaningful positive associations, sung in a context of familiarity, induces safety that encourages sleep, especially when musical elements such as repetition and cadence are included.

The sedation effect, a music therapy intervention designed from our research outcomes, developed from this study. It is a formalized protocol that has been further studied and implemented not only with infants and children, but also with adults. The "first do no harm" medical tenet supports a place for music therapy as a safety-first option for sedating in medical testing, or helping people relax and fall asleep as part of an anxiety-reducing "sleep health" protocol.

NEONATAL MUSIC THERAPY

The effect of entrainment in neonatal music therapy is substantial. When live music is entrained to the rhythm of an infant's vital signs, their internal regulation is strategically calibrated. This effect is even further pronounced when the rhythm is accompanied by a familiar voice and repeated as a ritual, which strengthens neural patterning. This therapeutic technique has led to improved vital signs such as heart rate, respiratory rate, sleep, and regulated sucking patterns.

Beyond a music therapist's matching of a patient's physiological rhythm of respiration, the effects of entrainment are deepened when attuned with the vibratory integrative mechanisms of pitch, tempo, dynamics, and tonality, eliciting homeostasis (equilibrium or internal stability) of the body. This can move a person's experience of "dis-ease" to ease, as the ultimate integrative experience of what we understand as vital calibration.

Our 2013 study of 272 neonates, in conjunction with our neonatologist and nurse practitioner, instituted a "song of kin" intervention. Compared to a control group presented with a well-known folk theme ("Twinkle, Twinkle, Little Star"), the study yielded interesting outcomes for participants presented with a song of kin. Culturally based, parent-selected, personalized musical tunes fostered an optimal, continuous quality of care and also reduced the parents' perception of anxiety during their infants' neonatal intensive care unit (NICU) stays.

We saw a parallel process at play as well in treating the parents with live music psychotherapy first, before demonstrating the similar impacts of entrainment on their infant's observed vital signs. After an assessment of the parents' potential for trauma, we could accompany and frame their voices, enhancing their strength and resilience. This fostered security and joy that the parents, in turn, offered their neonates through entrained song.

Our research led to the creation of First Sounds RBL (Rhythm, Breath, and Lullaby) training, which is implemented in NICUs globally and is aimed at enhancing bonding moments through live music therapy for infant-parent dyads and triads. Entrainment is likewise a key aspect of this work; music can instill a potent means of support, allowing for and then moderating expressions of fear or anxiety related to a premature birth. Typically, attention in the treatment of premature infants is directed primarily toward the fragile infant. Our training implements music to support parents' grief and assist in the expression of hope that can instill a sense of security and containment.

MUSIC THERAPY IN ONCOLOGY AND FRAGILE TREATMENT AREAS

Few messages strike such terror as a diagnosis of cancer. Siddhartha Mukherjee, in his seminal book *The Emperor of All Maladies: A Biography of Cancer,* stated: "Cancer is not one disease but many diseases. We call all of them 'cancer' because they share a fundamental feature: the abnormal growth of cells." Diagnosing, staging, and treating cancer is in itself complex, and engenders an equally complex set of changes in the lives of the people it touches. The burden of illness and the treatment resulting from a cancer diagnosis are devastating, life-altering events, and are often perplexing and overwhelming to patients and caregivers alike. However, music psychotherapy can lessen the effects of medical ailments and anxiety associated with radiation and chemotherapy. Music's capacity to mobilize thought, feeling, and experience, can be employed to treat and reduce anxiety, as the calming of the body changes the patient's perception of the treatment.

After providing music therapy in oncology units for many years, we opened an outpatient Music and Health clinic and began to receive referrals for patients who had received cancer treatments and wanted to continue maintaining their wellness beyond hospitalization. We received grants to set up services for patients in chemotherapy and radiation. We call these "fragile treatment areas" because patients often endure unpleasant side effects. Our research has demonstrated that music therapy before and during these treatments could lessen the anxiety associated with radiation. A trusting music therapy relationship during chemotherapy allowed patients to better endure the pain and discomfort, through integration of mind and body control.

MUSICIAN'S WELLNESS: THE FINAL FRONTIER

Musicians themselves represent a unique population in the field of integrative medicine and wellness. At one time or another many experience overuse or occupational injury. Others may be prone to chronic fatigue, depression, or performance anxiety. Musicians are also more likely to die from alcohol and drug abuse than nonmusicians; one study of 226 musicians in New York State found that substance use was "markedly elevated compared to general population samples." Job security is a concern in this field as well. With technological advancements, live bands and orchestras have been replaced by DJs or recordings, which has made competition among musicians ever fiercer. The past few years have been especially difficult in this regard, with many live performances canceled or reduced due to the pandemic.

The Louis Armstrong Center's Music and Health Clinic has specialized in the treatment of musicians since opening its doors in 2007. In 2010 our medical director, Stephan Quentzel, and I published the first Integrative Bio-Psycho-Musical Assessment Model for the Treatment of Musicians, which explores how live music and the relationship between therapist and musician work together as central agents of intervention and change. Composition, clinical improvisation, and exploration of nonprimary instruments provide opportunities that enhance creativity and spontaneity.

Distinct from verbal discourse in conservative talk therapy, musicians have opportunities to discover themselves more fully through music ther-

A MODEL OF INTEGRATIVE MEDICAL MUSIC PSYCHOTHERAPY
J. Loewy & B. Scheiby, 2001

MUSICAL
- Wellness
- Subjective response
- Intuitive learning / Clinical improvisation
- Construction of meaning
- Altered states of consciousness
- Physical / Emotional pain management through intervention from within

Letting go / Holding on   Transpiritual

Humanizing the medical experience   Intimacy / Safety

MEDICAL MUSIC PSYCHOTHERAPY

Wholeness: Music identity   Integration of mind - body

Imagination / Transformation   Relinquishing Control / Relaxing   Retaining / Redefining self

- Physical pain treatment through intervention from without
- Pharmacology
- Measurement
- External knowledge / Prescribed regimen
- Clinical objective
- Illness

MEDICAL

Loewy & Scheiby, 2001, used with permission, Satchmo Armstrong Press

apy, and in turn have taken advantage of the unique contexts in which their wellness can be achieved and maintained.

Our department of music therapy at the Mount Sinai Health System in New York City provides a yearly training for master's- and doctoral-level music therapists and medical doctors to explore current research and clinical case studies and learn more about the physical and musical domains of treatment. We work to treat both physical and emotional factors that impede the health and performance of musicians and performing artists.

KEY COMPONENTS OF MEDICAL MUSIC PSYCHOTHERAPY

Medical music psychotherapy is a growing discipline in music therapy. The figure demonstrates key psychotherapeutic areas that include imagination, transformation, relaxation, and the ongoing refinement and redefinition of a sense of self. Additionally, palliative care inclusive of spiritual practice can often come into people's experience when there are profound comfort needs that make them necessary. Music therapy interventions involving transspiritual elements of letting go or holding on are determined through exploration of resilience building—such as drumming or chanting to strengthen, versus relinquishing control and accepting the end of a disease process, whereby being played or sung to enhances comfort as one transitions in passage from life toward death, as an imagined place/condition of ultimate rest. Finally, the concept of wholeness and identity can be realized through integration of mind and body.

The common objectives of clinical, medical, and musical domains correspond to components such as illness-wellness, clinical objective-subjective response, and so on.

Our research and practice of medical music psychotherapy provides patients with ways to foster agency, incorporating elements of strength in the face of some of the most daunting challenges of disease treatment. Music therapy–based protocols can strengthen difficult regimens of medical treatment, with effects such as lessening pain after spine surgery, enhancing resilience during chemotherapy, and decreasing anxiety during radiation.

Our team has also addressed music therapy's benefits in helping patients and families prepare for their ultimate passage at end of life. We provide music grief groups that have helped families and staff after death has occurred. Music therapy can serve a critical role during these transitionary periods.

From illness to wellness, from disease to ease, from sleep to awakeness, in music and nonmusic experiences of daily living, surmised contextually from birth to end of life, our lives are driven and metered by our individual histories, our moods, our beliefs, our goals, and our dreams. Music psychotherapy in medicine provides numerous ways to gain control and insight into our bodies as instruments. At the same time, the music we experience and its effects in ordinary daily use—including prescribed, personalized playlists by a music therapist—can help to harvest our hopes and ambitions.

We are currently studying in partnership with Carnegie Hall's Weill Music Institute the potential of music and music therapy experiences to affect depression across vulnerable disease trajectories. The National Endowment for the Arts has provided support for this research lab, entitled AMEND (Assessing Music Experiences in Navigating Depression). We also received support from the NIH in partnership with Columbia University to study the impact of a culturally based live music intervention on the metabolic pathways associated with chronic stress and the risk of preterm birth in Black women.

Music offers ways both within our bodies and in concordance with a larger ensemble of players through which we can explore, reflect upon, and cultivate our well-being. Music therapy seeks to provide the tools and can facilitate the creativity we need to maintain our health through unique, personalized expression, prompting a reward pathway in the brain that enhances resonance and innovation. It is my hope that this chapter has illuminated some of the ways in which music psychotherapy can nurture, strengthen, and heal, assisting in life's transitions and acclaiming the essential aspects of "living" that each of us experiences.

"What we play is life," said Louis Armstrong. The sounds and silences of our bodies are indeed instruments, and our understanding and utilization of each system's musical role in fostering vitality, and how we integrate these systems as a harmonious ensemble, yield the potential for safe, efficient, and cost-effective treatments through music therapy.

The research and clinical descriptions provided in this chapter offer an orientation for further discovery. Readers are invited to subscribe to the international, peer-reviewed journal *Music and Medicine* (mmd.iammonline .com/index.php/musmed/index) to gain access to the current research, practice, and theory of many of the topics provided here and within this anthology.

HEALTH
IN THE
SPOTLIGHT

Artists and Leading Presenters
Discuss Key Health
and Community Initiatives

How to Fall in Love with Opera

ANN PATCHETT

Award-Winning Novelist and National Humanities Medal Recipient

In my late twenties, I spent a couple of years living with Mark, a poet who grew up playing the flute. As a child he read *Grove's Dictionary of Music and Musicians*, and, armed with those abundant facts, went on to be a winner on a show called *The New Quiz Kids*. When we were together, he belonged to the Opera of the Month Club, which functioned much like the Book of the Month Club. As soon as the CDs arrived in the mail, he would remove the tiny booklet with its microscopic type from the front of the jewel case, and listen. He would listen for hours while I went into the bedroom to read. The music changed constantly in our apartment, but I never asked him what he was listening to, nor did he ever say, "Sit down, I want you to hear this."

Years after Mark and I parted ways, the faintest notes of that music began to return.

On December 17, 1996, during a party to celebrate the birthday of Emperor Akihito, fourteen members of the Tupac Amaru Revolutionary Movement (MRTA) stormed the Japanese embassy in Lima, taking hundreds of businessmen, diplomats, and military officials hostage. The siege would last until April 22, 1997, when the Peruvian military tunneled into the compound and executed the revolutionaries. One hostage died of a heart attack during the siege.

That was as much of the story as I knew.

I didn't know any of the people involved. I'm not sure I even knew anyone who'd been to Peru. But day after day I followed the events in the newspaper. As the story unfolded over time—dropping from the front page, to the international section, and then to the last page of the international section— I found myself wondering about the logistics of daily life inside the embassy: How did they get food? Where did they sleep? Maybe I latched on to this particular crisis because the tragedies of the world seemed to fly by so quickly, earthquakes gave way to fires, school shootings became police shootings. I wanted to think deeply about one story, to stick with these people until the end. I also recognized that what was happening in Lima was what happened in the novels I write—a group of strangers are thrown together by circumstance—and so my imagination began to shape all the things I didn't know. I read the facts then came up with different scenarios. In real life, the majority of the hostages were released quickly, and all the women were released. I pictured the wives saying goodbye to the husbands they were forced to leave. It made me wonder what would have happened had the revolutionaries told one woman (at gunpoint) that she alone had to stay behind.

Novels arrive in a series of questions: Who is the most important woman at the party? Is she a diplomat? The president's wife? The president? Why has she come and what does she do? I decided she was an artist, the celebrated guest the wealthy Japanese businessman was hoping to meet. She was the unwitting bait for what other businessmen hoped would be a lucrative venture. What kind of artist was she? Not a painter, that wouldn't make any sense, and certainly not a novelist. A musician? Yes. A pianist? A violinist? No. She would be a singer. She would be an opera singer. I had seen a grown man transfixed by the voice of a soprano. I knew such things were possible.

I decided to write a novel about the most famous soprano in the world, trapped in the embassy of a nameless South American country. I went to an appliance store that had a small CD section (they sold stereos) and found a copy of *Madama Butterfly*. Everyone's heard of Madame Butterfly. When I got home I began to listen to the music while folding laundry.

Ignorance is a good place to start. Things I know a little bit about make me lazy, while things I know nothing about make me work. I knew nothing about opera. I knew nothing except that I didn't like it. For the first time I wondered if that was why I was always leaving whatever room Mark was in.

As a novelist, I consider listening to be an essential part of the job. I'm interested in other people's stories. I ask the person sitting next to me at a dinner party or on a long flight questions about their life, their work, their siblings. I have the kind of concentration suited to the long format—Russian novels, Swedish films—and yet I had no idea how to listen to opera.

Birds deprived of other birds will not learn to sing properly. I had grown up in a family where people had not played music, not on an instrument or on a stereo or in the car. There were occasional school trips to the symphony, the nuns saw to that, but those were opportunities to sit in the dark, suck on hard candy, and dream.

In my mind, I had already named my soprano Roxane after Edmond Rostand's famous heroine in *Cyrano de Bergerac*. Roxane would unite the international hostages and their teenage captors with the beauty of her voice. The fact that I didn't like opera didn't matter. The story was in motion.

Picture Yo-Yo Ma deciding to trade his violin for a cello somewhere around the age of four. His sister plays the violin, his mother is a singer, his father is a music teacher in Paris where they live. Picture Renée Fleming singing complex harmonies in the back of her family's station wagon with her younger sister and brother, their parents, both music teachers, in the front seat, leading them on. Picture me in my thirties, trying to unlock the language of music for the first time.

Because it was music, I thought that all I had to do was listen. But expecting that *Madama Butterfly* will make sense without any background or preparation is akin to hanging out on a street corner in Tokyo, thinking you'll pick up Japanese. A mother can say the word "dog" to a baby all day long, but without context—a dog, a picture of a dog—words are nothing more than sound.

There are many cases to be made for the importance of early music education, but my favorite reason is the simplest: like any language, music is more easily grasped by children. I wasn't trying to sing or play an instrument or read sheet music, I was only trying to learn how to listen to opera with pleasure and some intelligence. I bought CDs randomly, thinking I would eventually stumble on the composer or soprano who would speak to me, but none of them did because I didn't know how to hear them.

As it turned out, the key I was searching for was in a book. Fred Plotkin's tutorial masterpiece, *Opera 101*, was my answer. Chapter by chapter, opera by opera, he guides the reader on how to listen. He tells his students (and I was his student, as surely Plotkin was my teacher) to read the libretto, then to read the libretto again while listening to the opera, and then, finally, to only listen, as opposed to, say, listening while washing dishes. I opened the CD case and removed the tiny booklet, read the microscopic type of the libretto, then I sat on the couch and closed my eyes, forcing myself to stay present for what I was hearing. Plotkin taught me how to identify the singers' roles and explained the combining of voices, the use of chorus, and the orchestra. Everything he said connected to my novel, which I had begun to think of as operatic. The main characters would take parts equivalent to the soprano and tenor, followed by a tier of strong secondary characters, mezzos and baritones, and beneath them, two choruses, one of hostages and one of hostage takers. Over time these choruses moved closer together until eventually they sang with one voice.

Plotkin also extolled the importance of seeing live opera, saying that what came out of the stereo, or the radio, thanks to the Saturday broadcasts from the Metropolitan, would only take me so far. Opera, after all, is an art form both richer and more complex than singing alone. I started to use what money I had to fly to New York. I bought tickets at City Opera because they were significantly cheaper than the tickets at the Met. City Opera seemed to be enamored of Handel, and so I became enamored of Handel.

Slowly, the part of my brain that was studying music was overtaken by the part of my heart that felt it. I was moved by a scene, and later an aria, and sometimes a single note. (See: Juan Diego Flórez in *La fille du régiment*.) The longing and sorrow and anger and love of opera proved so much larger than the words being sung. It surrounded me, engulfed me, included me, until a space inside me had opened, a place that existed specifically for music.

I came to opera because I wanted to write about young revolutionaries who had never heard opera before. This was what we had in common, and so the music became a bridge. I came to love opera not only by listening, but by creating a character who loved opera more than his life. I had known a man like that once. By writing about what singing meant to Roxane Coss, I could almost imagine myself singing.

The publication of this novel opened doors for me that not even the most creative of writers could have imagined. I was asked to write about opera in *The New York Times* and to speak at music festivals. After I was interviewed on New York's classical music station, WQXR, Mary Jo Heath offered to introduce me to her friend Renée Fleming, and though I'm still not entirely sure how it happened, Renée and I became close friends. Over the years I've watched her sing the Marschallin in *Der Rosenkavalier*, the title role in *Rusalka*, and Violetta in *La Traviata*. I saw her in *Eugene Onegin* (my favorite) and *Rodelinda* (Handel!). We went to the opera together and sat through *Boris Godunov* in its entirety. When Renée was the creative director of the Chicago Lyric Opera, her first project was to commission an opera of my novel, *Bel Canto*. My long road to opera had become an opera itself.

That's how far music has taken me.

I couldn't begin to count the number of times I've been with Renée when someone stopped her on the street or in a restaurant to tell her it was her voice singing to them the day they married, or the day their child was born, or the day their father died. They felt that through her music she had stood beside them, celebrating their joy or giving them the strength to face their losses. They love her because she is the embodiment of the power of music, and she graciously accepts that love because she understands it better than anyone. In a smaller way, I understand it too. I remember the first time my husband and I went to the opera together, a beautiful, spare production of *Madama Butterfly* in San Francisco. I cried for the beauty of the singing, the tragedy of a tale well told, for the entire encompassing experience of having entered into another life. I cried because I understood how close I'd come to missing it, and because I was so grateful to have been welcomed in. Music, if we are in the habit of listening, can be the bright silver thread that stitches our lives together and makes them whole.

Our Symphony Orchestra: The People's Band and a Symbol of Civilization

BEN FOLDS

Emmy-Nominated Singer-Songwriter-Composer;
Artistic Advisor, National Symphony Orchestra

I've spent more than twenty years advocating for the symphony orchestra to be seen as a fundamental symbol of civilization. Why? Because growing up, I saw the very concepts of life put into literal practice onstage. The composer, the musicians, and the conductor all working in concert, harmony, and even sometimes dissonance to create something that's greater than the parts.

My strong belief is that it's very natural for people to communicate and relax through music. Our long-past ancestors connected through the rhythm and pulsing beat of drums. Today we have a chat at the bar under cover of a PA system. The "jam band" and the "techno kids" who would have thought of themselves as diametrically opposed were both simply creating a trance-like environment for people to congregate. Dissonance and harmony. The coming together with some sort of shared foundation.

A rock concert has diverged from that a bit, so the person onstage has established some sort of right to affect the dynamic. But if you encourage a communal environment, if you encourage people to sing together, my deep feeling is that it's human, natural, and almost a necessity. And it becomes that much more necessary when people are scared and unified by something, like 9/11.

My first solo record was released on 9/11, and I was performing on live radio in Washington, D.C., when the world changed. Driving through the streets of the city, I heard reports that the Pentagon was on fire. The highway was shut down. The day had suddenly become a lot bigger than just the release of my album.

Later that day about one hundred and fifty members of Congress gathered on the steps of the Capitol, and in that moment of grief and tragedy, they spontaneously started to sing "God Bless America." Music brought them together in strength and unity. They all felt the need to sing. And that's why I didn't cancel the remaining concerts on my tour. If ever there was a need for music, it was now.

It was really tough to forge ahead and keep playing gigs when something so catastrophic had happened in the world. But I felt that people needed somewhere they could find a moment of respite from what was going on outside. A sacred moment to come off the street into a small community and find relief in music. As I played, I could almost feel the psychic pain in the audience. The grief that silently reverberated around the room. And that was when I switched from thinking about me and my career to asking, What can music do for people?

I witnessed the rebirth of community in the days following 9/11, like a phoenix from the ashes of tragedy. I noticed that people started to behave differently at music events, and one night a magical sound unexpectedly filled the room. A perfect three-part harmony was echoing around the venue. Like the members of Congress, the audience felt the need to sing together. Suddenly it was no longer just a concert. It was a room full of people. And in that moment I saw myself as an advocate, not just for music, but for humanity.

But why do people turn to music in times of tragedy? Because music has a huge impact on the brain. Surveys have found that people who listen to or play music report higher levels of mental well-being, reduced anxiety, and even improved cognitive function.

I've often wondered if, when I sing a note and the audience sings it back, have I just communicated the note, or have I also communicated the emotion behind the note? And if everyone sings the same song, can that get our collective blood pressure down? While I can't scan the brains of everyone in the audience, I feel that the answer must be yes.

In studies, participants' brains have been scanned using MRI scanners.

They showed that music activates multiple regions of the brain, including areas associated with emotion, memory, movement, communication, and, of course, sound. The really amazing thing is that this response can be seen in patients suffering from severe neurodegenerative diseases, such as Alzheimer's or Parkinson's. If someone with late-stage Alzheimer's listens to their favorite music, they start moving, even singing, when moments before they had been unresponsive. And the rhythm of music can help improve gait and motion in sufferers of Parkinson's disease.

The importance of rhythm is not just limited to music therapy. The rhythm of breath is an essential part of meditation, a practice renowned for its healing qualities. Rhythm also brings people together, forming the basis of dance and the essence of the drum circle. It creates a feeling of togetherness. Community. No matter what your background is, or where you're from, music is something everyone can be a part of and enjoy.

Throughout my life I have seen this in practice. When music started to be removed from the educational curriculum, kids didn't stop seeking it out. They formed a cappella groups on their own time. They weren't getting credit for it, but they found coming together to sing healing. Necessary. And this can be seen throughout the world. Children and adults alike choose to devote their time to music, whether it's through singing, playing in bands, or dance. Why? Because it makes them feel good. It makes them feel like they are an integral part of a community.

But playing music goes beyond simply making people feel happier. Playing and performing music contributes to the development of an extraordinary number of skills that are essential in life. It increases interpersonal and motor skills, strengthens concentration, and boosts confidence and creativity. In fact, studies have shown that trained musicians display a dramatic improvement in verbal memory and are faster at learning new languages. And these changes aren't just superficial—they can be seen in the brain!

Playing music enlarges the region connecting the brain's two hemispheres, resulting in increased communication between them, enhancing problem-solving skills. MRI scans also reveal that musicians have increased connectivity between several neural circuits, including auditory and motor pathways.

This is exemplified by the experience of a young professional musician. Having picked up the clarinet from a young age, he went on to study music at university, becoming well known as a talented soloist and orchestral player. As he was starting to build connections and begin his professional career, he had a stroke at the age of twenty-seven. The doctors said that part of his brain was permanently scarred and would not recover, and he might need to get used to having loss of performance in his left side, which was then almost paralyzed. However, within days he could move his fingers a little. He was given his clarinet and was able to make some basic shapes. The doctors were amazed, but his recovery just accelerated, so that today he is earning a living both composing and playing music for a variety of audiences, from theater to TV. His brain had reprogrammed itself to bypass the damaged section and find new neural pathways.

While playing music has astounding advantages, the brilliant thing is that you don't have to be a trained musician to benefit from music. Just listening to music, from classical to pop, can have an amazing impact, decreasing stress and increasing concentration.

So, then, why does civilization still need the orchestra? Is it just a symbol of the elite, as some would have you believe? I would argue not—it's just a lot older than our current way of making and thinking about music. It's been shaped over time, inheriting several traditions along the way.

The word "orchestra" can be traced back as far as ancient Greece, where it referred to the area of the auditorium stage reserved for instruments and the chorus. In later eras, music formed an integral part of life, consisting mostly of small groups that played for select audiences. During the fourteenth to sixteenth centuries, while composers were writing ever more complex music, the parts could generally be played on an assortment of instruments—whatever they had available. But it wasn't until the 1600s that the Italian composer Claudio Monteverdi specified exactly which instruments he wanted to play for each part, forming the basis of the modern orchestra.

Tracking the progress of the orchestra through time, you can see how it has evolved and influenced contemporary music. From how to shape the timbre of a sound for a synthesizer and mixing multitracks, our basic understanding of such concepts come from orchestration. You can even think of the orchestra as being like a mixing console, producer, and arranger all wrapped up in a single package.

Playing in an orchestra is a surprisingly selfless discipline. While each member is a gifted performer in their own right, for an orchestra to work effectively, they all must pull together to create something even greater. But asking people who are so generous with their talent to perform something that doesn't take full advantage of their skill can lead to a very deflated group of people. It's not just bad for their mental health as part of an orchestra, it's also not fair to the audience either, as they don't get to experience the best of what the orchestra can do. It's like an old country producer I met one time who said, "Well, if we ain't having fun, how can we expect that the audience is having fun?"

And that's exactly right. If the members of a symphony orchestra aren't inspired, you can't expect them to inspire other people. They have to be inspired themselves.

I'm a passionate advocate of the excellence that's inside the symphony orchestra and of letting the tools that make it great shine through. One way to do this is to generate music that can reach new audiences while maintaining what's at the heart of the orchestra. As the artistic advisor to the National Symphony Orchestra (NSO) in Washington, D.C., I'm creating a treasure trove of scores, willing artists, and programs that work for both the orchestra and the audience, making this formula available to any symphony orchestra.

One of the big tasks we face in our creative meetings is how to get people to attend concerts. Symphonic music dominates big movie soundtracks because it's effective, and people have grown up familiar with this sound. Therefore, using the orchestra to play live music in front of a movie screen will fill seats. But it's not just about getting people in. What you want is for them to come back, and they come back because they establish a relationship with the orchestra.

Finding things that work for both the orchestra and the audience is challenging. At the NSO we collaborated with Grammy-winning singer Sara Bareilles to perform six of her songs with the orchestra, alongside a program of traditional classical music. It was amazing to witness teenagers being emotionally affected by music by Stravinsky and Pēteris Vasks, and this was happening because the music was being put into the context of real people. I want to help other orchestras and creative directors understand how important it is to program in this way.

Tying classical music and pop music together can be a challenge, and the first fault line is purely technical. Some might even say it's boring. Yet it's the most important thing I can think of: the public address, or PA, system.

Almost all pop and rock music is played through a PA system to make it audible, which isn't necessary for orchestral music. For that reason, the two don't easily sit on the stage together—one must come through speakers and the other comes acoustically from the stage.

So how do you bring these two together? You must understand that both types of music work in the environments they have evolved in, and it's the music itself that has to cross this virtual technical fault line. I think the first thing to explore is how to program music that's purely acoustic, because that's where the symphony orchestra sounds, performs, and feels most effective. It's important to allow an orchestra to perform in its natural environment and not take these critical aspects away. At the NSO, we are experimenting with these concepts, creating a blueprint that other orchestras can use.

Involving the musicians themselves in the process is also a huge part of bridging that fault line. If someone brings in a good, but flawed, new score that's a work in progress, it's important to give the orchestra an opportunity and a responsibility to be part of it. When I work with the NSO, I want them to ask questions and voice their suggestions. I want to hear what they have to say so I can create a score that works for them as well as for the audience. I feel how important that is to them, and when I give them that opportunity, I find that they are more energized. More inspired. And that's not just great for the orchestra, it's great for the audience.

While constructing the right program is an essential component of engaging new audiences, a certain element of education should be included as well. Understanding how the orchestra and its traditions developed can help create that connection, but it's also important to allow kids to experience music early in life. That can be done by creating concerts designed especially for kids. I recently collaborated with author Mo Willems to generate a symphonic take of his book *Goldilocks and the Three Dinosaurs*, writing original music for the NSO to perform. Instead of the traditional written program, we created an engaging online learning guide, which highlighted things to watch out for and interesting information about the other pieces performed in the concert—and we didn't stop there. We encouraged the families who attended to continue engaging with music after the concert by looking for inspiration in their own neighborhoods and lives. For example, we might ask them to choose a picture and share what instruments they hear in their minds, or to create a song based on where they live.

Storytelling through music isn't a new concept. Prokofiev created a symphonic fairy tale with *Peter and the Wolf*, in which each character is given a theme played by a specific orchestral instrument. And Mussorgsky's *Pictures at an Exhibition* depicts his tour of Viktor Hartmann's work, with each movement representing a musical illustration of the painted image. Sharing moments through the medium of a story is a very natural way to communicate. So using this concept helps people to engage with music and create a relationship with the orchestra.

The responsibility not to let our symphony orchestra rot on the vine belongs to everyone: the composers, the musicians, the creative directors, and the audiences. Although the orchestra is a symbol of civilization, it may be experiencing some atrophy. I don't think we should allow it to fade away. We need to cling protectively to our orchestras and replenish where we're anemic.

Music has the capacity to heal and inspire, and that's got to be something worthy of our attention. Throughout my career I've seen people come into a concert, leaving their anxiety behind them. They experience the opportunity to join with other people, who may have different backgrounds and opposite beliefs outside the building, but they are brought together through the medium of music. By connecting with real people in the audience and orchestra, they can escape from their daily lives and find a brief moment to relax and rejuvenate their mental well-being. I can see that when they go back out into the world, they are almost always happier.

So we need to ask the orchestras to be even more excellent than they've ever been. We need to ask and encourage audiences to come in. We need to plant the seeds and cultivate some new musical flora growth for the next generation. The orchestra is in fact the people's band. A symbol of civilization. And an essential part of life.

We don't want to ask what we can do for the arts. It's what the arts can do for us.

With the collaboration of Joanna L. Patterson-Cross, PhD, MBiochem

Arts for Non-Arts Outcomes

DEBORAH RUTTER

President, John F. Kennedy Center for the Performing Arts

Art is as much a part of our humanity as love, language, and the pursuit of knowledge.

—DEBORAH RUTTER

In December 1994 three French explorers squeezed through an opening in the Earth to discover a treasury of prehistoric art. They found cave paintings of animals—lions, woolly rhinoceroses, leopards, horses. It was an extraordinary find, not only because of its scale but because of the quality of the work. This Paleolithic art is breathtakingly beautiful, conceived with an incomparable mastery of line, form, and perspective. Among these paintings the modern explorers discovered one image that had been created by blowing pigment across the artist's fingers, leaving a perfect outline of a human hand, as if a Stone Age person had reached across thirty thousand years to say to us, "I am."

Humans have been creating art, spontaneously and simultaneously, as far back as we can measure. And around the world, across the ages, there is, perhaps, no message more persistent in art than that of resounding self-affirmation—the proclamation "I am." Art is as much a part of our humanity as love, language, and the pursuit of knowledge. If you don't believe me, look at your smartphone. Behind it and just about every manufactured good lies the inspiration of people who identify as artists—the professionals who create the look and feel of the phone, the sounds, the graphic interface, and its unbounded content.

Today's arts administrator is filled with stories that would put a lump in your throat. We help create and produce work that touches lives—profoundly—but it's not enough to dwell in the realm of emotion and anecdote. As we fight for every dollar and every program that might benefit a group of people, it's handy to come armed with good old scientific facts. With data collected using the MRI and the EEG, we can demonstrate how the arts stimulate the brain. For example, listening to music stimulates not only the auditory cortex but the motor cortex as well—it makes you want to dance.

At the John F. Kennedy Center for the Performing Arts, we exist to nurture the role of art in our daily lives. We excel as producer and presenter, launching everything from large-scale productions to intimate recitals. But the Kennedy Center is so much more than that. Each year approximately 1.2 million school students participate in live and virtual programming and online offerings. More than seven thousand college students participate in our annual theater festival. We provide material support to community-based arts programs and place teaching artists in schools all across the country. We train dancers, instrumentalists, and singers. We operate everything from yoga classes to dance classes for people with Parkinson's disease. And that's not the half of it.

I often find myself in the awkward position of having to describe the Kennedy Center. Always I feel obligated to rattle off long, unwieldy lists of its offerings (arts education, jazz, hip-hop, comedy, folk, popular music, theater, ballet, the National Symphony Orchestra, Broadway shows, the Washington National Opera, dance, international festivals, etc.). Clearly, our spoken language demands such specificity (and it helps us on the marketing end). But art often dwells outside these conventional terms. Art is increasingly multi- and interdisciplinary. Sometimes a work fits into more than one category or none at all, and we arts administrators must wrestle with the best way to present it.

Art pushes us out of our comfort zones. It encourages us to move outside our patterns of thinking and look at an idea from a new perspective. More than that, it binds itself to human beings on multiple planes simultaneously (when we dance to a favorite song, we become both the artist and the audience). It is this ever-expanding relationship to human beings that feeds into the vastness of the Kennedy Center's programming.

To further the appreciation of culture among all the people, to increase respect for the creative individual, to widen participation by all the processes and fulfillments of art—this is one of the fascinating challenges of these days.

—JOHN F. KENNEDY

The Kennedy Center as we know it came about for a couple of reasons. The first was the National Cultural Center Act of 1958. With it lawmakers selected a piece of land and stipulated that a facility "be constructed with funds raised by voluntary contributions." The second reason began with the general election of 1960.

On January 20, 1961, America's second-youngest president entered the White House. Riding a wave of optimism, John F. Kennedy advanced ideals that applied equally to the sculptor and the astronaut, to the scientist and the playwright. It was an age rocked by Cold War anxiety and racial segregation, yet President Kennedy lit the way to a better future, giving urgency to the creative genius and resourcefulness of the American people.

"The life of the arts," he said, "far from being an interruption, a distraction, in the life of the nation, is close to the center of a nation's purpose and is a test to the quality of a nation's civilization."

During their time in the White House, the Kennedys uplifted the artist to serve as the standard-bearer for America's highest aspirations, making the executive mansion a showcase for writers, jazz musicians, poets, dance companies, classical musicians, theater companies, and more. The First Family was a natural ally of the effort to build a National Cultural Center. On November 29, 1962, President and Mrs. Kennedy hosted a nationally televised benefit for the Center's construction. The performers included comedian Danny Kaye, "King of Calypso" Harry Belafonte, poet Robert Frost, and the seven-year-old cellist Yo-Yo Ma. On that night the president proclaimed the Center's primary mission: to call "forth creative genius from every sector of society, disregarding race or religion or wealth or color."

Kennedy uttered those words at the height of the civil rights movement.

It was a time when U.S. citizens suffered extreme acts of violence—simply for trying to vote. Americans were deeply divided, yet the president saw past party lines and racial animus to frame the problem as something that matters to each and every person living within our shores: the problem of untapped potential. Untapped potential is a drain on America's bounty, and he articulated this truth through his advocacy for the arts.

A year later President Kennedy fell to an assassin's bullet. In the wake of that horrific event, there followed a spontaneous outpouring of donations to the National Cultural Center. Two months after his death, Congress redesignated the space as a presidential memorial to John F. Kennedy— a "living memorial" that would pay tribute to his legacy through an endless stream of creative expression.

Today we have capabilities that JFK never imagined. He spoke of the arts as "close to the center of a nation's purpose." Indeed. We can now carry entire music libraries in our pockets. Our teenagers produce videos at a staggering (if not alarming) rate, and musicians are creating and sharing their songs without ever having to leave home. As an innate aspect of our humanity, the arts are deeply embedded in American culture. Yet everywhere I go, I'm reminded of President Kennedy's words. We have barely begun to tap America's potential. On a daily basis I see a life transformed because a kid attends a ballet or a deaf person picks up a drum. However, our work is far from finished.

This is my lived experience. Understanding it at a scientific level is a different matter. In 2016 American soprano Renée Fleming joined the Kennedy Center as an artistic advisor. Soon after coming on board, she approached me excited about a conversation she'd had with Dr. Francis Collins, then head of the National Institutes of Health (NIH). They had met at a dinner party where Renée bent his ear about her personal interest in music and wellness. Down the rabbit hole they went, talking about brain research and the therapeutic applications of the arts. Soon I found myself having long conversations with my new artistic advisor—not about concerts and composers but doctors and medical researchers. Over time Renée convinced me that the Kennedy Center needed to get involved in this area.

In 2016 we launched Sound Health, a partnership with the NIH in association with the National Endowment for the Arts. Under the leadership of Renée and Francis, we began bringing together various professionals, from music therapists to neuroscientists to people working in behavioral intervention, in a forum where they could discuss their research and clinical experiences—and I must say, their combined knowledge is staggering.

Whether you're looking at brain development in children or therapies for stroke victims, Parkinson's disease, PTSD, concussion, or dementia, music can rewire the brain and improve the quality of life.

Working with the NIH, the world's largest funder of biomedical research, we designed Sound Health to function not only as a think tank for all this acquired knowledge but as a platform to share it with the public. Over the course of several years we have produced a series of lectures and webinars on neurology and enlisted the help of medical researchers, the National Symphony Orchestra, Dr. Sanjay Gupta, Dr. Vivek H. Murthy, the singer-songwriter Ben Folds, percussionists Mickey Hart and Zakir Hussain, jazz artist Jason Moran, and others.

Our programs on music and the brain have sold out the Kennedy Center's Concert Hall—more than two thousand seats each time! Therein lies the genius of Renée's idea. If you increase public awareness of music and wellness by enlisting the help of a massive performing arts complex, more people get involved, more people benefit, and more resources become available for those who need them. In the wake of these presentations, the NIH announced $20 million in research grants over five years to study the potential of music for treating a wide range of conditions resulting from neurological and other disorders.

Although my background is in music, Sound Health has given me a new understanding of the human mind. A couple of tidbits really surprised me:

1. Human beings have what's known as malleable intelligence. Our intelligence is not fixed but can increase or decrease depending on how we use our brains. This has a psychological impact on learners. For example, if you explain to middle schoolers that their brains will grow (forge new circuitry) if they apply themselves, their math scores go up.
2. Our brains are naturally wired for music. When you concentrate, your brain produces rhythmic electrical impulses. Also, the perception of rhythm activates multiple areas of the brain. According to the Northwestern University neurobiologist Dr. Nina Kraus, "Probably the

healthiest thing we can do for our brains is to make music." Making music activates the corpus callosum, the nucleus accumbens, the amygdala, the cerebellum, the hippocampus, and the visual, motor, prefrontal, sensory, and auditory cortices. These regions impact movement, emotion, self-control, personal expression, decision-making, memory, our ability to read, and more.

It's easy to see why these factors would be beneficial to schoolkids, and the Kennedy Center has jumped into the arena with both feet. Turnaround Arts is one of my favorite programs within our Education Department, and it has impact and scope across the country. It began in 2012 as a pilot program in just eight schools, under President Obama's Committee on the Arts and the Humanities, and rapidly grew to become a major reinvestment in arts education—particularly in America's struggling schools—with a primary focus to boost attendance and academic achievement. As the name suggests, the program integrates the arts into the academic life of the school, guiding students to master the core curriculum through music, movement, visual art, and creative writing. While this approach may sound radical, if you've ever watched kids play, you'll notice that they love to make believe; they sing, they dance, and they create things. It makes one wonder why we ever decided it was a good idea to plant children at desks and then penalize them if they failed to thrive. This is precisely the system that was in place at the eight pilot schools that were all facing some tough academic challenges before Turnaround Arts.

"My school was in the bottom ten percent," said Principal Liam Dawson of Northside Elementary School in St. James, Minnesota.

"Pure chaos," said Andrew Bott, who was principal of Orchard Gardens School in Boston. "There was furniture flying. And staff turnover was fifty percent."

"When we had Parent Teacher Organization (PTO) meetings, we'd get four parents and a pot of coffee," said Principal Cynthia Fernandes of Hall Elementary School in Bridgeport, Connecticut.

At Andrew Bott's school, administrators had allocated $250,000 to security and discipline (for the "flying furniture" problem). "We had failed those kids," he recalled. After some long hours contemplating the problem,

Andrew stepped into the unknown. In 2012 he reallocated the $250,000 to hire arts teachers.

Turnaround Arts harnesses the child's natural creative instincts and offers an alternative path to learning. It creates a supportive environment for self-expression and builds community around the same activities that build community outside the school (music, dancing, sharing stories). The tricky part is the implementation. It requires a commitment from top to bottom. You have to get the math teacher to ask kids to paint pictures. You have to get the parents on board, and you have to build alliances with local arts organizations.

Turnaround Arts gives schools the tools to accomplish these things, starting with a blueprint for the program. We provide funding and teacher training. We help make introductions to local arts leaders and teaching artists, but ultimately it's the school community that has to do the work. They have to own it. That is where the magic happens.

Cynthia Fernandes flipped the script on her PTO. "I'd tell parents: come to the Parent Teacher Organization meeting and get a preview of our new play," she said. With that she "packed the house." She hosted special events celebrating the international makeup of the student body. The kids wrote stories about their family histories, held fashion shows, and created artwork around their diverse cultural backgrounds. She offered classes on arts and parenting and then embarked upon a school musical. That's where they encountered a typical problem at Hall Elementary: some of the kids couldn't read their lines.

Undaunted, Cynthia got the special education teacher involved, using the musical as a motivator to teach reading. The night of the performance, family and friends filled the auditorium. All the kids mastered their lines. One child, who had dyslexia and initially struggled with reading, served as the narrator.

Believe it or not, Hall Elementary was on the chopping block at that time. The Bridgeport school district faced a budget shortfall and was drawing up plans to close Hall and send its students across a busy thoroughfare to a larger school. This set off alarm bells for the newly energized parent community. They likened it to breaking up a family.

When the school board brought the measure to a vote, the student body of Hall Elementary descended on them in a frenzy of poetry, song, and dance. They made impassioned testimonials (including one from the young narrator). In the end the measure failed, and the Hall community saved their school.

Across the Great Lakes, Northside Elementary in Minnesota signed on to Turnaround Arts in 2012 and rose from the bottom 10 percent to win the coveted National Blue Ribbon Schools award. According to Principal Dawson, the school's success has become a source of pride in the community. The local newspaper now features an Art Student of the Week, and the face of Lisa Becker, the school's visual arts specialist, features prominently on an enormous mural in downtown St. James. At Andrew Bott's school, where the security budget had been diverted to pay arts faculty, the program became self-sustaining after one year.

Success breeds success. The total transformation of these Turnaround Arts schools has caught the attention of a number of celebrities who later became Turnaround Artists, from Herbie Hancock to Cameron Diaz, from Elton John to Jack Johnson. At Hall Elementary, Pritzker Prize–winning architect Thom Mayne started an extracurricular program on architecture. Google donated the computers.

After the initial period of implementation in the eight pilot schools, researchers found that, on average, math proficiency rose 22.55 percent. Reading proficiency rose 12.62 percent. Other indicators included a drop in expulsions and suspensions of students. Today sixty schools participate in Turnaround Arts.

The arts are both universal and individual. We make lots of guesses about who's going to like what. But the truth is, we never know. In Turnaround Arts schools we emphasize values: celebration (papering the walls with student work), antiracism, and its close cousin: culturally responsive teaching. This means celebrating the cultural wealth of a given community, which not only honors a child's identity but builds upon a child's natural curiosity, opening doors to a whole universe of creative expression.

Cultural responsiveness comes from the idea that cultural rights are human rights. Through culture, people "express their humanity, their world view and the meanings they give to their existence," according to the United Nations' Universal Declaration of Human Rights. This brings me to a segment of our population who very often find themselves on the outside looking in—people with disabilities.

According to the Centers for Disease Control and Prevention, sixty-one million adults in the United States live with a disability—that's one in four. According to the 2019 census more than three million kids in the United States are adapting to some form of disability. Given everything we know about the arts and wellness, given the idea that cultural rights are human rights, isn't it time we made a greater effort to give everybody in the community an entry point?

We have another Kennedy to thank for the Center's work in this arena. In 1974 the former U.S. ambassador to Ireland Jean Kennedy Smith founded the international organization Access/VSA (originally Very Special Arts) to "promote the inclusion of people with disabilities in the arts, education and culture around the world." In 2011 Access/VSA merged with the Kennedy Center. Betty Siegel, who heads up the division, passes our many offerings through the lens of inclusivity for people with disabilities.

We present sensory-friendly performances for people who are neurodiverse. We offer assistive listening devices that can interface with personal hearing aids. A number of our performances feature sign language interpretation and captioning. We have curb-to-seat service for visitors with issues of mobility. We provide audio descriptions for patrons who are blind or have low vision, and the Access/VSA team oversees the dedicated volunteers who create braille and large-print programs for some two thousand shows a year.

Recently someone asked me if it's practical to go to all this trouble for a handful of people with disabilities, and a few things come to mind: First, I am in the business of bringing the arts to people, and this is and has always been a one-person-at-a-time proposition. As arts administrators we make dozens of decisions every day to accommodate and appeal to people; we install theater seats, elevators, spaces for children. I don't see any difference between these efforts. Second, when you create access, people come. They tell their friends, and the next thing you know, there's a community growing around your public events. Finally, human beings acquire disabilities as we age, and America is aging. By 2030 there will be more "over sixties" than "under thirties." Improving access is good for the soul, and it's also good business.

Washington, D.C., is a collection of people from all walks of life, local and national. Since the founding of VSA in 1974 it has been clear that building relationships and proactively seeking guidance from people in that community with lived experiences of disability would be core to the success of the Kennedy Center. For us, improving accessibility to a traditional arts complex was like stepping into a new pair of shoes. Did we want high heels, flats, or my favorite . . . flip-flops? There was no checklist to guide us on this complex journey and account for the needs of the current audience, much less anticipate the needs of our future audience. With input and feedback from our disability community we had the freedom to try, occasionally to fail, but often to succeed in implementing accessibility initiatives. Thankfully our high volume of programs each year together with regular input from our engaged audiences has allowed us to work through the challenges. And we've learned a lot. Today we're in a position to share our experience and change our industry.

In the year 2000 the Kennedy Center created the Leadership Exchange in Arts and Disability (LEAD), a forum for sharing information with partner organizations across the country. With LEAD we aspire to nothing less than changing the status quo. To accomplish this, LEAD serves as a brain trust of professionals who work at parks, zoos, libraries, museums, and performing arts organizations. At our annual conference, administrators of these cultural spaces come together with the world's experts in the field to learn practical methods of designing inclusive experiences and environments. We also set goals from one conference to the next, so we can hold ourselves accountable.

If access for all audiences is a priority, so is access for the artists. The human story is partly written by artists with disabilities—Frida Kahlo, Beethoven, Toulouse-Lautrec, Ray Charles, John Milton, and on and on. They well understood the challenge of navigating a world designed for people without disabilities. The good news is that the success of these artists extends a thread of connection to people everywhere who have encountered similar experiences.

Through the programs of Access/VSA, the Kennedy Center has welcomed a number of extraordinary young-adult talents into its arena: playwrights, visual artists, and solo musicians. We've begun to learn from them about the challenges of building careers in the arts for people with disabilities. They all seem to have similar and still heartbreaking tales about missing out on jobs or getting penalized at school. And they are constantly butting up against society's perception of disability—that they are special, different, needy, or waiting to be rescued. In truth, these artists are part of the greater human struggle against structures and attitudes that prevent any person, for whatever reason, from fully participating in society.

Our Access/VSA programs offer a variety of practical experiences for the artists. Emerging Young Artists, the visual arts program produced in partnership with Volkswagen Group of America, comes with a cash prize along with Kennedy Center–sponsored exhibitions and training in public speaking and financial planning. It also offers some intangibles.

"When I saw the call for Access/VSA I was still very much hiding my disability wherever I could," said Will Copps. "I viewed art as the one place where I could express myself with full control of how I came across. My disability seemed a burden. By the time I'd gone through the Access/VSA experience, that same disability was a superpower."

"When I went to the Access/VSA program at the Kennedy Center," said Oaklee Thiele, "it was the first time that I was in a room with people who were like me, and for once, we were not treated differently or less than."

Whether Robert Schumann or Truman Capote, the circumstances of an artist's life sometimes shape what they have to say and how they go about their work. But this is true of all artists. And so, the Kennedy Center's work in Access/VSA comes down to two fundamentals: disability is human; the arts are human. And we must make room for the two to come together.

Back in the 1960s the Kennedy Center was established as a presidential memorial in a city replete with memorials. As such, we understand its meaning. Because it is the national cultural center, it's not enough that we stage great shows. We must use our national platform to ensure a better future.

When the Center first opened its doors in 1971, we did so with a new piece by a cultural hero of the time: Leonard Bernstein. He wrote for us his *MASS*, enlisting, among other things, a symphony orchestra, a chorus, a blues band, a rock band, a boy soprano, a children's choir, a marching band, kazoos, a banjo, and an army of "street musicians" who sing and play steel drums, bottled gourds, and tin cans. *MASS* was like the Big Bang for the Kennedy Center. It unleashed an ever-expanding cosmos of human expression that reaches all fifty states. Life around the Center has caused me to move away from the expression "art for art's sake." I now believe in art for life's sake. And I see the results of it every day.

With the collaboration of Noel Morris.
© 2023 John F. Kennedy Center for the Performing Arts

Musical Connections:
What Can Music Do?

SARAH JOHNSON
Chief Education Officer and Director, Weill Music Institute,
Carnegie Hall

For fifteen years I have had the privilege of leading the Weill Music Institute (WMI), Carnegie Hall's education and social impact programs arm. While Carnegie Hall is well known as one of the greatest concert halls in the world, few people are aware of its enormous commitment to educational programs that connect people of all ages and backgrounds with meaningful musical experiences. We run programs across a wide range of settings, from work with students and teachers in schools in New York City and around the world to programs in health-care settings, in the justice system, and with people experiencing homelessness. We also support young aspiring artists through the National Youth Orchestras—NYO-USA, NYO2, and NYO Jazz—all free programs for extraordinary teens from around the country who come together in the summer to perform and tour globally. We explore classical music and jazz, hip-hop, and music from regions and traditions globally. Our work is deep and broad, and over the years it has been co-created by more people than I can count—staff, artists, participants, partners, and researchers.

For most of my life, starting at age ten, I was an oboist. The thing I loved the most as a musician was being part of an ensemble, preferably an orchestra. The oboe sits right in the middle of the symphony orchestra, and there is not much in life like being a part of the sound made by nearly a hundred people playing together. Thinking about what that feels like kept me going at times when the frustration of learning to play an instrument as challenging as the oboe made me want to quit. (And there were many such times!) I also loved the feeling of making music with a small group of people, and when I was at Juilliard I cofounded a woodwind quintet. In that chamber music group I dug into the nuances of learning to play with other people, to blend, disappearing into a sound made with another person so that you couldn't hear the contours of either tone on its own, emerging from another person's line as you take over the melody, and passing that melody off to someone else while fading back into a supporting role. The collaboration and togetherness of that kind of music making were as powerful to me as orchestral playing.

As much as I enjoyed the challenges and rewards of performing with other people, throughout school and during my life as a professional musician I had a gnawing feeling that there was something else for me to do with music. I wasn't sure what that could be, but realized that I wanted to have a more direct impact on society than I felt I could as a performer, and I became increasingly interested in what music could do in the world. How could the use of music advance social goals and human development? I also started to wonder about the potential of large cultural organizations to support musical activity with this specific intention. How might the power inherent in those big institutions be brought to bear in alignment with the desires and needs of their surrounding communities? Those questions eventually led me to life as a teaching artist and then to management roles working within the education and community engagement departments of cultural organizations. After five years of holding these positions I came to Carnegie Hall.

When I started at the Hall, we provided the kinds of programs that you would think a large cultural organization would run at that time, focused on music in schools and projects giving young people the chance to learn from and collaborate with great artists. We had substantial resources, thanks to a generous endowment by the then chair of the Carnegie Hall Board, Sandy Weill, and the ongoing commitment of the Hall's leadership. Clive Gillinson, the executive and artistic director of the Hall, was and is a radical in his passionate belief in the power of educational programs. He prioritizes and champions this work far beyond the commitment of most of his peer leaders of cultural institutions.

When I arrived, the question was, What were we going to do with these resources, both human and financial? What should our priorities, philosophy, and approach be? How would we define and measure success? Clive believes that questions are more important than answers, and as an educator I have always been interested in juicy questions as a tool to engage people. We asked ourselves, What are we uniquely positioned to do? And Clive always asks, How can we serve people and music? When we asked these questions with respect to the specific communities and settings around us, the answers began to point in interesting directions.

We always come back to Carnegie Hall's mission statement, which includes "the creation of visionary education programs and sharing the transformative power of music with the widest possible audience." I think a lot about that word "transformative." It sets a high bar. It doesn't mean a small change, but a change in form. It's big, aspirational, a powerful idea. Our mission pushes us to think about how we can establish programs with the potential to support genuine transformation. In what scenarios is that most likely? What conditions need to be present to make that possible, and what can we do to create those conditions whenever we can? I have come to realize that designing, operating, and evaluating our programs over the years is like having an in-the-world music lab exploring the question, "What can music do that the world needs?"

I will tell you about two of these programs, the Lullaby Project and Musical Connections, sharing some of what I have learned from this work and how it has deepened my understanding of what music can accomplish. Both programs answer the questions I posed above, and they have a palpable impact on the well-being of participants and their communities.

Since I am going to talk about impact throughout, I need to introduce Dennie Palmer Wolf, a researcher who is a key thought partner to the staff and to me, and whose observations and brilliant "noticings" have played a major role in the development of these programs. When we started to do work in justice and health-care settings in 2009, we brought Dennie onto the team, before a single note was played or workshop planned, because I realized that there was much we didn't know about working in these areas. I wanted someone to help us look at and understand the results of the programs, who would observe things we didn't see, and who would ask great, provocative questions to help the work get better along the way.

STORY #1: THE LULLABY PROJECT

When I first saw your little face
Oh, how I cried to see your face
You were so small, yet you were
All I ever needed to erase my fears
You were yawning and smiling in the bright morning
Suddenly I saw the light open up in me
And you gave me the peace sign
So now I'm giving it back to you
I'm wishing you
Peace tonight

EXCERPT FROM "PEACE" BY TAMILLES AND DEIDRE

In the late summer of 2011 I sat in a big room at Jacobi Medical Center, one of New York City's public hospitals in the South Bronx, in a planning meeting about what we might undertake next in Carnegie Hall's partnership with the hospital. There were hospital staff, nurses, and doctors present, as well as teaching artists and staff from the Hall. We had all been working together for a couple of years, exploring different ways to bring music into the hospital setting to advance both musical and health goals.

The Jacobi team spoke about the pregnant teens they saw who were experiencing all the stresses that come with becoming a parent for the first time. These young women were having a hard time developing the kind of emotional attachment to their babies that is crucial for the long-term health and well-being of mothers and their children, and ultimately families. When we heard this, Thomas Cabaniss, a teaching artist and composer, and I looked across the table at each other and said, "Lullabies?" We wondered . . . what if young mothers had opportunities to work with artists to write lullabies for their babies? Might that creative time give those mothers the chance to step outside of their situations, to think and dream a little about what they hoped for themselves and for their children, and to put those hopes into lyrics and melodies? Could that intimate song build connections within and beyond that family? Might it move the needle in some small way to support the overall well-being of young families? In that moment, the idea for the Lullaby Project was born.

We piloted Lullaby twice that fall and winter at Jacobi in workshops co-led by Thomas Cabaniss and Emily Eagen, another teaching artist and singer, with powerful results. The lullabies that emerged were sweet, funny, and playful. Many were soothing and peaceful, in the traditional way of lullabies, but some parents wanted to write joyful, animated songs to reflect the energy they felt from their infants. As the project developed, we added recordings of the lullabies and celebration concerts, and over the next few years Lullaby expanded beyond Jacobi, past teens, to all kinds of settings and participants across New York City. Our commitment to communities most impacted by inequity and injustice led us to seek out Lullaby Project partnerships in the public health sector, the public education system, the correctional system, and settings with people experiencing homelessness. Eventually we started to partner with organizations outside of New York City, and we now work with nearly fifty organizations globally to bring Lullaby to refugee camps, health-care settings, schools, universities, and correctional facilities, reaching a more diverse range of places and people than any of us could possibly have imagined when we started.

These beautiful, personal songs work their simple magic in both directions. We hear from participants who wrote lullabies years ago, who share what those songs mean to their children. These young people continue to request their own lullabies at bedtime, birthdays, and when they want comfort. But lullabies also soothe the singer. In the early days and months of parenting, personal lullabies can be grounding and comforting to sleep-deprived parents who sing them to children at all hours of the day and night. Lullabies also capture and channel a parent's flood of feelings. As Solangie Jimenez, an early Lullaby writer explained, "Being part of the Lullaby Project impacted me to become a better parent because sometimes I get too emotional expressing my feelings and it's easier for me to write it down. This project will always be an important part of my life because many years from now, after I am gone, my child will have this song to remember me and the love I had for her unconditionally."

Participants involved in our studies of Lullaby have also told us that the songs they wrote have given them connections that result in more social support. This is crucial for the overall health and well-being of young families. Lullaby forges connections between parents and children, artists and participants, parents from different families, staff of community organizations and participants. Lullabies also sustain—or even mend—connections across generations. The "Ave Rojo" song, written in Philadelphia in both Spanish and English during COVID, is a lullaby featuring a red bird (a cardinal) who is the embodiment of a loving grandmother's spirit coming to visit a young family from whom she was separated by the pandemic. As Tamilles Fernandes, another lullaby writer at Jacobi Medical Center in 2013, shared: "Being a part of the Lullaby Project was truly a blessing. It has brought so many positive things and people into my life . . ." An anonymous participant commented, "I didn't believe that we would write a song in two hours. It was an amazing process of unfolding, mixed with the teaching artist's talent and intuition, along with what she called 'songwriting magic' that helped create this beautiful lullaby. It worked muscles that I haven't used in a very long time, and I'm so thankful for the opportunity. It is inspiring me to use my parenting life experiences to create more artistic endeavors." We have seen this added effect in many parents; at a time when all attention is focused on the promise of the baby, a parent's own sense of agency and creativity is bolstered by Lullaby.

Eighty percent of brain development happens in the first three years of a child's life. Language, social skills, and walking all emerge (among many other essential skills). But all this development requires a healthy pregnancy and a family that is safe and well supported through these early years. In the United States, with our astonishing wealth, technology, and knowledge, we currently fail to make sufficient investments in the well-being of young families. In 2015 the United States ranked 33rd out of 179 countries in the international State of the World's Mothers report. These terrible outcomes fall disproportionately on poor people, families of color, and those without the essential resources of stable, safe housing; proper nutrition; and good health care. The encouraging news is that positive change is possible through collective efforts involving diverse community stakeholders focused on making sure that mothers and young children have the support and resources they need to develop and thrive. We know from our observation and evaluation over the years that the Lullaby Project and related initiatives can contribute in small, low-cost ways to that larger imperative.

Based on the network of effects we were seeing in Lullaby, Dennie Palmer Wolf and Thomas Wolf urged us to start thinking about our programs in a wholly different way—as "360 degrees of impact." They observed that by focusing purely on the "audience" or participant in a program (caregivers in Lullaby, patients in a health-care setting, or residents of a correctional facility), we were missing much of the potential change brought about by our musical activities. With this reframing, we began asking teaching artists about what they experienced and learned that the work brought about profound changes in their health and well-being. Sarah Elizabeth Charles, a teaching artist who started participating in Lullaby early on, shared her perspective:

> When I started this journey almost ten years ago, I had no idea that becoming a teaching artist would change my life as an artist. My first Lullaby Project with Carnegie Hall was at Rikers Island Correctional Facility. Writing original music with this population of birthing people was unlike any other songwriting experience I'd had up to that point. The communication of love to their future and existing children was the sole purpose of the songs that were being created. The emotional world was at the center of both the writing process and the collaboration between "professional artist" and "participant." But with this focus, the walls between these roles broke down. Sure, I was the "professional artist," but I quickly learned that no one can communicate love for a child better than the person who has brought or is bringing the child into this world. I realized with this first project that my teaching artistry was about letting go of ego, and learning as much as any participant through the process. For me, almost ten years later, music has become all about the interaction, the sharing and the exchange with others. With each creative project I embark upon, I try to keep this as the focal point, and when I do, the potential for something beautiful to be created grows exponentially.

Once we began looking at the work in this holistic way, all kinds of opportunities for analyzing impact and thinking about program design emerged. For example, we noticed that staff at the neonatal intensive care unit asked to write a lullaby of their own to process the intensity, intimacy, and potential grief of the work they did daily. We saw correctional staff contributing to the songs incarcerated fathers and mothers were writing, and coming back on their own time to attend the concert at which their songs were featured. We started to see how a project might ripple out in all directions, touching people, communities, and even systems. We began to ask how we might deliberately design and carry out projects to have these kinds of expansive, inclusive effects. As I worked with this 360-degree-impact concept, I realized that some of my deeper aspirations for our programs— ones I had been hesitant even to voice—were now on the table as possibilities. I could see how we could touch individual lives and how we might begin to change systems.

Speaking of possible systemic change, one aspirational goal that has emerged for the future of Lullaby came from a participating father. He and his wife were part of a CenteringPregnancy program in Washington Heights. In Centering women go through prenatal care as a group, rather than as individuals. With their husbands/partners they develop relationships with their medical teams and one another, moving their care into a more relaxed and human environment than the hospital exam room allows. The medical team leading this particular Centering group had decided to incorporate Lullaby seamlessly into their regular monthly sessions. In one of the later workshops, a father who took part related a story about a recent conversation with one of his friends whose wife was also pregnant. In that conversation he had asked his friend what his lullaby was like, and was surprised that his friend had no idea what he was talking about. Because he encountered the Lullaby Project as an integral part of regular prenatal care, he thought that writing a lullaby for your baby was a normal part of what everyone experienced when preparing for the birth of a child. Hearing that story, the Lullaby staff team immediately started to think, why not? Why couldn't a simple Lullaby-writing workshop be part of preparation for birth for everyone? How might that idea be carried into the health-care system and spread across the country, contributing to parents' preparation for the arrival of a child and the overall well-being of young families? This is now one of our dreams, or moonshot ideas, for Lullaby, and I love that it came from a participant who thought that this was already a common practice.

I trust you
You know what to do
And even when it's dark
You have the light coming through

Always remember
You can be tender
Give and receive and lead with love
You can be open
You can be broken
You can be free, hold and be held

EXCERPT FROM "FOR NICO"—WITH ALEXIS CARIELLO

STORY #2: MUSICAL CONNECTIONS

When I was interviewing for my job at Carnegie Hall, I was asked to write descriptions of a couple of programs I would be interested in starting if I were hired in the role. One of the ideas I described was a creative compositional and performance program in a correctional facility. I had been thinking about work in the justice system for a long time, but hadn't had the opportunity to participate in it. Given the crisis of mass incarceration in this country, prisons seemed like a place where music could make a difference on many levels. So when Carnegie Hall started a new set of programs in a range of community settings in 2009, they included work across the youth justice system in New York City, and a new partnership with the Sing Sing maximum-security facility in Ossining, New York. This program at Sing Sing has come to be called Musical Connections. People are often surprised when I tell them about Musical Connections, which now represents fourteen years of collaboration between the participating men at Sing Sing and the artists and team at the Hall. This kind of deep work, evolving over time as we learned together and as the participants took an increasingly central role as co-designers of the program, is not what one might expect from a concert hall that is more than one hundred and thirty years old. But expectations and assumptions are made to be challenged and checked, as I learned in my initial trip to Sing Sing.

In the first year we focused primarily on presenting concerts for the population of men at Sing Sing in the facility's auditorium, which seats roughly four hundred men, and in the smaller chapel. I attended the program's second concert with members of our staff. The men started to come in for the performance, and a few stopped to say hello as they found seats. One of them asked me what was going to be performed, and I told him that it was a wonderful band led by Chris Washburne called SYOTOS that would play a Latin jazz show. The man seemed disappointed to hear this, and when I asked him why, he said to me, "It's Carnegie Hall, so I thought it was going to be classical music." I was surprised and asked him if he listened regularly to classical music, and he responded that yes, he and a number of other men listened to the local classical music station all the time and loved it. They ended up loving this concert as well, but it stuck in my mind that we needed to check our assumptions about a place and a group of people about whom we knew little. We had assumed that a performance of classical music was not the place to start at Sing Sing, but we have found that the population there, of course, has as broad a range of interests and preferences as any group of people. I have a feeling that over time we have learned as much from our work together as the participants have learned from us, and this work has informed my understanding and perspective as much as anything we do in WMI.

The program at Sing Sing evolved quickly into a music workshop focused on compositional work across genres for a group of about thirty-five men, as well as instrumental and vocal training supported by a core group of artist faculty who visit the facility twice a month for workshops and classes. Men in the group are writing classical instrumental chamber works, gospel, R&B, jazz, and hip-hop, and one man is working on an opera. Some of them have had musical training and experience before, but others did not, and they have embraced the opportunity to study instrumental and vocal technique and music theory, and to write their own music. A serious musical community has developed between the participants and visiting artists involved in this work. Three or four times a year we present concerts at the venue for the broader population of residents, and those performances feature music written by the men in the workshop, who perform alongside the artist faculty. Once a year we present a special performance at the facility by a major artist, with guests who have included Rhiannon Giddens,

Common, and Joyce DiDonato, who has returned repeatedly to work with participants and sing for the broader population. These artists are invariably blown away by the level of musicianship, creativity, and engagement of the participating men.

One thing that anyone attending a performance at Sing Sing notices immediately is the quality of listening among the men in the audience. This is not an audience in which people are checking their phones throughout the performance and rustling around in a state of distraction. Clive Gillinson regularly comes to hear the concerts, and I remember speaking with him after a chapel performance that had mostly featured chamber music and songs with a small accompanying ensemble. We were sitting on a bench along the side of the chapel, which was full to the allowed capacity of about a hundred men, and in the small space we could easily see the performers as well as the faces of men in the audience. Clive commented after the concert that you would never have that feeling of intimacy in the audience at Carnegie Hall, of such focus, the men listening to soak up every drop of what might be found in the music they were hearing. For much of the time you could hear a pin drop, and then when something surprising or funny or particularly beautiful happened musically, a sigh or murmur rippled across the room. Part of this reaction is due to scarcity. The options to experience live performance in the facility are sharply limited, so there is appreciation for any opportunity to hear live music. The other factor, though, is the quality of the performances. One year the workshop's focus was Duke Ellington's Sacred Music, and many of the new pieces that season were inspired by those works. The final concert was particularly accomplished, powerful, and moving. Clive looked at me at the end of the performance and said, "That concert could have taken place at Zankel Hall," the midsize concert hall within Carnegie Hall. And then he said, "Is there any way we could make that happen?"

Years later, on a Sunday morning I stood in the Parquet—the downstairs section of seats in Carnegie Hall's Isaac Stern Auditorium. I was watching the end of a rehearsal in preparation for a major WMI event. The Hall's Festival that year explored the 1960s, that tumultuous decade in which so much social change advanced, looking at ways in which music powered those movements for change. Across WMI programs that season, including at Sing Sing, we invited people to write music for the change they now wanted to see in the world, and this rehearsal was the last one before a major concert showcasing much of that music. It was a big, complex show featuring program participants alongside professional musicians, with major visual elements, all tied together by a moving narrative arc connecting the 1960s to what we were experiencing in 2016. As I watched the cast rehearse their bows, what I was witnessing started to sink in—numerous men we met at Sing Sing who had since come home were now standing alongside faculty artists who had worked with them inside the facility, other professional musicians, major artists, high school students and their music teachers, and even a class of first graders, sharing their vision for change in the world. I felt in that moment the scope of what we were doing and the number of people who had contributed to making that event happen so beautifully. I realized that while I wasn't playing the oboe, I was still in the middle of a huge ensemble, even bigger than an orchestra, and that it took the best creative energy and care for the effort from all of us to make that incredible performance happen. As this thought filtered into my mind, I began to speak with Manuel Bagorro, who has been centrally involved in the Hall's Musical Connections program since the beginning, about how amazing it was that this was actually happening. From our first steps into programming concerts at Sing Sing many years before, to a major event featuring performances by men who had formerly been incarcerated there, now so beautifully performing their own music on the stage of Carnegie Hall. It was quite a journey, and I don't think we could ever have predicted an event like this when we started.

I wrote earlier about the aspiration behind the word "transformative," and nowhere is that type of impact clearer than in Musical Connections. We know from personal journals the men shared with us and from interviews that the creation of the music workshop inside Sing Sing has formed a kind of musical community that has shifted the feeling of being incarcerated. Numerous men say that the program has changed their lives. It contributes in powerful and positive ways to participants' sense of self. The men develop connections and creative, collaborative relationships with people they didn't know previously, both inside and outside the facility.

Kenyatta Emmanuel was a participant in Musical Connections from the beginning, and he continues to work with WMI now that he is home in New York City. His return was spectacularly celebrated on the day of his release by a performance he gave in Carnegie Hall's Resnick Education Wing alongside other formerly incarcerated people and Musical Connections faculty. He spoke to the difference that music made for him and other men.

> For people who are incarcerated, freedom is a negative state; it is a state of *not* having a restriction or constraint. We are free *from* something. From fear, or danger, or shame or guilt. When the constraint is absent, we may be free to *be*—to be brave or confident or be the fullness of our actualized self. But in art—in music—there is a positive freedom, an additive freedom. I am freed to express in a language I did not have before, to express in a way that disregards artificial and ultimately futile attempts to stifle individuality, or to bury my voice beneath the Latin and High Speech of an entire legal system. I am freed to express in spite of the constant reminder that nothing I have to say is worth being heard. Marvelously, music frees me to sing of my captivity, to play my imprisonment in melodies that float through these dank halls to resonate with every human in hearing. Music makes me free to sing that our captivity is hard—the captivity of incarceration, or of expectation, or of family name or assigned gender or the color of my skin. Music infiltrates and sabotages all the ideas that steal freedom, that perpetuate captivity, and offers freedom that cannot be stolen or diminished or denied. The freedom of expression.

We know that a network of connections and sense of being part of a community is the single biggest factor in recidivism—whether a person returns to prison after release. So using our 360-degree frame, we do all that we can to build a sense of community and belonging. We share videos of Sing Sing concerts with participants' families as opportunities for connection and healing. Some families say that these videos helped them see their incarcerated family member in a positive, productive light, bringing the possibility of renewed hope and love. We engage men in performing. Most of the released men now participate in our Musical Connections Advisory Council. They meet monthly at Carnegie Hall with staff and artists to continue their collaborative musical pursuits and provide support and community as they navigate the complex and challenging process of reentering society. Not one of them has returned to prison.

There are other results from these programs that are also valuable and worthy of mention here, with credit again to Dennie Palmer Wolf's observations. I've mentioned the power of music to connect and communicate, from parent to child in a lullaby, from a man incarcerated to his family via concert video. Music can also provide a portable sanctuary for people to carry with them. Refugee families who have written lullabies talk about the safe space they can create for their children through singing a song they wrote in different locations as they move toward a new home. It's a beautiful idea that a song can be carried safely and never lost, to be sung at any time in any setting to help create a feeling of safety and home. The need for sanctuary, for respite from a challenging moment, time, or situation, extends to so many people in all kinds of situations around the world. Who doesn't need at some point in life that invaluable ability to create a comforting and safe space for one's family and oneself? Perhaps this sense of sanctuary plays a role for incarcerated men for whom playing music, alone or with others, might also make a safe space for rest and healing. Music can also provide a means of travel. When a person's freedom is restricted, attending a performance provides a chance to step outside of a situation into a place of freedom and exploration. We have learned from men at Sing Sing that a single concert can last far beyond the ninety minutes of the performance itself, through weeks of anticipation when people look forward to the event, and months after as they reflect on and savor memories from the experience. So, even attendance at a single concert for one of the residents who doesn't participate in the workshop can ripple outward.

I want to return in closing to the idea of 360 degrees of impact, and say that this work has provided to WMI and Carnegie Hall as an institution an open space in which to think and learn about the well-being of everyone the programs touch, from staff to artists, participants to families and partner organizations. Institutions are made up of individuals. In that major rehearsal at the Hall that I describe above, there was another overwhelming emotion that surfaced for me, which I wanted to say out loud at the time, but I don't think I actually did. And that thought was, "I hope that people in the audience love this performance, because that is my heart up there on that stage." We tend not to talk very much about love in professional or institutional settings. Emotions can be messy, and in a professional context it is safer to leave many of them unspoken. But there is no getting around the fact that this work is deeply emotional. In creative musical work, we get to hear other people's perspectives, their joys and struggles, fears and dreams, communicated without words through a brilliant emotional medium. Everyone involved learns from the process. We learn about ourselves as people, all connected in remarkable ways through music.

Holding out hope
This is all some passing temporary insanity, I'm
Holding out hope
Deep inside we'll recognize our common humanity, I'm
Holding out hope
The way things are is not the way that it has to be, I'm
Holding onto love, holding off despair
And I'm holding out hope, I'm
Holding onto love, holding off despair
And I'm holding out hope

CHORUS, "HOLDING OUT HOPE" BY KENYATTA EMMANUEL

Sing, Dance, and Play!

MARK MORRIS

Artistic Director, Mark Morris Dance Group

D ance and music are related in so many ways that I see them as aspects of one nonverbal need, a need that everyone has experienced, consciously or not. It is not just the specialists, the elite professional musicians and dancers, composers and choreographers, but every person on every folkway, everywhere. Music and dance are fundaments of world culture, the benefits of which cannot be overestimated. In my particular choreo-musical world as a choreographer, I respect and revere the magic of these lyric arts. And as much as I think I have learned, I never want to understand all of the mysteries. I don't really want to know why we can't live without these seemingly pointless activities. Sing, dance, and play!

Worldwide agreement on space/time organizing methods is a societal obsession that leads both toward and away from what we consider the performing arts. To organize our complicated lives and thoughts, we have come to accept these very specific measures of increasing precision in order to begin and end things with accuracy: simultaneity, duration, departures and arrivals; days, furlongs, millennia, hectares, fathoms, parsecs; the sand drains through the glass, the tides ebb and flow, the seasons rotate, the .001 second win; the pulse, heartbeat, breath; a blink, a generation, a lifetime.

Musics of everywhere have always presented the perception of time and tune in numerous valid and ingenious ways. Two universal musical "points," the tonic (#1, or home/root) and dominant (#5, perfect/open), form the scaffold that allows varying intervals to achieve the quasi-infinite pitch possibilities and harmony in music. You learn to sense it: you hear it, you feel it, you live in it, and your comprehension deepens. The music is a part of you. Therefore, you are more likely to fall into the mode or vibe or swing of the music you grew up with and have heard the most. It feels like home. You love it and you never forget it.

Rhythm isn't merely a sequence of numbers, nor need time be reduced to a series of ticks. One beat is an event, two beats imply a rhythm, time is a distance and a duration. In an infinite universe, every point is the center, and time/space radiates from . . . right there. So where are you? Not waiting in line, but in the center of an expanding sphere. Getting from here to there in a particular amount of time decides your speed and the rhythm implicit in walking, running, driving, throwing, shouting and its echo. Distance and a duration. Is it rhythm? Is it a tune? Is it dancing yet? I say yes . . . and it never stops. These multiple, multivalent activities seem so complex, and yet they become second nature, matter of fact, taken for granted. Until they aren't.

Bipedalism insists on bilateral symmetry and the general binary: right/left, front/back, up/down, on/off, 1/0. We depend on the limits these rules supply, and that are necessary for most of societal order and logic. We require the use of compatible measurements for so much of our daily communication. These "landmarks" are crucial to accept and internalize, but they also limit the range and scope of imagination. One can become lost by straying from the strict cues of rhythm and music and have difficulty living in what seems a disordered world. I take that to mean what the sad cliché tells us, too late, "Think outside the box!" (oh . . . *that* box!). Sing, dance, and play!

When one has a limited, decreasing capacity to control one's actions and must rely on external stimuli for cues to move, numbers and cardinal directions are reliably helpful but aren't necessarily adequate. A pulse without an assigned number, a tune's unpredictable contours, a speed bump on the highway: How far? How long? When do we start? Are we there yet? We decide and we obey. The elegant rules of natural logic that we find in music and dance, in choreomusical expression, in socialization, in community co-operation, in games, in cheers and chants, in the body's own rhythms, are extremely valuable and life-altering. That's what I have felt and seen in my involvement in the sanctuary of Dance for PD, as described in David Leventhal's concise and revealing article.

Dance and Parkinson's: Finding Humanity Through a Musical Road Map

DAVID LEVENTHAL

Program Director, Dance for PD, Mark Morris Dance Group

I started dancing at a friend's recommendation, but it was the music that kept me hooked. And it still hooks me, even now, a decade after I stopped dancing professionally and at a time when I inhabit an undeniably middle-aged body that emits many more daily protests than it used to. Music still has the power to lift me from my seat, without warning, and propel me into motion, aches and pains be damned.

As a young ballet student at Boston Ballet, I remember one pianist in particular—Joanne—whose musical choices and textured articulation pulled me in and made me feel that I was moving inside the music. Joanne often played the Menuet from Maurice Ravel's *Tombeau de Couperin* for pliés (knee bends that come at the beginning of a ballet class), and I was mesmerized by the gentle falling and rising rhythm, the satisfying but surprising harmonic path, the sadness and the beauty of Ravel's music. I knew very little (at the time) about Ravel, or about Couperin; I didn't know the piece honored friends of Ravel's who had died in the First World War; nor did I know Balanchine's eponymous dance. As I got older, those contextual layers of art and cultural history added to my appreciation of the music (which I still love), but without knowing any of these elements, it was still love—and transformation—at first sight.

As a professional dancer I witnessed choreographer Mark Morris—for whom I danced for more than fourteen years—with a score in hand, creating dances that exposed and expressed the inner life of dozens of musical scores, music I never heard the same way after I heard it through Mark's ears. Since his company, the Mark Morris Dance Group, performs almost exclusively to live music, I also spent fourteen years listening actively to music being created simultaneously to and in partnership with the movements I was executing—a rare symbiosis in the digital age of hi-fi recording.

Now I observe music's transformative powers every day as I create dance experiences for people with Parkinson's disease (PD), a degenerative neurological condition that can cause slowness of movement, balance impairment, tremors, and rigidity, along with a host of nonmotor symptoms like cognitive impairment and depression. Parkinson's affects more than one million Americans and an estimated ten million people worldwide; it is the fastest-growing neurodegenerative condition in the world, and nearly ninety thousand are diagnosed with it each year in the United States.

When I started teaching people with Parkinson's, I knew almost nothing of the clinical manifestations of the condition. Nor did I know much about how music, dance, and an artistic approach to movement, working in synchrony, can positively affect the physical, emotional, and cognitive experience of people living with Parkinson's. When I started, I knew nothing of the field called neuroaesthetics, which fosters research to understand the intersection between arts and the brain.

Olie Westheimer, the visionary who introduced the idea of a dance class for people with Parkinson's to the Mark Morris Dance Group in 2001, wanted it that way, at least to start. Olie adamantly maintained that we dancers, with years of training and stage experience, had all the information we needed to create a beneficial, joyful experience for members of the Parkinson's support group she facilitated in Brooklyn, New York. To a great extent she was right (though over the past twenty years, I've immersed myself in learning about Parkinson's and neuroaesthetics). When Olie pitched the groundbreaking idea of a Parkinson's dance class to MMDG's executive director, Nancy Umanoff, she knew that simply locating the program she had in mind within an active arts organization—which was dedicated to a vision of high-quality dance and music being available and accessible to the Brooklyn community in which it was based—would have transformative effects. At that time most movement programs for Parkinson's were housed in clinical settings.

Olie knew that with a condition like Parkinson's, for which there is no cure, each person's prognosis and timeline is different—some Dance for PD participants have been living with Parkinson's for more than twenty-five years—but each journey involves the gradual reduction in motor skills, independence, confidence, and quality of life. Although it is classified as a movement disorder, our participants and their families remind us regularly that Parkinson's is a holistic disorder that affects an individual's physical, cognitive, emotional, and social realms. Although it is primarily associated as a condition related to older age, approximately 10 to 20 percent of people with Parkinson's are diagnosed before the age of fifty.

Dave Iverson, a filmmaker, journalist, and person living with Parkinson's—and director of the award-winning documentary *Capturing Grace*, which features members of the Brooklyn Dance for PD group preparing for their first public performance in 2012—speaks of Parkinson's as a disease of subtraction. One by one, as he narrates in *Capturing Grace*, things go missing—arms that swing, a steady gait, even the ability to smile. The impact on individuals and their families can be devastating. As Iverson noted in a lecture he gave at Stanford University in 2015:

> When you're first diagnosed with Parkinson's, you start thinking about yourself, your body, differently. Who am I now? Am I my diagnosis? And what about this body of mine, what's going to happen to it?

Countering layers of subtraction, Iverson maintains, requires diligence and a focus on addition—what people living with PD can add back into their lives to maintain a sense of physical well-being, control, independence, and hope.

In October 2001, when I facilitated the very first Dance for PD class at the Mark Morris Dance Center for six people with Parkinson's, we had no idea that the program would go on to have a positive impact—measured anecdotally and in more than forty-five peer-reviewed studies—on tens of thousands of people around the world. We didn't know it would provide the kind of addition Iverson feels is so critical for people living with Parkinson's.

My teaching colleagues John Heginbotham, Misty Owens, and I created our methodology over the first three years through a process of trial and error, in partnership with community participants, and with Olie. We would mine various dance styles, techniques, and choreographic repertoire to craft classes that, at their core, provided satisfying artistic experiences while also addressing such PD-specific issues as balance, coordination, confidence, social connection, walking, and, as we'll see later in this chapter, musicality and rhythm.

Over time Olie, in consultation with us teachers, created eight points that we thought captured the unique intersection of dance and Parkinson's—in other words, the ways that dance seemed to fit Parkinson's like a glove:

1. Dance develops strength, fluidity, flexibility, stamina, and balance.
2. Dance helps us master skills through progressive training.
3. Dance is a stimulating cognitive activity that connects mind to body.
4. Dance helps us to forge social connections and a sense of belonging.
5. Dance harnesses imagery, rhythm, and music in the service of intentional movement.
6. Dance helps us express stories and emotions through our bodies.
7. Dance sparks creativity and develops problem-solving skills.
8. The essence of dance is joy.

We wrote these points to make sure their value and importance would resonate deeply with teaching artists, people with PD and their families, and medical professionals (and researchers) alike.

These pillars have underpinned our lesson plans for the past twenty years, and they've served as areas of inquiry for researchers studying the impact of Dance for PD and other dance-based programs on symptom progression and quality of life in people with Parkinson's. Since 2009 researchers conducting studies in the United States, Canada, Germany, the United Kingdom, Japan, China, Australia, and Brazil have seen measurable benefits related to gait, balance, functional mobility, executive function, social inclusion, self-esteem, mood, and self-efficacy. A study published in July 2021 showed that participation in a weekly class based on the Dance for PD methodology effectively slowed both motor and nonmotor Parkinson's symptoms over a period of three years. Though a limited, noncontrolled pilot study, the research—published in the journal *Brain Sciences*—is significant because it suggests that the rapid motor progression that might be expected in people with PD over the same period is not seen in those participating in consistent weekly dance training, and motor impairment progression remains much slower in those who participate in dance classes. "The reasons for our findings," note the authors, "could be due to the additive effects of training, socialization, support and group dynamics that putatively occur within and around the classes."

In other words, dance—a holistic, multifaceted, and multifocal activity that engages body, mind, and spirit—seems to be measurably effective in slowing the trajectory of a holistic, multifaceted, and multifocal chronic condition. These findings—which addressed dance's transformative effects on both motor and nonmotor outcomes—mirror what I've seen in our participants from the very first class. As one participant who completed a post-class survey anonymously noted:

> My experiences with this class have played a major role in reclaiming my physicality and mobility from the relentless ravaging of PD. It's helping me to keep in mind the significance of not permitting PD to define me, but rather for me to shape my own dimension in the struggle to maintain mobility and agility.

This dancer speaks to a direct, dynamic connection between the physical improvements they experience in class and the socioemotional benefits. Reclaiming mobility allows this individual to redefine their own identity and maintain a sense of purpose and control.

Other participants, like this family member who also completed an anonymous questionnaire, point to a sense of hope that comes from the feeling of accomplishment:

> The music and movement started, I was filled with great joy. I was able to take the whole class and walked out feeling accomplished. . . . Seeing the class participants enjoy music and movement and benefit from it was so thrilling. I saw the endless possibilities for those with Parkinson's and for myself.

When dance class is going on, as Reggie Butts observes in *Capturing Grace*, there are no patients, only dancers. As another class participant noted, "It's Carnegie Hall compared to Bellevue Hospital."

Every element of the Dance for PD experience emphasizes accessibility and inclusion. Most classes start with a progressive, seated warm-up. As participants move in a circle of chairs, they're able to immerse themselves in a fully aesthetic experience while maintaining connection (through eye contact, gesture, and touch) with their classmates. As the hour-long class continues, dancers have the option to stand to do activities at a ballet barre or behind the chair, and, if they're comfortable, to travel across the floor. However, on any given day, a number of participants enjoy the entire class in the comfort and safety of a chair. Group dances are designed to integrate standing and seated dancers together, without privileging the contributions of one over the other. At the end of class, dancers return to a circle for a *reverence*. Drawn from the tradition of classical ballet, the reverence is the physical embodiment of gratitude and provides a moment to reinscribe the dynamics of a mutually supportive community. Although the majority of Dance for PD classes follow this format, a new program—Dance for PD PRO—features an all-standing class and is designed for individuals (several of whom were diagnosed with early onset Parkinson's before the age of fifty) who want a more rigorous experience.

In a particularly compelling section of *Capturing Grace*, Cynthia (Cyndy) Gilbertson, a longtime participant in the Brooklyn Dance for PD program, speaks to the way dance has helped her value herself more, "which is quite a gift. When I'm schlumping, I say to myself, I'm a dancer . . . I have to sit up straight . . . it gives me motivation to take better care of myself."

Cyndy goes on to demonstrate what happens "when my feet feel like glue and they're stuck to the floor. I sometimes cannot walk but I can dance." Within seconds Cyndy's small, unsteady steps become elongated, graceful, and rhythmic as she moves to the jazz music on her stereo. Her entire physicality and mood change, and she enters a state of flow. "The music leads. So I'm following this wonderful leader who's so mysterious and has such a lovely sound and it's going to take me to some other place."

Iverson interrupts her to ask what that place is. Holding back tears, she responds: "It's a place where you're weightless. Your body just flies. It doesn't tug at you . . . pull you and push you and have you in these knots where you can't move and you can't think and you're struggling and fighting . . . you go above that."

Joy, freedom, motivation, transformation, and confidence. The experience of dancing directly addresses these human needs, adding them back into the daily experience of people living with Parkinson's, who are more accustomed to rigidity, anxiety, apathy, and the feeling of being trapped in their own bodies. The transformation Cyndy experiences in her Brooklyn living room echoes the story of tens of thousands of people around the world who participate in local Dance for PD classes in more than three hundred communities in twenty-five countries.

MUSIC, THE MYSTERIOUS LEADER

In every Dance for PD class I teach, I use music the way an Italian chef uses olive oil—it is the base for everything, brings out specific qualities in other movement components (like gesture and attack), and draws disparate elements into a cohesive and pleasurable whole, creating a movement *ragù*. As Carroll Neesemann, one of Dance for PD's original participants, noted, "Music is like a red carpet that rolls out in front of you and tells you what to do."

Neesemann's metaphor captures the essence of what music can do: it can make anyone, even those who might be shuffling or feeling clumsy out on the sidewalk, feel like royalty. Over the twenty years that I've been teaching Dance for PD classes, participants, journalists, and teachers-in-training have asked me what elements of music seem most helpful for people living with PD. As a music lover, and as someone who has had a Pavlovian response to music since I was two, I've always answered with one word: *everything*. Rhythm, melody, harmony, form, texture, and narrative combine in an inherent holism that underpins why essayist and critic Walter Pater famously stated, "All art constantly aspires to the condition of music." People react differently to different music, and we all have specific musical likes and dislikes, but I bet everyone who has access to music has at least one piece that exerts a powerful urge to move or smile, perhaps to sing, to feel happier, or to cry. We don't need to claim a complete understanding of music to feel its power—in fact, it's probably most effective when our initial response is visceral, spontaneous, and unacademic.

Music's role as a wonderful, mysterious leader, as Cyndy describes it, reminded me of an insight that significantly impacted my teaching practice. John Argue, who leveraged his theater background to create classes for people with Parkinson's in the Bay Area until he retired in 2016, told me, "Parkinson's is a disease that challenges automaticity—it makes automatic movements less reliable." John's comments struck a chord because they reflected exactly what Cyndy describes, and what I'd noticed in the participants I was teaching: movements like walking, turning, and getting out of or into a chair were notably challenging for our Parkinson's dancers. But when those same movements were choreographed as dance movements to music, our dancers suddenly found a sense of ease and flow, and they could execute those elements with less struggle. In the context of dancing—with its focus on imagery, sequencing, narrative, and expression—movements that were difficult in daily life became accessible, even enjoyable.

A student in our program might shuffle down the hallway on her way into the studio, as Cyndy does in her living room, but forty-five minutes later, she's strutting rhythmically across the floor with a longer stride length and swinging arms. To determine how much she was moving automatically, and how much she was consciously thinking about each step, we'd need to be able to see what parts of her brain she was leveraging in the service of movement. Lacking this technology and a neuroscience PhD, I find it helpful to consider ways all living beings (and dancers in particular) process internally generated and externally generated cues to execute movement.

If you, the reader, take a deep breath and allow your torso to rise and fall with that breath, you have generated a movement internally—your own body cueing itself from its core to create a movement. (To be fair, the purest form of this sort of internally generated movement would be prompted by your *own* internal need, whim, or decision, not by the words in this book.) However, if I asked you to find a window in your room and to reach for that window, you would be motivated by something outside your body— a task based on an external target. Similarly, if you hum a tune in your head and start tapping your foot, you'd be using an internally generated cue; tapping your foot to music on the radio constitutes an external cue—your body responding to something imposed by your environment.

To execute complex movements, dancers need to be able to draw from and react to both types of cues simultaneously. When you watch a dancer perform movement, the marriage of internal and external cues is seamless and exhilarating. That dancer is drawing on memory, emotional state, and learned patterns, and combines them with external inputs coming from the musician, the other dancers around her, and the audience's reaction.

We all experience this marriage to some degree when we walk down a busy urban street. Inside your head, you have thoughts, instincts, and motivations that inform your movement choices (running late or being on vacation might affect your walking speed, for example, while the presence or absence of anxiety might impact how much you're moving your eyes to look around). At the same time, you are inundated with external cues—people coming toward you, the throbbing pulse of music blaring from a store, cracks in the pavement, or cars cutting in front of you—that also shape your movements. Amalgamating these two sets of cues results in a distinct, spontaneous physical manifestation as you walk.

In this context I would expand John Argue's statement one dimension further: people living with Parkinson's have much more difficulty initiating movement through internal cues *and* rely almost exclusively on external cues to initiate and maintain movement. This is not a new or special discovery—it forms the basis of most physical therapy for Parkinson's, along with a number of well-regarded Parkinson's exercise programs, and is well documented in the research literature. Fascinatingly, this discovery places an inordinate amount of power and importance on certain types of external cues, particularly cues related to rhythm and music.

Nearly fifty years ago neurologist Oliver Sacks noted the power of music as an externally generated cue that sparked movement in people with parkinsonian conditions. In his seminal book *Awakenings*, Sacks writes, "The power of music to integrate and cure, to liberate the parkinsonian and give him freedom while it lasts . . . is quite fundamental, and seen in every patient." Sacks goes on to describe one patient, a former music teacher named Edith T., who states that her parkinsonism had forced her to lose the naturalness and "musicalness" of movement, "that—in a word—she had been 'unmusicked.'" Edith goes on to say, "As I am unmusicked, I must be remusicked . . . songs, tunes I knew from years ago, catchy tunes, rhythmic tunes, the sort I love to dance to" allow her to break out of this "motionless-helpless" state and to start moving again.

Vilas Joshi, who participates in Dance for PD classes in Pune, India—
a program led by teachers who trained with us at the Mark Morris Dance
Center—shared his observations about the potent marriage of dance and
music:

> I am suffering from PD for the last five to six years and the left side
> of my body has been affected especially the left leg and hand. Doctors
> suggested physiotherapy, but I heard about the dance class and was
> interested in pursuing this as I prefer music and dance over just plain
> exercise. I move more freely and confidently now. The music rhythm
> helps me to know when to start, when to stop and I can control my
> speed of movement.

In the context of Sacks's and Joshi's observations, Neesemann's red carpet analogy becomes even clearer: the cues that rhythm and music provide
a person living with Parkinson's invite, cajole, and coach that person from
a static or inert state into the state of liberating possibility. External cues
like music are prompts to begin, sustain, and control movement. These cues
serve as a road map for locomotion that, in the absence of a strong internal
drive, mean the difference between being frozen and being free.

THE BEAT AS A LANDMARK

Listen to most any musical selection on the radio, and if it has a recognizable pulse, you'll likely be able to tap a hand or a foot to what you're hearing.
Unless you're a percussionist by trade, you're probably inclined to accent
the strong beats of that music. Those beats are like musical fence posts—
they anchor the rhythmic structure of the piece. You might also start to
notice that one of those beats is stronger than the ones preceding or succeeding it. In the song "Happy Birthday," the words "birth" and "you" fall
on the downbeats of two consecutive measures. Each measure contains
less-accented beats ("day" and "to" in the first bar) that fill out a time signature of 3/4.

For dancers the audible downbeat serves as a strong external cue for
something to happen—often, one foot landing on the floor. It's common
for dancers to count an introduction before they start dancing or before they

enter the stage at a particular point by counting to themselves "five, six, seven, eight," with the next beat—considered count "one" of the next phrase—being the landing target. Dancers use many different systems of counting, depending on the style of dance they're executing, the time signature, and their own learning preferences, but hearing and interpreting beats is one of the strongest forms of external motivation dancers have. Dancers without Parkinson's can harness these counting systems whether or not there is actual music playing; it's one way they can rehearse movement phrases—more slowly, or in shorter sections—before they do them in "real time" with full musical accompaniment.

W. Tecumseh Fitch, an evolutionary biologist and cognitive scientist who has worked extensively on the evolution of cognition as it pertains to language and music, argues that many of the core aspects of musical rhythm are closely linked to, and possibly even derived from, forms of body movement. At its most basic level, Fitch argues, this relationship is visible in the way our bipedal nature informs a basic duple meter in music.

In the Dance for Parkinson's environment, highlighting and emphasizing the strong beats of the music we're using is critical to providing our Parkinson's dancers with landmarks and goals in their movement experience. Strong external beats provide our dancers with a goal or target—stepping on each beat, whether they are taking those steps in place, seated in a chair as our participants do during the first part of class, or standing and traveling across the space toward the end of the session—and the task-oriented nature of this prompt helps our dancers coordinate their movements and internalize the externally generated musical cues. There's nothing wrong with occasionally utilizing arhythmic, amorphous musical selections to create a specific mood in class (think music for yoga or meditation), but sparingly. If you want people with Parkinson's to move with confidence and to manifest the kind of steady rhythmic locomotion non-Parkinson's people do automatically, a strong beat is essential.

BEFORE ONE: THE ANACRUSIS ON-RAMP

From Dance for PD's early days, both of our lead musicians—Richard X Bennett and the late William Wade—drew from jazz or classical music in which the audible pulse was strong, consistent, and reliable. But there is much more going on before and after our musical fence posts. After all, just as the posts themselves do not make a fence, the beats themselves do not create music, and the landing of the foot on the floor does not in itself constitute dancing. What happens before and after that landmark is critical.

In the song "Happy Birthday," for example, the first word, "happy," actually starts on a "pickup," more formally called an anacrusis, that resolves on the downbeat ("birth"). Anacrusis, from the Greek words meaning "pushing up," feels to a dancer like an in-breath before an exhale, a slight rise before the fall. It is the time when one prepares to do whatever one needs to do on the strong downbeat. If your downbeat is a step, then the anacrusis will involve lifting the foot and leg in order to take that step—and so the anacrusis must contain all the information a dancer needs to know about when and how to lift that leg so that the next step is perfectly timed and phrased. If a rocket is scheduled to blast off exactly at eight o'clock, the engines must start revving up just at the end of the countdown; this is the anacrusis.

For our Parkinson's dancers, who may have difficulty initiating movement and who struggle to take that first step, a cued anacrusis is critically important to movement and, for standing participants, locomotion. "And-a-one," in dancerspeak, indicates the need to prepare to step forward on the first beat. As we've discussed, people with Parkinson's may have lost the executive function skills needed to plan action internally. By drawing our dancers' attention to the anacrusis, we invite them to recognize an external tool that can help ready them for movement. Hearing the anacrusis, no matter how brief, serves as an auditory directional arrow and a gentle kick in the pants.

In class we've used the theme from Henry Mancini's score for *The Pink Panther*, because its anacrusis clearly prompts the lifting of the foot in order to step on the first beat. The dotted chromatic three-note pickup, which happens twice before the entrance of the main theme, perfectly mirrors the kind of cue a dancer—particularly a Parkinson's dancer—needs to lift the leg and touch down on time. (There's more going on in this theme's rhythmic workings that we'll discuss in a moment.)

The anacrusis can also be a moment of stillness. In some cases the pickup can serve simply as the auditory ignition spark for movement that will start momentarily. The *Bourrée*, from J. S. Bach's Third Suite for Unaccompanied Cello, is also built around a short two-note rising anacrusis that we dancers hear as "and-a." At the invitation of Yo-Yo Ma, Mark Morris choreographed the *Bourrée* as part of *Falling Down Stairs* (1997), created to the entire Third Suite. In 2015 we started sharing movement material from the *Bourrée* with our Parkinson's dancers as part of a global Bourrée Project.

Mark's choreography for the *Bourrée* reflects the freedom, playfulness, and precision of Bach's rhythms—but Mark was adamant in his coaching that the dancers not "indicate" the imminent start of movement during the anacrusis (the equivalent of a musician taking an audible sniff before starting to play). In other words, he asked the dancers to hear the anacrusis, but to try to start and finish each move exactly on the downbeat. The result is movement that appears etched in its precision and playful in its unpredictable patterns. In this example the anacrusis is a purely mental preparation, but even in that form, it still offers a strong impetus to focus one's attention and be ready to arrive on the first beat, and it served as an aural cue card for our dancers with Parkinson's.

THE IN-BETWEEN:
GROOVE AND LOCOMOTION

In some cases, once a composer like Mancini or Bach begins with an anacrusis, that pickup motif continues in some form throughout the section. This phenomenon is true in the *Bourrée*, and to some degree in *The Pink Panther*—where the three-note anacrusis becomes a syncopated upbeat that reverberates throughout the piece before almost every downbeat. But whether an anacrusis is present or not, I gravitate toward music that has an accented upbeat as well as a strong downbeat when making selections for a Dance for PD class. Examples include a swinging jazz standard like Bart Howard's "Fly Me to the Moon," where "fly" and "to" fall on the downbeats and "me" and "the" fall on accented upbeats, or in "*Votre toast, je peux vous le render*" (aka "The Toréador Song") from Bizet's *Carmen*. Imagine for a moment that, in time with the music, you're seated in a chair, stamping your feet in alternation, or perhaps walking across the floor. One foot lands on "fly," the other lifts on "me" and lands with even more conviction on "to"; similarly, if you're dancing to Bizet, one foot falls on "Tor," the other lifts on the two syllables of "éa" and lands with full Spanish spirit on "dor."

It *sounds* far more technical than it is. We all recognize this rhythmic pattern naturally—it's the propulsive syncopated force that exists in any sort of music that makes us want to dance, and it's part of what we call the "groove." Fitch provides a clear and detailed definition:

> [S]uccessful syncopated rhythms add acoustic energy on upbeats, when the legs (or limbs, or whole body) are moving upward, between the downbeats. More technically, by adding acoustic energy to phases in the movement cycle where movements are directed away from grav-ity, syncopation makes the dancer feel these upward movement com-ponents as coherent with the musical surface. The net effect is that syncopations essentially "inject energy" into upbeats, adding an ex-citing, propulsive, and light "feel" to the rhythm that is absent in a "straight" rhythm that simply emphasizes the downbeats, when the feet strike the floor.

That injection of energy between each footfall is critical for our Parkin-son's dancers, who may, as we know, be lacking the same kind of internally generated, automatic initiation that comes from taking one step in front of the next. Instead, the auditory musical cue to lift the foot, and then to drop it, provides a clear road map and framework that, like a carpet, is consis-tently present, supporting a person throughout the seated or standing danc-ing experience. For a population of dancers who can be prone to absence of movement and shuffling, the qualitative and rhythmic prompt to lift the foot (or knee, as in a march) can make the difference between a strong, safe, balanced step and a potential fall.

By encouraging our participants to hear elements like anacrusis and groove in our classes, we heighten the importance and value of music's rich-ness and its role as a full-blooded, richly layered artistic partner—not just a beat. This may seem obvious, but it's an important framework when we compare the use of rhythm in standard physical therapy for Parkinson's. Physical therapists working with Parkinson's clients integrate rhythm using a metronome but don't typically utilize music. However, metronomic cues only focus on the fence posts themselves—the footfalls in a walking phrase—thereby limiting the opportunity to provide the full spectrum of helpful, nuanced rhythmic cues that are available in music and can be harnessed effectively by people in a studio and on the go, in the real world, using an MP3 player.

MUSIC AND DURATION

We've discussed ways in which rhythmic structures in music provide both an on-ramp and a traveling lane for people with Parkinson's on the movement highway. Music, through rhythm and melodic phrasing, can also indicate and guide the *duration* of a particular movement, a skill that, in my observation, can be more difficult for people with Parkinson's to access on their own.

If I ask one of our dancers to extend an arm to the side in the absence of musical phrasing, the movement might either happen in one abrupt, brittle movement, or may happen very gradually and effortfully. The dancer is at the whim of whatever speed or approach their internal Parkinson's "dial" is set to.

In the presence of music that has clear rhythm and melodic phrasing, however, our dancers can move beyond what feels normal to *them* and strive to control how long a specific movement takes, even if it means moving faster or slower than their parkinsonian normal. When the choreography demands the extension of an arm above the head (in ballet terminology, a *port de bras* to fifth position) in four beats, for example, the music can support this action by providing dancers with a starting point, several middle beats to check progress, and an end target beat. In other words, the music once again lays out a clear plan that the dancer can consciously execute—a clear outline or scaffolding upon which the dancer can then embellish.

In this scenario the melodic phrase can also dramatically help a dancer pace movement so it aligns with that phrase. In class, I'll often use the expression "sing your movement." Although participants in our class do sing along as they dance, my coaching is designed to encourage participants to let the melodic cues sustain and shape their action so that it matches the phrasing of the music they're dancing to.

In the second theme of the *Third Suite's Bourrée* (Bourrée II), Bach writes in a more improvisational vein with longer, more legato melodic lines, in contrast to the punchier, more energetic first section. In this section, Mark's choreography demands attunement not just to the dance's consistent rhythms but to changing durations of musical and movement phrases. For example, a corkscrewing turn takes the same amount of time as four quick weight shifts—and the dancer must be careful to calibrate timing appropriately, quickly changing gears from choppier movement in the weight shifts to sustained movement in the turn.

When we adapted this material for our Parkinson's dancers as part of the Bourrée Project, the music was slower and the dance was done seated in chairs, but the movement phrases and musical contours were identical—and our Parkinson's dancers practiced and embraced the contrasting durational and qualitative shifts with aplomb. As an aide-mémoire our Parkinson's cast utilized the same technique the Mark Morris Dance Group dancers used—movements were described in action words (run, turn, fall), and the words were then phrased into sentences that reflected the movement prompt. For example, for four movement ideas each taking the same amount of musical time, we would say in our heads, "Shift-shift-shift-shift, turrrrrrrrrrn, run run run, join hands." By singing these words to learn the choreography and match their movements to the music, our Parkinson's dancers—running with their hands, turning with their shoulders—were able to embody and physicalize Mark's choreographic vision and to live inside of Bach's score. Regardless of physical limitations outside of the studio or symptomatic differences among them, the dancers harnessed the choreomusical structure to manifest a unified understanding and embodiment of time.

MUSIC, EXPRESSION, AND COMMUNITY

As we saw in the Bourrée Project and witness daily in class, musical attunement results in greater physical control for people living with Parkinson's. From this sense of control emerges a world of movement possibilities. Not only can our Parkinson's dancers start to move beyond their everyday parkinsonian movement cadence, but they can begin to think about their movement qualities as artists, making choices to utilize a *staccato* (sharp, detached) or *legato* (smooth, flowing) quality at will, depending on what they'd like to express (or what the teacher or choreographer is requesting). Add to this music's more implicit cues—orchestration, mood, harmonic changes, anticipation, and personal associations—and you start to understand just how wide and long Neesemann's red carpet might be.

The rhythmic and durational values of music—stepping in time with the beat, moving in tune with the musical phrase—have significant personal repercussions that allow individuals to initiate and sustain their movement, but these elements also foster a broader sense of community. By responding to shared external cues (music), people with Parkinson's in a dance class become unified by a shared beat, groove, and understanding of duration. Through this process of gradual synchronization—called entrainment—people combine the music they're hearing with the dancers they see moving in rhythm around them. The resulting unity—a community moving in unison, together—represents a dramatic contrast to the varied, idiosyncratic walking patterns, cadences, and rhythms visible among our participants outside of class. Yes, there are stragglers and outliers, individuals for whom the activity is too fast or complex. But when entrainment is present, it's the human embodiment of the classic metronome demonstration in which five metronomes, each ticking separately, coalesce around a single, unison rhythm after they are placed on a rolling platform.

What's interesting about music's power to create social bonds is that it seems to be dependent on the rhythmic clarity we highlighted earlier. In their groundbreaking work on movement, music, and social bonding, Jan Stupacher and colleagues at Aarhus University in Denmark demonstrated that for social interactions taking place in the presence of music, "the ability to perceive a clear beat in music is central for assessing temporal social entrainment, which in turn is influencing affective social entrainment." The study continues, "Without perceiving such a structure, temporal self-other overlaps are reduced and social bonding decreases." In other words, for the deepest social connections to occur through group movement, the dancers must be moving together to a clear rhythm.

In March 2020, along with the rest of the world, we embarked on an uncharted experiment that would challenge every pillar of our work. As the world shut down in response to the rapid spread of COVID-19, we moved Dance for PD classes online, hosting daily Zoom sessions that aimed to simulate the physical, social, cognitive, and emotional experience of dancing together in a beautiful sunlit studio. Despite initial technical challenges, the online classes became a lifeline for our local Dance for PD community and for people well beyond the borders of New York. Before the pandemic our New York City flagship classes boasted an active pool of 650 Parkinson's participants at any one time; by the summer of 2020, our pool of online class participants grew to more than 2,100, representing six continents, with an additional 4,000 people accessing on-demand recordings of our classes each week. In the period of just a few months, Dance for PD entered the field of telehealth as an important player, providing critical digital resources for thousands of people trapped at home and struggling with the effects of the pandemic exacerbated by the Parkinson's-specific challenges of additional vulnerability, isolation, and anxiety.

In the Zoom sessions something surprising happened. The unifying experience of seeing dance and hearing music synchronously, in the same space with others, was shattered. Now, the natural lag present in video conferencing meant that people in thirty-eight countries were seeing and hearing things in slightly different ways. No longer were they entraining together in a single space; every single body in multiple Zoom rectangles appeared to be moving with slightly different timing. Everyone was experiencing their own micro reality. Remarkably, people adjusted to the slight delays and asynchrony, and dancing on Zoom didn't negate the impact of dancing almost together to the music as they heard it in their own living rooms. Noted one online participant: "I do a virtual class almost every day. . . . As you hear again and again these are lifelines for us all, movement and exercise being vital. And there is community spirit as well."

As a teacher I did have to remind participants to follow their musical instincts—dancing on the beat—rather than following exactly what they saw, and for this reason I marginally simplified the choreography presented on Zoom so that it was easier to be in sync.

It became clear, however, that in the online space, music connected participants in ways that went far beyond rhythm. Instead of the resonant rhythmic entrainment we witnessed in a studio setting—and that Stupacher notes as a key element to social connection—Zoom highlighted the value of music's shared emotional impact, its connection to memories that crossed borders, and the way music could unite people from around the globe in an appreciation of how much could be universally expressed physically through a single song. After class, as participants went into breakout rooms to discuss the class and their lives, music often came up as a topic of shared interest, and even online the sense of community deepened.

A number of elements in an in-person Dance for PD class had helped participants forge strong social bonds: the empathy that comes from experiencing shared challenges, choreography that emphasizes eye contact and touch, and line and circle dances. Emerging work in the field, combined with my own observations about the unifying power of a shared choreomusical experience, suggests that social connection, bonding, and belonging were enhanced and deepened in the presence of the very kind of clear, rhythmic music we utilize in the Dance for PD experience. Now, dancing on Zoom, I witnessed something else: the virtual space forced participants to dig deeper into their musicality, to find ways of expressing themselves by exploring the music's rhythm, meaning, emotional context, and connection to one's personal history. If anything, dancing online expanded participants' musical tool kits and encouraged states of individual, private musical bliss that were simultaneously shared with others in a global online community.

Music's ability to foster a nearly immediate response—which Oliver Sacks witnessed so dramatically in Edith—is what convinced me after the first class I taught in October 2001 to commit to this work, and it is what entrances me still in every class I teach. Music's impact forces me to think back again to my own early classes at Boston Ballet, listening to the rise and fall of Ravel's melodies and Baroque-inspired dance rhythms. The feeling was not so much that I was dancing dutifully *to* the music, but that the music was being expressed *through* my body—that as a dancer, I was a transistor that converted musical energy into movement. Each time I danced in Mark's work—which highlights and revels in the beauty of a community moving together—I was ever more aware of the way in which music was expressed through multiple bodies, moving together in space and time, attuned to one another and to the rhythm. To move together, we had to hear the music in the same way, in every moment. And because that music was live, the spontaneous synchronized coalescence of dance, music, and community created an experience as riveting for us performers as it was for the audience.

Music—its rhythms, phrasing, feelings, and structures—offers the same gifts to people with Parkinson's. By providing such powerful prompts; well-signed on-ramps, fast lanes, and exits; and a powerful sense of inclusive community, music provides a road map for movement, a gateway for expression and artistry, and an invitation to belong. Music supports the complete journey of a person with Parkinson's from a state characterized by inertia, freezing, and dis-ease into one of physical control, expression, and connection. In the face of a dehumanizing condition, music's red carpet offers a path that gets at the essence of what it means to be human.

CREATIVE
LEARNING

Educators and Researchers Illuminate
the Effects of Arts Engagement
on the Developing Brain

Humans Are Musical Creatures: The Case for Music Education

INDRE VISKONTAS, MM, PhD

Associate Professor of Psychology, University of San Francisco

Professor of Sciences and Humanities,
San Francisco Conservatory of Music

Director of Communications, Sound Health Network

INTRODUCTION

Some forty thousand years ago, when Neanderthals were competing with early humans for resources, our ancestors were fashioning musical in struments out of bones. Ten thousand years before they were making figurines from pottery, or weaving baskets, or even painting art in European caves, they were making music. Instrumental music making has been a part of humanity since prehistoric times, and it's highly likely that choral singing, dancing, and drumming were part of human culture long before that.

Music is a part of who we are: how we connect, how we learn, how we make sense of our world. It's a tool that we've used for tens of thousands of years, if not longer, for many different purposes. It's no surprise, then, that our musical experience is etched into our neuroanatomy, affecting not only how our brains function, but also how they are wired—how they develop. After all, human babies are unique among primates in one important way— their brains are woefully underdeveloped at birth, so that they can adapt to whatever environment they are born into. Music can be one of the driving forces of this bespoke development.

There are many ways in which musicians' brains are distinguishable from those of the general population, but you don't have to be professionally trained to reap the benefits of music, or even to inhabit a brain shaped by music. You need only to experience its power to move us, literally and figuratively. And the traces it etches into the brain follow a typical dose-response curve: the more engaged with music you are, the more often you play, listen to, or otherwise use music, the deeper and more widespread its signature on the brain will be.

FROM DAY ONE

Even while we are in the womb, our nervous system responds to music, in ways that are distinct from other types of stimulation, including nonmusical sounds. Newborns can recognize melodies that were played to them in utero, and there's even some evidence that playing soothing music for a fetus can settle its heart, decreasing heart rate variability, a measure of stress. Of course it's hard to separate the effects of music on the carrier from those on the fetus itself, given how intertwined their bodies are, but there is ample evidence that even in utero, musical sounds are special.

Once babies exit the womb, music continues to hold special power: premature babies in the neonatal intensive care unit (NICU) who are sung to or otherwise exposed to music in the hands of an informed, licensed music therapist show improvements on cardiac and respiratory measures, sucking behavior, faster weight gain, better-quality sleep, and quicker recovery from painful procedures.

But as in any other delicate situation, music in the NICU needs to be carefully curated: piping in any additional sound into an already acoustically saturated environment can do more harm than good. But when caregivers sing lullabies and adjust their volume and tempo in response to the infants' reactions, music can be highly effective—reducing stress in both the caregiver and the baby, promoting healing, attachment, and overall well-being.

MUSIC DURING THE FIRST THREE YEARS KICK-STARTS LANGUAGE DEVELOPMENT

Once out in the world, babies as young as six months of age can begin to use music to learn about themselves and the adults who surround them.

Music teaches how to take turns, share attention, pair emotions with gestures, and interpret facial expressions. Babies use songs to self-soothe and make sense of their worlds—they feel safer and closer to their caregivers through shared music making. And it's through the melody of speech that infants learn the emotions behind the words that are spoken to them—right from the beginning, music is a fundamental part of how we learn to communicate.

Laurel Trainor at McMaster University in Canada has led several studies investigating the effects of group music classes on babies' brains and behavior. She and her colleagues have found that even before babies can talk, they can learn to express meaningful gestures and use them more effectively if they've attended participatory music classes with their caregivers. But it's not just gestural learning that baby music classes kick-start—there are other features of language development that benefit as well.

Babies bounced to music in a slightly more complicated rhythm—say in triple meter, like a waltz, rather than a simple 4/4—and given shakers, sticks, and other tools that they can use to track the beat, learn to tune into unexpected tempo changes, building a model of temporal structure in sound. These babies, even after just twelve sessions lasting fifteen minutes each over four weeks, showed enhanced brain responses to sounds that violated an expected pattern—noticing when it doesn't sound "right."

These neural responses are part of how we learn to code speech—such as which sounds belong to the same syllable and which don't. These rhythmically sophisticated babies then transferred their superior temporal sound processing to other meaningful sounds. Even four weeks of music lessons boosted not just expressive communication, but language learning more generally. And another study of typically energized four-year-olds showed that joint drumming was effective at taming them, encouraging spontaneous cooperation, much to the delight of the adults who care for them.

BEYOND SOUND: MUSIC EDUCATION BENEFITS OTHER COGNITIVE DEVELOPMENT

As many frustrated parents have discovered, getting a young child's attention can be a challenge—repeating requests or instructions is a feature of daily parental life. It can be tempting to blame inattention on the distractible nature of a child's brain, but young kids also find it more difficult than adults or older kids to distinguish speech sounds from other environmental noises. Babies with typical hearing might be sensitive to sound in general, but parsing speech from noise is a skill that develops over time. Musical training can help.

You might have heard of the "Mozart Effect"—the idea that listening to certain types of music, Western classical in particular, can make a child more intelligent. This myth can be traced back to a study of undergraduate students at the University of California Irvine published in 1993, showing that when students listened to one of Mozart's piano sonatas, they performed better on a subset of IQ tests than peers who were listening to relaxation tapes, or who sat in silence.

The authors themselves were surprised at how quickly their results captured the media's attention and were overinterpreted. Without diminishing the genius of Mozart, it's become clear that this effect is mediated by overall arousal—how awake and engaged the students were when they completed the IQ tasks—rather than by anything specific to Mozart's music. After all, follow-up studies showed that a chapter from a Stephen King novel, or music by the British pop band Blur, was just as effective. This temporary boost in IQ performance is a result of a child's preferences for entertainment—if they're energized and entertained prior to taking the tests, they try harder and, as a result, perform better.

But participating in music making, taking music lessons, or actively engaging with music is a different story. Listening might be entertaining, engaging, and moving, but musical training is where the long-term benefits to cognitive and brain development lie.

As we've discussed, in the first few years of life, musical training can promote the development of a more sophisticated auditory system in the brain, and that enhancement can benefit the child's language skills. One study, for example, conducted in the lab of neuroscientist Nina Kraus at Northwestern University, tracked the effects of musical training on neural responses to speech in preschoolers.

The researchers found that preschoolers exposed to music early on had developed brains that were more efficient at responding to speech in noise, compared to kids who hadn't attended music classes. Over time the musical kids also showed more resilience to background noise—they found it less distracting—than nonmusician peers. Sadly, children raised in noisy urban environments learn to tune out sound early on, which can lead to difficulties in speech and language processing, including reading ability. But this study, along with others, demonstrates a pathway by which early music education can give kids an edge and accelerate their language learning, helping them overcome the challenges of growing up in noisy settings. That's because music training can strengthen the brain's responses to all meaningful sounds— not just musical ones—and this heightened sensitivity to sound gives children an edge when they are placed in challenging listening environments, where there's a lot of background noise. "What was cool about this longitudinal study in preschoolers," says study author Nina Kraus, "was the finding that with training, the brain's response to speech became increasingly resilient to the disruptive effects of background noise."

Kids who are better able to hear teachers' instructions, particularly in noisy classrooms, reap a wide variety of benefits over time, and thus it should come as no surprise that kids who take music lessons often outperform their peers on many educational measures. The music training helps them learn what to listen for, so that they don't shut out the teachers' instructions along with the ambient noise. But assessing the long-term effects of musical training on cognitive and other skills is challenging: music lessons are expensive, in terms of both the fees and the time that parents need to set aside to provide them for their children. Learning to play a musical instrument or to become a proficient singer takes time—and the benefits can take months if not years to outweigh the costs. That's why studies of the impact of music lessons track students over long periods of time.

Longitudinal studies are not only expensive for the researchers, but they also mean that parents need to commit to either music lessons or a control condition for a significant amount of time. Parents who are struggling financially are less likely to have the resources to give their kids access to a musical education, even if the cost of the lessons is covered. As a result, one of the biggest confounders of long-term studies evaluating music lessons is the socioeconomic status of the child's household. Wealthy parents often prioritize music education—and therefore, wealthy families, who might provide additional benefits to their kids, are overrepresented in many of these longitudinal studies. As a U.S. national profile by Kenneth Elpus and Carlos Abril showed in 2019, wealthy students are overrepresented among high school music students.

With that caveat in mind, let's review the evidence outlining how music lessons impact brain development in kids from kindergarten to high school, and whether skills gained during musical training have real-world applications in domains outside the music studio. One of the most commonly presented arguments against making music classes a part of every child's basic education is that there simply isn't time—music is seen as a luxury, one that most schools can't afford, both in terms of the costs of instruments, sheet music, and specialized teachers, and in terms of the time away from other subjects, like math and reading. Most kids aren't going to grow into professional musicians, but knowing how to read and write and knowing how to handle numbers are considered basic skills that every participant in a literate society should have the opportunity to develop.

But what if music lessons don't take time away from other subjects, but rather strengthen basic skills, such that it's easier to learn math, reading, and writing? What if even a cursory musical education has long-lasting benefits, giving kids an edge when it comes to many other life skills?

Or, put another way, what if there was an intervention that could sharpen kids' executive-function skills, help them set and meet their goals, equip them with a growth mindset—a belief that effort is the path to mastery—and sharpen their ability to multitask and make decisions? What if this intervention was also fun, something that the kids enjoyed, and that made it more likely that they would come to school? What if setting aside thirty minutes a week for an enjoyable activity that boosted classroom morale and social cohesion also improved students' performance on standardized tests?

DISTINGUISHING NEAR AND FAR TRANSFER

That's what a musical education can do, when it's most effective. Of course, there are many different approaches to musical training—from a strict conservatory setting, pairing lessons with music theory, to freewheeling improvisation, experimentation, and informal experiences. Some music teachers are better than others, and there are approaches that make music classes aversive rather than appetitive.

But several decades of research now point to the potential of individual music lessons or group participatory music making to be this magical intervention, the tide that lifts all boats, when it comes to its effects on learning in general.

Regardless of the approach, musical training involves some development of listening skills, fine motor coordination, and timing. And so it shouldn't come as a surprise that these skills improve with training. We call this *transfer*—when skills from one domain, say piano lessons, transfer to another, say penmanship. And transfer can be near—when the skills overlap quite a bit, or are similar to each other, as in playing the piano and writing in cursive—or far, when the overlap is less obvious, or the skills seem quite different, as in drumming and vocabulary.

Not surprisingly, near transfer of musical training is relatively easy to document, with studies showing that kids with musical training are better than their untrained peers in terms of pitch and rhythm discrimination, melody recognition, and learning new sequences of actions using the same muscles that are important for their instrument. That is, kids who take piano lessons would find it easier to tap out a new sequence of letters on a keyboard, for example, since coordinating their fingers is a skill developed in both cases.

But as few as two years of group music classes also helps kids distinguish speech sounds from other noises, as we've already mentioned. And the earlier the training starts, the more they benefit. With ongoing training, the ability to remember spoken words improves as do other phonological skills, such as rhyming and reading. In one study, five- to seven-year-old kids who are better at clapping in time to a rhythm, a skill that develops with musical training, showed neurophysiological responses that signal better literacy skills, including the ability to process information more quickly, recognize speech sounds, read words, and spell and use grammar accurately.

These kinds of far transfer effects aren't consistent across studies, because of the limitations of cross-sectional studies and the challenges of longitudinal research, as I've mentioned. But several studies have found far transfer in a variety of cognitive functions once a child has trained for at least two years. In these studies there is evidence that longer-term musical training improves spatial, verbal, and mathematical performance, in addition to accelerating general gains in IQ.

One of the most common IQ measures in school-aged children is the Wechsler Intelligence Scale for Children (WISC-III), and children who have taken more than a year of music lessons tend to score higher than their untrained peers. But once again it's hard to control for issues of access and even genetics, as parents who sign their kids up for music classes might themselves have more resources, both financial and otherwise. Two well-designed studies by Glenn Schellenberg, however, have shown that music lessons seem to correlate with better IQ scores in six- to eleven-year-olds even after controlling for family income and parent education. These effects are small but seem to be long-lasting.

Typically, the research shows that kids who already take or have taken lessons are compared to those who haven't, or kids are assigned to an experimental group and given lessons, and then their improvement on tests over time is compared with either kids who are not given any additional activities, or who take lessons or play sports that are not musical in nature, such as drama classes.

In these studies we find solid evidence of near transfer—skills that rely on improved listening, or auditory processing, or fine motor coordination tend to show benefits—but usually far transfer is absent. But even in these relatively short-duration studies, the seeds of change have been planted. Brain imaging before and after music lessons tracks how musical training shapes brain development in as little as fifteen months in primary school children.

To address some of these limitations and to gauge whether the benefits of music lessons on intelligence are also present in different cultures, Hossein Kaviani and colleagues randomly assigned sixty Iranian preschool children, age five or six, into two groups: kids in the experimental group received weekly music lessons for three months, and their scores on the Tehran-Stanford-Binet Intelligence Scale before and after those twelve weeks were compared with those of kids who were not attending music lessons, but who were matched for sex, age, and their mother's educational level. The researchers found that the kids in the experimental group showed bigger gains on the intelligence test, on subscales that assessed short-term memory and verbal reasoning. Both of these skills are part of a larger set of executive functioning skills, and there's ample evidence that musical training enhances executive functioning in general.

EXECUTIVE FUNCTIONING SKILLS:
A MEDIATOR OF THE EFFECTS
OF MUSICAL TRAINING ON COGNITIVE
AND SOCIAL DEVELOPMENT

Executive functioning refers to a set of cognitive skills and abilities that underlie many other aspects of thinking and behavior, such as holding multiple options in mind at the same time, shifting directed attention, planning, and inhibiting distractions. They are broadly separable into four categories: inhibitory control, including self-control of behavior, such as not saying the inappropriate thought that enters your head; interference control, such as staying focused on a task; working memory, or what you can hold in your conscious mind at the same time; and cognitive flexibility, such as shifting how you think or behave when you learn something new.

Each of these categories is associated with musical training, such that musicians often show improvement over time on executive functioning tests compared with nonmusicians, and researchers have argued that the gains we see on IQ tests are mediated by improvements in executive functioning. (For an alternative perspective, see Glenn Schellenberg's "Examining the Association Between Music Lessons and Intelligence.")

In one study, for example, children in primary school were exposed to either music training or enhanced natural science lessons. After eighteen months of the intervention, the music students outperformed their science-trained counterparts on measures of working memory, a "core" cognitive function that can affect performance in a number of different domains, from mathematics to creative writing. This improvement in working memory might help explain why practicing a musical instrument can lead to better performance on general intelligence tests.

And although musical training in early childhood seems to capitalize on the plasticity of little kids' brains, supersizing its effects, there is evidence that even in middle and high school, kids benefit from music programs. For example, one study across six Maryland school districts found that middle school kids who were enrolled in instrumental or choral music programs scored higher, on average, on algebra tests, with the largest benefits seen in Black students. Another study, this time conducted on Canadian high schoolers, found that music program participation correlated with higher academic achievement and better grades in eleventh and twelfth grades. It seems as though time spent in music class is time well spent, benefiting performance on the core curriculum, rather than impeding it. And a large-scale longitudinal study of more than twenty thousand American high school students supports this idea: Kenneth Elpus found that students who took music classes were just as likely to get into college, receive scholarships, and choose STEM (science, technology, engineering, and math) majors as their nonmusical counterparts, even when those counterparts took additional academic subjects to enhance their education.

COME FOR BAND PRACTICE, STAY FOR MATH

And if academic gains weren't sufficient to justify the costs of music programs, there's a U.S. study in which teenagers who participated in performing arts programs were less likely to engage in risky behaviors, especially alcohol use, than their athletically engaged peers. They were also more likely to report liking high school and had a higher GPA in the twelfth grade. Long-term follow-up showed that they were also more likely to still be attending college at age twenty-one.

As another case in point, an enhanced music program in Nashville public schools seemed to increase attendance and graduation rates for students who had participated in it, according to a 2013 report. The students themselves listed the music program as one reason they showed up to school, and also said they felt happier, less stressed, and more accomplished. Participating students also had higher GPAs and other test scores, and fewer reports of disciplinary action, compared with their peers. In a public school district in Virginia, the same gains in attendance and improvements in student conduct distinguished kids in music programs from their nonmusician peers. And a similar study of Chicago public schools also found that schools with music programs had higher attendance rates and higher test scores and GPAs, even when socioeconomic status was controlled for.

Teachers and music educators aren't the only ones to notice improvements in behavior when kids engage with music. In another chapter in this book, an ambitious in-depth study of the impact of the Youth Orchestra LA program, Heart of Los Angeles, on kids from a diversity of socioeconomic backgrounds, has tracked the neurological, cognitive, and behavioral changes that distinguish kids in the program from their peers. The researchers also surveyed their parents. And after only two years of the intervention, parents themselves reported that their kids were less aggressive and hyperactive and more emotionally stable. These observations were not made by parents of kids in the control group.

These kinds of programs, many based on the El Sistema approach pioneered by Maestro José Antonio Abreu in Venezuela in the 1970s, have blossomed in North America, with El Sistema USA now counting 118 member organizations across the United States and Canada. Abreu recognized the power of music to enhance social development, of both the children themselves and their communities. With this power in mind, member programs target the most vulnerable among us—those with the fewest resources and hence the greatest need—and use music to drive social change.

Across the Atlantic in the United Kingdom, high school students have told researchers that the social aspect of music making was what they loved most. Specifically, they reported that playing in an ensemble boosted their self-confidence, fostered a sense of belonging, and taught them the value of cooperation and compromise and how to be a team player.

CONCLUSION

Music connects us, brings us joy, and helps us navigate our emotions and those of others. Our brains tune into music even before we are born, and music kick-starts the development of fundamental human skills like language, empathy, and attachment.

But it also enhances our executive functioning skills, like paying attention, setting and meeting goals, inhibiting distractions, and delaying gratification. In short, the skills that help us get things done.

Instead of taking time and resources away from the core curriculum, music programs in schools motivate kids to attend, and drive up graduation rates, GPAs, and good behavior.

Every child has a right to a musical education—to learn the multipurpose tool that we've been using for myriad reasons for as long as we've lived in social groups.

State of the Art: National Statistics on Music in America's Schools

KENNETH ELPUS, PhD

Professor of Music Education and
Associate Director of the School of Music
University of Maryland, College Park

S upporters of public education in the United States often contend that "equality of opportunity" is one of our nation's most important social goals for schooling. The idea that each child, regardless of family background, should be afforded the same opportunities to learn and excel as every other child is compelling and uniquely American. This notion has long roots in music education as well. As far back as 1923, Karl Gerhkens, then president of the organization now known as the National Association for Music Education, declared that its slogan would be "Music for every child; every child for music." My decade-plus of work as a quantitative, statistical social science researcher in music education has centered around understanding how close the music education profession has come to achieving this ideal.

As is evident in many of the chapters in this volume, there are tangible social and academic benefits to the habits of mind, ways of thinking, and aesthetic engagement that are promoted by studying music. The intrinsic value to students of music learning is recognized in the Every Student Succeeds Act, the most recently enacted American federal elementary and secondary education law, which includes music specifically in its list of subjects that make up the "well-rounded curriculum" that public schools must deliver.

Although the value of music to American education has broad public support, growing evidence for positive benefits in the education research literature, and a legislative mandate from Congress, access to music education in schools is far from universal. Even in schools where music is available, there are some important disparities in music enrollment that researchers have begun to document and uncover.

In this brief chapter we will tour the statistical research exploring which students have access to music education, which students choose to participate in school music, and how music students fare when they move from public schools to colleges and universities.

WHAT SCHOOLS OFFER MUSIC?

The most recent data on the availability of music in the schools compiled by the U.S. Department of Education are becoming a bit outdated. Collected in the 2009–2010 school year, the National Center for Education Statistics (NCES) reported that music was available in 94 percent of public elementary schools and 91 percent of public secondary schools. However, it's important to do a little digging beyond those headline numbers. An elementary school was considered to have a music program available even if that program provided students with as little as one twenty-minute music class per week. Elementary schools would also "count" in the NCES report if the music class wasn't taught by a certified music teacher. As you might expect, the 6 percent of elementary schools that didn't provide even that small amount of music instruction disproportionately served students from poorer households. The situation at secondary schools in the NCES report was similar: the 9 percent of secondary schools without curricular music programs taught more students who lived in areas of concentrated poverty.

To get a more recent picture of the situation for music in American public schools, I led a research project funded by the National Endowment for the Arts and published in the journal *Arts Education Policy Review*. Using a nationally representative sample of American high schools, I found that 74 percent of high schools in the United States—including traditional public schools, charter high schools, and private high schools—offered at least one music course. The *kind* of school made a big difference: traditional public high schools (78 percent) and Catholic high schools (80 percent) were considerably more likely to offer music than were charter high schools (an astonishingly small 37 percent) or non-Catholic private schools (57 percent). Not surprisingly, schools serving students with lower socioeconomic means were less likely to offer even one music course: only 58 percent of schools with the highest levels of students eligible for free or reduced-price lunch offered any music courses. The only other characteristic that made a difference was school size (that is, the number of students enrolled). Even when accounting for socioeconomic differences, larger schools were considerably more likely to offer music courses.

Other school characteristics did not seem to be related to whether a school offered music. I found no differences in music availability at schools in rural, suburban, or urban locales. The region of the country didn't matter either. Nor did the proportion of students of color who attended the school. School scheduling (i.e., more traditional shorter class periods per day versus fewer, longer "blocks" per day) was also not relevant.

WHICH STUDENTS TAKE MUSIC IN SECONDARY SCHOOLS?

Because not all schools are equally likely to offer music, it stands to reason that not all students with access might end up choosing to take music classes. In most states taking at least some music in elementary school is a state requirement, so the research in this area focuses on middle and high schools, where music is most often an elective.

In 2016 the final Nation's Report Card in the Arts results showed how well American eighth graders performed on an assessment of music and visual art. Using its underlying data, I conducted a research study designed to understand which middle schoolers were taking courses in band, choir, orchestra, or general music. Band and choir were popular, with orchestra less so: 17 percent of eighth graders were in band, 16 percent were in choir, and 5 percent were in orchestra. Overall, 63 percent of eighth graders took at least one type of music class, leaving about 37 percent of eighth graders not taking any music in school.

Middle school ensemble students—those in band, choir, or orchestra—were more likely to be female (because choir is 70:30 female to male), more likely to be white, and more likely to have higher socioeconomic means than their nonmusic or general-music-only counterparts. Students who enrolled only in a general music class and not in an ensemble were more likely to be male, less likely to be white, more likely to be eligible for free or reduced-price lunch, and more likely to be receiving special education services than were nonmusic students or ensemble students. Troublingly, these results suggest that special needs students, poorer students, and students of color may be systematically prevented from enrolling in band, choir, or orchestra.

The situation in American high schools is quite similar to that in middle schools. My research colleague Carlos Abril and I investigated who takes high school music courses for a study we published in the *Journal of Research in Music Education*. We found that 24 percent of high schoolers had enrolled in at least one year of band, choir, or orchestra before graduating. Choir was the most popular high school class (13 percent), followed by band (11 percent), and orchestra in a distant third (2 percent).

Certain student characteristics were related to the probability that a student would be in an *instrumental* music ensemble. There was a sharp disparity by race/ethnicity: white students were overrepresented and Latinx (Hispanic) students were underrepresented. Students from higher socioeconomic statuses were overrepresented, while poorer students were underrepresented. Students whose parents had higher educational attainment were overrepresented. Band and orchestra kids also had better prior academic achievement than kids who didn't take part in those ensembles—an important consideration if we want to fairly compare academic outcomes of instrumental music and noninstrumental music students.

Importantly, and with one significant exception, choir kids mostly looked like everybody—we found no student characteristic to be related to enrollment in choir, *except* for birth-assigned sex. Just as in middle school, female students in choir outnumbered their male peers by a 70:30 ratio. But the racial/ethnic makeup, the socioeconomic backgrounds, the parental education levels, and the prior academic achievement of choir students and nonmusic students mostly looked the same. Our results might suggest that singing is somehow more attractive to a broader population of students—maybe because it takes less economic investment or less before-high-school experience to begin—than are the instrumental ensembles. It's interesting food for thought.

CONCLUSION

If we believe, as the research evidence suggests, that music making is an important and beneficial part of schooling, then determining who has access to music in school and who takes part in music when it is offered can help us target our advocacy efforts to push for more equity of opportunity.

Considered together, the research evidence suggests that students of color, students from poorer households, and students with parents who have lower levels of education are missing out on school music—especially in band and orchestra classes. These "missing" students might have been prevented from taking music—because no program is available at their school, because an adult has steered them to another choice, or because they didn't start an instrument earlier. It's also possible that these students might not be interested in the kinds of music made and studied in schools.

Exactly why students might be missing from school music programs remains an open question for researchers. Getting those answers can help music teachers improve their teaching and help schools create opportunities for all students to enjoy the benefits that studying and making music provide.

Rhythm & Rhyme: Supporting Young Children and Families with Musical Play

SARA BECK, PhD

Assistant Professor of Psychological Science, Randolph College

MIRIAM LENSE, PhD

Assistant Professor of Otolaryngology, Vanderbilt University Medical Center

She was smaller than I thought she would be. Even though she'd been inside my body for almost nine months, I somehow pictured a plump, happy seven-month-old in there instead of the red-faced, screaming newborn I now rocked endlessly through the dark nights of the long winter. But one night, in a desperate state of sleeplessness and failed efforts to shush, swaddle, and sway, I discovered something she responded to, something I always had with me. It was my voice. The same one she had been hearing on the inside for the last trimester. If I whispered to her quietly, with a hint of a melody tucked inside my words, her eyes sought mine. If I repeated the melodic words, her crying paused. We connected. She settled.

It was a revelation to me in my new role as a parent, but scientists have been interested in infant-directed speech for decades, recognizing that infants across cultures elicit and respond to a specific vocal and linguistic approach from adults. This approach is characterized by higher and more variable pitch, rhythmicity and repetition, elongated vowels, and greater emphasis on word boundaries than is typical of adult-directed speech. For example, a parent engaging in infant-directed speech with his or her baby uses a loving tone of voice and emphasizes the capitalized syllables when saying, *"Good MORning! Did you sleep WELL? Are you ready to PLAY?!"* by holding these syllables for longer duration, pausing after them, and raising the volume and pitch of his or her voice. Infant-directed speech supports early social engagement, as well as infants' language and communicative development. Parents all over the world speak in this characteristic way to their infants (with some variations cross-culturally), and they also habitually engage in a related interaction: infant-directed singing. Infant-directed singing shares many features with infant-directed speech, but it has additional characteristics, like repeating melodic structures and a temporally regular beat, as in the classic children's songs "Itsy Bitsy Spider" and "Twinkle, Twinkle, Little Star." Recent research explores the value of parent-child musical interaction for children, parents, and families, and a growing body of evidence suggests that there are social, emotional, and communicative benefits to parents and children making music together. It turns out that parents don't have to be trained or experienced musicians to make music meaningfully with their children.

We are developmental (Beck) and clinical (Lense) psychologists in the field of music cognition, and our research programs investigate the use and value of infant-directed singing and parent-child musical interactions for children, parents, and families of neurotypical children and children with

neurodevelopmental differences such as autism spectrum disorder (ASD).*
In this chapter we'll explore the mechanisms by which early musical experiences may impact social, emotional, and communicative skills in children
and parents and share stories from families who have participated in our
research over the years. We'll also consider how music can be harnessed for
therapeutic purposes to support children and families. We use different
genders/identities in our examples (e.g., mother, daughter) but the concepts
discussed are universal across these forms of caregiver-child relationships.

SHARED CAREGIVER-CHILD MUSICAL INTERACTION: WHAT ARE THE ACTIVE INGREDIENTS?

You might be thinking, *OK, but you've never heard me sing. It goes beyond a
lack of training! I can't even carry a tune.* Lots of people believe this about
themselves. But not being a pitch-perfect singer is fine! Pitch accuracy is not
a prerequisite for achieving a successful musical interaction with a child.
What do these interactions look like? Picture a father holding his nine-
month-old baby, speaking to her in soft and loving tones, making eye contact. The father's voice is slightly higher in pitch than it typically is when
speaking to friends or older children, and he is speaking more slowly, emphasizing each individual word. *We are going to the playground*, he says to her.
The playground is so much fun! He is engaging in infant-directed speech, automatically adjusting his communication to meet the developmental needs
of his infant. Now imagine he continues interacting with her as he carries
her around the apartment, getting her dressed for the outing. His words take
on the tune of "I'm a Little Teapot," a song he knows she likes. He sings:

> *Going to the playground, me and you*
> *Here comes a hat and here comes a shoe.*
> *When we're at the playground, what will we do*
> *We'll have some fun just me and you*

---

*We use both identity-first (i.e., "autistic children") and person-first (i.e., "individuals with autism") language, in line with preferences expressed by autistic self-advocates, caregivers, and professionals, and
American Psychological Association guidelines regarding language and disability.

Her eyes are meeting his, and they are both smiling. He nods his head and bounces his daughter on his hips with the beat implied by his sung melody. He repeats his song as they continue getting ready, and she claps her hands. This particular father is not much of a singer, but it doesn't matter. He and his daughter are having a rich exchange involving joint attention (look at this shoe!), shared intention (we are singing a song and getting ready together!), and predictable word sounds that repeat and rhyme in predictable patterns. Additionally, there is a spirit of play in their musical interaction, and this air of fun gives a positive emotional tone to the interaction, which is already shaped by the musical elements of the tune the father is singing (it's in a major mode with a peppy beat). These elements are the active ingredients of musical interactions between children and caregivers—not precise pitch accuracy or ability to play an instrument. No training necessary.

SHARED MUSICAL INTERACTION: WHY DOES THE MAGIC HAPPEN?

Musical engagement between a caregiver and a child benefits from the potency of the music itself as well as the social interaction inherent in sharing a musical experience. Infants' preferences for musical and rhythmic stimuli begin even before they are born. In one study, mothers read a nursery rhyme story repeatedly to their baby during the third trimester of pregnancy. When the fetus was played new recordings of a female stranger reading the familiar nursery rhyme or an unfamiliar nursery rhyme, researchers observed a decreased fetal heart rate to the familiar nursery rhyme, indicating that the fetus was orienting (or attending) to this story their mother had exposed them to. After a baby is born, researchers can test if newborns show preferences for these prenatal auditory experiences using a nonnutritive sucking paradigm: Newborns are given a pacifier and are played different audio recordings. If they change how they suck on the pacifier in order to hear one recording more than another, this indicates a preference. Studies conducted in the 1980s indicated that newborns in the first days of life preferred their mother's voice over a stranger's, as well as stories and music they'd been exposed to in utero, revealing that infants are shaped by these early auditory experiences. One mother in our studies recounted how she used to sing *The Mary Tyler Moore Show* theme song to her daughter when she was in the neonatal intensive care unit, receiving specialized care after being born prematurely. She notes that two years later, this is still the song that calms her daughter the most.

Indeed, emotion and arousal regulation is the main reason people of all ages engage with music. Adults all over the world use music to regulate their own moods and set the stage for different activities; think of a workout playlist guaranteed to motivate your run, or a dinner-prep playlist full of mellow wind-down vibes guaranteed to clear your head after a long workday. Without specifically trying, you have probably selected music for each playlist with particular features; your workout playlist likely features songs with a faster tempo and more upbeat feel created through a more salient (or noticeable) beat or rhythmic structure, as well as melodic and harmonic structures linked to happy or pleasant emotions. Even young children reliably associate faster tempos and major (as opposed to minor) melodies and chords with happiness, and cross-cultural research demonstrates that young adults from countries as different as India and Finland report using music in their daily lives to create a range of positive emotional experiences. The structural, rhythmic, and melodic characteristics of even the simplest children's melodies can be potent mood regulators.

A mother's own singing is particularly effective at soothing infants, even more so than her speaking voice. When mothers sing lullabies to their infants, it impacts the infants' production of stress hormones like cortisol and reduces the activity of their sympathetic nervous system (the part of the nervous system responsible for preparing for fight or flight). This is why some caregivers use songs to help with the "witching hour" and naturally use lullabies to help their child go to sleep. As one mother of a little boy told us, "We sing calm songs before bed every night, and when we added this to our bedtime routine, it was the first thing that resulted in successful attempts in putting my son to sleep within fifteen minutes."

Singing to an infant not only soothes the baby but also regulates the parent's emotions. Think about how your body feels when singing to your child, whether it be a calming lullaby or a favorite upbeat musical tune. When a caregiver sings to an infant, it reduces her own production of cortisol and regulates her sympathetic nervous system activity. Caregivers express the greater positive emotion they feel during singing in their facial expressions—smiling more when singing versus speaking to their infants. As we often share with families, it's tough to "sing angry," so when singing and musical games are part of routine parent-child interaction like cleaning up or brushing teeth, it helps to transform even the most mundane task into interactive, joint play.

Singing with a child also provides a rich multisensory experience for them. When you think about engaging in musical play with a child, you might be tempted to focus on the auditory elements like the sound of your voice and your ability to keep a steady beat and reproduce a familiar melody. But parent-child musical interactions are inherently multisensory, not just auditory. Think back to the father we imagined singing to his daughter while they dressed for an outing: He sits her down to put on her socks, positioning himself in front of her and lowering his face to be in her field of view. As he sings to her, he opens his eyes wide, unconsciously timing the movements of his face with the rhythm of his singing. Infants are highly sensitive to the synchronization of cues across multiple senses—they hear their father's voice, but they also see his mouth move and his facial expressions change predictably as he sings. They feel the rhythm in his gait as he walks around getting ready, baby bouncing to the beat on his hip. These multiple sensory components work together to keep the baby's attention on her father as they playfully get ready to go outside.

As children develop and make increasing attempts to participate vocally and rhythmically, the experience becomes richer still. In order to coordinate singing, clapping, or movement along with another person, we have to engage in a complex process of mapping sound—both our partner's and our own—to our own motor plans in order to approach any kind of synchrony or interpersonal coordination. In other words, we have to listen and match our movements to what we hear. Researchers refer to this as auditory-motor mapping, and it allows us to synchronize our own voices or movements to an external stimulus—a process known as entrainment. Moving to music provides one of the clearest examples of entrainment, because the regularly occurring, predictable beat that underlies most music provides a ready-made signal for synchronizing our behaviors. It turns out that entrainment to the beat of music is actually a pretty sophisticated skill that involves mentally representing the beat and predicting when it will occur. Imagine a concert where the audience spontaneously begins clapping along with the beat of the music. While it's true that everyone won't clap exactly together, people actually tend to clap faster than they should, in essence anticipating the predicted next beat. Some of our closest primate relatives respond to a beat-based entrainment task in a completely different way; rather than predicting where the beat will fall (and sometimes rushing as a result), they tend to wait for the beat and then respond. This is a qualitatively different process than the predictive auditory-motor mapping that humans do, even as children. Throughout the animal kingdom, only a few species are able to accomplish spontaneous beat-based entrainment to music.

Rhythmic entrainment occurs not only with large body movements such as dancing or clapping together but also with subtle behaviors used as part of social interactions. Eye contact is one of the earliest markers of social engagement and connection to another person, and parents and babies habitually use eye contact to connect with and communicate with each other. In one of our studies led by Miriam Lense, infants watched videos of caregivers engaging them with infant-directed singing. Infants' attention to the singers' eyes varied in time with the rhythmic structure of the singing, with increased eye gaze at the metrically strong beats. When we disrupted the rhythmic structure of the singing so that it was no longer predictable, infants were less able to coordinate the timing of their gaze. Shared rhythmic experiences like infant-directed singing may support social bonding by helping parents and children coordinate their social behaviors with each other.

Entrainment between social partners represents a type of interpersonal synchrony that is uniquely rhythmic, if not overtly musical. And interpersonal synchrony fosters prosocial behavior—behavior that is beneficial to others—and bonding in a vast range of contexts: from community choirs to pairs of children in synchronous swings, people are more helpful to their partners, more likely to coordinate their behaviors, and feel more connected to each other after moving in synchrony. This prosocial effect of movement synchrony begins in infancy. In a series of studies led by Drs. Laura Cirelli and Laurel Trainor, fourteen-month-old infants worn in baby carriers were bounced in or out of synchrony with an unfamiliar adult while listening to music. Subsequently, the infants who had bounced in synchrony with the adult were more likely to help that adult by spontaneously picking up items she couldn't reach than the infants who were bounced out of synchrony. Researchers are not entirely sure how interpersonal synchrony functions as a mechanism, but some believe that auditory-motor coupling across individuals blurs the perceptual boundaries we have between ourselves and others; we can't differentiate the sound of our own clapping hands from sounds made by our musical partners. Perhaps this is why we feel closer to people we've synchronized with in some capacity. As one six-year-old shared with us about why he enjoyed musical games like dance parties with his parents and siblings, "When we dance together, it shows that we love each other."

Infants and toddlers don't have the motor skills to precisely synchronize their body movements to the beat of music, but that doesn't stop them from bopping along to it, especially when there's a strong beat in the song. Infants move more to music with a beat compared with sounds that have rhythm but lack a beat (like infant-directed speech). Having a social partner also helps young children to synchronize their movements: in one study, preschoolers tapped on a drum to a metronome by themselves or with an unfamiliar adult; the preschoolers were more accurate at tapping to the beat

when there was someone tapping along with them. And even though young children don't have the skills to time their movements precisely to the musical beat, moving to music still has prosocial effects for them. In a study led by Sara Beck, preschoolers who participated in a musical play activity showed more joint movement with an unfamiliar adult compared to those who participated in a nonmusical play routine, and the children in the musical play activity were also more likely to help and share with the adult afterward. In other words, just *trying* to move along with another person created positive prosocial effects, even though most preschoolers weren't able to synchronize their movements very accurately. This effect has also been seen between children, who are more likely to cooperate and help each other after musical play that involves joint movement or synchronized movement.

MUSIC IN THERAPEUTIC CONTEXTS: ASSESSMENT, INTERVENTION, AND PARENT-CHILD INTERACTIONS

As musical interests and skills emerge in early childhood and are integral to early developmental experiences, there is increasing research on whether music can be used as part of assessment and intervention for children with or at elevated likelihood for neurodevelopmental disorders. We'll provide two examples here—one in which we focus on rhythm and its role across neurodivergent conditions, and a more focused discussion of how musical experiences may naturally be incorporated into therapy (including to support parents) for young children on the autism spectrum.

Rhythm and Neurodevelopmental Differences

Neurodevelopmental differences affect millions of children and include relatively common neurodivergent conditions such as ADHD, ASD, dyslexia, and developmental language disorder. While different disorders may have different causes and specific profiles of primary areas of strengths and weaknesses, there are substantial comorbidities (i.e., co-occurring conditions) across conditions. For example, ADHD commonly occurs in children with speech and language disorders. Some behavioral symptoms are also frequently shared across different neurodevelopmental conditions, and recent evidence suggests that atypical rhythm processing is one of these common areas of difficulty. Note that when we discuss rhythm in this context, we are referring to a broad range of tasks and skills related to rhythm and timing. For example, conversational turn-taking is related to timing and can vary across individuals: How long are the pauses between what one person says and another person's response? Do two conversing individuals match the timing of their conversational turns? How individuals coordinate their turn-taking timing turns out to be predictive of several cognitive, linguistic, and social outcomes. A more traditionally musical measure pertaining to rhythm is beat perception and continuation; individuals vary in their ability to detect, internally represent, synchronize with, and reproduce the beat of an auditory stimulus. Across a range of neurodevelopmental conditions, consistent and precise synchronization to beat-based auditory stimuli is frequently a challenge. A recent hypothesis emerging from our colleague Dr. Reyna Gordon's work is the Atypical Rhythm Risk Hypothesis, which predicts that atypical rhythm in a variety of contexts may be associated with increased likelihood of having a neurodivergent condition.

The idea of someday using atypical task performance on rhythm assessments as part of screenings to identify children at increased likelihood of developing neurodevelopmental conditions is exciting, particularly given that diagnosis of many of these disorders is often delayed. To move closer to this goal, some researchers are advocating for what they call "transdiagnostic investigations" into rhythm across different domains and conditions. In other words, if we can increase our knowledge of the neural and behavioral mechanisms by which particular rhythmic deficits relate to particular conditions and across conditions, we may be able to predict who has vulnerabilities for challenges in these domains and design more effective interventions to support these individuals. One example of an intervention that seems to support rhythm-related cognitive skills is called rhythmic priming. During rhythmic priming, exposure to a regular beat-based rhythm (as opposed to an irregular rhythm) facilitates children's performance on a subsequent language task, and this finding holds for typically developing children and those with dyslexia and developmental language disorder.

Use of Music to Support Autistic Children and Their Families

A two-year-old boy recently diagnosed as being on the autism spectrum, Peter has difficulty communicating and rarely plays interactively with others. Peter's attention to others tends to be very brief, but his mother notices that when she sings to him, especially his current favorite song, "Wheels on the Bus," he tends to stay involved in the play for a longer time and makes more eye contact with her. She begins incorporating the song into their play-time, pushing a school bus toy back and forth and around the room in rhythm with the song. At other times she and Peter sit across from each other and she sings "Wheels on the Bus" with its familiar gestures, rolling her arms for the wheels and honking an imaginary horn. She helps Peter make the gestures, too, practicing them one verse at a time until he learns to do them independently and they have a new shared game that delights them both. Sometimes his mother pauses during the song to see what Peter will do. The first few times she tries it, Peter doesn't seem to respond. But then Peter begins to look at her face when she pauses and to spin his arms to make the wheels gesture himself. When she responds by continuing to sing, Peter smiles at her, and they continue the activity.

Given the emerging importance of rhythmic differences underlying many neurodivergent conditions and music's power to support children's behavior and parent-child interactions during early childhood more generally, increasing attention is being given to how music may be used therapeutically for children on the autism spectrum. Autistic individuals have challenges in social interaction and communication, as well as differences in sensory and play behaviors. Early interventions for young autistic children focus on building children's social and communication skills such as eye contact, gestures, imitation, play, and spoken communication. Development of these skills is grounded in the interactions between two partners, sometimes called social transactions.

It turns out that clinicians and caregivers may incorporate songs and musical play into both standard behavioral and music-based autism intervention approaches for young children. These approaches build upon early childhood musical activities naturally involving many "active ingredients" of social interactions—like helping individuals regulate their emotions, share attention, and move together in predictable ways. Since musical activities are enjoyable for many autistic children, songs, musical games, and finger-plays can be a motivating platform for interacting with others and embedding therapeutic strategies. As one parent of a three-year-old son with autism described to us, music is his "way of letting us come into his world and share part of that."

The predictability of musical games and songs is likely one ingredient that makes them appealing in intervention activities. We discussed rhythmic entrainment earlier, and how, for example, the presence of a steady beat helps us to develop expectations for when events will occur and to time our own behaviors (like clapping to the beat). Many autistic individuals have difficulty with rhythm and timing during social interactions, in which the rhythms fluctuate (for example, the back-and-forth timing of taking turns in conversation). But autistic individuals often perform equivalently to their age-matched peers without autism on certain types of musical rhythm tasks in which there is a predictable rhythmic structure or pattern.

How can this be used in early interventions? When Peter's mother sings "Wheels on the Bus" with him, their interaction benefits from the familiarity of the nursery rhyme—Peter knows the song will repeat over and over (the repeating refrains)—but also provides opportunities for flexibility within the structure (such as from the different verses, singing at different tempos, or incorporating new gestures). The rhythm and melody of the song are predictable, so Peter has expectations for what will happen (the horn will beep) and when it will occur (on the next beat). When his mother pauses at the end of a phrase to see if Peter requests for the song to continue— through his eye gaze, gestures, or vocalizations—his mother is naturally using a powerful therapeutic strategy called communication temptations, pausing during a routine to give Peter an opportunity to communicate with her and then reinforcing (or rewarding) his communication by continuing the enjoyable activity.

Another area of difficulty for many autistic children is imitation, which is a building block of communication and language development. Imitation is a form of social and emotional exchange similar to the back-and-forth nature of communication, and also helps children to learn new skills, such as how to play with different toys or the meaning of different gestures. Imitating a child shows them that you are attending to, interested in, and approve of what they are doing. When using the therapeutic strategy of contingent imitation, the child's play partner (parent, therapist, peer) follows the child's play by imitating the child's actions, gestures, and sounds in order to increase the child's attention to them and demonstrate social reciprocity. Contingent imitation occurs very naturally during musical play— musical play partners may imitate and expand upon each other's gestures during song routines like "If You're Happy and You Know It" or "Baby Shark." Musical instruments can also be used as part of this practice: copying a child in making musical sounds as they play a xylophone or shake a maraca can help call their attention to the social aspects built into musical play.

The auditory-motor mapping that occurs during musical games may be another therapeutic component. In Auditory Motor Mapping Therapy, adapted and developed by Dr. Gottfried Schlaug and colleagues for autistic children, children link motor movements with speech by tapping on tuned drums in time with sung (or intoned) speech to support speech production. Preliminary studies comparing this therapy with a nonmusical speech repetition therapy are promising for increasing children's production of specific speech sounds (e.g., consonants and vowels). Another team of researchers, including Drs. Megha Sharda and Krista Hyde, conducted one of the first investigations of neural activity during music therapy for autistic children.

Compared to children in a nonmusical play therapy, children who participated in the music therapy had increased connectivity between auditory and motor regions of the brain at the end of therapy.

Outside of individual behavioral or music therapy, music is also often used during group and community activities. For example, think of circle time in a preschool classroom, where children may sing a hello song and call out to other children by name. There are also some integrated community-based parent-child music programs, such as the Serenade Program, which we developed, or the Sing&Grow early intervention program in Australia. These provide a shared community experience while also teaching and practicing therapeutic strategies within parent-child musical activities. A parent who participated in the Serenade Program when her son was three and a half years old reflected back a few years later about how pairing music with various activities during their daily life continues to support her son's engagement and learning:

> I learned that when you have a child who loves music, you can turn any activity into a song and get that interaction from your child. Just the other day he was in a bad mood and didn't want to come play with me or his

sister, so we started singing and dancing, and he slowly worked his way
over to us and began playing with us. He has now started taking the tunes
of songs and changing the words to make his own songs. When we have
something that has a long wait, like a car ride, singing songs can help keep
him calm and distracted from how long he is having to wait. He is learning
to spell words right now; when there is a harder word, like purple, we add
a little singing and clapping to help him remember how to spell the words.
I guess I never realized how much you could really use music for things until
we took this class.

Of course, every child is unique, and specific intervention approaches and strategies will vary depending on a child's developmental level, interests, and goals. Regardless of use within therapy, for many families of young children with autism and other neurodevelopmental conditions, the most important role for music and singing is as an enjoyable and shared form of play and social connection. In describing her two-year-old autistic son's relationship with music, one mother said, "He dances, and I feel so much joy seeing him so happy." Another parent of a not yet two-year-old described starting a lullaby routine with her child: "I make it a point to do this at least once a day with my son. Honestly, these are the times I feel most connected to him. It's like he and I are tuned into the same channel. . . . The feeling is truly breathtaking."

BOTTLING THE BEAT: HOW TO CREATE A MUSICALLY RICH HOME ENVIRONMENT

The research is clear: there are a host of benefits to caregivers, children, and families of intentionally sharing music on a regular basis. Paying attention to how your own child responds to musical play is critical; just like adults, children have musical preferences. So what songs should you use with your children? There's no right answer to this question. Simply put, you should use music that you and your child find engaging—whether it's hip-hop, musical theater, or folk music. The simple melodies and strong rhythmic structure as well as the movements associated with nursery rhymes like "Twinkle, Twinkle, Little Star" or "Itsy Bitsy Spider" have made them timeless classics for generations of children. But children also enjoy music that has a social value: infants in the first and second years of life attend longer and are more likely to help new people who sing the same songs that their parents sing to them. So sharing songs that are meaningful to you is a way to build family traditions with your child. For years we have both had a nightly ritual with our own children of singing the same handful of 1970s folk-rock tunes that we heard from our moms as children. "Love Is a Rose" by Neil Young and "Will You Still Love Me Tomorrow" by Carole King work beautifully as lullabies, as do most songs sung in the dark with a sleepy child!

Regardless of the specific song selection, everyday *active* and *informal* family music activities—singing songs together, family dance parties, sharing favorite songs, and attending music events in the community—provide powerful moments of social connection. Children who were sung to a lot when they were young are also more likely to then sing songs to their own children when they become parents. Incorporating musical routines and

activities can create family traditions that are carried on for successive generations.

Here are some music activities to try at home. Don't be afraid to add your own spin to personalize these games for your family.

- Dance Parties: Dancing and singing along to your favorite recorded music as a family builds shared familiarity with songs and encourages free movement to rhythmic stimuli. Dance parties are great spontaneous fun, whether the soundtrack is Stravinsky, the Rolling Stones, the latest Disney musical, or music from your family's cultural or religious background. Plus, your favorite dance party tunes can become the basis for other types of musical play, like imitation games and pretend play (below).
- Imitation Games: Try singing a song or refrain that you and your child both know and imitating each other's movements while you sing, using big, exaggerated gestures. Some children's songs are tailor-made to elicit movement, and "Shake Your Sillies Out" is a great place to try this out! You might also try using kids' percussion instruments or making your own instruments. (Make an excellent homemade tambourine by stapling together two paper plates with macaroni between them.)
- Pretend Play: Acting out the lyrics to a song can be a natural way to incorporate pretend play into musical engagement. "Baby Shark" is a great example of a song that elicits pretend play, but so is "Fly Like an Eagle" by the Steve Miller Band. Engaging in pretend play is developmentally valuable, as it allows children to let imaginary and everyday items function as symbols; imagine holding a pretend banana to sing "Bananaphone" by Raffi or pretending to be a monkey during "Brass Monkey" by the Beastie Boys.
- Using Music as Part of an Everyday Routine: Whether you have a playlist for getting ready for school on weekdays or a song that you and your child hum while brushing teeth, music can be a building block for establishing household routines. The predictability of a familiar song (or songs) can add consistency and fun to make potentially challenging daily activities go more smoothly.
- Following Your Child's Musical Lead: If your child watches *PJ Masks* and constantly sings the theme song, or loves to shout-sing "If You Have

to Go Potty, Stop and Go Right Away" from Daniel Tiger, roll with it! Sing along! Make up moves. Act out the lyrics! Create variations! Soon enough, your child will translate that affinity for rhythm and melody to a broader range of music. You can feel confident that developing a habit of active, shared musical play is rich with benefits.

Healing Arts

ANNA DEAVERE SMITH

Writer and Actress

University Professor, NYU's Tisch School of the Arts

I was the least likely person to wind up in a conservatory, full time, for three years, to study acting. My classmates pirouetted down the hallways of the school. They sang Broadway tunes as they strode up and down the hills of San Francisco, where the school was situated. As for me, I had no idea that people actually "studied" acting in the way that was unfolding in front of me. Granted, there was a deep cultural inhibition, growing up as I did among college-educated Black parents, aunts, and uncles who, though worldly wise, were one generation away from a cautious Negro hyperconcern about appearing to be immoral. My maternal grandmother was nearing the end of her life and had an undiagnosed form of what would now be diagnosed as dementia. Upon hearing that I'd decided to "study" acting, she wrote me a letter. There was a five-dollar bill inside. The letter, in jagged scrawled words, amounted to these few words: "I hear you want to become an actress. Please don't take off your clothes. Here's five dollars, buy yourself a new dress. Love, Grandma."

As it turned out, during my first year of studying acting I lived with my grandmother's niece. They were about the same age and had grown up like sisters. Sweetheart, they called her. Sweetheart had left Baltimore, gone to New York, "passed" as "Spanish," and been a chorus girl. They were awestruck by Sweetheart every time she came home with a different boyfriend and a fur coat. And then she moved to California. The stories about Sweetheart had abounded. And now I'd left Baltimore with eighty dollars and an overnight bag and headed to California, not to become an actress, but to join the revolution. It was 1973. The revolution was over. I ended up by fluke in an acting class. People were changing in front of my eyes. These were the same people I grabbed a cup of coffee with, sweated with in tap class, were terrified with as I looked at them upside down from a trapeze in circus class. And they were changing in front of my eyes as they attempted to morph into characters during Scene Study class. Well, before changing the world, how about watching this form of change up close and personal? The study of acting was for me a way of putting the pieces together and healing my soul.

The most likely person to wind up in the conservatory had a Main Line Philadelphia accent and a vocal resonance that comes not from nature but from substantive study. She was very connected with what was happening where in the San Francisco arts world outside the walls of our conservatory. We were eating a cheap meal on Geary Street. She intoned with her characteristic urgency, "Wanna go up to the Cathedral and hear Beethoven's Ninth? It starts in a few minutes." We bolted up five practically vertical city blocks to Grace Cathedral on Nob Hill. It only took the first two words of the "Ode to Joy": "O Freunde." My perpetual sense of nonbelongingness in the world was transformed into a sense of oneness. I was one with the chorus. I was one with the music. I was one with voice. I was one with it all.

The next morning, my forehead was on fire. I asked Bonita Bradley, our yoga instructor, "Can a performance give you the flu?" This was decades before we began to believe that entering a performance space could cause you to be exposed to COVID. This was decades before we began to believe that entering a performance space, charged with emotion as it usually is, could trigger a latent trauma.

But there was no pathology in my reaction to "Ode to Joy." We both assessed that in fact the flu *shot* I had been required to get that morning could have indeed given me symptoms. But upon hearing more about how I felt, Bonita reassured me that nothing was wrong. In fact, everything was more than right, and Beethoven was the cause! My chakras were opening.

I was hyperaware of everything I heard. I listened the way some people read. That experience of Beethoven love also primed me for my first Shakespeare class. While Bonita, in a colorful leotard, appeared to be sitting on a white cloud when we entered the hush of her studio, Pat, our yoga teacher, in army fatigue pants and seated on the windowsill, waited for us as if she were ready to pounce. Before we investigated a single word of Shakespeare, she introduced us to rhythm. Rhythm could evoke the psychological state of a character. She prevailed upon us to trust that Shakespeare would lead us to feeling; the words would lead us to psychological realities deep in the histories of these characters, even to their jokes.

This was in sharp contrast to what all the "Method"-based gurus at the school were pronouncing: that every character lived inside of us, and we should only present the truth from inside *ourselves*. "There's a Hamlet in YOU!" The "Hamlet in *you*" evangelism had perplexed me from the start. In that era, and at that school, which was led by men and in which men were the objects of desire, the girls in the class would never have been cast as Hamlet—and certainly not a Black girl like me. Pat's idea was a relief. Hamlet was *not* in me. Hamlet had lived in Shakespeare's imagination. If I would respect the words, words that had lasted centuries, words that had traveled the mouths and minds and hearts and ears of trillions of actors and teachers and preachers and plumbers and listeners who fancied them, then the words would transport me back to Hamlet, or in my case, the nurse in *Romeo and Juliet*.

This work did not privilege identification with the other, rather it required a reach *toward* the other. It's a highly creative state that requires technique and skill and constant refinement. Words were both the muscle of the reach and the bridge upon which you stood. Empathy, from this perspective, would be *active* work.

The power of words. This was all so mind expanding that I read Pat's entire PhD dissertation, which she had recently defended at UC Berkeley. By now my ear was so transformed that I was listening to speech in real life as if it were a series of rhythms and songs. I listened with the same intensity as I read French during the few years that I'd majored in French literature, with the same scrutiny as when I was working my way through beginning German. My many conversations with Pat left me with even more questions: Was this a chemical mystery I'd never understand? Was it coming from the same place as magic potions? Why were kind words healing?

Exactly why is speech *action* in drama? What was the relationship of language as speaking to identity? I was seeing what people said to me in my head as architectural drawings. I decided to give Shakespeare a rest and study words in real life.

THE EXPERIMENT

I met a linguist—a stranger at a cocktail party. I don't remember her name, but she gave me the secret sauce of the process that I'd dedicate myself to for four decades. She suggested three questions that would ensure unique rhythmic speech patterns, and drama, in the course of an hour's conversation—didn't matter who I talked to. The questions were: Have you ever come close to death? Have you ever been accused of something that you did not do? and "Do you know the circumstances of your birth?

I created an experiment out of the questions. I walked up to random individuals in New York City and invited them to see themselves performed: "I know an actor who looks like you. If you will give me an hour of your time, I will invite you to see yourself performed." The baseline of every interview was whatever they wanted to talk about. The lifeguard at the Sixty-Third Street YMCA talked about swimming lanes, stickball in the street, and Elgar. A hairdresser at a chic Fifty-Seventh Street salon talked about mirrors and narcissism. Meredith Monk, the composer, talked about New Mexico and Bartók. A casting director talked about English gardens and vacationing in Marbella. About thirty-five minutes into each interview, I asked the same three questions of each interviewee.

The linguist was right. When engaging those three questions, the interviewee used language that became more animated. Sentences broke into new rhythms, words broke up into sounds, patterns of "uhs" and "uhms" and stammers had a life that should not be ignored. Some even started to act things out—in effect, making little "plays."

Bertolt Brecht discusses this phenomenon in his essay "Street Scene." He assessed that if a person witnesses something like a car accident in the street, they will automatically resort to performance. Normal word structures that we learn when we learn to read and write will fail the storyteller who has just witnessed something out of the ordinary. Brecht spoke of this in relationship to what he called "gestus," which means persona. Persona is our performance of ourselves: how we present ourselves to the world. It is what makes us recognizable. Listening to answers to the three questions revealed that there was a link between rhythm, melody, gesture, and "persona." I trained the actors in my experiment to perform verbatim excerpts of the interviews. The key to becoming through words was (1) what I'd learned in my first Shakespeare class—let the words lead the way, and (2) something Deaver Young Smith Sr., my paternal grandfather, had said when I was a girl: "If you say a word often enough it becomes you."

I rented a loft in Tribeca for the performance. The real-life people paraded in with their entourages: friends and family. They sat on the floor in anticipation, having no idea what they'd see. It had all been abstract, and most of them had spent an hour with me only a month or so before. The actors appeared to be "somewhat" like, if not "just" like, the interviewees. At any rate, rhythmic and melodic patterns of speech were recognizable to loved ones.

I performed in the show too. My "real person" was Julia, who had been my boss at JCPenney—in a dark basement room where I had done temp work. From nine to five, I listened as she spoke on the phone, for the most part to friends. *Girrll lemme tell you 'bout this fool on the bus . . .* I was awestruck by the melody in her voice, by how bursts of her laughter disrupted her sentences. She had a sense of the absurdities in her daily life. I was able to listen so well because I made myself invisible, poring over the minimal amount of work she gave me. I got up the nerve to ask her for an interview. I say nerve, because one, well . . . Julia, via my performance, stole the show.

Julia and her friends waited as I paid the stage manager and turned off the lights in the loft. The minute we hit the street, one of them called out into the night: "Julia, you were the STAR." Her other friends joined: "You the STAR, girl. THE STAR!" Julia was tickled by it all. What if the character were to be the star, rather than the performer? In antiquity in all cultures, were the performers the stars? Or were the stories they passed down the stars? Who is the star in a hospital? The doctor? Or the patient?

The experiment and the performance were a success. Illusions of similarity between the actors and the real people had been made. But I knew that illusion was not enough to create a new form.

I was trying to create a theater form that would disrupt stereotypes. My friend Donald Bogle had written the groundbreaking book *Toms, Coons,*

Mulattoes, Mammies & Bucks, which vividly laid out the limitations of Hollywood's imagination. There were basically five potential roles, and he cataloged popular movies and shows according to those established role types. A lot has happened in the several decades since Bogle's book was published, and he was at the forefront of expanding what was possible.

Donald and I went to see Lena Horne on Broadway. Between songs she told stories about the ways in which racism stole opportunities from her. Within the first few minutes of the show, she told us that she'd chosen to wear all white, despite the costume designer's warning that she'd sweat under her arms and the audience would see a flawed white dress. We felt at home with her from that moment on. She made a welcome space. Lena Horne in a white dress with perspiration stains under her arms. Flawed like the rest of us. One of my friends said he felt so whole after the show. Lena Horne. A healer. And it started when the curtain went up. Ideally that is how one would be welcomed into any arts institution, not with wall-embossed mission statements about how they change the world, or chandeliers the size of airplanes, but with a resounding "You are home now." Ideally, that's when healing would start in a doctor's examining room, or a hospital. Not with portrait after portrait of men who undoubtedly did problematic things even as they gave billions, but with a sense that we all have something in common. In both art and medicine that commonness boils down to—vulnerability and mortality.

ASGHAR RASTEGAR, MD
Nephrologist, Yale New Haven Hospital

I have tried to look at this as a—actual being a journey that not one person is taking but two persons are taking. I look at some of the most probably maturing event in my life: it has been in that relationship with a patient. Having seen them through an acute illness. Having seen them accept that, having seen them then get over the p- self-pity, accept and move on. It is to walk into that relationship recognizing your own frailty and your own mortality. Walking into that and knowing that you could be that individual, sitting across table. Recognizing that. And in that recognizing, that while you do sense what they're going through you will never totally understand. We have become much better at diagnosis. We can look inside cells; we can look inside genes. We could never do that twenty years ago. We can define diseases with such power. But we lack the realization that there is human being, fully developed, sitting across who has his or her own dreams. Has his or her own beliefs, wishes, desires, and they're being ravaged by disease. Is not the disease. And so we often are caught with technology and miss the fact that there is an individual who has his own wishes, hopes, dreams that plays into their ability to defend themselves against the illness and recover. But it is really the recognition of that dignity that individuals bring with a total humanity caught in a crisis that makes opening that door so challenging.

Hospitality and hospital have the same etymological genes.

It seemed to me that one way to confront stereotype was to look at how people actually are—how many false starts they have when trying to tell a story. I wasn't interested in the smooth sentence any more than I was interested in the well-made play. If I want smooth sentences, I can read a book. If I want to get closer to a human, I want broken sentences.

The tape recorder gave me the necessary distance I needed to get closer and closer to strangers. Could this be an antidote to the scars left on me from growing up in a segregated town? Would this allow me to be closer to America? My grandfather had said, "If you say a word often enough it becomes you." I would try to become America using my methodology. The method I was creating required highly concentrated attention to minuscule specifics of what a person did and the sounds they made.

I left Carnegie Mellon, where I had a much sought-after tenure track position, after one year. I wanted to continue my experiment. I threw my new set of pictures and résumés—meant to secure me work as an actress—in the trash.

I worked as an assistant and dog caretaker for a famous coach of newscaster stars and some politicians. Among her clients: Oprah and George H. W. Bush, before he was president. I typed up her meticulous notes on their vocal performances. I spent off-work hours studying speech and interviews—courtly gracious ones, like those conducted by the musicologist Alan Lomax; frequently ungracious ones, like those conducted by Barbara Walters; hilarious ones, like the one conducted by Johnny Carson of Sophia Loren.

That was so off rhythm from the "bah da BOOM" of his show that Joan Rivers had to go to extreme bawdiness to bring the show back to its normal stasis. She had a long list of grievances about how poorly she was treated backstage because she lacked the physical endowments that Sophia had. This is not verbatim, but it went something like this:

Joan: She's thirsty, they're outside stompin' on grapes for her.

Johnny: Oh now . . .

Joan: No, John. No! I ask for a glass of water, they go (she spits in her hand), "Here!"

Johnny: Oh, come on now, you're too hard on yourself. . . .

Joan: No! No! No! I know I was not wanted.

Johnny: Oh now . . .

Joan: I was born with a hanger in my ear!

Sudden flash: Entire television shows were based on familiar rhythms. When disrupted the show didn't work. Well obviously, that's what sitcoms are. Rhythm is part of the illusion that we are all having a grand time.

I studied words as vehicles of influence, having come upon tapes of Franklin Roosevelt's fireside chats in an Upper East Side bookstore while heading to the crosstown bus after work walking BB the dog and no doubt typing up notes to a Lincoln, Nebraska, local newscaster hoping to make it nationally. His "Four Freedoms Speech," in particular, made you want to dance. I danced around my railroad flat. I realized I was waltzing! Was he using waltz-like rhythms to make the country waltz along the difficult times with him? Martin Luther King was a rock star of oratory. He had the solid rock of hope in his voice. Was this a part of how words became action? What is the impact of a word on one's being? ("If you say a word often enough it becomes you."—Grandpop)

During the three-questions experiment, I named the overall project "On the Road: A Search for American Character," and thus began the creation of a series of such shows. I continued to experiment with interview technique, storytelling technique, and performance technique, using myself as the sole performer and director—because I could not afford to pay actors. Until I could afford to have a troupe, I'd work on becoming America word for word. Years later I realized it was one way of reckoning with my segregated Baltimore upbringing; with my experience as one of seven Black girls in an otherwise entirely white all-women's college; and with the segregated, stereotype-ridden theater and film professions. In other words, being cast as the one who does not belong would follow me wherever I went. If belongingness were going to be a part of my life and work, I should understand that it was not a given, I'd have to move to experience it. Like having the wind at your back. The wind is not at your back for very long; you have to move to keep it there.

I was missing something. And then I met the poet.

COMMUNITY, BEAUTY, REALIZATION

It was in a beautiful setting that I found one missing piece of the puzzle. Intention. Intention as the backbone of dramaturgical structure.

Squaw Valley, California, recently renamed Palisades Valley, in the Sierras, near Lake Tahoe, was the exquisite setting for the Squaw Valley Community of Writers. I arrived in 1977 for a weeklong conference where wannabee writers like me met and had tutorials with big shot poets, novelists, screenwriters, and directors. Thirsty boots, cowboy hats, and ski bums in shades carrying hammers were what I saw that first day in the Valley. Somebody was fixing the huge wooden wraparound porch. We were greeted by a rainbow that went clear across the Valley. (What if a rainbow welcomed you on your way to surgery?)

Though some of the group were *Paris Review* types, *New Yorker* types, the gathering did not have an East Coast pedigree. A few years earlier I'd attended the Eugene O'Neill Playwrights Conference, a sought-after networking fest for New York actors and playwrights. It was held in and on the grounds of Monte Cristo Cottage—the actual boyhood summer home of O'Neill—sacred ground in American dramatic literature.

There was a path from the arrival area to the cottage. Upon arrival, an actress—my age but significantly more accomplished than I—was walking in front of me. One of the leaders of the conference—and one of the most influential men in all of theater at the time—walked toward her. With open arms he said, "Well, my dear, what have you been doing besides getting fat?" He laughed jovially and pulled her into a crushing hug, but I can't imagine she thought the greeting was funny. A few nights later, the ocean washing in the background and fog rolling into the living room, I spotted a director I'd admired and had always wanted to meet. He was moving from room to room in Monte Cristo Cottage, wearing a cape and puffing on a cigarette in a cigarette holder—in the middle of July. I did not approach.

Hierarchy is a friend of efficiency and necessary for those who need to make sure everyone is in their place. That's understandable if one is herding sheep or making tires for a car, but not if one is devoted to cultivating creativity. Eased hierarchical structures are essential to creativity. Creativity requires mobility.

In Squaw there was no need to genuflect. No hush fell when Sam Shepard ambled into the beat-up saloon where we drank cheap beer. He headed for the pool table and that was that.

I was standing on the wooden wraparound porch when the poet attracted my attention. In a wrinkled shirt, with thinning hair and a bit of a cowlick, wearing sunglasses, he stepped out of a car with two others. He looked like a fasting monk. Perhaps he was nourished only by words and thought. He had presence.

He gave a public reading that very day. I sat down in the front row, directly across from him—nothing between us but a music stand. One of his poems was quite brief. But it changed me. As with the "Ode," I had a dramatic physical reaction to it the following morning. All of the muscles in my body were sore, as if I'd just had a massive full-body workout. My endorphins were depleted, but I was alert.

I saw him across the room at a cocktail party given by a patron the next evening. Because genuflection was not part of the community etiquette, I went directly to him. I told him that I'd woken up with aching muscles after hearing his poem. His face lit up with a bit of surprise and lots of interest: "Well, that's because I wrote that poem as a curse against my ex-wife!"

The "Ode to Joy" had been full of *good* intentions, the poet's curse was full of *bad* intentions.

In this book we are dedicated to healing. I only bring up the power of the *bad* to give credibility to the power of the *good*.

To pretend that the power in words can only be for good, and that one can only learn about the power of words by studying words dedicated to goodness, would make my call for words as vehicles for healing nothing more than milquetoast. Any form of power in the universe has two sides: Fire can warm us or burn a city down; water can nourish us or destroy; medicine can heal or kill. Words carry the weight of our past. We use them to write and speak the prescription for our future.

The poet's intention opened my senses to words as potions. But understanding what it meant to be so focused on where those potent words were being sent led me to a dramaturgical understanding that eventually would make the fragments of my storytelling come together in one direct move. I was able to make disparate pieces of a story about the death of a Black boy in a Hasidic-Black neighborhood in Crown Heights and the riot that ensued into a whole. I was able to craft a story that looked like a Rorschach test, but what made it move dramatically was intention. Intention was the backbone of a performance architecture that moved from opinion to rage and finally to grief. Intention. This understanding, particularly while performing, helped me get my work onto the map with my play *Fires in the Mirror: Crown Heights, Brooklyn, 1991.*

"The word above all is truly magical, not only because of its meaning but by its artful manipulation." Can't remember the name of the author.

Manipulation has a dark connotation, yet the quotation suggests the potential of words as enchantment. Think of Ella Fitzgerald's scat singing. In Teatro Sistina, Rome, 1958, she sang "St. Louis Blues" and managed, in the course of singing the song, to reference *twelve* other songs. She pulled twelve other songs out of her psyche, out of her vast internal song catalog. That could be called manipulation, or association. Manipulation, or integration. Manipulation, or—magic.

DOCTORS AND PATIENTS

Ten or eleven years after my experiment came to an end, there was a letter in my mailbox on embossed stationery from Dr. Ralph Horwitz, the chair of Internal Medicine at the Yale School of Medicine. By this time I had created fourteen one-person shows and two multicharacter plays using the technique I'd developed. I had been credited with creating a new form of theater.

Horwitz's invitation was a Visiting Professorship at Yale Medical School. His proposal was that I'd do interviews of doctors and patients to learn about how doctors do and do not listen. Listening? *Listening.* I would then write a play using those interviews—which was what I was known for. He further proposed that I would perform that play using the real words of doctors and patients—at medical grand rounds.

Medical grand rounds? Wasn't that a *science* kind of gathering? Horwitz had a plan. The play would serve as a mirror on the subject of how doctors listen, or not. That brings us back to *Hamlet*: "The play's the thing wherein I'll catch the conscience of the king." *Performing at medical grand rounds? About something the docs presumably do not do well and possibly don't want to do well?* I'd feel like a clown, or worse, a crazy person amongst their white coats, pressed shirts, bright ties, and silk blouses. It took me a year to say yes.

Horwitz's invitation arrived in the nineties, well before "health care" became buzzwords in our society. In our first meeting he predicted that the nation would soon realize health care was a train wreck.

Horwitz provided intellectual inspiration. The drama lived in the words expressed by the patients. I only had to say three words, upon pressing the button on my tape recorder: "Well. What happened?" Stories upon stories came forth. Vulnerabilities were spread out across the room. One woman lifted her shirt to show her scar. A man who had needed a heart transplant and who had almost died while waiting for a heart brought both his wife and his preteen granddaughter to the interview. The granddaughter read to me from a pile of letters she'd written when she thought he was dying. One patient was among the first to be diagnosed with AIDS. She had not known her ex-husband was gay until her ex-mother-in-law knocked on her front door and told her that he was dying of a disease no one understood. That patient became a partner in her own healing and, with the doctor, became one of the frontier fighters in the battle against AIDS.

I asked Dr. Horwitz if he'd intended to invite the patients I'd interviewed to the performance. He had not thought of it. But he agreed to do so, and the place was packed, at eight a.m., with doctors, patients, and . . . uninvited students from the Yale School of Drama, who'd gotten wind of what I was doing. They thought they'd sneak by incognito—bless their hearts—but scarves and emotion busted their game. They were quite noticeable among the starched shirts, ties, and silk blouses of the doctors.

Later that week we convened third-year MFA students from the drama school and resident doctors. One actress sobbed as she discussed the pain and terror in James Baldwin's writings. The young docs in blazers and ties and polyester blouses looked at her as if she were from Mars. Perhaps they'd seen real pain and terror and suffering that day in patients. Yet an exchange of artists and docs in training could be fruitful. Now more than ever actors, like everyone else in the culture, are concerned about dramatic works triggering their personal trigger. From medical students they could learn useful lessons about how to be emotionally present and objective at the same time. There is that necessary distance. Medical students could learn from actors how to be objective and emotionally present at the same time. There is that necessary intimacy, if one is truly "taking care" of another.

Legendary playwright Anton Chekhov was a doctor. Dr. Abraham Verghese is not only a renowned physician, but a novelist. Francis Collins, former director of the NIH, is a musician and the proud son of a playwright.

A year after medical grand rounds, Dr. Horwitz asked me to come back to Yale and perform for a conference. Unbeknownst to me, he invited the patients again. After the presentation the patients came "backstage"—to a small, sterile room next to the auditorium. I wondered to myself, "Why would you want to come hear someone tell the story of the most traumatic moment of your life, a moment when you were in pain, a moment when you almost died?" I answered myself: "It's because you, a stranger, not their doctor, not their family, not their nurse, you—a stranger—saw them." There was very little discussion and none of the backstage hugging and kissing and "oohing" and "aahing." Their near-silent presence was intimate—a nonverbal hug. And I hope they felt that my portrayals were a very verbal hug of them.

I knew, from the minute I pressed the button on my tape recorder and asked the first question of the first patient, that medical care would be the subject of my next play. I presented at medical grand rounds in 2000. Nine years later Obama was addressing a joint session of Congress about his health-care plan. By then I had recently landed on a New York stage with a fully developed play, *Let Me Down Easy*. It was the result of an extensive research phase during which I conducted interviews at MD Anderson Cancer Center; at Stanford University Medical School; throughout South Africa at the time its president was an AIDS denialist; in Rwanda ten years after the genocide; at Mulago Hospital in Kampala, Uganda; in a Ugandan forest where traditional healers had a convening; in a northern Uganda rehabilitation center for escaped child soldiers; and at Landstuhl Army Hospital, where seriously injured American soldiers were sent from the Middle East to get patched up enough to be shipped to Brooke and Walter Reed. Horwitz and the patients and doctors I met at Yale had been the spark for it all.

LIFE AND DEATH

Let Me Down Easy was marketed as being about the vulnerability of the body and the resilience of the spirit. But it was about death. Theater, like the medical profession, explores the mystery of life and of death. Americans do not want to face death. That is one of the major tolls on our health-care economy.

PHILIP PIZZO, MD
Oncologist, former dean of the Stanford University School of Medicine, Oncologist

What are our expectations of what constitutes reasonable care at both ends of the spectrum—at the beginning and toward the end (of life) is gonna have to be part of this public debate because it tracks right back to the economics and what we're going to spend. The debate has to begin by a significant cultural frame shift, that is really quite encompassing. You know, there, in addition to being a pediatrician I'm also an oncologist. There was a study done just a couple of years ago that asks if *oncologists*, how often did they introduce to their patient that they were at the end of known therapy. Rare. Rarely done. Rarely does the dialogue take place that, you know, we, we have expended a reasonable a reasoned amount of treatment. And we need to move towards comfort and care. And I think that's a cultural phenomenon that doesn't exist throughout around the world. I mean you've traveled the world Anna and you know how people talk about death and dying in other societies. It's different than we do here. The kind of dialogue that I describe that a doctor may need to have with her or his patient about death and dying, may be one that a [medical] student, or even a resident, never really has organized supervision around. Shocking. Isn't it? Shocking. I think that there are probably at least two or more reasons that contributed to why that doesn't happen as much as it should. One of which is—the lack of skill and sophistication. The other is—in some ways the concern that if you begin to move toward that discussion, that you're taking away hope, you know, from a patient. And then a third, which I think is a hard one for me to say—is (*Brief pause*) that it takes a lot of time.

Pizzo calls for a "cultural" frame shift. Not a science frame shift. A cultural frame shift. In all critical social movements—the civil rights movements, the anti-apartheid movement in South Africa, the antiwar movements, the sexuality movements in particular—culture has played a crucial role. Perhaps science and medicine could use the help of artists too. Imagine the "healing arts" movement.

The simplest words in the many words I spoke in *Let Me Down Easy* were the last words of the show, and they came from the 14th Dalai Lama's translator, a French Buddhist monk. The gesture he describes is like speech as an action, though silent.

In the evening you s—
When someone is dead in Tibet you
you put you his cup upside down.
His cup.
Like his tea cup.
Finished.

—MATTHIEU RICARD, *BUDDHIST MONK*

COVID put death in our face. The medical profession was pushed to its limits. Hospitals were filled with doctors, nurses, and supporters who were champion healers. Yet, spiritual and emotional healing came from everywhere. Individuals were more prolific than institutions could be. Nonstop blasts of remarkably innovative, and often hilarious, videos shot across social media. "Laughter is the best medicine—it does the most and costs the least." We were constantly while quarantined sending one another memes and YouTubes that had popped up. It got us through that terrifying and dissembling time.

While writing *Let Me Down Easy*, I spoke to Susan Youens, PhD, a Schubert expert:

SUSAN YOUENS
Musicologist, University of Notre Dame

Well, if you mention the word mortality, the first place in [Schubert's] Quintet that I'm automatically going to think of is the Adagio movement? The slow movement? Now, Schubert lived in a city that has always been death-haunted. Vienna is the only city I know of that has a funeral museum? A museum for funeral coaches? And, uh, all, all of the funerary pomp—that was not only expended on the Hapsburg monarchs, but also on ordinary citizens who would compete with one another for magnificent burials of the dead. So, Schubert had always been, I think, very attentive to death—because he was Viennese.

Medicine and science have a vast and exciting frontier. So do those of us who touch on the threads of human identity. What's a male? What's a female? Why are we so tribal? It's a moment when a center for the study of the human being that could mesh art, science, and medicine should be in the works. May as well get some human touch on the blueprints made before AI takes over.

Play On Philly

STANFORD L. THOMPSON

Executive Director, Equity Arc

Founder, Play on Philly

The student who had a hard time fitting in. The student whose father was in and out of prison yet went into engineering. The one who was always behind but ended up at the Royal College of Music, and the one who found her way to the stage in theater after finding her own visibility. Then there was the student who most people thought wouldn't thrive because ADHD defined her. The other student, who was so shy that words only flowed from the instrument he played, an instrument loud enough that he could no longer hide, and is now, of all things, a sportscaster. And another student whose parent was deported yet who went on to get a degree in music education and is now a full-time teaching artist with the organization I founded, Play On Philly (POP), which provides high-quality music education to students who would typically lack access, as a vehicle for life skills and academic achievement. These students aren't isolated examples. They aren't exceptions to the POP norm. They are spectacular, but none of them is one in a million. They all sat in the same classes, played side by side in the same orchestras. They all started POP in the fourth or fifth grade and stayed with the program through twelfth grade.

These are the students POP has grown into their own destinies, but who have also contributed to, and even provoked, POP to grow as an organization.

These individuals were easy to give up on. They could have been statistics in an unfair mathematical puzzle. But they have made POP what it is, what it is now and will continue to be moving forward. But even as they turned statistics on their head, they still aren't mere numbers. The ones who thrive, defy all expectations, overcome supposedly impossible circumstances—there is not a set of data that can show who they really are, complete with names, hobbies, goals, triumphs.

Take the one who was bullied, and in return became a bully for the sake of survival. Let's call her Jeanine. Overweight—significantly taller and bigger than everyone else in fourth grade—she fought for herself, hurt others in the process, used her body to intimidate those who might shrink from her because of it. But what POP saw in her was a leader. We saw that the energy she had, if contained, could guide her classmates. In the time it took her to grow in maturity, into being comfortable in her own skin, she also grew into an understanding of what attention she could get if she directed it toward being a great clarinetist. Jeanine became an intern teaching the elementary students at the same school in which she started the program, and through her leadership, and her energy rightly focused, her personality and confidence flourished.

The student we'll call Anisha embodied, not just metaphorically, the grit of failing upward. In the way that music can chart the traits a student gains in the process of learning, practicing, and producing, Anisha was it from fourth grade all the way to twelfth before going to a conservatory. She started playing the violin later in life but worked her way to playing with musicians who began the instrument before they could even say complete sentences. In the group lessons that POP offered, she was well behind her peers and didn't get private lessons until seventh grade. Anisha was someone who consistently put in the work, someone who didn't let being behind discourage her. Instead, it fueled her. She always turned a negative into a positive. How does that student become the assistant concertmaster and then concertmaster of local youth ensembles? How does she get featured on NPR's *From the Top*, touring Asia with the National Youth Orchestra of the United States of America, and become violinist of the World Youth Symphony Orchestra before completing high school? And then how does she propel herself all the way to the Royal College of Music in London before returning to attend the Hartt School and teaching part time at

POP? It wasn't an accident. Anisha didn't get lucky. She worked hard through the structure and opportunities POP provided and moved well beyond them once she graduated from the program.

POP isn't about bringing in the most talented and disciplined students who have had the kind of instruction and training afforded by so few and nurturing them musically. By lottery, any student, with whatever struggles they're facing and with usually no skills in music, can participate. There is no grand narrative for the students coming to POP, which is what makes it unique. POP takes the students first, then helps them become the best and brightest with the kind of instruction and training that should be available to all.

For students whose home life is unstable, POP offers a family and community—a place where they can be recognized and applauded, encouraged yet challenged. The program is for the student—we will call him Isaiah—who wound up living in a small apartment with his grandmother and mother after his father was deported while Isaiah was still in elementary school. Isaiah had a lot of attachment issues, but now attaches himself to music. He falls in love with it. Isaiah was the student who brought his instrument home every day to practice after three hours at POP; the one who took part in all the local youth ensembles and orchestras and went to music camp every summer. He found a home for himself but also what students find when they finally have a home: a sense of identity. With the musicians now part of his life, Isaiah got to deal with things like his sexuality, attended college for a music education degree, and then returned to POP to teach full time. He makes it possible for students coming up in the same West Philadelphia neighborhoods that he grew up in to find a home too. And who was he in the same lessons with? Madison.

Madison, we'll call him, is the one who taught us at POP that going to a four-year college isn't for everyone, because he's now an engineer serving in the Air Force with the new United States Space Force. His parents didn't pass down the art of discipline, because one was in and out of prison and the other was hard to reach, hard to pin down, hard to incorporate into his training and education. To this day he frequently credits the discipline of practicing music as the foundation he needed to take on the discipline of the U.S. military.

On either end of the spectrum are students like the ones we'll call Corina and Robin. They are both superstars in their own way. Corina was a talented player—*very* talented. Robin, too, had a great deal of talent. They were both the most accomplished players of their instruments that POP has ever had. And yet their superstardom can be attributed to the same fundamentals: being recognized, being noticed—seen.

Corina understood immediately how to do something after being told. Sometimes kids don't take quick adjustments but require repetitions before they click. Yet techniques that took her classmates months to learn, Corina could master after the second or third time trying them. And as the techniques were piled on, getting more and more difficult along the way, she continued to progress incredibly quickly. She is exactly what we would call a child prodigy. Yet she wasn't being seen for what she could accomplish because she was known for her ADHD rather than for herself. Corina had a teacher who knew she could do better than her diagnosis. His patience left everyone in disbelief that Corina even had ADHD, because they assumed that someone with her condition wouldn't be able to catch on as well as she did. Maybe Corina just needed to be around people who didn't diminish what she was capable of.

POP learned some valuable lessons from Corina too. First, placing a diagnosis on her was limiting what she was capable of, simply because no one was giving her the chance to be capable at all. Second, Corina couldn't be removed from lessons to sit quietly by herself, as teachers sometimes need to do with disruptive students to continue their lessons. Corina had to participate, because that was when she focused—when she was playing music. And the third, but not final, lesson, Corina had an advocate. Her teacher supported her when others wanted to give up. This lesson reverberated throughout the program. When we encountered students who might have otherwise been released from POP, there was always one teacher, one adult to believe in them. And each time it happened, it became obvious that these students weren't simply floating around the school from music classes to orchestra rehearsals and back again. They had relationships with their teachers, conductors, administrators. They weren't invisible. Corina was seen.

And Robin found the visibility that she needed. Playing music helped her find her place by communicating through the arts. Starting in fourth grade, she could pick things up very quickly, and that gift thrust her into the spotlight. She was reaching for something through her instrument. Robin didn't always commit herself to what the instrument would require for long-term study, and where she ended up is exactly where she should be. Studying theater in college, she's onstage. Seen.

All the kids in POP come from difficult backgrounds with trauma and baggage in a city where, as of 2022, approximately 30 percent of youth drop out of school and violence and crime have significantly risen in the past decade. But POP doesn't lean into a problem-based strategy. Overall I don't look at the kids that way, because my mother and father never used our situation to determine whether my siblings and I would do extraordinary things. I do have a sense of the students' problems and families, but POP focuses on the musical interventions we're providing, giving these kids a sense of community and mitigating the effects of risk on academic achievement and prosocial behavior by fostering their executive functioning. And we all need it. I needed it.

I didn't at first realize that I was living the life that I wanted the young people in POP to have. My own parents were music educators in Atlanta—my mother an orchestra conductor, my father a band director. Our house had a revolving door for music students. My mother taught strings, flute, and piano, and my father taught saxophone, clarinet—really any wind instrument—and jazz theory. When my father turned his attention to teaching me is when I wanted to turn my ears off, but I couldn't; it's impossible to not listen to a father who cultivated hard work in everything I did. It meant raking leaves in the fall in our huge backyard filled with trees. It meant meticulously moving furniture to vacuum in all the places no one could see.

It meant that I and my seven siblings were taking music lessons every week, spending every day practicing alongside one another for the next one, and next one, and next one. Eventually I was practicing with them in the Dekalb Youth Symphony Orchestra, Metropolitan Youth Symphony Orchestra, Atlanta Youth Wind Symphony, and the Atlanta Symphony Youth Orchestra. My father, a jazz musician, was part of a jazz ensemble that two of my brothers were in before me and one of my sisters after me. It was led by a longtime friend of his who taught jazz at Spelman College. He brought together a few local music students to teach us how to hear music, even if we couldn't play it. Then he'd take the best of them, one of my brothers included, to play the stage at the Atlanta Jazz Festival in Piedmont Park each year. Every ensemble I played in was dotted with different siblings—a brother here, a sister there, or two brothers and two sisters, sometimes three. Older and younger than me, some playing with me in my own mother's orchestra at school and my father's band at his. It's an understatement to say that we all wanted to quit at different times in our musical journeys, but we couldn't. My parents knew something we didn't—that learning to play, practice, listen, travel, and stay busy would grow us as much as having the mortgage paid and food on the table. It's music that taught me the discipline, listening, learning, and accepting all at once. From music, through music, and everything surrounding music came my spiritual, emotional, and relational understanding that undergirds what POP does and is, what it represents and who it represents.

Now the kids in POP get what was generally hard to come by when I was growing up and is still hard today: growth. When they come to POP after school each day, they work on a personal development that isn't mandated by law, like going to school. They see the world and their place in it as an interconnected and interdependent existence, much like I came to understand by going to Interlochen Center for the Arts in Traverse City, Michigan, every summer for eight weeks. It ran just long enough to hit right up to the first day of school in the fall, leaving no time to cut up with my close, yet also careless, neighborhood friends. At Interlochen I moved in groups with different artists. Dancers, theater actors, singers, writers, visual artists—they all forced me to expand what the arts meant to me. Also, they demonstrated who would be cultivating the future. My father drove me and my siblings every year for eight years up I-75 to Traverse City, and would visit during the summer as well just to see how it was all going. He even drove our friends, musicians from Atlanta, who also started going to Interlochen.

The dreams I had as a kid were plentiful, just not relatable. Because of the youth groups I grew up playing in and places like the Interlochen Arts Camp, I got to dream about being the principal trumpet in the New York Philharmonic with kids who understood what it meant to me. But we couldn't all be the principal trumpet chair of the NY Phil. If I got that chair, my friend wouldn't. Neither would my competitor, which is who my friend might become as a result. Since those are often held for an entire career, I could be auditioning for the position that my teacher, David Bilger, at the Curtis Institute of Music, held for decades. I would be ready by now. Graduating thirteen years ago would put me well beyond the experience I would need to audition for the Philadelphia Orchestra, having played in orchestras all over the world. It wouldn't be like showing up to my all-state auditions in fifth grade and having the wrong music prepared, standing outside of the audition room and listening to other students playing, one after the other, and knowing before I even started that I wouldn't get in. Even though I was the youngest player in the Dekalb Youth Symphony Orchestra, sitting first chair in fifth grade, it didn't matter when I arrived at that audition with the wrong music. It's how I learned that being the best trumpet player wasn't as important as being the best *prepared* trumpet player. From this recognition of preparedness, I began to understand something about control— the control I don't have. I can't control something like showing up to an audition in the middle of a blizzard and finding out I only have ten or so minutes to warm up before standing in front of an intimidating judge panel. What I could get control over was making sure I had time to head into the bathroom to get the forty-five-minute warm-up that I'd usually get at other auditions.

It was when I visited Venezuela and saw how kids in El Sistema were fed directly into conservatories and professional orchestras that I had the redefining shock to imagine what El Sistema could be if introduced in the United States. The pipeline from vigorous study to profession was not disjointed, but rather support-guaranteed to a serious student making diligent progress. Those students were becoming the teachers at conservatories because their hard work was evident, not made invisible, and their experiences were valued, not measured in value. Those students were playing in concert halls all over the world because they play incredibly well. Those students are from the very program that cultivated Gustavo Dudamel, who has become the most recognizable conductor around the world, because even people not in classical music know his name.

I had visited Germany years earlier with the Atlanta Symphony Youth Orchestra and got to experience what it felt like sitting onstage with the orchestra. All the audience could see me in the percussion section. I felt the bass drum as if I were playing it myself, which wasn't as great as it sounds, but was also as great as it sounds. On my first night in Venezuela, I saw Claudio Abbado conduct. I had watched him years earlier when I sat in the choir loft of the Berliner Philharmonie, where he led the Berlin Philharmonic in a stirring performance of Gustav Mahler's "Tragic" Sixth Symphony.

Now it was as if he remembered my being in Berlin and wanted to take me further, moving me through that transition from being a student in ASYO to being a fellow of El Sistema with the hope of moving students of POP through progressive layers as well.

El Sistema made me ready to return to the communities I really cared about, finally understanding the communities that really cared about me. They, the mothers and fathers, the public school orchestra and band directors, and especially those who made it to financial heights who fund our communities, like Azira G. Hill, a Cuban immigrant, did for the Atlanta Symphony Orchestra Talent Development Program. The Talent Development Program for minority students was only a blip on an unattended radar when my siblings and I started in it with little outside support, but became abundant when we, meaning the plethora of minority musicians coming out of Atlanta, developed with little outside support. But in fact, we weren't without support, as we were community based. They taught us. They trained us.

Just like POP, we had to look inward before we were visible to those outward.

Preparing to start POP became a measure of practicing skills I had learned from a young age from people like Gordon Vernick at Georgia State University, then Christopher Martin at the time he was in the Atlanta Symphony Orchestra (ASO), and then Joseph Walthall, before getting to David Bilger at the Curtis. I took inspiration from all those teachers and many mentors in between. I had other supporters like Suzanne Shull, an advocate for the ASO's Talent Development Program, who introduced me to Doc Severinsen, the famous trumpet player who worked as bandleader on *The Tonight Show Starring Johnny Carson*, who also helped me get a piccolo trumpet. When my longtime POP mentor Elisabeth Babcock prepared me to meet our angel donor, Carole Haas Gravagno, I had to apply the lesson of allowing people who knew more than me guide my progress. Without such lessons, starting POP would have been impossible. Every day that the students in POP show up to work on their instruments, they have to accept the same guidance. Someone who knows more is training them in the lessons of humility, a musical instrument being the vessel to accepting that if they are going to get better at something, they can't do it alone.

Beth Babcock helped me secure our first $1 million donation with a succinct, one-page proposal detailing what we needed to grow POP: a sufficient budget to better compensate the staff; opening a new school site; implementing a robust evaluation process. Getting my first major donor wasn't a showcase of charm and finesse. Quite the opposite. It was dry, compact, and borderline uninteresting, to say the least. But Beth knew something I didn't, which is what motivates major philanthropists and what kind of team I would need to build to help achieve my vision. I had to be humble enough to trust her the same way POP students have to learn the humility of trusting POP and our teaching artists to craft their musical and personal growth.

Before we got that first $1 million donation, all I knew was charming donors and having the kids pull at their heartstrings. While those things brought me to the table with philanthropists, they wanted to talk business: How many kids and schools would be added? How would I sustain the organization financially when their funds ran out? How would my organization's capacity be expanded (staff, board, etc.)? If I didn't have Beth's guidance on exactly what to put on the funding request, I don't think we would have secured anywhere close to that same level of funding in our second year.

In the beginning I thought I needed to convert everybody. That was my control issue. I couldn't control who would actually understand what I was trying to achieve with POP, although I was certain that if I only communicated the right things in the right way, the donations would flood POP's coffers. Nor could I control the donors who pledged money to POP but didn't follow through. After I'd found Carole Haas Gravagno, I realized that it might be one person at a time, that one major donation might come in only once a year—from Carole to, later, Gerry Lenfest, and many more all the way to MacKenzie Scott. What Carole did as my first major donor went beyond money. She leveraged her privilege, swaying her friends to support, matching donations, and facilitating partnerships. She gave us money, but she also gave me validation—the other little thing that happens in the confines of a music lesson that ends up being even bigger than everything else. There were times I'd go to my lessons deflated with feelings of inadequacy, thinking I was in over my head in a field I didn't belong, and my high school private trumpet teacher, Christopher Martin, reassured me that I would be okay. That was followed by the validation that I could get into the Curtis, once I had overcome some technique issues in my playing. Carole opened doors for me that I didn't know were there, let alone how to get through them. It meant standing in her office a year and a half later with news that we had secured our first seven-figure donation. Why there was anything available to me with six zeroes at that point was possible only because of the people who were willing to train me beyond the practice room.

Yet checks like those were never the main prize. Being the principal trumpet of the Philadelphia Orchestra, or what I once dreamt when I was even younger, about playing principal chair in the New York Philharmonic, is no longer the main prize either. I didn't play with the Philadelphia Orchestra, but I have played for years in the Kimmel Center under the same batons that conducted Philadelphia's orchestra. I traveled around the world touring, playing in chamber orchestras and the Seoul Philharmonic and so much more that allowed me to shift my perspective on what the main prize really is, or should be.

As much a breakthrough as Curtis was and still is for me, I didn't know how to break through the barriers and boundaries at Curtis and those of the Philadelphia Orchestra. But now the students in POP have been at Curtis, more importantly *in* Curtis, in the Kimmel Center, rehearsing, performing, working with the most accomplished conductors and musicians in the classical music field. These experiences, I've come to realize for myself, built something much more expansive than sitting still in the back of an orchestra for possibly the rest of my life. I don't sit still anymore, and neither do the students at POP.

Among the many ways I identify with these students is in underestimating myself. While training them to believe in what they are capable of before they achieve it, I also fight it within myself. With every dream I have for my next steps come unreasonable expectations of myself and those around me. In my early years, my parents had to step up to support me. In my professional training, I needed a place like Curtis to fully support me in the ways they do for all their students. In my professional career at POP, I need staff, teachers, board members, donors, etc., to come along for the journey. I just can't set simple goals and plans like the vast majority of people around me, so when I dream, the exciting possibilities are always met with an equal force of skepticism and self-doubt.

The stakes aren't higher than those of my students—if anything, they're higher for them—but nonetheless, the stakes are there. When I underestimate myself, it comes with a lack of trust in what I'm capable of, and it shows. Funders won't make investments. Parents doubt the staff and POP's ability overall to keep their children engaged. Most importantly, people don't see what we're trying to create in advance. They don't get to envision being on a winning team ahead of the victory, which is what the students need the most. They need to be seen on the winning team before they can prove they deserve to be there. The students in POP don't pay tuition. They don't have to audition to get in. They don't have to buy their own instruments. They don't have to explain to anyone that they are worthy of winning. I however, do, and these were the disappointments I had to face, but pick myself up and keep trying. And this, among earlier disappointments like having good staff and teachers come into the program but not paid well enough to retain, or the disappointments that arise when working with school and community partners. The disappointments don't stop at structural issues. There are program leaders who are motivated by shallow outcomes and driven by their egos rather than providing equitable opportunities to students with the least resources. The people who disguise what they really want to say propose veiled ideas like having the students only do one day of lessons rather than five lessons a week, undermining what the kids and families are capable of or interested in because of who they are.

The truth is that I wanted to give up all the time. I got to the point of doing a lot of complaining to the people who were trying to help me, the ones on my side. Through the most unfortunate lessons, I've had to learn how to face getting stuck in those emotions. From the loss of my brother, Marcus, in middle school, to heartbreak after falling in love for the first time in high school—the rawest emotions there are, the ones that dig and cut so deeply. Eventually I admitted that someday, I would have to move on. As I reached a professional level of study and performing, my complaining didn't look the same, sound the same, when I did it in front of a mirror, so I resolved to stop believing it sounded different to other people. With POP, I didn't have time to be visibly upset. I had those moments, but just like in the practice room, I mostly had to move through them by myself. No one could learn to play the trumpet for me; no one could absorb and overcome my difficulties for me either. Pushing through various disappointments I learned what it took to achieve the long-term successes of POP and what it felt like to triumph. Imagine the impact of students getting to discover what that feels like for themselves. Knowing what it means to be good at something and learning the strategy of seeing it through to a glorious end. This is what kept me going in building POP, and it's the same thing that keeps many of these students pushing through their own disappointments, not just because they know how to fail, but because they know how to conquer.

POP doesn't revolve around my difficulties running it apart from the difficulties the students in POP have to live with every day. This was abundantly clear, if not already, after the murder of George Floyd. Over 90 percent of the students in POP are Black. They were no less affected by the visuals and resulting sorrows of Floyd's murder than I was. What POP has already been trying to do is solve the inequities in our education system. We didn't release a statement of solidarity with Black Lives Matter because POP has been in solidarity since it began. We didn't look systemically at what POP was doing, because systemically we are already working to tear down the barriers that exist between our students being able to live in an equitable society or not at all. We didn't go through diversity, equity, and inclusion (DEI) sessions to examine ourselves because we are inherently an examination of DEI efforts and practices. In the face of atrocities such as George Floyd's murder, it is clear that what POP does for the communities of Philadelphia extends far beyond classes, rehearsals, and performances. It is family and a place where our students can empty themselves, then refill with something better.

I fundamentally believe that all students have the potential to pursue a professional arts career, if they so choose. Many POP alumni have already realized these goals, being accepted to summer music programs at Interlochen, Brevard, and Kinhaven, and to prestigious music conservatories such as the Royal College of Music in London and the Peabody Institute in Baltimore. But if students do not have robust support in the form of dedicated parents, teachers, coaches, mentors, and training opportunities, they will never be able to realize their dreams. Despite the growth of many music programs such as POP in cities across the country, there is still a significant gap between music students who have sufficient supporting resources to pursue an arts career and those who do not. My work at POP has focused on using music education as a vehicle for personal growth for divested youth in Philadelphia. These next steps in students' careers have not been a essential part of POP's core mission, but it is something that gnawed at me over my thirteen-year tenure at POP.

So in January 2021, I led the launch of the then-named National Instrumentalist Mentoring and Advancement Network as the founding chairman. And in May 2023, I transitioned from my role as founder and executive director of Play On Philly to the executive director of the newly rebranded Equity Arc. This organization is dedicated to the vision of creating a level playing field for BIPOC (Black, Indigenous, and People of Color) classical musicians in the United States by aligning, promoting, and developing equitable opportunities and inclusive environments so they can thrive in classical music.

This work is critical, and only just beginning. But bringing the field together in this way is the next important step to providing all musicians with the mentorship to achieve their own artistic dreams—and to compose their own future.

Belonging Through Music: Investing in Our Children's Future

FRANCISCO J. NÚÑEZ

Founder and Artistic Director, Young People's Chorus of New York City

The Young People's Chorus of New York City (YPC) uses music as a hook: students come to the program for a creative musical outlet, and they stay for the friendships and community support. YPC participants are from diverse socioeconomic backgrounds and forge lasting relationships. The community we build offers them a strong framework of support and consistency that they may not find in their schools. Unlike the revolving door of classmates and teachers they will have in their formative education, students establish strong relationships with their YPC cohort as they grow and evolve. Moreover, whereas a school fosters a competitive atmosphere, the YPC program fosters collaboration toward a common goal: its students' efforts are rewarded by the same applause. Through this shared purpose, chorus members develop a deep sense of respect for one another that is further strengthened by their distinct backgrounds. As a diverse group, they feel that they are succeeding at creating the kind of community that the rest of society only talks about.

When I was six years old, my mother went to buy a spinet piano at the Salvation Army on Forty-Sixth Street in Manhattan and had it delivered to our house. We were living on Columbus Avenue on the Upper West Side during the 1970s, and she would not let me go outside. "It is too dangerous," she said. Maybe because I wasn't allowed to leave the apartment, she always invited music in. She often sang while I danced along with her. Of course, life was not all music. There were bills to be paid, and as a new immigrant, my mother took what she could get. During the day she looked for work in factories as a seamstress while I went to school. On the weekends and some evenings, she cleaned people's homes. Even then she found a way to let music in. In lieu of getting paid for housework, she asked some of the families with pianos to give me a piano lesson. This changed the course of my life. Not only did this begin my career as a musician, but it also gave me access to a whole new world. I was able to step inside the homes of people living in beautiful buildings surrounded by amazing views, with doormen who took care of the buildings and them. All this, just several blocks away from me, yet a world apart from the life I knew.

The piano became a refuge; it kept me away from the gangs in our neighborhood and allowed me to enter a world where children wanted to study and go to college. Both groups were seeking a better life, but in much different ways. I stood out in society for many reasons: my accent, my name, my appearance. But when I played the piano, I belonged. The perception of who I was changed, and the atmosphere in the room changed with it. In seventh grade I met a young girl who lived in a beautiful building and accepted me as her friend. That's when the learning began.

As a child musician entering a competition filled with other musicians, I found it obvious what we all had in common: a commitment, a passion, and a talent for music. We earned a palpable respect from others once we began to play. But while music was the equalizer, social norms remained a divider. I was not a typical child musician. I was not what people expected to see in these rooms.

I was the kid who walked in wearing different clothes. The one who spoke English as a second language, with an accent. The one whose family brought food whose aromas wafted into the room and smelled different, who then spoke and laughed louder than all the other families. As that nine-year-old kid, well, I needed a bit more to walk into those rooms. I walked in silently, avoiding the stares and whispers, and quickly found a corner to call my own. Here, as a young musician, I built grit, pride, perseverance, humility, calm, focus, and mental strength. But it was not easy. Because my mother dared to imagine a better life for me through music, my very existence disrupted social norms. I was interacting with children I would never have interacted with before, and they were interacting with me. They were learning from me as much as I was learning from them—and from there, education, understanding, and compassion grew.

I carried this lesson and this life experience with me into adulthood, determined to make the same difference in other children's lives, because I realized that my experience was not unique then, nor is it today. Youth everywhere feel the weight of "otherness" and a desire to find their voice and a place of acceptance. Music and the arts can provide this—but we must provide the resources for children to access them.

In 1988 I graduated from New York University as a piano major and immediately started a program at the Children's Aid Society on Sullivan Street in Greenwich Village. I wanted to create a space, a room, a program, an ensemble that represented the very best of New York City through its children. I wanted to fight racism and poverty. I wanted to build the very best children's chorus and harmonize the children of the city. New York City is considered one of the most segregated cities in the country, and I was told over and over again that bringing together a group of children from underserved and affluent neighborhoods was not going to work. But I kept going.

Voice was the instrument I chose. With voice I could reach thousands of students. I started with just nine children when I founded the Young People's Chorus of New York City; today, it serves two thousand children from ages eight to eighteen yearly. And in the span of thirty-five years, I have been able to reach and teach over twenty thousand children. Our mission: to provide children of all cultural and economic backgrounds with a unique program of music education and choral performance that seeks to fulfill each child's potential, while creating a model of artistic excellence and diversity that enriches the community. This begins with creating an environment where children feel safe and have the support and resources they need to build confidence. Our choristers learn to perform in public and lessen performance anxiety. They socialize and create networks of friends from all different backgrounds. These connections lead to a more well-rounded perspective about the world and students' choices for the future— a change that occurs among all the children over time. In conversations that take place over the course of years, friendships and trust are built that change everyone's perceptions of one another and slowly break down barriers. Since the earliest days of the program I have seen children inspire one another. Many choose to attend better schools and go on a path to higher education, which in turn has a ripple effect on their families and society as a whole. Students become leaders in college, in the workforce, and in their communities.

In many other types of music programs, the students are there to master their craft irrespective of others—clock in, clock out. In contrast, YPC rehearsals are designed to offer time for the singers to socialize—to learn from and support one another. If you put any group of children onstage together, they will push one another to succeed as one—to high-five, laugh, cry, and celebrate. As students gain respect for one another onstage, it changes how they interact offstage. Children look to the friendships they gain in YPC; when you receive care and positive affirmation every day from your peers instead of being bullied at your school, that connection of self-worth becomes very important. The arts are critical in this way—students aren't just being taught how to be excellent in their artistry, but to feel excellent in their self-worth, and to become inspiring members of society, ready to take on the world.

The impact that our choir program has on our students is transformative. A mother shared with me that her daughter started singing around the house, making her bed, and putting on her school uniform with a sense of pride. One of our singers lost her mom to cancer during her time with us at YPC. Her fellow singers planned a small performance and sang to her. They wanted her to know that she could lean on them as a support system. Many of the friendships from YPC continue on into adulthood. They attend one another's bar mitzvahs; they become each other's best men and maids of honor. We recently had a wedding party composed mostly of YPC alumni!

At YPC we care for our children beyond the performances. We nurture, guide, and inspire choristers and offer whatever they need to succeed. Ninety percent of our choristers receive program and tour scholarships as well as costumes and transportation, but a scholarship is not enough to build equity. We must invest in our children beyond financial support so that the arts are not just a possibility in their lives, but are central to it.

Our wraparound program includes hours of rehearsal, private vocal lessons, group performance classes, and national and international performance and touring. We are committed to new music, to the classical canon, to folk music and global music sung in many languages. We also draw on dance, acting, and movement to create a full-body experience. Dance allows us to sing more on the breath, and acting leads to connection with the audience. Working with living composers we have broken through the stigmatized barrier some may have about children's choirs. In 2000 we began a bold new initiative entitled Transient Glory—a program to commission, publish, record, distribute, and perform new masterworks for children by today's leading composers, sung gloriously during this ephemeral time before the choristers become adults. To date we've commissioned hundreds of new works from some of the most influential composers, most writing for the very first time for children. This project started an avalanche of new works from other youth choirs who started to commission living composers, changing the landscape for children's choirs worldwide.

We have been lucky to have great artists take part in master classes with our singers, from Renée Fleming to Denyce Graves and Anthony Roth Costanzo, among many others. And we've worked with great choreographers such as Ben Vereen, Frank Hatchett, Jacquelyn Bird, and Stephen Petronio.

But what we are building is not just success for the choristers while they are with us. We are setting them up for long-term success after they leave YPC. We offer private scholastic tutoring in core subjects from math to science. We offer college-bound workshops, essay writing and financial literacy courses, and SAT and ACT preparation. YPC students of all backgrounds prefer to study together and encourage one another. One hundred percent of our choristers graduate from high school and 100 percent pursue higher education. To date we have given over $1.2 million dollars in college scholarships to alumni. And like my mother did in our home, we always invite music in—into our classrooms, into our choristers' lives, and out into the world.

One of the ways our program weaves together our community is through the experiences our students share during our traveling expeditions. Students share snacks with peers who didn't have the means to bring money for treats. They experience culture shocks together and support one another when they feel homesick. Some of our students will be traveling for the very first time. It will be the first time they will get on an airplane and see what exists outside their own neighborhoods. From surviving jet lag to discovering foods with vastly different ingredients, the students get to experience an international world. Through this exposure, all the students will also look inward and ask: *Who am I? What is my identity?* As they work to succeed onstage together, they see a world with boundless possibilities—and get to figure out how they will want to fit within it.

YPC has been traveling to participate in major global choral competitions since 1997, when we received the Silver Medal at the Prague International Choral Competition. Awards such as these have competitive application processes, and finalist choirs from all over the world are invited to compete in person. YPC won gold medals in every category at the Golden Gate International Children's and Youth Choral Festival in 2015, and they have won first place in the children's choir category at the Euroradio Choral Competition (the first American choir to do so) and the Festival Internacional de Música de Cantonigròs in Barcelona, Spain. And at the biennial International Choral Kathaumixw in British Columbia, another of the most prominent global competitions, YPC was named "Choir of the World" in 2018—the top-ranked choir of *all* categories and age brackets, and the first North American choir to be named as such!

In 2013 the YPC was invited by the United Nations to perform a winter concert in Geneva with the Geneva Chamber Orchestra, in recognition of our choir's multiculturalism and excellence in singing. As part of the concert, conducted by Pulitzer Prize–winning composer Tania León, we prepared a new work by English composer Karl Jenkins that was highly rhythmic with nonsensical words. The American ambassador later recounted to me that, during the rehearsal, the other ambassadors started to argue about what the music was. The English ambassador could not figure out where my choir was from and didn't understand the (nonsensical) language, but the French ambassador said, "Look at them and listen to that sound—it can only be an American choir."

Imagine that, being called American! Children of immigrants from such diverse backgrounds representing our country. All this is to say that diversity is a strength that allows us to share in the beautiful sounds found in the accents and rhythms of the world.

We don't have to wait to invest in our youth. We don't need to wait for the prodigy to be found. With the right instrument and the right teacher, all children can be prodigies. That is our YPC mandate: creating a community that blends together children from diverse religious, socioeconomic, racial, and cultural backgrounds, from every borough and neighborhood in New York City, from private to public to home schools—and providing them with the resources they need to succeed. And because of the multicultural blend, it did not limit what we could sing—it expanded it and gave them the keys to their future.

MUSIC AS THERAPY

Experiences and Applications

Music and Mysticism

ZAKIR HUSSAIN

Grammy Award–Winning Tabla Virtuoso

In India all musicians are considered to be conduits to the spirits. Music belongs to the temples, and it comes from the temples. Many of the gods and goddesses whom people in India worship are shown with instruments. Lord Krishna with the flute; Ganesha, the elephant god, with the drum; Lord Shiva with the damaru, a small two-headed drum; and Saraswati, the goddess of knowledge and learning, with the veena, a stringed instrument. We revere and honor our musicians—our gurus and our elders—almost as if they were priests of music. This reverence is ingrained into our cultural and spiritual upbringing. Every young person must have a few lessons of spiritual music that is sung or played in the temple, not unlike traditions of churches and other religions.

Each year in India, during the full moon of the month Ashadha (June/ July), we journey to visit and honor our gurus, or teachers, for the holiday of Guru Purnima. It is a very important holiday for everyone, but especially for artists, and it is venerated diligently. We offer our respects and gifts and thank our gurus or teachers for the knowledge that they have transmitted to us. On each Guru Purnima I bow down to and ask for the blessings of my mentors, and those of my treasured musician friends, because musicians represent the spirits—and our upbringing and our music seek to honor that.

I normally travel to India for this holiday each year, but because of COVID, I instead spent the Guru Purnima of 2020 at home, placing a garland on my father's portrait and honoring him there. (Luckily, I was fortunate to spend that celebration remotely with two legends and friends, Renée Fleming and drummer Mickey Hart of the Grateful Dead!)

The tradition of Hindustani classical music (from the northern Indian subcontinent) has two types of sound: Aahat naad (struck sound) and Anahat naad (unstruck sound). Both of these are required in the creation of drone and vibrating frequencies. The most commonly used device for drone in traditional Indian music is the tanpura, a four- or five-string instrument with a wooden neck attached to a goad (a long stick). The basis for the Hindustani musical tradition is the raga: an extended melodic improvisation based around a musical mode. During the performance the strings of the tanpura, tuned to the tonic and the dominant notes of the mode of the raga, are gently plucked continuously by the fore and the middle finger, thus making the strings vibrate a sustained tone that we identify as drone.

Drone and vibration are two sides of the same coin. My instrument is a two-piece hand drum called the tabla, which is the main percussion instrument in the Hindustani tradition. When I strike my tabla, the sustained sound it produces depends on the vibration created by the black clay tuning paste, the syahi, that sits in the center of the skin. (This paste was originally added manually for each performance; it now remains as a permanent part of the instrument.) This vibration prolongs the resonance of the "struck sound," and, when played continuously, also creates a drone-like soundscape (like with the tanpura), hence the idea of drone and vibration as one. In fact, "sound" as we hear it is our brain's perception of a vibration's repeated oscillations of motion in the air. If you were to strike a wooden table with your hand, for example, it would create a dead sound. But if that dead sound is recorded and repeated a thousand times and replayed back at least twenty times per second, the dead sound transforms into a drone that we can hear. So the only difference between tone and rhythm is tempo—a fast-enough rhythm will produce its own audible tone.

Even the Earth creates a tone as it revolves around its axis—a B-flat, to be specific, though many octaves below what our ears could hear. And for some reason, our music has tuned in to it. The drone of the tanpura is often tuned to B-flat; when women sing in India, their standard tonic is the key of B-flat. It is considered that our Earth is Mother Earth; Shakti, the female energy of our life, comes from its very strong energy.

In India we take drone as a natural, everyday, living experience, not as a scientific phenomenon. Playing rhythms is almost like reading a novel while you imagine the story—or reading sheet music as you sing a song. That language must become like a second language; just as I have learned how to express myself in English, I had to learn to express myself in the language of tabla. There is a melodic and expressive element to the performance, almost like a question or a series of spoken phrases; the dynamics follow through naturally, like the inflection of a sentence. We first learn to recite and sing the rhythms before we get a chance to play our instrument, and fortunately it is able to show those dips and flows.

Music and rhythm were, in fact, my first language, before I even learned to speak. When I was two days old, I was brought home from the hospital. Traditionally your father is supposed to whisper a prayer in your ear. But when my father took me in his arms, instead of whispering an actual prayer with words, he sang rhythms. "Why are you doing that?" my mother asked him. "You're supposed to say a prayer."

"But this *is* a prayer!" he responded. "He's going to be praying through this for the rest of his life and leading the flock through, so I'm starting him right now." From then on that's what he did every day; he would hold me in his arms for an hour or two and sing rhythms to me, perhaps to prepare me for what was to come later in my life.

There is a deeper spiritual belief about drone and vibrating frequencies that flirts with mythology and unexplainable miracles. When I'm performing on the tabla, I feel myself traversing through a landscape—perhaps going uphill, downhill, diving into a river, or floating along somewhere. I might settle into a simple rhythm, before bringing in a little trill as I visualize a flock of birds flying overhead. The essence of the tabla, as an instrument, exists in this liminal space along with me in this very audiovisual experience. I don't need to make the tabla and the music follow me; rather, I'm following the tabla. I know that the essence is there, and I'm just flowing with it.

This energy exists inside of music. For example, singing from the Kundalini, the divine feminine energy at the base of the spine, leads the energy to rise with the tonal frequencies that align with your chakras (the focal points of meditation along the body). The ambience and everything that comes together, as it needs to be, are all part of the music that keeps you healthy. Joints often ache at age seventy—but my father was playing at eighty, and there was never a complaint at all about his fingers aching or his wrist not working. Ravi Shankar played concerts when he was ninety years old, pulling on the sitar strings—no issues with pain at all. And I have been tired and totally broken down after a twenty-two-hour journey to arrive at a concert. But when I get on the stage and start playing, just five to eight minutes into the performance, I have an injection of rejuvenation. This is the power and energy of the vibration of frequencies, which emerge from the musical instruments, and emerge from within.

Ustad Thirakwa Khan is considered one of the greatest tabla maestros ever by one and all in India. When I was fourteen years old, I used to watch him up close while he would practice every day, and I went to see him perform many times. He was in his eighties at that time; his hands would shake constantly from Parkinson's, and he could barely hold his walking stick as he would be helped up to the stage. But when he sat down to play a concert, all he had to do was make contact with his tabla. Slowly, the tipper-tapper, pitter-patter emerged—and the next thing you know, the weight has appeared, the sound has blossomed, the punch has arrived, the shaking is gone, and the hand is steady as a rock. His strength would arrive in full, and he would play an incredible concert for at least an hour. To see that phenomenon right in front of my own eyes was to understand the true healing nature of music.

Around this time my father, Ustad Allarakha, another legendary tabla player in his midseventies, would sit down to play a show with me accompanying him, arriving as a serious old man with glasses on. But as the concert began, I would see his face transform: a mile-wide smile would appear, an innocent playfulness would sparkle in his eyes, and he would become a child with his favorite toy in his playpen. The years would dissolve, the strength of a young man would run through his veins, and we were all swept away by his vibrating energy.

In the dressing room before these concerts, there would be two full-size tanpuras providing a drone for at least an hour. The maestros absorbed the vibrations of the drone, being bathed in the frequencies the drone produced, like a sonic jacuzzi. The vibration and drone frequencies entered their bodies: rejuvenating them, energizing them, and helping them focus on the task at hand. Their breathing would slow down, and they would settle on a tempo that their breath would establish, occasionally touching and reassuring the instrument—praying to the spirit inside the instrument to accept the contact and allow for the flow of thought, energy, and creativity. I was sixteen when I resolved to connect more deeply with the spirit inside my own instrument. This was precipitated by a very bad review of one of my concerts; my initial anger at the review slowly turned to clarity, as I realized that the critic was, in fact, correct. I sought to ask my tabla to help me see my way through to the next level of my apprenticeship with my father, who was my guru. For this I journeyed to a shrine of a revered saint and prepared myself for the rigors of the Chilla, a (very biblical) forty-day retreat in total isolation with just me and my instrument. The tradition calls for the guru to give his blessing and prepare the apprentice for the perilous journey through the Chilla—but my father was away on tour with Ravi Shankar, and I did not want to wait, so I went anyway. The shrine keeper arranged for a man who would bring food and leave it outside the door of the hut, and who would stay nearby in case I needed help. But otherwise, it was just me, alone with my music.

I began my quest by activating the drone, focusing on the vibration of the strings and the tone of the drone for many hours. The process of this sonic bathing—immersing myself into the vibration and frequencies of the drone moving through me—was to have the spirit understand that I had the patience required to learn what it had to teach me. I was ready to touch the instrument in total submission to whatever the spirit intended. For the next six or seven days, I communed with my tabla for fifteen, sixteen, seventeen hours a day, doing nothing but playing music. The drone of my instrument filled the room; the vibration and the frequencies bounced around every nook and corner of the space, building layers upon layers of sonic shelves. Negative space did not exist, and the energy was good. Alone with these sound waves and with no one to talk to, I found myself drowning, losing consciousness, entering a dreamlike trance. I reached a point where the worlds seamlessly meshed; time stood still, and I had no recollection of how long I had been playing. Had I taken a break? Had I eaten? Was I thirsty? Where was I?

Whatever experiences you've had in your life will manifest themselves in some sort of visual encounter, because once the rhythm and the vibrations are playing for all this time, for all these hours, it gets hypnotic, and you get caught into this dream world. And then things start to appear. There seemed to be a crossing with no sign, as I stood there, not knowing in which direction to go. And then, walking toward me was an elderly dervish (a type of Sufi Islam mystic known for choosing a life of austerity). The man asked me my name and asked if I was lost; I answered yes. He then started giving me direction—but not in human language; rather, it was instead the language of the drum, the language of rhythm. Surprisingly I was able to understand exactly what he was saying. When he finished, he blessed me, said goodbye, and walked away. I continued along the path he had shown me and completed my forty-day retreat without much difficulty, arriving home with a much clearer understanding of my craft.

A couple of weeks later my father returned, and my mother told him of my Chilla. Hearing this he became furious—not because I had gone without his permission, but because of the fear that something bad might have happened to me. After some time he asked me about my experience. I told him about my practice regime and the discovery of a new composition. He asked me to recite the composition, and when I did, he appeared stunned. He was quiet for a very long moment and looked quite flustered.

Finally, he spoke up. "Where did you learn this?" I told him of the elderly man who helped me and taught me the composition. My father asked me to describe the man; I did, and my father again went silent. He started pacing up and down, very serious, and then walked away. After a little while he came back—and he gave me a hug. "You know this composition now," he said. "I've never taught it to you, but I am so blessed that I got to see this moment.

"The man you met at the crossing was my great grand-guru that came to you; the composition you had learned was his."

The remarkable thing is that I had never heard the composition before the Chilla, and there was no photograph of the long-dead man—yet I had met him and learned this composition from him. And so, it came to me in that manner—the rhythm that brought me to the ethereal plane. I transcended into a world where I met beings of incredible light and energy and knowledge. This is what the rhythm is all about; it has that incredible impact on you, reinforcing your ability to face the world. An unexplainable

happening, initiated through the power of the drone; its vibration project-
ing frequencies, which, in a focused atmosphere, perhaps opened a doorway
to a crossing—where, for a fleeting moment, souls met and passed on the
knowledge.

We as humans are not any different; it doesn't matter where we are. We
all know that love is an important element in our lives. Whether you go all
the way back to Muhammad, Jesus, Moses, Abraham, Zoroaster, Confu-
cius, or Vyasa, they all have said the same thing: love thy neighbor, be at
peace with each other, do good, be happy, be pleasant. And one of the elements of music is that it injects a happy thought inside of you. Even when
you listen to a sad song, and there might be tears in your eyes, you smile
and appreciate how beautifully that emotion was conjured. This is the thought
process that has existed from time immemorial. We as human beings are
sometimes led astray and forget that; maybe this is the time when that's
happening, and we're on a different track. But somewhere along the line,
through music, we will come back to the mutual understanding of 'āmīn
(Quran), amen (Bible), and shanti (Gita or Ramayana)—peace, truth, and
trust in one another.

Healing Note by Note

TOM SWEITZER, MMT, MT-BC

Cofounder and Head of Music Therapy, A Place to Be

MUSIC SAVED MY LIFE

At eight years old I never knew if I would live to see the next day. I was an only child living in a small town in the midseventies, with a mother who was dying and a father with paranoid schizophrenia, and major abusive fights between my parents would constantly tear through the house. My eight-year-old self had few avenues for emotional or spiritual respite; music was mostly absent at home, and on account of my father's very damaging relationship with God, religion was too. But every Sunday morning music would pour out from the stained-glass windows of the church across the street—and every night, I prayed toward the church, begging God for any hope of sanctuary.

One day, in fear of the screaming that would not end, I fled to the church, as God had answered my prayer and moved me to finally cross the street. That fateful morning, stepping inside for the first time, I was greeted at the church door by Erdean, a Sunday School teacher in a mint-green three-piece suit, pink cat glasses, and a hairdo that seemed to touch the ceiling. She took me in, and when I entered her Sunday School room, there in the corner was a piano.

In that moment Erdean introduced me to music.

Growing up I had never heard of music therapy, nor could I have imagined that there was a career that used the power of music to help people live healthier, more independent, and more fulfilling lives. But when people ask me why I became a music therapist, Erdean is truly why. Throughout the next ten years, she taught me to play piano and encouraged me to sing. She took me into her Sunday School so that I had a safe place to go, to make music and to be myself. As I grew older, I would cross the street to the church as early as six in the morning, volunteering to stay until nine at night—anything to stay out of the house. Erdean and the music she shared with me were my saviors; music gave me a way to express my pain and my imagination. Long before I became a music therapist, or even knew that music therapy existed, Erdean gave me therapy through music without even knowing it—and I am alive today because of it.

I continued to bury myself in music through college and beyond. Music theater became my life: I acted, directed, and taught voice lessons. Instead of opting to try my luck on Broadway, like many of my classmates, I went directly into teaching, running a music and theater program at a small private school outside of Washington, D.C. I loved it, but I knew I wanted to do something more.

One day at thirty-two years old, I found myself teaching voice lessons when a student walked into the lesson with a bombshell—his father had just taken his life in front of him. In shock I stared at this young man, just fourteen years old, as he asked me to write him a song. That night, I was in an elephant outfit in a production of *Seussical the Musical*, pondering my life and asking myself, *What am I doing sitting on an egg?*

That was the moment. I recalled what Erdean had done for me, and I was compelled by the feeling that I had a larger purpose in life than just performing. I love acting, but that night, I applied to go back to school to become a music therapist. I wanted to take all I knew about music and theater, and my love for people, and combine them to make a difference in the world. Once I began to uncover the clinical and data-based research in the field of music therapy, my mind and heart opened to the endless possibilities music could have on a person emotionally, physically, mentally, cognitively, and verbally, as well as on their overall health.

FORREST

Forrest was in first grade when I met him as his music theater teacher in school. Throughout the next seven years, I taught him music, directed him in school productions, and became enamored with his charm and wit. I became a mentor of his, and although music and theater were not his favorite subjects, he always gave it his best shot. As he went off to high school, I connected with him only infrequently, but it was clear he had made some poor choices as a student, as many high schoolers do. By this time I had attained my graduate degree in music therapy. Given my professional skill sets and our familiarity with each other, his parents asked me to help guide him onto the right track, and so we began meeting again periodically for sessions.

Until a catastrophic accident nearly killed him.

When he was seventeen and a junior in high school, Forrest lost control of his snowboard and slammed headfirst into a fence, without a helmet. The accident split his skull in half, and he was flown directly to Shepherd Center for Rehabilitation. With Forrest in a coma and his future looking bleak, his family held on to prayers and hope and told themselves if he was ever to wake up, they would do whatever it would take to rehabilitate him and give him the best life they could offer him. Even so, it was clear that this swaggering, athletic, and charismatic young man's life, from that tragic day forward, would never be the same.

Forrest's mom called me when he finally awoke from his coma. The first time I entered the hospital room, I was shaken by the astounding physical damage to his body—only to be drawn to his wide-open eyes, the only part of his body he could still control. Tubes, wires, beeps, and bandages were everywhere. I entered cautiously, with a guitar, and after talking softly to him, I began to sing. His gaze tracked me, and although his face was unable to make an expression, he seemed to smile with his eyes.

A few sessions later, as I was singing, we watched a small miracle: his pinky finger kept rhythm to the Beatles' "Let It Be." Months later he was finally able to be moved around, so with the very limited ability of his gross motor skills, we worked on his swallowing and breathing. I brought a recorder with me and would put it on his lips, and we would hope for the tiniest blow of air, aspiring for a sound. Dozens of sessions later, in an atrium at the rehab center, I again placed the recorder up to his mouth. A few seconds later there was the small miracle of a puff of air, strong enough to produce a minuscule peep of noise from the recorder. His parents' cell phone captured it again, and we were all brought to tears. You could see the pride in Forrest's face. His moment of producing one musical sound echoed in the hospital halls and in our hearts as if it were played by an orchestra at Carnegie Hall.

Months later, after numerous surgeries, the miracles of modern medicine allowed him to move back home for his major rehabilitation. While there was hope for him to regain a portion of his physicality and cognitive ability, there was uncertainty about his ability to regain his voice. I used numerous music therapy methods to engage Forrest. He was able to use his fingers, so I created an original song that prompted him to give either one finger or two fingers for answers. One finger was a yes; two fingers meant no. This song was learned by all family members and caregivers for everyday decisions. I used my theatrical background and dressed up as characters and danced for him, sang for him, and did anything I could to get a response—any sort of connection of recognition and response. Working beside his physical therapist, I would play the score of *Pirates of the Caribbean* and with a foam sword and an eye patch on I would sword fight him. Using clients' preferred music in music therapy, as we did here, allows them to better connect to the music and to the moment you are working in, and helps reinforce memories and physical actions. For Forrest, I would give him choices of each song we would use. The mere ability to make a choice independently gives a person autonomy and agency.

Music also redirected his attention during painful intimate moments. We would play soft piano and harp music when he had to be turned over and when he had to be washed or dressed. We used music for deep breathing exercises for his overall relaxation. I also collaborated with his speech therapist to create original music for the interventions. In tandem we worked on helping Forrest regain his swallowing, his production of sound, and his ability to vocalize.

MELODIC INTONATION THERAPY

For years speech language pathologists have utilized Melodic Intonation Therapy, which uses rhythm, pitch, and melody to assist in speech recovery for those suffering from aphasia. This method takes advantage of the ubiquity of music processing throughout the brain, and of the brain's innate plasticity, to rewire speech capacity to undamaged areas of the brain, using singing. Those who have had a stroke—or a traumatic brain injury, such as Forrest—often have a form of aphasia or apraxia, which limits their ability to communicate on several levels.

This therapy uses musical phrases with the clients, starting with the simplest of hums or whatever sound they are capable of. They are asked to repeat or imitate the phrase, and all the while the clinician keeps a steady rhythmic beat with her fingers on the client's right hand. As the client achieves success with the vocalization and verbalization, the clinician fades out, allowing the client to sing the phrase on his own. This is followed by fading out the melodic component—the singing—to generalize it into normal speech. With Forrest I would start by humming a short sound, then have him hum that sound back to me. Then I would turn that hum into a short phrase. For the first ten months, I would only get the faintest hum returned. Months more went by, and he answered with longer hums and deeper, more intentional breaths.

Then one day, I sang the phrase "Good morning."

And in his most fragile, quietest voice, he sang back, "Good morning," and the world stopped.

The caregiving team and I stood there awestruck. Over the next months the short phrases turned into bolder ones, with greater volume and longer numbers of words. Within six months after the breakthrough, Forrest was able to sing short sentences, which turned into conversations. And then we took the music away—leaving Forrest with a "voice."

More than ten years later Forrest went to college, now drives a car, and has a full life of friends and adventures. He has spent most of the time after his intense recovery raising awareness for helmet safety and raising funds for music therapy. He has become a hero and light for many in the traumatic brain injury community and beyond. I am honored to be a part of his documentary *Music Got Me Here*. What I experienced with Forrest is a true miracle. I was only a conduit for the music, but watching how it healed so many parts of his body, mind, and soul made me realize that music can do more than we ever could have imagined.

A PLACE TO BE

In 2010 I conceived of and cofounded A Place to Be Music Therapy in Loudoun County, Virginia. We work with any and every kind of disability or life circumstance that holds people back from living life to its fullest, using music therapy to help them face, navigate, and overcome these challenges.

Performance is a centerpiece for our clients, giving them the platform to express themselves through recitals, concerts, and theatrical productions, including advocacy and awareness events. I have had the opportunity to work as a music therapist with thousands of clients: individually, in groups, and in performances. Every day, I continually experience music's magical power of metamorphosis for people who are most in need.

My focus in the initial years was geared toward clients with developmental delays, including children with autism. Ryan, for example, first came to me at age eight; despite being mostly nonverbal and with extreme communication difficulties, he was a brilliant musician, able to write out music by ear and identify the beats per minute of someone's speech. So we created "The Communication Song," with which he would add words to his vocabulary and learn phrases to use with his family. This kind of communication with his environment did begin with singing each phrase, but it evolved into speaking as we added common phrases used in everyday speech. We continued with over ten years of original songwriting, and had Ryan perform characters in shows that gave him outlets of expression. Touring in performances in front of thousands of audience members, he would share who he was as a person beyond his autism, which gave him the confidence to further develop his goals and ideas.

This led to an open job letter he wrote and posted on LinkedIn in 2021:

Dear Future Employer—

My name is Ryan Lowry. I am 19 years old, live in Leesburg, Virginia, and I have autism. I also have a unique sense of humor, am gifted at math, really good with technology, and a really quick [learner].

I am interested in a job in animation, or in IT. I realize that someone like you will have to take a chance on me, I don't learn like typical people do. I would need a mentor to teach me, but I learn quickly, once you explain it, I get it. I promise that if you hire me and teach me, you'll be glad that you did. I will show up every day, do what you tell me to do, and work really hard . . .

The letter went viral, reaching *The Washington Post,* CNN, *NBC Nightly News,* and more. Millions of people read the letter, and thousands reached out in support; job offers and internships abounded.

Amy, another early client at A Place to Be, also leads her life seeking to inspire others. She is a motivational speaker who educates the public about humanity beyond disability. But when I first started working with her, she was unable to verbalize more than one or two words in each breath, because of her cerebral palsy. We spent two years of dedicated sessions focused on building lung capacity and vocal strength through breath control. Slowly we increased her pulmonary stamina to up to six words per breath, then to eight. After two years she could sing the entire "Part of Your World" from *The Little Mermaid*—with proper breathing and musical phrasing.

As word spread about our work at A Place to Be, some clients started coming from far and wide, seeking out our music therapy programs. Thanks to the documentary *Music Got Me Here,* a family from Lake George, New York, had learned about Forrest and the story of his recovery. They came to me with their son Patrick, who had been run over by a four-wheeler all-terrain vehicle. Since the accident, he had remained in a wheelchair, with severe traumatic brain injury, no movement, and no voice. A hardworking middle-class family, they would save their money to be able to come down to Virginia every four to six months for Patrick to work with me.

When Patrick and I began our sessions, he could barely grunt, let alone speak. I started by helping him make his grunting stronger and more defined. Eventually he was able to create two distinctive grunt sounds, representing yes and no. Watching the joy on his parents' faces, with even the progress of this basic communication, was inspiring and bittersweet. Patrick and I continued to push forward in our sessions together. In order to allow him to take part in one of our concerts, we worked for two months on having him get just a single word out, which he could then contribute during the performance of a particular song.

On concert day the group of participants onstage sang:

"Jingle bells, jingle bells, jingle all the . . ."

Then the music paused. Everyone in the audience waited expectantly. Twenty seconds passed, with everyone on the edge of their seats. Finally, a weak but determined voice rose from the stage:

"Way."

Patrick beamed, as the entire audience clapped and hollered in joyous celebration.

MENTAL HEALTH

As the first few years of A Place to Be flew by, we began to serve clients from every walk of life. Many people who came to us were not classified as disabled, but rather were searching for a sense of belonging, to connect to something greater than themselves. Performances like the ones in which Amy and Patrick took part are the heart of A Place to Be's community. Participating children and teens are provided opportunities to perform for audiences—and even write and perform their own music—as we tour our own large theater productions around regional schools and venues. We produce animated videos and other online content, having local children voice the characters and guide the story. Members of the local community frequently ask if they can volunteer with A Place to Be for these performances and projects—and when they do, they often come out of the experiences with as much of a profound transformation as the clients themselves.

One of our most emotional productions at A Place to Be has been *A Will to Survive*. Two local parents, friends of mine, wrote a letter for their son Will after he had taken his own life, and asked me to read it at his funeral on their behalf. The show emerged as a visceral response to my looking out and seeing the hundreds of teens in pain remembering and grieving Will. Working with a co-writer, and with encouragement from Will's parents, we created a production for high school students, confronting realities about depression, suicide prevention, and mental health awareness. The show incorporates segments from Will's diary, as my co-writer and I pored over his thoughts, dreams, and internal struggles night after night and transformed them into rock opera songs. Will's own mother, Ann Charlotte, a regional community actress, even plays herself in the production.

Each performance of the musical is a cathartic experience for Will's family, the student performers, the audience, and the larger community—transforming grief, through music, into productive and tangible healing. Hundreds of students in an assembly often come up and hug our cast members and Ann Charlotte after the show; attendees share their own struggles, with many talking about suicidal thoughts that they or someone they know has had. A Place to Be has a responsibility to use its creative platform for the betterment of our community in projects like these. And while we have clients come to us from all over, our focus has mostly been on our surrounding Loudoun County. Imagine what we could do beyond that.

In recent years, especially, with nationwide increases in rates of depression and suicide, we have seen a significant increase in clients seeking mental health treatment. Many of these clients had been nearly written off in life, but music has allowed us to make connections even in the most challenging circumstances.

One day, a sixteen-year-old client, whom we'll call Derek, arrived at A Place to Be. His mother had reported to our office that he was always angry and had been kicked out of school for being a potential danger to others; at every psychiatric or therapy session that his mother would try to bring him to, he would angrily storm out. In the hallway before our session, his mother whispered to me, "Don't be upset; he's not going to stay in that room with you. Don't feel bad—and he will probably tell you to f*** off. He won't be with you for more than two minutes."

We started our session, sitting across from each other; Derek's eyes pulsed with anger, and he genuinely looked as if he wanted to kill me. The only other thing I was told about him was that he liked drums, guitar, and music. So without anything else to go on, I asked him, "What would you like to listen to?"

"You're not going to like it," he said.

"Try me," I responded.

"Metallica."

I just turned on the music—Metallica's first album. I was still expecting him to curse me out and leave at any moment. But four minutes went by—and there he stayed, silent, just listening. So I kept the music going—track two, then track three. By tracks four and five, he laughed as we were banging our heads to the music. Then we started talking about the guitar around tracks six and seven. We reached the end of the album, and Derek just sat there, silent again. Fifty minutes had gone by. I had not said anything except little comments about the song. With the music over, he stayed, still not getting up. "Well, thank you!" I finally said. "Thanks for coming in today!" And he had tears at the bottom of his eyes. I asked if he was okay, and he looked up at me and said, "I just don't want to be the next school shooter."

When I went out to the hallway, Derek's mother came to me, stunned, and asked, "What happened in there?"

"Metallica," I said. "I didn't do anything!"

Derek stayed with me for regular music therapy sessions for a long time. We found him drums; he joined the band at his school, and he started a rock band of his own. However, I recognized my limitations as a music therapist in this situation. He liked our sessions, so I told him that if he wanted to come back, we had to get him a real psychologist. And we did—we found one who worked perfectly for him. The psychologist and I would share notes and coordinate our respective sessions. If he was having a really bad day, all three of us would get on the phone and talk through it. Slowly, week by week, he would start to open up—telling me why he experienced such hatred, why he felt he was picked on, and how he was bullied. He's really healthy now—in his early twenties, going to college and playing in a band. The music was the portal for him to finally speak, and to finally feel okay.

TELEHEALTH

By 2020 I had been a music therapist for ten years, and our A Place to Be Music Therapy was expanding. I was fully entrenched in our strategic plan, with the goal of becoming one of the best nonprofit music therapy centers in America. I began to spend much of my time speaking on behalf of music therapy on many different platforms. I even created a one-man show about how music saved my life and how that brought me into music therapy, with the hopes of inspiring others to join the music therapy cause.

Then came COVID. In-person music therapy sessions ceased. During the thick of the quarantine, many of our clients—already isolated even before the pandemic—barely interacted with the outside world. We worried that many of them would sense a lack of progress in their treatment, in addition to significantly higher anxiety and social difficulties.

Facing this, we dove headfirst into telehealth music therapy. It's not something we would have thought to do on a large scale prior to the pandemic; performing live music online is inherently difficult because of the natural latency delay of remote communication. Music therapy is generally more effective in a face-to-face setting, but as we grew our online presence, we did see benefits and positive experiences. For some clients, the physical distance of telehealth music therapy allowed them to feel more confident during the sessions. Many clients with autism—who may have trouble being in an unfamiliar room or around too much noise—found the Zoom platform to be a more controlled and accessible safe zone for our interactions. For others, telehealth opened up music therapy as a possibility when in-person sessions were not, such as for those who are immunocompromised, or those with mobility issues or work schedule constraints. (A lot of parents have a much easier time making a 6:30 p.m. Zoom session than coming in person after work!) And with music, we were able to offer much-needed socialization to clients during this isolation period—including for a group of one hundred and fifty at-risk elementary school children with high emotional needs.

While it was odd not to go into the office and work during the periods of complete quarantine, there was something beautiful about the relaxed environment at home for music therapy sessions. Postpandemic, we have mostly returned to in-person sessions, but some telehealth does continue with clients for whom it is beneficial or necessary. Music therapy over long distances has become more feasible, allowing us to work with clients in other states. And it's more flexible for music therapists as well—for example, if one of our music therapists tests positive for COVID but has no symptoms, they can continue to work from home.

LONG COVID

One of the group sessions we offered during the pandemic was for "COVID long-haulers." After finding a support group and reading about their severe and intense bouts with this virus, I was moved one day to offer a free music therapy session for those who might need it. Within a week the group swelled to fifty faces on my Zoom screen. Each week COVID survivors from all over the nation would put aside an hour of their lives to work on their physical, mental, and emotional health. I would ask participants to suggest a song that makes them feel powerful or makes them want to dance. We breathed, we talked about the long-COVID journey, and we allowed music to work its magic, subsiding anxiety and allowing us to smile and experience a way to connect and feel validated. We create playlists and share them with the group: playlists representing music to calm, music to breathe to, music to pick you up when you are down. My biggest surprise is how the core group has never missed a Wednesday night, which has made me feel honored and responsible. Throughout the years, this group has transformed into more of a hybrid of music therapy, entertainment, and a place to share personal emotions. The horrible isolation that COVID created is even more severe for those who still suffer the aftereffects of the virus. The impacts for COVID long-haulers can include exhaustion, lung damage, brain fog, severe muscle and body pain, and other chronic conditions.

I should know. Because I am one of them.

On July 8, 2020, I contracted COVID. I was hospitalized for a little under a week, but I was told the night I was admitted that I was hours away from a ventilator. That night I was turned upside down onto a table with my tears falling onto the stark hospital floor. I prayed to stay alive and made plans in my head for how I could do more to help others, and I reflected on all the things I wanted to experience personally before I died. When I returned home, I was on oxygen for a month. For months after, my oxygen levels remained too low, and my heart rate was constantly racing; I couldn't take a full breath, and I couldn't sing. So I applied everything I knew from singing and music therapy to regain my breathing and oxygen level, and I began my own regimen of breathing exercises to expand my lung capacity. I would start my day with thirty minutes of stretching and deep breathing. Then I would turn to the music, singing for two hours every day. Just as I'd done with my clients, I used it to expand my phrases and to exercise my lungs, supporting them back to a healthy state—though it took almost eight months to improve my pulmonary capacity.

The effects of COVID persisted beyond just my lungs. Its greatest and most long-lasting impact for me was the brain fog—I no longer have the same brain I did before my bout with COVID. During my hospitalization I had a 105-degree fever for three days; imagine what that did to my brain tissues. In the year after my 105-degree fever I had difficulty with verbalization, persistent short-term memory issues, short but complete blackouts, and challenges with executive function. It literally felt like a brain fog; crossing the street, I would remember feeling as if I were drunk at one o'clock in the afternoon. One morning I woke up thirsty, and at the same time, I remembered I had not charged my phone. So in the kitchen I filled my glass up with water, and then I took my phone charger and promptly stuck it in the water. Another time, when I was barbecuing, I took a piece of chicken and stuck it in the washing machine. Each of these lapses lasted only a few seconds—but they were frequent, and often scary. At one point I dropped a utensil in a pot of boiling water—and proceeded to submerge my whole hand in the pot to retrieve it.

For the whole first year I was greatly impacted by these effects. Sadly, the neurological symptoms I experienced matched those of my clients who have had a stroke, traumatic brain injury, or chemotherapy. Fortunately, the similarities of the cognitive impairments allowed me to utilize the therapeutic tools I use with clients to help myself. I had never been afraid to speak before, but I found myself having to be slow and deliberate before doing so, and sing the words I wanted to say, just as my clients did. This was particularly difficult for me as a performer: my one-man show has 990 lines, and I needed to entirely rememorize about half of them. Though my brief memory blackouts when practicing would last only a few seconds, I would completely lose my place in the performance. Luckily the flow of memorized lines is like music and singing; with their flow and rhythm already deep in my memory, they came back with continued practice. I used my own show as a healing process for my brain.

Only after about eighteen months did my brain finally get back to a semblance of normal, with the small misfires and memory lapses becoming rare—but my brain is definitely different than before. Previously a constant multitasker, I have had to force myself to slow down and write everything down throughout the day, lest I triple-schedule myself. I continue to use music daily to help my memory and my focus, just as I do for my clients.

COMMUNITY

In addition to the COVID Zoom group, I started a weekly Facebook Live to document the progress of my recovery and connect through music with anyone who wanted to listen. Friends and neighbors would tune in, as would others around the country, as I demonstrated the singing and breathing exercises that I used to improve my own lung capacity. Hundreds of chats, messages, and emails poured in during and after the sessions, with notes that said things like "Thank you for getting me through nine o'clock today," and others who shared their own struggles with the virus. COVID, despite all its devastation, yielded an opportunity to come together online for people who needed a sense of home—and we came together with music.

I saw the strength of music's social bonds in my own community as well. A Place to Be is located in a very small town—Middleburg, Virginia. Our music therapy program and the concerts we put on are a prominent enough fixture in the town that I'm almost famous at the local Safeway supermarket! Everyone in town knows me, and always says hello. So when I was one of the first people in Middleburg to get COVID early in the pandemic, people noticed. Any hesitation about wearing masks and social distancing evaporated when they'd heard about what happened to me or saw me with my oxygen. I was the stark reminder of the seriousness of the pandemic.

And the community we have sought to bring together through music at A Place to Be came back around to support me—and all its members—as the world shifted around us. Every day, as I struggled to heal, a bag with soup and a bunch of flowers would appear at my doorstep. When we reached Christmas, I brought my keyboard out into the yard, and the community came together for a socially distanced sing-along. Amid the devastation of the virus, and the fears of grocery shelves empty and jobs and lives lost, music gave our community an outlet to dance, and even to laugh—and to bond with one another.

The online COVID support group continues on Zoom to this day, meeting every Wednesday in a deep seventy-five minutes of sharing; I make sure to rarely miss a meeting. I'm sad to see how many members still have severe physical and cognitive damage that lingers in their lives, constraining them from living life to its fullest. And since the group began, some of our members have passed away. Once in a Zoom square, and now gone. I have heard people's most intimate and vulnerable stories, and often I will pick a song to lift their spirits after what they shared. The music acts as the host during our sessions; it can dig deeper and faster than speaking can, and it fosters companionship. Sharing ideas and feelings through music has been a fantastic way to feel understood and to provide a sense of belonging. As I healed throughout the first year, this virtual group—just like my physical community—gave me validation and hope. Many of the members have told me that knowing they meet every Wednesday to fill themselves with music gets them through the week. I feel just as lucky as they do, and honored, to have an hour with friends and music to make my life a little better too.

Because, in the end, the healing comes from the music itself.

The Potential of Group Singing to Promote Health and Well-Being

JULENE K. JOHNSON, PhD

Professor of Cognitive Neuroscience, Institute for Health and
Aging, UCSF School of Nursing

Codirector, Sound Health Network

The idea that singing can promote health and well-being has been con-
templated for thousands of years. As early as 400 BC Hippocrates
and others theorized about the benefits of singing alongside the development of the practice of medicine. In his *Regimé*, Hippocrates discussed the
value of singing for helping balance the components of good health, using
singing to "warm and dry the soul and to rarefy the flesh."

During this time, singing and vocal exercises were broadly considered
under the health-promoting activity of "exercise." The act of singing also
was thought to bring air into the body and affect inner spirituality, which
in turn improved physical health. Other ancient Greeks considered music
as therapeutic in a broader sense—through the process of creating harmony. It
apparently was widely accepted during the Middle Ages (circa fifth to fifteenth
century) that singing could promote health. Musicologist Gretchen Finney
reflected, "There is no reason to believe that anyone throughout the Middle
Ages questions the belief that, prudently used, 'the exercise of singing is . . .
good to preserve the health of Man.'" Physician and philosopher John Case
wrote in *Apologia Musices* that singing was good for "agitating the lungs,"
which in turn would produce "generous heat and spirits in the heart and
dispose and dispels all vapors." In *The Principles of Musik in Singing and*

Setting, seventeenth-century musician and priest Charles Butler noted that singing could help prevent asthma, pneumonia, and wasting of the body.

An interest in studying singing and health expanded over time. As one example, the Swedish historian and poet Olof von Dalin provided one of the first observations of the preserved ability to sing after a brain damage. In 1745 Dalin published a short report of a man who had lost his ability to speak after a stroke; yet he could sing previously known hymns. Observations that some people living with aphasia were able to sing songs inspired scholars over the next three hundred years to examine the relationships between music, brain, singing, and language. Musicologist Amy Graziano and I were fascinated by these nineteenth-century clinical reports and have spent many hours searching for descriptions of music in eighteenth- and nineteenth-century neurology and psychology literature. We wanted to understand how prior scholars framed questions about music and the brain, which ultimately led to insights about how music (including singing) was processed by the brain. Over the past two decades, music has become an increasingly popular topic in neuroscience research. In parallel, there was increasing interest in studying the impact of group singing on health and well-being, in both clinical and nonclinical settings.

The more contemporary study of the impact of singing on health and well-being (in nonclinical populations) emerged in the early 1990s. Singing also has been actively used by music therapists in clinical practice since the founding of the profession in the 1940s. I became interested in studying the impact of group singing on health and well-being as a Fulbright Scholar in Jyväskylä, Finland, in 2010. This was the first time in my academic career that I could focus just on music research, after studying music for my undergraduate degree and cognitive neuroscience for my doctorate (investigating memory for music in Alzheimer's disease). While in Finland I collaborated with the departments of Music and Gerontology at the University of Jyväskylä to better understand the relationship between well-being and singing in a choir as an older adult. Lifelong involvement in music is a treasured cultural value in Finland, and many embrace community choir singing throughout their lives. Although a relatively small city (with approximately 125,000 residents), Jyväskylä had approximately fifty choirs for people of all ages, six of which were exclusively for older adults. Here I learned firsthand the potential of singing to promote health and well-being for older adults.

After returning to San Francisco I connected with the local government office on aging and a local community music center to explore the possibility of designing a research study to examine the effects of singing in a choir on the health and well-being of older adults from diverse racial/ethnic and socioeconomic backgrounds. At this time there were only two longitudinal intervention studies of group singing for older adults, but other promising studies about the impact of choir singing on health had been done. Research studies over the past twenty years have documented that singing in a community choir as an older adult was associated with multiple health benefits, but most of these were cross-sectional studies, and causality could not be determined. Around this time the National Institute on Aging (of the National Institutes of Health) called for grants that would test novel interventions that had the potential to help older adults remain active and independent in their communities. Our grant submission was successful, and a three-way collaboration between the University of California San Francisco, the San Francisco Department of Aging and Adult Services, and the San Francisco Community Music Center formed the "Community of Voices," the largest study to date about the impact of choir singing on health and well-being among older adults.

THE COMMUNITY OF VOICES STUDY

The Community of Voices study was a multisite, "cluster-randomized" trial that involved twelve senior centers (which functioned as the "clusters") in San Francisco County. Each of the centers was randomly assigned to receive the Community of Voices choir program immediately after enrollment or after a six-month delay. Random assignment of the senior centers allowed comparisons of those who participated in the choir (i.e., intervention group) with those who waited to start their choir (i.e., control group). The Community of Voices program involved taking part in weekly choir sessions for twelve months. These sessions were held at senior centers throughout San Francisco and were led by professional choir directors and accompanists who could promote health and well-being: cognitive, physical, and psychosocial engagement. The choir directors selected the music repertoire to address these core components and tailored it to be appropriate to different skill levels (from beginners to advanced) and to be challenging enough to facilitate growth and mastery over time. They also arranged the songs to be appropriate to the singing voices of older adults. The participants used folders to organize their song sheets (e.g., memorizing the music was not required). Each choir gave an informal performance every three months.

Three hundred and ninety adults aged sixty and above were enrolled into one of twelve choirs that were newly started for the study. The average age was seventy-one years, and participants reflected the rich cultural diversity in San Francisco. After all of the twelve choirs completed six months of weekly singing, we analyzed the main randomized trial results. The assessments in the Community of Voices study focused on three areas that were the hypothesized mechanisms of the choir intervention: cognitive, physical, and psychosocial engagement. For cognitive function, we assessed verbal memory (remembering a short list of words), attention (concentrating on a task), and executive function (shifting attention from one task to another). The physical function assessments focused on measuring lower-body strength, walking speed, and balance. The psychosocial outcomes included surveys about positive affect, interest in life, loneliness, depressive symptoms, and anxiety. To complete a cost analysis, we asked questions about use of health-care services (e.g., visits to doctor or nurse). Finally, we also collected descriptive information that included questions about prior experience with singing, other activities, and self-reported ratings of musical skill. When we analyzed the main randomized comparisons, we found that the older adults who sang in a choir had a significant decrease in feelings of loneliness and an increased interest in life. However, the cognitive and physical outcomes and health-care costs did not change. Although the health-care costs were higher in the control group compared to the experimental group, the difference was not significant.

GROUP SINGING AND AN OVERALL SENSE OF "FEELING GOOD"

After completing the cluster-randomized trial, we also conducted focus groups in which participants were encouraged to share their perspectives and experiences and react to others' during the group discussion. They highlight issues that are important to them and use their language and narrative styles to share their experiences. We hosted six focus groups after participants completed twelve months of singing in their Community of Voices choir. We interviewed thirty-one choir participants with an average age of seventy-one years; the majority represented diverse racial/ethnic backgrounds (e.g., Latino, Asian/Pacific Islander, Black/African American). Sample questions included: "Overall, what did you think of the choir program?" and "If you had to describe to a friend what singing in a choir does for you, what would you say?" We audio-recorded and transcribed the focus-group discussions and identified themes using content analysis. More details about the study can be found in our publication.

Participants in the focus groups identified several benefits that they attributed to participating in the Community of Voices choirs. An overall sense of well-being, often expressed as "feeling good," was overwhelmingly reported as a benefit. One older Latina choir participant shared, "The choir— it rejuvenates you. It gives you encouragement, more will to live. Music is medicine for the soul. It's helped me a lot."

Another participant in the Community of Voices study remarked, "Ever since I started here with the choir—with any music now—I can get the rhythm. I started feeling happy. Friends arrived; we sang. Now to me everything is music. I feel really good."

Participants also reported multiple positive emotions associated with singing in the choir. These included happiness, enjoyment, compassion, contentment, optimism, relaxation, peacefulness, unity, gratitude, and awareness of beauty. One participant explained how singing in the choir helped her find deep enjoyment and appreciation, which led to becoming stronger and braver, even in the context of life challenges. She also shared how she was changed with an encouragement to live life to the fullest, saying, "We are not the same as we were when we got here. I have loved it so much. I've always been involved with music, but I learned so many things here that I didn't appreciate before."

A deep sense of enjoyment and relishing good experiences has been described as "savoring" the moment. Psychologists Frank B. Bryant and Joseph Veroff describe savoring as the ability to notice and appreciate experiences, events, and feelings or, simply put, noticing the good in one's life. Singing in a choir seems to promote savoring, along with other emotions that are important for promoting health. For example, another participant described how singing in the choir activated previously dormant emotions, sharing, "Words came out of my heart that were dormant. But seeing my peers and singing, well, that has surfaced in me. I had plenty to offer, but it was dormant within me. I mean, it was awoken during this wonderful time that we have shared here."

Participants in the Community of Voices choirs also reported other psychosocial benefits, including improved self-esteem and self-confidence, increased social connection and support, and decreased loneliness. Singing in a choir promoted cultural identity and appreciation of other cultures. This was attributable, in part, to the fact that the Community of Voices study recruited socioeconomically and racially/ethnically diverse older adults, which differed from prior studies that involved participants who were predominantly white and from higher socioeconomic backgrounds. Future research could focus in more depth on the mechanisms by which singing affects well-being and be more inclusive by gaining more diverse perspectives about the benefit of singing on health.

GROUP SINGING AS A STRATEGY TO PROMOTE HEALTH AND WELL-BEING

As discussed above, it has long been hypothesized that engaging in music might be good for the mind, body, and community. Older adults who regularly sing in a choir often report high levels of self-confidence, enjoyment, and positive emotions. Group singing is also associated with a sense of belonging and higher levels of social interaction, social inclusion, and less loneliness, in addition to other mental health benefits, such as reduced symptoms of depression and anxiety. Researchers have attempted to categorize these benefits into broader categories, such as psychological (e.g., happiness, self-esteem), social (e.g., social inclusion), cognitive (e.g., attention), and physical benefits (e.g., breathing, posture, stamina), and emerging research is focusing on benefits to the immune system (e.g., cortisol, cytokines). Numerous studies have shown that higher levels of well-being are associated with healthy behaviors, longer lives, and people's perception of their health.

Singing engages multiple systems that are important to health, including physical, cognitive, emotional, and sensory systems. For example, singing relies on the body (e.g., vocal apparatus, motor system, chest-intercostal and neck muscles, diaphragm), sensory systems (e.g., auditory, visual, proprioception), and physiological systems (e.g., respiration). Singing also makes demands on vocal control (e.g., voice quality, voice to convey emotions). Singing also involves interactions among systems, including the coupling of sensory and motor systems. For example, singing involves hearing sounds, matching sounds with those of other people, shaping the vocal apparatus in a way that will produce the desired pitch, and then automatically coordinating the respiratory and motor sequences necessary to make sound. When producing vocal sounds, the singer receives auditory feedback about the accuracy of the note, often in the context of others, and can modify or maintain the ongoing production of the sound. This process occurs on the order of milliseconds and occurs thousands, if not hundreds of thousands, of times throughout a choir rehearsal and performance.

Choirs also have other advantages. They are practical and can be implemented in a variety of community settings (e.g., community centers, senior centers, faith-based organizations, schools). In addition, the music repertoire can be culturally tailored to reflect different cultural backgrounds and shared cultural traditions. Singing in a group has the added benefit of being something that can be done throughout the life course. As one older adult in the Community of Voices study remarked, "I used to sing when I was young. I would sing in my ranch, and the songs were Antonio Aguilar's, Miguel Aceves Mejía's. I would climb the trees and sit all the way up there and sing. And then people would poke fun at me and say, 'Hey, I can hear a little bird singing.' I would just laugh. I would sing all the time, singing and singing all day long. And I kept singing; when I married my husband, I had kids, and I would sing to my kids."

This quotation provides a reminder that music creates meaningful experiences throughout life. With older adults there is an opportunity to build upon these meaningful experiences earlier in life and to create new opportunities with music in later years. There are also opportunities to provide more precise recommendations and to tailor different types of music-based interventions based on specific needs of older adults. For example, if someone is concerned about feeling lonely, we might prescribe a choir, whereas if someone is concerned about their memory, we might prescribe a music training program. These questions and others need to be answered via the scientific method and well-designed scientific studies.

With recent societal challenges related to the COVID-19 pandemic and an increase in concerns about mental health and well-being, there are new opportunities to consider the potential of group singing and other types of music engagement. Although singing was considered a high-risk activity during the pandemic (because of aerosol transmission during singing), some choirs adapted by creating virtual choirs, with mixed success. However, several studies found that the benefits outweighed the challenges, suggesting that group singing could become more widely available and accessible in the future with the appropriate technology and supports. As such, group singing and other music experiences have the potential to more broadly help improve well-being and promote positive social experiences across the life span using old and new approaches.

Building on the need for more interdisciplinary collaborations among researchers, music therapists, musicians, music educators, clinicians, and others, the Sound Health Network was founded in 2021. This network is an initiative of the National Endowment for the Arts, in partnership with the University of California San Francisco, in collaboration with the National Institutes of Health, the John F. Kennedy Center for the Performing Arts, and Renée Fleming. It aims to promote research and awareness about the impact of music on health and wellness. The network built on the Sound Health Initiative, which grew out of a transformative partnership between the National Institutes of Health and the John F. Kennedy Center for the Performing Arts. Sound Health is currently following recommendations for building the evidence and infrastructure to support research about the use of music to foster health.

In summary, the potential for singing to promote health and well-being has been considered for thousands of years. Current efforts are poised to generate new scientific knowledge about the benefits of singing and music across the life span, ultimately advancing the potential of music to improve all our lives.

Sing Your Way Home:
How Music Therapy Taught
Me to Trust the Journey

STACIE AAMON YELDELL, MA, MT-BC, AVPT

Founder and Music Therapist, Amöntra Music and Wellness

The voice is a light. If the light becomes dim, it has not gone out; it is there.
It is the same with the voice. If it does not shine, it only means that it has
not been cultivated and you must cultivate it again and it will shine once
more.

—INAYAT KHAN

"Here comes Staaacie," the nurse announced in a singsong voice. As one of two music therapists in the Expressive Arts Department at the Children's Hospital Los Angeles, I could often be seen traipsing from floor to floor and room to room, with a guitar strapped to my back and rolling a crate full of myriad musical instruments: bells, shakers, small drums, a mini xylophone, to name just a few.

The hospital staff could actually *hear* me coming . . . shaking, rattling, and jingling all the way, even before I was in their line of sight.

I spent the majority of my time on the Bone Marrow Transplant unit, treating kids with varying stages of cancer. It was an intense place with a frantic pace, heavily laden with sorrow, laced with glimmers of hope. Years before KN95 masks would become a common accessory in a pandemic-stricken world, I had to suit up and boot up in thick rubber gloves, a hospital gown, and the mask before I could enter each kid's room. These patients' immune systems hung in a delicate balance—my hands were constantly peeling from the constant handwashing I had to do to keep them safe.

Typically I would see two to three patients a day. Each session would last anywhere from forty-five minutes to an hour. Afterward, I'd escape to the courtyard to reenergize under the rays of the California sun or maybe even dive into a bathroom to weep . . . especially after the more difficult sessions, like singing to a baby diagnosed with neuroblastoma or jamming with a family that was fighting back tears for a son or daughter whom they might lose.

I also had the luxury of retiring to my office from this heartbreaking reality. I couldn't imagine what it must've been like for the doctors, nurses, and families having to endure life on the unit, day in and day out.

My admiration for them is endless.

One day, while doing my daily rounds, a new patient popped up in my caseload: Sarah Ramos. When I arrived in Sarah's hospital room, she was curled up in the covers and surrounded by her parents, two sisters, and her brother. I immediately picked up on that familiar uncertainty and the incredulous concern that every parent experiences at the sight of their child in a hospital gown.

Even though I'd been working on this unit for almost a year, I never could get accustomed to the harrowing sight of a sick kid encircled by a frightened family.

Sarah, though, was a vibrant and very much alive sixteen-year-old, who, when she discovered she had cancer, had thick, flowing black hair. Like most teenagers she had an active social life and was already looking at dresses for her senior prom. She was diagnosed with myelodysplastic syndrome (MDS) after an attempt to donate bone marrow to her brother Samuel—who eventually lost his battle with the same disease.

Even in the wake of this, and sans her lustrous locks, Sarah's eyes sparkled with radiance and vitality when we met. Turns out, her other brother played guitar, so we spent our first session singing her favorite songs while he strummed along.

Typically our sessions began with sing-alongs and gradually evolved to composing original music and song lyrics. Thanks in large part to CHLA's family-centered healing approach, the entire Ramos family often contributed to the songwriting process.

As the weekly sessions continued, our work together deepened, and the songs we wrote became more personal and profound. Themes ranged from grieving the loss of Samuel to keeping the faith as Sarah continued to fight her own battle with cancer.

During one of our sessions, Sarah said she wanted to dedicate a song to Samuel. We gathered bedside and began to pen the lyrics:

"I cried for you . . . when you went to ICU . . ."

I suggested a few chords, put the finishing touches on the lyrics, and just like that, "Bravebird," an ode to Samuel, was born.

Sarah seemed pleased with our creation, but I sensed that she felt something was missing.

"Should we add a bridge?" I asked.

A bridge is a section of a song that's intended to provide contrast to the rest of the composition.

"Why not!" her little sister squealed animatedly.

"Sure," her parents agreed.

"What kind of a bridge?" Sarah asked.

I remembered that Sarah once played a recording of Samuel singing a lyric from a popular song. I suggested we build the bridge around it. I wasn't sure if this was the right intervention. It was risky—adding her deceased brother's voice to the song could be quite triggering.

Gratefully the Ramos family jumped at the suggestion.

Sarah's eyes blazed with a blend of excitement and sadness as we sang the completed song as a group. When we got to the bridge, Sarah pushed play on her phone's voice recorder, and Samuel's voice filled the room.

"So amazing . . . So amazing," he sang.

Turns out, something *was* missing. Samuel.

Our voices echoed his sentiment in unison.

"So amazing . . . So amazing . . ."

Miraculously, his ethereal voice was perfectly in key with the song. It felt as if he were in the room with us. Honestly, I don't know how I held it together. Even now, almost ten years later, I get choked up as I write this.

Through the healing power of music and an unconditional bond fortified by grief, the Ramos family were able to discover their collective voice and find solace in the crippling grief that is losing a child . . . and the prospect of losing another.

As a recording artist turned music therapist, I could have never pictured myself here in this brief, mystical moment in time.

I most certainly had a totally different version of how my life would play out.

Growing up in the early eighties, I idolized female singers with birdlike voices—sweet, shrill, and soaring. My own voice was wide, raspy, and deep-rooted. I spent hours after school playing classic twelve-inch records on the tiny stereo in my room. I would mimic Teena Marie's high notes in my mirror and make believe I could actually hit them.

Many years would pass before I would pierce the veil of my romanticized soprano dreams and behold my alto voice's true beauty.

One day, onstage, rehearsing for an upcoming show, my bassy teenaged voice bellowed the lyrics to Teena Marie's "Cassanova Brown" into the microphone.

"My baby's fine . . ."

"Stacie, stop playing around." That was my manager's cue for me to get back to rapping. This was his not-so-subtle way of "putting me in my place."

After all, I was the designated rapper. He already managed a singing group. I did sing in secret, though.

And so it went. Eventually the girl group got their record deal, and I almost got one of my own. The devastation of that "almost" left me disoriented and heartbroken, so I promptly shifted my focus to the business side of music.

But I never stopped my secret singing. Eventually I met a high-profile producer, and the wheel of fortune once again began its spin. This time it almost carried me to the steps of the Palace.

My dreams were within my grasp, yet just outside my reach. And this time, I wasn't rapping . . . I was singing.

No more secret songs.

But who could've foreseen what happened next? The ink had barely dried on the recording contract when I caught wind that my manager was skimming the finances, which meant he was literally taking money out of my pocket. I confronted him, and he denied everything.

Still, the rift had been opened, and there was no closing it.

The part of the story where I finally become a mega pop star deteriorated rapidly, and my Big Dream fell between the cracks.

Well, that was just about too much for me to handle. This turn of events set into motion the darkest days of my life.

In the depths of what felt like an insurmountable sorrow, I found music therapy.

Or it found me.

A few years later I stepped through the mahogany oak doors of the New York University Master's Music Therapy program, wobbly and wounded. As a classically trained cellist, I was stunned by the intuitive and psychological undertones of the audition process. I was expecting these folks to command me to play Beethoven or Mozart, but instead, they wanted me to play what "happy" and then what "indifferent" sounded like.

I was intrigued.

I showed up with the wrong guitar, with half a soul missing. But somehow those judges glimpsed the half that did show up, because a week later I received my acceptance letter. My heart leapt with joy.

By autumn, life had shifted on its axis. Suddenly I was catching the G train from Brooklyn to the West Village and strolling through New York City streets peppered with rainbow leaves.

My first day of class at NYU seemed surreal. The late and great Clive Robbins showed us videos of children diagnosed with autism singing at the top of their lungs, at-risk teens grinning and drumming together, and a sweet grandmother with dementia exhibiting a total recall of memory, just by listening to a song. By the end of the class I was misty-eyed and goose bumpy.

I had this inexplicable, innate knowing that I was about to become a part of something really special. It felt as if I were being initiated into some kind of mystery school.

Or Hogwarts.

As I matriculated at NYU, my experience would prove to be quite magical, indeed.

But on the inside I was still hurting. After all, my childhood dream of the stage had been deferred. What I didn't know yet was that becoming a music therapist would initiate the process of healing my inner-artist child.

Eventually I *would* be able to sing again—and from a much healthier place—without it consuming my entire sense of self. And somehow, some way, a Force—some call it Destiny—would pull me through the darkness.

And hurtle me forward.

As I approached the hospital room, the first thing I saw was a pair of wide eyes brimming with tears, peering from beneath the crumpled sheets of his hospital bed.

A round, chocolate face curved into a pronounced frown as I came nearer.

I checked the patient roster on my clipboard. His name was Jordan. He was eight years old and a patient on the Bone Marrow Transplant unit at the Children's Hospital Los Angeles.

I stood in the doorway and waved at him.

"Go away!" he screamed at me.

Clearly he had other places he'd rather be.

Turns out that Jordan had sickle cell disease and had been in and out of the hospital since he was four years old. Sickle cell is the most common genetic blood disorder in the United States, where it affects more than one hundred thousand people. Interestingly enough, people of African ancestry make up 90 percent of this population.

One of the more challenging experiences for those living with this disease is the pain crisis. When sickle cells travel through small blood vessels, they can get stuck and clog the blood flow. This causes pain that can start suddenly, be mild to severe, and can last for any length of time.

After enduring many of these crises and countless trips to the ICU, Jordan was preparing to receive a bone marrow transplant in the hopes of eradicating the disease completely.

"Hi," I introduced myself, "my name is Stacie. I'm the music therapist."

His walnut eyes sized me up. He pulled the blanket up to his chin.

"Can I come in? I brought some cool stuff with me."

Jordan didn't answer, but his eyes began to glisten with curiosity.

"Hello, Jordan . . . hello, Jordan . . . it's nice to meet you," I lightly sang while strumming the guitar.

This is the classic "Hello Song." It's one of the first techniques I learned in graduate school. Singing a person's name repetitively during a hello song can create a loving environment where healthy praise and a secure relationship can be developed. Additionally, as we've seen in so many romantic scenes in Hollywood movies, being serenaded can be a powerful experience in and of itself.

Jordan's face softened ever so slightly, and the previous hostility that permeated the room's atmosphere gradually dissolved.

I concluded the tune with a dramatic vocal flourish, pulled up a chair, and laid my instruments out on his bed, one by one.

So began our healing journey together.

Jordan had a robust support system. His mom visited every day and was an active and audible voice on his treatment team. He also had a cheerleading squad of siblings and cousins whom he would FaceTime with frequently, as well as a loving and supportive church community.

As for Jordan, he was your typical kid. He was into superheroes, video games, and sports. He said he missed playing with his brothers and sisters. His baseball team shouted him out at games, and despite the physical limitations his illness presented, he still walked and talked like a Little Leaguer.

In fact, I used to think of him as a big little man. On the outside he was this adorable kid who was into kid stuff. But the more time I spent with him, the more I noticed the very grown-up toll having to face a chronic illness on the daily took on his emotional state.

Jordan never seemed happy to see me. He would either sulk and ignore me, or participate in the session but refuse to follow cues. Or he would just hijack the iPad and play video games the whole time. Occasionally he would explode in anger when I would attempt to redirect him. Or just cross his arms in defiance.

The moments of authentic connection were few and far between. Another thing we had in common? We were both huge Marvel fans. In fact, the same day that Chris Pratt visited the hospital to promote his new *Guardians of the Galaxy* movie, Jordan stood up and danced in his bed during our session, in a rare moment of pure, unadulterated joy. To be honest, we were both pretty stoked.

But for the most part I didn't think I was making a difference.

Still, I leaned into my music therapy training and stayed the course.

Resistance, as it is commonly called, is a common occurrence in the treatment process. According to the *APA Dictionary of Psychology*, resistance is defined as "obstruction, through the client's words or behavior, of the therapist's or analyst's methods of eliciting or interpreting psychic material brought forth in therapy."

However, as noted by Pamela H. Steele in the article "Aspects of Resistance in Music Therapy: Theory and Technique":

> Resistance is an elusive concept to define for two reasons. First, it cannot be defined in terms of its objective content, that is, an act can be resistive or not, depending upon its context. Second, it can quickly and smoothly cease to be resistive when appropriate therapeutic techniques are used.

In addition, one must consider the obvious. What kid wants to be a patient in the hospital?

To make matters even more complicated, I experienced Jordan's seeming resistance as invalidation of myself, which triggered memories of similar experiences in my career as a recording artist. This increased my own personal resistance to working with him as a patient and amplified my experience of wanting to be "somewhere else"—both career-wise and quite literally. After all, I was still dreaming of singing on world stages.

This transferring of emotions is known as countertransference in the psychology world.

One of the ways I'd been soothing my own resistance to the unpredictable path that landed me in a children's hospital instead of an amphitheater was by finding ways to meet myself exactly where I was. In other words, to practice acceptance of my emotions and experience, free of judgment or overanalysis.

Ever since I was a child, I'd gotten into the habit of playing music to match my menagerie of moods, especially frustration, heartbreak, and disappointment. In my native land of Washington, D.C., I'd push record on my tape player and doze off to the sounds of the "Quiet Storm" radio station almost every night.

I didn't realize it at the time, but this was my way of utilizing music to self-soothe and to self-validate.

Remembering this, I delicately wove this practice into my work with Jordan.

On the days that were particularly rough for him, I would intuitively swing my guitar around from my back and walk in, strumming slowly. I can still picture his round cheeks, red with stinging tears.

After singing the "Hello Song," I would hum a familiar tune like "Twinkle, Twinkle, Little Star" and substitute a few of the chords with minor chords to match the sullenness of his mood.

Lightly and with intention, I'd begin to sing the words, oftentimes "directing" my vocal tones to his heart and any areas of his body that might be holding pain or tension.

S. E. Hale stated: "To sing is to use the soul-voice. It means to say on the breath the truth of one's power and one's need, to breathe soul over the thing that is ailing and in need of restoration."

I played the guitar in an arpeggio and alternating between two chords, which created a holding, lullaby effect. I'd watch intently as his breathing would deepen. His body would disengage and relax. He'd stretch out a bit in the bed. Once his affect began to shift, I would pepper in a few major chords and sing more brightly, in an effort to match the brightening of his mood.

One popular stereotype for music therapists is that our work primarily consists of cheering people up and goading folks into singing songs like "Kumbaya." That couldn't be any further from the truth. Try walking into a session with a patient who is mid meltdown singing Pharrell's "Happy," for example.

You just might catch a hospital tray to the head.

Think about it, though. How often do you want to hear an upbeat and jovial song when you are feeling down? The effect is most often cognitive dissonance.

Or more simply, extreme annoyance.

It's not to say that happy tunes aren't an integral part of the music therapy treatment process. But my primary role as a music therapist is to meet clients exactly where they are.

According to Ira Maximilian Altshuler, the *iso principle* is a "method of mood management in which the music therapist provides music that matches their client's mood, then gradually changes the music to help the client shift to a different mood."

Utilizing the human voice to validate Jordan's emotional state was a way of utilizing the iso principle. It was an invitation to fully experience what he was feeling, all the while giving him the space to organically move into a more expanded emotional state.

In addition, the use of the voice as a healing modality is a highly effective way to acknowledge, heal, and grieve loss, as well as varying levels of trauma.

In Jordan's case, numerous pain crises and consequently multiple trips to the hospital were traumatic in and of themselves. As our work together continued, it became more clear that Jordan was experiencing a myriad of emotions, including anger, sadness, frustration, and an overall sense of helplessness due to his prolonged hospitalization.

During one of our first sessions, I facilitated a music therapy assessment and asked Jordan what kind of music he liked to listen to. He said he was mostly into rap music and artists like Major Lazer, Bruno Mars, and Tyga. He also liked a few popular songs that were dominating the charts at the time.

One of the popular songs he asked me to bring in was "The Fox (What Does the Fox Say)" by Ylvis.

The song consists of repetitive themes with a predictable melody, with the first verse focusing on the sounds of specific animals. Jordan would sing the sound that each animal made, while I accompanied him on the guitar.

In the chorus, the lyrics ask the question, "What does the fox say?" This is followed by a cacophony of hilarious sounds that imply all the sounds a fox could make.

This seemed to be Jordan's favorite part. Each day he'd come up with a new sound. On some days he would just scream at the top of his lungs. The improvisational nature of the chorus created a bridge to the unconscious so that Jordan could express repressed or dissociated psychic contents through sound, words, and symbolic language.

This process of vocal improvisation holds tremendous therapeutic value.

According to Dr. Diane Austin:

> When we sing, our voices and our bodies are the instruments. We are
> intimately connected to the source of the sound and the vibrations.

We make the music, we are immersed in the music and we are the music. . . . The self is revealed through the sound and the characteristics of the voice. The process of finding one's voice, one's own sound, is a metaphor for finding oneself.

Unlike the piano, the drums, or other musical instruments, which act as extensions or expressions of our creative self, the voice *is* the self. Thus, it could be considered the most intimate musical instrument we have.

For instance, during the time I worked with substance abuse survivors, I had the opportunity to innovate a unique style of vocal improvisations that incorporated call-and-response chants. I coined these "Vocal Activations" and primarily utilized them to open and close a group.

As soon as we would begin to sing, I'd observe in awe as the energy in the room would palpably shift. It's like our cells would spin animatedly and the air would become rarefied. The fear and the pretenses hiding in the hearts of the brave souls whose journey led them to a treatment room would somehow mystically dissipate.

In the midst of life-shattering and body-shaking illnesses and maladies, I witnessed patients experience a seemingly immediate sense of safety: the activation of the human voice lovingly crafted for us a cocoon of sacred space.

As icebreakers and session starters, these "Activations" set the tone and gave us permission to allow the therapeutic process to actually begin. The discovery of one's voice can be powerful enough to open the seemingly locked door that traps us inside the mind's tyranny of thoughts. It can lovingly guide us back into our bodies . . . and into our hearts.

Considering the power of the voice, it makes sense that so many of us suffer from vocal trauma in our lives. In my case, as a young recording artist, I unconsciously gave away my power to the music industry. Without even realizing it, I hinged my entire sense of self upon the acceptance and validation of fickle and aloof A&R executives, and as a result, I suffered a severe creative injury.

Julia Cameron describes "creative injury" as the discouragement to be creative. She notes the importance of acknowledging our creative injuries and grieving them. If not, they can harden like scar tissue and block our growth.

Largely due to the popularization of competitive singing TV shows, we as a culture have become hardwired to consider singing as a "natural talent" and to equate it with judgment. Perhaps unknowingly, these types of shows have normalized harsh criticism of the human voice and posit that in order to sing, we must be "born" to do so. Fancy production and savvy editing can paint an unrealistic picture . . . we are led to believe that the contestants on these shows sprang forth from the womb with crystalline voices.

Even more damaging is the idea that if we aren't one of these "chosen ones," then we shouldn't sing at all. Or if we do dare sing, it should be confined to the shower . . . or our morning rush-hour commute.

It is not my intent to demonize these TV shows or the gifted people who create them. Most of these messages are subconscious, but they do have the power to affect our psyches in ways we may not realize. In the most extreme cases, I have worked with clients who unconsciously suppressed their voices by never singing at all, and in doing so, unknowingly suppressed their light.

If our human voice is a hallmark of our true character, our unique emanation in the world, then this vocal suppression could result in a type of character assassination.

By inviting Jordan to share his musical preferences and then providing vocal support, he was able to, much like the Ramos family, give a voice to feelings that had previously been voiceless.

Eventually, Jordan was discharged from the hospital, and our work came to an end. Our time together had been bittersweet. We both struggled with our own kind of resistance. Yet I had grown exponentially as a result of our collaboration. I had the opportunity to dig deeper within myself and examine the belief systems (the "BS") and the core doubts that had, for years, kept me chained to one version of what being a successful artist "looked like."

Personally I harbored concerns that perhaps my own personal struggle in accepting my "voice" in the role of music therapist had impacted my ability to help him find his.

A year later I walked away from my music therapy position at CHLA, never knowing if I had actually made a difference in Jordan's life at all.

In the years that followed, life became a magic carpet ride. I traveled to Salvador da Bahia, Brazil, and was invited to sing at the world-famous Carnaval, which helped me redefine the meaning of success and nullify my longing for fame and recognition. I became a soloist in the Agape International Choir in Los Angeles and sang inspirational songs, which further served to alchemize the evolving relationship with my voice.

One clear and crisp Sunday morning, I was singing at a local church when a tall, handsome, brown-skinned young man approached me as I exited the stage.

"Music therapy lady," he said matter-of-factly as he towered over me.

I blinked my eyes in bewilderment as I tried to place the face of the person standing in front of me.

It wasn't until I saw Jordan's mom enter from stage left that I realized it was him. The adorable, round-faced, chocolate-cheeked, frail boy that I remembered from CHLA had morphed into a full-grown teenager, bursting with life and vitality.

"Joooordan?" I drawled, in amazement.

He smiled and said, "Yep!"

I burst into tears. I couldn't believe what I was seeing.

His mom started crying, too, and before long there was a bit of a scene unfolding in the tiny lobby of this modest church.

Suddenly it dawned on me. The "church home" he mentioned in many of our sessions at the hospital . . . this was it. I was standing in it. I was *singing* in it.

A few of his siblings surrounded us, and I stumbled over a million questions that I wanted to ask.

Unbeknownst to me, the word was quickly spreading that I was the one who was a part of Jordan's "miraculous" recovery.

The preacher even wove our serendipitous encounter into the sermon.

"Look at God. We thought this woman was just here to sing. Turns out, she is here to heal."

I sat in the pulpit, speechless. I felt a hand on my shoulder. Jordan.

I glanced behind me, and he just nodded. This was our silent acknowledgment. Our work had made a difference. I *had* helped him find his voice.

And it just so happens, I found mine.

The preacher danced and shouted, repeating over and over: "You just don't know how God is going to use you . . ."

. . . & the Field: Re-membering the Hinterlands in Music & Health

MARISOL NORRIS & ESPERANZA SPALDING

We write this paper in the traditional, unceded territories of the Mult-nomah, Cowlitz, Confederated Tribes of Grande Ronde, Confederated Tribes of Siletz, and Lenni-Lenape peoples in the places commonly called Portland and Philadelphia, respectively. In sharing this, we bring to bear the historical vestiges of genocide, forced occupation, and erasure that continue to enact violence upon Indigenous peoples and the earth, water, and air they call home. In our Black bodies, marked with indigeneity—the confluence of Taino, Moor, African, and European peoples—we put metaphorical pen to paper and amplify the fullness of our present time and the interconnectedness of liberatory struggles. We invite you to join us in acknowledging all these things and our shared responsibility to make good use of our time and space together in text—to reflect on our roles in anti-colonialism, reclamation, reconciliation, solidarity, allyship, and partnership in shared struggle, and the ways our work is connected to radical resistance, imaginings, healing, and collective liberation.

PROLOGUE: ROOTS

It is like all the other things in creation that are truly themselves . . . all natural things really are strange and odd as beautiful too as they are.

—ALICE WALKER

In 1989, Indigenous scholar and music therapist Dr. Carolyn Kenny published *The Field of Play: A Guide for the Theory and Practice of Music Therapy.* Kenny's seminal book offered an overarching philosophy or pretheory of music therapy that centered aesthetic qualities across human experience and musicking as an energetic possibility. The flowing river Kenny divined considered the ecological conditions for musicking practices that moved beyond mechanisms of change toward a musical ethos of wholeness. In so doing, she amplified the relational space between musicking and co-creators, but most importantly, a focus not solely on doing but *being*—harmonious *being* with ourselves and with all living things surrounding us—and what it means to stay close to the earth. Nearly a decade later, Malidoma Somé, a revered teacher, knowledge bearer, and healer, published *The Healing Wisdom of Africa: Finding Life Purpose Through Nature, Ritual, and Community* (1999). In it, Elder Somé offered insights into the theories and protocol of his Indigenous Dagara culture and community. His work centered on the inherent value of healthy communities for persons, families, ecologies, and society at large. Amplifying the life of Indigenous and traditional peoples, he detailed multiple rituals designed for those within a journey of becoming—an ever-evolving, more relational *being* on a shared, sacred journey of healing, reclamation, and restoration. Though distinctly different in their lived experiences and occupational orientations, Kenny's and Somé's works poured from their personal stories, spiritual practices, and whole *beings* as Indigenous peoples—Kenny of Choctaw mother, adopted into the Haida Nation, and Somé of Dagara origin, from present-day Burkina Faso. After their respective passings, Kenny in 2018 and Somé in 2021, their lifework and journeys have continued to receive increased focus among minoritized communities across music and health and have been a continuous source of reflection as we, esperanza and marisol, consider healing trajectories at the margins, or as we prefer, the *hinterlands* of mainstream music and health discourse.

Our engagement in conversations converging music, healing, and transformation recognizes the sacred grounding of the hinterlands wherein Indigenous and traditional practices thrive. Entering this chapter, we are deeply influenced by and hold reverence for Dr. Kenny and Elder Somé, as well as the many teachers, healers, fields, and communities in the hinterlands— those thinly veiled, yet unknown, and those purposely cloaked. In many ways, they index the roots of fruit-bearing practices, unsevered from the energy of the undomesticated hinterlands—very much alive and well— grounded in ancestral legacies and communal wisdom, in reciprocal relationship with earth and spirit.

While roots are known to be vascular systems that supply nourishment to plant structures, we recognize their duality, also indexing genealogical mapping as a necessary resource that stories our current context. Existing underground, they are no less known, bearing fruit as *life force*. For these reasons, we could not help but enter with a posture of gratitude for how their work has seeded, nurtured, and rooted new possibilities in our individual and collective work across music and healing. To be rooted, for us, renders solitary *being*—often forebode by ancestral knowledge—as an unfathomable existence. Rootedness extends us beyond our personhood to recognize our connectedness as part of a reciprocal whole. Therein, naming our roots serves not only as acknowledgment but also as reclamation, recognizing origins, honoring the lands of our proud ancestors, touching the spiritual world, and returning to something otherwise deemed strange or unrecognizable by dominant culture.

MUCH OF THE FIELD

And then there are radical creative-intellectual amalgamations, the interdisciplines, the cross-discipline—the undisciplined—the matter that moves us beyond the academy, beyond the fields.

—FAHIMA IFE, *MAROON CHOREOGRAPHY*

The *field* explored across music and health discourse traces a convergence of multiple branches of study that yield insights into music's capacity to influence health and well-being. The fertileness of this discourse is often credited to the labor of merging fields, transgressing the sanctity of disciplinary boundaries to engender sound-based innovations that expand the applied use of music in medical and community-practice settings. Despite the growing body of cross- and transdisciplinary research and intervention-based approaches, commitments to "the field" have limited the possibility to deeply consider its multiplicity and those that have long existed outside its construction. Therein, the *fields* as a metaphor offers additional opportunities to consider (a) exclusionary practices that render those outside of mainstream discourses invisible; (b) constricting effects of culturally and spiritually denuded protocols dominating the professional work of music-based and capitalist constructions; (c) domains where undercompensated labor is permissible and industry-designated workers tend and till human or material source and resources, exclusively in accordance with the theories and designs of that industry; and (d) the *hinterlands* beyond the *fields*—thriving systems of healing and resiliency, beyond the domain of colonized and/or capitalist health industries.

Author and educator fahima ife, in her book *Maroon Choreography* (2021), centered Black Maroon traditions in contrast to the disciplinary trajectories typically upheld to underscore the magnitude of human experience. She lays bare the privileges these disciplinary trajectories are often afforded and attests to the limits of labor within walls. As we write our contribution to this book, our sensibilities are tuned to consider how entry into mainstream discourse often requires contorting to colonial constructs of personhood (who is deemed human, and the range of human experience), property or place (whose humanity precludes a possession of space and the capitalist consumptions that assumes the ownership of place), and narrative (the storying of one's humanity and relationship with beings and space).* We shed the need for contorting our subjective narratives and vying for validation. Instead, we wish to move away from the proverbial *fields* and participate in radical creative amalgamations, the communion of people—the interdisciplines, cross-disciplines, the intentionally undisciplined.

Imagination is the generative and intrinsic essence enlivening our collaborative devisings of how to help each other heal (much like Kenny's *field of play*). Radical imagining asserts the ability to conceive sociopolitical and spiritual possibilities not as they are but as they could be. May this writing be part of our practice embodying that shift. Through testimony from our lived experiences and seeds from our collective devisings for new possibilities, we hope to offer entryways for exploring the multidisciplinary methods we feel privileged to have encountered through our respective and shared experiences in music-informed healing. We offer a milieu of reflections and questions born from radical imaginings that are all in "undisciplined" conversation with one another. Of which we ask: What does it mean to be

---

*Elements of personhood, property, and narrative discussed in CharCarol Fisher and Hakeem Leonard's "The Agency of Hip Hop as a Force of Liberation and Healing in Music Therapy," in *Colonialism and Music Therapy*.

free (not solely freedom as an intellectual pursuit but deep, soul-flying free)? How does freedom look, feel, sound, sense? For the music and healing community: How may we facilitate the conditions of freedom within our work that support the liberatory aims of the communities we serve?

PLACEMAKING: INDIVIDUAL AND COMMUNAL STORYING

If one of my friends is ill, I'd like to play a certain song and he will be cured.

—JOHN COLTRANE

Us too.

—ESPERANZA AND THE SONGWRIGHTS APOTHECARY LAB

Over the past three years, we have embarked upon the sacred journey of communing in music. We strive to honor the multiple *fields at play*, radically imagining the possibilities for healing and growth as a continuous move beyond the walls of mainstream paradigms. At the center of this work has been a profound love for people—their full beings, their musical transformations and freedom; a love for the breadth of musicking and all the possibilities it holds; and for the work of deepening the healing potential of music that can only be done through communion. At the root of our/my (marisol's) imaginative searchings is a deep desire to understand the significance of (1) being made "the other"—Black alterity made commonplace in public space—the investments into *othered* existence by a dominant mass within globalized music and health contexts, and (2) the politics that were enlisted to substantiate this otherness across space and time. The desire to unpack otherness therein is a spiritual realigning, not solely the amplification of eliminatory violence but rather a centering of *power*, the expansion of influence. This conscious unearthing of the ways that Black *power* (read "influence") is appropriated across contexts to reimagine spirit, being in spirit, relationship to spirit, and the spirit of perpetual healing gives birth to liberation. The nucleus of our/my (esperanza's) interdisciplinary work is the living archive (and lineage) of improvisation-based, co-musicking practices that have nourished me and my friends, family, colleagues, and community. I/we have come to this work with the embodied need to center these modalities, notice where they already exist within our respective and collective cultural identity/lineage, and wade into deeper contact with the complex river of healing potential coursing persistently through our species.

esperanza: Origins of Songwrights Apothecary Lab

In 2015, a close friend plunged into an intense and urgent healing journey. I watched them, an artist and religious scholar, dredge up and engage with countless healing modalities. Their compassion, openness, and perseverance through their journey of recovery inspired me deeply. Their reflections about how their upbringing and socialization had affected their emotional well-being awoke in me a hunch that I, too, had unaddressed traumas that affected my wellness and way of navigating the world. During that season of deep growth and exploration, my friend introduced me to many books and methodologies, including Laurence Heller and Aline LaPierre's *Healing Developmental Trauma* (2012).

Heller and LaPierre spoke about how trauma lingers in our nervous system, and whether tended to or not, continues to affect us throughout our lives. The authors offered a paradigm for addressing the neurological aftermath of trauma. So much in that book struck me to my core and taught me that, indeed, I had developed very potent survival strategies for skimming over the effects of trauma in my life. I understand now that the "mental health" issues that many adults in my early life struggled with were brilliant survival strategies, allowing them to endure the aftermath of their harrowing upbringings. Of course, as a child, growing up with unwell caregivers was traumatic. Within the often chaotic milieu of my early life experiences, my mother set a profound example of hope and resiliency as she confronted and tended to her healing needs. My mother continues to inspire me through her ongoing efforts to learn about herself and apply relevant resources and structures to support healing and recovery.

Taking this preliminary inventory of my life, along with witnessing my friend's healing journey, eased me into a season of deeply investigating my well-being. Two seminal books I encountered during that period were Bes-

sel van der Kolk's *The Body Keeps the Score* (2014) and Alejandro Jodor-
owsky's controversial *Psychomagic: The Transformative Power of Shamanic
Psychotherapy* (2010). In quite contrasting or contrapuntal ways, these two
books alerted me to the potential of music and performance-based engagement to support the transmuting of deeply stored trauma. In that same
period, I experienced Reiki for the first time. Though I had no reference or
framing for what I was experiencing, I recognized in it a visceral sensation,
similar to my first experience with classical music. I felt immediately drawn
to it, committed to learning about it, and aspired to recreate the experience
for myself and others. In 2018, I began to integrate Reiki into my therapeutic and creative practices. Composing at the piano one morning, I felt
a rush of inspiration to write a body of music intended to prompt a particular experiencing of various body parts. The title, concept, and theme for
each song arrived all at once, and I immediately started developing what
would become the album *12 Little Spells*. While creating each song on the
album, I drew from Reiki, psychomagic techniques, and various books and
articles relating to the somatic dimensions of healing.

Over the course of creating, producing, and releasing these songs, I
recognized that this was more than an artistic concept or conceit. I truly
wished for these song spells to affect the listener's body, I truly loved (and
still love) the song-spells that took shape in my little laboratory with fellow
musicians, guided by my intuition and our developed musical instinct. But
I felt that for the salutary aspiration to mature, I would need guidance,
council, and accountability from practitioners with knowledge and understanding of how music and performance-based practices affect human
physiology.

In 2019, the compromised health of my mentor and collaborator Wayne
Shorter compelled me to pause all other creative and professional endeavors
and move to LA to finish the opera Mr. Shorter and I had been slowly developing for half a decade. During that year in LA, I received the gift of a
mental breakdown. Due partly to unaddressed and compounding traumas
emerging in my life, plus the stress and stakes of Mr. Shorter's health and
the opera project itself, my mind and body careened beyond my ability to
self-regulate. This breakdown was revelatory. People who didn't know me
intimately could not tell I was unwell. When I explicitly asked loved ones

for help, guidance, patience, and support, many friends and family played it down or didn't know how to respond. Though this was painful and isolating, it alerted me to the truth that I and my community didn't know how to show up for one another or where to turn for comprehensive support when internal wounds flared up.

The learnings this breakdown gifted me continue to influence my work today. I can never forget the tremendous and isolating effort it took to navigate daily life while in the throes of pain that are invisible from the outside. I recognize that having access to the financial and community resources I did is, sadly, a very rare privilege. Also, what I experienced as a mental breakdown felt wholly unhealed by the methods I attempted to employ alone from my arsenal of Reiki, one-on-one talk therapy, meditation, chanting, and psychomagic. (I didn't yet know to employ music directly to remediate personal struggles.) After months of physical and mental anguish, relief started trickling in as soon as I brought my struggle into council, community, and co-exploration.

One seminal environment for collective processing and co-exploring (not for exploring my personal woes, but at least the portions related to the opera) developed as an experimental opera lab, devised in collaboration with Carolyn Abbate in the Harvard Music Department. During the Spring 2020 semester, we invited opera-curious students to engage alongside the opera's creative team in collective problem-solving and devising around each outstanding phase of the opera's development. Though the lab was devised to work toward resolving the complex issues of the opera, and only members of the opera creative team knew about my mental breakdown, deep relief seeped into my being via this collective and council-supported process. This process alerted me to the power and benefit of a collective research and creation model, which then informed the design of what would come to be called Songwrights Apothecary Lab (SAL).

In February 2020, I sought to build a similar exploratory lab model to continue and deepen my learnings at the intersection of music and healing/restoration. I sought out practitioners and researchers working in the realms of music and healing and invited them to form a council for the purpose of collaboration with me on a new body of work guided by their respective expertise.

marisol: Joining Fields and Intentions

When esperanza invited me to be a member of what soon would be formally called the Songwrights Apothecary Lab (SAL) council, the COVID-19 pandemic was slowly becoming known across the city where we taught, and I had just made a necessary move to Florida to be with family as I worked remotely. My mother, a hospital chaplain, began seeing an influx of patients admitted with the yet unknown coronavirus. We all collectively began to grapple with navigating the urgency of life and death as these realities were made more evident against the increased weight of health inequities across Black communities. My work within the Black Music Therapy Network, Inc., began to attest to the physical and emotional labor demanded of Black communities as protest, refusal, and fugitivity became necessary acts of care. As universities also faced new realities that strained their existence, I chose to leave my academic position while transitioning to the next to tend to my family, as well as make a renewed commitment to healing from a sexual assault I had experienced two years prior. These compounded realities made way for deepened reflection, new ways of being, and an embodied reckoning that became the backdrop of my experience with SAL.

I grew up in a musical culture oriented toward African-derived spirituality and Christian faith, so my relationship to music often indexed the healing potential of communal musicking. Classical operatic training throughout my college years often drew me away from the relational improvisatory musical practices experienced with my family and community. Attending Oakwood University (then Oakwood College), a historically Black and religious institution, situated me within a musical history and culture that acknowledged the multiple ways Black musical traditions influenced musical engagement and production. Musicality, embodiment, legacy, and lineage were centered as a continual source of inspiration as well as resources to navigate daily life. Still, a classical vocal career trajectory, rooted in European classical music traditions, demanded an alignment to fixed composition, orientations away from the expansiveness of performers' creative autonomy. This was further reinforced as I transitioned into a graduate degree in opera performance as the politics of classical musical culture, as with any industry-driven profession, were made more evident. The decision to become a music therapist felt like a return home, not as a professional pursuit but a human and philosophical orientation toward a fuller potential of musicking as a healing space.

Music therapy became my opportunity to bridge nonamplified aspects of my musical culture with theory and praxis, honoring the range of aesthetic knowing that compels humans to make and enjoy music. As Carolyn Kenny readily discussed in her work, beauty was removed from elitist frames that solely focused on musical production and its characterization as high and low art to consider beauty and its inherent "value" as multidimensional aesthetic reality for *all* people, with transformative and restorative potential. The orientation toward human health-seeking practices shifted a deficit orientation that was often elicited and then cloaked in sentiments of classical rigor, training, and skill. The transactional nature of human relationships within classical contexts was contended by relational lenses that honored human wholeness. In music therapy, as in my musical culture, I found a place where skill and compassion meet to acknowledge the growth orientation of beings in a hyperproductive world that centers around competition, judgment, and marginally sought health.

As I became more familiar with music therapy, I began to learn that these spaces were also challenged by similar concerns. The singular white Eurocentric lens that permeated music therapy discourse minimally allowed for the detailed discussion of Black and Indigenous clients' musical engagement as a personal, aesthetic means of perceiving and being in their environments. Musicking, in the music therapy context, was rarely acknowledged as being informed by participants' lived experiences as sociopolitical beings, the implications of the clinical setting's social context, and the musicking cultures from which minoritized clients originated. Although theorists utilized various Black and Indigenous musical traditions undergirding foundational theories of improvisation, the postmodern commitments to Black musical aesthetics in music therapy were rarely explored. Consequently, the significance and political relevance of Black and Indigenous music on music therapy aesthetic construction were also omitted from music therapy discourse.

While music as a construct held multiple framings within music therapy theory and practice, reductionist attempts to define music as stimuli or even symbolic object amplified the perpetuation of dominant medical and Eurocentric constraints on musicking, relationships, and health. Within this framing, music is stripped of the spiritual fortitude and language to describe this work while other types of transactional meaning-making are prioritized, moving away from Indigenous conceptions of musicking that include people and their communal being. The un/intended ramifications of this type of centering forfeited the multidimensional, relational connections to musicking and led to the further displacement of minoritized communities within music therapy practice. Journeying within the music therapy profession as a Black woman music therapist demanded another return, a return home to my being—communal, transcorporeal, and spiritual—more fully aligned with the practices of the communities from which I am derived and in which I am engaged in a broader discourse of what it means to heal and be healed. My resonance with esperanza's commitment to deriving form-*wela*s that had the potential to bring about healing, abandoning the individualistic egocentrism that I often critique within the music therapy profession, sprang from a deep respect for music therapy as a discipline but also recognizing the ways Black and Indigenous voices have contributed to healing narratives in ways that were both known and unknown.

esperanza: For Keeping Us Well

When the pandemic hit, we prematurely tried to scale our practitioner + musician lab model. In a well-intentioned attempt to co-create therapeutic music for hospital patients recovering from COVID, we moved too fast, too broad, too soon, and stymied the actual process and outcome of our enthusiastic efforts. Though the first council ultimately dissolved, we learned many lessons and did succeed in devising a praxis for collaboration between student musicians, medical students, and practitioners. I realized during this iteration of the lab (then inaptly called "Sonic Healing Lab") that I was actually more interested in how musicians, utilizing their existing creative methods and delivery platforms, could collaboratively create and share songs with enhanced salutary potential, whether for an audience of millions or for friends and family gathered in the living room.

Integrating the knowledge from the previous iteration of the lab and resourced with a Harvard Dean's Competitive Fund for Promising Scholarship Grant, I invited a cohort of researchers, practitioners, professional musicians, and producers to work with me in a new formation of the lab, called Songwrights Apothecary Lab. I suggested we work toward creating a series of songs responding to isolation and stress in the home. Dancing with the framing of *apothecary*, we called the songs *formwelas*: specific musical ingredients combined intentionally to induce a desired salutary effect when ingested (aurally). Since the songs themselves are formulas that take shape only when they are musicked together, the word could also be understood as "form we la." As a cohort, we decided on three interconnected salutary themes, each with its own formwela that would connect and reflect the other two songs. The three formwelas were released on digital streaming platforms and YouTube in early 2021.

Inspired by Dr. norris's teachings on the importance of shared intention and consent when engaging with music designed for therapeutic effect, I integrated the practice, initiated with *12 Little Spells*, of including a written outline of each formwela's intended effect and suggested use. For example, "Formwela 2's" intended effect was to provide "gentle vibrational embrace as airs in the room soak in the latent undercurrent able to envelop and dilate the clench of interpersonal woe, grief, and/or aggression." The suggested use was "to be discreetly incorporated into a home scene where interpersonal dynamics are veering toward an all-out burn-down." Essentially, the formwela could be utilized as "background" music, re-reminding the listener/s that, despite the present clench or woe or ache or loss or fight or grief, their *back* is in fact "got" and the good *ground* is ever available. Each element woven into the final recording of the formwela was chosen for its potential to support the listener in widening "the aperture of receptivity to that omni-present field of restorative light, permeating all things at all times in all places."

The collective enjoyment, deep research, learning, and abundant music creation facilitated by the SAL model inspired me to facilitate a version of the lab as a course at Harvard during Spring semesters 2021 and 2022. In the Harvard course-style version of the lab—half songwrighting workshop and half guided-research practice—each student rotated and collaborated between the roles of songwright and researcher. Throughout the course, student researchers and songwrights practiced culling relevant music elements from their research, then creating songs/music with those elements. The council of practitioners who participated in the most recent iteration of the lab agreed to show up in a similar way, as a council of elders for students involved in the Songwrights Apothecary Lab. These four practitioners (Dr. marisol norris, Dr. Suzanne Hanser, Sam Curtis, and Chris Sholar) joined the class via Zoom every third week throughout the semester. They listened to what students were intending to create through their research and songwrighting, and as a council, offered reflections, feedback, research prompts, cautions, and paradigms that would support students' efforts. During both semesters of the lab, we prioritized music-devising through collaborative research + creation practice, rather than developing methods for measuring the songs' effect on the intended listeners. The council did, however, analyze, critique, and offer professional and personal reflections about the music's effect on them, and how the musical elements of each song might support the intended salutary effect. Through these semesters of SAL, we further refined our abilities as musicians, researchers, and practitioners to collaborate via creating music designed to offer enhanced salutary potential.

I carried these learnings into the Spring and Summer 2021 iterations of the Songwrights Apothecary Lab (in Portland, Oregon, and Lower Manhattan, New York, respectively). In both, we replicated a model where: (a) musicians and researchers identify the salutary intention for a song, (b) the research team situates the intention as their study directive, and (c) the researchers transmit or translate their findings to the musicians, who then (d) compose/songwright by combining the researchers' findings with their/ our intuition and musical sensibilities.

Since every iteration of the lab (before Summer 2021) happened remotely over Zoom, phone, and remote studio sessions, we never had the opportunity to explore musical elements and concepts in a live, responsive context with one another. So during the Spring 2022 semester, I curated a J.A.M. (Jentle Aggregation Maneuvers) each Tuesday night after our Songwrights Apothecary Lab class time. Students and affiliates of the SAL invited anyone they wished to invite—musicians and nonmusicians—with the only prerequisite being an openness to exploring themes of healing through music together. These sessions (which I curated at both Harvard and Berklee) formed the foundation for the current (and still emerging!)

co-musicking session model described later in this chapter. These J.A.M.s showed me that, for all our research-based, methodological practice, these improvisational co-musicking sessions, when supported by supple yet explicit structure and shared healing intentions, offered an immediate and powerful sense of renewal, connection, and wellness at a register never quite reached through devised songs (as potent as so many of them were/are). Current iterations of the Songwrights Apothecary Lab continue to invite practitioners, researchers, and musicians to collaboratively devise therapeutically inclined songs and music, and dedicate just as much time and interest exploring/formulating modalities and applications of J.A.M.ing, aka co-musicking.

RE-MEMBERING THE HINTERLANDS

Having participated in the intentional practice of not solely *doing* music but *being* communal musick, we learned new lessons about ourselves and relational possibilities for co-musicking, health, and healing. Our shared work has led us to confront the continued erasure and displacement of Black and Indigenous healing wisdom from music and health discourse and to tend to its reclamation and continued growth within healing spaces, acknowledging the many possibilities it currently holds, and may have held, uninterrupted by systems of colonization. Holding knowledge of medical models and Euro-dominant therapeutic perspectives often elicited to define theory across community music, sound-based healing, and music therapy, we more deeply situate ourselves in the re-membering, or the elemental re-construction, of collective memory, cultural aesthetics, spirituality, embodiment and their meanings within social contexts consistent with liberatory practices. Our radical return is not to the appropriation of pseudo-shamanic work commonly evoked across music and health but a recentering of Black and Indigenous improvisational practices of music within everyday life. In so doing, this return recognizes the interplay between the fields and that which has been displaced as hinterlands in broader discourses of music and health, as well as embraces the tending fields of labor and care, the radically reimagined fields where we re-member and dream, and the spaces of possibility and of play that we engage daily to garner more potent ways of being together.

We invite you to peer with us into these nondominant spaces, in sacred recognition of all those who surround and move through us and those we have the honor to move through as well. This invitation serves not as an overdue eulogy of those past (because they are very present!) but as a necessary recognition of the imaginative workings that we all stand in the stream of while *being* in creative synthesis. Together, our synthesis is a variegated quilt enveloping and forming our experiential selves. Here, we gently pry open a few of the countless seams of this quilt, for you to glimpse the vast cosmos aflow behind each thread. Everything written and perceived thus is a snapshot of this ever-churning process that will change and morph with the flow of learning and living. As we look out into these spaces, played within the hinterlands, may we carry this deep knowing in our daily lives.

Recentering Healing Locus as Community

The worldview of most traditional, indigenous societies is so completely relational that there is not a concept of self as individual. Rather, a person exists and acts on behalf of others. A sick person goes through a healing ritual for himself, but also acts symbolically on behalf of the entire community

—CAROLYN KENNY

In this space, we take to heart what Malidoma Somé and Carolyn Kenny have taught us, what our ancestors and families have passed on to us, and dare a full reorienting toward healing as being inherently rooted *in* community and culture. As we highlight some of the many teachings that have shaped our orientations within healing and music, we recognize that our own ancestral lineages and cultural circumstances are the locus from which our practices of reintegrating forgotten and latent community healing technologies must (re)root to (re)flourish. For us as practitioner-musicians these communal healing responses are not the hinterlands of center-mainstream but rather a central presence, perhaps only needing to be magnified as the vitalizing force within our work.

Elder Malidoma Somé taught passionately about the necessity of deindividualizing diagnoses of human ailment and illness. He offered that, when an individual is exhibiting signs of unwellness—physically, emotionally, psychologically, or otherwise—it is a signal to the community at large that something critical within the collective needs tending to. Outside of church or cathartic impromptu music sessions (which, by omission from the theories and pedagogies of various healing modalities, are often interpreted as "invalid"), dominant messaging around individual suffering reemphasizes the burden and responsibility of an ailing person to individually find help to resolve their issues. Accompanying this messaging (or reinforcing it) is the prevalent model of the dyadic patient-therapist session. What other shapes of supported healing might we co-devise if I/we presume an individual ailment carries a healing gift for the community? What shifts if we assume there is no such thing as "individual" treatment? What changes, starting with the sensations in our bodies, when we tune to what ails us as if it were a gift to our community? What might it look like for therapists to deindividualize themselves as facilitators of healing? What structures of support would need to be redesigned or newly devised to allow therapists to assess and do their work within an engaged constellation of practicing peers and mentors?

esperanza: As I wade into the sensations of this possibility, I remember multiple ways in which this philosophy and practice already manifest within my community. One example comes to mind in the work of Ekua Adisa, a liberationist medicine person whose work has helped many community members in my hometown of Portland, Oregon. Ms. Adisa periodically hosts community grieving rituals—in-person or online—in which she serves as a facilitator, using music, lighting, prompts, ceremonial objects, and spatial design to help participants touch into and constructively release pent-up grief. These sessions are not offered in response to the circumstance of any one community member's suffering. Rather, when Ms. Adisa recognizes that one or some people in the community are suffering from loss, or grief, she responds by offering a grief ritual for anyone who feels they may benefit from it.

Another example stems from a gathering hosted by Khadija Tudor, founder and director of Life Wellness Center in Brooklyn, New York. For this event, Khadija asked me to facilitate collective musicking for a small group of people connected with or working at the center. Khadija explained to me that she had a sense that "the community needed it." She is deeply involved in various roles of mentorship and healing-practitionership within her community, so when she voiced this, I trusted her assessment of need and was honored by the invitation. On a Friday night, Khadija invited about twenty people whom she sensed might benefit from an opportunity to express themselves musically together. Khadija, Baba Umpho (an elder drummer and Ifa priest), and I presented ourselves to the group as facilitators and supporting presences for the music that would emerge. Khadija—familiar to everyone at the gathering—oriented participants by inviting them to see themselves as part of and contributing to the broader effort toward expanding community wellness in that neighborhood. Baba Umpho oriented participants to recognize themselves as being within the lineage of African and African American ceremonial cultural practices, where music is made in community as a force for unification and healing. I then invited everyone to form a circle, and as they felt comfortable to do so, to share what they were going through, or what they wanted our music to attend to or support that evening. After hearing from everyone in the circle, we agreed to pool our musical intentions and strived to collectively make music that would respond to everyone's needs. Not everyone chose to stay for the evening, but those who did earnestly strived to show up musically for and respond to one another, and in so doing, be responded to themselves. The details of specific lyrics, calls, melodies, rhythms, and dancings that emerged among and through us that evening are too intimate to share here. But I can share that I felt a great sense of relief, support, and expanded possibility as the music took shape. For the most part, the music took shape without a clear leader, and when one person occasionally initiated a musical idea, it would morph and develop in response to what the collective decided they needed from it. After the event, I overheard the phrase "I really needed this" exclaimed many times from various participants. As a cofacilitator, I felt relaxed and supported throughout by the mature, experienced presence of Khadija and Baba Umpho as they equally chaperoned and participated in the unfoldings of that evening.

The two models above clearly shape themselves to meet the particular cultural identities and shared experiential affinities of the participating individuals. However, underlying the circumstantial particularities of these examples is an essential structure: members of community brought their ailments into collective restoration space, simultaneously receiving support and alleviation while extending their care and support to others. The efficacy of these structures hinges on each person touching into their potential to conjure and benefit from the healing power of music and/or collective gathering, as well as a willingness to extend trust and care to other beings convened—as community—for the duration of the ceremony/practice. Once shared intentions and supple structure have been expressed, most participants seem to contribute from an intuitive understanding of how to engage in these practices. We believe this understanding is born from an intentional repositioning of oneself in relationship to people and deep remembering of just how potent and available these communal healing technologies are and have always been—to us and the peoples comprising our various ancestries.

An Invitation: Tuning into the essential structures underlying the two examples above, we invite you to inventory your lived experience within community, and notice: Where and how have these communal spaces and modalities been accessible to you? If they have felt accessible, did they feel safe or valid? Why? Or why not? Are you curious about or do you long for collective care rooted in ancestral wisdom or communal healing? Can you sense the most restorative iteration of a collective-healing model you have encountered, or been involved in? How does this sense influence your aspirations and desires for further engagement with community healing?

The Extraction & Commodification of the Hinterlands

Musicking practices of marginalized communities, as an extension of their humanity, have historically been othered across the disciplines of music and health. Those assuming dominant Western ideologies that render minoritized communities illegible within healing discourse have often assumed proximal likeness as superior and those deemed "other" as inherently less human. In this manner, the severing from ancestral, culturally seated technologies of music healing that predate Western empiricism or scientific rationalism has impacted all peoples. Whether it be through primitivization, whereby non-Eurodominant cultures are perceived as wild, undisciplined, childlike, and uncivilized, or through exotification, whereby they are essentialized for consumption, the utility of ideological tools of dehumanization has severely impacted the ways the world comes to understand and relate with marginalized communities today.

Established practices of omission, objectification, and misrepresentation have, part and parcel, contributed to and reinforced the extraction and commodification of music technologies across disciplines. Examples of these practices can be witnessed through scholarly critiques, whereby Black and Indigenous peoples and their creative expression have been historically labeled as primitive and maligned as solely sensorial, lacking cognitive complexity, meaning, or virtue while simultaneously being rendered profitable when reproduced by European counterparts. Consequently, Black and Indigenous influences on current assumptions and practices of music and healing are erased.

As seen in the Negritude movement manifested throughout France and the Francophone nations in the late nineteenth century, consumers displayed a distinct shift toward African art as the fascination and fetishism of primitivism became profitable and trendy. In comparable ways, similar objectifications of African and Russian folk art could be seen in Igor Stravinsky's musical use of polyrhythms and additive rhythms, and rhythmic "chugging" in the early twentieth century. Scholars revealed that Stravinsky was notably influenced by these folk arts and musical structures to depict primitive conceptualizations of African objects introduced to him by Pablo Picasso (and Stravinsky's work would later be drawn upon by white music therapy forerunner Juliette Alvin, in her free, improvisatory music therapy practices). However, the original intention and context of the musical repertoires extracted from and coursing through their work were lost.

Scholars holding dominant perspectives at times galvanized around Black and Indigenous peoples' healing music discourse to further conceptualize their purpose, function, and value. Yet disciplinary and interdisciplinary constructions have unintentionally misrepresented the connections between elemental musical representations and their complex relationship to the communities from which they derive. The history and aftermath of extractive engagement with Indigenous music technologies thwart full recognition of the meaning-making potential within them, and circumvent the continued agency in the construction and development of a culture's musical lineage. The commodification of these therapeutic technologies therein shifts the relational trajectory of their healing potential, stripping and repurposing musical elements of their intended meaning and context, hoping it will have the same effect. Unsatiated, we long for healing from music technologies not allowed to do their work because the dehumanizing spirit of intrusion has taken its life force and healing potency.

marisol: Far from solely intellectual pursuits, the precipitation of these practices often holds real effect in the music and healing spaces. Facilitating music-based trauma processing and prevention groups, I often support culturally sustaining practices among community members and participants and witness their lasting influence. In these instances, group members' musical cultures and influences are centered in the healing discourse as we consider how they are a source of meaning-making and index communal knowledge, resilience, resistance, agency, and care. Through musical discussion, members consider the various ways personal and cultural narratives provide deep insights pertaining to the embodiment of trauma in their daily lives and serve as a catalyst of change, as needed. Group members utilize songwriting methods drawing from their personal well of creativity to compose healing narratives, and together with myself and community-centered musicians, engage therapeutically in music production. Black healing practices are amplified in their relationship to flow, groove, and tension and release, as well as spirituality, communal connectedness, and reciprocal being. The act of extraction, in this context, would displace the presence of Black music-based practices in health and healing traditions of participants' communities. However, group participants' identification with their musical cultures situates them as musical knowers within a lineage of creative healing reclaiming and embodying the power of their musical histories within their own healing narratives. As a therapist situated in culturally sustaining musical care practices, my role is not to hoard power and presume the authority to heal group members but to recognize the individual and collective ways that power already exists in their beings. Together, we exercise power by engaging autonomously as political subjects that hold personal agency to empower ourselves and be empowered through our communities. If participants were not supported in naming and claiming their Black music-based healing practices, therapeutic spaces can easily become sites for extraction, and the musicking potential could easily be treated as stimuli—as commodity.

An Invitation: The extraction and commodification of Black and Indigenous healing practices have supported the development and expansion of musicking and health throughout the Western world and beyond. Witnessing these realities we ask: What does it mean to release the assumed power held over minoritized communities? What has my field or therapeutic profession (including musicianship) standardized or methodized, which may have been taken or borrowed from other communities, without their permission or consent? How might we devise models for asking permission to learn, use, and translate what we learn from historically marginalized communities and their ancestral and living practitioners? How might we devise— in conversation with communities and their practitioners—a practice of reciprocation, as we begin to professionally or therapeutically benefit from their borrowed modalities? When permission to borrow, translate, or modify a practice or method is not granted, how do we help ourselves and one another release those methods? And in what ways does the repackaging of Black and Indigenous healing rituals stripped of their cultural-historical context and essence further the othering of minoritized communities that receive hyperfocus in the field of music and health? In what ways do we suppress the liberatory function of music processes that deepen its participants' access to freedom?

Co-Musicking/Communal Musicking

Because it's not in a paradigm, nobody owns it and it doesn't need to be explained.

—DR. MARISOL NORRIS

The "it" here is an energizing and renewing presence coursing through co-created sounds, movement, and compositional arcs common during a collective musicking session. Fortunately for anyone hoping to engage in these kinds of sessions, they are relatively simple to organize, facilitate, and participate in. Though the "it" is difficult to language around directly, we offer a transmutable map for journeying into "it," drawn from personal and collective adventures through this liminal terrain.

esperanza: These sessions are something I've been involved in and exploring my entire musical life—whether under the premise of "jazz" jam sessions, an Ornette Coleman ensemble during college, playing professionally with "free" musicians, making up songs as a child for my mother to harmonize with, or more recently, in carefully devised Songwrights Apothecary Lab co-musicking sessions. At the core of these musical experiences is an intimate exchange of mutual attunement, accompanied by seemingly miraculous collective acts of spontaneous beauty. There is also a profoundly renewing spiritual *something* underlying these music exchanges. That *something*, as I've experienced it, prefers to remain uncaptured by language. It shows up not by anyone's accurate playing of a certain chord, song, melody, or rhythm. Rather, it seeps in as enough people involved allow themselves to play and respond from a place of authentic presence. Some prompts, invitations, arrangements, and framings that have seemed to help participants tune in to this type of co-musicking are:

- Inviting a mix of people who are skilled improvising musicians, along with people who do not identify as musicians, or have minimal musical training.
- Participants offering willingness to make an emergent style of music *together*, unbound by the expectations of any particular vernacular or form.
- Setting up in a circle that includes everyone in the room, along with all instruments in the room.
- Opening with a reminder and invitation that everyone in the session is invited to participate as composer, arranger, musician, and listener.
- Offering the invitation and framing up front that during this session, we are entering a co-created music space, which means we can't predict exactly what will happen. So, during the co-musicking we ask all participants to earnestly show up as support, witnesses, contributors, and listeners to our collective and individual musical reflexive processes.

- Encouraging participants to try *not* to steer the shape of the emerging music, even as each person adds to or initiates sounds, phrases, lyrics, melodies, rhythms, chords.

- Facilitators explicitly and/or implicitly articulating that the session is an invitation to explore being deeply receptive to the total sound happening and contribute one's musicianship in support of the unfolding music's intention.

- Before the musicking begins, taking a somatically supported moment for everyone to notice how they're actually feeling in the moment. (That somatic support could be collective breath exercises, a short round of Pauline Oliveros's tuning exercise, group rhythming/stepping together, or others.)

- An invitation to the group to allow themselves to trust their knowing about how music can best support them right then, right there. And for those willing, to share out loud what they most need/wish music to support in that moment.

And music begins. Or as it seems to me, a latent current of music surfaces into and through the group. Swells and flurries and whispers of rhythms, harmonies, melodies, textures, turnarounds, vamps, lyrics, counterlyrics, choruses, and so forth emerge. In the unfolding milieu of music are ample moments of friction, seemingly arrhythmic pulses, awkward silences, clashing notes, senses of participatory trepidation and participatory overindulgence, and even sounds that are truly incomprehensible. There also emerge supremely subtle interpersonal musical dynamics I have no vocabulary for. Sometimes the music stops abruptly as if on cue . . . sometimes there's a feeling of coming to in the midst of an intricate rhythmic/harmonic richness that only seconds ago had sounded like myriad errant parts nonsensically interacting, which have all suddenly coalesced into a consummate groove. In all that describing of the musical happening, I haven't described the "renewing presence coursing through" (sigh). That presence, that "it" . . . is so much a feeling, a being-there-ness, a being-amid-ness, that perhaps one must be within to recognize. To feel the realness and effect of that renewing presence, it helps to be earnestly contributing to the music, as a part of its unsteered direction/expression. It helps to dare vulnerability in a responsive relationality to co-musicking in the complex reality of whoever is in the room, with whatever all is swirling among us musically, emotionally, interpersonally, and the rest. And when one is in it and feels it, recognizes it . . . *It doesn't need to be explained.*

What I can describe (kind of) is—after an hour or two of being wholly immersed in this type of co-created music—there emerges a visceral sense of release, renewal, battery-refilledness, "a subtle hunger whose pangs I grew numb to, now feeling fed and full" feeling. Sometimes, as the music winds down, there emerge impulses to abruptly joke or interject some coarse reality to cut the suspended, glowing feeling (maybe for fear that what we're feeling is untenable or unsafe in whatever post-session environment we each must move into).

Going from the connected, tender, cathartic sensations of a co-musicking session directly into, say, a bustling Lower Manhattan street can feel as jarring as leaving the optometrist with dilated pupils and no sunglasses. An intentionally crafted or co-devised wrap-up ritual or cadencing circle-up helps us transition more gently. I've learned that letting people know at the beginning of the session that there will be a closing ritual helps alleviate some of the angst (as I interpret it) of reentering our "normal" modes of engaging with our respective worlds. This post-musicking cadence could be a few breaths or an invitation to silently reflect on what happened. (I like to say *cadence* instead of *closing* because I hope it's possible outside of the co-musicking to remain open to that sense of fullness and expansiveness that the session cultivated.) It could be singing a simple song in unison, a round of gentle stretching, or a guided visualization of everything nourishing from this session being gathered together and brought to our hearts to be stored there and reached into anytime. Something I deeply revere about this practice is the way music emerges from everyone, equally. That even if certain individuals played or sang more notes than others, those notes were emerging in response to our collective creation, and were no more or less significant to the total musical phenomena. Even a soft scratching of a drum head is hearable as texture. No specific person, genre, pedagogy, paradigm, prompt, or practitioner ensured the success of what happened. *Because it's not in a paradigm, nobody owns it.* Therefore, everyone who participated "owns" it. And from different levels of awareness to that fact, we each came in already owning it. We merely helped each other remember, and allow ourselves to show up for, the propagation of this medicine we carry within and amid us.

Reckoning with Power & Legitimacy
in Current Contexts of Music and Health

Power and legitimacy have always been a central contention within contemporary discussion of musicking and health. Conceptualizations of health have historically negated the formidability of musicking practices to contribute to generative healing within Western constructed health paradigms. As cultural workers, artists, practitioners, and researchers alike attempt to expand their sphere of impact, our understanding of and relationship to power becomes a growing priority. Our performance of power and legitimacy must distinguish how power is named, extracted, or repurposed to meet diverse needs, and how commodification of power yields professional legitimacy. The exclusionary practices contended within the contemporary revitalization of music and health discourse ask us to not only consider the healing *power* of music previously discussed, but assess the *power*-ladened politics engendered within reimbursement-driven health-care systems. We must reckon with evidence based practice and the capacity of empirical research, which have perpetuated the marginalization of minoritized communities, to sufficiently determine the scope of music and health with its limited notions of music, health, healing, and evidence itself.

Distinguishing musicking's place within health care and broader discussions of health and wellness amplifies the ways power already exists within individuals, communities, and the musical representations they create. Moving toward wholeness underscores the way power is repudiated and the weightiness of bringing the margins to the center. Yet holding a scarcity mindset reproduces the false narrative that we are in an utter space of lack, that we must delegitimize others to meet our current goals or meet the needs of the communities we serve. In this manner, recognizing the relational wounding that separates care recipients, artists, community workers, practitioners, scientists, researchers, and the broader community agents who support this work must move beyond distinguishing similarities and differences to collaborative care. The call for acknowledgment of the hierarchical, dichotomous, and sometimes bifurcated existence centers the restorative communal knowing that presumes that we all collectively hold meaning and significance of our current music and health discourse and stand within streams of healing.

The Invitation: Consider how power and legitimacy are defined in your context. How are they communicated? How do power and legitimacy define your relationships and those of others around you? In what ways are power and legitimacy hoarded or sourced as a form of control? How do these practices lead to or reveal the devaluation of people or musicking practices in the hinterlands of music and health discourse? In what ways is power assumed to aid in legitimacy, resulting in the purposeful erasure of contributors to this work? When forms of care or healing are delegitimized, who bears the responsibility of making the work "whole"? When those who have been minoritized within music and health discourse are further marginalized, who bears the responsibility to ensure that minoritized communities' voices are heard and that they are supported with culturally sustaining and accessible practices?

WIDE ATMOSPHERES: THIS ISN'T FOR ANYTHING OTHER THAN KEEPING US WELL

There is something about participation that celebrates the human specialness that you will not see somewhere else. There's something in participation that says that the participating individual is not an individualist. You participate because you want to get out of the gated prison you're in, into the village square, to make yourself known, to make yourself seen. You participate because somehow there is a sacred dimension to the other participating individual that is significant in your total becoming. Which means, how you grow, how rich you become is proportional to the echo of participation that you encounter in a circle like this.

—ELDER MALIDOMA SOMÉ

When a something, a musical something, is not recognized by outside audiences as being worthy of analysis, commodification, or recontextualization, it is afforded an undomesticated continuance, growth, and evolution within the environment practicing and benefiting from it. In many ways, it is afforded a wide atmosphere, honoring its ancestral roots and reciprocal relationship with earth and spirit, to thrive within the existence of non-intrusion. Acknowledging the implications of "domestication" within the veins of co-musicking often referenced, we recenter unhindered existence whereby participants engage with music and each other via undetermined, instinctive, group murmuration. There is no way of predicting how each person's musicianship will behave within an environment of multiple individuals contributing their authentic musical sensibilities with the intention of helping each other. While shared intentions may influence the affective directives of musical responses within the group, there is no way of predicting how the music will move, leap, howl, take flight, taste, yield, intimidate, or scatter. Neither is a predetermined assessment of value prescribed or expected. Musical trajectories aren't pre-fixed to ensure a specific function, predetermined outcome, or preference. This allows expression and healing to emerge from the innate musical sensibility of each person.

One may presume that the unpredictability or nontransferability of the *experience* of collective co-musicking makes it unsavory to persons or paradigms that wish to fix, reproduce, or commodify it according to aesthetic values more preferable to their professions or industries. From the wide atmosphere of undomesticated musicking spaces, aka the *hinterlands* discussed above, we turn to look again at more prevalent contemporary fields, whether in the entertainment music industry or music and health industries. We perceive a glaring contrast of *being* there, as and among industry-designated "field workers," tending and tilling for profit the human and material source/resource of music, exclusively in accordance with the theories and designs of their respective industry. Messages about music's value and success, prioritizing individual proficiency and external validation, and therein legitimacy, seem nearly ubiquitous. These implicit and explicit messages prime people to contort and fix their musical and co-musicking aspirations and expectations. Like many, I/we (esperanza) received the message that once I have practiced enough, and am deemed good enough, I become worthy of sharing my musicianship via performance or studio recording. The implicit message is that rare exceptionality and highly technical proficiency entitle a person to be heard, collaborated with, and compensated (within prescribed rules of relational engagement) for making music deemed valuable. In this prevalent paradigm, the playing, practice, sharing, and cultivation of music become enmeshed with being evaluated by external critique, consumer/audience preference, and professional hierarchies. These enmeshments influence who feels entitled to embody music as a means for connection, pleasure, and wellness, and places stringent limits on how musical capacity and agency are to be used.

It grieves our hearts to imagine how many opportunities for healing connection through music are lost, when our innate need and right to be healed through music are contended by dehumanizing or exclusionary expectations for entering music with others. Fortunately, these ancient and innate musickal pathways to wellness are always existent; we are already in relationship with them and through them, more than ourselves. We can afford ourselves the intimate reprieve of communal knowing that allows personal and collective transformation through music—knowing that the music and musicianship offered, received, and exchanged in these contexts aren't for anything other than *keeping us well*.

During the process of writing this chapter, we stumbled upon a recording of Elder Somé (n.d.). In it, he speaks to the essence of reciprocal engagement and communing:

"You participate because somehow there is a sacred dimension to the other participating individual that is significant in your total becoming. Which means, how you grow, how rich you become is proportional to the echo of participation that you encounter in a circle like this."

A return to the hinterlands recognizes the communal locus of restorative healing practices that exist outside the purview of for-profit, dominant music and health fields. Even more so, a recognition that co-musicking practices of the hinterlands may only be effectively devised, enacted, or even measured by the folks directly involved in and benefiting from them, and whose embodiment and critique ensure direct passing on of the co-contributive process that delivers the essence of their efficacy. To engage in reciprocal relationship within these healing practices requires the active re-membering of the communal wisdom coursing through the work itself. It asks that we shift personhood toward a relational being that honors the breadth and complexity of this work, dismantles the colonial gaze, and turns toward compassionate witnessing of all that surrounds us.

remember the works of sun
towering within the blue
while we are stuck inside
wide atmospheres breathe and surround you

—ESPERANZA SPALDING, "FORMWELA 3"

Music and Memory: Exploring the Power of Music to Reach Those with Dementia and Other Neurologic Conditions

CONCETTA M. TOMAINO, DA, LCAT, MT-BC
Executive Director and Cofounder, Institute for Music
and Neurologic Function

> *The effect of music is so very much more powerful and penetrating than is that of the other arts, for these others speak only of the shadow, but music of the essence.*

—ARTHUR SCHOPENHAUER,

THE WORLD AS WILL AND REPRESENTATION, VOL. I

Music, indeed, is much more than the sum of its parts, i.e., vibration, pulse, tone, rhythm, melody, songs, lyrics. The idea that our brain can process all this information and allow us to appreciate music as a complete form has always amazed me. In fact my journey as a music therapist and in music brain research started in 1978 with this question: How can someone with supposedly no memory recognize a familiar melody?

My clinical training began that year at a skilled nursing facility where people with end stages of dementia were kept on a separate unit, a place that seldom received visitors. Almost all the residents had nasogastric (NG) tubes for feeding, and their hands were placed in mesh mittens tied to their wheelchairs to prevent them from removing the tube. For anyone this would be extremely uncomfortable, but for a person with dementia it was unbearable. Those who were awake were screaming and pulling to release their hands. The others were minimally responsive and slumped in their chairs. When I entered the unit for the first time, the nursing staff saw my guitar and remarked, "Don't expect anything from these people—we just feed and water them. They have no brains left. You can play for the staff."

My music therapy training was in the psychodynamic properties of music, and so I thought of a song that might have an emotional connection regardless of how far removed from reality these poor folks were. I started singing "Let Me Call You Sweetheart," and within the first few notes the bedlam stopped, those who were unresponsive lifted their heads, and those who were screaming became quiet. Half of them started singing the words of the song. What had just happened? Based on what the nurse told me there shouldn't have been any response, let alone their recalling and singing the correct words! This was more than an emotional response to music—this was a level of cognitive processing that was still available to these individuals. In order for them to recognize the music, their brains needed to process the sound vibrations in the air into musical tones comprehended as a melody and then not only recall the lyrics but sing them. I knew then that I had a way to connect to these individuals, who were otherwise lost to the world. I had to find out why music could still be processed by someone with severely impaired cognition.

Although I took many sciences courses as an undergrad premed student, there was nothing in science at the time that could explain what I just witnessed. Nor the potential improvements I observed as I continued to engage with this group using folk songs from their countries of origin, since many were immigrants, as well as songs popular in the early 1900s, when they were in their late teens and early twenties. They didn't recognize familiar voices or faces of their loved ones, but they did recognize music with which they seemed to have a personal connection. I discovered one book, *Music and the Brain: Studies in the Neurology of Music*, edited by Macdonald Critchley and R. A. Henson, that had been published in 1977. This work mainly focused on possible music processing with regard to the skills of a performer and the losses of function due to brain injury in such composers as Ravel. Although I couldn't find specific answers to what I had experienced with the nursing home residents, the book did make me wonder about music as a tool from a neurologic perspective to help patients with brain injuries.

In 1980 a full-time music therapy position opened at a chronic disease hospital near my home in the Bronx. I was excited because I was replacing a woman who was referred to as "the music therapist," something that was very unusual at the time. She was retiring and although not formally trained as such, she had kept abreast of developments in the field. The fact that this facility had an awareness that music therapy was different from music entertainment was extremely encouraging to me. Within my first week I received an interoffice envelope address to "the music therapist." Inside was a torn piece of loose-leaf paper with the following note written with a felt-tip pen:

"Every disease is a musical problem every cure a musical solution"—Novalis. Welcome, Ollie

"Ollie," I soon learned, was the attending neurologist, Oliver Sacks, who was somewhat eccentric and reclusive but who had written a book about some of the hospital's patients, and the BBC had made a documentary about it.

So you could imagine my delight when I received that strange torn note. The staff neurologist seemed to understand the role of music in medicine. It would be a few weeks before I met "Ollie" in person. I was assigned to the units where those awoken with L-dopa still resided. L-dopa, or levodopa, is a precursor to the neurochemical dopamine, which is essential for many human functions, including movement and memory. It is now a common drug treatment for Parkinson's disease, but back in the mid-1960s it was still relatively new, and Oliver was the first to explore using it for his patients immobilized for decades by an encephalitis-related disorder he chronicled in his book *Awakenings*. Most of these patients were in wheelchairs, totally dependent in their daily care, yet still could sing with full voice and lose their hyperkinetic movement when engaged in drumming or moving to music.

One day I saw one of my patients who was nonverbal, physically rigid, and with severe dementia waiting in line for her neurology evaluation. I stood there until the neurologist appeared. "Dr. Sacks," I told him, "I work with Mrs. B. Would you like to see how she responds to music?" "Oh, yes, do bring her in," he replied enthusiastically. Thus began our first session together. I observed as this somewhat quiet and socially awkward physician sat face-to-face with the patient, gently holding both her hands and softly singing "Daisy, Daisy la, la, la, la, la, la." She opened her eyes, moved her hands in his, and smiled. I told him I used a different song—"When the Saints Go Marching In." He asked me to sit with her and sing it. I, too, sat face-to-face, held her hands, and started to sing, "Oh when the saints," to which she immediately chimed in, "Go marching in." He was amazed and delighted. Soon I found that Oliver would include special notes "to the music therapist" within his exam chart notes—"How was she in music?" "Can she replicate a rhythmic pattern?" "Does she initiate movement?" I began to look at my clinical work more closely. What in the music enabled these responses to occur?

For the months that followed I had more opportunities to meet Oliver and share questions about music and neurology. I discovered that he lived near me in the Bronx. He invited me to his new home on City Island, where he shared the journals written by each of the *Awakenings* patients. These were people I was presently working with, who were now frailer. The journals were filled with their personal accounts during that magical awakening when they were able to move around and interact freely with others after more than forty years of immobility It also contained the not-so-nice accounts of what it was like to be spoon-fed and treated like a child. It opened my eyes to the inner worlds and minds of our patients. We began to discuss what it was about music that could reach them so quickly and deeply. For each question I had, Oliver pulled a book from his collection of first editions—Henry Head, Hughlings Jackson, Darwin—and introduced me to the founding fathers of neurology and evolutionary science. He recounted stories of his friendship with W. H. Auden, who shared ideas about music from other poets—like T. S. Eliot's "You are the music / While the music lasts." He gave me copies of A. R. Luria's book *The Man with a Shattered World* as my introduction to how a damaged mind has to reconstruct the world to be engaged with it. I shared information about the field of music therapy, of the potential for treating people with music. We were excited by the prospect that music was able to change and improve our patients' brain function in ways not yet understood. The fact that rhythm could provide a template for movement, could possibly jump-start the basal ganglia in someone with Parkinson's disease. That flickers of memories could return in those with dementia, and words and speech come back to those who lost the ability to communicate after a stroke. The concept of neuroplasticity was then very new, but we knew we were observing real change and, in some, recovery. In the mid-1980s we met with several scientists to see if they could help us study music and the brain, but they laughed and said music was too complex and the science of the brain still too new.

Oliver began publishing case studies for the *London Review of Books* and then *The New York Review of Books*. His own book *Awakenings* was out of print, and he couldn't even pay a publisher to reprint a few hundred copies. For years he had been working on other manuscripts, which lay in his desk drawer at home. In our weekly walks in the New York Botanical Gardens, he would talk nonstop about music—about being "remusicked" himself in his recovery from a leg injury—and how he was working again on a manuscript. I served as his sounding board as he tried out ideas and formulated what would become *A Leg to Stand On*. Oliver was not yet a public figure, but the literary world had taken notice, and he was invited to give lectures. Susan Sontag had a series at Cooper Union and invited Oliver to speak on his *Awakenings* patients. Still very shy and not comfortable in this role, Oliver asked me to accompany him. An hour before his talk he reviewed what he would say—scribbling notes with his felt pen on the inside of his arm. My job, he told me, was to remind him to look at his arm—if he started to stammer.

In 1985 his case studies were published in a new collection entitled *The Man Who Mistook His Wife for a Hat*, which became a *New York Times* bestseller. In 1989 I became the president of the American Association for Music Therapy and would invite Oliver to speak at several of our conferences. I wanted others to be inspired by his knowledge and insights into music and neurology. When the film *Awakenings* was released in 1990, it brought a flood of media attention to Oliver's present work, which now included interest in memory function.

The TV program *48 Hours* heard about our work with music and memory and asked if they could visit. There were several residents I was working with who demonstrated how deeply music could reach, engage, and improve function. Henry was one of them. Diagnosed with dementia, he was wheelchair-bound. If asked why he was a patient, he said he was recovering from an enemy bullet—believing that it was still World War II and that he was in the VA hospital. He had been a new resident when I first met him in my music therapy group on the unit. For these residents I would improvise, on my accordion, a variety of dance rhythms to encourage movement and social interaction. While I was playing a swing style of song, Henry, who I was told couldn't walk on his own, leaped out of his chair and started to dance. He legs were a little stiff, and his knees bent in, but nonetheless he danced for as long as I played—he "was the music while the music lasted"—and when I stopped, I saw that he was unsteady, looking as if he had forgotten why he was standing. I reached quickly for his arm to help him back to his chair.

Henry, I learned, had danced with his brothers at the Savoy Club in Manhattan. Although he couldn't walk independently, his motor memory for dance was still intact and easily accessible through music. Dancing became a way to use this preserved motor memory to get Henry on his feet every day to dance, with the encouragement of the unit staff, and eventually to walk on his own. His balance and his cognitive ability improved so much that he was discharged back to his daughter's home.

For Henry, as for others with movement challenges, music becomes a template for the movement—the initiation of movement as well as the timing in between each step. Following the music is an easier neurologic process than thinking about the necessary sequence of movements or initiating the movement itself. The hesitancy of not knowing what to do or the fear of falling disrupts the flow from thinking to doing. For people with cognitive impairment the thinking gets in the way of the doing.

At that time I found some possible explanations for my patients' responses in the work of Larry Squire, a neuropsychologist whose book *Memory and Brain*, published in 1987, introduced a tentative memory taxonomy. Declarative memory is information that could be brought to mind, and included episodic or working memory and semantic or referential memory. Whereas procedural memory, Squire explained, includes motor skills, simple classical conditioning, and other instances where engaging in specific cognitive tasks is improved by experience. I realized that so much of what I was doing with Henry and the others was finding ways to use music to cue or stimulate overlearned skills and then use music engagement consistently enough that these connections could be enhanced and lead to improvement. Today neuroscience research reveals that the auditory system stimulates motor areas of the brain into action, and that the pattern or rhythm of the music informs the timing of the movement.

Gary, on whom Oliver's case study "The Last Hippie" was based, was one of the younger residents. Gary was cortically blind following removal of a brain tumor and had no short-term memory. He also had some temporal-lobe damage that made it difficult for him to initiate interactions with others. He needed stimulation from the outside to turn on his ability to engage with the people around him. The surprising thing about Gary was his eidetic memory for the sequences of music tracks and cover images on his old albums. Listening to one of these songs would release a flood of remembrance. The film *The Music Never Stopped* is based on Gary and illustrates this beautifully. His memory recall was excellent for all events and music up until the 1970s, at which point it seemed to stop. He had lost the ability to encode new information. He often created rhymes of things he found interesting or amusing. Oliver and I wondered if Gary could learn to associate new information using music as a mnemonic device. We put names and other information to short musical phrases that Gary was able to repeat and then use to recall the names of the staff. This pairing of a musical phrase with information was similar to the rhymes he was creating spontaneously.

Both individuals show how clearly music could reach preserved function and how, through consistent engagement with music, those skills could be improved. Oliver and I still wanted to know why this was possible. In 1994 we received funding from the New York State dementia grants program, with which we investigated the impact of music-cued reminiscence compared to picture-cued reminiscence in people with moderate dementia. Different resident units were assigned to either the music or the picture groups, which focused on a specific topic each week and met three times a week for ten months. Those in the music-based groups were not only consistently on topic—each of the songs chosen for the session reflected the topic of the week—but also learned words to a new song used to open each session. Over time those in the picture-based group maintained or declined in memory function while those in the music groups improved in short-term memory, despite the diagnosis of moderate dementia. Not only did memory improve, but there was carryover outside the group. This became apparent when the wife of one of the music participants visited him. He had stopped recognizing her a while before his admission to the facility, but one day, several months into the study, when she came to see him, he called out, "Mary, where have you been? I've been looking for you." The consistent engagement in music had stimulated his memory recall, including facial recognition. The group from New York State overseeing the grants program was so impressed with the outcomes that they recommended that music be used in all memory programs for nursing home residents. One of the reasons people with dementia decline in memory so rapidly when admitted to a skilled nursing facility is that everything in the environment is new, and their minds struggle to make sense of it. Familiar music connects with preserved memory function and stimulates attention and other mental responses, allowing for a certain level of cognitive function to be maintained for a longer period of time.

With the success of this research grant we soon had the attention of our administrators, who recognized the importance of studying music and the brain, and thus the Institute for Music and Neurologic Function (IMNF) was established in 1995 to bridge the worlds of neuroscience and clinical music therapy to bring new knowledge about music and the brain and advance the practice of music therapy.

A great deal of my work since the founding of the IMNF has been to study and share knowledge about the importance of music and music therapy to help those with neurologic diseases and conditions such as dementia and movement disorders. Even before its founding in 1995, I had started presenting on therapeutic uses of music in the care of people with dementia at the newly formed New York Geriatric Education Consortium as well as at world conferences on aging, whose audiences included nursing home administrators, nurses, and certified nursing attendants. In 2002 we received a large grant from the Administration on Aging to develop best practices for music therapy and music-based interventions in dementia care and stroke rehabilitation. This led to lectures around the world to increase the use of music-based programs to enhance function and quality of life of people with memory issues and Alzheimer's disease as well as movement disorders such as Parkinson's disease.

In 2007 we received a grant to help build a program to educate nursing home staff on how to create personalized playlists installed on MP3 players so that people with dementia could have access to their music. This work was done in collaboration with a newly formed nonprofit, Music & Memory, which was the focus of the documentary *Alive Inside*. In dementia care it is crucial to understand the impact the right music can have on improving the quality of life of someone who seems difficult to engage with. Individuals with memory loss may still be able to make connections to others through the music they shared together. So often when a loved one has severe dementia, family members are at a loss for how to connect. I remember one of the residents with AD who was nonverbal. She was very well educated and often responded to classical music—especially piano works. She would spontaneously move her fingers in front of her as if she were performing the piece. Her husband, who was a physician, came to see her every day. One day he visited while I was playing the music for her. He was surprised and delighted to see that she recognized these works, as he had assumed that she had lost all memory. He said that they used to play together, she on the piano and he on the violin. He hadn't picked up the violin since her decline, as it brought back too many sad memories of all he had lost. I asked if he could bring his violin on his next visit. He did, and with his wife beside us he and I played songs that they had shared. She moved her fingers as if playing the piano. As he started to play she looked at him in a new way, and we could tell that she recognized him in this context of their shared music. For them, like many others, music became the bridge that enabled them to stay connected. This sense of knowing, sense of the familiar, is still present in people with dementia, even in very late stages of the disease. Familiar music, music that has a personal importance, stimulates and recruits multiple networks in the brain. This multiplier effect provides enough "cues" to enable this sense of knowing. The resilience of familiar, personally important music to evoke emotional responses and memory recall in people with late-stage dementia became the subject of my doctoral dissertation, completed in 1998. What I found was that at the most basic level, people, even those with severe dementia, will respond and move to the rhythm of music. It doesn't have to be a familiar song, it just needs to have an energetic beat. For music that holds a personal association of their own rich lived experiences, those with severe dementia showed recognition—a sense of knowing still available to each of them.

The importance of music and memory has gained much interest from the neuroscience community too. In 2009 University of California Davis neuroscientist Petr Janata published an interesting study. He had students listen to randomly selected popular songs from when they were eight to eighteen years old while in a brain scanner. After each excerpt, the student responded to questions about the tune, including whether it was familiar or not, how enjoyable it was, and whether it was associated with any incident, episode, or memory. Immediately following the fMRI session, students completed a survey about the content and vividness of the memories that each familiar tune had elicited. He found that when a song represented or evoked several memory associations—a person, time, and place—one area of the brain, the medial prefrontal cortex, was the most active, an area that may also be functioning better in people with AD. More recently, studies have shown that when people with dementia who are agitated and exhibit various behavior issues are provided with a personalized listening program of their favorite music, their behavior becomes calmer and the need for pharmacological treatment greatly reduced.

Research such as this is helping explain the areas of the brain involved in music and memory processing while providing validation for the clinical effects of music therapy and meaningful music-based programs to help those with neurocognitive deficits. Even with the growing evidence, access to the beneficial applications of music in all aspects of memory care is still lacking. There are over fifteen thousand skilled nursing facilities in the United States and millions of people with memory disorders. Of the ten thousand board-certified music therapists in this country, only 7 to 13 percent work in geriatric care. In other countries, access to professional music therapists in this area is even more limited, due to lack of financial support. The need for more music therapists is great, as is the need to train caregivers and health professionals in ways they can use music effectively in various aspects of geriatric care. There is still work to be done, not only in research to further demonstrate and validate the efficacy of music-based programs, but, and more importantly, in government agencies to increase financial support for music therapists to be able to lead in this effort. With such support, music therapists can impact all aspects of care, from pain management to reducing agitation and behavioral issues, which are often treated with psychotropic medications that are costly and have many negative side

effects. I am presently working with an international group of music therapists to advocate for increased support of music therapy services in geriatric
care. Everyone who cares for someone with neurocognitive deficits should
be aware of and have access to music therapy and music-based interventions, not only to enhance quality of life for themselves and those they care
for, but to preserve the meaningful connections and the sense of self that is
still possible. This continues to be my mission and that of the IMNF—to
share knowledge about the importance of music brain research and to educate on best practices in music therapy so that everyone can benefit from
the power of music to awaken and heal.

My Voice, My Song: Music as a Form of Self-Expression in Cancer Treatment

SHERI L. ROBB, PhD, MT-BC

JEFRI A. FRANKS, MS, CPC

This chapter shares the origins of a music intervention that was designed for adolescents and young adults with cancer and findings from a scientific trial investigating its benefits. More importantly, it provides the experience of Heather and her mother, Jefri, our first music video participants.

SHERI

Music as a therapeutic tool is not a new concept. In the United States the music therapy profession found its roots in serving wounded veterans in both world wars. At its core, music therapy is the blending of art and science, and music therapists use best available evidence to address the health or the educational needs of the individual.

Cancer is a leading cause of death by disease for adolescents and young adults in the United States, with an estimated 85,980 new diagnoses for 2023. Cancer treatment is complex, but it has been found that adolescents and young adults who use positive forms of coping* with strong social support systems have better health outcomes after treatment. We developed and tested a therapeutic music video intervention to help patients develop

---

*Examples of positive forms of coping include learning more about cancer; reframing the cancer experience from an insider perspective; adapting previous or learning new coping strategies to deal with cancer-related concerns, treatments, and procedures; and learning comfortable ways to share cancer-related experiences with health-care providers, family, or friends.

and use positive coping strategies and engage their social support systems during a high-risk and high-intensity treatment called hematopoietic stem cell transplant, also called stem cell transplant.

This treatment requires high doses of chemotherapy that cause a lot of unpleasant symptoms, like fatigue, nausea, weight loss, and painful mouth sores. In addition, uncertainty about outcomes from transplant causes emotional distress in patients and their parents. Transplant also requires a long period of hospitalization and protective isolation, during which adolescents are separated from extended family and friends.

The Stories and Music for Adolescent and Young Adult Resilience during Transplant (aka SMART) study used songwriting and video production as a way for patients to identify what was important to them, reflect on their individual cancer experience, and share that experience with other people. Every week during the transplant process, a credentialed music therapist worked with the adolescent or young adult to create lyrics and collate visual images before recording their voices to assemble the final video. It was during the first pilot study of this intervention that Jefri and I met. Jefri later became our parent adviser for this NIH-funded trial.

JEFRI

My daughter, Heather, was very excited to be involved in this study. We were on the Bone Marrow unit for a month, where there weren't a lot of choices. It was a constant adjustment to whatever was coming at you every day.

While Heather was working on the project, she had a completely different look on her face. It gave her something she could personally control. She could choose what song she wanted, the lyrics she wanted, what pictures she wanted to draw, and how she wanted to put it all together. It was her project. Her story.

SHERI

Adolescents and young adults get hit with a cancer diagnosis during a developmental period that is marked by tremendous growth and change. They're working to become more independent and less reliant on their parents, while strengthening peer relationships and making plans for the future.

During treatment they suddenly find themselves reliant on their parents for even basic forms of care. They're separated from their friends, and their life plans are put on hold while everybody else is moving forward. They are challenged to cope with side effects from treatment, maintain some semblance of independence, manage their emotions, and seek social support during a time of isolation. What makes this even harder is that they often lack the coping skills needed to navigate these complex social interactions, while also managing high levels of distress.

We wanted to offer adolescents and young adults a meaningful way to remain resilient in the face of a life-threatening illness. Information, family and peers, spiritual beliefs, personal resources, and music are sources of support identified by this age group as valuable during cancer treatment. However, very few supportive care interventions have been developed and evaluated for them.

JEFRI

I would spend Monday through Friday in the hospital with Heather while her father worked. On the weekends he would come to the hospital to spend time with her and I would go home. This meant that Heather had one of her parents with her every day. It was a double-edged sword. On the one hand, she needed that comfort and security. On the other hand, she was a preadolescent and was probably needing to break away from us a bit! Cancer made that difficult.

I was always concerned about how she was doing emotionally. When it was clear she was in turmoil, I would ask her to tell me how she was feeling. She would often respond that she didn't want to talk about it. Then I would ask her if there was anyone whom she would feel comfortable talking with, and she always requested Annie, one of the Child Life Specialists. When Annie appeared at our door, I would go down the hall to the Parent Room. Heather and Annie usually spent an hour talking. When Annie would come get me and we made our way back to Heather's room, I would ask if there was anything I was doing that I shouldn't be, and she would always tell me I might be hovering a little too much! When I asked her if there was something I should be doing that I wasn't, she always said no.

I will be forever grateful that Heather had ways to find space from her mom and dad. The making of the music video was another opportunity for her to talk with someone other than her parents and have time and space to be her own individual self.

SHERI

The therapeutic music video intervention is based on self-determination and motivational coping theory, which centers on creating supportive environments that encourage engagement with the environment rather than withdrawing or shutting down. Although social withdrawal can be a natural and adaptive response to stressful situations, over time it can inhibit the use of positive coping strategies.

The music therapist worked with adolescents and young adults to identify, explore, and express what was important to them using songwriting and creating a personalized music video over the course of six one-hour sessions. The first three sessions included brainstorming, lyric writing, and song recording. These activities were clustered in the early sessions when symptom distress was lower. The last three sessions included storyboarding for the video component, gathering and capturing photographs and artwork to complement their lyrics, and, if desired, hosting a "video premiere" to share their project with family, friends, and/or health-care providers. They worked privately with the music therapist during the first session and then had the option to keep their sessions and project private or to invite others to join in and help.

Having a safe space to explore and express what is important during a time of distress and uncertainty helped adolescents begin the process of making meaning of their experience. As one participant expressed it, "I think that with my video and the lyrics that I used, it kind of helped me realize that this is just a temporary thing and that I'm not going to be stuck in the hospital all the time or forever."

JEFRI

Heather was twelve, so it must have been tough, but the music therapist came in each day just for her, not for us, which gave her a little space.

I felt very blessed to hear the lyrics she wrote and that she felt comfort-

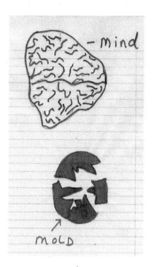

"... only your mind can break the mold"
~Heather, age 12

able sharing her experience, allowing us to see exactly how she was feeling. We didn't ask what she meant by each line. We just accepted her words and let it be the gift that she gave to us.

One of the things that was in my mind during the journey through cancer was "How much of Heather is this disease going to take away?" I saw her weight loss and her lack of appetite, but when she wrote the lyric "Only your mind can break the mold," I felt immense relief and comfort. She was saying that things may be happening to her body, but it wouldn't break her mind. That cancer wouldn't take her soul.

SHERI

We wanted each patient to derive benefit from the intervention, regardless of the amount of symptomatic or emotional stress they were experiencing. During transplant, patients often experience a lot of fatigue, nausea, and mood fluctuations, so it was essential that the protocol include strategies to tailor the experience.

Adolescents and young adults identified the music therapist as central to their sustained engagement and success. They shared that they felt valued, and this helped build trust and open communication. They also noted the therapists' flexibility in meeting their changing needs and described the relationship as collaborative.

We used the Resilience in Illness model to identify risk and protective factors that contribute to resilience. Significantly, we saw that adolescents and young adults who received our intervention reported more positive and courageous forms of coping throughout their cancer treatment. Our participants also reported significant benefits in the areas of family function and social integration, with better open forms of communication and higher quality of relationships with their families, friends, and health-care providers.

JEFRI

I definitely saw Heather's energy level increase throughout the project. It was something fun that she could work on, and she was at the helm.

As parents, you often don't realize how tired you are. You're watching constantly, you're looking at lab reports, you're listening to the doctor, you're listening to the nurse, and you're trying to make sure you're understanding everything.

To keep running the marathon that cancer is, you need to have some little breaks. The study didn't take the stress away, but it provided some time away from that. It helped us relax as a family.

SHERI

I've worked clinically in this area for many years, and I'm passionate about understanding the mechanisms that are responsible for the positive changes we see in our studies. Music therapy is becoming more widely available in pediatric cancer care settings, but a 2020 U.S. survey indicates we have far to go. Services tend to be limited to larger academic centers and freestanding children's hospitals, and when services are available, the ratio is about one music therapist for every hundred hospital beds. Often one music therapist is serving an entire hospital, and about half of music therapy positions are philanthropically funded.

In 2012, the Psychosocial Standards of Care Project was initiated to guide and improve care that patients and families receive during cancer treatment. Music therapy services address nine of the fifteen standards of care identified, and therapists are uniquely positioned to help ensure personalized, comprehensive care. As the body of research evidence grows, my hope is that music therapy will become a standard of care service that is available to more people.

So far we have developed two interventions: the SMART studies, focused on adolescents, and we are now studying an intervention that uses music play for younger children and parents. Music therapy is not a "one-size-fits-all" intervention, so we want to understand the optimal intensity level, the skills by which it needs to be delivered, and how we can create a better model of care with music.

Our goal is to also apply these learnings beyond cancer to help patients and families who are living with other devastating illnesses, such as sickle cell disease. Importantly, we need to make sure our music programs are culturally meaningful and align with the preferences and needs of individual patients and families.

While active participation in music is central to our studies, we're also working to disentangle the role of active music play compared to taking in auditory stimuli as a receptive experience. Listening to music isn't a passive

"Chemo Kid Rock" by Heather (age 12)

Verse 3
Somebody once asked, "How can you do this task?"
I said, "You just have to do it yourself . . ."
I have to be strong, I have to be tough
And I'll know when I've had enough
And we could all use some kind of CURE . . .

experience, as it evokes powerful emotions, and the selection of music can really reflect what you're going through.

JEFRI

Music has always been a huge part of my life, and after Heather died I would listen to songs in her room. It was almost impossible to describe how I felt in those times, but there was always music someone else had written that mirrored my emotions.

The music video project was the highlight of our four-week stay on the Bone Marrow unit, and it was such a relief for my husband and me to see Heather so happy and full of energy. It gave her control, choice, and the ability to say what she wanted, and we still have her words in her own voice.

ACKNOWLEDGMENTS

Research described in this chapter, specifically the therapeutic music video intervention, was funded by the NIH National Institute of Nursing Research (R01NR008583) and the National Cancer Institute (U10CA098543; U10CA095861).

Research is a team endeavor. I want to thank all the researchers, music therapists, health-care providers, patients, and families who have contributed to this work.

With the collaboration of Joanna L. Patterson-Cross, PhD, MBiochem

Achieving Body, Mind, and Soul Harmony with Multiple Sclerosis

COURTNEY PLATT

Courtney Platt, a dancer and choreographer who lives with relapsing multiple sclerosis (RMS), is spokesperson for MS in Harmony, a first-of-its-kind initiative to educate people with MS and their loved ones about achieving mind–body harmony through music therapy.

To me, music is *the* universal language. Whether tapping your foot to jazz, moving your body to hip-hop (my personal favorite), singing your heart out at a concert, or listening to your favorite ballad, it's amazing how a tune can get into your body, mind, and soul. And for as long as I can remember, music and dance have been a part of how I express myself. The rhythms and melodies coursing through my body have always been the most wonderful feeling, but about ten years ago, the sensations I felt while on tour with *So You Think You Can Dance* were different. There was numbness and shock, which worried me. At first I just thought I had injured my back. I was doing ten dances a night, six shows a week, so this was very much a possibility, but as time passed on, it became scary when it did not go away. When I started to do my own research, I realized many of the symptoms of a pinched nerve, like numbness and tingling, were also symptoms of multiple sclerosis (MS). That made me think twice, especially because my maternal grandmother had suffered from primary progressive MS.

While I spoke to my doctor, went through tests, and waited for a diagnosis, music was—again—there to soothe my nerves. At twenty-three, I was diagnosed with relapsing multiple sclerosis—all in the midst of embarking on my dream as a professional dancer, on tour with a leading TV show at the time. As one can imagine, being diagnosed with any chronic, debilitating illness is shocking and overwhelming. I couldn't help but feel as if my own body had turned against me, and I worried that it would hold me back from the future I had dreamed for myself, in both big and small ways. But rather than turning inward (and believe me . . . I tried to just deal with it myself), I found solace in my family and friends. I shared my fears about where I would go from here and ultimately, with their help, made a plan to confront my MS head-on.

The biggest question for me—since it impacted my career and my deepest passion—was "Will I be able to keep dancing?" My physician assured me that I should never stop dancing. That was exactly what I needed to hear, or shall I say, it was music to my ears! It is the core part of who I am, and I know myself well enough to know I could never go down without a fight. To hear that was a relief.

For me an important part of regaining my sense of control and empowerment was to learn as much as I could about MS. I have always believed knowledge is power. It's a progressive illness of the central nervous system that affects one million people in the United States. In MS the immune system mistakenly attacks the myelin sheath, a fatty substance that covers the nerves. This disrupts communication between the brain and the rest of the body, resulting in a wide range of symptoms that may change over time. MS can impact a person's physical and mental abilities, including motor skills, and cause fatigue, and trouble with memory and concentration, particularly divided attention. In the ten years that I've lived with MS, at some point I have experienced every one of these. My biggest symptom has always been fatigue. I have always been described as a person who seems like she has boundless energy, but being diagnosed with MS has caused me to be more aware of where I use my energy. In a way I view that as one of the silver linings. You have to find the good!

Before my diagnosis I didn't understand what was happening inside my body and didn't have the tools to keep my symptoms in check. As I learned more about the disease I wanted to jump in and take action, and so I got involved. I connected with the MS patient community nearby and began working with local MS organizations to drive awareness and support for people with MS. In 2021 I was given the incredible opportunity to expand my role as an MS advocate and launch MS in Harmony, a first-ever music therapy initiative by Bristol Myers Squibb and the American Music Therapy Association. The program is designed to help people living with MS achieve mind-body harmony and to become in tune with their body in a positive way, just as dancing has always done for me. Besides saying "I do" to my husband, this was the fastest YES I have ever said! I was so excited to be a part of such an important initiative. With an illness like MS, it is often hard to feel positive about your body, and the MS in Harmony program can help people to feel that again through music. Think about the goose bumps you can get from a certain song—that's a demonstration of how music can impact specific areas of your brain.

For me, practices like using music as a memory device for my grocery list or revisiting positive memories while listening to certain songs have helped me learn how to better manage certain symptoms that come with MS, like a low mood, forgetfulness, and brain fog. When you listen to music, different parts of your brain are engaged, and you can work on strengthening those connections.

That's because music has been shown to affect the parts of the brain that regulate emotion and behavior, as well as the areas that control memory and learning. Music therapy seeks to harness those effects to help people manage emotions, behavior, memory, and learning. It has been used to supplement treatment plans for people living with central nervous system diseases like MS for years.

In building the MS in Harmony program, I was paired with a board-certified music therapist to create interactive videos demonstrating music therapy techniques, all customized to address the unique challenges that can come from living with MS. These exercises include recalling sounds and writing song lyrics from pleasant memories.

MS in Harmony empowers people with MS—even those who don't consider themselves musically inclined—and allows them to take control of what moves them, engaging their friends and family in the process. My four-year-old might not understand why we have so many family dance parties in the living room, and he doesn't have to. It's fun for both of us, with the benefit of being good for me!

My journey with MS has also inspired me to double down on my personal and professional goals. At first I felt an almost desperate need to keep moving forward in life. I was determined that MS would not rob me of my dreams. Over time, as I continued to progress professionally, I started to let go of some of the anxiety about my career. I'm thrilled with where I am. I'm a professional fitness instructor, wife, and mother. I might need to rest sometimes. I might occasionally need to say no if I'm not feeling 100 percent. And I'm okay with that. In music and in dance, you have to have pauses. This is the dynamic of life itself. These rests are the context for an ongoing musical or dance number, just as they are the context in a well-spent life.

MS is a lifelong illness that I have to contend with, and I vow to always do that with a playlist at my side.

SCIENCE:
A DEEPER DIVE

Researchers Reveal Their Methodology
and Compelling Results

Arts-Based Therapies in Integrative Health

Affiliation: National Center for Complementary and Integrative Health (NCCIH) at the National Institutes of Health, Bethesda, Maryland

EMMELINE EDWARDS, PhD
Director, NCCIH Division of Extramural Research

WEN G. CHEN, MMSc, PhD
Branch Chief, NCCIH Basic and Mechanistic Research Branch

CATHERINE LAW, MTSC
Director, NCCIH Office of Communications and Public Liaison

MARK PITCHER, PhD
Chief of Staff, NCCIH

HELENE M. LANGEVIN, MD
Director, NCCIH

Disclaimer: The opinions expressed in this chapter are the authors' own and do not reflect the view of the National Institutes of Health, the Department of Health and Human Services, or the United States government.

INTRODUCTION

Music, dance, and visual arts and crafts have long been a part of the human experience, conjuring emotions and imagination, making us think and move, and enabling communication. They may also have roles to play in promoting physical and mental health and managing symptoms of illness.

In this chapter, we discuss how arts-based experiences can be incorporated into an integrative approach to health care. Integrative health means bringing conventional medicine and so-called complementary practices together in a safe, coordinated way to improve patient care, promote health, and prevent disease. By "complementary," we mean practices that originated outside of mainstream Western medical care. Examples of complementary practices include acupuncture, herbal remedies, massage therapy, meditation, yoga, and art, music, and dance therapies.

The National Center for Complementary and Integrative Health (NCCIH) was created as part of the National Institutes of Health (NIH) more than twenty years ago to facilitate the study of nonmainstream medical practices and to share the results of that research with the public. As time went on, we increasingly incorporated a focus on integration into our work. More recently, we have expanded our definition of integrative health to include whole person health, which we define as empowering individuals, families, communities, and populations to improve their health in multiple interconnected domains: biological, behavioral, social, and environmental.

Research on the arts and health fits into NCCIH's mission because it is relevant to our Center's research priorities, including health promotion and restoration, disease prevention, and symptom management. In addition, like many of the other approaches we study, arts-based interventions, if proven to be effective, may help decrease the need for drugs or other treatments that can have serious side effects.

Research funded by NCCIH has explored many complementary health approaches and found support for the benefits of some but not others. For example, studies that we funded showed that either mindfulness-based stress reduction or cognitive behavioral therapy is better than usual care for chronic low-back pain and that acupuncture improves symptoms of knee osteoarthritis. On the other hand, NCCIH-funded studies showed that *Ginkgo biloba* did not reduce the development of dementia in older people, and that echinacea did not decrease the severity or duration of the common cold. NCCIH works together with other NIH institutes and centers and other agencies to study topics of importance to all; for example, we are leading a collaborative initiative involving multiple components of NIH, the U.S. Department of Defense, and the U.S. Department of Veterans Affairs to study nondrug approaches for pain management in the military and veterans' health-care systems.

The symptoms of many current health challenges—for example, autism, chronic pain, stroke, cancer and its treatment, and Alzheimer's disease—have remained difficult to manage. In addition, mental and emotional health conditions, such as depression and stress, can coexist with chronic diseases or pose challenges all on their own. These disorders often arise out of or exist within a broader social framework that can and should offer more to improve people's health and well-being.

Research tells us that a combination of integrative therapeutic approaches is needed to address complex health problems. Employing the arts—such as music, visual arts and crafts, and dance—as therapy can be a beneficial strategy for managing a wide range of symptoms. NCCIH classifies "creative arts therapy" or "arts-based therapy" as a mind and body intervention that may play an important role in integrative health strategies for managing the symptoms of many conditions. Creative arts therapies often use art, music, drama, or dance/movement alone or within the context of psychotherapy, counseling, rehabilitation, or allopathic (mainstream) medicine to improve health and functioning.

Integrative health brings conventional and complementary approaches together in a coordinated way and emphasizes treating the whole person rather than, for example, one organ system. It emphasizes lifestyle changes and multimodal interventions with a combination of nutritional, psychological, and/or physical therapeutic inputs (see the figure below) that may

EXAMPLES OF ARTS-BASED THERAPIES WITHIN THE THERAPEUTIC INPUT FRAMEWORK

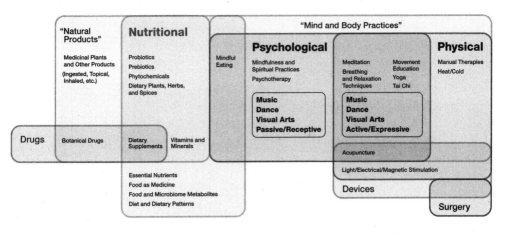

include art therapy, music therapy, and dance, often administered or taught by a trained practitioner or teacher.

This graphic shows the primary therapeutic input of approaches that may be studied within NCCIH's array of research interests. The specific modalities are meant to be illustrative of the types of therapeutic approaches that fall within these categories. The arts-based therapies are highlighted as examples of psychological, as well as combined psychological and physical, inputs of music, dance, and visual arts. This demonstrates the impact that the arts can have on the passive recipient, the audience member, viewer, or listener, as well as on an active participant who is engaging in the act of expressing oneself through music, dancing, painting, etc. Additionally, whether engagement in therapeutic arts is passive/receptive or active/expressive, engagement with others adds a social component that can enhance response. But what does the research say about how the arts can be used to help those dealing with the symptoms of chronic disease or pain? The fact is that rigorous, systematic investigation of the impact of arts-based therapies on health is just beginning. Researchers are currently exploring the potential benefits of arts-based therapies as a component of integrative health to develop the evidence base for supporting its use in multiple settings.

For music-based interventions, for example, much of the current evidence comes from observations by practitioners and studies on small numbers of people. These types of evidence are valuable for suggesting new ideas, but much larger, more rigorously designed studies are needed to clearly demonstrate an intervention's value, understand how it works, and support its adoption in clinical practice. Recently, NCCIH, other components of NIH, and the Renée Fleming Foundation brought together an interdisciplinary panel of experts to develop a set of guidelines and recommendations for high-quality, replicable studies of music-based interventions, focusing initially on those for brain disorders of aging. The resulting tool kit, published in 2023, provides standards and recommendations for study design and assessment of outcomes that will help investigators advance the development and testing of music-based interventions across the life span.

This chapter briefly describes what we know about the components of arts-based therapy that are beneficial and how we can measure and understand their effects on the brain and other parts of the body. It describes the results of studies of arts-based therapy as a component of integrative health approaches. These studies demonstrate its value in improving well-being through symptom management and in restoring health. It concludes with a discussion of the concept of "social prescribing" in health care, that is, offering patients nonpharmacologic interventions such as arts-based therapy in addition to conventional medicine to tackle wider determinants of health and to improve health and well-being. The more we know about which arts-based therapies work and for whom, based on evidence obtained through research, the more precise and tailored these interventions can be when delivered effectively to the appropriate individuals.

PSYCHOLOGICAL AND PHYSICAL THERAPEUTIC INPUTS OF MUSIC AND OTHER ARTS-BASED INTERVENTIONS

To understand the potential benefits of an arts-based therapy, it is important to understand the nature and characteristics of the intervention itself, beginning with its primary therapeutic input. For music and other arts-based interventions, this falls within the psychological and physical domains illustrated in the figure above. There are many ways to introduce these therapies where the participant is either active and engaged or passive and receptive. Active engagement will typically have both psychological and physical inputs (as in playing a musical instrument), while passive, receptive participation will be primarily psychological (as in listening to music). These distinctions are important for sorting out what the effects might be.

The psychological and/or physical inputs can be further characterized into components that may, individually or together, contribute to a therapeutic effect. For example, some forms of music therapy, including guided imagery, music-assisted relaxation, music and imagery, or therapeutic music listening, primarily target individual sensations, such as audition and vision, to potentially elicit therapeutic effects. In contrast, other forms of music-based therapy may simultaneously engage other functions, including movement/motor function, cognition, and even emotion, in addition to sensory functions such as audition and vision. Such therapy includes active singing or performing music, improvisational music therapy, composing one's own music, and dance therapy, as the individuals actively engage in the artistic process. Of additional relevance are the components of the music itself, such as frequency, tempo, and melody, and the volume at which the music is played. All these factors need to be understood and recognized when studying and implementing music-based therapies so that the right activity is prescribed.

Similar distinctions can be made for dance therapy, which is usually active, and thus involves a combination of physical and psychological inputs, or could be passive, such as observing others dancing, which would be primarily psychological. Components include the type of dance (e.g., ballroom, folk dance, contemporary), the length and frequency of sessions, and the interactive effect of music and movement during dance.

In the visual arts and crafts, components of active participation could include the activity itself (e.g., drawing, painting, knitting, pottery) as well as the medium employed (e.g., textile, clay), which could have different effects on one's visual and fine motor skills. As with music and dance, passive viewing of art would have a primarily psychological input. Research conducted on the effects of perceiving or engaging in art has uncovered the differences in the brain and mood and emotional responses based on whether one is viewing art or actively creating it.

Arts-based therapists and researchers also must consider the condition or symptoms of those who will participate, for example, their cognitive abilities, their age and socioeconomic status (which could be meaningful in terms of life experiences), where the therapy is offered (e.g., hospital setting, assisted living facility, classroom, home), and who is providing the therapy sessions. When conducting research on arts-based therapies, clearly defining the components of an intervention allows scientists to hypothesize about what aspects of the intervention are acting on one's health and well-being as well as to compare results across many studies and determine what does and does not work for certain individuals.

PSYCHOLOGICAL AND PHYSICAL THERAPEUTIC EFFECTS OF MUSIC AND OTHER ARTS-BASED INTERVENTIONS

Arts-based therapies may lead to multiple beneficial effects on health outcomes in terms of physical functioning, fewer or less severe symptoms, restored visuospatial skills (needed for movement, depth and distance perception, and spatial navigation), improved sense of well-being, and reduced stress, as discussed later. Scientists have developed multiple strategies for investigating when and if these benefits occur, how they occur, and for whom.

For example, art therapy has been shown to have a suspected or validated beneficial impact on symptoms of a wide variety of medical conditions, such as cancer, mood disorders, Alzheimer's disease and other dementias, schizophrenia and psychosis, post-traumatic stress disorder (PTSD), and other psychiatric and nonpsychiatric conditions. Developing the evidence base through research is critical in ensuring that arts-based activities offered to various populations actually work. Basic or fundamental research can be done in animal models or in the laboratory to see how exposure to certain stimuli relevant to arts-based therapy affects the brain or the body's chemistry. These ideas can then be tested in humans using a variety of scientific methods to establish cause and effect, usefulness, efficacy and effectiveness, and ease of implementation.

One example of the use of animal models is the investigation of responses to rhythmic stimuli in songbirds. Songbirds have specialized brain circuits for learning and producing rhythmically patterned sequences that are remarkably similar to the circuits that perform the same functions in people. Studies in zebra finches, the most studied songbird species, are helping us understand the biological mechanisms of rhythm perception and how they may be disrupted by damage to specific brain regions. The results of this research may aid in the design of interventions involving music or dance for the benefit of both healthy people and those with conditions that affect the brain.

Changes in the Brain

Understanding and identifying the brain processes involved when experiencing music and other art forms can strengthen the premise of why and how arts-based therapy works, and for whom. Neuroplasticity, also known as brain plasticity, is a term that refers to the brain's ability to change and adapt as a result of experience. Faced with different situations, our brains will continue to change and respond to environmental activity throughout our lives. The ability of the brain to adapt and adjust or to overcome "negative plasticity" from, for example, stress, disease, trauma, or anxiety, is an important concept behind a "brain-based" view of arts-based therapy. The results of numerous studies suggest that many neural processes are involved when individuals experience the arts. For example, studies of the brain in those participating in art therapy find that the experience allows the brain to integrate sensory-motor, visual, and verbal aspects of traumatic memories. Bringing these separate components of memory from the brain's left and right hemispheres together can enable people to form explicit, coherent verbal memories. This reformulation can facilitate processing of the memories in ways that promote the experience of flow (a state of focused attention associated with long-lasting positive feelings) and allow for post-traumatic growth. Other studies have shown that dance/music training can enhance functioning in parts of the brain that increase someone's ability to sense and absorb other people's emotions.

Understanding these neural mechanisms and outcomes can provide clues as to which music-based interventions might work best, and why, in populations with, for example, deficiencies or degeneration in key parts of their brain. Scientists can use noninvasive measurements of brain structure and function, such as magnetic resonance imaging (MRI), electrophysiology measurements of the heart or brain (e.g., EKG, EEG), and behavioral or cognitive tests to study short- and long-term brain plasticity associated with musical training or art therapy. Using these tools, scientists have demonstrated that engaging in an artistic activity with no clear evolutionary advantage, such as music or art, activates the same reward network in the brain that reacts to basic sensory pleasures, such as food or sex.

It is important to recognize that not all people respond the same way to the "higher-order stimuli" offered by arts-based therapies. Factors such as musical or artistic ability, familiarity with art or music, opportunities for engagement, demographics, clinical conditions, and personality play a role in an individual's emotional and physical response. Even the type of music and its tempo can elicit a variety of distinct responses with regard to physical performance.

In 2016 Matthew Sachs and his colleagues provided the first evidence of a neural basis for differences in how individuals respond to music, with greater connectivity found in certain parts of the brain among those who have a visceral reaction to music (e.g., chills, lump in the throat, tears). This observation might provide clues as to why music-based interventions affect and benefit some more than others. Similarly, in 2020, using imaging, Alexander Belden and his colleagues found varying levels of interconnectivity in two parts of the brain when engaged in music; one that is active when processing one's internal mental state and one that is active during memory, decision making, and problem-solving. A beneficial effect of music on brain connectivity has even been found in severely brain-injured patients, regardless of the level of consciousness. Differing degrees and strengths of the connectivity between specific brain regions have been found to depend on whether one was an improvising musician, a classical musician, or minimally musically trained.

Beneficial changes in the brain, such as increased cortical thickness, can even be found in school-age children who are trained in music. This is important because general intelligence is positively associated with cortical thickness in the brain. There is good reason to encourage your child to practice the piano or join the school choir!

Physiological Changes

Scientists are also studying how arts-based therapies alter the physical and chemical interactions in the human body (i.e., physiology). Music has been shown to be a powerful mood modulator. Understanding how music engages the neurochemical systems underlying mood, stress, and even immunity has received increasing attention in recent years. Stress and recovery from stress can be studied by looking at interactions between the central nervous system, endocrine (hormonal) pathways, and the immune system. Physiological measures, such as heart rate, blood pressure, hormone levels (such as cortisol), and immune system molecules that circulate in the blood, can serve as biomarkers for our body's reaction to art or music. For example, research has shown that when music induces a positive mood, certain hormones and proteins called cytokines change in a positive way, indicating a healthy stress response. The benefits of music therapy can even be felt by caregivers. For example, in a study of children receiving stem cell transplants, the cortisol levels of both the children and the adults caring for them were tracked and showed stress reduction after music therapy.

THE IMPACTS OF THE ARTS ON HEALTH AND WELL-BEING

As discussed above, listening to, performing, or dancing or swaying to music influences emotion, cognition, and the motor and sensory domains in the brain. Music, rooted in sound, engages the auditory system and hearing brain. This then engages multiple aspects of our biology, including not just classic auditory pathways but also how people feel about music, how they move with it or produce it, how other senses contribute to the sonic information, and what people know and feel about sound from their life experiences. Music strongly inspires rhythmic movement, and this has led to using music, dance, and rhythmic drumming for movement rehabilitation while also improving emotions and social connections. Rhythms are also central to the brain, and rhythmic processing is affected by many disabilities. As such, music-based therapies have been used to improve the symptoms of disease.

Parkinson's disease (PD), which affects movement, balance, walking, and speech, has been the center of much research on arts-based therapies. Music and dance have been shown to boost spontaneous rhythmic connection between one's sensory and motor systems, both of which are affected by PD. Persons with PD who regularly engage in weekly dance classes were found to improve their parkinsonian symptoms, with improved gait, balance, and mood. Additional research suggests that singing may improve and maintain vocal function and respiratory control in persons with PD.

Other research has focused on military service members experiencing PTSD and/or traumatic brain injury. Art therapy is increasingly accepted as a form of complementary care for military veterans with PTSD symptoms. Art sessions such as mask making have been shown to offer important psychosocial support for service members with these diagnoses. It is hypothesized that art therapy helps them sort through their issues of identity and self-expression (not typically a focus in the military culture) through visual self-expression. This allows them to communicate their lived experiences regarding grief, loss, guilt, and trauma. Researchers have concluded that using art making for nonverbal discovery can be beneficial in conditions where domains of the brain normally engaged in verbal communications have been compromised.

Arts-Based Therapies Improve Mood and Well-Being

Art therapy has been shown to assist with mood and well-being by allowing individuals to express their concerns and feelings through a creative and nonverbal format. Art sessions can provide a safe way to gain control and inner strength and learn new coping skills. Importantly, because art is an expression, it can foster communication with others through sharing, displaying, and giving of artwork to others.

Similarly, the pleasure people experience when exposed to music is believed to relate to emotions and its ability to change or enhance how someone feels. A review of fifty-five randomized controlled trials found that music therapy resulted in a significant reduction in depressive symptoms compared with the control group, and music medicine (i.e., music as therapy that is not managed by a music therapist and does not involve a therapeutic relationship) exhibited a stronger effect in reducing depressive symptoms. The specific music therapy methods were important, resulting in different effects on mood.

The following are a few examples of how arts-based therapies can improve or restore psychological and mental health. Other benefits have been found in terms of emotional well-being, enhanced quality of life, and improved sleep.

- Many people with Alzheimer's disease and other dementias will experience agitated or aggressive behaviors during the later stages of the disease. This causes significant stress for them and their caregivers, including nursing home staff. Research suggests that early musical memories are stored in the brain until the later stages of dementia. Studies have shown that eliciting those familiar musical memories can reduce agitated behaviors in this population, benefiting them as well as those who care for them.

- Persons with diabetes mellitus are more likely to suffer from depression because of their need to constantly comply with medication, exercise, diet, and other treatment requirements. This can then lead to poor control of blood glucose levels and further disability. A review of studies of painting therapy in this population found that it may have significant beneficial effects on the levels of depression and blood glucose for diabetic patients.

- Research is ongoing to determine if mindfulness-based art therapy offered to college students can protect them against the emotional and physical consequences of stress and anxiety.

- Suicide involves a variety of social and mental health factors. Emerging research that connects the arts to positive health outcomes is behind efforts to determine their value in suicide prevention and survivorship. Research is suggesting that factors that influence suicide risk and survivorship may be effectively addressed for some through arts-based interventions.

ARTS AND HEALTH: PRESCRIPTIONS FOR THE FUTURE

Conventional Western medicine and its reliance on pharmaceutical and medical approaches to treating chronic conditions remain central to improving health. However, complementary interventions, such as arts-based therapies, are increasingly recognized as useful tools to address wider determinants of health and disease that have not always been the focus of, or responsive to, conventional medicine. As described here, arts-based therapy has been shown to improve the management of both mental and physical health. The benefits accrue when the arts-based therapy is experienced or practiced alone or with others. Further, both active and more passive experiences, such as creating art or simply enjoying it, can yield substantial health benefits to the individual.

"Social prescribing" is an emerging concept used to promote and facilitate endorsement of and investment in collaborative and integrative care models by physicians, health-care organizations, communities, and policy-makers. In the United Kingdom, the social prescribing movement involves primary care physicians recommending arts-related interventions such as personalized music playlists, dance classes, or singing lessons to their patients. It is being studied as a means of addressing long-term physical health conditions and promoting mental health and well-being. Further, this practice gives general practitioners greater options when helping patients with complex social problems that may be contributing to their medical conditions.

Likeminded efforts are emerging in the United States. For example, in January 2020 the Mass Cultural Council launched CultureRx in Massachusetts, an initiative focused on advancing the role of culture as a protective factor for the health of everyone in the Commonwealth. The program was founded to address significant gaps in provision of care and to focus on the many health conditions that have not been addressed adequately or equitably, such as stress and trauma, chronic illnesses, and substance use disorder.

In 2016 the Rhode Island (RI) Department of Health partnered with the RI State Council on the Arts to support development of a State Arts and Health Plan, a public health road map for advancing the integration of arts and health for the state. As part of this process, an interdisciplinary team of arts and health practitioners, which includes researchers, artists, and clinicians, formed the RI Arts and Health Advisory Group. This body developed a strategy for fully integrating arts and arts-based therapies into health-care and community settings through innovative and sustainable policy, practice, and research recommendations.

Numerous other large health-care providers in the United States are incorporating arts-based therapies (see Table 1 below) into their integrated care management plans. These programs do not just focus on current symptoms; they are also oriented toward prevention using arts-based strategies to impact management of chronic diseases, stress-related disorders, and multiple health outcomes. There is also variability in how arts-based programs are integrated into care. Many such programs are offered as adjunct therapies to reduce stress and improve coping in patients undergoing complex and/or long-term treatments such as certain cancer therapies, but with limited integration of the arts-based therapy into treatment planning. However, some health systems are taking a much more integrative approach.

For example, the Department of Veterans Affairs (VA) provides veterans with comprehensive creative arts therapies incorporating creative modalities as well as evidence-based medicine that are both oriented toward restoring health and improving well-being. Arts-based approaches have been used by the VA for more than seventy-five years. In 1945 the U.S. War Department's Technical Bulletin 187 discussed its integration of music into recreation, education, occupational therapy, and physical reconditioning for service members convalescing in Army hospitals. The primary objectives of the VA's current arts-based therapy programs are to enhance cognitive and sensorimotor function as well as build emotional resilience and social and coping skills. The VA's Creative Arts Therapies program includes Art Therapy, Dance/Movement Therapy, Drama Therapy, and Music Therapy, all fully integrated into the VA's standard team-based practice to cover the full continuum of care among service members, veterans, and their families.

CONCLUSION

Over centuries every culture has used the arts as a means of communication, self-expression, and social bonding. Given the growing evidence of how arts-based therapies can improve patient outcomes, quality of life, and the health-care experience, greater advocacy for the arts in medicine is needed. In this chapter we have highlighted research studies that show that arts-based therapies are effective in reducing various adverse physiological and psychological health outcomes. However, the extent to which these psychological and physiological effects are sustainably health enhancing is an important area for public health investigation. The need for continued research and the generation of large datasets from randomized clinical trials using standardized protocols is certainly warranted. NCCIH's focus on whole person health fully supports the integration of arts-based therapies with conventional medicine approaches to improve patient outcomes and enhance health and well-being across the life span.

TABLE 1. EXAMPLES OF INTEGRATIVE HEALTH
AND ARTS PROGRAMS IN THE UNITED STATES

Covenant Children's Hospital provides developmental, educational, and expressive opportunities through play and the creative arts to help children and families better cope with illness, hospitalization, and recovery.

providence.org/locations/covenant-health/childrens-hospital/integrative-care.

The Georgetown Lombardi Arts and Humanities Program is conducting research, "Recovery in the ICU: An Investigation of Music-Induced Physiologic and Metabolic Changes That Promote Healing," to encourage a creative and constructive response to illness and to promote wellness.

lombardi.georgetown.edu/artsandhumanities.

The Center for Performing Arts Medicine at Houston Methodist offers music therapy to patients and their families specific to medical diagnoses, development and course of treatment, and discharge timeline.

houstonmethodist.org/performing-arts/music-therapy.

The Huntsman Cancer Center offers art, music, and writing sessions for cancer patients to reduce anxiety, depression, pain, loneliness, and stress.

healthcare.utah.edu/huntsmancancerinstitute/wellness-support/wellness -integrative-health-center/creative-arts.

Johns Hopkins Medicine offers art, dance, and music therapy to help distract from and ease symptoms from illness or disease.

hopkinsmedicine.org/health/wellness-and-prevention/art-dance-and-music.

The Louis Armstrong Department of Music Therapy at Mt. Sinai Beth Israel incorporates mind-body music therapy techniques for adults in pulmonary and cardiac rehabilitation and for children and teens with asthma.

mountsinai.org/locations/music-therapy.

At Montefiore, healing arts programs are available in the multiple pediatric and adult departments to complement patient care by helping to reduce pain and other physical symptoms, provide comfort and enjoyment, promote self-expression, and enhance quality of life.

montefiore.org/healingarts-programs.

University Hospitals offers art therapy to help cancer patients and caregivers cope with the diagnosis through self-expression.

uhhospitals.org/services/integrative-health-network/our-services/art-therapy.

Music therapy's seventy-year history in the U.S. military covers the entire continuum of care among service members, veterans, and their families. It is a vital part of treatment currently delivered in military treatment facilities and VA medical centers across the country, delivered by board-certified music therapists. The military's TRICARE program covers ancillary therapies including art, music, and dance therapy.

tricare.mil/CoveredServices/IsItCovered/MentalHealthTherapeuticServices.

Music, Memory, Aging, and Science

Affiliation: National Institute on Aging (NIA) at the National Institutes of Health, Bethesda, Maryland

CORSYE ST. HILLAIRE-CLARKE, PhD

Program Director, NIA Division of Neuroscience

DAVE FRANKOWSKI, PhD

Health Specialist, NIA Division of Neuroscience

LISA ONKEN, PhD

Program Director, Behavior Change and Intervention Program, NIA Division of Behavioral and Social Research

Disclaimer: The participation of these individuals or the materials should not be interpreted as representing the official viewpoint of the U.S. Department of Health and Human Services, the National Institutes of Health, or the National Institute on Aging, except where noted.

Music has a unique ability to impact us in multiple ways because it engages the entire brain. It activates emotion, stimulates us to tap our feet or get up and dance, and even possesses therapeutic potential. Scientists are continuing to investigate the effects of music on the brain and body and to unravel the mechanisms by which music may be used to improve health and well-being, particularly in older adults. Aging is an inevitable part of life, but there are many factors that influence how we age. Eating well, getting enough sleep, and engaging in physical activity and exercise are some ways to promote healthy aging. Playing an instrument, listening to music, and/ or singing may also influence healthy aging.

The National Institute on Aging (NIA), one of the twenty-seven institutes and centers of the National Institutes of Health (NIH), leads the federal government in conducting and supporting research on aging and aging-related diseases, including Alzheimer's disease (AD) and Alzheimer's disease–related dementias (ADRD), with the goal of improving the health and well-being of older adults. NIA is at the forefront of groundbreaking science on music and health and is well positioned to identify topic areas that deserve greater attention and to help stimulate research in those areas. Understanding how music may affect the brain to provide health benefits for older adults, and if and how music can be used to prevent or treat some of the symptoms of AD, is certainly one of those areas deserving further investigation.

Alzheimer's disease is a progressive brain disorder that slowly destroys memory and thinking skills and, eventually, the ability to carry out even the simplest tasks. It is the most common form of dementia and affects over 6 million people over sixty-five in the United States. According to the Alzheimer's Association, it is projected that this number could rise to 13.8 million by 2060 without new approaches to prevent, slow, or cure AD. Additionally, in 2023, Alzheimer's and other dementias were projected to present a significant financial burden to individuals with AD, those providing care to individuals with AD, and the nation's health-care system, which could cost about $345 billion. Even more alarming is that this number could rise to more than $1.1 trillion by 2050. Those with AD may experience behavioral and psychological symptoms such as agitation, aggression, anxiety, and depression. Later in the disease they often have difficulty with communication and performing routine activities of daily living such as dressing, eating, or walking independently. Because there is currently no cure for AD, it is especially important to find ways to ameliorate some of its behavioral and psychological symptoms, and to improve the overall quality of life for individuals with AD and those providing care for them. Music has great potential to contribute to this goal.

RESEARCH ON MUSIC, MEMORY, AND AGING

Memory is a process that allows one to encode, store, and retrieve information. As we age, we may find ourselves becoming a little forgetful, but this is normal. Misplacing your car keys is a good example. What isn't normal is when memory problems affect one's ability to clearly think, learn, and perform everyday activities. This could be a sign of dementia. Can music play a role in maintaining or improving memory? The short answer is, we don't know, but scientists are continuing to explore this question. Some evidence suggests that music may help with memory recall and enhance one's awareness of the current environment. This may be because musical memories are stored in a part of the brain that remains relatively undamaged by AD and other dementias. For example, you may have seen the 2014 award-winning documentary film *Alive Inside*, which shows nursing home residents with severe dementia, who are unable to speak but begin to move, sing, and interact with others when listening to their favorite music on iPods.

NIH has supported numerous grants on the effects of music on health, and many have been supported by the National Institute on Aging. For example, Dr. Vincent Mor was funded by the NIA to test the impact of preferred music on people living with dementia in nursing homes. Specifically he studied whether music could help to address the behavioral and psychological symptoms of AD (for example, aggression, irritability, depression, and anxiety) in residents with the disease. The NIA also recently funded a study led by Dr. Amy Belfi that explores music-induced reminiscence to better understand how music evokes autobiographical memories and associated emotions. There is hope that the research on music supported by NIH will be able to inform the development of music-based interventions to improve affect, well-being, and cognition—the ability to clearly think, learn, and remember.

There is some evidence to suggest that older adults who participate regularly in a choir may have improved health benefits compared to those who do not engage in choral singing. The NIA previously supported a study led by Dr. Julene Johnson to investigate the effect of older adults singing in a choir for ninety minutes each week over a period of a year. Her results showed that those who participated in the intervention reported decreased loneliness and increased interest in life. Dr. Johnson recently initiated a new study to examine whether music improvisation—the spontaneous generation of musical melodies and rhythms—training in older adults with and without mild cognitive impairment (an early stage of memory or thinking problems) can improve their cognition and brain function and late-life engagement in cognitively challenging activities such as playing a musical instrument or reading.

There is anecdotal evidence to suggest that music could be valuable as a therapy for some aging-related disorders, but, so far, there is little scientific evidence for this. In 2017 the NIA commissioned the Agency for Healthcare Research and Quality (AHRQ) and the National Academies of Science, Engineering, and Medicine (NASEM) to assess the state of the science regarding nonpharmacological approaches (including music) that might have benefit to quality of life of people living with dementia. Their report, published in August 2020, concluded from the thirty-five studies examined that evidence was insufficient to draw conclusions about music therapy for agitation, anxiety, depression, mood, and quality of life in people living with dementia. But an absence of evidence is not evidence of absence. One common thread across these studies is the small numbers of participants. To be able to draw definitive conclusions about the role of music in dementia, including AD, we need to improve upon the rigor of the design of the studies, which often includes significantly increasing the number of people taking part. Moreover, many of these studies have not been designed within a scientific and theoretical framework, so their results remain preliminary. Why is it important to improve the evidence base and understand the science of how music might be exerting its effects when evaluating its impact on health? Isn't it enough if we determine that music is having a positive effect?

STUDYING THE EFFECTS
OF MUSIC ON HEALTH

Music is universally viewed as one of life's pleasures. How could it *not* have positive effects on health? Who can deny that listening to music touches people . . . that it can, for example, help to soothe after a stressful day at work? Who can deny the way that music can inspire, and the way the rhythm seems to boost energy? It seems as if it can evoke feelings you didn't even know that you had.

It is difficult to appreciate music without appreciating the characteristics that define it: the tune, the pace, the rhythm, the beauty when notes are combined harmonically. In his 1722 book *Traité de l'harmonie*, Jean-Philippe Rameau noted, "Music is a science which should have definite rules; these rules should be drawn from an evident principle; and this principle cannot really be known to us without the aid of mathematics." The process of science, or the "scientific method," also has rules, and two of the most important parts of the scientific method are to form an educated guess or "hypothesis" and then to test this hypothesis. NIH's mission is a scientific one that seeks "fundamental knowledge about the nature and behavior of living systems and the application of that knowledge to enhance health, lengthen life, and reduce illness and disability," and the prevention and treatment of disease is one of its major goals. Those of us who appreciate music may find it hard to believe that music cannot contribute to these goals. But providing scientific evidence for the beneficial effects of music on health isn't easy.

Science involves asking a question and using an approach that answers the question while ruling out other explanations to your question. If your question is "Does music improve people's health?" and you compared the health of people who listen to music a great deal with that of people who don't listen to music very much, you wouldn't come close to answering the question. Even if you did find that the group of people who listened to music more had better health than those who listened less, it might have nothing to do with music itself. It could mean, for example, that people who listen to more music simply have more leisure time, and it might be that having more leisure time is what is making them healthier, not the music. Or it could mean that people who listen to music are wealthier than those who listen to less music, and it is the wealth that is causally related to the health effects. Or it could mean that those who listen to more music listen to it in the company of other people, and they are less lonely and less socially isolated than those who don't listen to much music. And it could be the effects of social isolation and loneliness that are responsible for the poorer health of the people listening to less music.

In science one must design a study that controls for other explanations such as these. But let's say that you design a study to determine whether music has health effects, and you control for all these variables, as well as any others that you believe might explain your results. Even then, wouldn't it increase the meaningfulness of the findings if a more specific question were asked? Let's say you were trying to improve the health and well-being of people living with dementia in a nursing home. Would it be better to tell a person providing care to a person with dementia, "Play more music," or would it help to know more about what kind of music should be played?

(Should the music preferences of the person with AD or AD-related de-mentias be considered? Should it be soft, soothing music? Should it be music with a strong beat?) How frequently and at what time should it be played? (Should it be played all day long? Twice a day? Three times? For fifteen minutes? Thirty minutes? An hour? Should it be played only in the afternoon?)

And what kind of effects are you seeking? Shouldn't this be specified? For example, are you trying to reduce feelings of depression or anxiety that sometimes go hand in hand with AD? Are you trying to improve cognition, and, more specifically, improve memory? Are you trying to reduce feelings of loneliness, which are all too often experienced by people in nursing homes, and are associated with increases in morbidity and mortality? What you're aiming to change is very likely relevant to what kind of music is chosen.

If you're trying to provide evidence for the beneficial effects of any and every type of music on any and every type of health outcome, it becomes exceedingly difficult to design a study that answers your question and also rules out other answers to your question. Rigorous scientific research re-quires that scientific questions be clearly articulated, and that studies are designed to provide clear answers to these questions. So, to answer a scien-tific question about the effects of music on health, it can be very helpful to have a very specific question.

There are many personal stories of how music has transformed the qual-ity of life for a loved one with dementia, or how music helped to ameliorate behavioral symptoms of dementia. These anecdotal stories can be exceed-ingly moving and compelling. For example, one of the authors recounted an experience with a family member with a malignant brain tumor. The tumor had rendered the loved one unable to speak. Although she clearly understood what she heard, she had been unable to generate language for over half a year. But when a song familiar to her was played, she was able to sing along. After six months of being unsuccessful in generating a sen-tence, she was able to sing *all* the lyrics. The joy she exuded was palpable, and it was impossible not to be convinced of the power of music. But as compelling as personal stories may be, they cannot substitute for rigorous scientific research. Nonetheless, they can propel the research by stimulat-ing ideas that help to generate hypotheses. Hypotheses related to music and dementia can ask this type of question: "Does this specific type of music, when played in this specific way, at these specific times, cause these specific effects?" In addition, such scientific studies are often well served to include specific hypotheses regarding *how* and *why* music might be causing these effects. Why does this serve science better? The answer is simple: If we know how and why music exerts its effects, we have the possibility of making the effects even stronger.

Consider this scenario: A study shows that an afternoon gathering of people with dementia where music is played is associated with improved physical health. But do we know why? Is it because it is increasing a feeling of social connection, and the increased social connection is improving mood, which improves physical health? If this is the case, we can make sure that the music is offered in this context, and perhaps even do things to maximize the effect. Is it because the music itself is improving mood, and the improved mood is improving health? If this is the case, we might find that the music doesn't need to be played in just a group setting but could have an additional positive effect when the individual is alone in his/her room. Is the music stimulating the reminiscence of events associated with it in the past that, in turn, has a positive effect on mood and leads to better health? The possibilities for capitalizing on the positive effects of music are limitless but would not be discovered if questions regarding the "how" and "why" a music intervention is working weren't asked within the context of rigorous research. Answering those questions could potentiate the impact of music on health, and this is why the NIH and its scientific collaborators are working to stimulate the relevant research.

THE EFFORTS AT THE NIH TO UNDERSTAND THE IMPACT OF MUSIC ON HEALTH

The Sound Health Initiative: A Partnership Between the National Institutes of Health and the Kennedy Center in Association with the National Endowment for the Arts

The Sound Health Initiative (SHI) is a partnership between the NIH and the John F. Kennedy Center for the Performing Arts, in association with the National Endowment for the Arts (NEA). This partnership is the brainchild of the renowned Renée Fleming and Dr. Francis Collins, former NIH director, and was established in 2017 to explore ways to understand the brain's relationship with music and the mechanisms underlying the therapeutic potential of music, and to create public awareness about how the brain functions and interacts with music. Just prior to its launch, an inaugural music and health workshop was convened at the NIH campus with twenty-five neuroscientists, music therapists, musicians, and educators from around the world in attendance to discuss the state of research on the interaction of music and the brain as well as how music can be used as therapy. As a result, a set of recommendations for further research to advance both the fundamental science of music's interaction with the brain as well as potential therapeutic applications of music were identified.

As part of the SHI, the Kennedy Center has focused on raising awareness of the science of music and its role in health and well-being through a series of Kennedy Center events. In addition, the National Endowment for the Arts, a federal agency that supports arts and arts education in communities across the United States, has contributed funds to new awards and provides consultation on the SHI to support research on music, neuroscience, and health through several projects nationwide.

Funding Opportunities for Researchers

One of the goals of the SHI is to promote research that increases our understanding of how the brain processes music, develop scientifically based strategies to enhance normal brain development and function, and advance evidence-based music interventions for brain diseases and human health overall. To this end, several funding opportunities for researchers have been made available by the NIH. Through the SHI, fifteen research projects (totaling $20 million over five years) were funded in 2019. The projects span the gamut from basic research, for example, understanding how brains are shaped by music over time from childhood to adulthood, to more clinical research, such as understanding the impact of singing interventions on cardiovascular health in older patients with heart disease. With so much still to discover about music and the brain, the NIH strongly encourages investigators to continue to develop their exciting research projects and to take advantage of these NIH funding opportunities. More detailed information on funding opportunities and the awards funded under the SHI

can be located at nih.gov/research-training/medical-research-initiatives/sound
-health/funding-announcements-opportunities.

Areas of Research to Be Explored

An orchestra is made up of many individual players who perform within
instrumental sections that all come together to produce a melodious symphony. The human brain can be thought of in a similar manner—individual
neurons perform their roles and form a larger regional network of the brain
that works together with other networks to create comprehensible thoughts,
emotions, and behaviors. The complexity of the brain's neuronal networks
within networks is truly incredible, and it poses a multitude of challenges
when attempting to understand how to maintain healthy brain functioning.
Adding to the complexity is the variety of routes music may take when
activating the brain. After all, music engages not only areas of the brain
that process sound, but also those involved in the elicitation of emotion,
recollection of memories, and (if it is really good) the generation of motor
movement (dancing!). Thus, given the complexity of brain function and the
nature of music therapy, there are many avenues of research to be conducted
within this emerging field.

When clearly defined music-based interventions are being developed
that can be used to lessen the severity of age-related illnesses, not only do
several factors need to be taken into consideration to improve upon the
rigor of the study design, but testing and retesting of these interventions
across the spectrum of disease states and diverse backgrounds are also critical. For instance, does a given music intervention benefit early onset dementia but not late onset dementia? Does that intervention benefit all racial
groups and genders equally? Other factors that are currently poorly understood relate to the level of engagement necessary for an intervention; can
an individual simply passively listen to music to benefit from a therapy, or
might actively moving/singing to the music be necessary (thus engaging
more brain networks)? Many factors must be considered when designing
effective interventions to combat age-related illnesses.

Because music engages a wide variety of neural systems (e.g., motor,
memory, reward systems), scientists face challenges in understanding how
and why a music-based treatment effect may (or may not) occur. For this

reason, it is important to promote studies that help deepen our understanding of the biological underpinnings of music therapy. Understanding how both the healthy and the impaired brain process music may enable researchers to uncover useful biomarkers that may provide an unbiased assessment of music therapy efficacy *and* help predict whether a therapy will work within a given individual. For example, a researcher may identify a neural pathway involved in processing music that is degraded by a particular condition, such as AD. In such a case that researcher might use the integrity of this pathway as a measuring stick to test how beneficial a given music intervention may be. In addition, that same hypothetical pathway may be particularly resilient in a specific population of people, which, therefore, would inform the researcher whether a music-based therapy may be useful in that population.

In conclusion, there is still much research needed to understand the effects of music on the brain to establish effective music-based treatments for age-related illnesses such as AD/ADRD. Researchers must be aware of what questions they are answering and, importantly, what questions they are not. In 2021 the NIH, in collaboration with the Foundation for the NIH (FNIH) and the Renée Fleming Foundation, sponsored a series of workshops (nih.gov/sound-health/events) with the goal of developing standards and tools that could be applied to all music-based interventions to improve the rigor with which they are conducted. The NIH published these standards and tools in a peer-reviewed journal, and we hope that researchers will find them helpful for their music-based studies. This is a very exciting time to be a music researcher, and anyone interested in pursuing this area is encouraged to seek support from the NIH. We are excited both to see how the funded NIH projects develop over the coming years and to see the types of new projects that come our way in the near future.

Art Therapy, Psychology, and Neuroscience: A Timely Convergence

JULIET L. KING, ATR-BC, LPC, LMHC
Associate Professor of Art Therapy, The George Washington University

ANJAN CHATTERJEE, MD
Director, Penn Center for Neuroaesthetics, University of Pennsylvania

*T*ypically the quietest member of the group, John muttered expletives while making his watercolor wash. When one of his peers asked him what was wrong, he looked up, smiled, and said he was fine. When told that he was cursing and his face and ears were red, he said, "Yeah, these paints are annoying and impossible to control . . . but I guess I am doing what I always do; I pretend that everything is fine, when it's not." Here, the art-making experience evoked in John a feeling of frustration, one that he did not recognize until others pointed it out. Through the interaction with his peers, John quickly became aware that his coping skill of avoidance did not necessarily make his pain disappear.

John was a participant in a mindfulness-based art therapy study for combat veterans. In this chapter we will refer to his experience to illustrate the convergence of art therapy, neuroscience, and post-traumatic stress.

In the pilot study all the participants were diagnosed with post-traumatic stress disorder (PTSD), and some also had traumatic brain injury (TBI). In one session the participants were given a large sheet of sturdy paper and watercolor paints with brief instructions for how to create a watercolor wash. Water is applied to a large surface and paint is added, allowing the colors to merge. The more water that is used, the lighter the colors; the more paint, the darker the effect. Watercolor wash is typically used to create an initial layer for a painting. The art therapist used this task as a warm-up exercise for participants to experiment with the art materials, move the paint around the paper, and get a sense of the look and feel of the medium. The clinical goal was to encourage participants to creatively express themselves through movement, play, and discovery. The art therapist also observed how the group members responded to the art materials to assess how they coped with stress. Watercolors are unwieldy and are theorized to evoke emotional responses because of the way they draw on a person's sensory-motor and emotional systems. People with PTSD, also called post-traumatic stress syndrome (PTSS), can be flooded by their emotions. Readily defined as symptoms consistent with PTSD, but that occur earlier than thirty days after experiencing the traumatic event, PTSS is now acknowledged to be a serious health issue. Their capacity to process and articulate uncomfortable feelings is often impaired. But the art therapist had established a relationship with the group and its members, the environment was safe, and paints are not as threatening as other events in their lives.

After the watercolor wash the participants were given the same size sturdy paper and asked to use the same paint set to create a symbol of themselves. The group was also offered a choice of Sharpie markers if they did not wish to use paints. No one chose the Sharpies. Although still encouraging free expression, this directive was more structured and centered around themes of identity. Often veterans and service members report feeling and being a different person after returning from war. Aptly stated by Tyler E. Boudreau, "Coming home has been more than just adapting to life in the aftermath of war; it has been very much about remaking myself. . . . All of my life's experiences have shaped my identity and perspectives but war, I

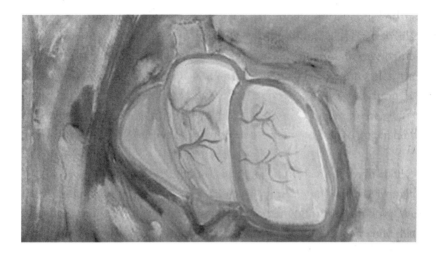

think, has made a disproportionate claim on me." For over eighty years art therapists have observed that images have symbolic meaning for people who create them. Making the artwork and then talking to it, about it, with it, and among others in the therapy group offer a chance to reflect on oneself in a way that is not afforded with words alone. Because of the neurobiological impacts of psychological trauma on language and emotional regulation, these methods are effective intervention strategies.

As the group engaged in the second directive, the chatter fell off to silence. John was focused and engaged. His posture gradually shifted from being hunched over his watercolor wash to sitting straighter in his chair. When the group discussed their artwork, John volunteered to go first, an unusual act for him. He said that his painting was called the Heart of Darkness *and that it represented his heart. He then explained that, unlike regular hearts, his didn't have any of those "things" on it. Another member of the group, a nurse, smiled and said, "You mean arteries?" He laughed and said, "Yeah . . . them. My heart doesn't have arteries, it is completely disconnected. Like me."*

Art is both universal and deeply personal. Initiatives combining arts and health to promote well-being through passive and active arts activities are under way. Being involved with art seems to have positive mental and physical effects. The World Health Organization and advocacy groups recognize the importance of the arts in contributing to improved health outcomes and see that the benefits of arts remain understudied and underfunded, and could be more highly valued in our health-care systems. Inter- and trans-disciplinary collaborations can help advance research, yet gathering evidence linking the arts and health can be challenging, because of different methods used and perspectives of what constitutes adequate evidence. These problems are exacerbated when linking psychological processes to artistic expression, a connection central to psychotherapy.

While therapeutic arts approaches can improve health and alleviate symptoms of distress and psychological injury, arts engagement differs from psychotherapy. Also trained in "talk therapy" (e.g., traditional psychotherapy), creative arts therapists (CAT) have a "definition of the profession, legally defensible scope of practice, educational competencies, standards of practice, code of ethics, and evidence-based research." Therapists within the disciplines of art therapy, dance/movement therapy, drama therapy, music therapy, poetry/biblio therapy, and psychodrama therapy are credentialed in accordance with national and state regulations and standards.

The American Art Therapy Association defines (visual) art therapy as an integrative mental health and human services profession that enriches the lives of individuals, families, and communities through active art making, creative process, and applied psychological theory, within a psychotherapeutic relationship. Art therapy integrates art and psychology and has been informed by medicine and the humanities since the 1940s. Decades of theory development and clinical insights have set standards of practice for the profession, and art therapists work with several core assumptions: (1) the art-making process and the artwork itself are integral components of treatment that help to understand and elicit verbal and nonverbal communication, self-awareness, and reflection within the therapeutic relationship; (2) processes of creativity are healing and life enhancing; (3) the materials and methods used affect self-expression, assist in emotional regulation, and are applied in specialized ways.

Despite the success of art therapy interventions, the biological mechanisms that explain the value of art therapy are not known and remain to be uncovered. Engaging neuroscience may offer insights into how the arts illuminate the connections between the mind, brain, and behavior, and broaden the scope of how the arts impact mental health and disease states. Collaborative partnerships between neuroscientists and art therapists contribute to conceptualizing, hypothesizing, and systematically testing the links between aesthetics, psychology, and brain function that will serve both disciplines and, crucially, the people we seek to support.

THE NEUROSCIENCE OF AESTHETICS

Neuroaesthetics is a subdiscipline of cognitive neuroscience that, as suggested by the name, investigates the neurobiology of aesthetic experiences. These experiences encompass events and interactions with objects such as artworks that evoke intense feelings, often linked to pleasure. Aesthetic experiences emerge from dynamic interactions of three neural systems referred to as the Aesthetic Triad. The triad involves sensory-motor, semantic-meaning, and reward-emotion neural systems. In its applied form, neuroaesthetics asks, Why do aesthetic experiences matter? Relevant to this chapter, How are aesthetic experiences relevant to disorders of emotion regulation?

Knowledge about how the brain relates to artistic experiences extends to art therapy. The art therapist uses tasks to help people express memories and feelings and process them verbally in a safe therapeutic relationship. In the United States, the most well-known theory for this application is the expressive therapies continuum (ETC) developed by Sandra Kagin and Vija Lusebrink in 1978. The ETC attempts to integrate art therapy and neurobiology. The ETC incorporates a set of contrasts in art making between kinesthetic and sensory processing, perceptual and affective depictions, and symbolic representations and cognitive processes.

At the sensory-motor level, the materials used are directly relevant. According to the ETC, the use of artistic materials such as pencils, or watercolors, or clay makes a difference. The resistive properties of these media and kinesthetics of movement required to make art have different effects on emotions. The clinical observation that resistance and receptivity to movement rendered by artistic media have an impact on emotional expression allows the art therapist to choose media based on the needs of specific therapeutic encounters. The body-mind model extends the ETC to emphasize the tactile experience of art making and ways in which it integrates emotions with verbal expression.

Semantic meaning systems refer to cognitive systems that store our personal and general memories and how thoughts and feelings are organized and expressed. For people with PTSS, as we describe below, traumatic memories often have a profound impact on how they view the world and how they interpret their present experiences based on past pain. Individuals with PTSS often have trouble describing their mental state. Some people's distress impairs their language to a point that they are unable to speak. Art therapy engages this system by helping people verbally express and ultimately regulate their emotions.

At the core of PTSS is a disconnection between the semantic-meaning system and a dysregulated affect and emotion system. Affect and emotions have three characteristics. Firstly, they have physiological components that are linked to interoceptive bodily responses serving homeostasis. The interoceptive system refers to internal sensations from different parts of the body that the brain apprehends. For example, our feeling of hunger is influenced in part by low levels of blood sugar. Peripheral glucose sensors relay this information to central integrative centers to coordinate neuroendocrine, autonomic, and behavioral responses to the condition that our brain helps us determine is a state that we *feel* hungry. The interoceptive system thus integrates such information about internal bodily states to influence our perceptions and emotions. Affect is inextricably linked to these physiological states.

Secondly, affect and emotions organize actions. This action principle represents a homeostatic role for emotions and contributes to understanding approach and avoidance behaviors. For example, pain and disgust make us withdraw. Delight and pleasure make us approach. Other cognitive systems, like attention, language, memory, and perception, can be co-opted by emotions to serve actions, whether driven by fear, anger, or desire. Thirdly, in humans, these physiological responses have a phenomenological counterpart. We have a subjective impression of what it feels like to have these emotions.

There is an important distinction between affect (or feelings) and emotions. Affect lies closer to our interoceptive experiences. Over a hundred years ago, psychologist Wilhelm Wundt recognized that affect has arousal and valence components. Arousal refers to how energized we feel. It fuels approach and avoidance behaviors. Valence refers to whether we feel good or bad and can vary in intensity. Emotions are appraisals of these interoceptive feelings and involve language and memory. We organize affect into categories such as fear or anger or joy, and nuanced emotions like shame or melancholy or amusement. People are typically more aware of arousal and valence than other internal sensations.

We can label high arousal and negatively valenced states as anger or fear, or low arousal negatively valenced states as boredom and depression. Emotional categories are constructed from appraisals of dynamic internal sensations. For example, we use language to distinguish between dejection, sorrow, and melancholy, or between awe, wonder, and delight.

John sat up straight by the end of the group. His flushed skin likely represented capillary dilation in a hyperaroused autonomic state that was linked to his feelings of frustration and anger. Making the artwork in the group context allowed John to experience his high arousal in a nonthreatening environment, which diminished the negative valence he associated with high arousal. Although he may have experienced the sensory aspects of using watercolors without thinking too much, valence was still attached to that activity. The art therapy intervention seemed to help him work through his approach-avoidance conflict and gave him a greater sense of agency, awareness, and insight.

Arousal and valence offer axes to understand approach and avoidance behaviors. High arousal is needed to act. Valence determines whether the action moves toward or away from objects and events. Animal and human studies show that our brain's reward systems engage with approach behaviors, and other regions involved in affect and threat assessments engage in avoidance. People with PTSS are typically hyperaroused and in distress. Their neural structures involved in threat assessment and avoidance are likely triggered easily, and their reward systems resist activation. These neural patterns are not confined to situations that evoke avoidance behaviors immediately but are also seen with anticipation of such situations. This observation means that recollection of traumatic memories is also likely to generate similar unhappy avoidant reactions.

John experienced novel enjoyment and pleasure from making art among others, and this experience generated insight and confidence. Although he was initially frustrated, moving from the watercolor wash to the painting task gave John the opportunity to test his new knowledge that when using less water, the paint was easier to control. Here, John's reward system was probably activated when he experienced the pleasure of making art and the sense of accomplishment of having learned to control the media. Presumably, these responses mitigated activity in structures implementing avoidance behavior that might have been generated by his initial feelings of frustration. While this insight might seem irrelevant to the untrained eye, John's mastering of the media illuminated his capacities for problem-solving and resilience.

THE NEUROSCIENCE OF CREATIVITY

The ETC framework identifies functional similarities between the cognitive and symbolic level in the model and contemporary ideas from the psychology and neuroscience of creativity. Pablo Tinio points out that artwork has purpose beyond what it looks like and how it is classified. Meaning drives *why* it was created. The artist-participant starts with the meaning they wish to convey and then refines their output in layers. Making art and talking about its creation help to externalize personal experiences and perceptions. The artist-participant is making creative choices for how to express their ideas and feelings.

Creativity is framed as the capacity to generate new and useful ideas and products. This capacity often involves making new connections between seemingly disparate domains. Many models of creativity invoke a generative phase (divergent thinking) and then an evaluative and selective phase (convergent thinking). Different neural systems underlying cognitive control coordinate aspects of the creative process.

Recent advances in neuroscience have shown that different parts of the brain work together in a series of functional hubs and networks. This organization helps us understand how many functions of the brain are a result of neural activity within and across brain networks rather than being attributed to one specific area. For example, while the hippocampus is a part of the brain that participates in retrieving memories, many interactions take place between it and other parts of the brain from which elements of the memories and their associations are constructed. Vinod Menon identified several brain networks that show coordinated neural activity when people are at rest and underlie different mental operations. Three of these large-scale brain networks (LSBN) most relevant to aesthetics and creativity are the central-executive network (CEN), the default mode network (DMN), and the salience network (SN).

In general the LSBNs work together to execute creative tasks. In creativity, the CEN and the DMN, which typically act antagonistically, increase their functional coupling. While the DMN is implicated in many mental states, most scientists agree that this network is active when one generates ideas. The CEN likely narrows the breadth of ideas generated and focuses behavior into useful outcomes. The SN helps switch attention between internal interoceptive feelings and externally directed stimuli, such as what happens when making art. As Vija Lusebrink and Lisa Hinz plausibly speculate, the symbolic level of idea generation (divergence) is likely to involve DMN activity. The CEN would evaluate and narrow production choices (convergence). Spontaneous and controlled processes interact fluidly when people express themselves creatively, with the SN facilitating switches between the DMN and the CEN. These large-scale networks at rest, and the way the brain responds to specific tasks, are relevant to PTSS.

After John returned from combat, his wife had suddenly died, and he was left to care for their five-year-old son. Like thousands of other veterans and service members, the tragedies he endured in his twenty-five years were horrifying, impacting his psyche at its very core. John's choice to carry on with his artwork without using Sharpie markers spoke to his developing autonomy, confidence, and agency. These nuanced effects of psychotherapy are made possible with the extra "tools" of art materials, process, and product, and allow the art therapist to reflect and support healthy coping strategies in people with PTSS.

Creating a symbol of oneself can be a challenge and is made even more difficult when people have endured profound trauma and loss. Creativity is different from self-expression—here, John engaged creatively when making a symbol of himself, which seemed to involve a different process than moving paint around paper in his watercolor wash. The goal-directed second task, presumably engaging his CEN, allowed him to reflect about himself, engaging his DMN, and evoked insights that he expressed in his Heart of Darkness. *Through therapy, his brain's interactive networks helped him integrate his interoceptive and exteroceptive stimuli. John could deploy meaning in response to his artwork, giving him distance and a new way to see himself. The art therapist and group members were witness to John's process. These social interactions are relevant to his long road ahead; the psychotherapy groups supported him along the way. Through the participation in the art therapy group, John became "more connected."*

PSYCHOLOGICAL TRAUMA: CLINICAL
AND NEUROSCIENTIFIC OBSERVATIONS

Psychological trauma is present in nearly 80 percent of people in mental health clinics. Symptoms after psychological trauma range from anxiety and depression to extremes of PTSS. Trauma reactions are often expressed behaviorally as startle and action (fight or flight); immobility and numbing (freeze); emotional reactivity; depersonalization and dissociation; and nonverbal, aberrant sensations. Intrusive memories and flashbacks of the traumatic event(s) may cause people to avoid their emotions and often keep them in a hypervigilant state.

PTSS is associated with specific patterns of neural activity. These patterns are seen in large-scale brain networks when a person is at rest and in neural activity evoked by specific tasks. Stress symptoms produce changes to activity and connectivity of the ventromedial prefrontal cortex (vmPFC), dorsal anterior cingulate cortex (dACC), and amygdala. Stress also affects connections between DMN, SN, and areas involved in memory (such as the hippocampus) and language (such as the left peri-Sylvian cortex). Generally, well-being correlates with a tight coupling of activity between the CEN, DMN, and SN, a coupling that is diminished for people in distress. People's affective distress correlates with altered activity in regions involved in executive function and reward processing, areas that normally inhibit inappropriate emotions and behaviors.

In task-evoked approaches to assessing emotional regulation, people are shown images that have negative valence (e.g., snakes, attack scenes) or positive valence (puppies, babies), or are neutral (books, silverware). Healthy people and people with PTSS show different neural patterns in response to these affectively charged pictures. Healthy people show greater engagement of the bilateral prefrontal cortices (PFC), cingulate, and temporal lobe when viewing positive-valence images. Negatively valenced images recruit the amygdala. Disruptions to emotional responsiveness to such images are also seen in people with PTSS. Similar patterns of amygdala activations are seen when people with PTSS imagine traumatic situations. People with PTSS who develop anhedonia (a form of emotional dysregulation in which they do not experience pleasure) have abnormal connections between the amygdala and the ventromedial prefrontal cortex, parts of their reward systems.

People with PTSS often ruminate. Rumination is associated with disrupted connectivity between the hippocampus and the amygdala, implying that the symptom occurs because of altered links between aversive emotions and memory. For these individuals, memories are often experienced in fragments and as images and sensations. Broca's area, responsible for speech and language production, shows reduced activity when people recall traumatic experiences, complicating patients' capacity to express themselves. When extreme, this verbal incapacity results in a "speechless terror," the essence of which is captured by a veteran saying, *It's like I am paraplegic in my mind.* Communicating traumatic memories is integral when working with people who have PTSS. The nonverbal expression of art making allows the client to gain distance and "step back" from the process of the making and what is being made. The observation and witnessing of the artistic productions within the therapeutic alliance allow for a safe space for the client and therapist to talk about and reflect on the art as a symbolic representation of its creator. Using language and words in psychotherapy allows the client to make meaning and construct a new narrative of their experiences. Art therapists, trained in both verbal and nonverbal psychotherapy methods, help to modify fearful memories with approaches that decrease stress and arousal, making art therapy a "treatment of choice" for psychological stress and trauma.

Emotional memories associated with fear are malleable. Animal studies show that they can be modified by blocking stress hormones (cortisol) and arousal neurochemicals (norepinephrine). The safety of the therapeutic encounter, which reduces stress and arousal and facilitates access to language while people with PTSS process their trauma, presumably modifies their fearful memories. This modification allows them to reconstruct their personal narrative of past painful events.

MOVING FORWARD

Nonverbal modalities help healthy self-expression by engaging physiological sensations, emotions, and cognitions in the creative-expressive process. Art therapists working with people who have been traumatized rely on nonverbal, symbolic communication. Specialized training provides the art therapist with a critical and perceptive eye to observe and help make sense of how art media are used and formal elements are understood through symbols and metaphors. Externalizing one's experience through art helps to develop a "visual voice," where emotions and experiences are expressed using imagery, symbols, and metaphor, and then verbally processed both within and outside of treatment. Imagery conveyed over time offers an external record that can be used to track progress and regression throughout treatment and to systematically test the correlations between psychological states and symbolism observed in artwork.

Observations made in clinical practice are important in the development and implementation of research methodologies that address trauma sequela, brain injury, and accompanying symptoms. Spearheading these efforts is Creative Forces®: NEA Military Healing Arts Network. Creative Forces® is an initiative of the National Endowment for the Arts, the U.S. Department of Defense, the Veterans Affairs administration, and state and local arts agencies. Creative Forces® places creative arts therapies at the core of care and leads nationwide research to advance the scientific underpinnings of creative arts therapy interventions with military service members (SMs) and veterans. The Creative Forces® flagship clinic at the National Intrepid Center of Excellence (NICoE) provides a standard clinical approach to treat "the invisible wounds of war."

The collaborative partnership between the NICoE and Drexel University's PhD Creative Arts Therapy Department highlights the interplay between clinical practice and research and has produced substantial scholarship to advance the understanding of how the expressive therapies impact the psychosocial health of veterans and SMs who experience PTSS and TBI. Using diverse methods, research has revealed the value of art therapy to assist with the processing of traumatic memories, emotional regulation, management of frustration tolerance, and guilt and loss associated with military experiences. Art therapy helps SMs address themes of identity and explore a changed sense of self when returning from combat. This research also provides insights into how to discover the ideal dosage (intensity, duration) of art therapy and what type of creative arts therapies will be most beneficial for certain patient groups. (To access these peer-reviewed research publications, see: creativeforcesnrc.arts.gov/.)

Mask making, a common art therapy directive, is embedded in the research protocols of Creative Forces®. The "trauma masks" made by SMs provide psychological distance to express personal experiences that are reflected in the formal qualities of the masks created. Mask making and clinical notes that document patient associations and therapist observations have been used as data sources to document case studies that have led to grounded theory and observational studies that explore the relationships between the imagery and subjective measures of anxiety, depression, and PTS symptoms. To date this is the first time a systematic examination of the associations between visual self-expression and how it relates to standardized clinical self-report measures has been made. Some examples of the masks and corresponding themes are seen below:

 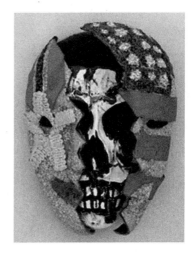

Initial case studies conducted by the clinical research team of Creative Forces® have also led to neuroimaging research that links neuroanatomy, functional connectivity, PTSS symptoms, and artistic productions. Thematic content of masks was correlated with patient report scales, symptom checklists, and functional magnetic resonance imaging (fMRI) scans that analyzed the resting state connectivity of the DMN and brain region connectivity in SMs with PTSS and TBI. While many factors are considered in analysis, this seminal study illuminated the potentials of correlating brain activity with visual elements of art therapy products and their subjective associations, and leads to a greater understanding of how art and science together provide a picture of one's "state of mind."

Efforts to build on existing research have recently been funded by the National Endowment for the Arts and the Henry Jackson Foundation. This research capitalizes on and extends the work done by Creative Forces®: NEA Military Healing Arts Network and aims to address a fundamental question: Does art therapy improve the emotional well-being of military populations (MPs)? To illustrate the promise and challenges ahead, several considerations need to be addressed:

Therapy protocols: A basic question for any art therapy intervention is what protocols to use. This study adapts an art therapy protocol developed at NICoE (as described above) that taps into the symbolic and affective levels of the ETC. Other art therapy sessions include drawing and painting tasks designed to engage SMs' expressive capacity, symbolic communication, and affective responses in the safety of the therapeutic relationship. The choice of protocol is based on clinical experience.

Participants and comorbidities: This study enrolls SMs with PTSS. However, many SMs with PTSS also have TBI. According to the Defense and Veterans Brain Injury Center, from 2000 through the first quarter of 2018, nearly 384,000 MPs were diagnosed with TBI. Together, PTSS and TBI present with more severe or with different symptoms than either alone. The difficulty of disambiguating the effects of TBI and PTSD complicates treatment strategies. These injuries might affect neural structures that implement art production and possibly the efficacy of treatment. One challenge for art therapy studies is sorting out the contributions of comorbidities that are present in almost any population who might benefit from art therapy.

Individual differences: Apart from comorbidities, people vary in personality characteristics and dispositions. For example, people who are most open to new experiences (one of five major personality factors) are more likely to engage with art and be creative and be better at regulating emotions. One might predict that, regardless of past trauma, people most open to experiences would benefit most from art therapy. Programmatic research would need to enroll sufficient numbers of participants to address how individual differences interact with the efficacy of therapy, and whether some protocols are better suited for some individuals, based on their personalities, than others.

Therapeutic relationship: The therapeutic alliance is considered a primary vehicle for change in most psychotherapeutic approaches. The therapist plays a critical role in art therapy. Does standardizing a protocol, which is necessary in any systematic intervention, diminish the efficacy of a talented therapist who might otherwise work flexibly, sometimes deviating from a standardized approach based on their clinical experience and acumen? This question is complicated by the rationale that practitioner choice is intentional, as it allows for therapist decision making that is necessarily inclusive of the client's phenomenological experience in treatment.

Measurement and prediction: In determining the efficacy of art therapy, what should we measure? For PTSS, including a standard questionnaire that measures anxiety, stress, and emotional processing would be needed. The actual art produced could be examined. For example, the emotions expressed in masks before and after treatment could be assessed using expert judgment by art therapists or by crowdsourcing methods. Are SMs better able to express their emotions in their art toward the end of treatment? Are those SMs who were better at expressing themselves at the beginning more likely to benefit from treatment? Participants in this study write about their experiences of making art. These qualitative responses could be subject to quantitative analyses when therapists code the themes being expressed, or in the near future by using machine-learning algorithms to conduct sentiment analyses of subjective reports. Neural biomarkers could be useful to predict outcomes and index change. Using resting state measures of large-scale brain networks, as described earlier, could help determine who might benefit most from therapy. Task-evoked protocols could be informative about emotional reactivity in SMs with PTSD and serve as a biological index of the degree to which SMs regulate their emotional reactions.

CONCLUSION

We are at a critical point at which the role of arts in health is being recognized widely. The arts contribute to human flourishing in health and in disease. Art therapy is poised to converge with psychology and neuroscience and make advances, yet more systematic research is necessary to establish its efficacy and advocate for its inclusion in mainstream health care. Capturing and clarifying *how* and *why* psychotherapy works is a challenge, one made even more difficult when the arts are involved. Collaborative partnerships and technological advances offer promising directions to advance transdisciplinary research at the intersection of neuroscience, arts, and related therapeutics.

Overcoming restrictions of traditional brain imaging technologies with mobile brain-body imaging (MoBI) could allow studying cognition in natural settings and provides an approach to investigating the connections between the brain, body, and behavior. MoBI combines different types of neuroimaging, including functional near-infrared spectroscopy (fNIRS), electroencephalography (EEG), as well as other physiological measures such as heart-rate variability and eye tracking to investigate brain dynamics in real-world environments. This integrative technology has potential to explore aesthetic and environmental experiences outside the confines of laboratory settings and provide insights into therapeutic potentials for clinical health populations.

Merging cognitive neuroscience with the arts might illuminate how people's embodied and physiological responses to artwork influence perception. For example, a museum exhibition could be curated to focus on social justice issues such as systemic and generational racism. MoBI could be used to explore how people from diverse demographics experience the imagery. Doing so could provide important insights into how people process traumatic material. Such a project could help clarify the many dimensions of trauma and move the needle toward developing therapeutic interventions within a broader sociocultural context.

The arts, traditional psychotherapy, creative arts therapy, and cognitive neuroscience all contribute and translate knowledge that informs best practices to treat trauma, stress, and related mental health problems. Prospective systematic studies are just beginning. While many questions remain to be answered, the promise and hope are to integrate art therapy into our health-care system and make it an essential part of treatment for people experiencing mental and emotional distress.

For what it's worth, John did paint arteries on the wall of his Heart of

Darkness. *He did have those "things." John's description of his heart was metaphorical. Metaphors, like arteries, are part of the human system and serve as routes for the connections between mind and body. They allow us to explore the abstract and investigate its contradictions in a way that makes sense at the time.* John's Heart of Darkness *was also symbolic; it represented a temporal, internal state that he was able to clearly articulate and communicate to others. Although it is unknown how John is doing now, we can have faith in his resilience and hope that he sees what was claimed to be missing has been there all along.*

Coda and Crescendo: How Neuroscience Created Neurologic Music Therapy to Help Heal the Injured Brain

MICHAEL H. THAUT, PhD

Professor, Faculty of Music, Faculty of Medicine,
Institute of Medical Sciences and Rehabilitation Science Institute

Director, Music and Health Science Research Collaborative
and Graduate Programs, Collaborator Scientist, CAMH Neuroimaging

Affiliate Scientist, St. Michael's Hospital

Canada Research Chair Tier I in Music, Neuroscience, and Health,
University of Toronto

RETHINKING THE ROLE OF MUSIC IN REHABILITATION

The role of music in therapy and its shift to music as therapy has gone through some dramatic shifts in the past twenty years, driven by new insights from research into music and brain function. Initially these shifts were not strongly reflected in public or even professional awareness, but there has recently been a large effort to bring new visibility for music as the language of brain rehabilitation into the public health arena. Starting in the early 2000s, the accumulating research led to the development of Neurologic Music Therapy (NMT), a standardized, evidence-based, and medically recognized treatment system. NMT techniques are being added more and more as standard treatments in rehabilitative care, and NMT certified therapists from all rehabilitation professions practice in sixty-five-plus countries. Three of the five top-ranked neurorehabilitation hospitals in the United States now have NMT teams.

Biomedical researchers have found that music is a highly structured auditory language involving complex perception, cognition, and motor control in the brain and thus can effectively be used to retrain and reeducate the injured brain. For example, all NMT techniques are based on processes involved in music perception (example: rhythm perception in gait training), music cognition (example: stimulating autobiographical memories in dementia), and music creation (example: practicing functional arm motions by using musical instruments such as percussion or keyboard). The first data showing these results were met with some skepticism, but the consistent accumulation of scientific and clinical research evidence from many different research directions and groups has replaced doubt with scientific assurance. Therapists and physicians use music now in rehabilitation in ways that not only are backed up by clinical research but also are supported by an understanding of some of the mechanisms of music and brain function.

A general estimate suggests an average of seventeen years as typical for new research findings to translate into a treatment ready for use in patients. Considering this timeline, the developments in music neuroscience research and the consequent establishment of NMT have been very fast. For over two thousand years, music was considered as much or more a science than an expressive art form. For example, the discovery of the Pythagorean school around 500 BC that sounding bodies vibrate in multiple frequencies (known in music as "overtones") led to the view that the frequency ratios of these overtones were a model of the physics of planetary motion traveling in vibrating ratios as celestial bodies across the sky. Around 500 AD, the Roman philosopher Boethius wrote a treatise that dominated music theory for the next thousand years, subdividing the study of music into three levels: *musica mundana*, as model for the physics of the universe; followed by *musica humana*, unifying body and soul; and finally *musica instrumentalis*, the actual performance of music. Starting with Plato's treatises of around 400 BC and formally practiced throughout the Middle Ages, music was assigned to the "quadrivium," the pairing of scientific subjects for advanced studies and learning together with arithmetic (numbers in the abstract), geometry (numbers in space), music (numbers in time), and astronomy (numbers in time and space). When the German astronomer and mathematician Johannes Kepler discovered that the elliptical ratios of planetary motion could be expressed as harmonic proportions in music (e.g., earth motion varies by a ratio of a semitone, 16:15), he wrote a book published in 1619 titled *Harmonice Mundi* (The Harmony of the World). The German polymath Leibniz (1646–1716) called engaging the mind into music "subconscious arithmetic." Many Baroque composers such as Johann Sebastian Bach and Philipp Telemann were members of musical science societies. And even the beginnings of modern music psychology in the late nineteenth century were initiated by physicists and experimental psychologists. Fascinatingly we are now observing the return of music as a science in the neurosciences and health. Evidence-based models of music as therapy have moved from soft science—or no science— to hard science.

WHERE IT STARTED

While the notion that music has healing powers over mind and body has ancient origins, its formal use as therapy emerged in the middle of the twentieth century. At that time music therapists thought of their work as rooted in social science: art had value as therapy because it performed a variety of social and emotional roles in a society's culture. Music was understood, as it had been down the ages, to foster emotional expression and support; to help build personal relationships; to create and facilitate positive group behaviors; to represent symbolically beliefs and ideas; and to support other forms of learning. In the clinic, patients listened to music or played it together with the therapists or other patients to build relationships, promote well-being, express feelings, and interact socially.

However, these concepts of early music therapy were viewed by the health-care industry, including insurers, as mostly accessories to core therapies. Hard scientific evidence was difficult to collect, because there was a lack of underlying scientific theory regarding how mechanisms in music were working to create behavioral clinical change or changes in the brain.

From a personal perspective, when I first became involved in basic and clinical brain research in music, my views were strongly influenced by my previous training and career as a professional musician. It requires an enormous amount of cognitive and motoric effort to learn to "speak" and understand music as a complex auditory language. I knew that musical training can drive high achievements in cognitive learning, e.g., memorizing music, as well as motor learning that involves executing with great precision in rapid succession large sequences of very complex movements. When exposed to the idea of therapeutic uses of music, my approach was to ask, Could elements in music that had helped me train for high levels of performance standards also be used effectively to retrain lost functions due to disorders or injuries? So my research became shaped by a search for mechanisms in music learning and performing itself that could become therapeutic or rehabilitative. And one of the first elements that seemed most critical in my experience as a musician was rhythm, as the element that creates temporal structure in music and binds all vertical and horizontal music events—i.e., melodies and harmonies—into time-ordered and rule-based comprehensible patterns. And this is where my first investigations started, to study the role of auditory/musical rhythm in retraining motor function in neurologic movement disorders.

NEUROSCIENCE STEPS UP

When new as well as older but more fully developed brain imaging came along roughly thirty years ago (functional magnetic resonance imaging, positron emission tomography, electroencephalography, and magnetoencephalography), it enabled explorations into rehabilitative uses of music that could be performed immediately in the fields of neuroscience.

From the beginning of imaging research, music was part of the investigation. Scientists used it as a model to study how the brain processes verbal versus nonverbal communication; how it processes complex time information; and how a musician's brain develops the ability for the complex integration of high-level perceptual and motor skills necessary to perform a musical piece.

Three findings now stand out as particularly important for using music in rehabilitation. First, the brain areas that music activates are not unique to music; the networks that process music also process other functions. Second, music enhances horizontal and vertical connectivity between many different regions and layers of the brain, from lower subcortical to higher cortical levels. Third, music learning changes the brain by inducing plasticity in its networks while connecting different brain areas.

The brain areas involved in music processing are also active in processing nonmusical functions in language, auditory perception, attention, memory, executive control, and motor control. Music efficiently activates these shared systems and creates complex patterns of interaction among these systems. An example of shared function is an area near the front of the brain that processes a problem in the syntax of a sentence as well as in a musical piece, such as a wrong note in a melody. This region is called Broca's area, after the nineteenth-century French neurologist who first described it. Broca's area is also important in processing the sequencing of physical movement and in tracking musical rhythms, and it is critical for converting thought into spoken words. Scientists speculate, therefore, that Broca's area supports the appropriate timing, sequencing, and rule knowledge that are common and essential to music, speech, and movement.

Key examples of the second finding, enhanced connectivity, have shown that intense music training builds and strengthens a rich network of nerve fiber pathways across multiple brain regions, such as between auditory, motor, and prefrontal regions, involved in executive functions, as well as parietal areas, involved in patterns perception. These cortical networks also have rich vertical connections into subcortical limbic regions for memory and emotional functions, the brain stem for processing auditory input, and the cerebellum, which is considered the brain system that shapes and optimizes all brain functions.

Plasticity induced by music learning has been clearly revealed in research showing that through such learning, auditory and motor areas in the brain not only interact more efficiently but also become reshaped and rewired by growing larger. After novice players have just a few weeks of piano training, the areas in their brain serving hand control enlarge and become more connected. Music—it quickly became clear—can drive plasticity in the human brain, shaping it through training and learning.

Interestingly, brain plasticity and connectivity have become very important concepts in brain rehabilitation. It is commonly accepted now that the brain changes in structure and function as a result of learning, training, and environmental influences. Exposure and experience will create new and more efficient connections between neurons in the brain in a sort of rewiring process.

This discovery fundamentally changed how clinical research and therapists developed new interventions. Passive stimulation and facilitation were no longer considered effective; active learning and training promised to be the best strategy to help rewire the injured brain and stimulate the recovery of as much ability as possible. Engaging in music-based interventions fit well into this new active learning and training paradigm.

By combining these developments in the brain's processing of music, the clinical neuroscience of music could emerge with theoretical foundations rooted in science. Research finally could build an overarching, testable hypothesis relevant for music in rehabilitation: music can drive retraining and reeducation of cognitive, motor, and speech and language functions via shared brain systems, altered connectivity, and enhanced plasticity. Once considered ancillary, music could now be investigated as a core language of brain rehabilitation. And there may be an evolutionary basis for that. Overwhelming archaeological evidence exists that rather sophisticated artworks and musical instruments (e.g., flutes with equidistanced boreholes) are tens of thousands of years old, supporting an argument that music is a hardwired biological language of the human brain.

MOVEMENT GOES FIRST

To explore this hypothesis in the early 1990s we were the first group that began to extract and study shared mechanisms between music and nonmusical functions in motor control. One of the most important shared mechanisms is rhythm and timing.

Timing is key to proficient motor learning and skilled motor activities; without it, a person cannot execute movement appropriately and skillfully. Rhythmic timing adds an anticipation component to movement timing. Rhythm and timing are also important elements in music. Rhythm, the necessary harness for all elements of musical sound architecture, is also important in learning the appropriate motor control to play music.

We hypothesized that by using musical rhythms as timing signals we might improve a person's motor control during nonmusical movement. To test this idea we used rhythmic auditory cues to give people an external "sensory timer" with which they could try to synchronize their walking. We chose walking (or, technically, gait) because it consists of naturally occurring rhythmic step patterns that are driven physiologically by central pattern generators in the brain stem and spinal cord. Next, we looked for a gait disorder where consistently asymmetric movements would occur. We decided on hemiparetic gait in stroke, where the step duration of the weak leg is consistently shorter than that of the strong side. We now could investigate whether an evenly rhythmic beat stimulus—by itself or embedded in rhythmically accentuated music—could modulate the asymmetric timing of stepping movements closer to symmetric timing. The underlying physiological question was whether information processed via the sensory system (the rhythmic auditory signal) could alter the motor system (hemiparetic gait). The results, which by now have been frequently replicated, were instantaneous and stunning. By synchronizing—or entraining—their stepping movement to the rhythmic cues, patients were able to walk faster and with better control over the affected side of their body. Some of the more complex measures of movement control, such as neuromuscular activation, limb coordination, knee and ankle angle extensions, and trajectories of the joints and centers of body mass, also became significantly more consistent, smoother, and flexible. A first rhythm music-based technique, which we called Rhythmic Auditory Stimulation (RAS), had emerged.

We followed up studying RAS with investigating another very prevalent movement disorder, Parkinson's disease (PD). PD is characterized by a very different pathology than gait in stroke, in that PD is not hemiparetic. PD patients are slow, shuffling, unstable, sometimes freezing, which often leads to falls. If we saw benefits of RAS in this very different disorder we could possibly postulate some universal effect of auditory rhythm and music on the brain. In several PD studies over many years we found that music and rhythm could quicken patients' movements; they could serve as an auditory trigger to keep the movements ongoing, to prevent freezing; and a longitudinal study found significant reductions in incidences of falling. These improvements held up over long-term training and also proved to be superior in comparison with other standard physiotherapy interventions. RAS is now state of the art in motor therapy for stroke and PD.

One of the most moving encounters in my research life came from a person who had participated in our first landmark RAS-PD study. He reported that the study had opened his eyes to the power of music to help him move again, and that he used a Walkman daily for walking tours he hadn't done in years. A few days later he called us again, telling us that when trying to turn around and walk home again at one of his excursions, the Walkman's batteries died. After the initial panic, he decided to sing his walking songs and was able to safely sing himself home without becoming immobile. This gentleman had by intuition spontaneously discovered the power of musical imagery, which interestingly is now a much-studied topic in music cognition.

We then applied the same concepts from gait to arm control and whole-body coordination with similar success. Timing of functional arm and hand movements and coordinated movements involving the whole body (e.g., standing up, sitting down) does not always follow simple symmetric beat patterns. For example, a movement of reaching, grasping, lifting, and releasing an object consists of several segments, each of which may have different durations. Therefore, rhythm-music-based cuing requires more complex rhythmic patterns. Additionally it became clear that other musical elements were successful cues for movement—for example, pitch height cuing high and low movement directions, or loudness translating into different levels of force when moving. Unlike RAS, this type of cuing required translations of all temporal, spatial, and force aspects of movement into a more complex sound architecture, creating sort of a "kinematic composition," consisting of rhythm, pitches, chords, different loudness, etc. This technique was labeled Auditory Patterned Sensory Enhancement (APSE).

We finally extended musical cuing of movement into more direct applications of music creation, where in parallel to the concept of playing musical instruments we mapped functional movements—for example, arm reaching or finger/hand movements—onto musical percussion and keyboard instruments. The produced sounds provided direct auditory feedback when moving correctly and in time with rhythmic cues. This technique—Therapeutic Instrumental Music Playing (TIMP)—has been very successful with many movement disorders. By creating augmented feedback and making movement audible, TIMP improves spatial and temporal accuracy in rehabilitative motor training. This process is technically called "sonification"—to sonify movement—and our research now looks increasingly into sonification of the entire movement and not just the point where the body strikes an instrument. Sensors on key body parts (e.g., joints) can generate sound when the movement is performed more accurately. Motor learning and movement accuracy become audible in music-based feedback—a very helpful strategy in many neurologic disorders where the inner sense of controlling movement (proprioception) or visual guidance is often distorted and not fast and precise enough.

Music as a powerful language in brain rehabilitation became established and medically recognized. But could this model be extended from sensori-motor rehabilitation into other domains of brain rehabilitation, such as speech/language and cognitive functions?

REACHING FOR SPEECH AND LANGUAGE

When we broadened our research into the speech/language domain, we discovered that the role of music in speech/language training already had amassed a considerable amount of research and documentation about shared functions, parallel brain processes, and behavioral overlaps.

Both speech and music are complex rule-based auditory communication systems. Both share acoustical parameters (e.g., pitch, rhythm, loudness, timbre) as well as anatomical networks for sound production. Brain research had shown shared and distinct features for speech/language and music perception and production, speech systems being more focal and lateralized than music. Furthermore, one performance domain in music, singing, is entirely voice based.

What was missing in this research—with some notable exceptions—was translational concepts of clinical applications. One most prominent notable exception was, of course, Melodic Intonation Therapy (MIT). MIT was developed by speech-language pathologists in the early 1970s, harnessing the centuries-old observation that certain types of post-stroke aphasics could sing but not speak words into therapeutic protocols. MIT has been successful, and brain imaging research has indeed shown that singing will access an alternative language system in the uninjured right hemisphere, with potential for later retransfer after extended therapy. MIT remains somewhat underused because it requires some musical skills from the therapist. This is where NMT-based therapists have been able to be helpful by stepping in and often collaborating with speech-language professionals.

Therefore, when asked by the medical profession and speech-language professionals to help translate music into this rehabilitation domain, we saw as our main task to help formulate clinical applications in some systematic fashion following the translational neuroscience model of music as therapy described earlier.

We proposed eight NMT-based techniques that address dysfunctions that fall into roughly four groups: central neurologic pathologies, pathologies of production, developmental language disorders, and alternative communication systems. Seven of the techniques involve either singing (or variations of it, like *Sprechgesang* or rhythmic chanting) or playing wind instruments. The eighth technique uses playing easily accessible musical instruments like percussion or keyboard with persons who have not acquired verbal speech to learn communication gestures through music, as an alternative sound-based language (e.g., dialoguing). In expressive aphasia, singing words (MIT) can also access uninjured brain networks to neurologically encode and produce words and sentences that have functional value for the patient. Over-learned lyrics in long-known songs can trigger reflexive speech as the first access to speech networks in severe cases of aphasia, a technique known as Musical Speech Stimulation. Persons with disorders of planning and sequencing speech (apraxia) benefit from speech training using melodic and rhythmic cues to improve planning and sequencing.

When studying music for production disorders we discovered how many tools music holds to improve the typical production challenges: rhythmic cuing and singing can help fluency; oral motor and respiratory exercises using music-based vocal exercises and simple wind instruments (e.g., harmonicas, blow melodicas) can shape articulation and pulmonary strength; and music-based vocal exercises can effectively improve pitch and volume range, modulate appropriate loudness, and reduce hoarseness and abnormal timbres. Music simply has an enormous and varied toolbox to address speech-language disorders that can be focused on specific dysfunctions or applied more globally in a larger context of practicing speech-language production in a highly integrated holistic fashion, e.g., in choirs and song circles.

A few years ago a former professional opera singer was recommended to our research center because he had had a stroke five years earlier and hadn't been able to speak due to expressive aphasia. He started working with one of our NMT faculty who was also trained in MIT. She played a well-known folk song to him and asked him to join. He spontaneously started singing loudly and clearly, and his sister, who hadn't heard his voice in years, started crying for joy. This was the beginning of his MIT-based therapy, which lasted for several years and resulted in his becoming conversational and performing in small settings and even at a music neuroscience lecture in front of eight hundred people. It brought the house down, no dry eye left. But all this didn't happen until music entered his rehabilitation.

COGNITION ENTERS

Cognitive rehabilitation was the last domain for music-based interventions to be established. Similar to sensorimotor rehabilitation, the role of music as intervention stimulus needed to be conceptualized first within a scientific paradigm. Typical areas for cognitive rehabilitation are memory, attention, and executive and psychosocial function. So, following our model of music as therapy on a neuroscience basis, we first had to ask the question of how music perception and cognition engage memory, attention, executive, and psychosocial systems behaviorally and physiologically. The follow-up question would center on defining and testing applications of those processes to clinical outcomes.

A brief review of seven studies we conducted to help unpack the role of music in cognitive rehabilitation may help illustrate this search.

As musicians we are very familiar with the ability to learn how to perform by memory long pieces of music that entail thousands of discrete arm, hand, and finger movements, or lyrics sung to music that would exceed usual memory performance outside of music. This ability is usually associated (e.g., in music psychology research) with the intrinsic structure of musical gestalts consisting of motivic patterns, short and long phrases, extended thematic patterns, repetitions and variations, etc. Based on this knowledge, we wondered if music's architecture could also serve as a scaffold to train a person's memory for nonmusical information—the ABC Song Model. We tested this using standardized verbal learning tests consisting of word lists with patients with multiple sclerosis. We found highly significant advantages for sung versus the typical spoken presentations. Brain wave analysis via EEG showed almost immediate synchronizations between different brain regions that were not present during the spoken condition.

We recently extended this "memory for music" research to long-term musical memories in patients with Alzheimer's disease (AD) and Minimal Cognitive Dysfunction (MCD) using functional brain imaging (fMRI).

We wanted to first learn what brain mechanisms in music helped preserve musical and associated autobiographical memories often far longer than many other memory functions in these patients. When patients were listening to familiar music (as opposed to only briefly exposed music), a widely distributed network of cortical and subcortical brain regions was activated, characteristic of what can be described as a "deeply encoded" memory network, which also included regions that are not affected by the disease. In a follow-up study we had these persons listen daily to their long-known favorite music, focused for one hour. After three weeks, scores on the memory subsection on a highly established cognitive assessment tool showed small but significant increases accompanied by increases in brain network connectivity and white matter density. Two hopeful conclusions for music-based interventions may be drawn from these studies: first, long-known favorite music can create a neural memory network that has some embedded sparing or preservation mechanisms; second, although listening to this very personalized music cannot reverse the disease, it can provide cognitive boosts to persons with dementia that are reflected in brain plasticity. Remarkably, although the studies required several brain-scanning sessions in tight MRI tubes that can make even healthy persons quite uncomfortable, we didn't have a single dropout in our group of persons with AD and MCD. They expressed great commitment because they felt the benefits of the studies.

In a recent pilot study of persons with acquired brain injury, we found that music-based attention exercises, where individuals were asked to follow and respond to musical cues requiring different attention efforts, such as for sustained, selective, or divided attention, were in some assessments better and others equal when compared to standard neuropsychological tests. We know from music cognition research how musical elements can direct a listener's attention to different musical events. So our translational model of music as therapy—structuring musical events to activate functional attention systems—may also benefit persons with auditory attention deficits. Similarly, recent studies, one of ours among them, have shown that when persons suffering hemispatial neglect (i.e., not processing visual information in the left visual field) engage in musical tone bar exercises, where they have to complete melodies extending into the neglect visual field, they can experience significant reductions in their neglect syndrome and improved activations in the injured brain regions causing neglect.

Finally, we tested another translational model regarding music effects on executive functions. We engaged persons with acquired brain injury into guided elementary music composition exercises on pitched and nonpitched percussion instruments. In the study, clients were asked to create and arrange simple musical melodies or rhythms that might be inspired by nature scenes, paintings, sculptures, or moods. In this creative process, clients were asked by the NMT therapist to practice decision making, problem-solving, planning ahead, initiating, and other executive skills to build a spontaneous composition. Post-test assessments showed significant improvements when compared to a nonmusical treatment condition.

A few years ago our research group was asked to scientifically accompany a community-based music study with the local symphony orchestra. Twenty-three couples with a spouse with Alzheimer's disease were invited to attend a full concert season (concerts once a month for seven months), and we would do comprehensive cognitive tests at the beginning and end of the season, as well as shorter tests after each concert and call-in interviews the following morning. To our astonishment, this music exposure of very moderate intensity showed highly significant cognitive benefits on several neuropsychological test batteries. However, the qualitative part of the study may have been even more impressive. Couples—especially the healthy member—reported responses from their spouses that they hadn't seen, sometimes in many years: emotional responses while sharing the music, smiling and holding hands, remembering the concert the next morning, enthusiasm about attending the next concert, staying alert and awake throughout the event, talking about shared memories triggered by the music, even planning a date night.

This last study can serve as a coda connecting the science of music in rehabilitation and the quality of life of persons in very rewarding, yet scientifically grounded, ways. The brain mechanisms we discovered in our research benefited persons in need through a community-based music program designed for them. Biomedical research in music has come a long way to open up new and effective doors for music to help reeducate the injured brain. The research evidence for music's clinical effectiveness and the brain mechanisms underlying these effects is no longer speculative. What no longer needs to be done is prove that music as therapy and language of rehabilitation works, in principle and in practice. NMT is medically recognized. RAS is included in official medical stroke care guidelines in the U.S. (Departments of Veterans Affairs and Defense) and Canada (Heart & Stroke Foundation). The NMT Academy is an institutional member in the World Federation for Neurorehabilitation. It is a fact: music shows evidence for helping heal the brain.

Musical Enjoyment and the Reward Circuits of the Brain

ROBERT ZATORRE, PhD

Cognitive Neuroscientist, Montreal Neurological Institute,
McGill University

How is it that we have this miraculous thing called music? What allows us humans to make it, to understand it, and—most remarkably of all—to enjoy it? Musicians and music scholars might have their own quite valid answers to these questions. But in recent decades cognitive neuroscience has provided great insights into the brain mechanisms that allow music to exist in our species. This understanding of *how* music is enabled by our nervous system can help explain the fundamental question about *why* it gives us pleasure, and maybe even why we have it.

In particular there has been progress over the past couple of decades in unraveling the neural mechanisms of how music—in essence an abstract pattern of sounds, often devoid of any propositional meaning—can produce intense pleasure. In turn this understanding builds upon prior knowledge about the biology of rewarding experiences, together with knowledge derived from music perception and cognition. We are now at a juncture where this knowledge can be brought together to synthesize our current understanding and to propose a unifying idea about how and why music gives us pleasure.

The central thesis of this chapter is that the enjoyment of music arises from the functional organization of the human brain via the interaction of two broad neural systems: the auditory perceptual system on the one hand,

and the reward system on the other. The perceptual system analyzes patterns in general and, in the case of music, is able to generate predictions about how sounds will unfold in time. This system is relatively recent in terms of evolution, as it involves some of the most advanced parts of the human brain, especially the frontal cortex, that set it apart from the brains of other primates. On the other hand, the reward system is phylogenetically ancient, and has a very different function: it evaluates the significance or importance of patterns and generates positive or negative signals according to how they play out. That is, it signals whether the event experienced (the face of another person, the taste of a piece of food, the sound of a series of tones) is better or worse than what had been expected, in terms of its capacity to enhance fitness and well-being. These ideas are developed in much greater depth in my recent book, but here I will present a global overview of these systems and then discuss how they work together to generate pleasure, as well as more complex emotional responses.

PREDICTION AND ANTICIPATION

Before we delve into the description of the neural systems, I would like to introduce the concept of prediction, which is crucial to understanding how perception works, but also to understanding the corresponding brain processes. It used to be thought that perception was a passive process: a sound comes into the ear, it is sent up via the nerves to certain brain structures, and some kind of interpretation happens. But that idea has been replaced by the concept of predictive coding. In a nutshell this term refers to the idea that the brain makes active inferences—a best guess, or prediction—in order to interpret events in the environment.

Thus, the brain tries to anticipate what is about to happen, rather than merely reacting to what has already happened, which allows comparison of incoming signals with the expectations. If the input is as expected, all is well; but if the input differs from the expectancy—whether better or worse— then that means something important may have happened that requires attention and evaluation. These situations generate a so-called prediction error signal, because what happens is not what was anticipated. It seems obvious that such a function would be beneficial for basic survival, because it is critical to prepare an appropriate response to any given event, and that can be done much more effectively if the event can be predicted in advance. But how can we ever make predictions about what will happen, since mental crystal balls don't exist? The answer is that our brain can make an educated guess about what is going to happen next, based both on what just happened recently, and also based on accumulated knowledge, or learning via experience in the environment. If you notice dark clouds on the horizon, and a cool wind, plus an earthy smell, you can predict, based on having gotten soaked in the past, that rain is coming, and that you might want to take shelter. Similarly, if based on your experience you can tell when the ripest apples will be available in an orchard because of their color and the season of the year, you will get a delicious treat.

These learned expectancies, part of our long-term memory store, play a huge role in music, as elaborated by the musicologist David Huron in his book, *Sweet Anticipation*. In music, as is also the case for language, there is a rich statistical relationship between patterns of sounds that we internalize. Every musical system, just like every language, has a set of rules, or syntax, about how patterns of sounds are organized. These rules are usually a matter of probability: if you hear the sentence "My cat got caught in a . . ." it's a good guess that the next word could be "tree," although less likely options could occur. Maybe it got caught in a laundry chute, or a lobster trap, etc., but you would not expect the next word to be, say, "wrist." Similarly, if you hear a pop song with the major chords C, F, G, and G7, it is most likely that the next chord will be another C, although, again, less likely options can and do happen (an A minor, for instance, known as a deceptive cadence; or, less likely, a D6, etc.); but based on the preceding chords, you would hardly expect to hear a tone cluster consisting of, let's say C#, D, F#, and G (and if you did, you might assume that the cat got off the tree and onto the piano keyboard).

It turns out that the human auditory brain is exquisitely sensitive to these kinds of syntactic regularities, and is able to learn statistical relationships quickly and efficiently when exposed to relevant patterns. This learning starts in infancy and continues to be reinforced throughout our lives as we hear more and more patterns that contain statistical regularities. We are not necessarily conscious of the rules; they tend to be implicit. But once the probabilities are learned, they form part of what psychologists call internal models, that is to say, a kind of mental road map of sound expectancies.

Different models are associated with different learning experiences; so the internal model of a Baroque specialist is different from that of a jazz musician, and different still from an expert sitar player. It is thanks to these models that our brains can generate predictions based on known relationships and their likelihood of appearance. The model is not entirely static, because every time an error signal occurs, it is an opportunity to update the internal model (i.e., to learn), to try to make better predictions next time. This capacity to represent both the incoming sounds from the outside world, and the expectancy of what those sounds are, is built into the very structure of the auditory system, and so we turn to that next.

AUDITORY SYSTEM BASIC STRUCTURE

The auditory perceptual/cognitive system consists of several different components. Early components of the system, including brain stem nuclei and the more primary parts of the auditory cortex, encode basic acoustical features, such as sound onsets and frequency. But there is a gradient from more veridical representations (closer to the acoustical properties) at earlier levels to more abstract representations (patterns, relationships between sounds, categories—closer to our conscious understanding of sounds) at higher levels. So the brain performs a transformation on incoming sounds, first comput ing the physical elements present in the signal, and then through successive stages, figuring out how those elements combine into meaningful patterns.

This hierarchical organization means that different kinds of predictions can be made at different levels of analysis. The way this works is via a two-way communication system between two anatomically distinct sets of connections: the ascending, or "bottom-up," input pathways, and the descending, or "top-down," control pathways. The former are responsible for sending information coming into the ear rapidly and accurately to higher centers, while the latter are responsible for sending down the predictions stored and generated at higher levels. The descending signals are thus often referred to as prediction signals, while the ascending ones are often thought of as prediction error signals, because they are stronger when an error occurs— that is, when the input does not match what was expected.

These error signals have been extensively studied in human neurophysiology via the mismatch response, which can be easily measured with electroencephalography (EEG). The mismatch response in its simplest form occurs when a sequence of repetitive sounds is interrupted by a new sound (for example, after several repeated Cs, a C# unpredictably appears). Under those conditions, a change in the electrical potential measured from auditory areas is elicited because the C#, in this case, was not expected. However, this response is also sensitive to more complex situations, in which the stimulus features themselves don't change, but only their order does, such as tone pairs that are ascending/descending. In this case the brain can anticipate that the pairs of tones will be ascending, irrespective of their frequency, but generates a "surprise" signal when the tones are descending. So it's no longer just the individual pitches that count, but rather the interval formed between them. Even more complex patterns can also elicit a mismatch response, including musically relevant ones like the contour of a melody. The mismatch response depends entirely on the preceding context, so that the identical sound will either elicit a response or not depending on how well it fits the context.

The reason these effects are important is because they prove the existence of predictive mechanisms. If the brain were responding only to each sound as it comes in, independently of whatever came before, and therefore without any expectation of what might come next, it would not show sensitivity to these violations of expectations. The fact that the mismatch responses are sensitive in a hierarchical manner to changes in both simple aspects (like pitch) as well as more complex ones (like intervals or melodic structure) also means that they are highly relevant for understanding how music is processed.

THE AUDITORY VENTRAL AND DORSAL CORTICAL PATHWAYS

Once sounds reach the auditory cortex, they undergo further processing along two major pathways. The first one, referred to as the ventral stream, leads from the primary auditory cortex along the temporal lobe toward the inferior part of the frontal lobe; the second one, called the dorsal stream, leads from the primary auditory cortex back and upward toward the parietal lobe, and from there to motor structures in the superior part of the frontal lobe.

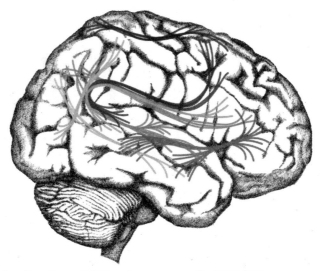

Diagram adapted from Zatorre, 2023. Brain drawing courtesy of Emily B. J. Coffey; overlay courtesy of Ahmed Farhan. Designation of fiber tracts after Petrides, 2014.

The figure above provides a schematic of the fibers that connect auditory cortical areas with the rest of the brain, showing both the ventral and dorsal streams. These two pathways perform many complex functions that make our rich auditory mental world possible. In this chapter I will focus only on a few salient aspects of how these systems are relevant for music.

The ventral pathway is especially important for operations that enable us to understand relationships between sounds and how these form patterns, leading to the internal representations discussed earlier. To accomplish this goal, one critical function of the ventral stream is its capacity to maintain sounds in memory over time. Since sounds disappear from the environment instantly, we need a mechanism to hold them in mind. The interactions between auditory areas and the inferior frontal cortex seem to be especially critical in this regard, as shown by neuroimaging studies. This mechanism allows sound patterns to be knitted together and predictions to be made about what sound will come next based on the pattern just heard; the mismatch response mentioned above is an index of this operation and originates in auditory and inferior frontal regions that are part of the ventral stream.

The importance of the ventral stream for musical processing is demonstrated dramatically by the condition of congenital amusia (sometimes referred to as tone deafness), in which people with otherwise normal auditory perception have great difficulty with most musical tasks, especially those requiring understanding of pitch-based patterns. Careful analysis of their brain responses has shown that people with amusia have diminished communication between the right frontal and auditory areas, and that this disruption is especially related to an inability to maintain pitch information over short periods of time. Amusia is also associated with a reduced anatomical connection in the ventral stream. Congenital amusia seems to be largely associated with dysfunction in the right cerebral hemisphere, as is also true for musical processing deficits that manifest themselves after stroke. This relative hemispheric specialization arises at least in part from an enhanced resolution for fine frequency information in the right auditory cortex, which is especially relevant for music, as compared to speech processing.

Turning next to the auditory dorsal pathway, it, too, is responsible for many different processes that make music—and other complex auditory cognitive functions—possible. Cortical regions in the parietal lobe are the first stop for auditory information going through this pathway. The parietal cortex is a multisensory integration region, where inputs from different senses converge and are converted into motor-related codes for the next step in the pathway, the premotor cortex. It's easy to see that this process, then, is critical for the production of music, since to play an instrument or sing, it is necessary to activate the muscles in certain ways to produce certain sounds, and to monitor whether the sounds produced are what was intended or not.

Plenty of evidence from neuroimaging implicates these dorsal structures in music performance, including studies in which musicians are scanned with functional MRI while they are playing a real or simulated piano keyboard, trumpet, cello, or singing. But these and other studies go beyond merely indicating the recruitment of these dorsal regions; they point to an important temporal prediction component. In order for actions to be properly timed in a musical performance, it is necessary to anticipate the next movement. If the drummer in a rock band waits to hear the next chord from the guitar before moving to hit the cymbals, the sound will come too late and be off the intended beat. It must be planned in advance.

This temporal predictive component is also related to the fact that the dorsal stream is especially important for the tracking of rhythms and for processing of the musical beat. Several studies have shown that the premotor cortex, together with other motor structures, such as the basal ganglia, is active when beat structure is present, or is modulated by the strength of the beat. These sorts of findings have motivated several important theoretical models about the relationship between motion, beat perception, and their neural substrates. The most prevalent current explanation for these phenomena has to do with top-down signals coming from premotor and other dorsal cortices and influencing auditory cortices to provide predictive cues about when to expect sounds, and sending commands to motor systems to generate predictive actions to enable accurate rhythmic production. As we shall see below, these predictive signals also play a role in musical pleasure.

THE REWARD SYSTEM

All of the foregoing discussion dealt with the cortical pathways related to perception of music, and how these pathways enable prediction mechanisms. But that does not immediately explain why we experience pleasure, and emotion more generally, from music. To understand this essential phenomenon we turn to a different neural circuit, known as the reward system. The reward system mediates our subjective hedonic experience of pleasure; but its responses are not confined solely to pleasure, as it is also critically involved in other phenomena, especially learning, motivation, and action. One way to think of the reward system is that it provides information about the value of an event that is processed in the perceptual system. These reward computations happen after a perceptual analysis has been carried out. The reward system thus guides our behaviors based on how well our actions lead to positive outcomes that enhance survival, well-being, and fitness.

The reward structures are quite distinct from the cortical circuits described above. Along with the orbitofrontal cortex, which is considered a major part of the reward system and is involved in valuation of stimuli, several subcortical structures play a critical role in the reward system, especially nuclei in the midbrain and basal forebrain. The striatum, found within the gray-matter nuclei of the basal forebrain, is one of the more important structures that is related to reward processing. It may be subdivided into dorsal and ventral regions, which have different connectivity. The more ventral portion of the striatum receives inputs from the orbitofrontal cortex, and as one ascends toward the dorsal striatum, inputs shift to more dorsal parts of the brain, including the cingulate and dorsolateral frontal cortex.

This topographic distribution of inputs is directly relevant to the cortical systems described above, so that the more ventral striatum responds to musically related inputs coming from the ventral auditory stream, via the orbitofrontal region, whereas the dorsal striatum responds to musically related inputs coming from the dorsal auditory stream. This organization means that the two types of predictions generated by the two cortical streams, related to patterns and timings, map onto the ventral and dorsal subregions of the striatum, respectively. This concept fits well with music theory ideas about anticipating *what* events will occur versus *when* they will occur.

The reward system was initially thought to be strictly related to biological, or primary, rewards, as shown with countless animal studies in which food or water was used to elicit activity in the striatum. Such findings were extended to brain imaging research in humans, in which biologically important stimuli, such as food or sexual images, were shown to activate the striatum and other reward structures; in addition, money—a secondary reward, because it can be exchanged for primary rewards—was also shown to engage the same circuitry. Importantly, more abstract stimuli can also generate reward activity, most notably information that serves to reduce uncertainty. Even when there is no primary reward involved, the reward system responds to novelty, for example, in the context of a trivia game when the information has no particular relevance for daily life, but nonetheless satisfies one's curiosity.

Beyond the response to a rewarding stimulus itself, whether primary or more abstract, a wealth of evidence has also shown that responses from the striatum are also elicited by the cues that signal the presence of a reward (such as a light that goes on to inform an animal that food will be available). If the food reward occurs as expected, there is little or no response, because it was predicted; but if a larger or smaller reward occurs, reward neurons show higher or lower activity, respectively. This pattern is highly compatible with the reward prediction error concept, such that reward neurons compute the error, or difference, between expected and obtained rewards. A positive reward prediction error, when the reward is better than expected, yields the greatest response in the reward system, and this effect has been verified not only in animal studies but also in human neuroimaging.

THE REWARD SYSTEM AND MUSIC

Starting about two decades ago, our lab began to ask whether musical stimuli would engage the reward system. At the time there was no evidence that the reward system would mediate the pleasurable response to music, a truly abstract stimulus, and therefore quite different from the primary and secondary rewarding stimuli that had been used until then. So it was exciting to discover that these previously identified reward structures, especially the striatum, were indeed active when people listened to music that they found pleasurable. In those first studies we took advantage of the musical "chills" phenomenon, a sensation experienced by many people when they feel pleasure induced by music. Musical chills are useful because they can be measured objectively with psychophysiology (heart rate, respiration, skin conductance) and therefore serve as a verifiable index of peak pleasure. For these studies we asked listeners to select their own music that they found most pleasurable, which is important because music preference varies a lot from one person to another, depending on many factors (age, culture, musical training, and so forth). These findings that the reward system responds to pleasurable music regardless of the style or genre, as long as people report liking it, have now been replicated by many subsequent studies, as shown in a recent meta-analysis.

Although the results have proven very reliable, many questions remained, especially *why* certain patterns of sound without specific meaning would elicit these responses. One important hint that helps us answer this question comes from a study in our lab in which we divided brain activity according to the moment at which peak pleasure was experienced. We scanned people with functional MRI as they listened to favorite pieces of music, and we also asked them to indicate when they felt a chill by pressing a button. When we looked at the few seconds just before the chills occurred, we saw the largest response coming from the dorsal striatum, but when we examined the brain activity during and just after the chills, most of the activity was coming from the ventral striatum. This temporal and anatomical dissociation fits well with the ideas mentioned above, because the dorsal striatum is associated with the anticipation of the upcoming rewarding moment, in keeping with its role in temporal predictions and its connections to parts of the brain involved in higher-order cognitive processes, including planning, anticipation, and decision making. Conversely, the ventral striatum is more responsible for the hedonic emotion associated with the pleasing sound itself, rather than its anticipation, which is why it is most active at the peak pleasure moment.

Although this study was important in demonstrating the role of the subdivisions of the striatum, it did not attempt to test a central idea of our model: that interactions between the perceptual and reward systems are responsible for musical pleasure. To examine that question we carried out another brain imaging study, in which listeners were presented with new music they had not heard before, but that they might like based on music recommendation software. In this experiment we preselected people who indicated that they liked indie/electronic music genres, which then allowed us to confine our selections to songs that were new, but that were within the style that was likely to be pleasurable to these particular listeners. This approach also has the advantage that any pleasure response elicited cannot be related to memories or associations with the music, since it was all novel. The paradigm involved asking listeners to indicate how much money they would be willing to spend to purchase a recording of each musical excerpt after they heard it. The amount of money serves as a proxy for how much they valued that item. Analysis of the functional MRI results revealed, as expected, that the higher the monetary amount, the greater was the response in the ventral striatum. But even more interesting is that the functional coupling between this structure and the auditory cortex also increased as a function of increasing value. In other words, the more activity in the reward system, the more cross talk there was between auditory and reward systems, which is exactly in line with the concept that musical pleasure emerges from the interaction between these two systems.

This model generates certain specific predictions that we can test directly. If it's true that hedonic responses elicited by music depend on the interaction of these two systems, then people who don't experience pleasure from music should not show the interaction. To test this prediction, we began to study people with specific musical anhedonia.

MUSICAL ANHEDONIA AND MANIPULATION
OF MUSICAL PLEASURE

People with musical anhedonia are defined as those who have no perceptual difficulties with music or other sounds, and who do not have generalized anhedonia to other pleasure-inducing stimuli (food, sex, exercise, money, etc.), but who report experiencing very little or no pleasure from music, and who do not show the characteristic psychophysiological responses indicative of pleasure. When we studied their neural responses with functional MRI, we discovered that although their striatum responded normally to a gambling task (monetary reward), they had reduced activity to music. More importantly, the amount of functional coupling was strongly reduced in this population when they heard music compared to that of a control group. Further relevant evidence comes from analysis of the anatomical pathways that link the auditory system to the reward system, which pass through the orbitofrontal cortex as explained above. In persons with specific musical anhedonia these pathways are not as well organized compared to those of controls. This anatomical alteration explains why there is a lower functional interaction, which in turn is consistent with the hypothesis that such interactions underlie musical pleasure.

Musical anhedonia provides a powerful test case for our theory, but one could argue that it does not apply to people who have normal levels of musically induced pleasure. Furthermore, we are lacking direct, causal evidence that changing the way that the reward and auditory systems interact would actually change musical pleasure. To really test this idea rigorously, we carried out further experiments with healthy volunteers using a brain stimulation technique, transcranial magnetic stimulation, that allows us to modulate the dynamics of neural activity. When applied over the frontal cortex at certain frequencies, this stimulation modulates the activity of deep structures, including the striatum. We therefore applied this technique while listeners made judgments of music, using both excitatory and inhibitory stimulation protocols. We found that musical pleasure ratings, along with psychophysiological responses, either increased or decreased with the positive or negative stimulation, respectively. This finding is pretty remarkable, because it shows that we can influence subjective pleasure by actively changing the brain. To see where exactly the neural changes were happening, we repeated the experiment while volunteers were being scanned, and sure enough discovered that the brain stimulation changed the functional coupling between reward and music circuits, just as expected from our model.

A Model of Musical Pleasure

Having shown rather definitively that musical pleasure derives from the interplay between perception and reward circuits, we now turn to addressing the question of *why* music has this effect. All of the foregoing information in this chapter cues us to the idea that musical information is transmitted from auditory pathways, where patterns are processed and predictions about musical events are made, to reward circuits where value is assigned. In other words, a sensory prediction error is detected in the auditory system, and it is then propagated to the reward system, where a reward prediction error is computed. Recall that the strongest reward response comes when an event is better than anticipated, such as when the payout of a gambling game is higher than usual on a given trial. It's easy to see how winning ten dollars when you expected one dollar is better than winning ten dollars when you expected to win fifty dollars. But how does that concept translate into the domain of music? What is the equivalent of "better than expected" in music?

The answer, I submit, has to do with the informational value of a musical event. We saw above that information, even when not directly relevant to anything specific, has its own reward value, because it serves to reduce uncertainty and hence improve our internal model of the environment. In the case of music, each event as it unfolds can be thought of as providing information. Both what event happens and when it happens serve to inform us of the harmonic, melodic, or metrical structure of a piece of music; when music takes a particularly unexpected turn it often delights us, and often generates pleasurable chills. Musicologists have also noted that certain conventional patterns (trills, repeated notes, rhythmic motifs) are very often used in different musical systems to signal the end of one section and the start of another, thus providing information. So the idea is that the more information is conveyed, the better than expected the event will be perceived to be.

However, the relationship between the expectedness of a musical event and its reward value is not a simple linear function. Many investigators have proposed that there is a curvilinear (inverted-U shape) relationship between expectedness and reward. In the 1970s, Daniel Berlyne suggested that hedonic value would be maximal at intermediate levels of complexity, where the stimulus is optimally engaging—neither too simple, leading to boredom, nor too complex, leading to confusion. This idea has been confirmed in music under certain circumstances, and has recently been shown to be specifically linked to complexity as formally modeled using computational approaches for different kinds of musical materials. The inverted-U has now been shown for melody (everything from Celtic tunes to Bach to Chick Corea); harmony (taken from pop music hits between 1958 and 1991); and rhythm (drum breaks from funk/soul music). In all these cases, intermediate complexity leads to the highest ratings of pleasure. When examined in the context of brain imaging, these studies also demonstrated a link between the hedonic pleasure response and the engagement of reward structures in the brain. This result supports the concept that an appropriate balance between expectedness and surprise is at the heart of musically induced subjective pleasure, which in turn is mediated by the engagement of the reward system.

Research on how musical pleasure arises from the structure and function of our nervous system has important implications for our understanding of how music can be applied to many different circumstances. The engagement of the reward system is linked to positive mood states and general well-being. Music does not simply generate a mindless state of euphoria. Rather, its effects emerge from the interactions of perceptual, cognitive, social, and memory mechanisms with prediction and reward processes, as I have tried to show in the present brief survey of the neuroscience literature. These complex interactions between various mental functions allow us to move beyond the context of mere pleasure, and move toward the rich emotional world that music elicits in us.

MUSICAL REWARD AND APPLICATIONS

The knowledge gained from music neuroscience provides a more solid scientific basis to consider the many therapeutic applications of music that are currently the focus of intense study, as described in many of the other chapters in this book. Many behavioral surveys have previously shown that people from diverse countries spontaneously use music as a way to self-regulate their moods, including in older age groups. But we've achieved a better idea of how such effects might emerge. Music is under active study in different clinical settings as a means to improve mood, reduce anxiety, and enhance well-being, including in psychiatric disorders, depression, stroke, and dementia. Understanding the neural mechanisms behind these effects will lead to better development of targeted strategies, and evaluation of the neural changes associated with therapeutic interventions. Recent moves in this direction suggest that music listening training can change the connectivity between auditory and reward structures. There is also new research developing neurofeedback interventions to modify neural circuitry associated with mood disorders.

A dramatic demonstration of music's power is provided by the COVID-19 pandemic. Several studies examined how music was used as a coping mechanism during the worst of the confinement that was imposed during the early waves of the virus. One survey of over five thousand people from three continents documented that music was used extensively for social cohesion and emotion regulation. Another survey, from Brazil, found that music was especially beneficial for mood management among those who were most depressed during the pandemic. Yet another study comparing responses across countries reported that music was the most effective activity for enjoyment, venting negative emotions, and self-connection, and that cultural differences were relatively minor. Our group also studied people in lockdown in Italy, Spain, and the United States (three countries badly affected in the first wave), and found that music was the single most highly rated activity used for coping with the stress of COVID, followed by entertainment (movies/books), exercise, and food/cooking. Importantly, only music and food/cooking-related activities were specifically related to reductions in symptoms of depression associated with the pandemic lockdown: those people who listened to more music and/or cooked more had healthier psychological outcomes. We also found that the people who most benefited from music during the pandemic were the ones who indicated that they experience pleasure from various stimuli in general (i.e., greater reward sensitivity). This finding is important because it links the positive influence of music directly with the engagement of the reward system.

CONCLUSION

Music has been around probably for as long as humans have been around. It exerts such an influence on us that there must be a good reason why it exists and flourishes in essentially all human societies. The explanation I wish to offer of music's persistence in and importance to our lives hinges on an understanding of neurobiological mechanisms. It is notable that the reward system is phylogenetically ancient and preserved across many species, whereas the cortical systems responsible for pattern perception and prediction are relatively recently evolved and most highly developed in humans. So music is enabled by links between our most basic biology on the one hand, and our most highly developed cognition on the other. This explains perhaps why music has such a primal pull, yet also depends on learning, experience, and culture. We still have much to learn about the neural basis of music and how it may be applied for helping, healing, and happiness. But it is exciting that we are well on our way in this scientific journey that will continue to yield new insights and knowledge.

The Benefits of Musical Engagement Across the Life Span: Education, Health, and Well-Being

ASSAL HABIBI, PhD
Affiliation: University of Southern California

HANNA DAMASIO, MD

ANTONIO DAMASIO, MD, PhD
USC Brain and Creativity Institute

BEATRIZ ILARI, PhD
USC Thornton School of Music

INTRODUCTION

Musical engagement takes many forms but is invariably associated with some benefits. It may be as simple as a decorated war veteran who describes how playing the ukulele and singing songs from his native Oah'u helped him cope with PTSD. Or it may be the group of teenagers who exchange music online during the lockdowns imposed by the COVID-19 pandemic, and as they do this, they also talk about their feelings and emotions. Or U.S. Rep. Gabby Giffords, who suffered a traumatic brain injury and works on her speech and singing skills with a music therapist. In all these examples, no matter how simple, musical engagement results in some increase in well-being and often in some remediation of a health problem. We have been exploring the possibility that more formal ways of musical engagement in an educational setting result in benefits to brain function that underlies cognitive development.

In this chapter, based on our collective efforts over the past twenty years, we offer our perspective on the relationship of musical engagement and health and well-being over the life span. After providing a brief review of the current state of the literature, we focus on our past and ongoing research programs on musical engagement and well-being, highlighting the aims, design, and findings from each study along with the implications of our findings for the health and well-being of children, adults, and older adults. We conclude the chapter with reflections on the current limitations and future directions of music research and its impact on public health and education policies.

CURRENT RESEARCH TRENDS ON MUSIC, HEALTH, AND WELL-BEING

It is reasonable to think that music might be effective in the promotion of health and well-being because it is ubiquitous, emotional, engaging, distracting, physical, social, communicative, and semantically ambiguous. Music also affects core aspects of our lives, including behavior and identity construction.

The idea that music may promote health and well-being is not new. In ancient Greek culture, for example, music was perceived as central to the health and well-being of individuals and communities. This is well documented in both iconographical and literary sources. During the Middle Ages and Renaissance, writings of Aristotle and Galen were used to present music as capable of restoring the balance between the soul and its faculties due to its emotional reach. The effects of music on different medical pathologies were explored with emphases on music therapy and approaches such as vitalism. Music was seen as having a powerful influence on a vital fluid that could help manage diseases.

In recent decades we have seen a resurgence of interest in the links between music, mind, and well-being. Penelope Gouk and her colleagues attribute this renewed interest largely to the advances in brain science, in particular the imaging technologies that have allowed us to advance our understanding of how the human brain processes music, thus inspiring scholarship in a wide range of areas from psychology and medicine to education and policy. A growing body of knowledge demonstrates the association of music with well-being, as related to health, psychology, and education. For example, music-based interventions have been shown to reduce stress levels, to reduce aggressiveness in children, and to build self-confidence, well-being, and engagement in youth from underserved communities. While a meticulous review of the effects of music on health and well-being is beyond the scope of this chapter, it is important to mention some findings that have emerged recently, as a response to the challenges imposed by the COVID-19 pandemic.

Since 2020 several studies have been published concerning the role of music on mental health and well-being during the lockdowns imposed by the pandemic. A large study with over five thousand participants from eleven countries found that musical engagement was effective in the promotion of three out of five well-being goals, namely, enjoyment, self-connection, and venting negative emotions. While the authors found some minor cultural and age differences, altogether the results reinforced the central role of music in people's lives during that challenging time. A review of studies conducted worldwide during the lockdowns revealed the important role of music in emotion and mood regulation, and in psychological coping. Niels Hansen defined musical engagement during the lockdown as a "compensatory source of hedonic pleasure," and suggested that it was used to satisfy the human need for "eudaemonistic meaning in life during socially and psychologically impoverished times." In our group, we investigated how individuals worldwide utilized music to cope with pandemic-related stressors. We surveyed approximately one thousand participants across four countries—India, Italy, the United Kingdom, and the United States—at the onset of the pandemic, using online methods, and observed a significant relationship between engagement with music, well-being, and emotion regulation.

Prepandemic, several research initiatives and networks emerged with a focus on music, health, and well-being. In the United States, the Sound Health Initiative is a partnership between the National Institutes of Health, the Kennedy Center for the Performing Arts, and the National Endowment for the Arts. It is meant to expand our current understanding of how engagement with music, whether it be the listening, performing, or creating of music, involves neural mechanisms that might be harnessed for health and wellness applications (nih.gov/research-training/medical-research-initiatives/sound -health). Led by British scholars Neta Spiro and Kate Sanfilippo, the Musical

Care Throughout the Lifecourse—An International and Interdisciplinary Network is aimed at focusing on research on music as an act of care. Spiro and Sanfilippo define musical care broadly, as "music listening as well as music-making in supporting any aspect of people's developmental or health needs." They add that musical care can be applied to physical and mental health, cognitive and behavioral development, as well as interpersonal relations. While these networks have different goals, a common element to them is musical engagement. But what exactly is musical engagement?

DEFINING MUSICAL ENGAGEMENT

Music is central to human life. Humans come into the world endowed with musical inclinations that to a larger or lesser extent develop over the life span. These inclinations develop through social interactions that take place in a wide variety of settings—the home, school and other educational settings, and community spaces, including those in the virtual world—through a process known as "musicking." "To music" is to engage in performing, listening, composing, dancing, and improvising, and to generate meaning from such experiences. Modes of musical engagement vary considerably: musical engagement can be unintentional and implicit (for example, when music is playing in the background and the listener does not make much of it), or reactive (when one dances or sings in response to music), or deliberate (when someone with more expertise teaches a song to a novice), or self-initiated (when one resorts to inventing a tune or dancing).

Modes of engagement, in turn, are related to three main learning processes, known as formal, informal, and nonformal. While formal learning is perhaps easier to define, given its preplanning, goals, assessment tools, and focus on teachers as the experts, the boundaries between informal and nonformal learning are less clear. Typically, research on informal and nonformal learning often focuses on the early and late years of life, whereas many studies on formal learning tend to focus on the formative years of schooling, which coincide with middle childhood, adolescence, and early adulthood. Our research efforts have centered on both formal and informal music programs. Investigating these two approaches to music studies is important due to their relevance in everyday life and across the life span.

MUSICAL ENGAGEMENT IN COMMUNITIES

In everyday life, humans engage with music in multiple ways and with varied companions. A major issue associated with music engagement through formal learning is access. Instruments and lessons in formal spaces like conservatories and music schools are expensive and not always accessible. Likewise, not all schools offer comprehensive music education for their students. Formal spaces aside, many people (perhaps most) learn music within the social spaces that they navigate in everyday life, through listening experiences and opportunities afforded by their families and communities. Drum circles, community choirs, New Horizons bands, garage bands, and taiko drumming ensembles are some of the possible forms of musical engagement within communities. Unsurprisingly, research on community-based musical experiences has been carried out by scholars from different fields, such as community music, music therapy, community psychology, gerontology, and public health, each with its own epistemologies and methodological approaches. These studies have focused on a wide variety of musical offerings, including youth orchestras, community choirs, after-school music programs for children and adolescents, and songwriting workshops for incarcerated youth and adults, to name only a few. While these studies show encouraging findings in terms of the impact of community-based music programs on health and well-being, there are several gaps in our knowledge. In other words, existing evidence is fragmented and in need of further substantiation.

One area that has received considerable attention in recent years is group singing, especially in amateur musicians. Several initiatives, including the ten-year Canadian project known as AIRS (or Advancing Interdisciplinary Research in Singing), had health and well-being as their main focus. In the United Kingdom, the workshop "Setting an Agenda for Best Practice Choir Singing Research" led to a set of recommendations for future research in terms of study designs, randomization of participants, ethics, theoretical frameworks, and analytics. But one should ask, why singing and not instrumental music?

Singing, a complex multimodal behavior, is often described as a music universal, given its omnipresence. Singing is arguably more accessible than instrumental music, as everyone with a voice can sing. Humans sing across the life span, and singing is a powerful means of human communication and expressivity. Group singing is especially powerful because it often taps into positive emotions, increasing prosociality and group cohesion, although such effects may be short-lived. According to Susan Maury and Nikki Rickard, it is likely that the level of engagement rather than the expertise is the key to accruing benefits from participation in group singing. The same is probably true for other forms of collective musical engagement. But before delving further into the phenomenon of singing and its connections to well-being, we turn to an introduction and review of our ongoing work on the effects of musical engagement in children and adults.

MUSICAL ENGAGEMENT AND CHILD DEVELOPMENT

At the University of Southern California's Brain and Creativity Institute, we have been investigating the effects of music engagement on child development. This research required a series of cross-sectional and longitudinal studies to focus on neural, cognitive, and social development. The studies were carried out over the last decade in partnership with the Los Angeles Philharmonic and its Youth Orchestra program, YOLA. The program involved a multiyear longitudinal study of children from underprivileged communities of Los Angeles who participated in the Youth Orchestra of Los Angeles at the Heart of Los Angeles program known as YOLA at HOLA. YOLA is inspired by the Venezuelan approach to community-based music education known as El Sistema. It offers free, high-quality, group-based music instruction four to five days a week to children. The program focuses on ensemble practice with the goal of promoting social interaction and inclusion. The curriculum focuses on critical elements of music learning, including rhythm, melody, and harmony, and the practices include group string instrument practice, group singing, and musicianship, totaling five to seven hours of music instruction per week. Children enrolled in the program were selected by lottery, typically up to a maximum of twenty students per year per grade, from a list of interested families who lived within a five-mile radius of the program.

To account for the contribution of nonassisted general development, we assessed this group of children against two comparison groups. One group of children participated in a community sports program. The sports program was selected as a comparison to control for aspects of performance that may not be unique to music learning per se and result from participating in an enrichment program, such as social engagement, group motivation, and learning reward. In addition, a second group of children from the same neighborhoods were selected from public school and community organizations and were not engaged in any organized and systematic enrichment programs at the time of enrollment in the study. In total, eighty-eight participants with an average age of 6.8 years were enrolled in the study and visited our laboratory at the USC Brain and Creativity Institute once a year. All three cohorts were from equally underserved minority communities, including primarily Latino and Korean families, and lived in low socioeconomic neighborhoods in Central and South Los Angeles. All children were raised in bilingual households, but all attended English-speaking schools and spoke English fluently. Compared to the rest of the nation, the communities where most participants lived have lower incomes, larger household sizes, lower levels of education, and a higher percentage of Latinos and residents born outside the United States. In addition, participants' communities had higher rates of community violence and limited access to health-care services, healthy food, and nearby adequate schools compared to the rest of Los Angeles.

Recruitment, retention, and data collection from young participants were not without obstacles. To succeed we had to overcome several challenges, including but not limited to building a trusting relationship with the community, accommodating individual circumstances such as transportation and childcare, and developing child-friendly testing protocols to keep the young participants interested and engaged. Each year they participated in a series of psychological and behavioral testing designed to assess their cognitive development and socioemotional maturation.

For example, we were interested to know if music engagement can support development of important social skills such as empathy and compassion in children, and if it helps them to achieve more successful social interactions. In addition, we used two neuroimaging methods, magnetic resonance imaging (MRI) and electroencephalography (EEG), to examine systematically the development of their brain structures and associated functions.

EEG is a noninvasive method to measure electrical activity of the brain, and has an excellent temporal resolution (in milliseconds range). This high temporal resolution allows for tracking the rapidly changing pattern of brain activity that underlies processing of unfolding speech or music. In addition, EEG is quiet and more tolerant to movement artifacts. However, EEG has poor spatial resolution, because the skull distorts the underlying brain electrical activity over a large area of the scalp. In contrast, MRI has excellent spatial resolution, which refers to its capacity to locate specific foci of activation with millimeter precision in the brain. MRI allows for examining the brain's macrostructure and microstructure and how the brain functions in response to different stimuli. Using the two methods combined allowed us some powerful measures of brain development in relation to music engagement during childhood.

FINDINGS FROM THE MULTIYEAR LONGITUDINAL STUDY

We summarize the general findings of the study first in general and then focus on specific aspects of singing, creativity, and socioemotional well-being. Although at baseline assessments there were no differences among the groups, after two years of training, the children who received music training not only were better at fundamental auditory abilities, such as pitch perception, but also showed increased functional development of corresponding auditory brain regions compared to those in the two control groups. For example, children who received music training showed better ability to detect changes in pitch and displayed more mature-like auditory processing abilities as measured by EEG. But the benefits of music learning were not limited to auditory skills. Children who received music training were also better at an earlier age at controlling their impulses. For example, in an experiment where they could choose between a small immediate reward versus a large but delayed reward, compared to the two control groups, children who received music training systematically discarded a small reward in favor of larger and better rewards at a later time. Moreover, they also showed a greater engagement of their brain's planning and decision-making network—prefrontal network, including the anterior cingulate cortex and the inferior frontal gyrus—at an earlier age, as the performance of a decision-making task inside the MRI scanner demonstrated. Another significant finding concerned neuroplastic changes in brain connectivity, particularly in the corpus callosum. The corpus callosum is composed of nerve fibers that connect the two hemispheres of the brain. Using diffusion-weighted magnetic resonance imaging, we observed that children who received music training showed more robust connections in the corpus callosum as measured by fractional anisotropy.

It was important to determine if the improvements in auditory and cognitive skills were accompanied by benefits to socioemotional well-being. We used both qualitative and quantitative assessments to examine socioemotional well-being among participants in the study. For example, we conducted annual interviews with the family members to obtain their perspective on whether participating in enrichment programs had had an impact on their children's well-being. As judged by their parents/legal guardians, participating in music learning as well as in the sports program had a protective effect. They rated their children as less aggressive and less hyperactive. These reports, combined with the absence of such differences in parental views of children's aggression and hyperactivity at the beginning of the study, suggest that music learning benefited the child's social development and the family. When asked if they saw any benefits associated with participation in the music program, parents/legal guardians also spoke about issues of mobility and visibility. In the words of two mothers:

"Our family had the opportunity to visit new places like the Hollywood Bowl and recently went to the opera."

"My child meets new musicians and has a role model in the program. One of these days, a music group from Colombia visited the program, signed my child's T-shirt, and took a photo with him."

SINGING AND IMPROVISATION SKILLS

Turning our focus specifically to singing and improvisation, we used quantitative data to examine the roles of age, biological sex, and music training on children's pitch matching and vocal improvisation skills. We also used qualitative inquiry tools to shed light on the musical contents of vocal improvisations, the strategies used by children when improvising, and children's responses to different improvisatory prompts over time. These tasks were based on two components from the AIRS Test Battery of Singing Skills (ATBSS).

The pitch-matching tasks from the ATBSS included intervals, arpeggios, and an ascending and a descending major scale. Children were asked to listen to the experimenter and sing back what they heard. When we examined data from the first three years of our study, we observed that girls outperformed boys. Girls were not only more accurate in matching pitch, but also more willing to sing than boys. Children in the music group specifically showed the highest improvements in pitch-matching tasks over time, which suggests some near transfer effects from instrumental music education.

To gain some insight into children's creative improvisatory processes, we asked them to complete four melodies sung by the experimenter. We started with the vocal improvisation task from the ATBSS (a 4/4 melody in major mode) and added three new prompts with varying key and time signatures, to examine the direction of change in children's vocal improvisation. Prompts were recorded and then analyzed in terms of melodic embellishment and tonal/stylistic properties. This approach to the analysis of children's vocal renditions was warranted, because few studies to date have examined children's vocal improvisations using a longitudinal design.

Although we found developmental effects for the entire sample, we note that girls, irrespective of group, outperformed boys in their vocal improvisation task as well. Their vocal renditions were more musically sophisticated. The laborious musical analysis—pitch, rhythm, and conformity to rules of Western tonal music—of over four hundred vocal renditions revealed six different strategies that child participants used when creating vocal endings to a melody: exact imitation, slight variation but in time and ending on the tonic, playing with form but maintaining much from the original melody, long creation without any reference to the original melody, long creation within the same tonality and with a sense of form, and potpourri or mixing the original melody with a known song such as "Joy to the World." Such knowledge extends beyond music cognition and development and adds to the body of literature on vocalizations and invented melodies by young children. The latter are known to play important roles in language and musical development, interpersonal communication, and self-regulation.

Improvised vocalizations are also linked to human creativeness and agency, which are associated with components of well-being, including accomplishment and engagement.

We also examined children's preferences for songs and singers/groups over the course of five years. Musical preferences have been linked to personality and identity work, and are often used in health, educational, and community settings as a means to strengthen interpersonal links and group affiliation, both important for well-being. Using case-study methodology, we analyzed song preferences of five Latinx children. Our findings suggested that children's musical preferences were robust and fairly stable. Although all children were bilingual, their preferences for popular music in the dominant language (i.e., English) emerged very early. Children reported listening to a variety of genres, including movie soundtracks, hip-hop, pop, rock, and gospel, to name a few. These findings raise many questions about the role of technology, media, and popular culture in the development of musical preferences in childhood. Given the easiness with which music can be accessed these days, for how much time and what music do children listen to in daily life? What is the role of musical videos and film music transmitted through online platforms (e.g., YouTube) in shaping children's musical preferences? How do these multimodal music listening experiences (i.e., through musical videos) shape the developing brain? These questions highlight the need for future research to examine musical engagement with multiple musical genres.

MUSICAL ENGAGEMENT AND AGING

By 2060 nearly one in four Americans will be sixty-five years and older, and the number of adults older than eighty-five will be three times higher than currently. With these increasing numbers, there will be more demand for innovative and novel interventions to support the quality of life and well-being of older adults. One such intervention depends on engagement in the arts. Arts-based interventions are relatively low cost, are engaging, and can be culturally tailored and offered in the community.

In an effort to better understand the role of participation in accessible music-based experiences on health and well-being beyond childhood, our research group at USC Brain and Creativity has expanded its research program to include the role of music in the lives of older adults. Because music is integral to most cultures, engagement in music is an opportunity for older adults to remain active and socially connected. In addition, engagement in music is correlated with improved hearing abilities and cognitive functions.

A common problem of aging is hearing loss. According to the National Institute on Deafness and Other Communication Disorders (NIDCD), 25 percent of adults over age sixty meet the diagnostic criteria for moderate hearing loss, and by age seventy-five, approximately 50 percent of adults meet this criterion. Age-related hearing decline is associated with reduced social interactions and related loneliness and depression. One consequence of hearing loss is the reduction in the ability to understand speech in noisy environments, and existing hearing aids are not effective at remedying the problem. As a result, older adults are often unsatisfied by their limited ability to hear clearly and communicate effectively in loud environments and incline to avoid social gatherings altogether.

Music making involves multiple components, which include the engagement of the auditory, cognitive, and socioemotional skills that can confer important health benefits in older adults. Engagement in musical activities also has been shown to correlate with better auditory abilities and cognitive skills in children and adults. Accordingly, we predicted that engagement in music programs, even for a short time, but group based, can be an innovative intervention to assist older adults with improving their cognitive function and hearing abilities, and consequently enhancing their quality of life. Following models of community choirs, in a series of studies we enrolled older adults to participate in short-term community-based choir training that was designed to promote music engagement, social interaction, and overall well-being. Participants in the study were members of the community who did not have prior formal training in music. We selected choirs because most people can sing, even without formal music training, and because singing is an accessible and widespread form of expression. To evaluate the impact of music engagement through choir singing, we incorporated a battery of assessments designed to measure musical abilities, auditory skills, and quality-of-life outcome before and after participation in the choir. Here we summarize the design and findings from two of these studies.

In one study we randomly assigned adults aged fifty to sixty-five either to participate in a twelve-week choir training program or to take part in a music listening activity. By randomly assigning participants to either the music intervention or comparison music listening activity, we opted for a rigorous design that allows for examining cause-and-effect relationships between the music intervention and the outcome and to reduce biases of preexisting differences and motivational factors. The choir-singing group participated in two-hour weekly group choir singing sessions for twelve consecutive weeks, and were given at-home vocal training and music theory exercises to complete outside of class. The choir was directed by a professionally trained choir director, who was assisted by an accompanist who provided the music accompaniment for the songs, and four section leaders who provided musical leadership for each of the choral sections (soprano, alto, tenor, and bass). The choir rehearsals took place at the Cammilleri Hall, a world-class music hall at USC Brain and Creativity Institute, and each week followed a general routine, beginning with announcements and warm-ups, work on the repertoire, a break, additional work on the repertoire in sections, and a short group practice at the end. Although some of the participants were hesitant to sing at the beginning of choir program, the support and encouragement by other members and mentoring by the choir director and section leaders facilitated their full participation after just a few weeks. The control passive-listening group received twelve weekly three-hour musical playlists that they were asked to listen to throughout the week. Playlists were curated to reflect a variety of musical genres that would be enjoyable to participants in this age group. We evaluated performance of both groups on perceiving speech and communication in noisy environments and the associated neurophysiology using EEG measures. We also evaluated socioemotional well-being using related standardized classes and open-ended well-being interviews on the impact of the intervention on quality-of-life outcomes. After the twelve-week period of the intervention, we observed in the group who participated in the choir neuroplastic changes—as measured by EEG—in the brain's auditory system associated with better sound encoding.

Qualitatively, through open-ended questions and interviews, participants in the choir perceived greater social benefit and indicated that singing together was a more effective way to gain a sense of social belonging and consequent wellness. One participant shared the experience of participating in the choir:

> Yes, I believe the singing and participating in the music intervention has influenced my confidence level and sensitivity to others. I am especially able to recognize emotional tone in music more now that I did before. I am thinking this carries over to how people express themselves also. Often find myself listening longer to people than I would before so perhaps my participation has also improved my empathy for others too.

Another participant shared the influence of music training on his confidence and self-efficacy: "I think that I am more prone to stepping out of my comfort zone after experiencing the increased bravery and confidence I derive from learning to sing."

While individuals in the passive-listening group did participate in online group discussions about the playlists, qualitative results demonstrate that singing together was a more effective way to gain a sense of social well-being. However, we did not observe differences between groups in quantitative measures of well-being. This could be related to our small sample size or short duration (twelve weeks) of intervention.

In a second study we expanded upon the previous work to determine the effects of short-term virtual choir and mindfulness training on speech-in-noise perception and well-being in middle-aged and older adults (aged fifty to sixty-five) during the COVID-19 pandemic. We used a randomized-control trial design with an active comparison group to determine if the differences in speech-in-noise abilities and well-being that we had previously observed were due to specific qualities of either mindfulness or choir or simply to participating in a known psychologically beneficial communal activity. Again, we randomly assigned sixty-seven adults (aged fifty-five to sixty-five) to a ten-week virtual choir program. For the control comparison group, we opted for a virtual mindfulness program. We selected mindfulness because it was readily accessible, was feasible to be implemented in groups with older adults, and had previously been shown to result in significant benefits to cognition and well-being in the aging population. Because of the spread of COVID-19 and associated restrictions at the time of this study, both programs had to be delivered virtually over Zoom. A virtual platform is not an ideal format for choir training, as there are challenges with singing in sync with others when online. However, considering the possible benefits of engagement in an activity for older adults who were suffering significantly because of the pandemic disruption, resulting in isolation and loneliness, we chose virtual interventions that were accessible to older adults and had shared structural and social environments. We found that although both interventions were effective in improving communication and social skills, choir training was advantageous to mindfulness in speech-in-noise perception, particularly in challenging conditions where the relevant difference between the speech and the background noise was small. We also observed that participating in choir was advantageous in reducing anxiety, an important component of well-being.

Our findings from these studies provide evidence that musical engagement during older adulthood can improve cognitive and auditory function, reduce feelings of stress and anxiety, and thus increase quality of life. Growing evidence is also now available that engagement with music during childhood benefits multiple cognitive domains that typically decline with higher age. For example, musicians with extended practice across the life span displayed better cognition in advanced age (sixty to eighty-three years of age). And at least ten years of musical participation across the life span has been shown to have a strong predictive effect on preserved cognitive functioning across both verbal and visuospatial domains, and for executive processes. Given the demographic shift toward an increasingly older population, these findings have broad implications for public health and for the identification of cost-effective and sustainable music-based intervention to support the aging population.

CONCLUDING REMARKS

Engagement in music can be beneficial as detailed in the research we describe. While most people engage with music at some level on an individual basis mostly through listening, it will be important to gain access to more formal and prolonged musical engagement through lessons and collective musical experiences.

THE ROAD AHEAD

Integrated Approaches to Arts, Technology,
Community, and Health for the Future

Nature, Culture, and Healing

YO-YO MA

Grammy Award–Winning Cellist

Shortly before dawn on a June day last year, I stood in the middle of a field in Acadia National Park in Maine. Beside me were my hosts: elders, storytellers, and musicians from the Wabanaki peoples who have lived in this place—which they call Moneskatik—for thousands of years. We were gathered to celebrate a centuries-old tradition of music and story. Roger Paul began by sharing the legend, first in Wabanaki then in English, of Koluskap, the first man, who had placed their ancestors on the eastern edge of the American continent for a purpose: to welcome the sun each morning. We listened to Lauren Stevens sing against a background of the softly breaking waves of the Atlantic. And as the sun rose through the pines, I was invited to take out my cello. I played a Mongolian tune, a piece that tells of the grasslands that my ancestors may have wandered, long before they came to the concrete of Hong Kong and Paris and New York.

We humans have been cultural beings since our beginning. Each of our creations—music or dance or stories or visual art—is an elemental act of culture that plays a vital role in our lives and our environment. They are the tools we have for making sense of our most basic relationships: with the world around us, with one another, and with the metaphysical.

As an artist and a traveler, I've had the great fortune to see culture fueling relationships and meaning all over the world. For decades, I have found joy in the connections between performers and audiences in concert halls and among friends sharing food at the dinner table. I've been inspired by meeting strangers, and by learning about and sharing the cultural practices we have built over millennia that continue to shape our everyday lives. But I have also been worried by signs that we are increasingly struggling to find meaning in these connections. Our relationships with others seem to feature too much distrust and division; our relationship to metaphysical questions seems to become an unnecessary contest between reason and emotion. On that morning in Moneskatik, though, what I was thinking about was our relationship with nature. The Wabanaki artists I was working with, and the members of the local community who joined us—scientists, artists, tribal and government leaders—displayed a profound empathy for the natural world and, above all, a strong sense of our membership in it. Their sense of stewardship for the earth is a contrast to the dualist vision of humanity and nature we can too frequently fall into, a vision in which we see the nonhuman part of the world as a resource to be sampled, consumed, or tailored to meet the needs of the human project rather than as an integral part of our existence. If this attitude is taken too far, the consequences for individuals, for societies, and for the planet are potentially disastrous. But I believe we can find a solution in culture.

Over the last few years, I've started to understand how culture helps us not only to understand one another and to connect to the transcendent, but also to make sense of our place in the natural world and our responsibilities toward it. Science, business, and politics have their own important roles, but culture is essential: it codes our consciousness, it creates some form of order from chaos, it helps us create narratives that navigate our path forward, and it can restore our sense of belonging in and responsibility to the world around us. The early morning Wabanaki ceremony welcoming the sun was more than an encounter in a beautiful setting; it was an act of culture, a renewal of tradition, an acknowledgment of humanity's place in nature, and a message of hope.

CULTURE AND COMMON NATURE

We have always used literature, art, science, and music to mediate our place in the world around us, not only to understand nature but also to learn ways to be in relationship with it. We create rituals rooted in the cycles of the natural world and our need to navigate its transitions: harvest festivals, New Year's traditions, and rites of spring. We depict nature in cave paintings of animals, the decoration of Egyptian tombs, Japanese textiles, the sound of a nightingale in a piece of music. In creation stories and throughout literature—from the Kalila wa-Dimna, to Aesop's Fables, to the poetry of Walt Whitman—we have used nature as metaphor to help us understand our place in the world and illuminate human concerns.

The inseparability of our cultural creation and the natural world codes a crucially important truth: humans are a *part* of nature, not separate from it.

When we live with this in mind, many other good things follow. We move from a world dominated by separateness and competition to one that instead recognizes the interdependence of living things and prioritizes coexistence. We make decisions not only on a human time scale but on a natural time scale, and we find ways to accommodate rather than force or exploit nature. I believe that when culture strengthens our empathetic connection to our planet, it's easier to remember that our senses and emotions are as important as our reason, and that we all have a fundamental connection through the natural world. This is my—our—cause for hope, even as we face great challenges.

UNNATURAL TIMES

I am deeply concerned when I think about the world I will leave behind for my children and grandchildren. Innovations like instant communications, rapid travel, and large-scale industry—so often the measures of human progress—bring us many benefits, but also detract from our sense of place, reduce our time for reflection, and make change so fast that it outstrips our capability to process it. Nature is all around us, even in cities and human-made environments, but if we do not recognize this, we cannot feel connected with it. Despite our inborn curiosity about the world, I worry that it has become too easy to stop thinking intentionally about our connection with and place in nature.

Losing our empathetic connection with the world around us would be bad at any time, but the problem is particularly acute today. As we watch heat waves and wildfires, flooded rivers and melting permafrost, we understand that what is happening to nature is happening to us. Some agricultural practices are exhausting the soil's delicate balance, and there is an ever-increasing demand for one resource that sustains us all—water. These issues require urgent reconnection with our natural home, not just for our health but to ensure our common survival.

I do not believe that this crisis is without hope. Over the past two years, the COVID-19 pandemic has led to tragic losses and exposed serious stresses in our society. But we have found new forms of connection and created many "wet cement" moments, where people have decided to make different choices about their professional and personal lives. I hope that this newly released energy and refocused purpose will make it easier for us to address seemingly overwhelming challenges such as this one.

RESTORING OUR HEALTH

What if we *could* restore the balance between ourselves and nature? What if more of us had a stronger empathetic connection with the nonhuman world around us?

We know that a harmonious relationship with nature contributes to a healthier society. Over the past five years, I've spent time in Indigenous communities from New Zealand and Peru to Taiwan and Canada, communities that have practiced a reciprocal relationship with the natural world for many, many generations. I've come to believe that this mindset—one that recognizes our part in an interdependent world—is essential if we are to have any chance of leaving a better world to our children.

Nature can also give us a healthy dose of perspective, bringing a different understanding of time and distance. The astronomers I met at the Paranal Observatory in Chile's high desert told me that the vastness of the universe taught them to value both the insignificance and the potential impact of their individual actions. Standing on the rim of the Grand Canyon last November, I felt something similar in the sweep of "big time"—the millennia and generations that came before me and those to come. Knowing that the Canyon has existed for millions of years didn't make my life feel trivial; instead, it let me focus on the present and freed me from worry about personal outcomes. When we allow ourselves to stand in its embrace, the natural world reminds us that even the largest-scale change begins with each of us doing our part, one person building on others' work and creating something for those who will come next.

Finally, a stronger empathetic connection between humans and the world around us also helps the planet. If we consider our relationship to the natural world as a familial bond (like parent and child, or sibling and sibling), we instinctively take our responsibility to it more seriously. We reject selfishness in favor of nurture, exploitation in favor of regeneration, scarcity in favor of abundance.

How do we restore this balance? Policy and economic investment can and do make important contributions, but there is a complementary power, just as strong: humanity's oldest tool, culture. Culture is uniquely well suited to help us learn, empathize, and make resolutions; it gives us the tools to imagine and create a symbiotic relationship with nature.

In 2018, I began a journey to ask artists and scientists on six continents how culture can help us imagine and build a better world, and I've spent the last four years listening to their answers. I've met AI scientists in Montreal, DJs in Beirut, furniture makers in Pittsfield, coders in Sydney, chefs in Lima, and fashion entrepreneurs in Jakarta. When I look back on those experiences, there's a single thread that runs through them all: an urgent desire to use culture to restore a healthy relationship with the world around us.

In Lima, I was hosted by artists from the Shipibo-Konibo tribe, whose paintings and weavings reimagine the flow of the Amazon in intricate geometric forms, a stunning map of our collective future. On the coast just south of Cape Town, where two great oceans converge, I played with musician-scientists whose instruments were an organ made from hollow kelp and a drum constructed from a whale's eardrum, a reminder that purposeful sound and music are phenomena we share with all the world. And in Ōtautahi Christchurch, New Zealand, I heard the songs of the Ngāi Tahu iwi, emphasizing the central vitality of water to all living things, a metaphor that helped their community recover its health after a series of traumatic natural and human events.

When I think back, I realize that stories like these have always been part of my cultural life. The instrument I play is a product of nature, soft pine resonating against harder maple, horsehair on steel string. The first music I learned, Bach's first cello suite, to me contains all the variety of nature at play: symmetry and asymmetry, regularity and irregularity, and the joy of infinite variety. The compositions of Antonín Dvořák, including his cello concerto, are inseparable from the riverbank of his youth in Bohemia and from the natural sounds he found while traveling in America. Among the songs that I have played with my colleagues in the Silkroad Ensemble are references to our great rivers, galloping horses, and birds soaring toward the sun. So many of our greatest cultural creations are celebrations of our living planet; they give life and voice to the truth that *we* are part of the energy and health that surrounds us.

A recent "sonification" of the pressure waves from a black hole at the center of the Perseus galaxy is an extraordinary example—it translates the image of something many times bigger than the sun and impossibly far away into something we can internalize, knowledge that can transcend distance to become an extension of us. And that sits very comfortably beside Pablo Casals's "Song of the Birds," a musical portrayal of animals much smaller than us that brings alive our shared freedom.

To me, all of these creations—not the work of our ancestors but what is happening among us today—show how culture can strengthen an empathetic bond between us and our geography, the plant and animal life around us, and the planet itself. And when we are emotionally and empathetically tied to the natural world, we are reminded at a more profound, instinctive level of our interdependence with it. Culture has a vital role to play in this most existential moment in the history of our species, a responsibility to restore our connection. It reflects our care and our love for this world, a love that will lead to better health and more long-term, sustainable thinking.

There is an opportunity for each of us to be part of a movement, one that draws upon the millions of stories and cultural practices that have connected us to nature over time. We need to create new stories, illustrations, and understanding inspired by our current knowledge and experience of nature, like the "music" recently captured from the black hole at the center of our galaxy. We need to use the broad and deep perspectives of culture to imagine a different and better future for our planet and our relationship with it, drawing on the same spirit of creativity, collaboration, and innovation that helps us imagine new technologies and new worlds. We need to reconnect with the inspiration that wakes us up at four a.m. to welcome the sun, to play music and share stories with our communities, and to care enough about our natural home to rescript this chapter of the human story.

The late Richard Feynman wrote that "the imagination of nature is far, far greater than the imagination of man." Let us be part of that greater imagination, as we are among the wonders of nature—growing, adapting, evolving, and all connected.

—Yo-Yo Ma, writing in June 2022

Over the next several years, as he continues to explore the many ways in which culture connects us to the natural world, Yo-Yo Ma will visit sites that epitomize nature's potential to move the human soul, creating collaborative works of art and convening conversations that seek to strengthen our relationship to our planet and to one another.

Composing the Future of Health

TOD MACHOVER

Muriel R. Cooper Professor of Music and Media, and Director of Opera of the Future Group, MIT Media Lab

RÉBECCA KLEINBERGER, PhD

Assistant Professor of Humanics and Voice Technology, College of Arts Media Design and Khoury College of Computer Sciences, Northeastern University

ALEXANDRA RIEGER

Doctoral Candidate and Researcher, Opera of the Future Group, MIT Media Lab

If you are reading this book, you are probably already convinced that music has the power to shape our minds, stir our emotions, and heal our bodies. We, as members of the Opera of the Future group at the MIT Media Lab, certainly believe this as well. However, our investigations over the past twenty years have shown that much remains to be discovered about exactly *how* music affects us, and whether not-yet-created music—based on emerging theories and techniques—could exert even more powerful medicinal benefits than what we have heard so far. In this chapter we share examples of our interdisciplinary approach to musical research, demonstrating the interrelationships between the investigation into fundamental sonic properties, with a focus on the power of the human and nonhuman voice; the blending of interactive music making and medical practice into a new field of MediMusical Instruments; and the experimental creation of musical compositions designed to calm the spirit, focus the mind, and establish profound human connection. In doing so we hope to show that such a process that combines sounds, science, circuits, and societies can significantly contribute to establishing the future practice of musical medicine that so many of us seek.

VOICE, MUSIC, AND HEALTH

Music shares a profound and ancient bond with voices. Over the past decade Dr. Rébecca Kleinberger's research in the Opera of the Future group has focused on exploring the voice beyond words, connecting fields in a holistic manner to create voice-based interventions and technologies for physical and mental health. The voice is one of the most natural tools for expression, but we may not be aware of exactly how much we truly express through our voice. Because it is the result of complex processes involving both the body and the brain, the voice can reveal various physical and mental health conditions, from Parkinson's to Alzheimer's, as well as hormonal imbalance, lung diseases, and mental health conditions. In addition to its potential for diagnosis, the voice can also be used to influence health from the outside in. Vocal practices and voice-based, technologically mediated interventions have potential applications in contexts ranging from stuttering to emotion regulation to eating disorders. In this context Dr. Kleinberger's research explores the music of the voice as a marker of our fluid identity and highlights how it can be used in medicine, as both a flashlight to reveal health issues and a tool to help with various physical and mental health conditions.

The Voice Is Richer and More Complex Than We Think

For most of us the voice feels like a very familiar instrument. It follows us from birth to death, from our first cry to our last whisper. After only a few years of life, most of us control our voices virtuosically, without so much as a thought. It may seem obvious, common, simple. And yet, the voice is also full of paradoxes. For instance, the voice distinguishes us from other primates while also revealing profound similarities to communication patterns in other mammals and birds. Chimpanzees, our closest living evolutionary relatives, share 96 percent genetic similarity with us. Some of the very few differences between our species lie in our descended larynx, giving us a wider range of tonalities, and in the fine control of facial and throat muscles that allows us to articulate sounds with high accuracy and precision. However, such precision can undoubtedly also be witnessed in the nightingale's singing abilities, even though its vocal apparatus—called a syrinx—is markedly different from the mammalian larynx.

The paradoxical qualities of the voice also appear within our own species. Indeed, the human voice is a near-universal ground with which humans have built common languages. Inversely it is also a unique signature that we associate with specific individuals. Humans typically have the same number of voice-related muscles and use the same mechanism for vocal production. Those same muscles have just marginally different shapes and sizes, and we use them with slight variations, creating a unique tone that is exclusively ours. The sound of a human voice is immediately recognizable, as our brains categorize and process human vocalization in a unique way. Therefore, we are able to distinguish human voices from any other sounds within a fraction of a second. However, within this same fraction of a second, we can usually tell *who* made that sound, discerning age, familiarity, and more. In the grand scheme of sound source recognition, quickly identifying whether a vocal sound was uttered by your mother, father, colleague, favorite actor, third-grade teacher, or someone you have never met is no small feat.

The apparent contradictory qualities of the voice permeate all facets of the human experience, even on the most personal and intimate level. Whether they are smooth, screamed, whispered, silent, or expressed through ASL, our voices are indeed central to how we participate in the social sphere. Many common metaphorical English expressions can attest to this—whether or not the act of speaking is involved, we often seek to "be heard" or "have a voice." In other words, the voice is the way we express ourselves and project who we are to the world around us. However, despite this intimate relationship with our own self-expression and the power our voice holds for making others hear and recognize us, we are estranged, almost alienated, from our own voices. Ask anyone around you, and most might report that their own vocal recordings sound strange or unfamiliar. We do not hear ourselves the way other people do—the way we think our voice sounds is very different from how we *actually* sound to everybody else. When others hear us, sounds are transmitted through the air, whereas when we hear ourselves talk or sing, part of the sound is transmitted through the bones, especially the lower, richer frequencies and harmonics. Beyond this bone-conduction phenomenon, various other filters in voice perception and processing further reinforce this estrangement of the voice. Our body, ears, and even brain seem to be conspiring to keep our voice hidden from us, creating an uncanny and sometimes uncomfortable feeling when we listen back to our voicemail greeting.

With its many facets, hidden by a veil of apparent familiarity, the voice is truly paradoxical and complex in a way that surpasses even the meaning of the words it carries. Its precise sonorities, prosody, individual tonalities, and paralinguistics reveal who we are and can be seen as markers of our fluid identity. Such sonic richness could be called the "music of the voice."

What the Voice Reveals: Voice as Marker of Our Fluid Identity

Although there is a lot we still do not know about voices, current research reveals that they contain crucial social information. Our identity, or at least a projection of it, is imprinted in our voice. Most of us are experts at identifying voices we have heard before. In fact, even when hearing the voice of a complete stranger, we are often able to estimate the age of the speaker and their gender, or at least their hormonal identity, which may sometimes be at odds with biological or gender identity. We may even be able to predict their height, weight, health, and facial features. We can also detect accents, which give clues about cultural background and upbringing. In this context "who we are" is embedded in the music of our voice at many different levels, ranging from physiological to biological to hormonal to upbringing. In addition to carrying markers of physical and biological identity, the voice also yields insight into emotion. Just by hearing the voice of a friend, we may recognize if they are excited, angry, sad, or depressed, even if their words tell a different story. The fact that our emotions are recognizable from our voices also highlights the important temporal variability of our identity.

Indeed, our body, like our mind, is not static. In this way the music of the voice is as fluid as our identity itself, changing over time, throughout life, and even throughout the day. Some changes result from a willful decision, such as a gender transition, while others result from diseases or the regular process of aging. Some major drivers of such changes are hormones. The voice box, our larynx, is packed with hormone receptors. This is quite noticeable in men's voices during puberty, and is also reflected in women's voices during menstrual cycles. Beyond physiology the fluidity of the voice is also seen in context-dependent variations, consciously and subconsciously, depending upon with whom we are speaking. This phenomenon is known

as "subconscious interlocutor-based voice variability." For instance, women often unconsciously lower their voice in the workplace to appear more assertive, sometimes to the detrimental extent of damaging their vocal cords. Additionally, when talking to babies, toddlers, and young children, adults often change their prosody and tone of voice to more exaggerated and musical forms of speech known as infant-directed speech or "motherese," which appears to help children acquire language faster.

As such, the fluidity of the voice, part intentional, part subconscious, reveals the fluidity of the self, identity, and mind. Beyond these intangible, though vitally important, features, the voice also provides insight into bodily function. For instance, in the context of health, listening to subtle changes of vocal sonority can shed light on various medical conditions.

The Voice as a Flashlight for Diagnosis

Due to its deeply rooted connections with the body and the brain, as well as the insight it provides into who we are as people, the voice can be used as a flashlight to illuminate health-related conditions. The voice is the result of complex, interconnected, and multifactorial processes in the body: when we make a vocal sound, we are precisely controlling up to a hundred muscles, from the face to the throat, voice box, diaphragm, abdomen, and chest. This careful balance of vocal, respiratory, and digestive processes is precisely controlled by the brain, both consciously and subconsciously. Any abnormal functioning of these systems might be reflected in the voice. Indeed, very subtle biological, physical, and mental conditions influence the music and sonority of the voice, which could be used as a diagnostic tool to reveal nascent health issues, whether through human listeners or trained automatic detection systems. In fact, the art of listening to the voice and the body to understand illnesses is not new. The term "auscultation," derived from the Latin verb *auscultare* (to listen) and defined as the action of listening to the internal sounds of the body, was introduced in the early nineteenth century by René Laënnec, though the process itself originated as early as ancient Egypt.

Thus, listening to specific prosodic features of the voice can give insight into characteristic biological, physical, and mental conditions. For instance, the timbre of the voice contains information about the respiratory airflow, tissue health, and muscle control. Parkinson's disease (PD), which affects muscle control, provides an interesting case study for this concept. Patients often report that, at later stages of PD, difficulties in vocal control and vocalizing loud enough to be heard are among the most profound handicaps. However, even at early stages, PD affects the acoustics of the voice by creating unique patterns of nonlinearity and non-Gaussian turbulence that can be detected long before other symptoms, likely because the voice requires fast, precise, and sustained control of small muscles that shape the vocal sound, as well as strong support from respiratory muscles like the diaphragm. Respiratory conditions and lung diseases also affect the timbre of the voice, allowing for the use of specific acoustic features as diagnostic markers. For instance, since COVID-19 reduces lung capacities and, therefore, leads to insufficient airflow through the vocal tract, researchers have identified specific voice signatures that may indicate the presence of COVID-19 in patients. Even in patients whose vocal timbre appears unchanged, subtle variation in volume can help identify precise conditions: voice dosimetry monitoring, defined as measuring the volume of vocal production in dB, helps predict the probability of bronchial stenosis.

The prosody and tempo of the voice can also aid in the identification of important mental health crises, including depression and other such conditions that often affect timing elements in the vocal production mechanism. Though depressed patients can purposely adopt a joyful or neutral voice, subtle elements in the relative timing between words or sentences can still be otherwise revealing. Alcohol and drugs affect muscle control and response time, which consequently affect voice timing and prosody. Alcohol specifically is a multifactorial disturbance, since it affects vocal range, rhythm, and formant shape, creating a recognizable vocal signature in the short and long terms. Certainly the most apparent vocal effect of alcohol is slurred speech, caused by the increased production of gamma-aminobutyric acid (GABA) in the brain, leading to slow reaction times and movement control. Beyond alcohol, marijuana and cocaine are known to slow down and speed up time perception in rats respectively, suggesting further impacts on affect speech timing and rhythm. In addition, cocaine abuse often induces vocal tics, while smoking marijuana can lead to hoarse, breathy, and weaker voices. Smoking tobacco has been shown to alter the jitter, frequency, and tremor of the voice in younger adults. In all of the aforementioned cases, the use of the voice as a diagnostic tool could help patients find help in their journey to recovery while informing medical knowledge on voice variations and the potential use of generalized recognition systems. However, despite this potential benefit, the dystopian risk of automatic monitoring also raises important ethical questions related to privacy and medical confidentiality.

Voice Practices and Interventions— To Heal, Influence, and Affect Health

Though the vocal signal does carry a plethora of meaningful health information, it is important to remember that the voice is also an *action* that we may be able to leverage to impact health. Voice practices, rituals, and even therapy techniques are potential ways to actively shape and use the voice as a form of healing.

Chanting, mantras, chorus, and solo singing have been associated with various physical, physiological, mental, and neural health correlates, including affecting cerebral blood flow and improving mood and social cohesion. Furthermore, the use of the voice seems to affect us beyond the benefits of meditation and prayer. The past century has also seen the development of the field of speech pathology, which has provided patients with proactive techniques to change their voice, improve their intelligibility, and, for some, improve the ability to express themselves. Ancient traditions, cultural practices, and therapies have advocated for the proactive use of one's voice in a multitude of additional ways for positive health benefits, beyond what could be discussed in a single chapter. As such, we thought it pertinent to bring modern technologies into conversation with these ancient practices, to focus on the potential to leverage newer developments to open new perspectives into impacting physical and mental health with the voice.

There is great potential for using voice-based technologies to affect health by combining advancements in signal processing with modern developments in the understanding of the neural basis of voice production, perception, and inner processing. In fact, over the past ten years, our research team has developed new technological devices, software, and experiences based on the voice to affect physical and mental health. Modulated auditory feedback, or changing the way we hear our own voice, provides an exciting avenue for further study in this field.

The perception of one's own voice appears to follow a different neural pathway than the perception of others' voices. When hearing someone else, we subconsciously analyze their identity, intent, and state, and all this informs our conscious reactions toward them. When hearing our own voice, our brains appear to constantly readjust our prediction and perception of the world, our body, and our mind instead of simply predicting how to react to others. Indeed, when we produce a vocal sound, our brain creates an intended prediction signal of what we *should* sound like. If we happen to sound slightly different—maybe due to room acoustics, a cold, or signal filtering—this prediction is updated and adjusted in a process that can have broad and surprising consequences.

By disrupting the brain's expectation, modulated auditory feedback can strongly affect speech motor control, for better or worse. Numerous studies have demonstrated that speech motor control is heavily dependent on sensory feedback, meaning that our ability to speak fluently also relies on external clues such as sonic feedback, tactile feelings in our jaw muscles, and the way we can feel that our skin tenses and relaxes when we open our mouths. By slightly changing the way we hear our own voice, we can, under the right delay conditions, fool the brain into adopting the modified audio signal within its internal model of the self. For instance, hearing one's own voice pitch-shifted to sound artificially lower will make you involuntarily speak with a higher voice as your brain attends to offset the difference between expectation and perceived reality. Some applications of modulated auditory feedback are rather deleterious. In 1950 it was discovered that adding a precise delay to someone's voice can desynchronize the voice production mechanisms so badly that it renders them almost incapable of speaking. The military used this technique both in the development of nonlethal speech jammer guns and as a way to detect malingering in drafted soldiers pretending to be deaf. If someone claimed a draft exemption for deafness, they had to take a special test consisting of reading a text while hearing their voice with a delay of 100 milliseconds. If they could speak normally, it meant they indeed couldn't hear any sound, including the sound of their own voice. However, if their speech started to blur and slow down, it meant that they could hear their voice, and the delay added was producing its desynchronization effect. Although adding a delay to the voice can lead to disfluent speech, a slightly different delay can inversely help people who stutter to speak more fluently. Research dating back to the 1960s has shown that adding delays or simple pitch shifts to the voice of a person who stutters can help them speak more fluently. Beyond delays or simple voice transformations, Rébecca Kleinberger's research has highlighted the potential of music to help with stuttering. Our studies have indeed indicated that voice musification—consisting of capturing a subject voice and processing it in near real time to make it sound more musical to the person talking—can bring even stronger fluency-evoking effects than simple delays or pitch

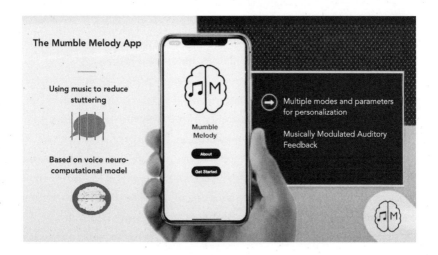

The Mumble Melody App

Using music to reduce stuttering

Based on voice neuro-computational model

Mumble Melody

About

Get Started

Multiple modes and parameters for personalization

Musically Modulated Auditory Feedback

shifts did in the past. Based on advances in neurology and recent developments in audio processing, such musification modes include adding multiple harmonies or changing timbral qualities or room acoustics.

Research from our group and from others has shown that hearing one's own voice modulated can influence a speaker's self-reported feelings. In one of our studies, participants were instructed to invent stories based on neutral images while hearing their voices transformed musically, layering either minor or major harmonies. Subjects exposed to the major condition invented stories with more positive vocabulary than those with the minor condition, suggesting potential applications for emotion regulation. Beyond this, musically modulated auditory feedback shows exciting promise across disparate domains. Eating is a highly multisensory experience, and it has been shown that filtering of eating sounds can affect texture perception of food. Bringing richer treble harmonics to the sound of eating potato chips makes them appear fresher, while amplifying lower harmonics makes them taste more stale. Our group has explored a wider space in the auditory and musical transformation of chewing and eating sounds, and our preliminary results suggest that musical feedback of these sounds can also affect flavor perception and satiety, opening the door for music-based intervention for eating regulation and disorders.

With its paradoxical mix of familiarity and mystery, the voice has been a tool to listen to the body and affect health for millennia. With scientific advances, multidisciplinary approaches, and new technology comes the potential to explore the space of health-based vocal experiences. Kleinberger's broad spectrum of applied research shows that the wide-ranging potential of voice technology opens the door to the next generation of tools and approaches for mental health and physical health. As a unique result of the fusion between brain and body, the voice can guide us in tuning into the ailing body and open doors to access and soothe the mind.

Beyond the noted interventions, music and the voice can also help us connect with our nonhuman counterparts. Kleinberger's research has explored new systems and technologies based on the voice to enrich the lives of animals and extend the pursuit of interspecies understanding. She has led the design, deployment, and evaluation of numerous voice- and music-technology-based interventions for interspecies research. These interfaces include an augmented wooden branch to allow a macaw from the San Diego

Zoo to control music in his environment, a boat-mounted acoustic apparatus to enable real-time singing dialogue between orca whales and humans,
a sonically augmented incubator for mother hens to communicate with their
unhatched eggs, and a tablet-based system to allow pet parrots to talk to
other parrots remotely.

SENSORY MEDICAL INNOVATION: MUSIC-BASED TECHNOLOGIES FOR HEALTH APPLICATIONS

Our voices reach beyond words as modes of expression, containing the richness of our experiences, backgrounds, conditions, hormonal balances, and
general health. The complexities of the human voice reveal extensive possibilities for creative expression, scientific inquiry, and therapeutic impact.
The very voice we inhabit, which we think we know well, remains a frontier
for continued research and investigation. The human senses are another field
our lab explores, which present a similar paradox of being both familiar yet
vastly undiscovered.

From the memorable petrichor scent of summer rain on the pavement
to hearing a song that lets you step into a memory or even how you precisely

know the position of your feet at this moment, without lifting your eyes from this page, our senses are a deeply ingrained part of how we experience the world. By targeting the senses, researchers, providers, and engineers can positively impact health.

Inspired by her early experiences as a young multi-instrumentalist and youth ambassador performing in hospitals and elder-care facilities globally, MIT doctoral candidate Alexandra Rieger extended her research as an undergraduate at Stanford University and graduate student at Dartmouth College, exploring sense-based health care through neuroscience, engineering, and music. Her current doctoral research intersects medicine, music, and accessible design engineering, expanding our understanding of the senses within clinical applications.

We know that, as humans, we perceive the world through our senses, but there is less awareness that the senses can provide information about our physical and cognitive health. For example, individuals with Alzheimer's disease (AD) perceive hues differently and see less of the color blue. Viruses such as COVID-19 can cause olfactory changes. Many individuals on the autism spectrum hear less of the 85 to 180 Hz human speech spectrum, and tactile object recognition timing can provide insights into dementia. Further studies reveal that engaging the senses in ways specific to the diagnosis can be an effective intervention. Given this framework, the senses should be—must be—leveraged to promote early diagnoses and to support rehabilitation. Despite this, the sensory bandwidth is not yet fully leveraged as a clinical tool to effect biological change or to measure cognitive health. Rieger's research focuses on the implementation of music-based medical devices specifically developed to override, effect, and examine the scope of the human sensory spectrum to create and measure neurobiological change. Her research has established the function of the senses to operate as a "bidirectional interface," receiving and providing information.

How many senses do we have? Many readers might answer five. In truth, however, we have many, many more senses. Why are our other senses often ignored? The idea of five senses is traceable to circa 335 BC, when Aristotle, in his philosophical theories, identified humans as having only five senses. Now, over 2,356 years later, the fields of medicine, rehabilitation, and humancentric design remain stymied by this model, although evidence reveals that many more senses exist, such as proprioception, kinesthesia, interoception, and thermoception. If you know the position of your hands at this moment without looking, that's proprioception. If you know where they are directionally according to space, that's kinesthesia. If you know whether you're thirsty or not, that's your sense of interoception, and if you know that the room you're reading in has the perfect temperature for your comfort level, that's thermoception. Despite our finely tuned senses, our devices, diagnostic procedures, and care systems tend to exclude these to our detriment. However, our senses are vital indicators of the state of our health, and changes in sensory experience alert us to illness before disease progression, highlighting the importance of crafting a more comprehensive perspective. Rieger's research has developed the term "Omnisensory Cognition" to establish this area of neuroscience, extending the limited concept of humans possessing only five senses to include the broader spectrum of senses and sensory differences.

Experiential and Perceptual Associations

One aspect of Omnisensory Cognition highlights the importance of examining sensory differences and similarities across individuals. Experiences, both culturally modulated and learned, can cause impactful cognitive adaptations. Oftentimes, familiar scents can evoke specific visual memories of a place. When learning the English alphabet, one learns to associate the triangular shape, aka the letter A, with a particular sound, phoneme, and grammatical usage. This pointy shape gains both sound and meaning, revealing how higher-order cognitive processes modulate our senses. The phenomenon of cross-modal association details how humans can associate or connect one kind of sensory stimuli with a completely different sense. Studies have revealed that we prefer matching higher pitches with blue over yellow. Similarly, we associate paler hues, smaller objects, and elevated motions with higher notes, and deeper colors, larger objects, and lower hand motions with lower notes. Researchers have even discovered that humans associate taste intensity with particular music pitches and shapes with sounds.

Some sensory reactions reach beyond culture, region, and era, such as the "Kiki, Bouba" study initially conducted in 1929 and revisited in 2013.

The study presents two forms; one is spiky, and the other is rounded and cloud-like. Using your creativity, if you heard the shapes were named "Kiki" and "Bouba," which names would you assign to which forms? If you said that Kiki was the spiky shape and Bouba the round, you'd agree with the majority of individuals who have participated in this research worldwide since 1929. By researching the bandwidth of sensory differences and commonalities, we can understand more about humanity within an inclusive and global context. These understandings could demonstrate where we as humans are "more alike than we are unalike," as well as how we are distinct. For example, the "Kiki, Bouba" associative connection is theoretically due to active and passive neuronal interactions, showing that cognitive and biological predispositions also impact sensory associations across continents. This conclusion is further supported by understanding patients with sensory differences. Individuals with sensory processing disorders (SPD) utilize less sensory integration. Synesthetes have an additional layer of sensory associations, where stimuli in one sense can elicit consistent, automatic cross-sensory experiences within another. Individuals with disabilities or sensory differences may not utilize all of their senses for perception. Even one's ear shape can change how a specific musical piece will sound to them, it is something to consider when a friend or partner does not share the same taste in music!

Sensory Integration

Our perception is modulated by how our brains process information through our senses. Therefore, it seems logical to assume that more multimodal stimuli will always cause greater stimulation and engagement. Audio/visual pairings are a common expression of multimodal stimuli. From Wagner's concept of the leitmotif to the music accompanying silent films or classic cartoons, this pairing is well established in the arts and media. Sometimes the music accompanying a film amplifies the scene; other times, it is distracting. How well the music interacts with the visuals determines the congruency of the pairing. This effect within the brain can be visualized and monitored through numerous scanning methodologies, such as EEG. Although combining stimuli *can* elicit a more robust cognitive response, some stimuli pairings are so incongruent that the sum of the whole experience is less than the additive parts; researchers refer to this as "subadditive processing." "Superadditive processing," on the other hand, occurs under specific conditions where stimuli pairs are so congruent that the sum of the elicited response is greater than the individual parts assembled. For stimuli to yield the most effective patient response, their arrangement must support a patient's ability to process them with superadditivity. In an experiment, researchers noted that stimuli—for example, sounds presented from varied locations in a room—resulted in subadditive processing. The processing of any given stimulus (i.e., temperature, sounds, visuals) is based upon a participant's attention, perception of congruence, internal drives, memories, decision making, and emotions.

Three main factors contribute to superadditive processing: timing, stimuli location, and congruence. If stimuli are synchronous, patients are more likely to process them with superadditivity. Second, if the stimuli stem from the same location in space or seem to stem from the same trigger or object, they will have a more robust perceptual pairing. When sounds seem to emanate from various places, our brains assume there are different sources; thereby, we do not integrate them with superadditivity. Sounds from multiple parts of the room may not seem to coordinate at all with one another. Imagine being in a studio apartment with your eyes closed and hearing hands clapping in one corner, a piano playing in another, a radio on in another, and water pouring in the last. Would you assume these sounds are all being made simultaneously by one source? Likely not. When performing sensory integration, our brains assemble various stimuli into likely perceptual scenarios.

Third, if the stimuli are congruent, they will also be processed with superadditivity. What is a congruent match across senses? In the scope of Omnisensory Cognition, congruence of stimuli depends on numerous factors ranging from neurobiological to cultural. In one study, researchers found that individuals associate more pleasant music with sweet tastes. Another showed connections between the letter A and the color red. Determining congruence for each patient can expedite rehabilitation and treatment through a more personalized medicine approach.

Impacting and Measuring Human Health Through the Senses

While we can study the senses to measure and track health conditions such as AD, researchers and providers can target the senses to cause brain and body changes. Numerous findings have revealed which sensory pairings elicit novel reactions. In one study, participants were asked to hold a researcher's cup. The participants holding the warmer cups versus the colder cups were more likely to feel positive about the researcher. Researchers have also found that walking on softer surfaces can establish greater behavioral flexibility in decision making. Moreover, when stimuli are paired based on cross-modal associations, individuals tend to feel a stronger sense of congruence.

Combining sensory stimuli allows for broader brain region activation, emphasizing the efficacy of music, which already has the capacity to stimulate multiple brain regions simultaneously. Researchers attribute the conduction of this multisensory process to the frontotemporal-parietal brain regions. Neurologist Gottfried Schlaug, MD, PhD, asserts that in stroke rehabilitation or aphasia music has the potential to "provide an alternative entry point into a 'broken' brain system to remediate impaired neural processes or neural connections by engaging and linking up brain centers that would otherwise not be engaged or linked with each other."

Brain Entrainment, Cortical Preservation, and Music

The aforementioned findings are essential to brain entrainment research. In introductory neuroscience classes, brain entrainment is often linked to explorations with pendulums, all starting at different times and speeds but alighting eventually upon a common rhythm. Similarly, brain-wave synchronization describes the widespread electrical neural oscillations that can fall into synchrony with both internal and external stimuli. Over the past several years our lab has supported MIT's Aging Brain Initiative, spearheaded by Dr. Li-Huei Tsai, director of the Picower Institute for Learning and Memory at MIT. As part of the initiative, the institute is exploring novel, noninvasive brain-entrainment-based approaches to AD treatments. Brain entrainment allows external stimuli to override a patient's current brain wave state, for example, from alpha to gamma. The initial Aging Brain

Initiative study demonstrated that flickering lights in the 40 Hz spectrum could induce gamma frequencies in the brain, which recruit microglial cells for successful beta-amyloid plaque removal, potentially helpful for AD. Early studies found that humans required greater brain region activation to support increased possible plaque clearance. While experiments continue to examine replicating this effect in humans, our lab has contributed to this initiative through multimodal and music-based approaches. As part of our lab's participation, Rieger designed a series of interactive devices and instruments to support multimodal entrainment, leveraging music to deliver entrainment stimuli. One of these devices is the Modular Omnisensory Orbital Neuroinstrument (MOON Instrument). As research reveals that multisensory stimuli can increase entrainment, the MOON Instrument can translate a grating tone in the required frequency into congruent sonic, visual, and haptic vibratory stimulation while surrounding the signal in a chorus of meditative harmonics.

The MOON Instrument includes music, as studies show a substantial likelihood of brain preservation in the auditory cortex regions, highlighting another benefit of music-based intervention. The music-processing regions of the brain are so widespread that even if a patient has memory loss and amnesia, they may still remember familiar songs. Incorporating music within designs allows tools to follow the principles of Cognitively Sustainable Design, supporting patients through various life and health phases.

MediMusical Instruments for Medical Contexts

Rieger's innovations leverage principles of Omnisensory Cognition to create a positive change in the landscape of human health. These devices, known as MediMusical Instruments, combine a medically purposed device within the experience of music creation by synthesizing the benefits of a participatory therapeutic musical experience with sensor-based medical technology. These devices support multisensory medical intervention in at-home telehealth settings while ensuring patient enjoyment, comfort, compliance, and duration of use. Developed through patient pilots with our stakeholder-informed approach, our lab is now exploring these devices in hospital-based outpatient settings. In collaboration with Harvard University's Massachusetts General Hospital, a full-scale telehealth implementation of the Medi-Musical Instrument devices is launching within its Cardio-Neurology department in partnership with director and heroic frontline physician Dr. MingMing Ning, MD, MMSc.

Whether in hospital or telehealth settings, the MediMusical devices provide more biofeedback to patients and data to physicians than are usually available, even in physical visits. Numerous MediMusical devices target different patient requirements throughout the diagnostic, treatment, or rehabilitation process. The Sensiturn is a recent invention by Rieger. It is a small, portable instrument designed to implement music and sound to cue a cognitive bridge over affected motor-cortex brain regions. The Sensiturn guides patients toward motor recovery after a stroke. Without sensation, physical and tactile milestones are hard to reach. With the Sensiturn, patients with hemiparesis or loss of feeling can use the instrument's auditory cues as a guide to regaining their hand function. The Sensiturn plays a continuous note interwoven within a soundscape of harmonic tones. Patients can change the pitch through the motion to play familiar tunes or compose their own, ensuring the experience is highly flexible and broadly appealing. This device is an example of a rehabilitative MediMusical Instrument specifically engineered to help the recovery of stroke patients. This device allows patients with hemiplegia to engage their fine motor connectivity, using music as a guide to restore sensations such as proprioception and movements, including lateral and medial rotation, as well as circumduction and diadochokinesis. Since each internal system network connects via the patient's or clinician's laptop, computational data collection supports detailed progress documentation.

Patient sensory-motor data can be captured, analyzed, and applied to precisely track fluctuations or red flags in patient health and alert the practitioner when to adjust difficulty settings as a patient improves. The Sensiturn captures and relays information from the slightest flutter of a hand to a purposeful, coordinated turn, making it easy for providers to track improvement. The device shares this patient data with clinicians, allowing doctors to closely monitor patient recovery from a distance. Patients lacking sensation or proprioception can benefit from the device's multisensory feedback and engaging musical interface, attaining dignity and delight throughout the recovery process.

Perhaps one of the most compelling features of these MediMusical devices is their sonic quality. The harmonious music emitted through interaction promotes creativity and enjoyment while guiding patients through specific cognitive-motor exercises, wrapping the arduous process of medical procedures into an emotionally rich and comforting experience. The pleasant interaction is one of the most powerful reasons patients and participants benefit from these instruments, thereby facilitating compliance and continued engagement, allowing for longitudinal observation and deep rehabilitation mediated by pleasure. Thus, rightly so—"as music is a strong multimodal stimulus that simultaneously transmits visual, auditory, and motoric information to a specialized brain network consisting of fronto-temporoparietal regions whose components are also part of the putative human mirror neuron system." This system refers to neurons that are part of mirroring behavior and play a vital role in social and emotional neuro-cognitive systems, including empathy, language acquisition, and other aspects we group within EQ. The importance of music in medicine has been revealed and confirmed consistently throughout neuroscientific research and is a critical element of our lab's approach. The Sensiturn is an excellent example of the musical range of these devices designed to emit compelling, sonorous, and melodious tones that are not limited by a patient's musical expertise or current range of motion. The instrument design allows growth, so improving patients will find they can even play specific familiar melodies through their expressive, rotational gesticulation. This responsive device enhances the healing experience for a patient, encouraging movement and proprioception through music.

Some patients rehabilitating from strokes lack proprioception or bodily awareness, in addition to suffering from weakness and hemiplegia. A patient may retain sensations in their affected limb while still losing track of that limb in space when not directly observing their movements. The Sensiturn can help by providing associative anchors, connecting space with sound, thereby transforming intangible goals into measurable milestones. The Sensiturn's immersive experience increases through multimodal, sound-responsive lights and colors, which congruently and concurrently change in time with the music.

MediMusical Instruments have undergone extensive pilot and user testing with patients, caregivers, clinicians, and other stakeholders, with initial data already revealing beneficial aspects. Our collaborators at MGH support this effort, as it is poised to fill a significant gap in providing health care from a distance during this telehealth "new normal." During the COVID-19 pandemic we have seen extensive equity disparities in health care and the detrimental impact of this on our communities, nation, and world. Accessible, customizable telehealth devices such as MediMusical Instruments could play a central role in providing accurate diagnostics and individualized treatment for patients in low-resource populations. Even in prepandemic studies, research has shown that despite efforts to make medicine more accessible, socioeconomic and systemic factors, including distance to medical services and the ability to go to appointments, impact patients on a daily basis. In fact, since telehealth visit options have expanded postpandemic, doctors have noted "dramatically reduced no-show rates among minority patients" and "an increased percentage of Medicaid enrollees seen via telehealth." A 2021 McKinsey & Company survey revealed that "telehealth utilization has stabilized at levels 38 times higher than before the pandemic," increasing accessibility. With over 83.4 percent of the world's population owning a smartphone and many more possessing mobile devices, these devices will make it easier to access higher-quality care from wherever home is. Regular access to the internet is not even required for patients to utilize their devices. Rieger's work also focuses on improving medical access and health equity, especially for patients whom the health-care system has historically marginalized. Our lab envisions that the telehealth MediMusical Instruments could be part of reducing this gap.

Looking to the future, we hope remote-health devices like MediMusical Instruments can ultimately support medical collaborations and standardized, equitable access to cutting-edge clinical interventions worldwide. We are also excited about the potential for music-based connections facilitated by these recuperative devices. Musical experiences can become even more immersive when shared. We envision that these devices could one day support the sonic collaborations of patients globally.

COMPOSING FOR HEALTH: BALANCING RESEARCH AND PRACTICE

As highlighted through these descriptions of vocal investigations and MediMusical Instruments, the MIT Media Lab's Opera of the Future group has long pursued a multipronged approach to expanding the power of music to increase self-awareness, build connection, and positively influence health and well-being. A core conviction has always been to deliver these audio-based advantages through custom-crafted musical compositions that attempt to strike a productive balance between experiments built from new research findings and "musical visions" that might inspire future research directions. In navigating this continuum, the group's philosophy has been closer to Schoenberg's open-ended, creative-oriented theories than to Hindemith's harmonic-series proscriptions, an approach further affirmed in Charles Rosen's seminal *Sonata Forms*. Rosen argues that musical form— even for something as supposedly canonical as the classical sonata—can only be explicitly described *after* the creation of the works, not used as preexisting templates during the creative process. This dynamic relationship between musical research and practice has been influenced by methods developed at Pierre Boulez's IRCAM in Paris in the 1980s, where Tod Machover was the inaugural director of Musical Research. These techniques have been further expanded at the MIT Media Lab, where the degree of interdisciplinarity and the potential for art-influencing-life (as well as the inverse) are viewed through a much wider lens.

Researchers at Opera of the Future firmly believe that the physical and mental health benefits of music composition can be used to greatly improve the lives of the general public. Long interested in increasing the potential for music to play a transformative role in the lives of individuals and societies, we started work on health and well-being applications in 2004, as a direct result of the strongly positive response to our international Toy Symphony project. Toy Symphony was designed to allow children to actively perform and participate in music creation through the use of specially designed Music Toys (some of which were subsequently commercialized by Fisher-Price, as well as prototyped for potential release by Mattel, Hasbro, and LEGO), as well as Hyperscore graphic composing software. The project successfully enabled kids to collaborate with major soloists, such as violinist Joshua Bell, and symphony orchestras, including BBC Symphony, Deutsches Symphonie-Orchester Berlin, and others, stimulating an interest in music learning as well as leading to the development of more general skills in communication and expression. On the basis of these results, we were invited by the Mass Cultural Council to see if such tools and techniques could be beneficial in a medical context, for both physical and mental illnesses. We conducted an intensive series of workshops and experiments at Tewksbury State Hospital from 2004 to 2008, with powerful results. Using Hyperscore primarily, which allows for sophisticated, highly personal musical compositions to be created through an intuitive, accessible-to-all graphical interface, we found that individuals with various conditions such as schizophrenia, bipolar disorder, and depression reported personal benefits of composing and sharing personal music. The process of using Hyperscore has allowed many—such as Dan Ellsey, a young man with cerebral palsy who has become a long-term collaborator—to express themselves through music when most other forms of communication were prohibitive. As Dan Ellsey said from the stage of the 2008 TED Conference, through the use of a laborious mechanical speaking machine, "I am thirty-four years old and I have cerebral palsy. I *have* always loved music, and I am excited to be able to conduct my own music with this software." Indeed, when Dan then performed his Hyperscore-created composition *My Eagle Song*, the TED audience erupted into a extended standing ovation; they had seen and heard Dan in a way that only music could convey. These and other Tewksbury experiments have been well documented in Adam Boulanger's master's and PhD work developed in our group. As Boulanger writes, "By bringing accessible composition tools to residential hospital communities, patients emerged as composers, instead of merely participants in music groups. . . . [For example,] when Pam came to Tewksbury Hospital she was clinically depressed and homeless. Her treatment team deemed it impossible to consider discharge at the time. . . . Pam excelled in the Hyperscore sessions [and] when the final concert was held, she was able to say she was moving into a new apartment and being discharged. . . . In Pam's words, 'there was new hope' thanks to the Hyperscore interventions."

VOCAL VIBRATIONS: FINDING YOUR SOUND IN AN OCEAN OF COMPLEXITY

In addition to inventing tools to enable others to create their own music for potentially powerful therapeutic effects, both mentally and physically, the Media Lab's Opera of the Future group has been devoted to producing its own original music. Such compositions—through both active and passive audience participation—have the potential to calm and stimulate the mind and to encourage creative contributions at the individual and collective level. *Vocal Vibrations* is an experiment in combining listening, singing, and vibratory feedback to fully engage the participant in an emotionally rewarding, mentally focused, auditory journey. Tod Machover designed the *Vocal Vibrations* composition as a game to stimulate careful listening. The piece has various forms and lengths that adapt to different situations: for live performance by a vocal ensemble, meditative listening, and active participation. In each version, there is a musical pitch—the D above middle C—that remains constant throughout. All of the musical material is derived from recorded singing voices, provided by soprano Sara Heaton and the Blue Heron vocal ensemble, conducted by Scott Metcalfe. The voices were processed to obscure beginnings and endings of notes, so that boundaries between sounds could blend magically, reminiscent of the blurred borders—or lack thereof—in a Rothko painting. The work starts and ends with a solo D, developing more and more complex harmonies and textures upon this base note—a kind of *cantus firmus* in the very middle of the texture. The invitation to the public is, first, to try to focus on that D no matter the sonic surroundings, and second, to match the D with one's own voice, in any comfortable octave. Though this is quite possible for any listener, participants may find difficulty in identifying a volume level where one's voice complements and reinforces the accompaniment without obscuring it. To augment listener immersion, we designed and built the Orb, a ceramic, handheld device that translates the sound of one's voice into accurate vibrations in the object, allowing you "to hold your voice in your hands." The listener is instructed not only to reproduce the D, but to "follow" it as closely as possible, imitating its changing tone quality and spatial placement. Doing so creates a kind of "vibratory massage" inside one's head, which is reinforced by the vibrations in the Orb.

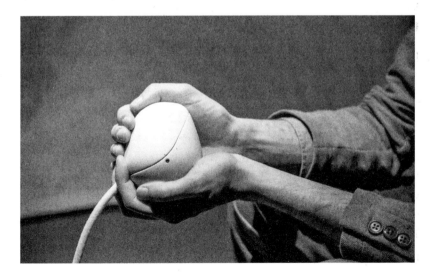

In this way, the composition is an invitation—in both five-minute and twenty-minute versions—to practice calm focus in the midst of increasing distractions. Resulting data, collected through surveys and interviews with participants, as well as by the use of specially designed vibration sensors applied to different facial regions, strongly suggest that *Vocal Vibrations* did indeed increase concentration, reduce anxiety, and connect listening, vocalizing, and experiencing physical sensation in powerfully satisfying ways.

GAMMIFIED: HIDING HEALING FREQUENCIES IN A MUSICAL LANDSCAPE

If the musical goal of *Vocal Vibrations* is to allow listeners to hear and imitate a simple sound in complex surroundings, the goal of *Gammified* (2019) was the opposite: to embed a complex, curative sound in musical surroundings so that it could produce healing effects while being almost inaudible—felt but not heard. The hidden sound was based on the gamma 40 Hz frequency, with a modified, time-variant square wave that was shown to most effectively entrain the brain to regenerate its own gamma signals. This audio signal—while having been demonstrated by our MIT colleagues Li-Huei Tsai and Ed Boyden to stimulate microglial cells that would in turn eliminate plaque and reverse the effects of Alzheimer's disease among other conditions—proved to be rather aggressive and unpleasant to listen to. We experimented with varying the signal spectrum to produce more interesting variety, and then augmented it with processed recordings of acoustic double bass (as 40 Hz is almost equivalent to the lowest E on the bass), as well as with specially crafted electronic sounds. Just as Tod Machover created *Vocal Vibrations* with a single D always constant, he composed *Gammified* so that the low E 40 Hz pedal tone would always be present. Beyond this, because numerous harmonics are necessary in order to deliver the full therapeutic effects of gamma, Machover decided to base his entire composition on this complex spectrum. As this work was created for the Kronos Quartet, he exploited the great timbral variety that string instruments are capable of producing through controlling the speed, pressure, and position of the bow as it courses over the strings. Indeed, at its core, *Gammified* is a compositional exploration of a complex spectrum based on low E that blends a live string quartet, specially crafted gamma tone, and audio electronics to invite the listener to experience the meditative calm that is induced through the constant low frequency, while becoming increasingly aware of the individual harmonics of this sonority. Over the course of the work, harmonics become more and more independent, branching out into overlapping melodies, and finally blossoming into a unison melody played by all four instruments. This feels like a homecoming, a kind of full acceptance of the presence of this gamma tone and a recognition of its power to provide continuity and subvocal grounding. Importantly, while the ear was following the spectral variations of gamma harmonics, the ever-present gamma tone was stealthily delivering its therapeutic entrainment and mental stimulation.

In 2021, Machover created a version of this work—at the request of

soprano Renée Fleming—that adds a vocal line to the texture. As with *Vocal Vibrations*, the voice adds an extra element—sometimes calm, sometimes cascading—that the ear can follow as the gamma frequencies sink into the mind.

WELL-BEING IN BILBAO: A CITY SYMPHONY DESIGNED FOR COMMUNAL HEALING

A third direction of compositional work undertaken by the Opera of the Future group to promote health and well-being is the City Symphony series. It is well established that creativity helps young people develop a sense of agency, open-mindedness, and optimism as potential antidotes to alleviate despair, depression, and destruction, and we have sought to expand on these qualities through our City Symphony projects. The series was launched by Tod Machover in collaboration with the Toronto Symphony Orchestra in 2012, with the goal of creating sonic portraits of cities worldwide, through listening to and collecting real sounds in each city, in addition to traditional means such as instrumental, vocal, and electronic resources. Our group invites all city residents to collaborate on the resulting symphony, sparking a communal investigation of problems and potentials unique to that place and creating new connections among people of extremely varied backgrounds. We develop special tools—such as Hyperscore, Constellation,

Media Scores, and Repertoire Remix—to allow people with any level of musical training, or lack thereof, to contribute.

At the time of writing, we have recently launched a new kind of City Symphony—one devoted to an exploration of how to build communities that support health and well-being—but this time on a global scale. Invited by the Paris-based Wellbeing Project to develop such a project for its inaugural summit in Bilbao in June 2022, we began by asking young people in that city to create Hyperscore pieces that reflected their feelings about well-being: What does it sound like to feel healthy? What does it sound like to be ill? What sound reflects an experience you had during the pandemic? What does it sound like to be well taken care of when you are ill? What does it sound like to be alone? What would be the sound of a community where well-being was a high priority, deeply and equitably shared? We collected these Hyperscore pieces and showed them to graduate students in our Opera of the Future group back at the Media Lab, who in turn created electronic mini compositions in response. Some of the outcomes of this process were shared in Machover's keynote address at the Wellbeing Summit and further developed through a series of public workshops in Bilbao. The process will continue for the next two years, by collaboration with regional Wellbeing Summits around the world, leading to the presentation of *Wellbeing of the World: A Global Symphony*—cocreated with both the local community and the international community of health professionals, social entrepreneurs, civic leaders, and artists assembled for the first time at this conference—at the next Wellbeing Summit in June 2025. In this way we will experiment with combining access to musical creativity with sonic reflections on the goals and potentials for a "healthy society" as interdependent means for activating awareness and producing positive outcomes, leading—we hope—to greater well-being for all. As Leonard Slatkin, conductor and then music director of the Detroit Symphony Orchestra, said of our *Symphony in D* project, "The concept of using the sounds of our city, both those found and those submitted by others, and then incorporating them into an orchestral work is quite amazing. . . . Clearly this is a project of unique interest to all those interested in the power of collaborative thinking." We expect the City Symphony concept to become even more powerful when scaled to connect people worldwide through shared music and common concerns.

TOWARD PERSONALIZED MUSICAL MEDICINE

Our experience with the work described in this chapter reinforces our conviction that music—whether produced by our own voices, experimented with through therapeutic tools and interfaces, created and shaped by anyone, or simply listened to actively and fully—has enormous potential for promoting individual and communal well-being on an unprecedented scale. At the same time we are humbled by the many mysteries that remain about how music actually works its magic, and about how specific music might be designed and shared to address targeted physical and mental ailments for maximal human benefit. However, we remain convinced that an integrated program of fundamental audio research, therapeutic tool design and testing, and visionary composition creation is the most fruitful path toward establishing a new field of Personalized Musical Medicine. No musical endeavor is more promising or more urgent, and none more deserving of our attention, collaboration, and support.

Porous Density

::

LIZ DILLER

Founding Partner, Diller Scofidio + Renfro

In October 2018, New Yorkers were invited to an unprecedented cultural experience, an immersive, free choral work, stretching along a mile of public park built atop an abandoned elevated railroad spur. The Mile-Long Opera: a biography of 7 o'clock was co-created by architects Diller Scofidio + Renfro and Pulitzer Prize–winning composer David Lang, with texts by poets Anne Carson and Claudia Rankine. The work shared personal stories from hundreds of New Yorkers about life in their rapidly changing city, in the setting of the High Line, perhaps the most renowned cultural project of Diller Scofidio + Renfro.

After working on the design of the High Line for over a decade and witnessing the rapid transformation of the surrounding area, I thought a lot about the life cycle of the city—its decay and rebirth—full of opportunities and contradictions. This vantage presented an opportunity for creative reflection about the speed of change of the contemporary city and the stories of its inhabitants. We had a thousand New York singers, both professional and nonprofessional. Having this sort of collective public event by and for New Yorkers created a novel sense of community and citizenship.

Human health and human behavior are undeniably, inextricably linked to the spaces and structures in which we live, work, and move. I believe absolutely in architecture as a discipline elevated to the status of an art form, one that plays a crucial role in our well-being. It is far more complex than the pursuit of creating beauty. Beauty is undefinable, subjective, and cultural, not always something that is an agreed-upon aesthetic, and aesthetics change over time. I find beauty in things that are unresolved—an intriguing mathematic equation or physics problem, for instance. Beauty might be a space that you can't quite understand, that triggers your imagination in some way. But reaching beyond beauty or aesthetics, architecture is generative, with enormous impact on our physical and mental health, and virtually unlimited potential for improving the quality of our lives as individuals and communities. Architects, when permitted, can safeguard open space, green space, cultural space; encourage activity and participation; give people experiences of awe, novelty, community; help balance work and life modalities, and advance the cause of equity. In the context of rapid city growth, and the increasing commodification of every inch of buildings, these are crucial values. When you create a great public space and make it open and inviting to everyone, people behave differently. Rather than being defensive about public space, we must be generous in providing more of it. When we are, people will be good citizens, active, engaged, and healthier.

Modern architecture and medicine are bound together in an endless battle against illness. For architects and planners practicing at the turn of the twentieth century, urban density was the enemy of health. As urban populations exploded in industrialized cities, the working poor were condemned to overcrowded and unsanitary slums, susceptible to diseases like tuberculosis, cholera, typhoid fever, yellow fever, and the Spanish flu. At the same time, a revolution in public health and mass production was handing architects unprecedented tools to confront public health challenges. Massive sanitariums, towers rising in the park, and wedding cake buildings stepping back into zoning envelopes became the monuments to a modern crusade against density and disease. By the 1950s cities had thinned out as populations fled in droves to the suburbs. At the scale of the building, the modernist architect's moral obsession with hygiene prompted an aesthetic of clean lines, platonic forms, and minimal ornamentation, smoothing out any nooks and crannies where germs might lurk.

In the late 1990s and early 2000s, urban density made a comeback, but with all its positive social and economic benefits: demographic diversity, cultural vibrancy, reduced dependency on cars, concentrated educational resources, positive environmental consequences, and a sharing economy that promised to democratize access to goods and services. Architects and planners also rediscovered the advantages of the mixed-use compactness championed by Jane Jacobs. As young professionals started streaming back into cities in search of like-minded talent, dilapidated neighborhoods were redeveloped into creative, tech, fashion, and finance clusters. New buildings rapidly infilled formerly vacant lots, and an embrace of adaptive reuse transformed derelict industrial structures into everything from co-working incubators to luxury housing to parks—for example, the High Line, created atop an abandoned elevated railroad. With this pressure on the real estate market, developers became increasingly speculative and started turning to AI-based algorithmic design to squeeze every last dollar out of every last square inch of space. Meanwhile, engineering technology was catching up to reurbanization, making it possible to build supertall towers on sites barely larger than the footprint of a townhouse. Medical studies validated this urban renaissance: urbanites have enjoyed longer, healthier, and more intellectually engaged lives than their counterparts outside of cities.

It was not until 2020 that urban density once again became a threat to human health. COVID-19 defined the metrics of human safety as the throw of a sneeze. Apocalyptic predictions about the future of in-person work, learning, cultural institutions, and shopping all called into question the benefits of the city. Architecture seemed impotent in the face of a microscopic pathogen that preyed on all facets of urban life. The densest cities became ghost towns. Yet if medieval Florence thrived after losing 80 percent of its population to the plague, it was not unrealistic to assume that the modern-day metropolis could rebound. And it has. People continue flocking to cities despite ever-stronger viruses, which medicine and architecture must be prepared to confront. The future of the city depends on a paradigm shift. It calls for a new public-private-community approach to civic space. This is a challenge in our increasingly privatized, land-scarce, and cash-strapped cities afflicted by political short-termism. How can we promote density without breathing each other's air?

THOUGHTS TOWARD A POROUS DENSITY

- To survive and prosper, cities must adopt a new ethos of oxygenation. We must aerate rather than fortify the built environment.
- Buildings must be oxygenated in three dimensions—punctured, staggered, slipped, stepped, sheared, and cantilevered to produce more outdoor space.
- Access to terraces, courtyards, and rooftops can no longer be treated as a luxury but a human right.
- Amended building codes must force developers to bury mechanical equipment in the bodies of new buildings to clear rooftops for accessible green space.
- A terrace is to a building as a park is to a city. Like any complex organism, as a city grows, so must its lung capacity. This is not just a question of acreage but also equitable distribution: green spaces should be evenly spread out and scaled up from pocket parks on every block, to neighborhood-level gardens, to citywide central parks.
- As building lots fill out, new buildings should incorporate publicly accessible green space cascading up and through buildings to parks in the sky.
- A democratic public realm should extend through the lobbies of office buildings to allow free pedestrian flow in all directions. This imperative also extends to other construction. At the Tianjin Juilliard School, a building composed of four pavilions, glass bridges span an expansive public space that extends the surrounding park into the building, inviting students, visitors, and concertgoers to mingle, relax, and experience the students practicing and giving informal performances.
- As cities move away from dependence on cars, parking lanes should be reclaimed as neighborhood porches.
- Buildings could be utilized in the fourth dimension. Micro-timeshares can allow double and triple use of space according to staggered work shifts that track the twenty-four-hour global day.
- Floor area bonuses, tax breaks, and other financial incentives should encourage developers to build permanent voids and unprogrammed space.
- To protect our mental health, we cannot condemn our shared cultural institutions to a future of cyclical lockdowns. All institutions should

own inflatable pop-up venues equipped with baseline acoustics, lighting, and environmental controls. The post-COVID cultural citizen can forgive the imperfect sound diluted by the drone of the city if it allows for uninterrupted engagement with the arts.

- New schools, concert halls, museums, and libraries must be supple and responsive to transcend the physical limits of their geo-fixed buildings. (The Shed at Hudson Yards, a 200,000-square-foot cultural space with a telescoping outer shell, is one of our projects that responds to this imperative.) Institutions should be mobile and travel the city—anywhere, anytime.

- Abandoned office buildings and storefronts that are the casualties of the retail apocalypse should host institutional pop-ups.

- Waterways should be considered part of a mobility infrastructure supporting floating institutions that visit up- and downstream communities.

- City streets should be embedded with power, data, and strong points to enable all types of outdoor plug-and-play events.

- Underused, uninviting existing cultural spaces should be reimagined to welcome everyone. One example would be our physical and philosophical update at Lincoln Center for the Performing Arts, reinterpreting the modernist campus to speak to a more diverse audience after decades of social change. These public space projects include a new grand entrance to the campus; a redesigned main plaza and fountain; a bosque and redesigned reflecting pool; a network of smart technologies to deliver real-time information throughout the campus; a grass hillside atop a new restaurant and screening rooms for the Film Society; the Lincoln Center Pedestrian Bridge; and the opening of Sixty-Fifth Street from a service corridor into the new "Avenue of the Arts."

- Equity must be prioritized. It is a global phenomenon that the poor are often concentrated near factories or industrial use areas where rates of asthma or cancer are disproportionately high.

While still a contentious topic, "it is not density that is the enemy, nor is it the virus; it is greed." In the face of privatization where every square foot is commodified to be bought, sold, and profited on, there is little room left for air. Cities have been seized by extremes, vacillating from explosive densification, to sudden dedensification, to speculative redensification—all the while forfeiting the windfalls to real estate developers. There is a third way that does not succumb to this zero-sum cycle: a porous density that embraces both the nature of cities and nature in cities.

Blueprint for Cultivating the Field of Neuroarts

SUSAN MAGSAMEN, MAS
Executive Director, International Arts + Mind Lab (IAM Lab)
Center for Applied Neuroaesthetics, Johns Hopkins University
School of Medicine

RUTH J. KATZ, JD, MPH
Executive Director, Health, Medicine and Society Program (HMS),
Aspen Institute

Codirectors, NeuroArts Blueprint

Imagine a world in which music and the visual arts, dance and movement, theater and storytelling, architecture and design, and many other art modalities are as common in the clinical arsenal as drugs and surgery. Consider a time when doctors routinely write prescriptions for museum visits, health insurers reimburse arts practitioners for their clinical skills, and anyone seeking a pathway to personal or community health and well-being has ready access to evidence-based arts practices.

In the fall of 2019 the Johns Hopkins International Arts + Mind Lab Center for Applied Neuroaesthetics (IAM Lab) and the Aspen Institute's Health, Medicine & Society Program (HMS) came together to begin making that a reality. There was already so much happening at the intersection of science, arts, technology, and health, but no center of gravity existed to bring the strands of accumulating knowledge together. We and many others believed it was time to cultivate the field of neuroarts, defined here as the transdisciplinary and extradisciplinary study of how the arts and aesthetic experiences measurably change the body, brain, and behavior—and how this knowledge can be translated into specific practices that advance health and well-being.

Just as bioethics and climate science have evolved into widely accepted, well-funded areas of study and practice because people from many disciplines came together as partners, neuroarts can coalesce and be sustained only by transdisciplinary collaboration and commitment. As we work to solidify the field, we honor the energy, creativity, and leadership that others have already dedicated to using the arts to promote health and well-being. Indeed, it is only because such a deep bench of pioneers has shown the way that the need to bring them together across their many disciplines and experiences has become apparent.

A FIELD READY TO COALESCE

Armed with ever more sophisticated scanning technology and deepening knowledge of the brain, researchers across disciplines are shedding light on how the arts can improve physical and mental health; amplify the ability to prevent, manage, or recover from disease challenges; enhance brain development in children; and foster well-being through multiple biological systems.

Consider how a growing body of scientific evidence is already being deployed. Music is helping people recover from depression and improving the memory of those with Alzheimer's disease. Creative arts therapists are using mask making to help traumatized military veterans confront long-hidden wounds. Virtual reality is proving to be a mobility aid for people with physical disabilities, and a tool to manage pain. Dance can reduce the symptoms of Parkinson's disease, while drawing bolsters social and emotional well-being in young people. Along with their value in improving the health of individuals, the role of the arts in strengthening communities is also coming into sharper focus.

The combination of scientific information and practice experience has created an unprecedented opportunity to transform the way in which we approach health and health care in the United States and around the globe. The goal of the NeuroArts Blueprint: Advancing the Science of Arts, Health, and Wellbeing, the initiative described in this chapter, is to cultivate that opportunity.

The synergy between the two institutions guiding the NeuroArts Blueprint is unparalleled. IAM Labs is a multidisciplinary translation research-to-practice initiative that brings together brain scientists and arts practitioners to accelerate the field of neuroaesthetics, with the goal of amplifying human potential. A commitment to both art and science as tools for building a just and equitable society is a founding principle of the Aspen Institute, while HMS, the Institute's health policy program, has a stellar reputation for identifying cross-disciplinary strategies to address some of the nation's greatest health challenges.

From the outset of our partnership, we recognized the need for a stewardship role. In the research realm, advances are being made in basic scientific discovery, translational and clinical investigations, and evaluation. Across disparate settings—in clinics and hospitals, community health centers and group care settings, community arts, social service and advocacy organizations, workplaces, and public spaces—practices that elevate the connection between arts and health are coming into widespread use.

In the United States substantial federal resources are dedicated to their convergence, especially within the National Institutes of Health and the National Endowment for the Arts. State and local public agencies are also engaged, as are numerous professional and cultural associations. A great deal of work is taking place in global settings as well, notably in Australia, Canada, Cuba, Finland, New Zealand, Sweden, and the United Kingdom. The World Bank and the World Health Organization have also taken up the cause with their own activities.

Yet neuroarts is far from realizing its potential. The overarching challenge has been fragmentation at every turn. Prior to the NeuroArts Blueprint initiative, there had been no dedicated effort to define the ecosystem, nurture an interactive network of stakeholders, or foster vigorous institutional commitments to the field. Lacking opportunities to connect in professional circles, scientists and arts practitioners have remained unfamiliar with one another's terminology, priorities, and norms. Implicit biases have tended to assign greater worth to certain disciplines, experiences, and sources of knowledge over others, and the voices of community advocates and healthcare consumers have too often been left out of the neuroarts conversation altogether.

There is a litany of other barriers as well. Published research typically remains within the confines of a single scientific discipline, and lack of communication has resulted in duplicative studies, prevented discovery from building on discovery, and limited generalizable conclusions. The absence of common reporting guidelines, an inflexible view of what constitutes rigor, a narrow understanding of how to measure success, and inconsistent methodological approaches are further impediments. Molecular-level analysis and placebo-controlled, multisite trials produce vital evidence, but without consensus on other study designs, protocols, and outcome measures that can also generate valid knowledge, many stakeholders are excluded from making full contributions.

In the practice arena, disciplinary silos have discouraged cross-fertilization, too often forcing practitioners to experiment and innovate alone, observing results that are neither evaluated nor shared. Sparse opportunities for trans-disciplinary educational and training opportunities, a dearth of supportive public policies and insurance reimbursement, and the lack of robust funding add to the difficulty of scaling and sustaining the neuroarts field. As a result of all this, neuroarts has yet to be adequately recognized by mainstream medicine or public health, let alone fully integrated into either of them.

The NeuroArts Blueprint initiative is working to change all of that. Following its launch in 2019, a stellar twenty-five-member advisory board came together under the leadership of co-chairs Renée Fleming, renowned soprano and arts advisor to the Kennedy Center; Eric Nestler, neuroscientist, dean for Academic Affairs at the Icahn School of Medicine at Mount Sinai, and chief scientific officer of the Mount Sinai Health System; Michael Paseornek, originator and longtime president of Lionsgate Films Productions; and Anna Deavere Smith, actress, playwright, author, and professor.

Over the next eighteen months the Blueprint embarked on a vigorous information-gathering process, exchanging ideas with hundreds of experts and stakeholders. The work began with an in-depth literature review that led to the publication of "Neuroarts Today: State of an Emerging Field." We also held eight stakeholder convenings to explore communications, policy, practice, research, and technology, including two with a global focus; commissioned KPMG to conduct an economic analysis ("Alzheimer's Disease and Music Engagement Economic Impact Analysis"); published findings from a three-hundred-person survey of neuroarts stakeholders, conducted by Lake Research ("Findings from an Online Survey of Stakeholders"); and published a World Bank report that linked art to economic development ("Human Capital and the Arts at the World Bank Group"). All of these stage-setting publications are available on the NeuroArts Blueprint website.

As an argument for policy change, the potential economic value of neuroarts had particular resonance. While more research is needed, KPMG's independent economic analysis suggested that using music to ease symptoms of Alzheimer's disease could have a significant payoff. If 30 percent of the population diagnosed with this devastating form of dementia engaged with music, the analysts concluded, it would generate a total economic output of $996 million, contribute $830 million to GDP, sustain 7,784 jobs across the United States, generate $369 million in labor income, and produce $126 million in government tax revenues.

Our legwork also uncovered significant enthusiasm for neuroarts across fields that included science, health care and health policy, the arts, philanthropy, technology, and business. In the three-hundred-person survey, stakeholders agreed by a solid majority that they were interested in engaging in or helping to cultivate the field. Significantly, 77 percent of the surveyed population under age fifty said they were "extremely" or "very" likely to engage. Respondents also broadly agreed that collaboration across disciplines is the way to progress.

Building on our analyses and findings, in December 2021 we released the NeuroArts Blueprint: Advancing the Science of Arts, Health, and Wellbeing, an ambitious and far-reaching plan for cultivating the field of neuroarts. In laying out both a five-year strategy and a longer-term action plan, the Blueprint spells out the steps necessary to change the narrative about what drives health and ultimately to transform the culture.

MEETING THE CHALLENGES

The explosion of knowledge about neuroarts, and the consensus recommendations for applying that knowledge to individual and community health and well-being make this an optimal time to promote transdisciplinary collaborations.

The Blueprint highlights revolutionary advances in imaging capacities, biomarkers, and other noninvasive technologies that allow us to map and measure what happens as we take in the world through the portals of sound, sight, scent, touch, and taste. We have learned that the brain is agile, changing nanosecond by nanosecond in response to stimuli, and that the interconnected neuronal networks engaged with reward, motor activity, perception, and the senses are activated by the arts in ways unmatched by anything else.

The Blueprint gives equal attention to the army of arts practitioners who are driving practice forward. Validated by a combination of professional experiences and a growing body of quantitative and qualitative evidence, they are applying the power of creative expression to some of the world's most formidable health challenges.

Scientists and artists actually have much in common. Skilled at exploring provocative questions that can generate valid learnings, the work of both sectors demands discipline and rigor while also rewarding the ability to improvise. But disparate training and professional experiences, combined with their unique traditions and evidence-gathering approaches, mean the two sectors have not always paired seamlessly. Structural issues related to differentials in power, funding, and status have kept stakeholders in their separate silos. To foster effective collaboration between science and the arts, the Blueprint acknowledges the need for a level playing field. Only then can pioneers across sectors who share a commitment to neuroarts forge partnerships that generate a multiplier effect.

By working together to drive innovation on behalf of individual and community health and well-being, they can cultivate new approaches to longstanding and seemingly intractable problems. In recent years challenges have piled upon challenges, contributing to unprecedented declines in longevity among Americans. The twenty-first century has been scarred by the greatest economic crisis to strike since the Great Depression and the first global pandemic in one hundred years. Worldwide, preventable chronic diseases are taking a terrible toll, vast numbers of children and adolescents are struggling with unrecognized and untreated mental illness, the dementia caseload is rising, and communities are fracturing.

For all its power, clinical medicine cannot solve these problems alone. Even with so many needs unmet, the cumulative economic burden of trying to grapple with them is enormous. In the United States, chronic diseases and mental health conditions consume 90 percent of the nation's $3.8 trillion health-care budget. Worldwide, the cost of dementia alone was $818 billion in 2015, representing more than 1 percent of the global gross domestic product that year.

To improve the health of individuals and populations, strengthen communities, and tackle the many other threats to well-being, we need more tools in our arsenal. A long-overdue reckoning with racism has further underscored the need for new narratives to challenge entrenched norms. In fostering the collective intelligence necessary to advance the emerging field of neuroarts, the Blueprint recognizes that equity must be at its core—a nonnegotiable commitment to dedicating the tools and sharing the power of the arts with all populations and in every community across culture, racial and ethnic backgrounds, socioeconomic status, skill sets, and more. Diversity, equity, and inclusion are woven into the fabric of the Blueprint initiative and the recommendations it embraces.

PRINCIPLES AND RECOMMENDATIONS

Although neuroarts as a widely recognized and broadly influential field will take many years to develop fully, knowledge will continue to build as we learn more about what works, in which settings, at what dose, and for whom. Based on iterative agreements of how we define and achieve success, measurable short-term wins and long-term milestones will be essential to track progress, guided by goals, objectives, and timelines.

Driven by a sense of urgency and inspired by the unprecedented opportunity at hand, the Blueprint lays out a systematic strategy for bringing science and the arts together in service to health and well-being. As we move along many parallel tracks to implement that strategy, the growth of neuroarts will also depend on developing educational and training pathways, dedicated funding, supportive public sector and private sector policies, effective leadership, well-crafted communications strategies, and infrastructure capacity.

Five Core Principles

These are the core principles on which the Blueprint is based:

- Experiencing art is fundamental to being human, a common thread across cultures, racial and ethnic backgrounds, age groups, income levels, and skill sets. The arts offer a shared language, a means of elevating diverse voices, and a catalyst for action.

- The arts, as expressed through many modalities, have demonstrable, evidence-based impacts on physiological and psychological health and well-being.
- Science and technology make possible the ability to understand and measure the biological effects of the arts and aesthetic experiences on individuals and populations.
- Neuroarts provides the connective tissue to bring together science, the arts, and technology as equal partners to advance health and well-being.
- The benefits of the neuroarts field must be readily, consistently, and equitably accessible to all populations across the life span and in every community around the world.

Five Core Recommendations

Rooted in these principles and the findings from our in-depth research, the Blueprint sets out the following core recommendations to guide the process of developing a neuroarts ecosystem, one that aligns stakeholders around common goals at the intersection of science, arts, technology, and health:

- **Strengthen the research foundation of neuroarts.** A synthesis of existing findings is the launching point for determining what we know, identifying gaps, and building on the evidence to learn more. Beyond the imperative of collecting, integrating, and sharing existing work, a rigorous quantitative and qualitative agenda will allow new scientific questions to be identified in the realms of basic, translational, clinical, and community-based research. Defining the core elements of arts-based interventions and developing consistent study design and evaluation protocols will enable comparisons and allow each set of findings to inform others. This approach requires a consensus among stakeholders on terminology, reporting requirements, high-quality methodology, outcome measures, and platforms on which to exchange knowledge and scale success.

Importantly, the neuroarts community will need to stretch its thinking about what constitutes rigor, respecting the many ways of knowing that can help determine the value of an intervention. In addition to traditional research designs, we need to identify innovative ways to understand the influence of arts on health and well-being that are equally exacting and replicable. A number of validated evaluation tools can contribute to measurement.

- **Honor and support the many arts practices that promote health and well-being.** To contribute their full potential to the growth of neuroarts, arts practitioners should be recognized and empowered as equal partners with scientists. They need opportunities to explore the biological underpinnings of their work, contribute to the growing body of evidence for the field, and share practices.

As well, the practitioner voice needs to be heard in conversations and convenings that explore taxonomy, articulate priorities for developing and testing interventions, consider the degree to which diverse arts practices can meet on common ground, and identify tools and techniques to adapt and scale effective interventions. When practitioners are embraced as co-designers of strategies, standards, and structures to advance the field, they gain the authority and visibility to pursue positive outcomes and inspire interest in their work.

Broad-based input at all levels helps to elevate practices that resonate with diverse populations. Ensuring that interventions are developed and implemented to meet the needs and goals identified by the individuals and communities they purport to serve requires intentionality, a commitment to inclusiveness, deep listening, and flexibility.

- **Expand and enrich educational and career pathways.** Well-defined educational and training pathways, course and curriculum development, and strategies for career advancement encourage entry into the neuroarts field and help retain those already working there. The establishment of a new field provides a rare opportunity to prioritize equity throughout the educational pipeline, with particular attention to race and gender.

To build capacity and expand scholarship and its translation, neuroarts education in some form should begin in early childhood, continue through secondary school, and offer well-defined on-ramps with undergraduate coursework and graduate-level degree programs. Although no single curriculum can ever serve an entire field, a package of synergistic courses and case studies can provide a shared grounding to link disciplines. The ultimate goal is to allow individuals to enter the field of neuroarts from almost anywhere.

In addition to traditional academic routes, new models that embrace multimodal delivery should be considered, including online courses and workshops, grand rounds, internships, and mentoring. Opportunities for collaboration and rewards, including scholarships and prizes targeted specifically at new and early-career investigators, can also widen interest. Deliberate educational boundary-busting is called for to encourage cross-cutting collaborations within and across the various scientific and practice disciplines that intersect with neuroarts.

- **Advocate for sustainable funding and promote effective policy.** As the neuroarts ecosystem evolves, dedicated and consistent funding and sound and innovative policies are essential to grow a broad-based transdisciplinary and extradisciplinary field. While individual champions will likely jump-start engagement, institutional commitments from a network of diverse public sector and private sector partners will ultimately be necessary for neuroarts to flourish.

In the public sector, establishing positive economic and social impact, whether by documenting systemwide cost savings or measurable effects on individual and community health and well-being, is likely to have particularly strong appeal. Globally, more information is needed about how nations are assigning public dollars, or blending public and private resources, to advance neuroarts. Evidence that engaging in arts activities will reduce demand for more costly health care could encourage insurers to provide coverage for arts-related interventions, while other incentives should be identified to attract philanthropies and employers. Social-impact investing, crowdsourcing, and other entrepreneurial opportunities are also potential entry points.

- **Build capacity, leadership, and communications strategies.** The neuroarts ecosystem requires a solid infrastructure that allows stakeholders to convene, connect, and partner. That infrastructure includes a clearing-house for information, aggregated data, research findings, case studies, and other resources. It also requires a center of gravity that draws together advocates, influencers, and champions; elevates voices that often go unheard; and fosters experimentation and innovation.

This developing field will need many kinds of leaders—early-career investigators and practitioners who think fluently across disciplines, dynamic institutions prepared to take center stage as momentum builds, and champions at every level and of every age. Comprehensive framing, messaging, and communications strategies using clear and accessible language are key. Rigorous data need to be presented, as do compelling stories that capture the vibrancy of neuroarts globally and the power of carefully implemented and evaluated interventions to achieve sought-after outcomes. Recruiting high-profile messengers, influencers, and local advocates to spread the word will also increase the field's reach.

LOOKING FORWARD

The NeuroArts Blueprint is a road map to the future. All of its recommendations and accompanying action steps are designed to draw in new champions, grow knowledge and translate it into use, innovate and scale effective pilot programs, and attract sustainable funding. To drive that process forward, we visualize creating a NeuroArts Resource Center to serve as a steward. Within this virtual hub, knowledge will be aggregated and action catalyzed; basic, translational, clinical, and community-based researchers will have opportunities to work hand in hand with practitioners to grow and apply findings; and all stakeholders will have a voice in shaping the direction of neuroarts.

Specifically, we are pursuing three core sets of activities in the first five years that follow publication of the Blueprint: building infrastructure, building evidence, and building community. The NeuroArts Resource Center will be a core tool. This highly interactive and continually updated compilation of neuroarts-related research, clinical findings, and arts practices from around the world, in all art modalities and for all outcomes, will enable intuitive searches and inquiries across a curated and dynamic landscape. Accompanying asset maps, including maps tracking research and practice activities, will draw on the aggregated data to define the field's reach.

The planned infrastructure also includes an Academic Research Consortium to foster transdisciplinary education, and a Community Arts Coalition, a virtual watering hole for artists and arts practitioners interested in neuroarts. To expand the evidence base, we will develop a consensus-driven research agenda, commission a series of field-building white papers, conduct further analyses of the economic benefits of neuroarts, and explore the feasibility of a comprehensive Neuroarts Mechanism Map that depicts the circuitry and systems of the brain that are engaged by art. The third priority area, building community, will launch with a framing strategy and a global communications plan to inform the outreach needed to bring diverse stakeholders on board.

Over time, as more transdisciplinary research flows through the pipeline and evidence-based pilot programs begin to scale, the synergies between science and practice will inform an interdependent ecosystem dedicated to using the arts to drive health and well-being. To evolve into a mature, sustainable field, neuroarts will need to align the incentives that foster institutional commitments—from governments; across global organizations; among scientific and arts bodies; and in academic, workplace, health-care, and community settings. From there, we can expect to see dedicated funding; degree programs and other educational opportunities that produce a diverse, well-trained workforce and career pathways that allow them to grow; and public and private policies that accommodate structural change.

Our long-term goal is that it becomes standard practice to use the arts to promote health and well-being—an expected part of discussions between patients and their doctors and a core component of clinical care and community building. Social workers, educators, local activists, employers, and consumers are among the constituents we expect to turn to arts interventions routinely. By fully integrating the arts into health-building activities that are accessible to all, we can foster individual health and well-being, strengthen our communities, and fulfill a human birthright.

Acknowledgments

So many remarkable people have contributed to the creation of this anthology. I would like to extend my sincere thanks to:

The many brilliant scientists, practitioners, and artists who authored chapters, for their invaluable contributions to this field and their willingness to share their work;

Dr. Francis Collins, former director of the National Institutes of Health, who brought the NIH into the conversation about the therapeutic power of music and welcomed collaboration with the Kennedy Center;

Deborah Rutter, president of the John F. Kennedy Center for the Performing Arts, for my appointment as Kennedy Center Artistic Advisor, for her support of these initiatives, and for her commitment to the collaboration with the NIH and NEA to share this science with the public;

The dedicated members of the NIH Music and Health Working group, who continue to advance this research, including Dr. Emmeline Edwards and Dr. Wen Chen from NCCIH, and Dr. Bob Finkelstein and Dr. Tom Cheever from NINDS;

The National Endowment for the Arts (NEA) for its continued collaboration, including Sunil Iyengar, head of research; Ann Meier Baker, director of Music and Opera; and Chair, Dr. Maria Rosario Jackson;

Susan Magsamen and Ruth Katz of the NeuroArts Blueprint and Christopher Bailey at the World Health Organization, each visionary leaders with whom I am fortunate to collaborate;

Executive editor for Viking Books, Rick Kot, for coming on this journey eighteen years after *The Inner Voice*, and for the integrity and quality he brings to every project he undertakes;

In my office, Chason Goldschmitz, who tirelessly kept track of every detail, working hand in hand with the publisher to shepherd this project forward; both Chason and Paul Batsel for editorial contributions, patience, and good humor;

And finally, Tim, Amelia, and Sage, who make life worth living.

About the Contributors

ABOUT THE EDITOR

Renée Fleming is one of the most highly acclaimed singers of our time, performing on the stages of the world's greatest opera houses and concert halls. Honored with five Grammy® awards and the US National Medal of Arts, she has sung for momentous occasions from the Nobel Peace Prize ceremony to the Diamond Jubilee Concert for Queen Elizabeth II at Buckingham Palace. In 2014 she brought her voice to a vast new audience when she became the first classical artist ever to sing the US National Anthem at the Super Bowl. A Kennedy Center Honoree in 2023, she was appointed by the World Health Organization as a Goodwill Ambassador for Arts and Health the same year.

Renée is known as a leading advocate for research at the intersection of arts, health, and neuroscience. As artistic advisor to the Kennedy Center for the Performing Arts, she launched the first ongoing collaboration between America's national cultural center and the National Institutes of Health. She has presented her own program *Music and Mind* in more than fifty cities around the world, earning Research!America's 2020 Isadore Rosenfeld Award for Impact on Public Opinion. In 2023 she received the David Mahoney Prize from the Harvard Mahoney Neuroscience Institute. During the pandemic, she created *Music and Mind LIVE*, a weekly web show amassing nearly 700,000 views from seventy countries. She is a founding advisor for major initiatives, including the Sound Health Network at the University of California San Francisco and the NeuroArts Blueprint, a project of Johns Hopkins University and the Aspen Institute.

Known for bringing new audiences to classical music and opera, Renée has sung not only with Luciano Pavarotti and Andrea Bocelli but also with Elton John, Paul Simon, Sting, Josh Groban, and Joan Baez. She has recorded everything from complete operas and song recitals to indie rock and jazz, and she has hosted a wide variety of television and radio broadcasts, including the Metropolitan Opera's *Live in HD* series and *Live from Lincoln Center*. She earned a Tony Award nomination for her performance in *Carousel* on Broadway, and her voice is featured on the soundtracks of Best Picture Oscar winners *The Shape of Water* and *The Lord of the Rings*.

Renée's memoir *The Inner Voice* was published by Viking in 2004 and has since been published in France, the United Kingdom, Germany, Japan, Poland, Russia, and China.

In addition to her work with the Kennedy Center, Renée has held artistic and consultancy roles for major arts institutions, including the Aspen Music Festival and School, Carnegie Hall, LA Opera, and Lyric Opera of Chicago. Other awards include the 2023 Crystal Award from the World Economic Forum, the Fulbright Lifetime Achievement Medal, the Polar Music Prize, the Order of Merit of the Federal Republic of Germany, and France's Légion d'honneur. She holds honorary doctorates from eight leading universities. reneefleming.com.

ABOUT THE CONTRIBUTORS

Christopher Bailey is the Arts and Health Lead at the World Health Organization and a cofounder of the Jameel Arts and Health Lab. The lab focuses on rigorous evaluations of arts-based health interventions with an eye to scalability and reach to vulnerable populations. Its Healing Arts brand focuses on outreach and has supported municipal Arts and Health activations around the world. A trained actor as well as a twenty-year WHO veteran, Bailey uses his theater skills not only to communicate the health benefits of the arts but to exemplify them.

Sara Beck, PhD, is an assistant professor of psychology as well as a lifelong singer and songwriter. She got her PhD from Vanderbilt University in Nashville, Tennessee, and currently teaches at Randolph College in Lynchburg, Virginia. There, she leads an interdisciplinary undergraduate lab focused on children's musical engagement and continues to release new music and work professionally as a studio vocalist and producer. Her musical output spans two decades and eight albums, with highlights including singing the theme song for Kevin Costner's Emmy-winning mini-series, *Hatfields & McCoys,* and touring internationally as a solo artist. She is also a parent to two daughters, both of whom inspire her research and creative writing. [sbeck@randolphcollege.edu; sarabeck.net]

Joke Bradt, PhD, MT-BC, is professor and program director of the PhD in Creative Arts Therapies program at Drexel University (Philadelphia) and a board-certified music therapist. Her federally funded research is focused on the development and testing of music therapy interventions for chronic pain management. She has presented her work extensively at national and international conferences and has authored and coauthored many music therapy articles and book chapters. She is the lead author of several Cochrane systematic reviews on music interventions with medical patients.

Rosanne Cash is one of the country's pre-eminent singer-songwriters. She has released fifteen albums of extraordinary songs that have earned four Grammy Awards. Cash is also an author whose four books include the bestselling memoir *Composed*. Her essays have appeared in *The New York Times*, *Rolling Stone*, *Oxford American*, *The Nation*, and many more print and online publications. In addition to regular touring, Cash has partnered in programming collaborations with Carnegie Hall, Lincoln Center, SFJAZZ, the Minnesota Orchestra, and the Library of Congress. Cash received the 2021 Edward MacDowell Medal, awarded since 1960 to an artist who has made an outstanding contribution to American culture. She is the first woman composer to receive this prestigious honor.

Anjan Chatterjee, MD, is the founding director of the Penn Center for Neuroaesthetics. He wrote *The Aesthetic Brain* and coedited *Brain, Beauty, and Art*, *Neuroethics in Practice*, and *The Roots of Cognitive Neuroscience*. He received the Geschwind Prize in Cognitive Neurology from the American Academy of Neurology and the Arnheim Prize for contributions to Psychology and the Arts from the American Psychological Association. He was the past president of the International Association of Empirical Aesthetics, and the Behavioral/ Cognitive Neurology Society.

Wen G. Chen, MMSc, PhD, is branch chief for basic and mechanistic research in the Division of Extramural Research at the National Center for Complementary and Integrative Health (NCCIH), NIH, overseeing fundamental science research, translational research, mechanistic clinical research, and methodology and technology development related to all complementary and integrative health approaches. Dr. Chen is also the chair for the Trans-NIH Interoception Research Working Group and the program lead for the Trans-NIH Music and Health Working Group. Dr. Chen received her master's degree from Harvard Medical School, PhD from Harvard University, and postdoctoral training at MIT. Prior to NCCIH, she worked at Cell Press/ *NEURON*, National Institute of Mental Health, and National Institute on Aging.

Francis Collins, MD, PhD, is a physician-scientist known for his leadership of the International Human Genome Project that read out the first copy of the human DNA instruction book in 2003. He subsequently served three US presidents as director of the National Institutes of Health (NIH) from 2009 to 2021. His own research has led to new insights about cystic fibrosis, diabetes, and progeria, a rare disorder of premature aging. His love of music led to his bringing together NIH scientists, Renée Fleming, and the Kennedy Center to cofound the Sound Health program, providing research opportunities for performers, music therapists, and neuroscientists to work together in new and creative ways.

Antonio Damasio, MD, PhD, is Dornsife Professor of Neuroscience, Psychology and Philosophy, and director of the Brain and Creativity Institute, University of Southern California. Damasio has made seminal contributions to the understanding of brain processes underlying decision-making, affect, and consciousness. He is one of the most highly cited scientists of his generation. His books include *Descartes' Error, Feeling of What Happens, Looking for Spinoza, Self Comes to Mind, Strange Order of Things,* and *Feeling and Knowing,* which are translated worldwide. He is the recipient of major scientific prizes, and holds honorary doctorates from several leading universities, including the École Polytechnique Fédérale de Lausanne [EPFL] and the Sorbonne.

Hanna Damasio, MD, is University Professor, Dana Dornsife Professor of Neuroscience, and director of the Dana and David Dornsife Cognitive Neuroscience Imaging Center at the University of Southern California. She is a highly cited neuroscientist and the author of the award-winning *Lesion Analysis in Neuropsychology* (Oxford University Press) and *Human Brain Anatomy in Computerized Images* (also Oxford University Press), the first brain atlas based on computerized imaging data. Hanna Damasio is a Fellow of the American Academy of Arts & Sciences and the American Neurological Association. She is the recipient of numerous scientific prizes and honorary doctorates.

Elizabeth Diller cofounded Diller Scofidio + Renfro with Ricardo Scofidio in 1981. Their studio led two of New York's largest recent architectural and urban planning initiatives: the adaptive reuse of an obsolete, industrial rail infrastructure into the High Line, a 1.5-mile-long public park, and the transformation of Lincoln Center for the Performing Arts' half-century-old campus. Her work has reshaped the cultural landscape of New York with the renovation and expansion of the Museum of Modern Art and The Shed. Diller also cocreated, produced, and directed *The Mile-Long Opera,* an urban choral performance featuring one thousand singers and a promenading audience atop the High Line. She is a professor of architectural design at Princeton University.

Emmeline Edwards, PhD, is the director of the Division of Extramural Research, National Center for Complementary and Integrative Health (NCCIH),

NIH. In that capacity, she is responsible for the development and implementation of all scientific and administrative programs of the Center. Dr. Edwards is co-chair of the NIH Music and Health Working Group, where she helps to galvanize and develop evidence-based research exploring the role of creative arts in health practices and policies. Prior to joining NIH, Dr. Edwards was a tenured associate professor of pharmacology and neuroscience at the University of Maryland, where she developed a genetic model of depression. She currently chairs World Women in Neuroscience, an international mentoring and networking group.

Kenneth Elpus, PhD, is professor of music education and associate director of the School of Music at the University of Maryland, where he prepares pre-service music educators to teach secondary choral music, teaches graduate research methods, and conducts the Treble Choir. He earned his PhD and master's degree in music education at Northwestern University and his bachelor's and K–12 teaching credential at The College of New Jersey. His research is funded by the National Endowment for the Arts and the Institute of Education Sciences. That work appears in the *Journal of Research in Music Education, Arts Education Policy Review*, and other scientific venues. He coauthored the book *Design and Analysis of Quantitative Research in Music Education*.

Ben Folds is an Emmy-nominated singer-songwriter-composer with an enormous body of genre-bending music that includes pop albums with Ben Folds Five, multiple solo albums, and numerous collaborative records. An active performer and *New York Times* bestselling author, Ben advocates for arts and music education funding, and serves as artistic advisor to the National Symphony Orchestra at the Kennedy Center in Washington, DC. He also launched a charitable initiative in his native state of North Carolina that provides free or affordable piano lessons to interested school-age children.

Dave Frankowski, PhD, earned his neuroscience doctorate from the University of Georgia. Dr. Frankowski joined the National Institute on Aging in 2020 and is serving as a health specialist in the Behavioral and Systems Neuroscience Branch, where he supports extramural research in the areas of cognitive neuroscience, affective neuroscience, and sensory and motor disorders of aging. In addition, he has been a member of the multi-institute Music and Health working group and is a NIA representative at the Interagency Modeling and Analysis Group. Prior to joining NIA, Dr. Frankowski conducted his postdoctoral research at the University of Texas, MD Anderson Cancer Center, focusing on neural mechanisms of cue-related behavior and their role in obesity and tobacco use.

Jefri A. Franks, MS, CPC, lost her only child, Heather, to cancer in 2001.

While Heather was in the hospital, Jefri was approached by Sheri Robb, PhD, about Heather participating in her SMART study. Jefri and Sheri have been working together ever since on studies and presentations pertaining to childhood cancer. Jefri has a master's degree in counseling; she is a certified life coach, and she is certified in trauma. She resides in Kansas City, Missouri.

J. Todd Frazier has spent thirty-plus years supporting education, research, and accessibility collaborations between education, medicine, and arts and culture communities in America. A composer and graduate from the Eastman School of Music and The Juilliard School, he serves as the Gerald H. Dubin, MD Presidential Distinguished Centennial Director in the Art of Medicine at Houston Methodist Hospital's Center for Performing Arts Medicine (CPAM). The mission of CPAM, now one of the largest and most comprehensive arts in health hospital-based programs in the world, is to effectively translate the collaborative potential of arts and medicine to the holistic health-care environment of Houston Methodist.

Rhiannon Giddens has made a singular, iconic career out of stretching her brand of folk music, with its miles-deep historical roots and contemporary sensibilities, into just about every field imaginable. A two-time Grammy Award–winning singer and instrumentalist, MacArthur "Genius" Grant recipient, and composer of opera, ballet, and film, Giddens has centered her work around the mission of uplifting people whose contributions to American musical history have previously been overlooked or erased, and advocating for a more accurate understanding of the country's musical origins through art. Giddens is co-founder of the Black string band Carolina Chocolate Drops and Black female banjo supergroup Our Native Daughters; she received the 2023 Pulitzer Prize in music for her opera, *Omar*.

Assal Habibi, PhD, is an associate research professor of psychology at the Brain and Creativity Institute at the University of Southern California. Her research takes a broad perspective on understanding the influence of arts and specifically music on health and development, focusing on how biological dispositions and learning experiences shape the brain and development of cognitive, emotional, and social abilities during childhood and adolescence. She is an expert on the use of electrophysiologic and neuroimaging methods to investigate human brain function and has used longitudinal and cross-sectional designs to investigate how implementing music training programs within the school curricula impacts the learning and academic achievement of children from under-resourced communities.

Zakir Hussain is one of the world's most esteemed and influential musicians and the preeminent classical tabla virtuoso of our time. The foremost disciple of his father, the legendary Ustad Allarakha, Zakir has elevated the status of his instrument both in India and globally with his brilliant performances. A Grammy Award winner and widely considered a chief architect of the contemporary world music movement, Zakir has led many historic and groundbreaking collaborations, including with Mickey Hart, Charles Lloyd, Eric Harland, Dave Holland, Chris Potter, Béla Fleck, Edgar Meyer, and Herbie Hancock. Zakir is the recipient of countless awards and honors, including Padma Vibhushan, Sangeet Natak Akademi Award, the USA's National Heritage Fellowship, and Officier in France's Order of Arts and Letters.

Beatriz Ilari, PhD, is associate professor of music education and chair of music teaching and learning at the University of Southern California. Using both quantitative and qualitative approaches, she has conducted extensive research with infants and children to examine the intersections between music, child development, cognition, and culture. Ilari is a research fellow at USC's Brain and Creativity Institute and collaborates regularly with colleagues from various fields in Brazil, Portugal, Spain, the UK, the US, and Hong Kong. Her research has appeared in the *Journal of Cross-Cultural Psychology, Journal of Research in Music Education, Music & Science, PNAS,* and *Psychology of Music.*

Julene K. Johnson, PhD, is a cognitive neuroscientist with an undergraduate degree in music. She is a professor in the UCSF School of Nursing's Institute for Health & Aging and codirector of the Sound Health Network. She has a long-standing interest in studying music and health in both healthy older adults and persons living with dementia. She previously studied preserved music skills in persons with Alzheimer's disease. She is currently studying the impact of music-based interventions on health and well-being of older adults with and without cognitive impairment. In 2010 she was a Fulbright Scholar in Jyväskylä, Finland, where she studied how community choirs help promote well-being among older adults.

Sarah Johnson, as Carnegie Hall's chief education officer, directs the Hall's Weill Music Institute (WMI), the illustrious concert venue's education and social impact arm. Programs created by WMI serve more than 800,000 people annually, and millions more digitally, including children, students, teachers, parents, young music professionals, and adults in New York City and globally. She has received numerous leadership awards, including from Americans for the Arts and Independent Sector. Ms. Johnson received her bachelor's and master's degrees in oboe performance from The Juilliard School.

Ruth J. Katz, JD, MPH, is executive director of the Aspen Institute's Health, Medicine & Society Program (HMS), which grapples with some of the toughest health challenges facing the US. She also leads Aspen Ideas Health, the opening three-day event of the renowned Aspen Ideas Festival, and serves as codirector of the NeuroArts Blueprint, a partnership between HMS and Johns Hopkins University School of Medicine. Prior to joining the Aspen Institute, Katz was chief public health counsel with the Committee on Energy and Commerce in the US House of Representatives and held leadership positions at The George Washington University Milken Institute School of Public Health and at Yale University School of Medicine.

Juliet L. King, ATR-BC, LPC, LMHC, is associate professor of art therapy at The George Washington University and adjunct associate professor of neurology at the Indiana University School of Medicine. Professor King's research explores the systematic integration of art therapy and neuroscience with a focus on contemporary neuroimaging to explore and test the psychological mechanisms of change in the creative arts therapies. She is pursuing a PhD in translational health sciences and her dissertation is the development of a neuroscience-informed art therapy tool kit for the treatment of psychological trauma. In 2016 she wrote and edited *Art Therapy, Neuroscience and Trauma: Theoretical and Practical Perspectives* and is currently coediting a second edition, set for publication in 2024.

Rébecca Kleinberger, PhD, is an assistant professor of music, humanics, and AI at Northeastern University. She obtained her PhD from the MIT Media Lab and conducted research at the McGovern Institute for Brain Research at MIT. She leads holistic and applied research to reveal the power and mysteries of the voice, tackling questions about health, music, assistive technology, neurology, perception, and the inner voice. She also codirects the INTERACT Animal Lab for mediated interspecies enrichment. Her work has been reported by *The New York Times*, *The Washington Post*, *BBC News*, *The Guardian*, CNN, CBC, NPR, and other news outlets.

Nina Kraus, PhD, is Hugh Knowles Professor of Communication Sciences, Neurobiology, and Otolaryngology at Northwestern University. As a biologist and amateur musician, she thinks about sound and brain health. Her research has found that our lives in sound, for better (musicians, bilinguals) and for worse (concussion, hearing loss, language disorders, noise), shape how our brain makes sense of the sounds we hear. Her book, *Of Sound Mind: How our Brain Constructs a Meaningful Sonic World*, was conversationally written for the intellectually curious. Kraus advocates for biologically informed choices in education, health, and society. See brainvolts.northwestern.edu.

Jacquelyn Kulinski, MD, FASPC, is director of the Preventive Cardiology Program and associate professor of medicine at the Medical College of Wisconsin with a secondary appointment in the Graduate School of Biomedical Sciences. She is a board-certified cardiologist with a strong interest in preventive cardiology and lipidology and provides individualized and comprehensive cardiovascular risk assessment to patients. She is a fellow of the American Society of Preventive Cardiology. She holds a certificate in clinical and translational science and has been an NIH-funded investigator since 2019. She has experience with running clinical trials in medical research, typically involving nonpharmacologic interventions, such as singing.

Helene M. Langevin, MD, is the director of the NIH National Center for Complementary and Integrative Health. She was previously director of the Osher Center for Integrative Medicine at Harvard Medical School. Dr. Langevin's research centers on the role of connective tissue in musculoskeletal pain. Dr. Langevin received an MD degree from McGill University, Montreal, post-doctoral studies at the MRC Neurochemical Pharmacology Unit in Cambridge, England, and Johns Hopkins Hospital in Baltimore.

Catherine Law, MTSC, is the director of the Office of Communications and Public Liaison at the National Center for Complementary and Integrative Health, NIH. The communications team is responsible for disseminating information about the research supported and conducted by NCCIH to the Center's many stakeholders. The team develops content for, maintains, and utilizes many communications channels, including the Center's internet and intranet websites, social media channels, information clearinghouse, exhibits program, and other outreach efforts. Ms. Law holds a master of technical and scientific communications degree and a BS in chemistry.

Miriam Lense, PhD, is an assistant professor and clinical psychologist at Vanderbilt University Medical Center. As codirector of the Vanderbilt Music Cognition Lab, she leads an interdisciplinary research program on music, social engagement, and well-being for children and families. Her research includes investigation into basic processes and clinical applications of music and rhythm, including for individuals impacted by neurodevelopmental conditions such as autism and Williams syndrome. vumc.org/music-cognition-lab.

David Leventhal is a founding teacher and program director for Dance for PD®, a program of the Mark Morris Dance Group, which has been used as a model for classes in more than three hundred communities in thirty countries. A recipient of multiple awards for his community teaching work, David leads classes for people living with Parkinson's disease around the world and has written and presented extensively on the intersection of dance and Parkinson's. As a dancer, he performed with the Mark Morris Dance Group from 1997 to

2011, appearing in principal roles in some of Mark Morris's most celebrated works and receiving a 2010 Bessie Award for his performance career.

Daniel Levitin, PhD, FRSC, is James McGill Professor Emeritus of Psychology at McGill University and Dean Emeritus at Minerva University. He is the author of the five consecutive international bestselling books: *This Is Your Brain on Music, The World in Six Songs, The Organized Mind, A Field Guide to Lies,* and *Successful Aging.* Levitin is credited with fundamental discoveries about the nature of musical memory and absolute pitch, the neural correlates of musical structure, and the role of the cerebellum in mediating musical emotion. Prior to entering academia, Levitin was a record producer and engineer with artists such as Blue Öyster Cult, Santana, and Stevie Wonder.

Joanne Loewy DA, LCAT, MT-BC, director of the Department of Music Therapy and the Louis Armstrong Center for Music and Medicine, is an associate professor at Icahn School of Medicine at Mount Sinai and a founding member of the International Association for Music and Medicine. Her federally funded research focuses on music therapy and stress (NIH) and depression (NEA) in vulnerable populations. She specializes in NICU music therapy, children and teens with emotional issues, and adults with pulmonary needs and neurologic disorders. Dr. Loewy is the coeditor in chief of the international, peer-reviewed journal *Music and Medicine.*

Yo-Yo Ma's career is testament to his faith in culture's ability to generate trust and understanding—from his iconic performances and recordings to original undertakings such as the Bach Project and Our Common Nature, a cultural journey to celebrate the ways that nature can reunite us in pursuit of a shared future. Yo-Yo was born to Chinese parents in Paris, where he began to study the cello with his father when he was four. Three years later, he moved with his family to the United States, where he continued his cello studies before pursuing a liberal arts education.

Tod Machover is a composer, inventor, and Muriel R. Cooper Professor of Music and Media at the MIT Media Lab, where he directs the Opera of the Future Group. Called a "musical visionary" by *The New York Times,* he has had his critically acclaimed compositions commissioned and performed by the Philadelphia Orchestra, the Ensemble intercontemporain, the Royal Academy of Music, Boston Lyric Opera, the Kronos Quartet, Yo-Yo Ma, Renée Fleming, Joyce DiDonato, and many others. He is particularly known for his groundbreaking operas such as the *Brain Opera* and *Death and the Powers,* and for developing new musical technologies for enhanced expression and creativity as well as for promoting health and well-being.

Susan Magsamen, MAS, is the founder and executive director of the International Arts + Mind Lab (IAM Lab), Center for Applied Neuroaesthetics, a pioneering neuroaesthetics initiative from the Pedersen Brain Science Institute at Johns Hopkins University School of Medicine. Susan's work focuses on how the arts and aesthetic experiences measurably change the brain, body, and behavior and how this knowledge can be translated to inform health and well-being. She is the author of the Impact Thinking model, an arts-based interdisciplinary translational research model, the codirector of the NeuroArts Blueprint, in partnership with The Aspen Institute, and the coauthor of the *New York Times* bestseller, *Your Brain on Art: How the Arts Transform Us.*

Mark Morris founded the Mark Morris Dance Group (MMDG) in 1980. In addition to creating over 150 works for MMDG, he conducts orchestras, directs opera, and choreographs for ballet companies worldwide. Live music and community engagement are vital components of the Dance Group. It has toured with its own musicians, the MMDG Music Ensemble, since 1996. The Mark Morris Dance Center, opened in 2001, provides a home for the dance group, subsidized rehearsal space for local artists, free programs for the community, and dance classes for people of all ages, with and without disabilities. Morris's memoir, *Out Loud*, cowritten with Wesley Stace, was published in paperback by Penguin Press in October 2021.

Marisol Norris, PhD, MT-BC, is a cultural worker, music therapy practitioner and educator, and scholar-activist whose work centers on musical placemaking in Black communities. She is the founder and CEO of the Black Music Therapy Network, Inc., and director of the Music Therapy and Counseling master's program at Drexel University. A leading scholar of Black aesthetics in music therapy, Dr. Norris teaches the liberatory function of artistic processes, expanding the applied practice of radical healing frameworks within music and health spaces. Her clinical and supervisory experience has spanned medical and community health settings, centering the agented portrayals of Black service recipients' health practices across chronic illness and mental health and emancipatory research that eliminates inequities within Black communities.

Francisco J. Núñez, a MacArthur Fellow and Musical America's 2018 Educator of the Year, is a composer, conductor, visionary, leading figure in music education, and the artistic director/founder of the Young People's Chorus of New York (YPC). His commitment to the arts, youth, and diversity has been recognized through numerous awards and honors, including an ASCAP Victor Herbert Award; the New York Choral Society's Choral Excellence Award; *Hispanic Business Magazine*'s 100 Most Influential Hispanics; ABC-TV's Person of the Week; Musical America Worldwide's 30 Influencers; Bang on a Can's Visionary Award; NYU Steinhardt's Distinguished Alumnus Achievement

Award; and honorary doctor of music degrees from both Ithaca College and Gettysburg College.

Lisa Onken, PhD, has a PhD in clinical psychology from Northwestern University and has worked as a psychotherapist and a researcher. She joined the National Institute on Aging's Division of Behavioral and Social Research in 2015, where she directs a program of research on behavioral change and interventions and leads NIA's Edward R. Roybal Centers program. Dr. Onken has been instrumental in the development of the NIH Stage Model, which helps to guide the development of maximally potent and scalable behavioral interventions that are defined by the mechanisms through which they work. Prior to joining NIA, she was chief of the Behavioral and Integrative Treatment Branch and the associate director for treatment at the National Institute on Drug Abuse.

Ann Patchett is the author of novels, works of nonfiction, and children's books. She has been the recipient of numerous awards, including the PEN/Faulkner Award, the Women's Prize for fiction, and the Booksense Book of the Year, and was a finalist for the Pulitzer Prize. Her work has been translated into more than thirty languages. She was named one of the 100 Most Influential People in the World by *Time* magazine. President Joe Biden awarded her the National Humanities Medal in recognition of her contributions to American culture. She lives in Nashville, Tennessee, where she owns Parnassus Books.

Aniruddh (Ani) Patel, PhD, is a professor of psychology at Tufts University, where he researches the cognitive, neural, and evolutionary foundations of musicality. His book *Music, Language, and the Brain* won the ASCAP Deems Taylor Award, and he wrote and presented *Music and the Brain*, a set of eighteen lectures produced by The Great Courses for a general audience. He is writing a book on the evolution of human musicality to be published by Princeton University Press. He has served as president of the Society for Music Perception and Cognition, and his evolutionary research has been supported by fellowships from the Radcliffe Institute for Advanced Study, the Guggenheim Foundation, and the Canadian Institute for Advanced Research.

Joanna Patterson-Cross, PhD, MBiochem, studied biochemistry at the University of Oxford before being selected as a scholar for the Wellcome Trust and National Institutes of Health (NIH) PhD program. While completing her post-doctoral fellowship, she combined her love for music and science by performing with NIH Philharmonia and writing several articles for the NIH newsletter. She is now a professional scientific writer, producing both commercial and technical content for life scientists.

Mark Pitcher, PhD, is the chief of staff at the National Center for Complementary and Integrative Health (NCCIH). Prior to NCCIH, Dr. Pitcher was the director of Interprofessional Health Sciences Research at the University of Bridgeport, where he led the university's health science research program, provided administrative oversight and coordination of UB's Institutional Review Board (IRB), and served as the university's Research Integrity Officer (RIO). Dr. Pitcher completed his graduate training in McGill University's Integrated Program in Neuroscience, where he studied pain neuroanatomy and neurophysiology, followed by multidisciplinary post-doctoral research as a Visiting Fellow at the National Institutes of Health.

Courtney Platt is a professional dancer, choreographer, and actor who lives with relapsing multiple sclerosis (RMS). She was diagnosed in 2012 at the age of twenty-three after experiencing unsettling symptoms while on Season 7 of the *So You Think You Can Dance* tour. Courtney is a spokesperson for MS in Harmony, Bristol Myers Squibb's first-of-its-kind initiative to educate people with MS and their loved ones about achieving mind-body harmony through music therapy. In addition, Courtney is a spokesperson for the National Multiple Sclerosis Society. Courtney lives in Los Angeles, California, with her two young children and husband, Jonah Platt.

Richard Powers is the author of thirteen novels, including *Bewilderment*, *The Overstory*, *Orfeo*, *The Time of Our Singing*, and *The Echo Maker*. He is the recipient of a MacArthur Fellowship, the Pulitzer Prize, and the National Book Award. He lives in the foothills of the Great Smoky Mountains.

Alexandra Rieger is a doctoral candidate at the MIT Media Lab in Tod Machover's Opera of the Future Group and a doctoral student researcher at Harvard Medical School's Mass General Hospital (MGH). She is a cognitive neuroscientist, designer, mechatronic engineer, multi-instrumentalist folk musician, and an instructor dedicated to leveraging her multidisciplinary background to develop medical interventions to reimagine health care and access for patients globally. Rieger received her BS at Stanford University, is an Oxford University Bing Alumna, completed her MS at Dartmouth College, and her second MS at MIT. She is collaborating with MGH on a stroke-patient study and is a recently appointed Morningside Academy of Design Fellow.

Sheri Robb, PhD, MT-BC, is a Walther Professor of Supportive Oncology in the Indiana University Schools of Nursing and Medicine and a full member of the Indiana University Simon Comprehensive Cancer Center. Dr. Robb is an established investigator with fifteen years of continuous funding from the National Institutes of Health. Her program of research focuses on development and testing of music interventions to manage distress and improve positive health outcomes in children and adolescents with cancer and their caregivers.

Deborah Rutter is president of the John F. Kennedy Center for the Performing Arts and is a leading voice in arts administration. As leader of the national cultural center, Rutter oversees programming across all genres. In 2019 Rutter opened the REACH, an expansion of the Center's campus designed to bring audiences into the artistic process. She's expanded programming to fully represent the diversity of art in America and introduced many programs across local, national, and international communities. Rutter has held executive leadership roles with the Chicago Symphony Orchestra Association, the Seattle Symphony, the Los Angeles Chamber Orchestra, and the Los Angeles Philharmonic. Rutter is a graduate of Stanford University and holds an MBA from the University of Southern California.

Anna Deavere Smith is a writer and actress. She lives in New York City.

esperanza spalding (aka irma nejando) is an eaabibacliitoti* artist, trained and initiated in the North American (masculine) jazz lineage and tradition. Her work interweaves various combinations of instrumental music, improvisation, singing, composition, poetry, dance, therapeutic research, storytelling, teaching, restorative urban land and artist-sanctuary custodianship, and growing in love as a daughter, sister, cousin, niece, auntie, great-auntie, friend. She is cofounder and curator of Prismid Inc., a 501(c)(3) that ushers and stewards restorative artist residency and workshop space in Portland, Oregon. With her dance company Off Brand gOdds (cofounded with Antonio Brown) and the Songwrights Apothecary Lab she leads multiweek performance, workshop, teaching, and therapeutic-arts research residencies.

Coryse St. Hillaire-Clarke, PhD, joined the NIA Division of Neuroscience as a program director in August 2016. She oversees the Sensory and Motor Disorders of Aging Program, which supports research on mechanisms of normal aging and disease-related changes in motor, visual, auditory, somatosensory, proprioceptive, vestibular, and chemosensory functions. She also represents the institute on a number of trans-NIH working groups, including Brain Research through Advancing Innovative Neurotechnologies (BRAIN) and the Music and Health working group. Prior to joining the NIA, Dr. St. Hillaire-Clarke worked as a health program specialist at the National Institute of Neurological Disorders and Stroke (NINDS), where she helped manage the Parkinson's Disease Biomarkers Program (PDBP) and engaged in several NINDS strategic planning efforts.

Tom Sweitzer, MMT, MT-BC, is the cofounder of A Place to Be, Amer-

---

*European-African ancestored being influenced by American cultures living in Indigenous Territories of Turtle Island.

ica's largest nonprofit music therapy center. He is a subject of the documentary *Music Got Me Here*, about his work with a client who suffered a traumatic brain injury. He has written several musicals, including cowriting *A Will to Survive*, a rock-opera about suicide prevention. Tom has worked closely with Renée Fleming and the NIH as a speaker and panelist for Sound Health. He is an actor as well, and his one-man show, *20 Seconds*, has an Off-Broadway run Fall of 2023. He uses his real-life story of how music saved his life to teach people the real secret, magic, and science behind music therapy.

Michael Thaut, PhD (Michigan State 1983), holds a Tier I Canada Research Chair endowed by the Federal Government of Canada. He has appointments as professor in the Faculty of Music and the Faculty of Medicine at the University of Toronto. His research has been pioneering in music neuroscience and clinical translations to brain rehabilitation. The discoveries of the effects of auditory rhythm on rehabilitating motor control in PD and stroke and the neural mechanisms underlying autobiographically salient musical memory preservation are credited to his research. As a former professional violinist in classical and folk genres he brings foundational musical knowledge and training into a context of neuroscience brain research.

Stanford L. Thompson, a principal of Goldsmith Strategies and executive director of Equity Arc, is a leading voice in promoting cultural equity and leading change for arts nonprofit organizations. Stan founded and led the internationally recognized Play On Philly organization and served as the founding board chairman of El Sistema USA. He serves on the faculty of the Global Leaders Institute and earned degrees in trumpet performance from The Curtis Institute of Music and New England Conservatory's Sistema Fellows Program.

Concetta M. Tomaino, DA, LCAT, MT-BC, is the executive director and cofounder (with renowned neurologist and author Oliver Sacks) of the Institute for Music and Neurologic Function (IMNF). Internationally known for her research in the clinical applications of music and neurologic rehabilitation, she received the Music Therapists for Peace Award at the United Nations and the Lifetime Achievement Award from the American Music Therapy Association. Her work has been featured on *48 Hours*, *60 Minutes*, and internationally on the BBC and CBC. Dr. Sacks's book *Musicophilia* is dedicated to her. Dr. Tomaino is past president of the American Association for Music Therapy, a founding board member for the International Association for Music and Medicine, and adjunct professor at Lehman College, CUNY.

Indre Viskontas, MM, PhD, is a neuroscientist, musician, and opera stage director. She is an associate professor of psychology and director of the Creative Brain Lab at the University of San Francisco. Dr. Viskontas has published more than fifty original papers and chapters related to the neural basis of memory and creativity and is currently the president-elect of the Society for the Neuroscience of Creativity and the director of communications for the Sound Health Network, an initiative of the National Endowment for the Arts. She has written and filmed ninety-eight lectures across four courses for The Great Courses, from "Essential Scientific Concepts" and "Brain Myths Exploded" to "How Digital Technology Shapes Us" and "Your Creative Brain."

Stacie Aamon Yeldell, MA, MT-BC, AVPT, is the founder of Amöntra. She is an award-winning vocalist, speaker, and music psychotherapist with over fifteen years of experience in mental health treatment. As a consultant, Stacie has worked with a range of organizations, including The Grammy Foundation, LA Opera, GoogleArts and Culture, Netflix, and YoungArts. In addition to being a faculty member for UCLArts & Healing and California Institute of Integral Studies (CIIS), she has spoken at events like Women in Music, National Arts Policy Roundtable, and Sound Health Summit. She has also appeared on CBS News, in Renée Fleming's "Music and Mind Live," and is featured in the documentary *Proven*. Stacie holds a master's degree in music therapy from New York University and certifications in Sound and Music Healing from the Open Center, and Vocal Psychotherapy (AVPT) from the Vancouver Vocal Psychotherapy Institute.

Robert Zatorre, PhD, is a cognitive neuroscientist at the Montreal Neurological Institute of McGill University. His laboratory studies the neural substrate for auditory cognition, with special emphasis on two characteristically human abilities: speech and music. He and his collaborators have published over three hundred scientific papers on topics including pitch perception, auditory imagery, brain plasticity, and musical pleasure. He cofounded the International Laboratory for Brain, Music, and Sound Research (BRAMS), a unique multi-university consortium dedicated to the cognitive neuroscience of music. He tries to keep up his Baroque repertoire on the organ whenever he gets a chance.

Note on Notes

For source notes to all essays in *Music and Mind*, please see

prh.com/musicandmindsourcenotes

Credits

CONTRIBUTOR CREDITS

Grateful acknowledgment is made for permission to print the essays in this book. Each contributor holds the copyright to their own essay:

"Music and Mind" by Renée Fleming.

"Sounding Joy" by Christopher Bailey.

"Rhythm & Rhyme" by Sara Beck, PhD, Randolph College, Lynchburg, Virginia, and Miriam Lense, PhD, Vanderbilt.

"Music for Chronic Pain Management" by Joke Bradt, PhD, MT-BC.

"Rabbit Hole" by Roseanne Cash. "Rabbit Hole" copyright © 2023 by Rosanne Cash.

"Art Therapy, Psychology and Neuroscience" by Juliet L. King and Anjan Chatterjee.

"Nurturing New Horizons for Science and the Arts," Francis S. Collins, MD, PhD.

"The Benefits of Musical Engagement Across the Life Span" by Assal Habibi, Brain and Creativity Institute; Beatriz Ilari, University of Southern California, Los Angeles, California; Hanna Demasio and Antonio Demasio, Brain and Creativity Institute.

"Porous Density" by Elizabeth Diller.

"Arts-Based Therapies in Integrative Health" by Emmeline Edwards, PhD, Director, NCCIH Division of Extramural Research. Wen G. Chen, PhD, Branch Chief, NCCIH Basic and Mechanistic Research Branch, Catherine Law, M.T.S.C., Director, NCCIH Office of Communications and Public Liaison, Mark Pitcher, PhD, Special Assistant to the Director, NCCIH, Helene M. Langevin, MD, Director, NCCIH. Affiliation: National Center for Complementary and Integrative Health (NCCIH) at the National Institutes of Health, Bethesda, Maryland, USA.

"State of the Art" by Kenneth Elpus.

"Our Symphony Orchestra" by Ben Folds and Joanna Cross.

"Music, Memory, Aging, and Science" by Coryse St. Hillaire-Clarke, Dave Frankowski and Lisa Onken. The participation of these individuals or the materials should not be interpreted as representing the official viewpoint of the U.S. Department of Health and Human Services, the National Institutes of Health, or the National Institute on Aging, except where noted.

"My Voice, My Song" by Sheri L. Robb, PhD, MT-BC, Jefri A. Franks, MS, CPC, and Joanna L. Patterson-Cross, PhD, MBioChem.

"Music Across the Continuum of Care" by J. Todd Frazier with coauthors Shay Kulha and Jennifer Townsend.

"How Music Shows Us What It Means to Be Human" by Rhiannon Giddens, Joanna L. Patterson-Cross, PhD, Mbiochem.

"Music and Mysticism" by Zakir Hussain.

"The Potential of Group Singing to Promote Health and Well-Being" by Julene K. Johnson, PhD.

"Musical Connections" by Sarah Johnson.

"Blueprint for Cultivating the Field of Neuroarts" by Susan Magsamen and Ruth J. Katz.

"Composing the Future of Health" by Tod Machover, Rébecca Kleinberger, Alexandra Rieger.

"Sound Connects Us" by Nina Kraus, PhD.

"Can Singing Touch the Heart" by Jacquelyn Kulinski, MD, FASPC.

"Dance and Parkinson's" by David Leventhal.

"What Does it Mean to Be Musical?" © 2022 Daniel J. Levitin. Updated and adapted by the author from Levitin, D. J., "What Does It Mean to Be Musical?" *Neuron* 73, no. 4 (2012): 633–37.

"I Sing the Body Electric: Music Psychotherapy in Medicine" by Joanne Loewy, DA, LCAT, MT-BC. Loewy independent.

"Nature, Culture, and Healing" by Yo-Yo Ma.

". . . & the Field" by marisol norris & esperanza spalding.

"Belonging Through Music" by Francisco J. Núñez.

"How to Fall in Love with Opera" by Ann Patchett.

"Musicality, Evolution, and Animal Responses to Music" by Aniruddh D. Patel, PhD.

"Achieving Body, Mind, and Soul Harmony with Multiple Sclerosis" by Courtney Platt, Dancer and Choreographer; spokesperson, MS in Harmony.

"The Parting Glass" by Richard Powers.

"Arts for Non-Arts Outcomes" by Deborah Rutter. © John F. Kennedy Center for the Performing Arts.

"Healing Arts" by Anna Deavere Smith.

"Healing Note by Note" by Tom Sweitzer, MMT, MT-BC.

"Coda and Crescendo" by Michael H. Thaut, PhD.

"Play on Philly" by Stanford L. Thompson.

"Music and Memory "by Concetta M. Tomaino, DA, LCAT, MT-BC.

"Humans Are Musical Creatures" by Indre Viskontas, MM, PhD.

"Sing Your Way Home" by S. Aamon Yeldell, MA, MT-BC, AVPT.

"Musical Enjoyment and the Reward Circuits of the Brain" by Robert Zatorre, PhD.

Index